THE CONCEPT OF WOMAN

THE CONCEPT OF WOMAN

The Aristotelian Revolution
750 BC–AD 1250

Sister Prudence Allen, R.S.M.

William B. Eerdmans Publishing Company
Grand Rapids, Michigan / Cambridge, U.K.

First published in Canada 1985 by
Eden Press

The first edition was published with the help of a grant from
the Canadian Federation for the Humanities,
using funds provided by the Social Sciences
and Humanities Research Council of Canada.

This edition published in the United States of America 1997 by
Wm. B. Eerdmans Publishing Co.
255 Jefferson Ave. S.E., Grand Rapids, Michigan 49503 /
P.O. Box 163, Cambridge CB3 9PU U.K.

Printed in the United States of America

02 01 00 99 98 97 7 6 5 4 3 2 1

Library of Congress Cataloging-in-Publication Data

Allen, Prudence.
The concept of woman : the Aristotelian revolution
750 B.C.-A.D. 1250 / Prudence Allen.
p. cm.
Originally published: Montreal : Eden Press, c1985.
Includes bibliographical references and index.
ISBN 0-8028-4270-4 (alk. paper)
1. Femininity (Philosophy) — History. 2. Women — History.
3. Sex — History. I. Title.
BD450.A4725 1997
305.4'01 — dc20 96-9102
CIP

DEDICATION TO THE FIRST EDITION

In gratitude for being the initial catalyst for this historical study of the concept of woman, the first edition was dedicated to Reverend Mother Benedict Duss, O.S.B., Abbess of Regina Laudis, Bethlehem, Connecticut.

DEDICATION TO THE SECOND EDITION

In gratitude for their personal example of the lifelong dedication to learning I dedicate this second edition to my parents, Mildred and Henry Allen.

TABLE OF CONTENTS

LIST OF ILLUSTRATIONS

A CHRONOLOGICAL TABLE OF THE PHILOSOPHERS CONSIDERED

Hesiod	c. 750 BC
Sappho	c. 600 BC
Anaximander	c. 540 BC
Pythagoras	c. 530 BC
Heraclitus	c. 540–480 BC
Parmenides	c. 539–500 BC
Anaxagoras	c. 500–428 BC
Empedocles	c. 450 BC
Aspasia	c. 440 BC
Protagoras	c. 490–420 BC
Gorgias	c. 490–386 BC
Prodicus	c. 470–3?? BC
Hippocrates	c. 460–377 BC
Democritus	c. 460–370 BC
Socrates	c. 470–399 BC
Xenophon	c. 430–357 BC
Plato	c. 428–355 BC
Speussipus	c. 410–339 BC
Perictione I	fourth century BC
Theano I	fourth century BC
Phyntis	fourth century BC
Aristotle	384–322 BC
Hipparchia	c. 300 BC
Theophrastus	c. 370–286 BC
Epicurus	c. 341–270 BC
Zeno of Cittium	c. 333–261 BC
Chryssipus	c. 282–206 BC
Melissa	third century BC
Perictione II	third century BC
Aresas	third century BC
Myia	second century BC
Theano II	second century BC
Cicero	106–43 BC
Lucretius	98–55 BC
Philo	13 BC – AD 54
Seneca	AD 4–64
Pliny the Elder	AD 23–79
Musonius Rufus	c. AD 30–101
Epictetus	born c. 50
Plutarch	50–125
Juvenal	60–140
Marcus Aurelius	121–180
Galen	131–201
Plotinus	205–270
Porphyry	235–305
St. Catherine of Alexandria	c. 307
St. Augustine	354–430
Hypatia	370–415
Boethius	480–524
Hilda of Whitby	614–680
John Scotus Erigena	810–877
Roswitha	c. 935–1002
Avicenna	980–1037
Avicebron	1020–1070
St. Anselm	1033–1109
Abelard	1097–1142
Hildegard of Bingen	1098–1179
Peter Lombard	1100–1160
Heloise	1101–1164
Averroes	1126–1198
Herrad of Landsberg	1130–1195
Maimonides	1135–1204
Walter Map	c. 1140–1209
Andreas Capellanus	c. 1186
St. Albert the Great	1193–1280
Roger Bacon	1214–1292
St. Bonaventure	1217–1274
St. Thomas Aquinas	1224–1274

ACKNOWLEDGEMENTS

The financial support of Supplemental Research Grants and a Leave Research Grant from the Social Sciences and Humanities Research Council of Canada from 1979 to 1982 have enabled this book to be researched and written. In addition, a grant from the Canadian Federation for the Humanities in 1982 supports its publication. I am extremely grateful to these agencies of the Canadian government for the opportunity to pursue the subject of this text with significant breadth and depth.

In addition, I wish to acknowledge the continued support of the administration of Concordia University in Montreal, which enabled me to be on leave of absence from 1979 to 1981 in order to work at the Library of Congress in Washington, D.C., and which has also allowed time during the academic year to continue research.

The final form of this book was aided greatly by the opportunity to study and work under the auspices of the Kroger Institute in Michigan. I would like particularly to thank Mother Mary Honora Kroger, R.S.M., president, and Sr. Mary Christine Cremin, R.S.M., chairman of the board, for their continued support.

There are many individuals who have given a great deal of their time towards the completion of this book. I would like to mention the following research assistants: Flora Kaplan (1979), Christine Teasdale (1979–80), John McCarthy (1980–81), Fr. Michael Hall, O.S.B. (1981–82), and Dominique Deslandres (1982–84). Their fidelity and ingenuity in searching out important texts and passages has given this book its breadth of analysis.

In addition, Delise Alison, Teresa Crawmer and Margaret Blevins laboured faithfully to type the lengthy manuscript, and Leo McGillvray, Sr. Mercedes Lockerd, R.S.M., Ingrid Birker and Anne Huette executed the difficult task of proofreading its several hundred pages. I am very grateful for their devoted service to the project. Anne Huette is also responsible for the excellent index that accompanies the text, and for many important editorial suggestions. The exceptionally professional quality of the book is due to the outstanding work of Evelyne Hertel and the staff at Eden Press. It has been a pleasure to work with them on the production of the text.

A work of this size and scope, however, could not have been accomplished without the tremendous support of librarians, whose ability to be superb detectives often uncovered unexpected treasures. In particular I would like to mention Sarah Pritchard from the Library of Congress in Washington, and Wendy Knechtel from the Georges Vanier Library at Concordia University. Other libraries that have been particularly useful to this project were: the National Library of Medicine, Bethesda, Maryland; Dumbarton Oaks, Washington, D.C.; Michigan State University, East Lansing, Michigan; the University of Michigan, Ann Arbor, Michigan; and the Folger Shakespeare Library, Washington, D.C.

I would also like to express my gratitude to the following persons who have, through their teaching, personal examples, or research, helped to shape my thought and confirmed my decision to a life committed to philosophy: George Davie, Elizabeth Boyd, Lewis White Beck, Hope Emily Allen, John Lemmon, Josiah Gould, Greta Nemiroff, Henry Allen, Mildred Allen, Raphael Paul Garside, Julian David Garside, Jude Dougherty, Fr. Andrew Murray, O.M., Sister Sarah Doser, F.S.E., Sister Mary Timothy Prokes, S.S.N.D., Jacqueline Dunlavey, Ronald Dunlavey, Kathleen Stief, Kevin Foley, M.D., Mother Mary McGreevey, R.S.M., and Mother Mary Quentin Sheridan, R.S.M.

PREFACE TO THE SECOND EDITION

In the intervening eleven years since the publication of the first edition of *The Concept of Woman: The Aristotelian Revolution (750 BC–AD 1250),* the philosophical field of women's studies (or gender studies, as it is now more often called) has literally exploded beyond its previously limited boundaries. In many respects this is a positive occurrence, and it has opened wide a new area for reflection and research about the respective identities of women and men.

At the same time, such a rapidly synergetic change in a field of study poses many complex challenges for scholars. It becomes less possible to read and digest all the relevant material on a particular topic. In order to master a particular area of thought, one's focus must become increasingly narrow. Thus, in many ways, *The Concept of Woman,* with its sweeping time span of nearly two thousand years and its analysis of original works of more than sixty authors, goes against the trend of the times.

Therefore, the question must be directly asked: Do the conclusions reached in the first edition remain sound in such a rapidly changing field? It is my firm conviction that the fundamental lines of analysis in the text are still valid and the conclusions reached through them are true.

Much new primary and secondary material about authors writing between 750 BC and AD 1250 has been published since 1985. While it has been tempting to engage with the interesting arguments of other scholars in this second edition, I decided instead to provide an updated bibliography so that readers can study these sources themselves and evaluate the relative weight of different arguments. My decision was based on the desire to forge ahead into further historical periods of analysis of the concept of woman, and to leave the in-depth continuing analysis of ancient and medieval philosophy to those who have special expertise in those areas.

As a consequence, a second volume in this series, to be entitled *The Concept of Woman: The Early Humanist Reformation (1250–1500),* is projected for release in 1998. This text, which builds on the foundations of the first volume, traces the interaction of Platonic and Aristotelian foundations for theories of sex identity in both academic and satirical literature, and considers new approaches to woman's identity articulated by early humanist and religious writers. It also considers the importance of intergender dialogue in the new foundations for theories of sex complementarity.

While the fundamental structure of the original argument in the first edition of *The Concept of Woman: The Aristotelian Revolution* remains relevant for contemporary debate about the history of woman's identity, contemporary language used to speak about this topic has changed significantly. I would like to address briefly three specific areas: (1) the difference between sex and gender, (2) the difference between the concept of woman in relation to man and the concept of woman in relation to woman, and (3) developments in theories of complementarity.

SEX AND GENDER

In the first edition of this text I used the word "sex" to include all aspects of what is more recently divided into categories of sex and gender. I chose to do this at the time because all the texts considered between 750 BC and AD 1250 referred to differences between men and women as differences in sex identity. The distinction between sex and gender, being a contemporary (primarily English-speaking) distinction, certainly valid in many respects, was not operative in the concept of woman in these early centuries.

The more recent claim that sex denotes a biological entity (male or female) and gender a psychosocial construct (including masculine or feminine characteristics) was made first in anthropology in the mid-1970s and then entered into philosophical arguments in the mid-1980s.[1] At first there was an effort to keep sex and gender as equally valuable dialectical concepts when describing women's and men's identities, but by the late 1980s, especially through the influence of postmodernism, there was a gradual separation of sex from gender.[2] This division eventually led to a claim by many theorists that sex is an imaginary construct and gender ought to be denaturalized and contain no reference to male or female identity.[3]

While these developments mark the more extreme thinking of some philosophers about the topic, in general we find in North America a tendency to use a bifurcated reference to a sex/gender system, with gender denoting the psychosocial aspects and sex the biological aspects of women's and men's identities. It is odd that this common use of gender places such an emphasis on the psychosocial aspects of women's and men's identities and excludes the biological, because the historical root of gender is associated with "gens," "engender," "generate," "generation," and other words which explicitly refer to the biological sexual aspects of human identity.[4] It would seem that gender, with this root meaning, should evolve into a concept which includes sex rather than excludes it.

In addition, I have a concern about the bifurcation of the two terms "sex"/"gender" because it seems to create a fissure in the core of the human being. My own view is that the human being is unified, and that our language ought to reflect this

1. See, for example, Gayle Rubin, "The Traffic in Women: Notes on the 'Political Economy of Sex,'" in *Towards an Anthropology of Women* (New York: Monthly Review Press, 1975), pp. 157-210; and Sandra Harding, "Is Gender a Variable in Conceptions of Rationality? A Survey of Issues," in *Beyond Domination: New Perspectives on Women and Philosophy* (Lanham, Md.: Rowman and Allanheld, 1984), pp. 43-63.

2. See Jane Flax, "Postmodernism and Gender Relations in Feminist Theory," *Signs: Journal of Women in Culture and Society* 12, 4 (1987): 3-19; and Allison Jaggar and Susan Bordo, eds., *Gender/Body/Knowledge: Feminist Reconstructions of Being and Knowing* (New Brunswick and London: Rutgers University Press, 1989).

3. See Michael Foucault, *The History of Sexuality,* Vol. I (New York: Random House, 1980); Vol. 2. *The Use of Pleasure: The History of Sexuality* (New York: Random House, 1986); Teresa de Lauretis, *Technologies of Gender* (Bloomington and Indianapolis: Indiana University Press), 1987; and Monique Wittig, "The Mark of Gender," *Feminist Issues* 5, 2 (1985): 3-12.

4. See another argument for the priority of gender in Ivan Illich, *Gender* (New York: Pantheon Books, 1982).

ontological reality.[5] Currently, the philosophical debate about the meanings of sex and gender has expanded, and it would take more time than available in this limited introduction to the second edition of this book to articulate my own views on the many different aspects of the debate, particularly as they have evolved since 1985. Consequently, I am leaving the use of the word "sex" as it was originally employed in the first edition, while in subsequent volumes I will enter more directly into the debate and begin to use gender in a more inclusive fashion. For example, in the nearly completed second volume, *The Concept of Woman: The Early Humanist Reformation (1250–1500),* the theories of identity will be no longer identified as sex unity (unisex), sex polarity, and sex complementarity, but rather will be identified as gender unity, gender polarity, and gender complementarity.

THE CONCEPT OF WOMAN IN RELATION TO MAN AND IN RELATION TO WOMAN

For those readers who wonder why I titled the book *The Concept of Woman* but actually wrote about the concept of woman in relation to man in the history of western philosophy, I would like to reiterate that my goal was to describe systematically what the philosophers themselves said about the concept of woman. During this early period most of the philosophers were men, so they wrote about woman's identity relative to their own identity. There are a few exceptions to this, such as the early Greek poet Sappho, some of the Pythagorean women philosophers, and some women religious philosophers such as Herrad and Hildegard. In every case where the author being considered did reflect on the concept of woman in relation to woman, this information is included in the analysis.

My purpose in focusing the title and approach on the concept of woman is to emphasize that we are going to study human identity from the starting point of woman's identity in the four areas of opposites, generation, wisdom, and virtue. By placing woman's identity in the foreground and men's identity relative to it, I hoped to gain a perspective on human identity different from the usual philosophical approach which places man's identity in the foreground and woman's in the background. The chapter on Hildegard's analysis of the concept of woman in relation to man considers one of the most innovative theories in the entire text because she opens up relations among four different types of women and four different types of men, and she refers in her analysis to aspects of the whole human being, including body structure, character, and dynamics of interaction with others.

In the next volume, *The Concept of Woman: The Early Humanist Reformation,* which focuses on developments in the thirteenth through fifteenth centuries, I give considerable attention to dialogue among women about women's identity, as well as intergender dialogue about women's identity. In addition, I compare differences in conclusions reached in these cases from those reached in the academic world of exclusively men's dialogue. It is during this time in history that self-conscious reflection on sex and gender identity becomes the preoccupation of several philosophers. Without wanting to anticipate too much the

5. Some examples of this unified approach include Kenneth L. Schmitz, "The Geography of the Human Person," *Communio* 13 (Spring 1986): 27-48; "Selves and Persons: A Difference in Loves?" *Communio* 18 (Summer 1991): 183-206; Edith Stein, *Essays on Woman,* in The Collected Works of Edith Stein, Vol. 2 (Washington, D.C.: ICS Publications, 1987); and Norris W. Clarke, S.J., *Person and Being: The Aquinas Lecture, 1993* (Milwaukee: Marquette University Press, 1993).

arguments of the subsequent volume, I will note that some remarkable developments do occur when the concept of woman is articulated in these new dialogical contexts.

One of these significant developments is the embryonic articulation of philosophical grounds for communities of persons. While Greek and medieval philosophy had articulated these grounds for communities of men, or male persons, in Renaissance philosophy we begin to find the grounds articulated for communities of women and for intergender communities of women and men. Much of my own research and that of other philosophers during the past several years has focused on contemporary philosophical grounding of such communities.[6] Once again, it would be beyond the limits of this introduction to the revised edition of the text to elaborate such theories. However, it should be noted that this particular text considers only the earliest formulation of such interpersonal communities, and in most cases, since the philosophers are men, the communities being looked at are those of women in relation to men.

DEVELOPMENTS IN THEORIES OF COMPLEMENTARITY

When we return to our initial focus in *The Concept of Woman (750 BC–AD 1250)* we can see how limited the development of the concept is in this early period. Men and women were considered primarily from the single point of maleness and femaleness. Later on, beginning in the Renaissance, we see the introduction of the further factor of masculinity and femininity. This augments woman's identity as female, feminine, and masculine, and man's identity as male, masculine, and feminine.

By the nineteenth century the notion that a man or a woman is a self-defining individual brings with it an awakening of interiority so that a woman can make herself a particular kind of woman within the nexus female, feminine, and masculine, and a man can make himself a particular kind of man within the nexus male, masculine, and feminine. Finally, in the twentieth century a further evolution in human consciousness occurs with the articulation of theories about women-persons and men-persons in acts of self-giving to other persons to build authentic communities of persons.

When we look back to the ancient Greeks from this contemporary vantage point, we can see that their way of articulating the concept of woman is very limited. At the same time, this limited focus on woman as female and man as male provided the starting place for all subsequent analyses of the concept of woman and the concept of man. That is why it is so important to consider the first structure of the concept of woman so carefully. We need to understand how the concept of woman in relation to man was first identified in the pre-Socratics, how it was elaborated theoretically within a theory of sex unity or sex polarity by Plato and Aristotle, how it was further developed in its original form or within

6. Sr. Prudence Allen, R.S.M., "Analogy and Human Community in Lublin Existential Personalism," *The Toronto Journal of Theology* 5, 2 (Fall 1989): 236-46, and "A Woman and a Man as Prime Analogical Beings," *American Catholic Philosophical Quarterly* 66, 4 (1992): 456-82; Jacques Maritain, *The Person and the Common Good* (Notre Dame, Ind.: University of Notre Dame Press, 1985); Mary F. Rousseau, *Community: The Tie That Binds* (Lanham, Md.: University Press of America, 1991); Charles Taylor, *Sources of the Self: The Making of the Modern Identity* (Cambridge, Mass.: Harvard University Press, 1989); and Karol Wojtyla, *Person and Community: Selected Essays* (New York: Peter Lang, 1993).

the subsequent theory of sex complementarity in medieval philosophy, and what factors led to the dominance of the Aristotelian elaboration of sex polarity and sex unity at the end of the Middle Ages.

Thus, my goal in this volume is simply to bring into focus the ways in which the philosophers themselves wrote about the concept of woman. It is not to demonstrate the limitations of their thought from the perspective of a contemporary theory—a project I have undertaken elsewhere.[7]

There are, of course, the limitations of individual philosophers and of the language and manner in which these early philosophers considered the topic of sex identity. One example of a historical limitation can be seen in the elemental forms of sex complementarity that begin to emerge in Christian thought. In the early forms in Hildegard we see foundations for claims that men and women are significantly different at the same time that they are fundamentally equal in dignity and worth. However, complementarity is understood primarily in the limited way of being a male or a female human being, and it only begins to include the further incorporation of masculine and feminine characteristics. It does not evolve to include understanding of the interior activity of self-definition as a woman or a man. These further developments in theories of complementarity took many centuries to be articulated in western philosophy. For those readers who are interested, I have tried elsewhere to describe the metaphysical and anthropological foundations for developments from theories of fractional complementarity to integral complementarity.[8]

There is one further aspect of a development in complementarity which needs to be noted in this introduction. This concerns the discussion of the relation between education and sex identity, especially in Chapters IV and V of the original text. We noted that in early western education, within the Benedictine tradition, there emerged some outstanding philosophers who contributed to knowledge in many fields of study. For example, Hildegard made original contributions to science, music, literature, art, and theology as well as philosophy. She did this, as did so many others, as an individual who had talents in many different fields of study. She also studied and wrote in collaboration with men.

When the universities were established in cities in the mid-thirteenth century, women were excluded from them, and sex complementarity in scholarly research ceased. In addition, the fragmentation of the faculties and disciplines also occurred during this important period. The importance of establishing faculties and disciplines each with a proper set of methodologies and premises should not be underestimated. However, they also began to focus the contributions of individuals toward a single field or discipline. Furthermore, these developments had devastating effects on the concept of woman because women were excluded from professional training in these single fields or disciplines.

7. See, for example, Sr. Prudence Allen, R.S.M., "Fuller's *Synergetics* and Sex Complementarity," *International Philosophical Quarterly* 32, 1 (March 1992): 3-16, and "Metaphysics of Form, Matter, and Gender," *Lonergan Workshop* 12 (1996): 1-26.

8. Sr. Prudence Allen, R.S.M., "Integral Sex Complementarity and the Theology of Communion," *Communio: International Catholic Review* 17 (Winter 1990): 523-44, and "Rationality, Gender, and History," *American Catholic Philosophical Quarterly*, Proceedings of 1994 Annual Conference, 68 (1994): 271-88.

It is common knowledge that in contemporary interdisciplinary studies scholars are working toward building up new forms of complementarity among disciplines as well as among persons of different gender backgrounds; it may be of interest to the reader to see exactly how these divisions originally occurred and what impact they had on sex and gender identity.[9] In addition, it is important to realize that contemporary authors no longer can attempt, as did Hildegard and others, to write from the perspective of many different disciplines. It is for that reason that my own work in this text seeks only to offer an analysis of the philosophical aspects of the concept of woman. Others who are trained in the disciplines of history or theology, for example, are better suited to provide their complementary analyses. In this way, we can each do our part, in cooperation with others, to hopefully contribute something to the advancement of knowledge about the human condition, and particularly about women's identity in the world.

MINOR CHANGES IN THE SECOND EDITION

In conclusion, then, I hope that this second edition of *The Concept of Woman: The Aristotelian Revolution (750 BC–AD 1250)* will prove useful once again to scholars from different fields by providing a broad outline and description of the origin and development of the concept of woman in nearly all philosophers during the first two thousand years of western thought.

The sections on Islamic philosophy have been revised because of the important suggestions of Thérèse-Anne Druart, Faculty of Philosophy, Catholic University of America. In addition, factual, typographical, and interpretative errors in the original edition have now been corrected. Many suggestions for these changes were given to me by students and friends who carefully read the first edition. Those changes will further strengthen the original presentation. Comments in reviews by Linda Damico (*Hypatia)*, Mary Tiles (*Philosophy*), and Beatrice Zedler (*Speculum*) were also helpful in preparing this introduction to the second edition.[10]

In a special way I would like to acknowledge Michael Thompson, previously a philosophy student at Concordia University and presently at Eerdmans Publishing Company, whose initiative led to this 1997 printing of the text. Finally, I would like to thank graduate student research assistants Claudia Spencer, Sr. Mary Veronica Sabelli, R.S.M., and Mary Troxell for their help in the preparation of the updated bibliography. The updated bibliography is divided by chapter to provide easy access to further sources on each historical period. The sources have been limited to include those with direct relation to the philosophical study of the concept of woman in philosophers between 750 BC and AD 1250.

9. See, for example, Diane L. Fowlkes et al., eds., *Feminist Visions: Toward a Transformation of the Liberal Arts Curriculum* (University, Ala.: The University of Alabama Press, 1984); and Julie Klein, *Interdisciplinarity: History, Theory, and Practice* (Detroit: Wayne State University Press, 1990).

10. Linda Damico, *Hypatia: Journal of the Society for Women in Philosophy, American Philosophical Association* 4, 1 (Spring 1989): 171-75; Mary Tiles, *Philosophy: The Journal of the Royal Institute of Philosophy* 61, 237 (July 1986): 414-18; and Beatrice Zedler, *Speculum: A Journal of Medieval Studies* 62, 4 (October 1987): 898-900.

INTRODUCTION

What is to become of woman and man? Today, this question has assumed an urgency which must be met by a full and considered response. All too frequently those answering this question have given superficial and polemical analyses which seek to persuade more by emotion than by the slow and painful search for truth. My aim is to begin to remedy this situation.

Philosophy has a particular perspective to bring to the question of the identity of the sexes. Through the exercise of human reason and the observation of the senses, philosophy seeks to find and lay bare fundamental structures of thought, one kind of which can be referred to as a concept.[1] Consequently, the central concern of this book is to use philosophy to uncover the basic concept of woman in its relation to the concept of man as first articulated by the great thinkers of the west.

It is often incorrectly assumed that philosophers have concerned themselves with the intertwining concepts of woman and man only during the last two centuries. Certainly it is true that we have recently seen an explosion of interest in the subject. Careful research reveals, however, that nearly every single philosopher over the first two thousand years of western philosophy thought about the identity of woman in relation to man. This astonishing discovery means that the concept of woman has been a fundamental area of philosophical research since the sixth century BC.

When further reflection on the evolving history of philosophy reveals that a radical change in direction took place in the thirteenth century, the obvious questions that spring to mind are: Why? What happened around 1250 to bring about a new situation in which the concept of woman slipped out of its central position within general philosophical reflection? The answers to these questions are to be found in the history of the influence of Aristotle on the western mind and in western institutions. In this book I will show the specific way in which the "Aristotelian Revolution" worked its effects on the concept of woman.

Ordinarily, the word *revolution* implies the overthrow of one power structure by another. However, the Aristotelian Revolution is not an overthrow in this sense; it is more properly understood as the first takeover of the western mind by a single theory of the concept of woman. It is, therefore, a revolution in the sense that it created a definitive context within which the subsequent development of thought about woman and man took place. Articulating the truth about the identity and relations of the sexes today requires reference to this revolution in western thought.

In examining the structure of thought, philosophy seeks to gather information provided by a variety of fields of study. It searches for the common pattern in concepts used by different disciplines. Philosophy is perhaps uniquely capable of integrating and evaluating central concepts in human knowledge. Therefore, it can bring much insight to the question: What is to become of woman and man?

Today, several studies of an individual philosopher's thought about the concept of woman have emerged.[2] At the same time, there are also a large number of good anthologies that have begun to uncover the neglected historical sources for the study of sex identity.[3] Also, works that treat systematically of a specific theme in relation to sex identity are coming more and more in evidence.[4] What has not yet appeared, and what I am presenting in this book, is the first systematic study of the ways in which the concept of woman itself emerged, developed and influenced western philosophy. To set forth systematically the questions asked and the theories developed about this topic, is to establish the groundwork for a twentieth-century approach to the concept of woman within the broader field of philosophical anthropology.[5] The concept of woman in relation to the concept of man must be understood as a central concern of the philosophy of the person.[6]

Questions that the pre-Socratics asked about the concept of woman fall into four broad categories having to do with opposition, generation, wisdom, and virtue. The following four questions can be used to differentiate these categories:

1. In what way are woman and man opposite?
2. What were the respective functions of mothering and fathering in generation?
3. Do women and men relate to wisdom in the same or in different ways?
4. Do women and men have the same or different virtues?

Each question delineates a traditional area of thought that was developed in the fields of metaphysics, natural philosophy, epistemology, and moral philosophy. In fact, these four questions appear to establish a central philosophical framework for the concept of woman.[7]

If we accept as a starting point these very questions, we can construct a visual schema for the concept of woman that will enable us to make comparisons between different philosophers. The general schema looks as follows:

	Man	**Woman**
Generation		
Opposites		
Wisdom		
Virtue		

As far as we can tell from the fragments that remain, most pre-Socratics considered the concept of woman in one or two of the above categories. From the eighth to the mid-fifth centuries BC, we have no record of any systematic attempt to answer the questions across all four categories. The great contribution of the pre-Socratics was the original delineation of the categories themselves. The development of systematic theories about the respective identities of woman and man had to wait for later thinkers.

In western philosophy, after the original questions were asked, certain philosophers emerged as having developed a concept of woman in relation to man that covered all of the four categories of opposites, generation, wisdom, and virtue. In the present text, Plato, Aristotle, St. Augustine, Hildegard of Bingen, St. Albert the Great, and St. Thomas Aquinas fully articulated such a concept. As a result of the breadth and depth of their systematic thought, the philosophical analysis of the concept of woman moved in new directions. These philosophers, therefore, serve as turning points in the history of the concept of woman.

A study of these turning points reveals a limited number of alternative theories that emerged historically to explain the concept of woman in relation to the concept of man. Alternative theories about the identity and relation of the sexes revolve around the two traditional philosophical issues of equality and differentiation. The first issue concerns whether women and men are considered to be equal in human dignity and worth; the second issue concerns whether there are any philosophically significant differences between women and men. The different decisions that various theorists reached about these two issues lead to three basic theories of sex identity. I have named these theories *sex unity, sex polarity*, and *sex complementarity*. A short description of the three theories, with two derivative forms, is given below.

Sex Unity: This theory claims that women and men are equal, and that they are not significantly different. In contemporary discussion, it is often referred to as the "unisex" theory.

Sex Neutrality: This theory, a derivative form of sex unity, also assumes that women and men are equal and not significantly different. However, it differs from sex unity in that it ignores differences rather than arguing directly for the equality of women and men.

Sex Polarity: This theory claims both that women and men are significantly different and that men are superior to women.

Reverse Sex Polarity: This theory, a derivative of sex polarity that did not emerge until the sixteenth century, claims that women and men are significantly different and that women are superior to men.

Sex Complementarity: This theory claims that women and men are significantly different and that they are equal.

Using the two factors of differentiation and equality, the following chart reveals the basic structure of the above theories:

	Differentiation	Equality
Sex Unity		X
Sex Neutrality		X
Sex Polarity	X	
Reverse Sex Polarity	X	
Sex Complementarity	X	X

As can be seen from the above summary, the five different theories can be reduced to three basic types with a sex unity, sex polarity, or sex complementarity framework. It must be emphasized here that the delineation of these theories of sex identity ought to be interpreted as loose guidelines rather than rigid models of thought. By a careful examination of the arguments in the history of philosophy, certain patterns of thought about sex identity tend to emerge. These patterns, when examined through the two issues of equality and differentiation, reveal the structure of a theory. Since much of this structure repeats itself in contemporary debate, it is very important to recognize its first articulation even though it was at times vague and imprecise.

The historical repetition of structures of theories of sex identity is a crucial discovery for the systematic study of the concept of woman in relation to the concept of man. By studying these historical repetitions it is possible to uncover certain tendencies within philosophical anthropology that recur in a particular theory of sex identity. For example, it appears that there is a fundamental tendency within sex unity theories to devalue the materiality of the human person. This tendency to devalue the body is evident in Plato, as it is in a contemporary sex-unity theorist such as Shulamith Firestone.[8]

In sex-polarity theories we find the same kind of continuity of tendencies. In the earliest articulation of sex polarity, in Aristotle, one particular aspect of human materiality is selected as the key to all valuation of sex identity. This isolated aspect of the body is used as the fundamental philosophical basis for the evaluation of one sex as superior to the other. Aristotle chose the ability to concoct seed as the basis for a claim that man is fundamentally superior to woman. The most recent sex polarity theorists follow the same pattern of selection and inflation of the importance of a single material characteristic. The male sexual anatomy was chosen by Freud, the activity of the male sexual organ by Sartre, and the hormone testosterone was selected by Stephen Goldberg as the foundation for a claim that males are superior to females.[9] Reverse sex-polarity theorists follow the same pattern. The general material of a woman's body was chosen by Henrich Cornelius Agrippa, the female chromosomal structure by Ashley Montague and Valerie Solanis, and the capacity for giving birth was selected by Jill Johnson.[10]

Therefore, it can be stated as a general hypothesis that the tendency in sex-unity theories is to devalue the materiality of the person, while the tendency in sex-polarity theories is to give too much value to one particular aspect of the materiality of the person. Sex complementarity seems to avoid these two extremes in its earliest articulation, by Hildegard of Bingen, where considerable attention is given to an integration of human materiality in human identity. Hildegard avoids both of the extremes of the sex-unity and sex-polarity theories by insisting on the importance of human materiality while presenting a comprehensive view of the nature of this materiality.

The question naturally follows whether later sex-complementarity theorists achieved the same balance. One of the most striking facts in contemporary philosophical debate about sex identity is that there has been very little attempt to develop a systematic foundation for a theory of sex complementarity.[11] In a recent article entitled "Sex Unity, Polarity, or Complementarity," I have sought to begin this process in a context of contemporary debate among academic philosophers who are caught in a false polarization between sex polarity and sex unity, or among feminist philosophers caught between reverse sex polarity and sex unity.[12]

One of the goals of this book is to uncover the historical reasons for this deadlock between sex unity and sex polarity within philosophical debate. As will be seen, this development is due in part to the role of the philosophy of Aristotle in the development of the teaching of academic philosophy at the University of Paris, and of the subsequent infusion of Aristotelian thought throughout Europe.

At the same time as there has been little philosophical interest in establishing a secure foundation for a theory of sex complementarity, several theorists in disciplines other than philosophy have moved towards sex complementarity. Contemporary works by Carol Gilligan in psychology, Jean Bethke Elsthain in political science, and Jessie Bernard or Betty Friedan in sociology, all lean towards the fundamental principles of sex complementarity, that is, towards a belief in the equality of dignity and worth of women and men that at the same time recognizes significant differences between the two sexes.[13] If we can judge from these examples of sex complementarity outside the field of academic philosophy, a balanced view of the significance of materiality in the human situation is present in all of their work. Therefore, it is distinctly possible that the tendency towards a balanced integration of human materiality, which was first articulated in Hildegard of Bingen's philosophy of sex complementarity, would be repeated in a contemporary philosophy of sex complementarity.

It must be obvious by now that my own preference within the options of theories of sex identity is for a philosophy of sex complementarity. It seems to me to be the only theory that presents an integrated view of the place of materiality in human identity and for this reason it also seems to offer the greatest possibility for fertile and creative relations between women and men. I also believe that it is not a mere coincidence that this theory was first articulated by Christian philosphers. Sex complementarity is perfectly compatible with fundamental Christian theological beliefs in the creation and the resurrection of the body.[13]

The relation between philosophy and religion has always been complex. It is often difficult to differentiate philosophical from religious theory within the writings of a philosopher who is also a religious person. In the present text, while my personal religious perspective is Christian, I have tried to use the following criteria to decide which references to include from historical sources. Arguments defended by an appeal to faith, to the scriptures, or to religious authorities, such as the early Church Fathers, have generally been excluded. On the other hand, arguments that appeal to the evidence of the senses, the reason, or to ancient philosophical authorities have been included. Since one aim of the text is to demonstrate the way in which philosophical arguments have been used by non-philosophers to defend certain theories, there are times when the philosophical foundation of religious arguments is examined. In these cases, a reader might be misled into thinking that the argument itself is religious. Although the subject being considered might be religious, such as Mariology or the resurrection of the body, the arguments themselves are primarily philosophical.

It is important to mention that I have tried not to distort any philosopher's views to create a false defence of a philosophy of sex complementarity. The use of distortion is all too common among those writers who select certain passages to defend a position of sex polarity, reverse polarity or sex unity. I have sought throughout the study to present an integral and comprehensive view of the philosopher under consideration. By searching out every passage in a philosopher's written text(s), I tried to discover the totality of the person's theory even if it contained many unsolved ambiguities.

One interesting aspect of these early articulations of theories of sex identity is that several philosophers appear to have held more than one theory at the same time. Usually this double, or even triple theory of sex identity occurred when a philosopher failed to achieve a total integration of thought about the issue. Certainly it must be maintained that consistency about a theory of sex identity is a desirable goal for a philosopher. However, it may be that at times, tensions between more than one theory within a given thinker reveals progress in the philosophy precisely because it indicates a movement towards better direction on this issue.[15] In other words, consistency *per se* is not the ultimate value; a philosopher may be consistently wrong! Therefore, accepting the guidelines for a sex-unity, sex-polarity and sex-complementarity framework as loose, rather than rigid, allows us to begin to map the historical terrain of this area of philosophy without falling victim to creating "straw men" or "straw women." We are genuinely seeking to understand how some of the greatest philosophers have perceived the respective identities of woman and man.

The book is divided into five sections that follow the chronological development of the concept of woman in western thought. Each section considers the thought of individual philosophers divided by basic orientation or school. At the end of the section is a summary and evaluation that brings out the central philosophical issues that these philosophers have raised for the concept of woman.

The five sections of the book are divided as follows.

Chapter I, Precursors to Aristotle: This early phase of western thought reveals that four basic questions and three different theories of sex identity were proposed in primitive form by the philosophers of this era. At the end of this phase, Plato developed the first complete foundation for the theory of sex unity.

Chapter II, Aristotle: The next articulation of a philosophy of sex identity is found in Aristotle's systematic defence of sex polarity. In this theory metaphysical distinctions were applied to the process of generation. The conclusion that woman is opposite and inferior to man is seen to have consequences for wisdom and virtue.

Chapter III, The Adoption of Aristotelian and Platonic Concepts: In this phase, some basic ideas previously expressed in Greek thought began to extend their influence. Aristotle's and Plato's effect on Stoicism, early Jewish philosophy, neo-Platonism, and early Christian philosophy is examined in reference to the concept of woman. At the end of this period, sex unity, sex neutrality, sex polarity, and sex complementarity are seen as interwoven alternatives with no one theory predominating.

Chapter IV, The Adoption of the Aristotelian Arguments: This phase of the Aristotelian Revolution occurred when the details of Aristotle's arguments became available to the Latin west. Through translations and commentaries, Aristotle's thought was incorporated into Islamic, Jewish and Christian philosophy. At the end of this period, Hildegard of Bingen's attempt to develop a complete rationale for sex complementarity was overshadowed by St. Albert's and St. Thomas's defence of sex polarity in the Aristotelian tradition.

Chapter V, The Institutionalization of Aristotelianism: In this final phase of the revolution, Aristotle's thought was incorporated into the structure and content of the curriculum of the western university system. Through the adoption of Aristotle's works at the University of Paris and the simultaneous exclusion of women from this centre of higher education, sex complementarity lost any impetus it might have developed within the monastic educational setting. As a consequence of this revolution, Aristotle's rationale for sex polarity spread throughout Europe, while sex-neutrality theory became institutionalized through the use of Aristotelian logic in academic philosophy.

The selection of 1250 as a finishing date for this book on the concept of woman was made because Aristotle's writings became required reading at the University of Paris in 1255. Therefore, it signals a moment of institutional victory for the Aristotelian Revolution.

Finally, it may be useful to make a few remarks about the endeavour to engage in "conceptual history" or "the history of ideas." Today, historians are sensitive to the need to place the writings of a thinker in a specific historical and social context. Social history or cultural history is extremely important for trying to understand the way in which people thought about their lives and values. The history of mentalities searches for a wide variety of sources to reveal the thought and actions of the ordinary person within a social group. The particular approach used in this text in no way seeks to substitute itself for these broader studies. Instead, it attempts to extract the arguments and theories developed from philosophers through the ages precisely in order to see the similarities and differences in their structures. In taking this approach of systematically comparing concepts of woman across different cultures and through different time frames, it is possible to see the patterns of thought that appear to perpetuate themselves throughout western history. Therefore, the history of the concept of woman in relation to man will provide a useful index for cultural and social historians to use in their more detailed analyses of specific peoples.

By a careful examination of the way in which women and men have used their reason and the observations of their senses to uncover and articulate a theory of sex identity, I hope to re-establish within the heart of philosophical study the central questions about the concept of woman in relation to the concept of man. When this area of thought is again given the rightful place that it held from 750 BC to AD 1250, the field of philosophical endeavour that has been referred to simply as the Philosophy of Man will be opened up to reveal what it has included from its beginnings, namely, the Philosophy of Man and Woman.

I

PRECURSORS TO ARISTOTLE

Today there is a renewed interest in the insights generated by western philosophers who lived in Greece between 750–350 BC.[1] The cause for this renewal is the belief that these original thinkers of the west reflected on the nature of reality without interference of centuries of abstract ideas, which tend to block the immediacy of perceptions. Philosophy, from its beginnings, sought to make distinctions, to develop explanations, and to promote theories about the respective identities of women and men. From this discovery we can conclude that sex identity was a central area for reflection from the beginning of western philosophy.

The breadth and depth of the thinking about the concept of woman in relation to the concept of man raised by these western thinkers are impressive indeed. These philosophers struggled to understand whether male and female were opposite, whether the contribution of the mother and father to generation had consequences for sex identity, whether women and men were wise by knowing the same or different things, and whether women and men were virtuous by doing the same or different things.

The first western philosophers offered a variety of answers to these questions. For this reason it was not clear from the outset how the philosophy of woman and man would evolve. Just as in other areas of philosophical reflection, a variety of theories developed to explain the basic experience of sexual differentiation in the world. Sex unity, sex complementarity and sex polarity all vied for a central place. Within the movement to develop a consistent set of answers to the question of sex identity, Plato was the first philosopher to shift the balance; at the end of the period of Aristotle's precursors, sex unity emerged in a strengthened form.

In the following section, the specific ways in which the pre-Socratics thought about the concept of woman will be examined. Then, the careful attempt to develop a foundation for the theory of sex unity by Plato will be analysed. As will be seen, these early thinkers opened up the struggle for truth about woman and man that is still going on today.

THE PRE-SOCRATICS RAISE THE FUNDAMENTAL QUESTIONS

By developing the four categories of questions and naming them as opposites, generation, wisdom, and virtue, I have sought to underline the common ground of the questioning of the pre-Socratics as it relates specifically to sex identity. Before examining the specific way in which the respective philosophers wrote about this topic, a few words about the categories themselves are in order.

In What Way are Male and Female Opposite?

A fact immediately apparent about the human race is that it is divided into two sexes. While there are any number of races, religions, economic classes, and nationalities among human beings, there are only two sexes. Therefore, it is an important philosophical task to determine the precise way in which women and men divide human existence.

If two things are to be considered opposite, they must be members of the same group; woman and man are both human existents. More broadly, female and male are the categories that divide animals into the two sexes. Therefore, woman and man are the human example of the opposition of male and female common to all higher forms of animal life.

The earliest philosophers considered the nature of opposites within what is now considered to be the area of metaphysics. [2] In this context they examined the opposition of male and female. Beginning in approximately the fourteenth century, philosophers began to study the opposition of the masculine and feminine. Today, the subject is approached more in terms of the way in which woman and man are opposite as persons. This change and evolution of the way in which opposition has related to sex identity reflects a deeper change in the history of philosophical anthropology. At first, humanity was understood primarily as a higher form of animal life, later an emphasis was placed on individual and personality characteristics. In the twentieth century, this evolution has continued with a new focus on what it means to be a person.

Today, the question of how woman and man ought to relate to one another is being given a great deal of attention. Is woman opposite to man? If so, what might be the nature of this opposition? Is it a relation of hostility, of indifference, or of fulfillment? The reflections of the pre-Socratic philosophers on these important questions are a very important source for people who are struggling with the same issues today.

What Are the Respective Functions of Mothering and Fathering in Generation?

The earliest philosophers considered the ways in which the union of male and female generated a new being that is separate from them both. They recognized that this capacity for generating a separate entity made the opposition of male and female different from that of other opposites such as hot and cold, or day and night. The uniqueness of generation through the opposition of the male and female led the pre-Socratic philosophers to use this example to explain other kinds of creativity in the world. Their analysis focused on three different areas: cosmic generation, the generation of first parents, and continuity of generation.

When the early Greek philosophers reflected upon the cosmos they asked how it came to be ordered. Were there specific elements? Did these elements interact as male and female? Did cosmic generation reveal the superiority of any one of its elements or forces over another? Today, theorists are still concerned with the question of the nature of cosmic forces. Are they best described as neutral energies, or as being created by God as the Father of the universe, or as springing from a cosmic maternal source?

The second area of consideration, the generation of first parents, is also philosophically significant. How did woman and man come to be? Was there a basic equality in their evolution, or was one sex superior to the other from the first moment of their appearance in the world? The early Greek philosophers pondered these questions and offered some interesting answers.

The third area of questioning concerned the continuity of generation through the conception and birthing of children. Answers to these questions considered various options, such as reincarnation or different ways of mixing seeds. Some of these early thinkers (Empedocles or Hippocrates, for example) joined philosophy with the study of medicine; this brought a great deal of intensity to specific reflections on the process of generation and its relation to sex identity. Today, discussions about sex identity frequently refer to the reproductive capacities of woman and man. These contemporary studies in the philosophy of science focus on the interaction of genes, hormones, anatomy, and childhood experiences of sexual identification; many of the same kinds of questions originally posed by the pre-Socratics are still being considered. Some of the earliest philosophers proposed theories that would be considered correct by today's standards of empirical investigation.

Many theorists today question the role of generation in sex identity. How important is it, they ask. What consequence does the different relations that woman and man have to generation carry over into the broader issue of sex identity? There can be little disagreement that this issue is central to the concept of woman in relation to man.

Do Women and Men Relate to Wisdom in the Same Way?

The early Greek philosophers were fascinated with the activity of human thinking; they analysed its processes and consequences. Excellence in thinking was called wisdom. Philosophy derived its name from the Greek words *philo* and *sophia*; it was characterized from the beginning as love of wisdom, *philosophia*. Consequently, philosophers were known simply as "lovers of wisdom."

Within this context, wisdom was not equivalent to just any kind of knowledge, it was associated with the right kind of knowledge. The early philosophical poets emphasized knowledge of deities and of human character; then Greek philosophers suggested that wisdom consisted in knowledge of the natural world; and finally, other philosophers suggested that it consisted also in knowledge of mathematics and the foundation of moral values.

The study of early Greek thought reveals that several of these philosophers were women. Some famous male philosophers also had female teachers and disciples. It is not surprising then that the question was asked whether women and men had the same capacity for wisdom. Another question that is related to but different from the question of capacity for knowing concerns whether or not women and men were wise by knowing the same or different things. Once again, we find a variety of answers given by the pre-Socratics.

Today, serious consideration is being given to these very same questions. Do girls have different capacitites for learning than boys? Should girls and boys be taught exactly the same things? Companion to these questions is the issue of the place of women's studies within academic institutions. Sex-unity theories tend to argue that all education should be the same, without any differences justified by sex. Sex-polarity theorists argue that the sexes ought to be separated sometimes; they always believe that the knowledge or wisdom of the more highly valued sex is superior to the knowledge and wisdom of the less valued one. Sex-complementarity theorists usually try to find a combination of common- and sex-differentiated education. In the light of these developments, it is interesting to assess the particular insights of the earliest thinkers to consider the relation of thought, education, and sex identity.

The question of the relation of sex identity to thought falls under the area of philosophy that is now called *epistemology*. Within recent developments in this field, the use of the term *wisdom* has fallen off somewhat. However, philosophers such as Karl Jaspers have insisted on its centrality to the endeavour of philosophy.[3] Arguing that philosophers ought always to search for fundamental truths about the world, the search for wisdom necessarily involves considering What ought I to think about? and How ought I to think? In this context, then, the questions whether women or men have different capacities for thinking or different data in the search for wisdom are central to any philosophy of sex identity.

Do Women and Men Have the Same or Different Virtues?

The fourth important category of relation between woman and man follows from their identity as conscious human existents. In addition to the capacity for wisdom or excellence in thinking, consciousness also brings forth the possibility of action. Persons are capable of moving forward into the future through specific decisions and acts. Therefore, women and men not only think about their relation to the world, they can also seek to change the world.

Many of the pre-Socratic philosophers were deeply concerned about human action. They began to classify different kinds of action. Virtue—the practice of good acts—became distinguished from vice—the practice of bad acts. Since the identity of women and men had also been distinguished, it was natural to consider whether women or men had the same or different virtues.

The two key areas where thought about the relation of sex identity to virtue emerged were the following: 1) Are there separate spheres of virtuous activity for women and men? 2) Are men virtuous by ruling and women by obeying? Considerable amount of discussion today focuses on precisely these areas as delineated by the earliest western philosophers, namely, on the public-private distinction, and on the relation of sex identity to structures of power and authority within society. Therefore, it is useful to consider the specific ways in which the answers to these questions were framed from the outset.

This category of human identity, which I have called *virtue*, has also fallen into some lack of use by contemporary philosophers; in part, perhaps, because of its over-use in ancient and modern philosophy. However, philosophers such as Peter Geach are re-asserting the centrality of this subject for contemporary ethics by arguing that the question How ought I to act? is crucial for any formation of a philosophy of person, and that the practice of virtue is needed by women and men in order to achieve the fullness of their human identity.[4] Once again, it is valuable to understand the way in which the question of virtue specifically touched upon the struggle to understand the concept of woman in relation to the concept of man.

In this first part of the book on pre-Socratics we will now turn to a consideration of the specific way in which questions were originally raised about sex identity, and to the first attempts to articulate answers to these fundamental questions of sex identity.

THE PHILOSOPHER POETS

The earliest record of a western theory of sex identity is recorded by poets who wrote from inspiration rather than from the careful exercise of reason and observation of the senses. For this reason, these writers are not usually considered to be philosophers. However, since both Hesiod and Sappho do include some passages about the concept of woman in their writings, and since their work forms a kind of context of images of sex identity within which later philosophers emerged, and against which these latter philosophers asserted their own thought, it is important that they be included in this systematic study of the relation of the concept of woman to the concept of man.

Hesiod (c. 750 BC)

The Greek poets believed that their thoughts about the world sprang directly from the inspiration of the nine Muses. Hesiod describes the Muses' request that he write the *Theogony*:

> They breathed into me their divine voice, so that I might tell of things to come and things past, and ordered me to sing of the race of the blessed gods who live forever, and always to place the Muses themselves both at the beginning and at the end of my song.[5]

The Muses, who sprang from the union of Zeus (the head of the Olympian gods) and Mnemosyne (Memory), inspired Hesiod with several images with specific reference to sex identity. The images described cosmic generation, the relation of the gods and godesses, and the generation of the first human parents.

The first cosmic generator to be described was Mother Earth (Gaia): "First of all, the Void came into being, next broad-bosomed Earth, the solid and eternal home of all."[6] This cosmic female principle gave birth to a cosmic male principle called Sky (Uranos): "Earth first produced starry Sky, equal in size with herself, to cover her on all sides."[7]

The union of Earth and Sky, or the cosmic male and female principles, was described by Hesiod as full of hostility, intrigue and violence. After generating the mountains, the sea and several gods, excluding Zeus, Father Sky tried to halt the process of generation after the birth of Cyclopes and three monsters: "Their father hated them [the monsters] from the beginning. As each of them was about to be born, Sky would not let them reach the light of day."[8] Earth Mother then convinced her child Chronos (Time) to castrate his father:

> My children, you have a savage father; if you will listen to me, we may be able to take vengeance for his evil outrage; he was the one who started using violence.[9]

In this early description of the relation of cosmic generation to sex identity we find a vivid account of polarization and hostility between male and female. Mother Earth and

Father Sky are driven by a desire for revenge and struggle for power in specific relation to the children they have generated.

The description of the Earth Mother as the first generator in the *Theogony* supports the claim of some scholars that the most original divine image in the western Greek consciousness was a cosmic female principle.[10] The subsequent development of the genealogy of the gods in Hesiod's work then asserts an emergence of Zeus as the king of the Olympian deities.

> When the Olympian gods had brought their struggle to a successful end, . . . Mother Earth advised them to invite Zeus . . . to be king and lord over the gods.[11]

In Hesiod's description, the cosmic female principle, Mother Earth, freely passed her authority to the immortal male deity, Zeus.

Hesiod continues to describe a power struggle on the cosmic scale; Zeus swallows the pregnant goddess Metis because he was warned that her son would rise to overturn his own power. As a result of this act Zeus "gave birth" to the goddess Athene, the "bright-eyed Tritonian goddess, the equal of her father in power and prudent understanding."[12]

For philosophers, Athene holds a particular place of importance because she was known as "the goddess of wisdom" in early Greek consciousness. Along with the Muses, Athene served as a source of inspiration for those who thought about the nature of reality—until philosophers later discovered that they were capable of exercising their powers of reason and observation of the senses independently from divine inspiration. Athene also served as the goddess of the self-defence of Athens and was the spiritual centre of the construction of the Parthenon by Pericles in 447 BC, some three hundred years after Hesiod first described her origins. In the *Theogony*, Athene's relation to her father Zeus is described as follows:

> Zeus produced out of his own head the bright-eyed Tritonian goddess, the terrible queen who loves the clash of wars and battles, who stirs up the fury and leads the armies and never retreats.[13]

As a female goddess, Athene served Zeus as a wise judge and protector for his domain.

The polarization and hostility found in the relation of the cosmic principles Mother Earth and Father Sky is further repeated in the relation between Zeus and his wife, Hera. Hesiod reports that in reaction to Zeus's generation of Athene from his head, "Hera in turn, in resentment and jealousy, without union with her husband, produced famous Hephaestus, the master craftsman in the line descended from Father Sky."[14] In another description of the early Greek myths we find a more detailed account of the power struggle and ultimate victory of Zeus over Hera:

> A time came when Zeus's pride and petulance became so intolerable that Hera, Poseidon, Apollo, and all the other Olympians, except Hestia, surrounded him suddenly as he lay asleep on his couch and bound him with rawhide thongs, knotted into a hundred knots, so that he could not move. He threatened them with instant death, but they had placed his thunderbolt out of reach and laughed insultingly at him. . . . Briareus, . . . swiftly untied the thongs, using every hand

> at once, and released his master. Because it was Hera who had led the conspiracy against him, Zeus hung her up from the sky with a golden bracelet about either wrist and an anvil fastened to either ankle. The other deities were vexed beyond words, but dared attempt no rescue for all her piteous cries. In the end Zeus undertook to free her if they swore never more to rebel against him; and this each in turn grudgingly did.[15]

In this description, the triumph of Zeus over Hera through a hostile series of interactions gives a very dramatic negative image of the concept of woman in relation to the concept of man.

The gods of Greek consciousness were considered to be part of the universe, they were not outside of it or transcendent, as was the God of Hebrew consciousness. The Greek gods were simply a higher form of human life with greater powers and immortality. For this reason, Hesiod's description of the relation between the sexes in the Olympian deities serves as a reflection of images of man and woman that were undoubtedly present in Greece at the time. Hesiod appears to be describing an attitude of sex polarity in which the sexes were differentiated and, on the first cosmic level, the female was superior to the male, much as Mother Earth was superior to Father Sky; while on the second cosmic level, the male was superior to the female, that is, Zeus was superior to Hera.

In Hesiod's description of the first parents or the generation of the first man and woman we find a reinforcement of the second pattern of images. Prometheus, the friend of man, born from the union of Iapetus and Clymene, had tremendous personal courage and cunning; he risked everything to steal fire from the gods:

> He stole the radiant light of all-consuming fire in a hollow stalk. This bit deeper into the heart of Zeus the thunder-god: he was enraged when he saw mankind enjoying the radiant light of fire. In return for the theft of fire he instantly produced a curse to plague mankind. At the orders of the son of Cronus, the famous lame smith-god (Hephaestus) shaped some clay in the image of a tender girl. The bright-eyed Athene dressed and decked her in silvery clothes. . . . When Zeus had completed this beautiful curse to go with the blessing of fire, he displayed the girl in an assembly of gods and men. . . . This was the origin of the damnable race of women—a plague which men must live with. . . . Zeus the thunder-god made women mischievous in their ways and a curse for men: he dispensed a curse to go with the blessing.[16]

Woman is described in her origin as a punishment for man. This clearly negative valuation of the generation of the first female parent in the *Theogony* is repeated in Hesiod's *Works and Days*, this woman is named Pandora:

> (Zeus) planned sorrow and mischief against men. . . . He bade Hephaestus make haste and mix earth and water and to put in it the voice and strength of human kind, and fashion a sweet, lovely maiden-shape. . . . And he charged Hermes . . . to put in her a shameless mind and a deceitful nature. . . . And he called this woman Pandora.[17]

The characterization of Pandora as shameless and deceitful is carried forward in *Works and Days* to include the image of this first woman as responsible for evil in the world.

> For ere this the tribes of men lived on earth free from ills and hard toil and heavy sicknesses which bring the Fates upon men. . . . But the woman took off the lid of the jar with her hands and scattered all these and her thought causes sorrow and mischief to men.[18]

This view of woman as a deceiver and the cause of sorrow in the world is restated by Hesiod in a later epigram in the same work: "The man who trusts womankind trusts deceivers."[19] This general thesis about woman's nature even extends to taboos about bathing in water a woman has previously used: "A man should not clean his body with water in which a woman has washed, for there is bitter mischief in that also for a time."[20]

Hesiod's images of the sexes as hostile to one another and his recurrent negative valuation of the female sex in relation to the male sex are most likely simply reporting general images of sex identity present in the Greek culture at the time. However, in another work entitled *Catalogues of Women and Eoiae*, Hesiod traces the geneology and "life stories" of the gods and goddesses.[21] There appears to be no particular valuation of one sex as superior to the other in that collection of myths. Both male and female deities involve themselves in constant intrigue and the struggle for power.

Hesiod is important to this study because he presents a context of images and an example of the poetic thought over and against which the first philosophers began to assert their own thinking. The philosophers sought to free their thought from the control of outside forces such as Muses or deities. They also appeared to struggle against the sex-polarity valuation of the female as inferior to the male, which is so common to the images Hesiod presented. In this way, the early Greek philosophers sought to establish a new ground for a philosophy of sex identity.

Sappho (born c. 612 BC)

It is interesting to compare the poetic images of Hesiod with a female poet of the same early period in Greek consciousness. Like Hesiod, Sappho understood her thought to be the direct result of the influence of the Muses:

> I tell you, they have been generous with me, the violet-weaving Muses.
>
> And they made me famous by the gift of their own work.
>
> Yes they gave me true success the golden Muses.
>
> And once dead I shall not be forgotten.[22]

Sappho is thought to have written nine books of poems, although the first written record of her work is not dated until approximately the third century BC, nearly a hundred years after she lived. Fortunately, the recent discovery of several fragments of her poems in the *Oxyrhynchus Paphri* (1897–1906) makes it possible to uncover some of her images of woman and man.[23]

While Sappho wrote many poems to the deities, the most interesting aspect of her work for philosophers is contained in her descriptions of the priority of desires over reason in human interaction. In one fragment Sappho writes: "Aphrodite's words were

'Eros my slave and of course you too Sappho.' "[24] Sappho's constantly recurring image was of a woman driven for union with someone she loved. In this theme, she represents a radically different mode of interaction than we found in Hesiod's image of the hostility and struggle for power.

Sappho uses Helen of Troy as an example of the irresistible power of human desires that would lead a person to forsake husband, parents and even children in order to fulfill a desire for a union with the beloved:

A cavalry corps, a column of men,
A flotilla in line, is the finest thing
In this rich world to see—for some . . . but for me
It's the person you love.

There's nothing more easy to prove than this:
Helen whose beauty far outshone
The rest of man's chose to desert
The best of men:

Willingly sailed away to Troy;
Thought nothing of child and nothing of fond
Parents, but was herself led astray
By a love far away;

(For woman is always easy to bend
The moment she's bent on her heart's desire).
Now Anactoria's in my mind,
Far from us here.

The way she walks, her loveable style,
The vivid movement of her face—
I'd rather see than Lydian horse
And glitter of mail.[25]

In this poem, Sappho asserts the priority of desire for union with the beloved over reason and duty. She describes this situation first in the love of a woman for a man, and secondly in the love of a woman for a woman. Nearly all of the extant poems of Sappho reflect one woman's experience of love, and a great many of her poems focus specifically on the love and friendship between women. At the same time, Sappho nowhere suggests that only women allow their desires to overcome their reason. She does not polarize the sexes in her descriptions by the implication that women are driven by their love attachments, while men are under the more restrained guidance of reason. Instead, it seems that Sappho, while giving voice to women's experience of love, nonetheless spoke of a great tendency in both women and men to follow the intense desires of love for union with the beloved.

At the same time, Sappho did not always view the total submission to the desires of the heart as a good choice for humanity. In addition to her hint that Helen was "led astray," Sappho says in another poem that too much intensity of desire can interfere with her capacity to create poems:

I cannot write
Heart, be still!
No jet of spellbound song, no Adonis-hymn
streams from you beautifully,
to please the goddesses:
Desire the disconcerter,
Aphrodite the dictator of hearts, has made you dumb;
and Peitho the enticer from her flagon of gold
has flooded your thinking soul with nectar.[26]

As a disciplined poet, Sappho had to integrate her reason and passions in order to achieve the goal of a perfectly constructed poem. At the same time, however, Sappho does accentuate the importance of the emotional intensity of love for a particular person. In the subsequent development of philosophy, this choice will be systematically criticized in the assertion of the importance of reason in human identity.

Philosophers' discovery of reason and the independent powers of the mind usurped the intellectual priority previously given to the poets in western thought and led to a new situation where human identity was praised for its capacity to think about the world independently from the external tyranny of the gods or the Muses, or the internal tyranny of the passions.

THE MILESIANS

The first Greek philosophers sought natural explanations for the changes they saw in the world. Significantly, from the beginning, these philosophers of nature reflected on the concept of woman in relation to the concept of man.

Anaximander (c. 540 BC)

The first written record we have of a specific reflection about sex identity is found in the writings of Anaximander, a student of Thales, the first philosopher of the west. Anaximander interpreted the origin of the world as a process in which the opposites hot and cold broke off from a vast undifferentiated mass called "the unlimited." Next came a second pair of opposites, wet and dry.

Everything in the world was subsequently explained through the interaction of the two pairs of opposites, hot and cold, and wet and dry.[27] In this way cosmology, which had previously been explained by myths, was de-sexualized and described as the interaction between natural opposites.

Anaximander described the origin of the planets, the earth and then animal life in terms of the interplay of opposites. "All living creatures arose from the moist element as it was evaporated from the sun."[28] In the significant passage for the philosophy of sex identity, Anaximander describes the first appearance of women and men:

> In these [fishes or fish-like animals] men were formed and kept within as fetuses until maturity; then at last the creatures burst open, and out came men and women who were able to feed themselves.[29]

Anaximander's naturalistic explanation posited an origin of equality and differentiation of the sexes. There is none of the valuation of one sex as superior or prior in origin to the other, as we saw in Hesiod's description of myths about the origin of humanity. Instead, Anaximander simply states that women and men appeared in the world at the same time and in the same way. However, he also notes that there is a difference between the sexes when he specificially mentions that both men and women appeared in this way.

Anaximander's use of the fish-like creatures was not meant to imply that men and women evolved from fish, or from a lower kind of animal existence; rather, he thought that the first human beings needed some kind of protection in order to be able to develop to maturity. Once women and men were in the world to protect their own infants, generation continued in the normal way.

Unfortunately, we have no further record of reflection on sex identity by this important philosopher. However, even in the pure simplicity of the single fragment recorded above, it is clear that this philosopher sought to explain the generation of women and men from a foundation of natural equality.

Heraclitus (c. 540–480 BC)

A description of the origin of human life in terms of the interaction of natural elements was continued by the philosopher Heraclitus. He understood that all things came from the primary element, fire; so the body evolved when fire moved towards moisture, and the soul when the movement changed back towards fire.[30]

For Heraclitus, the world was a dynamic cosmos of creative tension between opposites. He was particularly fascinated by the way in which opposites combined to create a third entity that was separate from the two original opposites. In one passage in *De Mundo*, Aristotle describes Heraclitus's view as follows:

> Perhaps Nature has a liking for opposites and produces concord out of them and not out of similars, just as for instance she brings male together with female and not with members of the same sex. . . . It was this same thing which was said in Heraclitus the Obscure.[31]

In this analysis, male and female are added to the more fundamental parts of opposites, the hot and cold, and dry and wet. In another passage where he reflects on the creative nature of opposition, Heraclitus suggests that the tension between wooden frame and string that in the bow gives flight to the arrow, is similar to the tension between the wood frame and strings that produces music on the lyre. "The harmony of the world is a harmony of oppositions, as in the case of the bow and lyre."[32]

The specific recognition that male and female are a fundamental category of opposition in the world appears to have been first expressed by Heraclitus. The opposition is described as a creative tension between two different but equal things. There is no indication, for example, that the wood frame is superior or inferior to the strings, although Heraclitus does give preference to the nature of the hot and dry over that of the cold and moist through the priority he holds for the element fire.

In another passage included in Aristotle's *Eudemian Ethics*, Heraclitus is again cited for recognizing the fundamental opposition of male and female:

> Heraclitus blamed the poet who said: "Would that strife were destroyed from among gods and men." For there would be no harmony without sharps and flats, no living beings without male and female, which are contraries.[33]

This insight of Heraclitus refers especially to the fundamental need for some kind of opposition in order for creativity to occur. Recognizing that new life depends upon the differentiation of male and female, Heraclitus interpreted the universe at large as needing a similar kind of dynamic between opposites. Heraclitus did not leave behind enough writings to enable us to go further in our understanding of the specific way in which male and female are opposite. For example, the Greek word used in the above quotation about male and female as contraries is *enantion*. This word contains within it two different meanings of contrary: 1) it can imply the hostility of two soldiers facing one another in battle; or 2) it can imply the openness of two persons simply standing face to face. Within this double meaning of *enantion* we already find the tension between sex polarity and sex complementarity in the basic question of how women and men are opposites.

Heraclitus's use of the opposition of male and female seems to refer primarily to the biological interrelation of the sexes. Two males or two females are not able to produce new life, just as the strings by themselves or frames by themselves would not be able to produce music or launch an arrow. The analogy of male and female with the harmony of sharps and flats simply carries forward the fundamental thought that tension between opposites is creative, while lack of tension is sterile. As with Anaximander, there is no reference in Heraclitus to a superior valuation of one of the pair of opposites over the other. Male and female appear to be equal in the relationship.

THE PYTHAGOREANS (c. 530 BC)

The collection of philosophers called the Pythagoreans belonged to a religious sect founded by Pythagoras in the mid-sixth century BC. Pythagoras left no writings; therefore his philosophical views about sex identity have to be gleaned from what others have reported about his teachings. Since most of the information about Pythagoras was written several hundred years after his death, it is difficult to assess its accuracy. From the evidence preserved, however, it appears that Pythagoras (or the Pythagoreans) held a combination of theories about the concept of woman in relation to man that contained elements of sex polarity, sex unity, and sex complementarity. Since it is impossible to know whether these discrepancies came from the many different sources that reported Pythagoras's thought or from his own thinking, we will consider the fragments about sex identity simply as Pythagorean in origin. In the analysis we will study fragments that fall into the four categories of opposites, generation, wisdom, and virtue.

In the *Metaphysics*, Aristotle recorded a table of opposites attributed to the Pythagoreans:

limit and absence of limit	odd and even
one and many	right and left
male and female	rest and motion

straight and curved	light and dark
good and bad	square and oblong[34]

The primary Pythagorean pair of opposites was limit and absence of limit. The previously mentioned natural opposites of hot and cold, and wet and dry, are not even present in the above table. Pythagoras chose a mathematical, rather than a natural model to interpret the world. The two primary opposites of limit and absence of limit formed the basis for an ordered distribution of points in space, which in turn generated material bodies. The number 10, as a basis for the determination of the precise number of fundamental opposites in the table above, probably evolved because the Pythagoreans believed that 10 was the perfect number since ten points arranged in space, in ascending order, formed a triangle.[35]

The Pythagorean Table of Opposites is extremely important for the concept of woman in relation to man. First, male and female are included as a primary category of opposites in the centre of the table. Second, the first member of the pair of opposites is given a superior valuation over the second member. In this way, the male became associated with limit, odd, one, right, rest, straight, light, good, and square; while the female became associated with absence of limit, even, left, many, motion, curved, dark, bad, and oblong. In the *Nicomachean Ethics*, Aristotle explicitly approved the Pythagorean association of the one with the "column of goods" and of evil with the "class of the unlimited."[36]

The Pythagoreans have left no further records interpreting the relation of sex identity to the Table of Opposites. As will be seen, however, subsequent philosophers explicitly developed various associations of the pairs of opposites with male and female identity. The male association with right and the female with left is mentioned in Parmenides, Anaxagoras, Hippocrates, Galen, Pliny, Maimonides, and Giles of Rome in specific reference to the formation of the sex of the fetus. The association of male with light and good, and the female with dark and bad, lurks more in the background of poetic images of sex identity than directly in philosophical theories of the concept of woman in relation to the concept of man. At the same time, however, it must be recognized that the Pythagorean Table of Opposites explicitly presents a metaphysical basis for the theory of sex polarity; here, the male and female are viewed as significantly different and the male is valued as superior to the female.

Pythagoras's explanation for generation appealed to a theory of transmigration of soul, or reincarnation. According to Diogenes Laertius, Pythagoras was the first western philosopher to mention the theory of reincarnation:

> He was the first, they say, to declare that the soul, bound now in this creature, now in that, thus goes on a round ordained of necessity.[37]

While there is no explicit reference in Pythagorean writings to the generation of woman or man through reincarnation, the implicit consequence of such a theory is that the same soul could at one time be born in a male body and at another time in a female body.

The key to Pythagorean theory is the superiority of reason in human nature: "Reason is immortal, all else is mortal."[38] Reason has no sexual identity, therefore the immortal part of human identity is free from a direct association with male or female identity. This view of human nature implies a theory of sex unity because the differences between men and women have a minimum significance for personal identity.

Within this context, then, it is not surprising to discover that "Pythagoras addressed himself to women as well as to men, and women were from the first admitted to the School." [39] Historical records suggest that there were several women among the early Pythagoreans:

> Iamblicus, in his *Life of Pythagoras*, after having cited one hundred-and-eighteen Pythagoreans, left us the names of sixteen women, who were, he added, the most illustrious of those who counted among the happy number of disciples of the wise man Pythagoras. [40]

Indeed, it is perfectly consistent with a theory of human identity that places a primary importance on a sexless soul identified with the highest function of reason, that women as well as men would be called to the study of philosophy. Pythagoras is considered to be the first to officially call himself a philosopher, or a lover of wisdom; women and men who followed his teachings were seeking to becomes lovers of wisdom by developing their capacity for reason. [41]

Evidence suggests that even though Pythagoras believed that women and men were equally capable of philosophy, they did not study philosophy together.

> Pythagoras, when he disembarked in Italy and reached Croton, . . . so moved the magistry of elders that they bade him pronounce an exhortation suitable to that age to the young men, and then to all the boys assembled from their schools. Then an assembly of women was arranged for him. [42]

If this report of Pythagoras's teaching is an accurate indication of his practice, then it could be said that he developed a practice of separate schools for women and men. In this way, he would apply his basic philosophical theories to the different situations of women and men within society at the time. This practice would imply a kind of sex complementarity in which differentiation by sex would be considered an important aspect of the search for wisdom while men and women were challenged equally to seek wisdom.

Apparently Pythagoras was very successful as a teacher of women:

> As a result of these meetings his reputatiuon rapidly grew, and he gained many disciples, men and women as well—the name of one of the women, Theano, has come down to us. [43]

Diogenes Laertius gave the following information about Theano:

> Pythagoras had a wife, Theano by name, daughter of Brontinus of Croton, though some call her Brontinus's wife and Pythagoras's pupil. [44]

The Theano referred to above, who was either Pythagoras's wife or student, must be distinguished from a later philosopher within the new-Pythagorean Hellenic school of the third century BC who wrote under the name Theano. The female Pythagorean philosophers—Perictione, Melissa, Phyntis and Aescara—who also fall into this later development of Pythagorean thought, left several fragments of their writing, which will be studied later in this text.[45] The presence of female philosophers in the Pythagorean school is a logical consequence of Pythagoras's high priority for the search for wisdom by both women and men. It also follows from his basic understanding that the primary seat of human identity is in the highest part of the soul or immortal reason. In this way, the early philosophers rejected Sappho's poetic affirmation of the priority of desire over reason.

It should also be mentioned that Pythagoras is reputed to have been taught by a woman: "Aristoxenes says that Pythagoras got most of his moral doctrines from the Delphic priestess Themistocles."[46] It is important to note here that a priestess does not teach in the same way as a philosopher. The priestess teaches by way of inspiration, much as a poet does. She does not develop reasons or propose arguments in defence of her views, but rather a priestess offers pronouncements that gain validity as having come to her directly from the gods. Therefore, even though Pythagoras may have sought counsel from Themistocles, it cannot be concluded from this that he was taught by a female philosopher.

Pythagoras was the first philosopher to emphasize the importance of virtue in human life. He said, "The most momentous thing in human life is the art of winning the soul to good or evil."[47] The ultimate moral value was harmony in the soul and in society. Following from this fundamental precept, Pythagoras argued that both women and men ought to be chaste and monogamous.[48] In this way, the lower passions of the soul came under the direction and control of reason.

Pythagoras believed that women and men who lived in this virtuous way were capable of friendship: "Pythagoras taught very clearly friendship towards all by all . . . of a man towards his wife."[49] The elevation of the role of reason in the identity of both women and men brought about a fundamental relationship of harmony rather than one of hostility or strife.

Pythagoras argued that harmony between men and women demanded the obedience of the female to the rule of the male. "He taught the women . . . to be obedient to their husbands."[50] Further, in discussing obedience:

> He urged them to consider that this virtue alone can and should be striven after by boys as well as girls, by married women and by elderly persons.[51]

The specific obedience of wives to husbands was described as absolute virtue:

> It was therefore right either not to oppose their husbands at all, or to consider that they would achieve a victory if they gave in to their husbands.[52]

Therefore, Pythagoras taught that women and men had a different specific virtue; man's virtue was to rule while woman's virtue was to obey. This view of separate virtues for men and women, when coupled with the claim that it is a superior function of reason to rule rather than to obey, is consistent with sex polarity.

In summary, if the reported theories attributed to Pythagoras and the Pythagoreans are correct, then this school of philosophy gave a great deal of consideration to the concept of woman in relation to man. At the same time, there also appears to be a variety of responses that indicate different kinds of theories of sex identity. If we summarized these views, using the structured concept of woman in relation to man that was proposed in the introduction, the following schema would emerge:

	Man	Woman
Opposites Sex polarity	limit, odd, one, right, male, rest, straight, light, good, square	no limit, even, many, left, female, motion, curved, dark, bad, oblong
Generation Sex unity	*Same by reincarnation*	
Wisdom Sex complementarity	Different learning context	Different learning context
	Same by exercise of highest reason	
Virtue Sex polarity and sex unity	By ruling	By obeying
	Same by harmony and chastity	

It is possible to suggest an explanation for this variety of Pythagorean theories of sex identity. Sex polarity appears to arise when the Pythagoreans are considering the concept of woman in relation to man from the perspective of the body, or human materiality. In the category of opposites, male and female occur as one way of dividing animality, or material existence, which is a principle of nature extending beyond women and men into all animal life. In the category of virtue, the Pythagoreans are focusing on human action that involves human materiality as well. So the emphasis on materiality leads to sex polarity in both the categories of opposites and virtue. In generation, on the other hand, only the highest level of reason is being described as capable of reincarnation in either the male or female body. Therefore, when human identity is considered from the perspective of reincarnation, sex is a relatively unimportant aspect of the identity. Here, sex unity arises when the material aspect of human identity is de-emphasized. Finally, wisdom demands the exercise of the reason through the study of mathematics and the study of general principles of thought. The search for wisdom is equally possible for women and men. At the same time, however, given their different incarnational states as male and female, education is separated to allow for the specific application of the principles of wisdom to the situation of women or of men. In this way, the equality, derived from the common presence of reason, is modified through a differentiation of the sexes in the learning process itself. So the category of wisdom leads to the basic principles of sex complementarity; there is equality and differentiation.

In conclusion, it is important to emphasize that the above analysis is drawn completely from a reconstruction of the Pythagorean theory. Because Pythagoras left no fragments of his own writings, it is not possible to verify the accuracy of statements attributed to him, statements that may have been distorted by those who wrote them down. At the same time, however, there does seem to be strong evidence suggesting that Pythagoras and the Pythagoreans gave serious consideration to the concept of woman in relation to man. By the inclusion of female philosophers in this process, the Pythagorean school represents a fundamental opening in the history of the west to the cooperative search for truth about sex identity by both men and women. For this reason, Pythagoreanism marks a significant increase in the intensity of western philosophy in its search for the truth about the concept of woman in relation to man.

PARMENIDES (c. 539–500 BC)

The next central question to be raised about the concept of woman concerned whether opposites were merely appearances. Parmenides, in suggesting that all opposites were appearances, relegated the differentiation of male and female to false opinion. Consequently, sexual differentiation had no significance for philosophical truth.

Parmenides left a complete work, entitled *On Nature*, which was divided into three parts—Prologue, Way of Truth, and Way of Opinion. In the Prologue, we are introduced to a goddess (Thea) who calls on Parmenides to learn how to exercise his reason by following her example:

> Young man . . . Welcome! . . . Thou shalt inquire into everything: both the motionless heart of well-rounded truth, and also the opinion of mortals, in which there is no true reliability. But nevertheless thou shalt learn these (opinions) also—how one should go through all the things-that-seem, without exception, and test them.[53]

This description of a female deity who teaches through the specific use of her reason is the first example in western writing of a female philosopher on the cosmic level. We have a further development of the same image of a female philosopher later in Socrates' description of Diotima in the *Symposium*, and in Boethius's description of the Lady Philosopher in *The Consolation of Philosophy*. In these texts, the imagined female philosopher is differentiated from a priestess or poet because she teaches by way of arguments or the free exercise of discursive reason rather than through simple pronouncements. This association of the cosmic feminine with the wisdom of discursive reasoning is an important addition to the history of the concept of woman.

Thea leads Parmenides first through a Way of Truth in which she claims that the world contains no divisions: "Nor is Being divisible, since it is all alike."[54] The practice of dividing reality into opposites is simply a false way of naming an indivisible truth. "Therefore all things that mortals have established, believing in their truth, are just a name: Becoming and Perishing, Being and Not-Being."[55] The implication of this Way of Truth for the concept of woman in relation to man is that a stated difference between male and female is simply an example of one of these false names.

The development of the Way of Opinion supports this implication, for here the goddess Thea describes sexual differences. There is considerable controversy about why Parmenides bothered to write out a Way of Opinion when Thea implies that it is full of deception:

> At this point I cease my reliable theory (Logos) and thought, concerning Truth; from here onwards you must learn the opinion of mortals, listening to the deceptive order of my words.[56]

Some critics think that Parmenides believed that the Way of Opinion brought partial truth through the use of his senses, while others claim that he rejected it as totally false.[57] The views Parmenides presents in the Way of Opinion were found among various philosophers familiar to him.

As soon as the philosopher examined appearances, distinctions between opposites emerged:

> For the narrower rings were filled with unmixed Fire, and those next to them with Night, but between (these) rushes the portion of Flame. And in the centre of these is the goddess who guides everything; for throughout she rules over cruel Birth and Mating, sending the female to mate with the male, and conversely again the male with the female.[58]

The goddess in the above passage, who rules over the sexual union of male and female, is not Thea the philosopher, but rather a lower force of erotic love, or a daimon. Thea represents the higher functions of reason, while daimon represents the lower sexual drives.

Parmenides gives a further description of the "cruel process of birth and mating." Both the mother and the father provide seed during sexual intercourse. This early statement of a double-seed theory is combined with an adaptation of the Pythagorean Table of Opposites, in which Parmenides reports the opinion that the placement of the fetus in the uterus determines the sex of the child: "On the right, boys, on the left, girls."[59] The view that the sex of males has something to do with the right and of females with the left was not that of Parmenides himself, but was probably believed by some philosophers and physicians who were seeking to explain sex determination at the time.[60]

In the following passage, the mixing of seeds in mother and father is described:

> When a woman and a man mix the seeds of Love together, the power (of the seeds) which shapes (the embryo) in the veins out of different blood can mould well-constituted bodies only if it preserves proportion. For if the powers war (with each other) when the seed is mixed, and do not make a unity in the body formed by the mixture, they will terribly harass the growing (embryo) through the two-fold seed of the (two) sexes.[61]

This passage is perplexing because the nature of the "harassed embryo" is not clear. While some commentators have suggested that the embryo might be a hermaphrodite, or a person with a homosexual orientation, the most common interpretation is that it refers to a child of one sex who resembles in some way the parent of the opposite sex.[62] If this interpretation is a correct account of Thea's arguments about the roots of sexual identity in the Way of Opinion, we can construct the following diagram to indicate the various alternatives generated through sexual union.

		Testicles (male seed)	
		right	**left**
Uterus (female seed and place)	**right**	boy resembling father	boy resembling mother
	left	girl resembling father	girl resembling mother

In this case, the right-right combination and the left-left combination will be examples of unity in the combination of double seed, while the right-left combinations would be disharmonious.

As stated at the outset of this discussion of Parmenides, it is difficult to assess the statements he presented through the goddess Thea concerning the Way of Opinion. These views, if taken at face value, imply an equality and differentiation of male and female. Both sexes provide seed to generation; both sexes are equally involved in the mating of male with female and female with male. Therefore, the face value of the pronouncements of the Way of Opinion indicates a kind of sex complementarity.

It appears much more likely, however, that Parmenides rejected the philosophical significance of any differentiation between male and female. By emphasizing only the undifferentiated One, he appears to be moving towards and even beyond a sex-unity theory. That is, for Parmenides, the pure use of reason would not discover any differentiation between women and men, or indeed any differentiation between everything that exists in the world. Opposites were simply appearances, and named differences between women and men are simply false. By taking this approach to questions of sex identity, Parmenides stood out against a period of intense intellectual activity that continued to press further towards an understanding of how the concept of woman related to the concept of man.

THE PLURALISTS

In contrast to the previously mentioned Greek philosophers who attempted to give a natural explanation of the world by appealing to the interaction of opposites, several other early philosophers believed that the most fundamental categories of reality were seeds, atoms, or elements. These thinkers, loosely referred to as Pluralists, viewed opposites as secondary to a more basic category of material existence. The concept of woman in relation to man continued to receive attention within this new metaphysical approach to the world.

Anaxagoras (500–428 BC)

This philosopher of nature was imprisoned for stating that the sun was not a god but a stone.[63] Anaxagoras, an astronomer who wrote *On Natural Science*, envisaged the world as composed of millions of tiny seeds that combined to form everything that exists. "There was a great quantity of earth in the mixture, and seeds infinite in number, not at all like one another."[64] The organizing principle that gathered the seeds into material objects was called Mind. Anaxagoras described Mind as being totally immaterial: "Other things all contain a part of everything, but Mind is infinite and self-ruling, and is mixed with no Thing, but is alone by itself."[65]

The generation of the first parents was given a purely naturalistic explanation. Mind gathered some seeds together to generate the first women and men, after which human beings continued to generate through sexual intercourse:

> The living beings . . . to originate (first) out of moist and warm and earth-like (substances), but later one from another.[66]

Anaxagoras did not explicitly mention men and women as had Anaximander in his description of the generation of first parents. However, there is no implication that men were generated before women. The phrase "living beings" appears to implicitly include women and men in simultaneous generation.

In Anaxagoras's description of the continuity of generation, however, Aristotle records a shift from theories that had previously attributed seed to both sexes. Aristotle states in the *Generation of Animals* that instead, Anaxagoras argued that only the male sex produced seed:

> It is a moot question whether or not the sex of an animal is determined before it can be clearly distinguished by observation—that is, whether sex is differentiated in the mother's womb, or before. For example, Anaxagoras and some other natural philosophers hold that sex is already determined in the sperm. They say that while the father provides the seed, the mother only provides a place for the fetus to develop; that male offspring come from the right testis and female from the left; and that furthermore, male offspring develop in the right side of the womb, females in the left.[67]

If this theory of sex determination is summarized, using a chart similar to the one used for Parmenides, it would appear as follows:

		Testicles (male seed)	
		right	**left**
Uterus (place only)	**right**	boy	X
	left	X	girl

Aristotle's claim that Anaxagoras believed that only males produced seed is contested by other philosophers. For example, Censorius records that although Anaxagoras held that male seed determined the sex of the child, female seed contributed to the physical appearance of the offspring:

> Anaxagoras and Empedocles argue that males are born from semen emitted from the right testicle, and that females are born from semen emitted from the left. Their opinions, although they coincide here, diverge in regard to the resemblance of children to their parents. . . . Anaxagoras thinks that children resemble that parent who has contributed the most seed.[68]

The description of this interpretation of Anaxagoras is summarized as follows:

		Testicles (male seed) right	Testicles (male seed) left
Uterus (place and seed)	right	boy	girl
	left	boy	girl

If the mother contributes more seed, then the boy or girl would look more like her; if the father contributes more seed then the boy or girl would look more like him.

In still another description of Anaxagoras's theory, Plutarch records a different view:

> How are male and female progeny formed? . . . Anaxagoras and Parmenides say that when the ejaculation from the right testis falls into the right side of the womb males are formed, and similarly for the left. If, however, the paths are crossed a female results.[69]

Plutarch's interpretation of Anaxagoras is summarized as follows:

		Testicles (male seed) right	Testicles (male seed) left
Uterus (place and seed)	right	boy	girl
	left	girl	boy

This view interprets the "crossing of seeds" as the production of females, rather than of a child of one sex that resembles the opposite sex.

What can we conclude about Anaxagoras's theory given these conflicting historical sources? It is difficult to know whether he believed that only males provided seed or whether both sexes provided seed. In a way, it is not surprising that Aristotle attributed the view that females lacked seed to Anaxagoras, since he came to the same conclusion himself. In any event, two of the three historical sources appear to agree that the male seed determined the sex of the offspring for Anaxagoras. They associated the right side of the testicles with male offspring. This association simply integrated the Pythagorean Table of Opposites into the theory of generation. In a slight shift from the Parmenidean theory, which emphasized the right or left side of the uterus, Anaxagoras emphasized the right or left testicle. So the shift in his thought moved from an emphasis on the specific location of the fetus in the female body to the place of origin of the male seed.

In spite of the difficulty of ascertaining exactly which theory of sex determination Anaxagoras believed, it is clear that he considered this question to be central to philosophical speculation. In fact, from the remaining fragments, it would appear that Anaxagoras's prime contribution to the concept of woman occurred in the category of generation. He raised fundamental questions about the relation between seed and sex identity. For that reason he is significant to the history of the concept of woman in relation to man.

Aspasia (c. 440BC)

While Anaxagoras did not found a school of philosophy, he did have two famous disciples: Pericles and Aspasia. The historian Thenistius claimed that Anaxagoras had a deep personal influence on his followers.

> Only Pericles and Aspasia received your praise for being public speakers perfect in action and lofty in thought—because they got this perfect action and lofty thinking from Anaxagoras's everyday conversation and added to it the art of rhetoric.[70]

Aspasia appeared to accept Anaxagoras's scientific approach to the universe. As a result, she was accused of impiety towards the gods and was tried; Pericles intervened and Aspasia was acquitted.[71]

Unfortunately, Aspasia left no permanent record of her thought; our knowledge of her philosophy is therefore completely second-hand. We know that she was Pericles' mistress, or *hetaira*, in part because Pericles had passed a law in 451 BC that inadvertently denied Aspasia the right of citizenship because of her foreign birth (at Miletus). In spite of this legal impediment to full citizenship and rights of marriage to the general-in-command of Athens, Aspasia held a position of great importance in Athenian society. She founded institutional educational structures for women because she believed that women who were going to be hetairas of the great men of Athens ought to have training in arts and sciences as well as in etiquette. She was, therefore, the first philosopher after Pythagoras to give serious attention to the philosophical education of women.

The writings in which other philosophers describe Aspasia tend to satirize her relationship with Pericles. In one it is implied that Aspasia secretly wrote Pericles' speech in praise of Athens. Plato reports the following conversation in the dialogue *Menexenus*:

> MENEXENUS: And can you remember what Aspasia said?
>
> SOCRATES: I ought to be able, for she taught me, and she was ready to strike me because I was always forgetting.
>
> MENEXENUS: Then why will you not rehearse what she said?
>
> SOCRATES: Because I am afraid my mistress may be angry with me if I publish her speech.
>
> MENEXENUS: Nay, Socrates, let us have the speech, whether Aspasia's or anyone else's, no matter.[72]

In spite of Plato's suggestions, there is no evidence that Aspasia was a teacher of Socrates in a formal way.

Socrates, in the dialogue, complies with Menexenus's request and repeats the entire speech, which consists of a lengthy description of the history of Athens, ranging from its contemporary political struggles back to its origins. In this latter section, Socrates offers a metaphor of Athens as a mother of her citizens:

> And a great proof that she brought forth the common ancestors of us and of the departed is that she provided the means of support for her offspring. For as a woman proves her motherhood by giving milk to her young ones . . . so did this our land prove that she was the mother of men, for in those days she alone and first of all brought forth wheat and barley for human food, . . . And these are truer proofs of motherhood in a country than in a woman, for the woman in her conception and generation is but the imitation of the earth and not the earth of the woman.[73]

The claim that woman takes her identity as a generator from the cosmic generator, Mother Earth, reaches back to the poetic image found in Hesiod's *Theogony* rather than towards a naturalistic explanation more likely to spring from a disciple of Anaxagoras. Therefore, the attribution of this speech to Aspasia is extremely unlikely. The dialogue concludes:

> SOCRATES: You have heard, Menexenus, the oration of Aspasia, the Milesian.
> MENEXENUS: Truly, Socrates, I marvel that Aspasia, who is only a woman, should be able to compose such a speech—she must be a rare one.[74]

Even if the particular content of Plato's dialogue is questionably attributed to Aspasia, there is no doubt that she had a reputation as an intelligent woman who studied and taught philosophy. Two other Socratic philosophers referred to her in their writings: Aeschines wrote an entire dialogue called *Aspasia*; and Xenophon referred to her as a teacher in the *Oeconomicus*.[75] Consequently, Aspasia holds an important place in the beginnings of a delineation of the category of wisdom in relation to the concept of woman. She exercised her powers of reason and the observations of the senses, and she taught other women to do the same. In this way, Aspasia moved the potential for women to become philosophers one step forward from the poetic inspirations of Sappho.

Empedocles (c. 450 BC)

A philosophy of sex complementarity was first articulated by Empedocles, who combined a knowledge of medicine with a capacity for creative reflection in considering a wide range of questions about sex identity. His thoughts have been preserved in two texts entitled *On Nature* and *Purifications*. In addition, several other secondary sources have left a record of his views.

Empedocles' greatest contribution to the concept of woman in relation to man occurred in the categories of opposites and generation. He was the first philosopher to limit the number of elements to four: earth, air, fire, and water. All created beings were generated out of these four elements, which combined and separated through the cosmic forces of Love and Hate:

> I shall tell you of a double process. At one time it increased to be a single One out of Many; at another time it grew apart so as to be Many out of One—Fire and Water, and Earth and the boundless height of Air, and also execrable Hate apart from these, or equal weight in all directions, and Love in their midst, their equal in length and breadth.[76]

As a philosopher, Empedocles de-anthropologized God, or the One out of which all things flow:

> For he is not equipped with a human head on his body, nor from his back do two branches start; (he has) no feet, no swift knees, no hairy genital organs; but he is Mind, holy and ineffable, and only Mind, which darts through the whole universe with its swift thoughts.[77]

For Empedocles, sex identity entered in the cosmic world as a force of union. Love, a goddess or daimon, is called Aphrodite. "She it is who is believed to be implanted in mortal limbs also; through her they think friendly thoughts and perform harmonious actions, calling her Joy and Aphrodite."[78] The force of Love, on both a cosmic and an individual level, seeks to unite; while the force of Hate seeks to separate. Empedocles does not name a male deity similar to Aphrodite as a male incarnation of the force of Hate. Therefore, it is not possible to conclude that he understood the cosmic female to be a force of union and the cosmic male to be a force of separation. At the same time, however, he states clearly that the Force of Love and the Force of Hate are "equal in length and breadth." So there does appear to be a cosmic force, opposite and equal to Aphrodite as the Force of Love.

Empedocles developed a complicated description of the ways in which women and men are generated through the cycles of Love and Hate. The recurring cycles of generation take place as follows:

Increase of Love	**Increase of Hate**
separate limbs	men and women
hermaphrodites	hermaphrodites
men and women	separate limbs[79]

These differing cycles of love and hate lead to a double generation of groups of women and men:

> There is a double creation of mortals and a double decline: the union of all things causes the birth and destruction of the one (race of mortals), the other is reared as the elements grow apart, and then flies asunder.[80]

In the cycle of Love, which combined the elements, various human parts emerged:

> On it (Earth) many foreheads without necks sprung forth, and arms wandered unattached, bereft of shoulders, and eyes strayed about, needing brows.[81]

These separate limbs, again through the force of Love, combined into hermaphrodite-like monsters:

> Many creatures were created with a face and breast on both sides; offspring of cattle with the fronts of men, and again there arose offspring of men with heads of cattle; and (creatures made of elements) mixed in part from men, in part of female sex, furnished with hairy limbs.[82]

Finally, the monsters combined in new ways to generate women and men:

> And trees spring up, and men and women, and beasts and birds and water-nurtured fish, and even the long-lived gods who are highest in honour. For these (Elements) alone exist, but by running through one another they become different; to such a degree does mixing change them.[83]

Significantly, Empedocles describes this process as an evolution of equal and differentiated human beings. For this reason, his theory of cosmic generation can be considered as a rudimental theory of sex complementary.

The cycle of Hate simply reverses the process. Men and women disintegrate into limbs:

> In turn they get the upper hand in the revolving cycle, and perish into one another and increase in the turn appointed by Fate. For they alone exist, but running through one another they become men and the tribes of other animals, sometimes uniting under the influence of Love into one ordered Whole, at other times again each moving apart through the hostile force of Hate.[84]

Aetius records that Empedocles thought that the evolutionary process took place in four stages:

> The first race of animals and creatures were born in no way complete in all parts, entire, but disjoined, with parts not grown together; the second, like shapes of parts grown together; the third of undifferentiated shapes; the fourth no longer from like things as earth and water, but now separated from one another.[85]

The third stage, or that of "undifferentiated shapes," has caused considerable controversy. It is also recorded in the following fragment:

> At first, undifferentiated shapes of earth arose, having a share of both elements Water and Heat. These the Fire sent up, wishing to reach its like, but they did not yet exhibit a lovely body with limbs, nor the voice and organs such as is proper to man.[86]

The question that puzzles scholars concerns whether the stage of "undifferentiated shapes" is a higher or lower form of generation than woman and man.[87] If it is lower, then how does it relate to the hermaphroditic creatures that have parts of both sexes? If it is higher, does it then signify some sort of physical creature that has an intelligence but no sexual identity? This latter question would imply that Empedocles envisaged a further phase of evolution beyond that of human beings. It is impossible here to determine the exact place that undifferentiated forms play in Empedocles' philosophy. For our purposes, it is enough to note that Empedocles had an evolutionary theory of generation that placed the evolution of women and men on an equal but differentiated basis.

Empedocles considered the continuity of generation from two perspectives: reincarnation of the soul, and the mixing of male and female seeds in the body. He believed that he had been reincarnated several times in different forms: "For by now I have been born as boy, girl, plant, bird, and dumb sea-fish."[88] Therefore, for Empedocles, the soul had no sex identity; it was able to be incarnated in either a male or female body. He does not appear to conclude from this, however, that the body is a prison for the soul, or that material life devalues the soul. There is a kind of cooperation between the material elements and souls through the cycles of Love and Hate that allow for recurring births and deaths to take place.

Empedocles was fascinated with the philosophy of medicine, and it is in the area of the concrete way in which generation continued through sexual intercourse and the mixing of seeds that he made some outstanding contributions to the concept of woman in relation to man. In fact, Empedocles was one of the few before the seventeenth century to have proposed the correct theory of reproduction, namely, that the mother and father each provide one-half of the seed needed for the production of the fetus.

> The substance of (the child's) limbs is divided (between them), part in the man's (body) and part in the woman's.[89]

This double-seed theory gave an equal role to the mother and father, thereby developing a crucial foundation for a theory of sex complementarity. It is precisely through the union of differentiated and equal male and female seeds that the child is generated.

In addition to proposing a double-seed theory of generation, Empedocles developed an elaborate explanation for the selection of the sex of the child. Avoiding the Pythagorean association of the opposites right and left, Empedocles chose instead the opposites hot and cold. The temperature involved three different factors: male seed, female seed, and the uterus.

> And the (male and female seed) were poured into pure parts. Some of it forms women (namely), that which has encountered Cold (and conversely, that which encounters Hot produces males).
>
> The divided meadows of Aphrodite.
>
> For in the warmer parts of the stomach (i.e., the womb) is productive of the male, and for this reason men are swarthy and more powerfully built and shaggy.[90]

From the chart on the next page it is evident that the theory of generation reached a new level of sophistication with Empedocles. Struggling to understand the biology of the body, Empedocles sought to explain the various genetic inheritances as well as sex determination. Significantly, his explanation maintained a balance between the sexes that included the necessary differentiation and equality of women and men.

Aristotle later remarked about his predecessor in the *Generation of Animals*:

> Empedocles—the two parents do not both supply the same portion, and that is why they need intercourse with each other.[92]

Significantly, Aristotle recognized the basic presuppositions of sex complementarity that Empedocles proposed. However, he completely rejected them in favour of a theory of sex polarity. Borrowing the use of hot and cold from Empedocles and Hippocrates,

	Testicles (male seed) one-half	
Uterus (female seed) one-half	**hot seed**	**cold seed**
hot uterus	boy If both seeds hot, resembles father	boy If mother's seed hotter than father's, then resembles mother
cold uterus	girl If father's seed hotter than mother's, then resembles father	girl If both seeds cold, then resembles mother[91]

Aristotle developed a theory of sex identity that argued that the female provided no seed in generation because she was by nature colder than the male. This lack of heat was a deficiency in the female sex that had far-reaching consequences for Aristotle's concept of woman. At this point in the analysis, however, it is important simply to recognize that Empedocles recognized the presence of seed in both the male and the female, and that he also realized that both parents contributed only half of the needed structure for the fetus. This means that Aristotle's view depended upon the rejection of the correct double-seed theory of generation, rather than on a simple lack of information present at the time.

Before passing to the last of the pluralist philosophers to be considered, it should be pointed out that Empedocles achieved considerable fame in his life. He also appears to have accepted women as well as men as followers; in the *Purification* he wrote:

> I go about among you as an immortal god, no longer a mortal, held in honour by all, as I seem (to them to deserve), crowned with fillets and flowing garlands. When I come to them in their flourishing towns, to men and women, I am honoured; and they follow me in thousands, to inquire where is the path of advantage.[93]

When Empedocles taught, he sought to give reasons for his views, "Come, listen to my discourse! For be assured, learning will increase your understanding."[94] Even though he had recourse to the invocation of the Muse, Empedocles makes it clear to his listeners that they are to accept his teachings on the basis of the evidence of reason and the observation of the senses, rather than simple inspiration: "As the trustworthy evidence of my Muse commands, grasp (these things), when my reasoned argument has been sifted in your innermost heart!"[95] In this way, Empedocles continued to advance philosophy over territory previously held by the poets and oracles.

Democritus (c. 460–370 BC)

With the last of the Pluralists to be considered, we find a beginning of the formulation of a theory of sex polarity. For Democritus, the male was superior and significantly different from the female. His views of sex identity sprang from a more fundamamental philosophy that interpreted the world as filled with small atoms colliding with one another. "Everything comes about by way of strife and necessity." [96] (Not surprisingly, this theory of a universe of atoms at war attracted Karl Marx, who wrote his doctoral dissertation on Democritus in 1841.)[97]

Democritus travelled widely and wrote a great many texts in philosophy on natural science, economics, ethics, and politics. [98] Only a few fragments of his considerable writings remain today. However, from these fragments and from records of secondary source writers familiar with his thought, it is possible to reconstruct Democritus's concept of woman in relation to man.

Following the pattern of natural philosophers, Democritus gave a description of the first parents as evolving from water:

> Democritus of Abdera thought that men were originally produced out of water and mud. . . . (Democritus says that) animals were produced by union, first from animal-producing water. [99]

While he did not specifically refer to the generation of woman as distinct from man, it would seem that he thought they appeared in the world at the same time. Once generated, human beings continued to generate through the production of seed.

Democritus believed both parents produced seed that contained parts of the body of the fetus. Aetius records the following claim: "(Democritus says that) from whole bodies and the principal parts such as bones, flesh and muscles (that is, the seed is produced)." [100] The fetus was formed by a combination of parts of the seeds from the parents, with the exception of the selection of sex identity. Aetius records:

> (Democritus says that) the common parts are produced from either (parent), but the peculiar parts (i.e., sexual anatomy) according to the mastery (of the parent whose sex identity is the same as the fetus). [101]

Therefore, Democritus rejected both the appeal to the opposites right and left, and to hot and cold to explain the sex determination of the fetus. Instead, he had recourse to the sheer strength of the seed of the mother or father. According to Aristotle in *Generation of Animals*:

> Democritus of Abdera holds that the difference of male and female is produced in the womb, certainly, but denies that it is on account of heat and cold that one becomes male and another female; this is determined, he asserts, according to which of the two parent's semen prevails, the semen, that is to say, which has come from the part wherein male and female differ from one another. [102]

For Democritus, the collision of seeds of generation paralleled the collision of atoms in the universe: "Man is a universe in little (microcosm)." [103] If the father's seed dominated this collision, the child would be a boy; if the mother's seed dominated, then the child would be a girl. Democritus appeared to have grasped the basic idea of dominant and recessive genes, while mistakenly identifying sex determination with the seed of the parent of the same sex as the child. If this view is charted, it would look as follows:

		Male seed	
		dominant	subordinate
Female seed	dominant	X	girl
	subordinate	boy	X

Aristotle noted that it is difficult, on the basis of this theory, to explain how a girl might physically resemble the father or a boy the mother.[104]

Democritus appealed to the timing of the collision of the seed to explain the generation of the deformed child:

> Now Democritus explained the form of monstrosities thus. Two semens fall into the uterus, one of them having started forth earlier and the other later, and the second when it has gone out goes into the uterus with the result that the parts grow on to one another and get thrown into disorder.[105]

Significantly, Democritus's theory gave voice to a fundamental antagonism between the seeds of the mother and father whose resolution depended on the strength and timing of the factors in the collision. It is not possible to uncover the sex polarity in Democritus's thought simply by examining his theory of generation, for he ascribes seed to both sexes and he allows the female to dominate the male, or the male to dominate the female, without concluding that one sex is biologically superior or inferior to the other.

However, when other fragments from the area of wisdom and virtue are added to his theory of generation, it becomes clear that for Democritus, the male is a superior kind of human being who ought not be dominated by the female.

Democritus valued the search for wisdom highly. He believed that "Medicine heals diseases of the body, wisdom frees the soul from passions."[106] The search for wisdom involved learning how to distinguish reason from the deception of the senses. Therefore, a wise person learned how to live in conformity with the higher part of self. Within this context, then, it is significant that Democritus claims that women should not develop their higher capacities of thought: "A woman must not practise argument: this is dreadful."[107] The practice of argument was an indispensable tool for philosophical thinking, so Democritus obviously believed that women ought not attempt to be philosophers.

Furthermore, speech was the tool with which philosophers realized their reflections. Democritus argues: "An adornment for a woman is a lack of garrulity."[108] This fragment could be interpreted as a prohibition against too much speech rather than of any speech. However, Democritus does single out woman in a censure that leaves the impression that public speech and argument, indispensable tools for the philosopher, were not appropriate to women.

Another possible interpretation of this passage is that Democritus believed that women ought to remain silent because their speech might reveal a less virtuous kind of thought. He says, "A woman is far sharper than man in malign thoughts."[109] This interpretation would imply that the weakness of the female sex could reveal itself in moral as well as epistemological areas. However, it is not possible to prove this from the simple fragment mentioned. The only certain conclusion is that Democritus believed women ought not to strive for wisdom in the same way as men, that is, through public participation in argumentation and speech.

In a similar way, Democritus draws out separate and unequal virtues for women and men. In particular, he places a great deal of importance on the virtue of ruling, both of the self and of others, for the virtuous person. "Rule belongs by nature to the stronger."[110] If we draw any conclusions about ruling from Democritus's theory of sex determination it would appear, from the division of the sexes in the world, that half of the time males ought to rule and half of the time females ought to rule. However, Democritus states explicitly, "To be ruled by a woman is the ultimate outrage for a man."[111] It is clear that he considers man to be stronger and more capable of ruling than woman.

Consequently, Democritus can be seen as suggesting a valuation of woman as significantly different and inferior to man. It is not surprising, then, that he gives an extremely negative description of the relations of the sexes through intercourse. He interpreted it as a kind of disease:

> Coition is a slight attack of apoplexy. For man gushes forth from man, and is separated by being torn apart with a kind of blow.[112]

Democritus's view of a war of dominance between the two sexes, with an ultimate humiliation for man if the female wins out as the stronger of the two, is completely consistent with the theory of sex polarity. It is interesting to contrast this early formulation with that of Empedocles, whose views of the equality and complementarity of the sexes contained a very positive interpretation of sexual union.

Democritus's views on sex identity conclude with the judgement:

> I do not think that one should have children. . . . Whoever wants to have children should, in my opinion, choose them from the family of one of his friends. He will thus obtain a child such as he wishes, for he can select the kind he wants.[113]

In a way, it seems as though the rejection of children can be considered as a logical consequence of the theory of sex polarity. If one sex is valued as superior to the other, then the devalued sex would not be desired as the outcome of sexual intercourse. This tendency is found in contemporary reverse-polarity theories, in which women are considered superior to men. Sexual intercourse is also rejected, and artificial insemination is regarded as a possible way to produce female children. Therefore, it is not surprising that traditional sex polarity, as expressed in Democritus's theory, leads to a similar conclusion. In the traditional situation, it is male children that are preferred.

THE SOPHISTS

The name "Sophist," which was originally applied to the wise poets of ancient Greece, slowly evolved to represent more specifically a person who was a teacher and/or a writer. Eventually, its meaning changed to refer to a professional educator who received payment for teaching.[114] The names of approximately twenty-six Sophists are recorded as having taught during the years 460 to 380 BC.[115]

There appear to be no women who were publicly known as Sophists. It is interesting to note, however, that Aspasia shares a common characteristic with the Sophists in that she taught philosophy for a fee. Also, Socrates described his own teacher, in the *Symposium*, as follows:

> I was astonished at her words and said: "Is this really true, O thou wise Diotima?" and she replied with all the authority of an accomplished sophist: "Of that, Socrates, you may be assured."[116]

However, since there is no record of an historical woman who represents Diotima, it is not possible to draw any positive conclusions from this passage about the existence of female Sophists.

The Sophists left several fragments that touch in some way upon the concept of woman in relation to man. In addition, some of their general theories of human nature had consequences for theories of sex identity. Therefore, we will now turn to a consideration of their individual views.

Protagoras (490–420 BC)

Plato suggests that Protagoras was the first philosopher to publicly proclaim himself as a Sophist: "You openly announce yourself to the Greeks by the name of Sophist and set up as a teacher of culture and virtue, the first to claim payment for this service."[117] Plato subjected Protagoras's thought to much criticism and even ridicule, for the Sophist argued that there were no absolute values. The belief that all value is relative was expressed by Protagoras in the famous maxim: "Of all things the measure is man."[118]

Protagoras is reputed to have written many works, of which the following may have had reference to sex identity: *On Sciences; On Virtues; On the Original State of Things; On Incorrect Human Actions; On the Gods;* and *On Truth.*[118] The view that values are conventional and relative, coupled with the belief that human beings equally emerged out of the elements, gave Protagoras a basis from which to argue for the potential equality of all persons. This view obviously could have implications for the concept of woman in relation to man. However, there are no existing fragments of his theory that draw out this consequence.

In a myth recorded by Plato, Protagoras is reputed to have described the origin of human life as follows:

> Once upon a time there existed gods but no mortal creatures. When the appointed time came for these also to be born, the god formed them within the earth out of a mixture of earth and fire and the substances which are compounded from earth and fire.[120]

While referring to gods in the passage, Protagoras nonetheless describes human generation in a scientific way. In addition, he does not separate the generation of woman from man, as Hesiod had done previously. Instead, the sexes had an equal origin.

Protagoras then suggests a social explanation for the origin of society. Men and women lived at first in scattered groups, then because of the danger of attack from wild animals, they moved together into fortified cities. Finally, they began to form themselves into communities based on a common sense of justice. Protagoras argued that virtues are acquired by convention rather than by nature. Education therefore becomes the key to a just society; and "the one who lacks it, man, woman or child, must be instructed and corrected until by punishment he is reformed."[121]

Protagoras believed that virtue can be taught, and he argued very strongly that people ought to strive for this form of excellence. However, he did not think that there was a single definition of virtue. Because virtues are relative, Protagoras thought that different people had different virtues. It would follow that men and women are differentiated by achieving their respective virtues in different ways. However, since no written record exists of this conclusion, Protagoras's views of separate virtues for woman and man must be accepted with qualifications.

The one area in which we have a clear record of Protagoras's thoughts about sex identity is in his theory of language. According to Aristotle, Protagoras was the first philosopher to divide Greek words into categories of masculine, feminine, and neuter: "The fourth rule consists in keeping the genders distinct—masculine, feminine, and neuter, as laid down by Protagoras."[122] These categories referred to the categories of things being referred *to* and not simply the words themselves, so that masculine should be used to refer to male things, feminine words to female things, and neuter words to inanimate things.

Protagoras apparently attempted to make speakers consistent in the use of gender words during a time when the Greek language was fluid. Words may have been given a certain kind of ending because of the way it sounded, instead of any sex identification of the thing referred to. Aristotle discusses some of the consequences of Protagoras's theory of language:

> If, as Protagoras used to say, *wrath* and *helmet* are masculine, according to him, he who calls *wrath* a "destructress" commits a solecism. . . . Almost all apparent solecisms occur owing to the word *this* or *it* and when the inflection denotes neither the masculine nor the feminine but the neuter. *He* denotes a masculine, *she* a feminine, whereas *this* or *it*, though meaning to signify a neuter, often signify either a masculine or a feminine.[123]

Protagoras accused a person of making an ungrammatical combination of words in a sentence when either words of one gender were mixed with words of another, or when a word of one gender was used to describe a thing of another gender. "In the one case it happens that we commit a solecism in the category of actual things, so in the other we commit it in that of names."[124]

One of the interesting questions being asked by philosophers today concerns the effect of gender identification in language on sex identity.[125] For example, what is the effect on female and male children learning French grammar when it is revealed that the presence of one male person among a large collection of women forces any descriptive word of the group to have a masculine rather than a feminine ending? How does the hidden reference of the gender identification of words affect the development of gender identity in women and men? Even though the pre-Socratics focused on the correctness of grammar itself—while today it is on the question of what constitutes masculine and feminine identity—it must be recognized that Protagoras first raised the important philosophical issue of the relation between sex and sex identity and language.

Gorgias (c. 490–386 BC)

The application of the extant writings of the Sophist Gorgias to the concept of woman falls completely under the category of virtue; his works include *On Nature, Technai* (including *Encomium of Helen*), and various orations.

Plutarch records that Gorgias emphasized the importance of a woman's character over her physical appearance: "Gorgias seems to us in better taste when he demands that 'a woman's fame rather than her form ought to be known to many.' "[126] Gorgias gave considerable attention to woman's character in the lengthy *Encomium of Helen*, where he argues that Helen is not to be blamed for her actions because they did not proceed from the exercise of her discursive reason. At the beginning of the text Gorgias states:

> Man and woman and speech and deed and city and object would be honoured with praise if praiseworthy and incur blame if unworthy, for it is an equal error and mistake to blame the praisable and to praise the blamable. . . . Thus it is right to refute those who rebuke Helen, a woman about whom the testimony of inspired poets has become univocal and unanimous as had the ill omen of her name . . . For my part, by introducing some reasoning into my speech, I wish to free the accused of blame.[127]

As a philosopher, Gorgias is interested in seeking the criteria for judgements of praise and blame for virtue or vice.

Gorgias then sets forth four hypotheses for the cause of Helen's voyage to Troy: "For either by will of Fate and decision of the gods and vote of Necessity did she do what she did, or by force reduced or by words seduced (or by love possessed)."[128] Working through each hypothesis in turn, Gorgias shows that Helen was not culpable:

> 1. It is right for the responsible one to be held responsible; for god's predetermination cannot be hindered by human premeditation. . . .
> 2. If she was raped by violence and illegally assaulted and unjustly insulted, it is clear that the raper, as the insulter, did the wronging, and the raped, as the insulted, did the suffering. . . .
> 3. What cause then prevents the conclusion that Helen similarly, against her will, might have come under the influence of speech . . . The persuader, like a constrainer, does the wrong, and the persuaded, like the constrained, in speech is wrongly charged. . . .
> 4. If, therefore, the eye of Helen, pleased by the figure of Alexander, presented to her soul eager desire and contest of love, what wonder? If (being) a god (love has) the divine power of the gods, how could a lesser being reject and refuse it? But if it is a disease of human origin and a fault of the soul, it should not be blamed as a sin but regarded as an affliction.[129]

Gorgias's analysis, sounding something like Sappho's description of Helen as following the power of the lower part of her soul, goes further to suggest that only when the soul is ordered by reason can a person become virtuous or vicious. To follow the lower desires is to fall prey to a false belief in the validity of the senses or in the power of external forces. Gorgias claims: "The things we see do not have the nature which we wish them to have, but the nature which each actually had." [130] Helen was on a pre-virtuous level of existence because she believed in her sensory impressions. Gorgias concludes: "For she came as she did come, caught in the net of Fate, not the plans of the mind, and by the constraints of love, not by the devices of art." [131] As a person who has not yet arrived at a virtuous level of existence, he concludes Helen ought to be absolved from all blame:

> How then can one regard blame of Helen as just, since she is utterly acquitted of all charge, whether she did what she did through falling in love or persuaded by speech or ravished by force or constrained by divine constraint? I have by means of speech removed disgrace from a woman. [132]

Although Gorgias has exonerated Helen, he has not described her as a virtuous person. Instead, he represents her as a pre-virtuous or pre-vicious person. Therefore, his analysis does not contribute to the view that women are capable of philosophy through the exercise of reason in its application to virtue.

Gorgias's view that there are separate virtues for women and men is explored in more detail by Plato in a dialogue entitled *Meno*. Here, the implication is that women can be virtuous, but the ways in which women practise virtue will differ from the ways in which men practise virtue.

In the dialogue, Meno introduces himself to Socrates as a follower of the Sophist Gorgias's particular view that virtue can be taught.

> SOCRATES: What do you yourself say virtue is? . . . I shall be only too happy to be proved wrong if you and Gorgias turn out to know this, although I said I had never met anyone who did.
> MENO: But there is no difficulty about it. First of all, if it is manly virtue you are after, it is easy to see that the virtue of a man consists in managing the city's affairs capably, and so that he will help his friends and injure his foes while taking care to come to no harm himself. Or if you want a woman's virtue, that is easily described. She must be a good housewife, careful of her stores and obedient to her husband. Then there is another virtue for a child, male or female, and another for an old man, free or slave as you like. . . . For every act and every time of life, with reference to each separate function, there is a virtue for each one of us, and similarly, I should say, a vice. [133]

The above passage is crucial for the concept of woman in relation to man. If it accurately expresses Gorgias's views, then it is the first record of an attempt to develop a theory of virtue with specific reference to sex identity. Previously reported fragments simply stated that women and men had specific virtues, but Meno is claiming that there is an important reason for this view, namely, that persons with different functions had different virtues in relation to those functions.

The notion that a function had its particular virtue is connected with the meaning of *areté*, which contains within it the double meaning of virtue and excellence. From this it follows that if a person has a specific function, then his virtue would be to perform that function well. Gorgias's view, as reported by Meno, implies that groups of people in society had different functions, namely men, women, and slaves, and that each group, therefore, had its particular way of performing that function excellently. Plato through the efforts of Socrates in the dialogue *Meno*, will attempt to refute this theory, but at this point it is important simply to recognize that the Sophist Gorgias appears to have publicly argued for the separate virtues of woman and man. The dialogue continues:

> SOCRATES: Well, does this apply in your mind only to virtue, that there is a different one for a man and a woman and the rest? Is it the same with health and size and strength, or has health the same character everywhere, if it is health, whether it be in a man or any other creature?
> MENO: I agree that health is the same in a man or a woman.
> SOCRATES: And what about size and strength? If a woman is strong will it be the same thing, the same strength, that makes her strong? My meaning is that in its character as strength, it is no different, whether it be in a man or in a woman. Or do you think it is?
> MENO: No.
> SOCRATES: And will virtue differ, in its character as virtue, whether it be in a child or an old man, a woman or a man?
> MENO: I somehow feel that this is not on the same level as the other cases.
> SOCRATES: Well then, didn't you say that a man's virtue lay in directing the city well, and a woman's in directing her household well?
> MENO: Yes.[134]

Here, Meno stipulates that women and men have different spheres of activity according to their different functions in life and, therefore, they have a different excellence or virtue in respect to the functions. The claim that women and men have a different sphere of virtuous activity because they have different functions is one that held a place of central importance in later theories of sex identity. While it is not *a priori* evident that this kind of differentiation should lead to a devaluation of one sex; in fact, historically the sphere of activity associated with the household was considered to be inferior to that associated with public life in the *polis*. Therefore, this particular separation of spheres of activity for woman and man contains a hidden tendency towards a theory of sex polarity.

The second kind of differentiation between the virtuous activity of the sexes mentioned in *Meno* concerns the interconnected virtues of ruling and obedience. The dialogue continues after Socrates has tried to convince Meno that there must be only one virtue for women and men as there is one health or strength for the two sexes:

> SOCRATES: Seeing then that they all have the same virtue, try to remember and tell me what Gorgias and you, who share his opinion, say it is.
> MENO: It must be simply the capacity to govern men, if you are looking for one quality to cover all the instances.
> SOCRATES: Indeed I am. But does this virtue apply to a child or a slave? Should a slave be capable of governing his master, and if he does, is he still a slave?
> MENO: I hardly think so.[135]

Significantly, Socrates left out the question of whether a woman might rule a man, as he later concluded that indeed she should, if she were wiser. However, in the first passage considered from the dialogue above, we are told that woman must be "obedient to her husband"; this implies that the separation of virtue for the Sophist Gorgias includes the specific theory that a woman ought to obey her husband and the husband ought to rule his wife. The view that it is a virtue for a man to rule and a virtue for a woman to obey also became incorporated into a theory of sex polarity. For within the tradition of Greek philosophy that places a high value on self-governance and the subsequent capacity to govern others, it follows that obedience, when consistently applied to a particular group of people—in this case women, slaves and children—devalued the obedient group in a way directly contrary to the superior valuation given to those who are virtuous by ruling.

However, it is important to note here that Meno—and by implication, Gorgias—does not imply that there is a natural origin for this difference of function and virtue. Later, Aristotle will argue for the separation of virtues and for the superiority of man's virtue over woman's virtue from a theory of the different natures of woman and man. The Sophists, however, viewed all value as conventional, not natural. Therefore, the reasons for the virtue of obedience for women were different in the two theories. The Sophists simply stated that woman's function in society as conventionally structured is to obey; while Aristotle will argue that woman, by nature, *ought* to obey. A third variation on this theme will be introduced by the neo-Pythagoreans and Hildegard, who will argue that women are virtuous by *choosing* to obey. So the Sophists simply introduced the question of the relation of the virtue of obedience for women and of ruling for men, given the conventional values of society.

In conclusion, Gorgias developed Protagoras's theory that man is the measure of all things and he applied it to a theory of separate virtue for separate functions of society. For this reason he is an important contributor to the history of the concept of woman. Gorgias began to deepen the questions asked about sex identity and to present theoretical arguments for their defence. Insofar as he seemed to accept the traditions of sex polarity as they manifested themselves in Greek society at the time, he must be classified as falling within the sex-polarity tradition.

Prodicus (c. 470–3?? BC)

As a Sophist famous for his public teaching, Prodicus was the first philosopher to explicitly develop a female personification of virtue and vice. Xenophon recorded Prodicus's important "composition on Heracles, which he recited to a large audience." [136]

Prodicus is reputed to have written three works: *On the Nature of Man; On Nature;* and *Horae*, which includes "The Choice of Heracles." [137] His main areas of contribution were in the correct use of language, in cosmology, and in the importance of virtue in human life. Since no detailed account of Prodicus's cosmology remains, his only contribution to the concept of woman falls under the category of virtue.

In Prodicus's text on Heracles, the young man is described as having to make a choice between following the advice of a female personification of either virtue or vice. While there is a suggestion that Heracles is simply being seduced by one or the other female figures, these personifications are in fact presenting detailed arguments to help Heracles come to a reasoned decision about a life of virtue or vice. Therefore, the female personifications are representing philosophical principles rather than irrational erotic attractions.

Xenophon describes Prodicus's text as follows:

> As I recall it, the story went this way. Heracles, he said, when he was growing from childhood to man's estate, at that time of life when young men are beginning to make their own decisions and thus to show whether they are embarked on the path of virtue or that of vice, went off to ponder in seclusion which path he should choose.
>
> And there appeared to approach him two tall female figures. One had a noble address and a bearing untouched by servility, with skin fair and pure, her glance circumspect, her person modest, dressed in white. The other's figure bespoke softness and luxury, her countenance showing the exaggerated whites and red induced by cosmetics, her carriage unnaturally lofty and stilted, her eyes darting about restlessly, and wearing a costume such as made her physical ripeness easy to estimate.[138]

Vice is the first to present her arguments:

> If you should accept my friendship and follow me, I shall show you the path of greatest enjoyment and ease, and you shall not fail to experience every last pleasure, while living quite free from trouble.[139]

Vice continues by promising Heracles the absence of war, fullness of the pleasures of the senses, and the freedom to exploit the labour of others. Virtue then offers her counter arguments:

> If you should take the path to me you will achieve honorable and wonderous deeds, and . . . you will come to think me still more admirable and estimable because of the excellence you attain. But I shall not deceive you with overtures promising pleasures, rather I shall truthfully disclose to you the face of reality as the gods themselves have constituted it. The gods give no real benefits or honours to men without struggle and perserverence.[140]

Virtue then gives specific examples of values that require struggle and perseverence, such as friendship, community, service, farming, warfare, and physical vigour. Therefore, while Vice offers a quick and easy way to pleasure, Virtue offers him a slow and arduous path to excellence. The discussion then continues with a further debate between the two female personifications. In this discussion, Virtue claims that Vice inverts the natural life of man by seeking to satisfy desires even before they arise; for example, by sleeping not from tiredness, but from boredom; and from inverting the real purpose of day and night. Virtue concludes with the following characterization of a life of vice: "Though you are immortal you have been denied the company of the gods, and you gain no honour among decent men either."[141]

Finally, Virtue proclaims her own value:

> I, on the other hand, am a companion of the gods as well as of upright men; no great deads are done, in heaven or on earth, except through me. I am honored more highly than all else both among gods and among those men who have virtue; I am the favorite spirit of the skilled, the faithful guardian of households, the ready helper of servingmen, the active promoter of the works of peace and a strong ally in the toils of war, and the best possible sharer of friendship.[142]

This use of the device of female personification is significant for the concept of woman because it externalizes both a positive and a negative female principle. At this point, in its earliest articulation, philosophical arguments in favour of virtue or vice are identified with a feminine cosmic principle. Philosophers would continue to use this device throughout the centuries (see, for example, Boethius). Although the female personification of virtue and vice is first articulated by male philosophers, it is later used by female philosophers (see, for example, Herrad of Landsberg).[143] While this female personification leaves open the question of whether individual women can relate to virtue in the same way as individual men, its use at this point in the history of philosophy is a step forward in the slowly evolving consciousness in which discursive reasoning becomes associated with the concept of woman. Prodicus, therefore, in this popular speech about the choices of Heracles, began in a rudimentary way to articulate arguments for and against the virtuous life, arguments expressed through a cosmic feminine principle.

Antiphon (c. 470–411 BC)

Judging from the extant fragments, this Sophist had nothing significantly new to add to the concept of woman. Antiphon is reputed to have written *On truth, On Concord, Politics,* and *On Dreams*. The only fragments with some application to the concept of woman concern generation and marriage.

Certain fragments of Antiphon's theory of generation exist in extremely short form: "Antiphon too has said 'that in which the fetus grows and receives nourishment is called the membrane' and 'Ambloma' (abortion) as Antiphon."[144] All that can be concluded from these references is that Antiphon considered the theory of generation to be of philosophical interest.

In the fragment on marriage, Antiphon appears to be suggesting that man ought to take the easier path by remaining single:

> From Antiphon: Well then let his life progress further, and let him want marriage and a wife. That day, that night, is the beginning of a new life, a new fate. For marriage is a great gamble for a man. If the wife turns out to be incompatible, how can he deal with the situation? Divorce is difficult, to make enemies of your friends, men who have the same ideas and the same background, who have thought him worthy of an alliance, and have been thought worthy by him. But it is difficult, too, to keep such a possession, to have troubles at home when you expected to have joys.[145]

Antiphon continues his analysis of marriage by suggesting that the sexual pleasures it offers compensate for the difficulties:

> Well then, let us not speak of the dark side, but speak of the most compatible of alliances. What is more delightful for a man than a wife after his own heart? What is more pleasant especially when he is young?[146]

However, the value of sexual pleasure is undermined by the fact that children follow upon intercourse. Antiphon concludes by emphasizing once again the difficulties of marriage:

> In that very place where the pleasure lies, dwells close the smart as well. For pleasures do not come alone, but are accompanied by pains and toils. . . . Well then, suppose there are children born. Now indeed is the world full of worries and the mind loses the bounce of youth, and the countenance is no longer the same.[147]

Antiphon seems to suggest a view similar to the philosopher Democritus concerning the negative value of marriage. There appears to be no positive aspect to the relations between the sexes in Antiphon.

In conclusion, the Sophists left a rather diverse set of fragments about the concept of woman in relation to man. Protagoras considered the relation of sex identity and language, Gorgias developed a theory of separate virtues for separate functions in society, Prodicus described a female personification of virtue and vice, and Antiphon questioned the desirability of marriage. For the most part, the Sophists simply reported conventional views about sex identity.

With subsequent developments in Greek philosophy, theories of sex identity began to examine the relation of nature and convention much more carefully. This analysis will now turn to one approach in this new tradition, an approach that considered sex identity as flowing from the natural identities of the respective bodies of woman and man as discovered through the study of medicine.

THE HIPPOCRATIC WRITINGS

The dates of the life of Hippocrates are presumed to be approximately 460 to 377 BC. A large corpus of over seventy works that have remained attached to the name of Hippocrates were probably written by several different writers over a period of three centuries and gathered into a library of medical texts. There is considerable controversy about the exact authorship of these texts in the Hippocratic collection. However, of those books with specific reference to sex identity, the following can be suggested for authorship: 1) genuine works of Hippocrates—*Aphorisms and Airs, Waters, Places;* 2) Hippocratic School at Cos—*Regimen;* 3) works of other Hippocratic disciples—*On Generation.*[148] A systematic study of the different works reveals no fundamental contradiction about woman's identity in relation to man. Although different texts chose to emphasize different aspects of sex identity, there does appear to be a continuity of theses. Consequently, in the subsequent analysis Hippocratic theory will be presented systematically, with the recognition that all the views presented cannot be directly attributed to Hippocrates himself.

Hippocrates is universally considered to be the Father of Medicine because he was the first to present a systematic methodology for the diagnosis and treatment of disease. Although the practice and study of medicine began earlier, with the Pythagoreans, it was Hippocrates who established the rigorous approach to the field that enabled it eventually to become independent of its philosophical origins. At this early time in western history, however, philosophy and medicine were closely intertwined. The impact of the study of medicine on the concept of woman was great, and the Aristotelian Revolution had some of its most important origins in the Hippocratic writings. Therefore, it is necessary to give close attention to the Hippocratic approach to sex identity.

In *Aphorisms*, an association found in the Pythagorean Table of Opposites is repeated: the male is related to the right and the female to the left.

> XXXVIII. When a woman is pregnant with twins, should either breast become thin, she loses one child. If the right breast become thin, she loses the male child; if the left, the female.
>
> XlVIII. The male embryo is usually on the right, the female on the left.[149]

The Pythagorean association of female with bad and male with good is also repeated in *Aphorisms* XLII: "If a woman is going to have a male child she is of good complexion; if a female, of a bad complexion."[150]

Far more important to the Hippocratic theory than these two Pythagorean opposites was the association of hot and dry with the male, and cold and moist with the female. This same association articulated in the works of Empedocles was reasserted in the Hippocratic text *Regimen*:

> The males of all species are warmer and drier, and the females moister and colder, for the following reasons: originally, each sex was born in such things (the elements fire and water) and grows thereby, while after birth males use a more rigorous regimen, so that they are warmed and dried, but females use a regimen that is moister and less strenuous, besides purging the heat out of their bodies every month.[151]

The Hippocratic text appears to suggest a progressive change in the history of sex identity. The natural association of the female with cold and moist and the male with hot and dry is aided by social habits:

> Males and females would be formed, so far as possible, in the following manner. Females, inclining more to water, grow from foods, drinks, and pursuits that are cold, moist, and gentle. Males, inclining to fire, grow from foods and regimen that are dry and warm. So if a man would beget a girl, he must use a regimen inclining to water.[152]

However, it is crucial that there be a balance of hot and cold, and moist and dry, because too much of any extreme will destroy all conception. The *Aphorisms* reports:

> Women do not conceive who have the womb dense and cold; those who have the womb watery do not conceive, for the seed is drowned; those who have the womb over-dry and very hot do not conceive, for the seed perishes through lack of nourishment. But those whose temperament is a just blend of the two extremes prove able to conceive. Similarly with males.[153]

Hippocrates intuitively recognized the important role of body temperature in reproduction in stating that the opposites hot and cold are significant both for conception and for the determination of sex. For example, today it is recognized that female body temperature rises just before ovulation, and that the male testicles are outside the body in order to have the lower temperature necessary to generate seed.

In *Airs, Waters, Places*, the influence of the weather on the sex identity of adults is considered. Men of the Scythian race, who were negatively influenced by too much cold and moist weather, developed effeminate personalities: "The men have no great desire for intercourse because of the moistness of their constitution and chill of their abdomen, which are the greatest checks on venery."[154] The discourse considers other causes of this characteristic and then concludes: "The great majority of Scythians become impotent, do woman's work, live like women and converse accordingly . . . They put on women's clothes, holding that they have lost their manhood."[155]

In an interesting parallel analysis of Scythian girls, we find a medical description of the Amazon myth:

> In Europe is a Scythian race, dwelling around Lake Maeotis, which differs from other races. Their name is Sauromatae. Their women, so long as they are virgins, ride, shoot, throw the javelin while mounted, and fight with their enemies. They do not lay aside their virginity until they have killed three of their enemies, . . . They have no right breast; for while they are yet babies their mothers make red-hot a bronze instrument constructed for this very purpose and apply it to the right breast and cauterize it, so that its growth is arrested, and all its strength and bulk are diverted to the right shoulder and right arm.[156]

The analysis does not explain the relation of the opposites hot and cold or wet and dry to this phenomenon. However, it concludes with a generalization about the influence of these opposites on character and conception:

> Such is the condition of the Scythians. The other people of Europe differ from one another both in stature and shape, because of the changes of the seasons. . . . Wherefore it is natural to realize that generation too varies in the coagulation of the seed, and is not the same for the same seed in summer as in winter nor in rain as in drought.[157]

The Hippocratic theory then places a tremendous emphasis on the influence of hot and cold on women and men. In *Ancient Medicine* the author states: "I believe that of all the powers none hold less sway in the body than cold and heat."[158]

The Hippocratic theory also recognized that both the mother and the father contributed seed to generation. In the *Regimen* we find:

> For growth belongs, not only to the man's secretion, but also to that of the woman, for the following reason. Either part alone has not motion enough, owing to the bulk of its moisture and the weakness of its fire, to consume and to solidify the oncoming water. . . . On one day in each month it can solidify, and master the advancing parts, and that only if it happens that parts are emitted from both parents in one place.[159]

Hippocrates recognized that there was a limited amount of time each month for conception. However, he confused ovulation with glandular secretions that occur during intercourse. He believed that women ejaculated seed similar to man during intercourse.

The seed was thought to be developed from the heating up of the humours of the body: blood, yellow and black bile, and phlegm.

> The law rules everything; as for man's seed it comes from all the humors which are in the body; it is the strongest part which has separated itself from the rest. The proof that it is the strongest part which separates itself is that, after coitus, one becomes weak in spite of such a small ejaculation. . . . Because of the rubbing of the genitals and this movement, the humors heat up in the body, become fluid, agitated because of the movement and foams as all agitated fluids foam. . . .
>
> In woman when the genitals are rubbed during coitus and the uterus is moving, . . . the woman too ejaculates from all of her body, sometimes inside the uterus, and the uterus becomes wet, sometimes outside, if the (opening to) the uterus is wider than necessary. . . . If she experiences orgasm, she ejaculates before the man and her pleasure is not at the same time; if she does not experience orgasm, her pleasure finishes with the man's.[160]

Hippocrates' claim that the seed is drawn from the humours in all parts of the body helped to explain what we would call the genetic inheritance of the child.

> The seed comes into the uterus from the whole body of the woman and the whole body of the man, weak from weak parts, strong from the strong parts. These qualities are permanently given also to the child. If some part of the man's body gives more to the seed than some part of the woman's body, then the child's corresponding part more resembles the father; if it is some part of the woman's body, the child's corresponding part more resembles the mother.[161]

The double-seed theory of the Hippocratic corpus certainly tends towards a theory of sex complementarity. That is, it describes both parents as being equally significant to the generative process. In addition, the theory posits a mixing of the parts of the seeds so that both parents are necessary to the process. Neither parent alone can accomplish the generation of new life. However, as the theory is unravelled in greater detail, it tends to slide towards a sex-polarity interpretation by concluding that the male comes from a stronger seed and the female from a weaker seed.

> Sometimes the woman's secretion is stronger, sometimes weaker; it is the same thing for the man's secretion. The man has both female and male seed; the woman as well. The male is stronger than the female; he must therefore come from the stronger seed. It is like this: if the strongest seed comes from both partners, the embryo is male; if it is the weakest, it is female. Which ever prevails in quantity, the embryo corresponds to it. If the weak seed, indeed, is much more abundant than the strong which is dominated by and mixed with, the weak one, it becomes a female seed; but if the strong seed is more abundant than the weak one, and the weak one is dominated it becomes male seed.[162]

The following chart will help to clarify this theory of reproduction as developed in *On Generation*.

<table>
<tr><th></th><th></th><th colspan="2">Testicles</th></tr>
<tr><th></th><th></th><th>male seed
strong seed</th><th>female seed
weak seed</th></tr>
<tr><td rowspan="2">Uterus</td><td>male seed
strong seed</td><td>If both parents give equal amounts of strong seed and if it dominates, then a boy results</td><td>a) If there is a greater quantity of strong seed, then a boy results
b) If there is a greater quantity of weak seed, then a girl results</td></tr>
<tr><td>female seed
weak seed</td><td>a) If there is a greater quantity of strong seed, then a boy results
b) If there is a greater quantity of weak, seed, then a girl results</td><td>If both parents give equal amounts of weak seed, and it is not dominated by the strong seed, then a girl results</td></tr>
</table>

The notion of weakness associated with the female sex and strength with the male sex—which is a devaluation of the female—is balanced by a theory that either sex can dominate the other through the quantity of seed. Therefore, the tendency in Hippocratic writings to devalue the female is countered by a desire to explain the facts of generation as they appear to the disinterested observer. The following passage gives further evidence of this struggle:

> It is possible to conclude from evident facts that both the woman and the man possess at the same time male and female seed. Many women, indeed have had girls with their husband, but, after relations with other men, have had boys. And the same men, with whom these women had had girls, after relations with other women had boys; and those who have had boys had girls, after relations with other women. This argument proves that both the man and woman possess at the same time female and male seed. In those who had girls, the strongest seed was dominated, the weakest being more abundant, and the embryos were female; in those who had boys, the weakest seed was dominated and the embryos were male. The secretion of the same man is not always strong, or always weak; it is sometimes the one way, sometimes the other way, and it is the same thing for women.[163]

Once conceived, the male embryo was stronger than the female embryo. Consequently the Hippocratic theory concluded that the male fetus developed more quickly than the female fetus.

> Formation for the girl is forty-two days and for the boy thirty. Miscarriages and the lochia prove it. The female embryo hardens and becomes articulated later. This is because the female seed is weaker and wetter than the male seed.[164]

In addition, *On Generation* concludes that male fetuses move earlier than the female:

> When the extremities of the child's body are externally branched out, and his nails and hair are rooted in, then he starts moving, which happens for the boy at three months of age, for the girls at four months. . . . The boy moves earlier because he is stronger than the girl, and he hardens sooner because the male comes from a stronger and thicker seed than the female.[165]

These theories, which carry out a logical consequence of the principle that girls are formed from weaker seeds than boys, indicate a tendency towards a sex-polarity rationale that exceeds the bounds of empirical observation.

This tendency towards sex polarity as articulated in *On Generation* gets a slightly different expression in the *Regimen*, where the relation of seed to intelligence and character is considered. As a basic principle, the Hippocratic theory develops a correlation between the elements of hot and cold, wet and dry, and intelligence. "The moistest fire and the dryest water, when blended in a body, result in the most intelligence."[166] As it turns out, the male seeds generate male children with the highest intelligence.

> Now if the bodies secreted from both happen to be male, they grow up to the limit of available matter, and the babies become brilliant men in soul and strong in body, unless they be harmed by their subsequent diet. If the secretion from the man be male and that of the woman female, should the male gain mastery, the weaker soul combines with the stronger, since there is nothing more congenial present to which it can go. . . . And these, while less brilliant than the former, nevertheless, as the male from the man won mastery, they turn out to be brave, and have rightly this name. But if the male be secreted from the women but female from the man, and the male gets mastery. . . . [t]hese turn out hermaphrodites ("men-women") and are correctly so-called. These three kinds of men are born, but the degree of manliness depends upon the blending of the parts of water, upon nourishment, education and habits.[167]

The correlative characteristic of the dominance of the female appears to be physical beauty rather than intelligence. For the Hippocratic theory develops a parallel theory of three kinds of women:

> In like manner the female also is generated. If the secretion of both parents be female, the offspring proves female and fair, both to the highest degree. But if the woman's secretion be female and the man's male, and the female gain the mastery, the girls are bolder than the preceding, but nevertheless they too are modest. But if the man's secretion be female, and the woman's male,

and the female gain the mastery, growth takes place after the same fashion, but the girls prove more daring than the preceding, and are named "mannish." [168]

If this theory were summarized in a chart it would appear as follows:

Uterus / Testicles	**male seed** strong seed	**female seed** weak seed
male seed strong seed	Brilliant man	a) If male seed gains mastery over female seed, then hermaphrodite results b) If female seed gains mastery over male seed, then "mannish" woman results
female seed weak seed	a) If female seed gains mastery over male seed, then bold, modest woman results b) If male seed gains mastery over female seed, then brave man results	Beautiful woman

As is evident from the above development of the various ways in which male and female seed can interact in generation, an association of male seed with intelligence and strength, and female seed with physical beauty is developed. In an interesting quotation from *Aphorisms* we find the suggestion that the female is limited in the skill of using both hands: "A woman does not become ambidextrous." [169] It would appear, therefore, that a subtle tendency towards sex polarity is found in the Hippocratic corpus, even though there is an acceptance of the double-seed theory of generation.

In conclusion, the Hippocratic writings stand out as the first systematic attempt to develop a theory of generation in western thought. Rejecting theories of cosmic generation as "akin to painting," the medical philosophers sought to explain and give reasons for their theories through the observations of the senses. [170] Not surprisingly, some of their insights would be considered correct and others false by contemporary medical standards. By insisting on empirical investigation, the Hippocratic writings set the stage for the Aristotelian Revolution, for Aristotle sought to establish his theory on similarly empirical grounds. Before we turn to Aristotle's use of the Hippocratic methodology, it is necessary to examine the thought of his two Socratic predecessors: Xenophon and Plato.

THE SOCRATIC PHILOSOPHERS

Socrates, who lived circa 470 to 399 BC transformed philosophical discussion by his introduction of a dialogue in the form of questioning. As will be seen, he is reputed to have given serious consideration to the question of the concept of woman in relation to man. Since Socrates left no writings of his own, we are dependent upon the records of two of his most famous disciples. Ironically, the two disciples developed slightly different theories of sex identity: Xenophon began a systematic defence of sex polarity, and Plato began a systematic defence of sex unity. It is difficult to know how to separate the thought of the master from that of his disciples. However, it would seem that the words attributed to Socrates in both Xenophon's and Plato's dialogues indicate that he raised serious questions about the practice of sex polarity in Greek society of the time. Socrates appears to have believed that sex identity was an important philosophical issue, especially within the categories of wisdom and virtue.

Xenophon (c. 430–357 BC)

While Xenophon was most famous for military writings, his dialogue *Oeconomicus*, on estate management, contains a great deal of information of interest to the concept of woman. It is one of the earliest records defending a theory of sex polarity against questions about its validity. It is widely believed that the figure of Isomachus in this dialogue represents the thinking of Xenophon himself.[171]

The first question to be considered concerns who is responsible for the quality of work of the wife on an estate:

> I can show that husbands differ widely in their treatment of their wives, and some succeed in winning their co-operation and thereby increase their estates, while others bring utter ruin on their houses by their behaviour to them.
>
> And ought one to blame the husband or the wife for that, Socrates?
>
> . . . If she receives instruction in the right way from her husband and yet does badly, perhaps she should bear the blame; but if the husband does not instruct his wife in the right way of doing things, and so finds her ignorant, should he not bear the blame himself?[172]

Socrates asserts that a person is responsible for his or her actions after having received the knowledge necessary for this practical wisdom. If the woman knows what to do and does not do it well, then she is to blame; if the man knows, but does not teach this knowledge to the woman, then he is to blame.

The dialogue continues with Socrates developing the theory of the complementarity of the husband and wife in estate management:

> I will introduce Aspasia to you, and she will explain the whole matter to you with more knowledge than I possess. I think that the wife who is a good partner in the household contributes just as much as her husband to its good; because the incomings for the most part are the result of the husband's exertions, but the outgoings are controlled mostly by the wife's dispensation.[173]

It is at this point that Isomachus enters the dialogue and begins to develop a slightly different line of argument. While Socrates had differentiated the work of husband and wife as related to the incoming and outgoing of goods, Isomachus begins to draw a rigid distinction between the public and the private spheres of activity. Socrates asked him, "I want very much to learn how you came to be called a gentleman, since you do not pass your time indoors, and your condition does not suggest that you do so."[174] Isomachus responds, "I certainly do not pass my time indoors; for, you know, my wife is quite capable of looking after the house by herself."[175] For Isomachus, work in the private sphere should be undertaken only when there is failure on the part of the woman to accomplish her specific tasks.

Isomachus develops an argument defending separate spheres of activity with an appeal to the gods in the following description of a conversation with his wife:

> It seems to me, dear, that the gods with great discernment have coupled together male and female, as they are called, chiefly in order that they may form a perfect partnership in mutual service. . . . And since both the indoor and the outdoor tasks demand labour and attention, God from the first adapted the woman's nature, I think, to the indoor and man's to the outdoor tasks and cares. For he made the man's body and mind more capable of enduring cold and heat, and journeys and campaigns; and therefore imposed on him the outdoor tasks. To the woman, since he has made her body less capable of such endurance, I take it that God has assigned the indoor tasks.[176]

This natural division of the sexes into private and public spheres of activities through their bodily potential had consequences for their specific virtues. Isomachus continues:

> And since he imposed on the woman the protection of the stores also, knowing that for protection a fearful disposition is no disadvantage, God meted out a larger share of fear to the woman than to the man; and knowing that he who deals with the outdoor tasks will have to be their defender against any wrong-doer, he meted out to him again a larger share of courage.[177]

The separation of the "virtues" of fear for woman and courage for man is balanced somewhat by Isomachus's insistance that they both share equally in memory, attention, and self-control:

> Because both must give and take, he granted to both impartially memory and attention; and so you could not distinguish whether the male or the female sex has the larger share of these. And god also gave to both impartially the power to practise due self control, and gave authority to which is the better—whether it be the man or the woman—to win a larger portion of the good that comes from it.[178]

It is at this point in the argument that Isomachus begins to draw far-reaching consequences from the theory. Since the division of labour is ordained by the gods, it becomes a serious error to transgress these dictates.

> Now since we know, dear, what duties have been assigned to each of us by God, we must endeavour, each of us, to do the duties allotted to us as well as possible. The law, moreover, approves of them . . . the law declares those tasks to be honourable for each of them wherein God has made one to excel the other. Thus, to the woman it is more honourable to stay indoors than to abide in the fields, but to the man it is unseemly rather to stay indoors than to attend to the work outside. If a man acts contrary to the nature God has given him, possibly his defiance is detected by the gods and he is punished for neglecting his own work, or meddling with his wife's.[179]

In the *Oeconomicus*, Xenophon has articulated the first rationale for a separation of spheres of virtuous activity for men and women. His argument begins with a statement that these roles are divinely ordained, next they are integrated into law, and finally they are subject to reinforcement by punishment when transgressed. What began as a descriptive enterprise ended up as a prescriptive command for the differentiation of virtues for woman and man.

Xenophon continues his argument with an appeal to an analogy with nature. He argues that the queen bee has a similar feminine task:

> I think that the queen bee is busy about just such other tasks appointed by God.
>
> And pray, said she, how do the queen bee's tasks resemble those that I have to do?
>
> How? She stays in the hive, I answered. . . . Those whose duty it is to work outside she sends forth to their work; and whatever each of them brings in, she knows and receives it, and keeps it till it is wanted. . . .
>
> Then shall I too have to do these things? said my wife.
>
> Indeed you will, said I, your duty will be to remain indoors and send out those servants whose work is outside, and superintend those who are to work indoors. . . . For it is not through outward comeliness that the sum of things good and beautiful is increased in the world, but by the daily practice of virtue.[180]

The virtues, therefore, receive their primary differentiation by the gods who develop certain patterns of activity in nature. Xenophon considers this divine ordination of the separate spheres of activity to be justification enough. Socrates, however, repeatedly asks Isomachus whether or not his wife was convinced by the arguments.

Subsequently, Isomachus develops a theory that a good household is best modelled after a military campaign.

> My dear, there is nothing so convenient or so good for human beings as order. . . . An army in disorder is a confused mass. . . . And so my dear, if you do not want this confusion, and wish to know exactly how to manage our goods, and to find with ease whatever is wanted, and to satisfy me by giving me anything I ask for, let us choose the place that each portion should occupy.[181]

After developing within the dialogue a detailed description of how to order the possessions of a household, Socrates again asked Isomachus whether he was successful in his teaching:

> Was your wife inclined to take heed of your words?
>
> Why Socrates, he cried, she just told me that I was mistaken if I supposed that I was laying a hard task on her in telling her that she must take care of our things. . . .
>
> Now when I heard that his wife had given him this answer, I exclaimed: Upon my word, Isomachus, your wife has a truly masculine mind by your showing.
>
> Yes, said Isomachus, and I am prepared to give you other examples of high-mindedness on her part, when a word from me was enough to secure her instant obedience. [182]

The military model of order in a household in the arrangement and care of possessions also carried over into the separation of the virtues of ruling and obedience according to sex. The wife who understood these principles was characterized as having a "masculine mind" or "high-mindedness."

Isomachus describes a situation in which he criticized his wife for wearing make-up:

> Well, one day, Socrates, I noticed that her face was made up. . . . So I said to her, Tell me, my dear, how should I appear more worthy of your love as a partner in our goods, by disclosing to you our belongings just as they are . . . or by trying to trick you with an exaggerated account . . .? How then should I seem more worthy of your love in this partnership of the body—by striving to have my body hale and strong when I present it to you, and so literally to be of a good countenance in your sight, or by smearing my cheeks with red before I show myself to you and clasp you in my arms, cheating you and offering to your eyes and hands red lead instead of my real flesh?
>
> Oh, she cried, I would sooner touch you than red lead, would sooner see your own colour than rouge, would sooner see your eyes bright than smeared with grease.
>
> Then please assume, my dear, that I do not prefer white paint and dye of alkanet to your real colour. . . . People who live together are bound to be found out if they try to deceive one another. . . .
>
> And pray, what did she say to that? I asked.
>
> Nothing, he said, only she gave up such practices from that day forward. [183]

The significant aspect of Xenophon's analysis here is that he is presenting detailed arguments about the different areas of activity of man and woman. He uses this example to indicate how obedient his wife is in this particular situation. Obedience is simply assumed to be the virtue of woman in relation to her husband. It follows directly from the military model of the estate in which the husband, like a military commander, assumes the responsibility of ordering everything under his care, of delegating areas of responsibility, and of insuring that they are carried out.

In conclusion, then, Xenophon is the first philosopher to offer detailed arguments for the separation of virtues for woman and man. In as much as obedience and the private sphere of activity is considered less important than ruling and the public sphere of activity, Xenophon can be considered as suggesting a rationale for sex polarity. His theory can be charted as follows:

	Man	**Woman**
Virtue	ruling	obeying
	public sphere	private sphere

Socrates functions as a questioner in the background, continuously asking whether or not Isomachus's wife agreed with the arguments that were presented. At the end of this section of the dialogue, however, Socrates appears to give his approval of this theory of virtue: "I think your account of your wife's occupations is sufficient for the present—and very credible it is to both of you."[184] Ironically, in Plato's dialogues, Socrates reaches precisely the opposite conclusion, namely that women and men have the same virtues. Therefore, while Xenophon uses Socrates to support sex polarity, Plato uses him to support sex unity.

PLATO (c. 428–355 BC)

This important Greek philosopher was the first to develop a systematic analysis of the concept of woman in relation to man that considers all four categories of questions related to opposites, generation, wisdom, and virtue. In addition, Plato can be called the founder of the sex-unity position because he was the first to defend this theory of sex identity in all four categories mentioned above. Therefore, Plato shifted the debate about sex identity to a new level of depth. Previously, the pre-Socratic philosophers, judging from the extant fragments of their writings, simply thought about the subject in one or another category. There appears to have been little attempt to develop an analysis that covered several different categories of human existence. Therefore the pre-Socratics raised the fundamental questions that Plato then sought to answer systematically.

It must be stated at the outset, however, that Plato did not develop a theory of sex identity that was completely consistent. In fact, Plato's contrasting orientations to philosophical questions about sex identity have led many theorists to develop confusing or even contradictory analyses of his views. Therefore, a careful analysis of Plato's philosophy of sex identity will help sort out these difficulties of interpretation. It will be seen that Plato argued for a sex-polarity theory of male and female on the cosmic level while he argued for a sex-unity theory of man and woman in the world. The following diagram may help to orient the reader to the subsequent analysis.

Plato's Theory of Sex Identity

	Male	Female
	Sex Polarity on Cosmic Level	
Opposites	Forms active like a Father	Receptacle passive like a Mother
Generation	Souls first fall into male bodies	Souls of cowardly or immoral men fall into female bodies
Wisdom	Forms are source of Wisdom	Matter is source of ignorance
Virtue		
	Man	**Woman**
	Sex Unity in the World	
Opposites	*Same identity by nature of the soul*	
Generation	*Same generation through reincarnation*	
Wisdom	Starts off stronger	Starts off weaker
	Same knowledge and education	
Virtue	Starts off stronger	Starts off weaker
	Same function and virtue	

To consider Plato as the founder of the sex-unity position is to focus primarily on the arguments he presented about the identity of woman and man in the world. However, since he also developed a rationale for sex polarity on the cosmic level, both aspects of his thought will be described. Plato's sex-polarity arguments were incorporated by subsequent philosophers even though his most significant contribution to the theory of sex identity flows from his breakthrough analysis of philosophical foundations for sex unity. The subsequent analysis will consider each of the categories of opposites, generation, wisdom, and virtue in turn.

Opposites

The complexity of Plato's views is underlined by the *Timaeus*, in which he suggested arguments in support of sex polarity, and by the *Republic*—written at the same time— in which he suggested arguments in support of sex unity.[185] In the consideration of opposites this conflict will become manifestly clear.

In the *Timaeus*, Plato describes a great Mother Receptacle who is totally passive:

> Wherefore the mother and receptable of all created and visible and in any way sensible things is not to be termed earth or air or fire or water, or any of the elements from which they are derived, but is an invisible and formless being which receives all things and in some mysterious way partakes of the intelligible and is most incomprehensible. In saying this we shall not be far wrong; as far as we can attain to a knowledge of her from the previous considerations, we may truly say that fire is that part of her nature which from time to time is inflamed, and water that which is moistened, and that the mother substance becomes earth and air, insofar as she receives the impressions of them.[186]

It is important to note that Plato has brought about a major shift in thought about the cosmic female principle. The vibrant and dynamic cosmic Earth Mother of Hesiod's *Theogony* has now been reduced to an abstract cosmic female principle. The Earth Mother in Hesiod had generated sky, air, and fire by herself. Plato's cosmic mother simply receives the forms of elements. Plato's description of the Mother Receptacle continues:

> She is the natural recipient of all impressions, and is stirred and informed by them, and appears different from time to time by reason of them. But the forms which enter into and go out of her are the likeness of eternal realities modelled after the patterns in a wonderful and mysterious manner.[187]

The claim that the cosmic principle was completely passive in her nature is repeatedly defended. Plato argues that if the cosmic female principle had any nature of her own "it would take the impressions badly, because it would intrude its own shape."[188] Therefore, the powerfully dynamic cosmic female principle of the poet Hesiod was reduced to a completely passive cosmic female principle by the philosopher Plato. The Earth Mother has become simply the metaphysical concept of Prime Matter.

Plato carries forward his analogy to include a description of the cosmic Father as being like Forms when he uses the generative process as an analogy for the interaction of form and matter:

> For the present we have only to conceive of three natures: First, that which is in the process of generation; second, that in which the generation takes place; and third, that of which the thing generated is a resemblance naturally produced. And we may liken the receiving principle to a mother, the source or spring to a father, and the intermediate nature to a child. . . .[189]

We must ask: What is it that Plato saw in the relation of male to female that allowed him to use this example as a simile for the relation of matter and form in the world? Obviously, there are similarities among the three factors in the two relations: men and women together generate children, just as Plato thought that form and matter interact to generate physical objects in the world. The third thing generated partakes of the two sources in a similar way; the child of its parents, and the physical object of a specific union of form and matter.

Plato also appears to be suggesting that the entry of true forms into matter is similar to the father's act of depositing seed during sexual intercourse when he says that the mother receptacle "is stirred and formed by the forms which enter into and go out of her." He does not give a further development of this image, but simply lets it rest as suggested. However, it is clear that Plato did associate fathering in some way with forms, and mothering with the reception of forms by matter. So on the cosmic level, he introduced a kind of sex polarity through his subsequent affirmation of the value of forms over matter. The cosmic male is superior to the cosmic female in that it is the source of all activity and is an "eternal reality" that contains everything with enduring value for wisdom and virtue; while the cosmic female is a passive receptacle with no identity of its own, which would cease to be of use when no longer needed by the forms. Therefore, in Plato, the historical identification of the cosmic male with form and the cosmic female with prime matter received its first philosophical formulation.

When this theory of sex polarity of male and female in the *Timaeus* is compared with the theory of sex identity as developed in the *Republic*, an entirely different perspective is suggested. In this dialogue, Plato uses the character of Socrates to open the debate on a different level:

> And we must throw open the debate to anyone who wishes whether in jest or in earnest to raise the question whether female human nature is capable of sharing with the male all tasks or none at all, or some but not others.[190]

The analysis then proceeds to consider the nature of woman and man, for Plato believed that activities flowed directly from nature. Socrates continues:

> We did agree that different natures should have differing pursuits and that the natures of men and women differ. And yet now we affirm that these differing natures should have the same pursuits . . . but we did not delay to consider at all what particular kind of diversity and identity of nature we had in mind and with reference to what we were trying to define it when we assigned different pursuits to different natures and the same to the same.[191]

Socrates presses his listener, Glaucon, to be specific about how women and men are the same and how they are different. The argument discerns first that bald and long-haired men have the same nature because the length of hair has nothing to do with their specific work, which, in this example, is cobbling. The dialogue continues:

> . . . [A] man and a woman who have a physician's mind have the same nature. Don't you think so?
>
> I do.
>
> But that a man physician and a man carpenter have different natures?
>
> Certainly, I suppose.
>
> Similarly, then, said I, if it appears that the male and the female sex have distinct

> qualifications for any arts or pursuits, we shall affirm that they ought to be assigned respectively to each. But if it appears that they differ only in just this respect that the female bears and the male begets, we shall say that no proof has yet been produced that the woman differs from the man for our purposes, but we shall continue to think that our guardians and their wives ought to follow the same pursuits.[192]

In this crucial passage, Plato indicates the direction that the argument in the *Republic* will take. The identity of a woman or man comes from their mind (or soul) and not from their body. The material aspects of generation, which played such a crucial role on the cosmic level of male and female identity, have no role at all on the level of actual human existence. The generative process is simply irrelevant to the respective identities of woman and man in the world. A woman's or a man's nature flows directly from the character of her or his soul, which is an immaterial and therefore non-sexual entity. Since the soul or mind is neither male nor female, when Plato considers the question of how woman and man are opposite, he concludes that when they are considered from the perspective of their real nature, they are the same. More specifically, it is the sexless soul and not the material body that determines the identity of the woman or man. The implicit key to Plato's theory is the belief in reincarnation, which will now be considered under the category of generation.

Generation

Plato described the reincarnation of the soul in the *Phaedrus, Republic* and *Timaeus* through the introduction of myths. In the *Phaedrus*, Plato described the soul as originally being in union with the immortal world of forms:

> All soul has the care of all that is inanimate, and transverses the whole universe, though in ever-changing forms. Thus when it is perfect and winged it journeys on high and controls the whole world, but one that has shed its wings sinks down until it can fasten on something solid, and settling there it takes to itself an earthly body . . .[193]

In this myth Plato describes the soul as falling into a series of reincarnations in descending degrees of wisdom: as philosopher, king, statesman, athlete, physician, prophet, poet, artisan, farmer, sophist, and finally, tyrant. In the *Phaedrus*, there is no mention of differences of sex within these categories, or of why the soul originally fell from its state of perfection. However, it is clear that the material incarnation of the soul was considered to be inferior to its original state in union with the immaterial forms. In the *Timaeus*, Plato asserts the priority of soul over body:

> Whereas he made the soul in origin and excellence prior to and older than the body, to be the ruler and mistress, of whom the body was to be the subject.[194]

The question of reincarnation is also considered at the end of the *Republic* in the myth of Er. Here the process of continuing incarnations is described as following from a choice with direct relation to the quality of a past life:

> . . . [I]t was a sight worth seeing to observe how the several souls selected their lives. He said it was a strange, pitiful, and ridiculous spectacle, as the choice was determined for the most part by the habits of their former lives. He saw the soul that had been Orpheus', he said, selecting the life of a swan, because from the hatred of the tribe of women, owing to his death at their hands, it was unwilling to be conceived and born a woman. . . . Drawing one of the middle lots the soul of Atlanta caught sight of the great honours attached to an athlete's life and could not pass them by but snatched at them. After her, he said, he saw the soul of Epeus, the son of Panopeus, entering into the nature of an arts and crafts woman.[195]

Plato described the same soul living at different times in male and female bodies. The soul itself had no sexual identity, it was only the material body that gave it a specification as male or female. Since the identity of the person was derived from the soul, and the soul could be incarnated in either a male or female body, the fundamental identity of woman and man was the same. It is precisely this thesis of the soul as a sexless identity with the potential of being incarnated in either male or female bodies that gave Plato a metaphysical foundation for sex unity. Reincarnation leads to the logical conclusion that there are no philosophical differences between woman and man.

In the *Timaeus*, Plato suggests a further qualification of this view when he gives a decidedly inferior valuation to female incarnation:

> Of the men who came into the world, those who were cowards or led unrighteous lives may with reason be supposed to have changed into the nature of women in the second generation.[196]

While Plato cautions the reader not to accept the details of the myth proposed, there is little doubt that he envisaged an inferior status for a female incarnation. He implied that animal incarnation followed a similar pattern:

> Thus were created women and the female sex in general. But the race of birds was created out of innocent light-minded men. . . . The race of wild pedestrian animals, again, came from those who had no philosophy in any of their thoughts. . . . The inhabitants of the water . . . were made out of the most entirely senseless and ignorant of all. . . .[197]

Plato seems to be suggesting that women and men, when considered from the perspective of soul, have similar natures. Nonetheless, when considered from the perspective of their bodily nature, the woman is inferior to the man. In fact, to be incarnated as female is an indication of a kind of punishment for a less than perfect previous life.

In the *Republic*, Socrates appears to agree that women are, generally speaking, weaker than men:

> Do you know, then, of anything practised by mankind in which the masculine sex does not surpass the female on all of these points? . . .

> You are right, he said, that the one sex is far surpassed by the other in everything, one may say. Many women, it is true, are better than many men in many things, but broadly speaking, it is as you say.
>
> Then there is no pursuit of the administrators of a state that belongs to a woman because she is a woman or to a man because he is a man. But the natural capacities are distributed alike among both creatures, and women naturally share in all pursuits and men in all—yet for all the woman is weaker than the man.[198]

Significantly, Socrates is suggesting that even though women begin with an inferior kind of incarnation, they should be considered from the perspective of their souls rather than the limitations of their bodies. Indeed, he is accepting a cosmic view of sex polarity in the inferior incarnation of woman, while also suggesting a theory of sex unity for the actual lives of women and men in the world. It is precisely in this way that Plato's philosophy can be seen as supporting sex polarity on the cosmic level while supporting sex unity in the world. The greater degree of importance that can be given to the theory of sex unity arises from Plato having devalued the material world in general and the body in particular. In the *Phaedo,* Plato describes Socrates teaching his disciples that the body leads to error and the soul to the truth:

> . . . [T]he body fills us with loves and desires and fears and all sorts of fancies and a great deal of nonsense. . . . We are in fact convinced that if we are ever to have pure knowledge of anything, we must get rid of the body and contemplate things by themselves with the soul by itself.[199]

Socrates concludes that philosophy is the practice of dying and death, or more specifically, it is the practice of separating the soul from the body:

> The desire to free the soul is found chiefly or rather only, in the true philosopher. In fact the philosopher's occupation consists precisely in the freeing and separation of soul from body.[200]

Therefore, if a woman achieves this practice of the separation of soul from body, she is living in terms of her most perfect identity. In this sense, the woman and man have the same goal, namely to become separate from all bodily aspects of their identity, including the sexual differentiation as male or female.

Before turning to a discussion of the specific way in which Plato develops his sex-unity theory in the categories of wisdom and virtue, some mention should be made about another cosmic myth of generation, which is often incorrectly taken as the view of Plato.[201] In the *Symposium*, the figure called Aristophanes introduces a myth about the origin of love that goes back to an original state of humanity where there were creatures that could be described as man-man, man-woman, and woman-woman:

> . . . [I]n the beginning we were nothing like we are now. For one thing, the race was divided into three; that is to say, besides the two sexes, male and female, which we have at present, there was a third which partook of the nature of both, and for which we still have a name, . . . "hermaphrodite." . . .

> . . . [E]ach of these beings was globular in shape, with rounded back and sides, four arms and four legs, and two faces . . . and two lots of privates. . . .
>
> (Zeus) cut them all in half just as you or I might chop up sour apples for pickling, or slice an egg with a hair. . . .
>
> Now, when the work of bisection was complete it left each half with a desperate yearning for the other. . . .
>
> The man who is a slice of the hermaphrodite sex, as it was called, will naturally be attracted by women. . . . But the woman who is a slice of the original female is attracted by women rather than by men . . . while men who are slices of the male are followers of the male. . . .[202]

Plato was not using this myth to describe his own view, but rather to report a theory believed by some members of the population.[203] This myth was possibly a characterization of Empedocles' theory of the recurring cycles of generation. In any event, Aristophanes provided his story at the pre-critical phase of the dialogue before Plato suggested his own view through Socrates' report of the teachings of Diotema. It can be safely concluded that Plato did not intend to suggest that the myth of the hermaphrodite was his own view.

It is significant that Plato did not appear to give much attention to the continuity of generation. Indeed, it is difficult to know whether he believed that both women and men produced seeds. That Plato considered the material aspect of the person to be less important than the soul was perhaps a factor in his neglect of an area of study that had so fascinated the pre-Socratics. In the *Timaeus*, we find him describing the sexual act in terms that reveal its danger to the ordered mind:

> The seed having life, and becoming endowed with respiration, produces in that part in which it respires a lively desire of emission, and thus creates in us the love of procreation. Wherefore also in men the organ of generation becoming rebellious and masterful, like an animal obedient to reason, and maddened with the sting of lust, seeks to gain absolute sway, and the same is the case with the so-called womb or matrix of woman. The animal within them is desirous of procreating children.[204]

While it is not clear from the above passage whether or not woman produced seed, Plato argues that the act of intercourse for both sexes is the result of the lower or animal instincts gaining dominance over the higher functions of reason. In the *Laws*, Plato develops his theory of how these lower parts of the soul should be ordered:

> Our third and most imperious need and fiercest passion arose later, but most of all fires men to all manner of frenzies—I mean lust of procreation with its blaze of wanton appetite. These three unwholesome appetites, then, we must divert from the so-called pleasant towards the good; we must try to check them by the three supreme sanctions—fear, law, true discourse. . . .[205]

The first ordering of the sexual instinct suggested by Plato in the *Laws* was to limit its expression to heterosexual relations:

> We must not forget that this pleasure is held to have been granted by nature to male and female when conjoined for the work of procreation; the crime of male with male, or female with female, is an outrage on nature and a capital surrender to lust of pleasure.[206]

Plato, through the Athenian, suggests that this argument be backed up by law:

> . . . [I] knew of a device for establishing this law of restricting procreative intercourse to its natural function by abstention from congress with our own sex, with its deliberate murder of the race and its wasting of the seed of life on a stony and rocky soul where it will never take root and bear its natural fruit, and equal abstention from any female field when you would desire to harvest. Once suppose this law perpetual and effective . . . the result will be untold good.[207]

The second ordering was to limit heterosexual expressions of sexual intercourse to marriage. The Athenian proposes a law that would force men and women to marry:

> A man to marry when he has reached the age of thirty and before he comes to that of thirty-five; neglect to do so to be penalized by fine and loss of status.[208]

Women were to marry between the ages of sixteen and twenty.[209] Even within marriage the sexual act was to be regulated so that it occurred only when procreation was desired. For Plato, in contrast to Democritus, the sexual act was not always bad; when it was ordered and strictly regulated it was good for society.

Plato believed that there were higher goals for the individual than the generation of children. In the *Symposium*, he traces the evolution of love from that which is directed towards a single beautiful person to the love of the Form of Beauty, and finally to a love of the Good itself.[210] In the *Phaedrus*, he recounts the rewards of people who have been able to achieve this internal ordering where all instincts have been placed under the higher direction of reason. For these people will "recover their wings" by stopping the cycles of reincarnation, and they will lose all need for bodily existence:

> If the victory be won by the higher elements of mind guiding them into the ordered rule of the philosophical life, their days on earth will be blessed with happiness and concord, for the power of evil in the soul has been subjected, and the power of good liberated; they have won self-mastery and inward peace. And when life is over, with burden shed and wings recovered, they stand victorious. . . .[211]

Plato's theory of the relation of sexual intercourse to sex identity is clearly tied up with his devaluation of the material world and of the body. He gives equally strict guidelines to men and to women, and in both cases demands a regulation and ordering of the sexual instinct. Plato's ultimate objective is for women and men to achieve the highest degree of wisdom and virtue so that they may escape the cycles of reincarnation and achieve an eternal union of soul with immaterial Forms. As will be seen, in these two categories he develops detailed arguments to prove that both women and men ought to strive to meet this objective in the same way.

Wisdom

On the cosmic level in the category of wisdom, Plato continued the movement of preceding philosophers to take control of the source of wisdom away from goddesses and Muses and to place it firmly in the power of the minds of the philosophers themselves. For Plato, the philosopher becomes wise not so much by worshipping the goddess Athena as by studying the Forms and achieving a vision of the Good itself. In the *Republic* we find:

> This reality, then, that gives their truth to the objects of knowledge and the power of knowing to the knower, you must say is the idea of the good, and you must conceive it as being the cause of knowledge, and of truth insofar as known.[212]

The philosopher must assume active responsibility for achieving this goal of wisdom.

In the *Ion*, Plato offers a devastating critique of the dependence of poets upon the Muses: "One poet is suspended from one Muse, another from another; we call it being 'possessed,' but the fact is much the same, since he is held."[213] The poet is not in control of his own reasoning process, but is held in bondage to the lower part of his soul. In a similar way in the *Republic*, Plato argues that poets attempt to sway others by appealing to their lower instincts:

> . . . [P]oetic imitation is the same. For it waters and fosters these feelings when what we ought to do is to dry them up, and it establishes them as our rules when they ought to be ruled. . . .[214]

As a consequence, Plato suggests that poets be excluded from an ideal Republic:

> For if you grant admission to the honeyed Muse in lyric or epic, pleasure and pain will be lords of the city instead of law and that which shall from time to time have approved itself to the general reason as the best.[215]

With Platonic theory, then, the dependence upon the Muses for inspiration, which was present in early poets such as Hesiod or Sappho, has been totally pushed aside. Philosophers henceforth were to depend upon the powers of their own reason, upon arguments and the observations of the senses.

Before passing on to a consideration of the relation of Plato's theory of the lives of women and men, mention should be made of a passage in the *Timaeus* that had later implications for male and female identity. Plato developed a theory of the mind that clearly gives a superior valuation to the higher powers of reason over the lower instincts. Although Plato nowhere argues that these distinctions have direct reference to male and female identity, i.e., that the higher reason is male and the lower female, the following passage was later interpreted in this light:

> And in the breast and in what is termed the thorax, they incased the mortal soul, and as the one part of this was superior and the other inferior they divided the cavity of the thorax into two parts, as the women's and men's apartments are divided in houses, and placed the midriff to be a wall or partition between them. That part of the inferior soul which is endowed wth courage and passion and loves contention, they settled nearer the head, midway between the midriff

> and the neck, in order that being obedient to the rule of reason it might join with it in controlling and restraining the desires when they are no longer willing of their own accord to obey the word of command issuing from the citadel.[216]

The use of the analogy of women's and men's apartments may suggest to some readers that the female identity is tied up with the inferior part of the soul, or with the passions, while the men's apartments are like the higher or ruling part of the soul. Indeed, the Platonist Philo draws just such a conclusion. However, the passage in the *Timaeus* does not reach that far; it simply describes a partition of the apartments into two separate areas. As will be seen, Plato's philosophy argues that women and men have the same capacities of soul.

In the *Republic*, Plato develops his view of the state as having the same three-level structure as the soul itself. The state of a soul "writ large."

Soul	*State*	*Virtue*
Reason	Philosopher-guardians	Wisdom
Will	Soldiers	Courage
Desires	Workers	Temperance

Plato argues that women and men have the same three capacities of soul, the same three possibilities of role in the ideal state, and the same three correlative virtues:

> Shall we, then, assign them all (the pursuits of the state) to men and nothing to women?
>
> How could we?
>
> We should rather, I take it, say that one woman has the nature of a physician and another not, and one is musical and another unmusical?
>
> Surely.
>
> Can we, then, deny that one woman is naturally athletic and warlike and another unwarlike and averse to gymnastics?
>
> I think not.
>
> And again, one a lover, another a hater, of wisdom? And one high-spirited and another lacking in spirit?
>
> That also is true.
>
> Then it is likewise true that one woman has the qualities of a guardian and another not. Were not these the natural qualities of the men also whom we selected for guardians?
>
> They were.

> The women and the men, then, have the same nature in respect to the guardianship of the state, save in so far as the one is weaker, the other stronger.[217]

The natural weakness of women is consistent with an inferior bodily incarnation. This weakness can be seen as a kind of handicap in the race to wisdom. However, it does not prohibit women from entering the race; it simply means that the struggle for wisdom takes somewhat longer for women than for men. Accordingly, in *Laws*, Plato stipulates: "[The limiting age] for official appointments shall be forty for a woman, thirty for a man."[218] The weakness of a woman's body simply means that she will need to study longer before achieving the height of wisdom necessary for her to become a philosopher guardian of the state.

Plato placed a great deal of emphasis on education. In the *Republic* he explicitly argued that girls and boys ought to receive the same education:

> If, then, we are to use the women for the same things as the men, we must also teach them the same things.
>
> Yes.
>
> Now music together with gymnastics was the training we gave the men.
>
> Yes.
>
> Then we must assign these two arts to the women also and the offices of war.[219]

This view is repeated in *Laws*: "And mind you, my law will apply in all respects to girls as much as to boys: the girls must be trained exactly like the boys."[220] Perhaps even more significant, this view was repeated in the introduction to the *Timaeus*, in which the inferior incarnation of the female was postulated:

> Neither did we forget the women, of whom we declared that their natures should be harmoniously developed by training, equally with those of the men, and that common pursuits should be assigned to them all both in time of war and in their ordinary life.[221]

Plato was the first philosopher in the west to offer extensive arguments for women and men receiving the same education. His rationale for this position was an appeal to the same nature. A person's nature had nothing to do with his or her sex, but simply with the quality of soul. Therefore, Plato's sex-unity position in the category of wisdom drew implicitly upon his belief that personal identity was primarily a characteristic of soul in separate existence from the body. It was not until the philosopher Porphyry wrote a philosophical letter to his wife, Marcella, that the link between potential reincarnations of the soul and the sex-unity position was explicitly stated in western thought. Plato, however, laid the philosophical foundations for this development.

By combining Plato's suggestions from the *Symposium, Republic*, and *Laws*, it would appear that the entire process of education would take approximately thirty years for men and forty years for women. Education would begin with the study of concrete physical objects and then proceed to the search for knowledge of the nature of the physical world in general. This period of focus on physical things was associated with the practical study of gymnastics and military skills. Next, the student would proceed to a study of higher Forms, especially through learning the principles of music and mathematics—with a special emphasis upon the discovery of invisible realities and harmony. Moving further into a study of the motion of the planets through the science of astronomy, the student would become attuned to the existence of eternal physical bodies. Finally, through a careful study of the principles of dialectic, the student would reach an understanding of the relations of eternal Forms to the Good that is the source of all knowledge and existence. For Plato, all learning involved a movement from matter to form, from the physical to the immaterial, from the temporal to the eternal, and from the illusory to the true. Women as well as men were expected to proceed along this path to wisdom.

Plato offers an example of a woman who achieved the heights of wisdom in the intriguing role that Diotima plays in the dialogue *Symposium*. Although Socrates implies that Diotima was an historical person, there is no corroborating evidence for her existence. Therefore, it is safe to conclude that Diotima was developed by Plato as a female personification of wisdom, or *sophia*. Significantly, Diotima is the embodiment of dialectic and discursive reasoning. She is able to offer reasons for her views, and Socrates even credits her with having invented the "socratic" method of question and answer:

> . . . [I] want to talk about some lessons I was given, once upon a time, by a Manitinean woman called Diotima—a woman who was deeply versed in this and many other fields of knowledge. . . . I think the easiest way will be to adopt Diotima's own method of inquiry by question and answer.[222]

Throughout the dialogue Socrates refers to Diotima as knowing more than he does about the subject. At one point Diotima asks Socrates a question about the proper activity of Love:

> Can you tell me that, Socrates?
>
> If I could, my dear Diotima, I retorted, I shouldn't be so much amazed at your grasp of the subject, and I shouldn't be coming to you to learn the answer to that very question.[223]

Diotima is presented as being able to give reasons for her views, reasons that can then be used to teach others:

> Don't you know, she asked, that holding an opinion which is in fact correct, without being able to give a reason for it, is neither true knowledge—for how can it be knowledge without a reason—nor ignorance.[224]

Diotima then gave lengthy descriptions of the theory of Forms and of the philosopher's relation to true knowledge. Of the content of her speech, two different themes bear mentioning in reference to sex identity.

First of all, Diotima is recorded as having introduced a cosmic differentiation between wisdom and ignorance that has reference to sex identity. She argues that Love has two parents: Resource and Need. Perhaps reflecting the cosmic identification of the

Forms with fathering and the passive receptacle with mothering, Diotima continues:

> Love is a lover of wisdom, and being such, he is placed between wisdom and ignorance—for which his parentage also is responsible, in that his father is full of wisdom and resource, while his mother is devoid of either.[225]

The cosmic father of love, therefore, is associated with resource, plenty, and wisdom, while the cosmic mother of love is associated with need, poverty, and ignorance. This sex-polarity interpretation is repeated in the writings of later neo-Platonists such as Plotinus. That Diotima is the one who propounds this view simply points out the ironic combination of sex unity and sex polarity in Plato. On the cosmic level, he suggests a sex-polarity theory, while on the level of women and men living in the world he argues and presents a model of sex unity. Diotima is as wise a figure as any in Plato's dialogues, and Socrates affirms his support of her teaching at the end of the dialogue:

> This, Gentlemen, was the doctrine of Diotima, I was convinced, and in that conviction I try to bring others to the same creed.[226]

The second part of Diotima's speech with reference to sex identity is her view of two levels of conception, of the body and of the soul:

> Well, then, she went on, those whose procreancy is of the body turn to women as the object of their love, and raise a family. . . . But those whose procreancy is of the spirit rather than of the flesh . . . conceive and bear the things of the spirit. And what are they? you ask, Wisdom and all her sister virtues. . . .[227]

The philosopher, preferring the soul to the body, chooses to conceive in the soul rather than in the body. Diotima asks, . . . "[W]ho would not prefer such a fatherhood to merely human propagation . . . ?"[228]

The radical separation of soul and body in the philosophy of Plato, coupled with a devaluation of the body, led to a situation where wisdom called for, in the first instance, a search for giving birth to true ideas. In the *Theaetetus*, Plato carried this view of intellectual conception forward in his description of the role of Socrates as a midwife:

> SOCRATES: How absurd of you never to have heard that I am the son of a midwife, a fine buxom woman called Phaenarete! . . . Have you also been told that I practise the same art? . . . My art of midwifery is in general like theirs; the only difference is that my patients are men, not women, and my concern is not with the body but with the soul that is in travail of birth.[229]

In this dialogue, Socrates describes the situation in Athens where he is the practical teacher of philosophy to young men. However, he does not imply that the arguments of Plato in the *Republic* in favour of women being given education in philosophy is wrong. Rather, the *Republic* suggests the nature of a just society, what ought to be done, while the *Theaetetus* simply describes the way in which philosophy is actually practised. In both situations the goal is to encourage the student to move from concerns with the body and the material world to a higher concern with the immaterial forms and to an eventual vision of the good as the source of all knowledge. After such a goal has been achieved, the philosopher should return to the world, whether man or woman, and begin the practice of external virtue. In the *Republic*, Plato suggests that this movement from wisdom to virtue is like passing from inside a cave of deception to a vision of the sun, and then back to the cave to carry out actions for the benefit of society at large.

Virtue

Plato's theory of virtue systematically supports sex unity in the context of a world that embodies the theory of sex polarity. He achieves this in three distinct areas: first in his arguments against the Sophist position that different functions of men and women have different virtues; second in his arguments against the universal prescription of the virtue of ruling for men and obeying for women; and third in his arguments against separate spheres of activity for women and men. These arguments for sex unity will now be considered in turn.

In the dialogue *Meno*, Plato argues against what is presumed to be Gorgias's view that man's virtue "consists in managing a city's affairs capably," while woman's virtue is "to be a good house wife, careful with her stores and obedient to her husband."[230] Socrates responds with irony to Meno's descriptions of different virtues for men and women, children and slaves: "I seem to be in luck. I wanted one virtue and I find you have a whole swarm of virtues to offer."[231] Socrates continues by trying to prove that Meno's theory of different virtues for women and men rests upon the deeper foundation of a single virtue for both sexes:

> SOCRATES: Well then didn't you say that a man's virtue lay in directing the city well, and a woman's in directing her household well?
> MENO: Yes.
> SOCRATES: And is it possible to direct anything well—city or household or anything else—if not temperately and justly?
> MENO: Certainly not.
> SOCRATES: Then both man and woman need the same qualities, justice and temperance, if they are going to be good.
> MENO: It looks like it.[232]

Since virtue for Plato sprang from the part of the soul that directed the acting of the person, both women and men needed the same virtues to carry out their work. Wisdom is the virtue of reason, courage of the will, temperance of the desires, and justice is the virtue of harmony between the three parts of the soul. By pressing the notion of virtue deeper, Plato has defeated the Sophist argument that different functions for woman and man demand different virtues. Significantly, in the *Meno* no more reference is made to the obedience of woman to man. Plato never discussed the specific question of the relation of obedience and ruling to woman and man. He was primarily concerned with the obedience of the lower part of the soul to the higher part, or reason, which was conceived as harmony or justice in the soul. However, he offers an implicit answer in the *Republic*, where he argues that women are able to be guardians of the state.

> Women of this kind, then, must be selected to cohabit with men of this kind and to serve with them as guardians since they are capable of it and akin by nature.
>
> By all means.
>
> And to the same natures must we not assign the same pursuits?
>
> The same.[233]

Female guardians would rule over male and female soldiers and workers. They would rule together with male guardians. Therefore, Plato clearly did not set up obedience as a specific virtue of women or ruling as a specific virtue of man. It may be that within the two lower classes of society, that is, of soldiers and workers, the traditional differentiation as proposed by the Sophists would hold. Plato gives no enlightenment on the subject. However, he is explicit about women's potential to become guardians, and in this situation it is clear that the virtue of ruling would be specifically theirs. Plato's sex-unity theory distributes virtues according to class or position in society and dominant quality of soul, not according to the sex of the person under consideration.

In a similar way, Plato also rejected the theory of separate spheres of activity for women and men. This view, which had been so carefully articulated by Xenophon, was questioned by Socrates in the *Republic*:

> In this matter, then, of the regulation of women, we may say that we have surmounted one of the waves of our paradox and have not been quite swept away by it in ordaining that our guardians and female guardians must have all pursuits in common. . . . This, said I, and all that precedes has for its sequel, in my opinion, the following law.
>
> What?
>
> That these women shall all be common to all these men, and that none shall cohabit with any privately, and that the children shall be common, and that no parent shall know its offspring nor any child its parent.[234]

The separation of the household into indoors and outdoors, women's quarters and men's quarters, and female and male work was abolished by Plato in the ideal Republic. Plato went even further than breaking the distinction between the public and private spheres when, in the *Republic*, he suggested that all private property ought to be abolished: "They, having houses and meals in common and no private possessions of any kind will dwell together."[235]

In *Laws*, Plato insisted on the importance of the common life for women to be able to overcome the disadvantage of their weaker natural state:

> In fact, my friends, your public table for men is an admirable institution, miraculously originated, as I was saying, by a true providential necessity, but it is a grave error in your law that the position of women has been left unregulated, and that no vestige of this same institution of the common table

> is seen in their case. No, the very half of the race which is generally predisposed by its weakness to undue secrecy and craft—the female sex—has been left to its disorders by the mistaken concession of the legislator.[237]

The claim that women were "generally predisposed to secrecy and craft" is consistent with the view proposed in the *Timaeus* that women were reincarnated from men who lived cowardly and immoral lives. The argument in the *Laws* continues to draw out this theme:

> Through negligence of the sex you have then allowed many things to get out of hand which might be far better ordered than they are if only they had come under the laws. Woman—left without chastening restraint—is not, as you might fancy, merely half the problem; nay, she is a two-fold and more than a two-fold problem, in proportion as her native disposition is inferior to man's. Hence it would be better from the point of view of the good of the state, to submit this matter to revision and correction and devise a set of institutions for both sexes alike.[237]

Therefore, for women who begin life with a slight disadvantage, the challenge to become virtuous is as important, if not more so, than the similar challenge to men. For Plato, everyone ought to strive to be virtuous to the ultimate limit of their ability:

> Our unanimous pronouncement was, in sum, that whatever the way promises to make a member of our citizen body—male or female, young or old—truly excellent in the virtues of soul proper to human character—that and no other shall be the end, as I say, towards which every nerve shall be strained so long as life endures.[238]

Before concluding this section on Plato's theory of virtue in relation to sex identity, it should be mentioned that he concerned himself, in both the *Republic* and *Laws*, with one of the consequences of the abolition of the public and private distinction, namely with the care and upbringing of children.

> [Nurses] will also supervise the nursing of the children, conducting the mothers to the pen when their breasts are full, by employing every device to prevent anyone from recognizing their own infant. . . . [T]hey will take care that the mothers themselves shall not suckle too long, and the trouble of wakeful nights and similar burdens they will devolve upon the nurses, wet and dry.
>
> You are making maternity a soft job for the women of the guardians.
>
> It ought to be, said I. . . .[239]

Female guardians are to be released from the daily care of small children in order to pursue the studies that lead more directly to wisdom of mind. In this way, Plato changes traditional virtues for women of the guardian class from those normally associated with women and their activity in the home. He drew out the logical consequences of a sex-unity position in his decision to go beyond the traditional bodily related activities that flow from the experience of mothering a child.

In *Phaedo*, Plato describes one kind of problem that occurs when a woman is too attached to her family. While Socrates is waiting for his execution, Xanthippe, his wife, is allowed to visit him:

> When we went inside we found Socrates just released from his chains, and Xanthippe—you know her—! sitting by him with the little boy on her knee. As soon as she saw us she broke out in the sort of remark you would expect from a woman, "Oh, Socrates, this is the last time that you and your friends will be able to talk together!" Socrates . . . said, "Someone had better take her home." Some of Crito's servants led her away crying hysterically.[240]

In the history of philosophy, particularly among the Stoics, Xanthippe was characterized as an emotional, possessive woman. Socrates, in contrast, was characterized as the epitome of self-control.

In spite of the contrasting example of male and female success or failure in achieving a virtuous life in the particular example of Socrates and Xanthippe, Plato believed that in an ideal society all men and women of the guardian class would root out their attachments to private possessions of any form. In the *Republic* he stated:

> Is it not true, then, as I am trying to say, that those former and those present prescriptions tend to make them still more truly guardians and prevent them from distracting the city by referring to *mine* not to the same but to different things, one man dragging off to his own house anything he is able to acquire apart from the rest, and another doing to same to his own separate house, and having women and children apart, thus introducing into the state the pleasures and pains of individuals? They should all rather, we said, share one conviction about their own, tend to one goal, and so far as practicable have one experience of pleasure and pain.[241]

It was this strict abolition of any form of private property or bonding along familial lines that Aristotle questioned in his rejection of Plato's arguments for sex unity. Aristotle saw in Plato a tendency to devalue totally the materiality of existence to such a point that individual identity was threatened. As will be seen, Aristotle argued that the total destruction of the concept of "my" or "mine" would eventually lead to the destruction of the basis of the utopian Republic itself.

It may be that Plato himself recognized some of these difficulties, for in the *Laws*, where some of the more radical suggestions of the *Republic* are modified, he suggested that private homes be allowed: "He that has marriage in mind must . . . keep house and home for himself and his children."[242] For the purpose of this study, however, the crucial point is that Plato raised the possibility of massive changes in social structures, and he argued for these changes by appealing to a sex-unity theory of male and female identity.

In conclusion, we have seen that Plato raised a whole series of new questions about sex identity and that he proposed a range of new possibilities for a shift in social structures to achieve his goal of constructing a world where the equality of women and men could be achieved through the study and living out of basic principles of philosophy. His defence of the principles of sex unity, that is of the equality and non-differentiation of woman and man, occurred in all four categories of sex identity. Therefore, he can rightly be considered the founder of the sex-unity position.

SUMMARY AND EVALUATION

It is useful in the present study to step back somewhat from the detailed analysis of pre-Aristotelian thinkers given above, and to consider the significance of these philosophers as a whole for the history of the concept of woman in relation to man. The purpose of the summary and evaluation section found at the end of each chapter is to draw out the major themes that arise in the close analysis of texts, to reflect on some of the systematic issues that are posed, and to suggest some tentative hypotheses about the significance of these issues for contemporary thought about sex identity.

THE SIGNIFICANCE OF THE PRECURSORS TO ARISTOTLE

The four hundred years of thought and writing in Greece from 750 to 350 BC mark an extraordinary beginning for the philosophy of man and woman. The pre-Aristotelian philosophers raised the fundamental questions that set the direction of numerous subjects for centuries to come. As soon as these philosophers thought about human identity, distinctions between male and female, woman and man emerged. Nearly every single philosopher in this period of intense intellectual activity thought about the concept of woman in at least one specific area of enquiry. This means that the concept of woman has been part of philosophical reflection from its beginnings in the west.

The questions that these early philosophers raised fell under the following broad categories: How are male and female opposite? What is the relation between sex identity and generation? Are women and men wise in the same or different ways? Are women and men virtuous in the same or different ways? If we classify the pre-Aristotelian philosophers according to the questions considered, the following ordering occurs:

Metaphysics:	**Opposites**
	Heraclitus
	Pythagoreans
	Parmenides (Way of Opinion)
	Hippocratic writings
	Plato
Philosophy of Science:	**Generation**
	Anaximander
	Parmenides (Way of Opinion)
	Anaxagoras
	Empedocles
	Democritus
	Antiphon
	Hippocratic writings
	Plato

Epistemology:	**Wisdom** Pythagoreans Parmenides Aspasia (reports) Democritus Protagoras Hippocratic writings Plato
Ethics and Politics:	**Virtue** Pythagoreans Democritus Protagoras Gorgias Prodicus Antiphon Xenophon Plato

The key questions within these same areas can be rephrased as follows:

Opposites

1. Are male and female opposite or the same?
2. If male and female are opposite, is their relation one of creative tension or hostility?
3. If male and female are opposite, are they like other pairs such as right and left, hot and cold, good and bad, moist and dry, or a bow and string?
4. If male and female are opposite, is one of the pair superior to the other or are they held in equal balance?
5. Is a claim that male and female are opposite really only a theory about how they appear rather than how they are?

Generation

1. What is the role of male and female identity in cosmic myths of generation of the universe?
2. Is there any differentiation according to sex identity in theories of the evolution of the first parents? Is woman or man given a superior status within the myth?
3. What is the relation between a mother's and father's contribution to generation and sex identity? Do both parents produce seed or only one?
4. How is sex identity determined in the fetus?

Wisdom

1. Can both women and men become philosophers?
2. Do women and men have the same capacities for reasoning?
3. Do women and men become wise by learning the same or different things?
4. Is there any relation between the biological constitution of women and men and their capacity to use particular kinds of reasoning?

5. What is the relation between language and sex identity?
6. What kind of education should girls and boys receive?

Virtue

1. Ought women and men to practise the same or different virtues?
2. Ought virtuous activity of women and men be divided into private and public spheres?
3. Is ruling and obedience necessarily related to sex identity?
4. Are these separate virtues for separate functions in society? And are functions determined by sex identity?
5. How ought society to be restructured to reflect a particular theory of sex identity?

The above questions are still being considered by many philosophers with a contemporary interest in the question of sex identity. The pre-Aristotelian philosophers posed these questions in a primitive and often pre-reflective fashion. In a sense, they opened up the field by making elementary distinctions and, in some cases, they began to raise some of the deeper issues that would lead to reflective answers to these questions.

Another way of expressing this specific contribution of the pre-Aristotelians is to say that they discovered the basic categories within which questions of sex identity could be posed. Most of these early thinkers, however, did not make a link between the categories, as far as we know from fragments of their writings. Therefore, their responses to the questions and their discernment of the questions themselves simply sketch out a primitive structure for analysis. Their legacy to subsequent philosophy is the questions themselves; the later philosophers would make the field of enquiry deeper by beginning to develop the interelations between the questions.

In conclusion, the main significance of the precursors of Aristotle is that they raised fundamental questions about the concept of woman in relation to man, and therefore they opened up a field of study that could be called the "Philosophy of Man and Woman."

PHILOSOPHICAL ORIGINS OF SEX POLARITY

The early Greek philosophers did not develop any systematic theory of sex identity, as far as we can determine by the extant fragments of their writing. Instead they left pronouncements that invite the reader to reflect on issues in relation to sex identity. If we use the basic contemporary criteria of equality and differentiation, it is possible to classify some of the early claims under three broad trends in theories of sex identity. The first theory, or sex polarity, claims that there are philosophically significant differences between the sexes and that one sex is superior to the other.

There is no question that Greek society at the time of these writers was structured on a sex-polarity model. Women were, in general, considered to be significantly different from and inferior to men. Therefore, it is not surprising that the poet Hesiod incorporated a sex-polarity model in his description of the generation of the universe and of the generation of the first parents.

However, sex polarity sprang up in the statements of several philosophers as well. The following is a list of the particular philosophers who stipulated, in at least one category of questioning, that the male was significantly different and superior to the female:

Opposites	Generation	Wisdom	Virtue
Pythagoreans	Democritus	Democritus	Democritus
Plato (cosmic)	Hippocratians	Hippocratians	Gorgias
	Plato (cosmic)	Plato (cosmic)	Xenophon

Rarely do these early thinkers make any link from one category to the other. There does not appear to be any overt attempt at this early point in western thought to develop a consistent theory of sex polarity or to argue for it over and against another theory of sex identity. It will take a further development in the field of Philosophy of Man and Woman before this occurs. So the pre-Aristotelians simply posited some basic tenets of sex polarity without developing systematic arguments for their validity outside of the single category within which they thought.

Plato is the only philosopher to suggest a framework for sex polarity that involves a theory of sex identity that falls under several of the categories of questions. As mentioned previously, his theory of sex polarity is basically on the cosmic level of existence. In summary once again, his views can be expressed in the following chart:

	Male	Female
Opposites	Forms active like a Father	Receptacle passive like a Mother
Generation	Souls fall first into male bodies	Souls of cowardly or immoral men fall into female bodies
Wisdom	Forms are source of Wisdom	Matter is source of ignorance
Virtue		

There is an implicit spill-over effect of Plato's theory of cosmic sex polarity into the actual world of women and men in his views that in the categories of wisdom and virtue, men begin life stronger and women weaker. This strength and weakness sets the situation in which men and woman have to struggle to achieve the highest wisdom and virtue. Practically speaking, this differentiation means that women take longer to learn the same things as men. Plato was careful to argue that the polarity of strength and weakness is not a factor that bars women from achieving the same goals as men. Rather it functions as a handicap during the race to achieve wisdom and virtue.

As will be seen, factors of Plato's cosmic theory of sex polarity become integrated into the rationale of subsequent philosophers for a sex polarity for women and men in the world. This is ironic in that Plato himself made significant efforts to argue for a theory of sex unity for women and men in the world. Before summarizing this aspect of his contribution, we will first look briefly at the history of the theory of sex complementarity.

PHILOSOPHICAL ORIGINS OF SEX COMPLEMENTARITY

Most of the early pronouncements of philosophically significant differentiation and equality of woman and man occur in isolated categories. There is no attempt to consider a cohesive rationale for a theory of sex complementarity across all the categories of questions asked about sex identity. However, it is significant at this point that the suggestion of sex complementarity even occurs, given the background of sex polarity in the structure of Greek society itself. Therefore, in a way, sex complementarity can be interpreted as an effort to move thought forward somewhat in the context of the society that lives by different principles.

The following is a list of the pre-Aristotelian philosophers who appear to suggest something of the principles of sex complementarity:

Opposites	**Generation**	**Wisdom**	**Virtue**
Heraclitus	Parmenides	Pythagoreans	
Empedocles	Anaxagoras		
	Empedocles		
	Hippocratian		

Sex complementarity considers the opposition of male and female as a positive dynamic of equals in interaction, rather than as a relation of superior to inferior. The male and female components of the interaction are differentiated, but have equal value and worth.

In a similar way, generation was interpreted by these philosophers as demanding the equal but differentiated contribution of mother and father. Simply put, these theories suggested a double-seed theory of generation in which the contributions from mother and father were equally significant. Perhaps only Empedocles and the Hippocratic writers suggested further that generation demanded the contribution of both parents, each of whom contributed part of the resulting fetus, but the general idea of differentiation and equality was found in all of them.

Sometimes there are inconsistencies in the theories. The Hippocratic writings, for example, can be classified as falling partially under sex complementarity—because of their double-seed theory—and partially under sex polarity—because of the characterization of the male seed as inherently stronger and female seed as inherently weaker. However, in the subsequent context of Aristotelian theory, in which the inferiority of the female is defended by the claim that the female is incapable of contributing seed to generation, the Hippocratic view does aim in some way towards a sex complementarity.

In the categories of wisdom and virtue there are hardly any views that can be considered as contributing to sex complementarity at this early stage of thought. It may be that the Pythagoreans practised some form of complementarity in their development of separate but equal schools of education for women and men. However, there is insufficient evidence to know whether this occurred. It will take many more centuries before a philosophical foundation for sex complementarity in the areas of wisdom and virtue will be uncovered. At this early point in western thought, sex complementarity remains as a suggestion primarily in the categories of opposites and generation.

PLATO AS THE FOUNDER OF THE SEX-UNITY POSITION

Plato stands out among all the pre-Aristotelian philosophers for his attempt to develop a theory of sex unity that included all four categories of sex identity. Even though he had suggested a theory of sex polarity on the cosmic level of existence, when it came to the question of how women and men ought to live in the world, Plato consistently developed a rationale defending the claims that men and women are not significantly different, and therefore men and women are fundamentally equal. These two criteria, namely non-differentiation and equality, are the two fundamental poles of sex unity. Therefore, Plato can be rightfully identified as the founder of the sex-unity position.

In summary, Plato's theory of sex unity appears as follows:

	Man Woman
Opposites	Same nature
Generation	Same soul reincarnated
Wisdom	Same mind and knowledge
Virtue	Same function, pursuit, and excellence

Plato's metaphysics established the sex-unity position through a body-soul dualism. The soul was the true nature of the person; it was neither male nor female. Bodily existence was merely an appearance of the true reality. Even though woman's incarnation was a weaker kind of existence than man's, it was not different in kind. Plato concluded from this that women and men ought to seek the same wisdom and virtue. Since the capacity to achieve wisdom or virtue was due to the nature and quality of the soul, Plato argued that there was no difference between woman and man with respect to these two categories of existence.

Plato, as founder of the sex-unity position, developed a rationale for the equality and non-differentiation of woman and man that included all four categories of the central concept of person. He argued that women and men were not really opposite; their equality flowed from this sameness, which, in turn, was derived from their fundamental nature as souls, capable of existing independently from the body. The material world, with its physical distinction between female and male, merely revealed an apparent differentiation between the sexes that, upon philosophical analysis, was seen to be unimportant. For Plato, the philosopher had to pass beyond the objects and distinctions of the material world to the eternal realm of Form. In this way, the soul achieved its eventual reunion with the perfection it sought. All distinction between male and female, woman and man, no longer existed. In Plato's formulation, sex unity resulted in the ultimate disappearance of the sex distinction altogether. For when women and men achieved the highest wisdom and virtue, they were freed from further incarnations in human bodies and they became simply sexless souls forever, united to the eternal Forms.

The connection between Plato's theory of reincarnation and a theory of sex unity is implicit, rather than explicit in his writings. The neo-Platonist Porphyry is the first to state explicitly this metaphysical foundation for sex unity. However, even in Plato's implicit formulation there is an obvious relationship between the two views. Particularly since Plato repeats his theory of reincarnation in the *Timaeus* and in the *Republic*, where he presents his most forceful arguments for sex unity, it would seem that the metaphysical theory of reincarnation, with its view of the soul as an independent sexless entity, is perfectly consistent with the sex-unity thesis that women and men are fundamentally the same, and that differences between the sexes are the superficial aspects of their material existence. Plato's cosmic theory of sex polarity allows him to explain the apparent inferiority of women in Greek society at the time, while his careful arguments for sex unity in an ideal society allow him to suggest a way of reforming society to better conform to true reality. Sex unity better corresponds to Plato's views of the way the material world ought to be and the way the immaterial world is. Therefore, Plato has a rightful claim to the important title of founder of the theory of sex unity.

RATIONALITY AND MATERIALITY FRAGMENTED

At this point it is useful to reflect on a significant consequence of this first formulation of a theory of sex unity. In Plato's articulation, the theory appears to contain a radical body-soul dualism. Plato identifies the two aspects of rationality and materiality as belonging to the human condition; at the same time he devalues the material aspect of existence. Philosophy, said Socrates, is the practice of dying, or of the separation of the soul and body. The body, for Plato, is an unimportant and negative aspect of human existence. The obvious question that springs to mind, then, is whether sex unity is necessarily associated with the devaluation of the body.

To express this question another way, we can say that in the first articulation of sex unity we also find a radical devaluation of human materiality. Plato suggested that women and men were the same because their body was not an important aspect of their human identity. For Plato, male and female bodies simply led to an appearance of important differences between women and men. When the body was recognized as the prison of the soul and as the true centre of human identity, then women and men would be understood as being exactly the same. The philosopher's task, for Plato, lies precisely in this movement away from the materiality of human existence and towards the truths of the immaterial world. Therefore, for Plato, the basic tenets of sex unity follow from his body-soul dualism and his devaluation of the body within that metaphysic. Women and men are equal and the same because their bodies have nothing to do with their true human identity.

This consequence, then, leads to a paradoxical situation where those factors that differentiate the sexes are excluded from a consideration of the true nature of the identities of women and men. In fact, one could say that there is a tautology in Plato's view, namely, that the theory of sex identity dissolves into a theory of human identity because differences between men and women disappear when they are considered from the perspective of soul alone. In this way it would be a contradiction to speak of sex unity, for there would no longer be a sexual differentiation to unify. However, from the perspective of the history of the concept of woman, it would seem that Plato's articulation is not that unusual. For we will see that when new attempts at defending a theory of sex unity arise, they nearly always involve a devaluation of the materiality of human existence and, in particular, of male and female bodies. Appealing to the soul, or reason, theories of sex unity seek to find a neutral focal point of identity that reduces sexuality to an insignificant aspect of personal identity. Therefore, Plato is extremely useful to the history of the theory of sex unity for the clear-cut arguments he presents about the priority of soul over body. His simple defence of sex unity reveals to us the general lines of argument that various sex-unity theorists would take for centuries. Plato, as the founder of the sex-unity position, uncovered a fundamental way of thinking about human existence and about the respective identities of woman and man. His discoveries in this area of thought, as in so many others, originated a pattern of reflection that appears to be fundamental to the history of philosophy. The challenge to contemporary defenders of sex unity would be to find a way to defend this theory without devaluing the body and fragmenting the rationality and materiality of human existence. The question that Chapter I raises, and that still remains to be answered is: Does a defence of sex unity always imply a devaluation of the body?

II

ARISTOTLE

Aristotle (384–322 BC) was the first philosopher to develop a completely consistent set of answers to questions about sex identity that previous philosophers had raised. His theory developed a comprehensive rationale for the theory of sex polarity. That is, Aristotle argued that differences between women and men were philosophically significant and that men were naturally superior to women.

While impulses towards sex polarity had been found in previous writings, Aristotle was the first philosopher to provide a comprehensive framework for sex polarity that covered all four categories of the relation of woman and man in the world. The diagram on the next page summarizes Aristotle's theory of sex polarity.

The most striking aspect of Aristotle's analysis is that he sought to develop a theory of sex identity that drew upon conclusions in one area of thought to make premises in yet another. In particular, Aristotle's description of the female as the privation of the male in the category of opposites, as considered in the area of metaphysics, was the foundation for the devaluation of woman in the area of generation. Further, the theory of the inferior generation of the female fetus offered the rationale for the devaluation of woman under the categories of wisdom and virtue. In this way, Aristotle's drive for consistency led to the first systematic attempt to defend a single theory of sex identity. As will be seen, Aristotle's particular theory of sex polarity laid the foundation for the subsequent revolution in the philosophy of sex identity, which I have called "The Aristotelian Revolution."

Before the stages of this revolution can be traced, it is necessary to follow the careful development of sex polarity within Aristotle's philosophy itself. In this chapter, each of Aristotle's answers to the questions raised by his predecessors will be studied, the specific arguments for his conclusions will be uncovered, and the interconnection between his various answers will be demonstrated. The success of the Aristotelian Revolution was due in large part to the highly systematic method he used and to the internal cohesiveness of his thought.

ARISTOTLE'S CONSIDERATION OF HIS PREDECESSORS

Philosophers frequently build a foundation for their own theory by criticizing the contributions of previous thinkers; Aristotle is no exception. In order to develop a

	Man		Woman
Opposites	like form	*woman contrary to and privation of man*	like matter
Generation	hot, fertile perfectly formed; contributes soul	*woman passive in relation to man*	cold, infertile deformed; contributes body
Wisdom	knowledge	*woman irrational in relation to man*	true opinion
Virtue	to rule	*woman unequal friend of man*	to obey

strong position for sex polarity, Aristotle questioned the effectiveness of arguments that had been presented for both sex complementarity and sex unity.

Since one of the primary bases for the equality of the sexes emerged through the double-seed theory of generation, it is not surprising that Aristotle directly attacked the philosophers who maintained this theory. He claimed that previous philosophers were intuitive in their arguments, while he was offering scientific evidence that woman did not contribute seed to reproduction. It is ironic that the intuitive insights of his predecessors have turned out to be correct while Aristotle's "scientific" evidence has turned out to be false.

Aristotle's most vigorous arguments were directed at Plato, as founder of the sex-unity theory. Aristotle ridiculed Plato's suggestions for the reorganization of society within a sex-unity model. Indeed, he argued that it would lead to the destruction of society itself. Furthermore, Aristotle developed many arguments against the metaphysical foundation for sex unity; reincarnation. His main attack involved the claim that the soul could not be reincarnated because it could not exist separately from the body. Having redefined the past, Aristotle was in a position to develop and promote his own theory of sex polarity.

ARISTOTLE'S REJECTION OF THEORIES OF FEMALE SEED

The claim that both women and men contribute seed to generation has been described as a foundation for the equality of the sexes within the contexts of sex unity and sex complementarity. It is not surprising, then, that Aristotle's defence of sex polarity should seek from the outset to eliminate arguments in support of female seed.

Aristotle's method usually concentrated on what he perceived as basic weaknesses in his predecessors. He referred to these earlier philosophers as "untrained boxers," who hit erratically, without scientific order, or as children "with lisps," who had not yet learned how to think maturely.[1] Aristotle's disdain for the method of his predecessors was accompanied by a rejection of the conclusions they reached. Specifically, Aristotle's rejection of the theory of female seed had far-reaching consequences for the concept of woman in relation to man. Aristotle developed concrete arguments against the different justifications for the double-seed theories of conception in Anaxagoras, Empedocles and Democritus.

First, Aristotle rejected the association of right and left with male and female identity by arguing against Anaxagoras's claim that the sex of the child was determined by the position of the fetus on the right or left side of the uterus. Aristotle asked:

> By what cause, then, will the uterus be present in those which come from the left side but not in those which come from the right? Supposing one comes (from the left) without having got this part, there will be a female without a uterus—and if it so change, a male with one![2]

In addition to this ridicule of Anaxagoras's theory, Aristotle correctly argued that male or female fetuses have been observed to be on the opposite side of the uterus than that suggested by Anaxagoras, that is, females on the right and males on the left, thereby providing a counter-example to the previous philosopher's hypothesis.

In the following criticism, Aristotle rejected Empedocles' association of the heat of the uterus with a double-seed theory of conception. Empedocles had claimed that after the seeds of male and female mixed, the child became female when the uterus was cold and male when it was hot. Aristotle, begging the question, implied that Empedocles meant that the sex could actually be changed from male to female, or female to male, by the degree of heat in the uterus:

> After all, Empedocles was really rather slipshod in his assumption, in supposing that the two differ from each other merely in virtue of heat and cold, when he could see that the whole of the parts concerned—the male pudenda and the uterus—exhibit a great difference, for supposing that once the animals have been fashioned, and one has got all the parts of the male and the other all the parts of the female, they were to be put into the uterus as though it were into an oven, the one which has the uterus into a hot oven, and the one which has no uterus into a cold oven, then it follows that the one that has no uterus will turn out a female and the one that has a uterus a male. And this is impossible.[3]

Aristotle continued his criticism of Empedocles' theory on more solid empirical grounds when he mentioned that the existence of male and female twins in the same part of the uterus disproved the pre-Socratic's theory:

> Further, male and female twins are often formed together in the same part of the uterus. This has been amply observed by us from dissections in all the Vivipare, both in land-animals and in the fishes. Now if Empedocles had not detected this, it is understandable that he should have made the mistake of assigning the cause he did; if on the other hand he had detected it, it is extraordinary that he should still continue to think that the cause is the heat and

> cold of the uterus, since according to his theory the twins should both turn out male, or both female; whereas in actual fact we do not observe this to occur.[4]

Finally, Aristotle argued against Democritus's double-seed theory by criticizing his claim that it is the greater quantity of seed of the mother or father that determines the sex of the child:

> They cannot explain with any ease how it is that at the same time a female offspring takes after the father and a male offspring takes after the mother.[5]

A theory that places the total responsibility for sexual resemblance on the quantity of seed, Aristotle believed, would lead to the logical consequence that all female children would look like the mother, and all male children would be like the father.

After Aristotle rejected the arguments of preceding philosophers for the double-seed theory of generation, he turned to an analysis of Plato's arguments for sex unity. His rejection of all previous foundations for the equality of woman and man then opened the possibility for Aristotle to develop a new foundation for sex polarity.

ARISTOTLE'S DIRECT REJECTION OF PLATO'S THEORY OF SEX UNITY

That Aristotle took Plato's proposals about woman's identity in the *Republic* quite seriously is reflected in his efforts to reject them in Book II of the *Politics*. First, he attempted to isolate Plato by mentioning that he was the only philosopher to suggest a community of women as well as public tables for women.[6] Next, begging the question, he argued that Plato's communal marriage would not allow for the practice of the virtue of abstaining from adultery.[7]

More importantly, however, Aristotle argued that Plato was unable to defend his proposal properly:

> There are many difficulties in the community of women. And the principles on which Socrates rests the necessity of such an institution evidently is not established by his arguments. Further, as a means to an end which he ascribes to the state, the scheme, taken literally, is impracticable.[8]

The basic claim here was that the state should be a plurality and not a unity. Aristotle believed that the state was not comparable to a military alliance among similar kinds of people, but rather, was a hierarchy of different kinds of groupings. He argued that Plato's scheme would lead to the eventual dissolution of the state:

> Is it not obvious that a state may at length attain such a degree of unity as to be no longer a state?[9]

However, Aristotle once again begged the question by arguing from his own definition of the state to the exclusion of Plato's Republic from this concept.

Aristotle was far more convincing when he based his criticism of Plato on practical considerations. He argued that Plato founded his Republic on a concept of extended family. The guardian class would see all children as their sons or daughters. Aristotle correctly pointed out that the original capacity for response as mother or father is formed in particular family situations. When the Republic destroyed these familial bonds, it would be impossible, beyond the first generation, to have the necessary experiential basis for the extended family:

> In a state having women and children common, love will be watery; and the father will certainly not say "my son," or the son "my father." As a little sweet wine mingled with a great deal of water is imperceptible in the mixture, so, in this sort of community, the idea of relationship which is based upon these names will be lost.[10]

Aristotle multiplied the effects of this loss:

> Each citizen will have a thousand sons individually, but anybody will be equally the son of anybody, and will therefore be neglected by all alike.[11]

He argued further that criminal acts against natural parents would no longer be guarded against and that there would probably be an increase in crime.[12] In a final irony, Aristotle argued that the presence of this weaker bond in parenting would be better applied to the workers than to the guardians in the Republic because it would make them weaker in their ties to one another and therefore more able to be controlled by the ruling class.[13]

Aristotle also correctly pointed out that, in practice, it would be difficult for Plato to hide the identities of children from their natural parents:

> Again, the transfer of children as soon as they are born . . . will be very difficult to arrange; the givers or transferrers can not but know who they are giving or transferring, and to whom.[14]

Furthermore, that children often grow up looking like their parents complicated the situation:

> How much better it is to be the real cousin of somebody than to be a son after Plato's fashion! Nor is there any way of preventing brothers and children and fathers and mothers from sometimes recognizing one another; for children are born like their parents, and they will necessarily be finding indications of one another.[15]

Finally, Aristotle raised an important issue that is frequently discussed today. Ostensibly, he was criticizing the qualifications of Plato's suggestion in the *Laws*, where private property was allowed. If women were given the same function as men in society, then who would look after the home?

> If Socrates makes the women common, and retains private property, the men will see to the fields, but who will see to the house? . . . Once more; it is absurd to argue, from the analogy of animals, that men and women should follow the same pursuits, for animals have not to manage a household.[16]

Plato probably could have worked out some cooperative approach in the household, but Aristotle did not foresee this possibility. In this way, Aristotle directly rejected Plato's sex-unity model of family life.

ARISTOTLE'S INDIRECT REJECTION OF PLATO'S THEORY OF SEX UNITY

A claim of this book has been that Plato based his theory of sex unity on an implicit metaphysics that contained a body-soul dualism and that postulated the separate existence of a sexless soul that could be reincarnated in either a male or a female body. Plato concluded that even though women and men appeared to be different, they actually had the same nature.

Aristotle indirectly undermined Plato's theory of sex unity by also challenging the implicit metaphysical assumptions upon which it rested. First, he argued that the primary entities in the world were individual substances composed of matter and form. In Book I of the *Metaphysics*, Aristotle argued against earlier philosophers who had believed that the basic metaphysical categories were opposites or contraries by stating that contraries always had to be predicated of things that existed in their own right. Therefore, these existing things were the primary entities.

One of the consequences of Aristotle's claim was that form could not exist separate from matter. This meant that the basis for Plato's body-soul dualism was destroyed. Aristotle argued for the total unity of soul and body.

> The soul is the first grade of actuality of a natural body having life potentially in it. The body so described is a body which is organized. This is why we can wholly dismiss as unnecessary the question whether the soul and the body are one: it is as meaningless to ask whether the wax and the shape given to it by the stamp are one, or generally the matter of a thing and that of which it is the matter.[17]

Since the person was a specific kind of substance, it embodied the same unity of form and matter found in all other substances. The soul was the form of the body. It gave life and shape to the specific matter of human beings.

For Aristotle, individuality was explained by the presence of matter. Therefore, he believed that it would be impossible to have an individual soul existing separate from the body. Reincarnation, then, was excluded as a metaphysical possibility; women and men were born only once as a male or as a female human being. Aristotle's theory of sex identity rested upon the rejection of reincarnation as a theory.

One consequence of Aristotle's concept of person was that differences between women and men were philosophically significant. Since women and men appeared to be different in body, Aristotle concluded that they really were different. The separation of appearance and reality found in Parmenides and Plato was rejected by Aristotle's theory of substance. The rejection of the dualism by which Plato developed a rationale for the sex-unity position allowed Aristotle to lay the groundwork for a sex-polarity theory that enshrined differences between women and men as absolute.

ARISTOTLE'S DEVELOPMENT OF SEX POLARITY

IN WHAT WAY ARE MALE AND FEMALE OPPOSITE?

Aristotle answered this question by stating that male and female are opposite as contraries. For two things to be contrary, they must both be in the same genus and species. Male and female were contraries within the species. Furthermore, Aristotle claimed that in a pair of contraries, one must always be the privation of the other. Subsequently, the female was interpreted as the privation of the male.

Since the concept of privation involves a negative valuation, it follows that this description of the female as the privation of the male provided the metaphysical framework for sex polarity. In fact, Aristotle concluded, quite directly, that the female is inferior to the male; the female became identified with the properties of matter, with passivity, and with the lowest of elements. The male, correspondingly, became identified with the properties of form, with activity, and with the higher elements.

For Aristotle, contraries also involved a mutual hostility. Consequently, he concluded that male and female are opposite in a hostile way. Aristotle grounded this relation of hostile opposition between women and men within the most fundamental of his metaphysical categories. Within this framework, he gave sex polarity the power eventually to dominate all of western philosophy.

Female and Male as Contraries

In Book X of the *Metaphysics*, Aristotle devoted an entire chapter to considering the way in which male and female were contraries. It is significant that he thought this question to be central to first philosophy (metaphysics). This fact must be remembered in light of the exclusion of this issue from the later academic study of philosophy.

Aristotle began his inquiry by asking:

> One might raise the question why woman does not differ from man in species, when female and male are contrary and their difference is a contrariety.[18]

The central issue with which Aristotle struggled was: How different are women and men? Aristotle stated that sometimes contraries did indicate a difference in species. He asked whether colour of skin in light and dark people led to a difference in species, and he concluded that it did not, because colour was contrariety in matter and not in form. Contrariety led to a difference in species only when the form of one thing was contrary to the form of another.

In applying this general principle to the question of woman and man, Aristotle concluded that the contrariety of male and female was a contrariety, not of form, but of matter:

> But male and female, while they are not modifications peculiar to "animal," are not so in virtue of its essence but in the matter, i.e., the body. That is why the same seed becomes female or male by being acted on in a certain way. We have stated, then, what it is to be other in species, and why some things differ in species and others do not.[19]

In this significant conclusion, Aristotle integrated biological and metaphysical principles.

Aristotle was, of course, correct in his claim that as members of the human species, woman and man share the same nature. He delineated this nature as being that of a rational animal. He was wrong, however, in his belief that the same seed could become a male or female fetus depending on how it was acted upon.[20] He underestimated the extent to which the differences were a functional aspect of male and female identity.

A further interesting aspect of Aristotle's theory was his application of the notion of contraries to the individual substances, a woman and man:

> Just as *mother* is the opposite of *father* as a general term, so also the individual mother is the opposite of the individual father.[21]

Therefore, even though, technically, Aristotle limited the concept of contrariety to attributes of substances, it turned out that individual substances with contrary attributes were often themselves taken to be contrary. Aristotle, by implication, considered woman to be contrary to man.

Female as Privation of the Male

Aristotle maintained that within every pair of contraries, one of the two could be considered as a privation of the other:

> For every contrariety involves, as one of its terms, a privation, but not all cases are alike.[22]

Privation was an inability or incapacity that prevented one contrary from becoming its opposite. The Greek word that Aristotle used for *privation* was *steresis*. This word, which is the root for *sterility*, implied an emptiness, or total passivity. Aristotle accused Plato, in the *Physics*, of confusing privation with matter in his description of the mother receptacle:

> Now we distinguish matter and privation, and hold that one of these, namely the matter, is not-being only in virtue of an attribute which it has, while the privation in its own nature is not-being . . . but they make it one.[23]

Aristotle, in separating privation from matter, suggested that while privation has no identity at all, matter had to have a specified nature; pure matter could not exist independently from form. Aristotle then applied the Platonic cosmic association of mother to matter in the world:

> For the one which persists is a joint cause, with the form, of what comes to be—a mother, as it were. But the negative part of the contrariety may often seem, if you concentrate your attention on it as an evil agent, not to exist at all.[24]

Therefore, ironically, Plato's cosmic association of mothering with the passive receptacle was transformed by Aristotle into an association of mothering with specific matter in the world.

Aristotle, in the *Metaphysics*, further argued that whenever there is a pair of contraries, that one is to be considered the privation of the other. Privation, then, determined the characteristics of the two contraries; indeed, since privation was complete non-being, with no identity of its own, it could only be found in something that had a nature. Therefore, matter was interpreted as the privation of form, and the female as the privation of the male. This aspect was shared by all contraries:

> Therefore, it is evident that one of the contraries is always privative; but it is enough if this is true of the first—i.e., generic—contraries, e.g., the one and the many; for the others can be reduced to these.[25]

The female also became associated with the many, and the male with the one through their respective relation to matter and form. Matter provided the basis for a division into the many, while form provided the basis for the oneness of similar things. Matter, privation, and the female, then, were integrated into the foundation of Aristotle's metaphysics of sex polarity.

Female Compared to Matter, and Male to Form

In Aristotelian theory, matter and form were found in individual substances. Any material existent had matter and form. Therefore, women and men alike, as individually existing persons, were composed of the union of matter and form. In this framework, it would not make sense to speak of one or the other as having more matter or form *qua* female or male.

However, Aristotle also developed a clear association of woman with matter and man with form. He believed that the sexes were differentiated precisely by their respective relation to matter and form in the process of generation:

> The female always provides the material, the male that which fashions the material into shape; this, in our view, is the specific characteristic of each sex.[26]

Aristotle believed that when the difference between the functions of two things was stipulated, this difference constituted the basis for a distinction in nature. The presence of a rational faculty differentiated human beings from other kinds of animals; and the relation to matter and form differentiated women from men:

> We may safely set down as the chief principles of generation the male (factor) and the female (factor): the male as possessing the principle of movement and generation, the female as possessing that of matter.[27]

Just as form activated matter and gave it a certain shape, so the male becomes the source of movement and shape for the female. By a further process of association, man initiated a relationship with woman, and man attempted to develop the identity of the woman to conform to his own ideas. Just as matter itself was lifeless and unformed, so woman by herself needed man to be awakened. A passage where Aristotle commented on Plato's concept of matter concluded as follows:

> The truth is that what desires the form is matter, as the female desires the male and the ugly the beautiful—only the ugly and the female not *per se* but *per accidens.*[27]

Aristotle argued that the lifelessness of matter was not a complete emptiness, but rather a specific kind of emptiness; matter was always a specific kind of matter. Nonetheless, it still needed to be shaped by form to become what it had the potential to achieve.

In the association of female with matter and male with form, and with Aristotle's belief that form was superior to matter, the metaphysical structure for sex polarity was established. The male was defined as superior to the female:

> As the proximate and motive cause, to which belongs the *logos* and the *form*, is better and more divine in its nature than the matter, it is *better* also that the superior one should be separate from the inferior one. That is why whenever possible and so far as is possible the male is separated from the female, since it is something *better* and more divine in that it is the principle of movement for generated things, while the female serves as their matter.[29]

The sex polarity within Aristotle's theory of generation became the basis for a sex polarity in metaphysics. The female, in her identification with matter, was defined as both opposite and inferior to the male.

Female as Passive, and Male as Active

One of the most far-reaching consequences of the Aristotelian Revolution in the concept of woman in relation to man was the association of the female with passivity and the male with activity. Plato's association of "prime matter" (as the receptacle for forms) to mothering was the original philosophical statement of this association on the cosmic level. For Plato, matter was pure receptivity, or total passivity. This concept was carried over into Aristotle's metaphysics through the concept of the female as privation, as sterility, in relation to the male.

Aristotle, however, did not view matter only as passive in relation to form; he also thought of it as potency in relation to act. Potential, or *dynamis*, contained a denotation different from matter as privation or *steresis*. To interpret matter as passivity implied a separation between matter and form in which matter was in no way dynamic, while form was fully active. On the other hand, the concept of matter as potential implied an existent in motion, a dynamic energy in natural things, which moved towards full actuality or *energia.*[30] Therefore, by introducing the notion of matter as potential, Aristotle brought an entirely new perspective to the categories of form and matter.

It is important, therefore, to determine how Aristotle interpreted his comparison of the female to matter and the male to form. Did he invoke active-passive or actuality-potentiality as categories to explain the relationship? The following passage demonstrates his decision:

> Now of course the female, *qua* female, is passive, and the male, *qua* male, is active—it is that whence the principle of movement comes. Taking, then, the widest formulation of each of these two opposites, *viz.*, regarding the male *qua* active and causing movement, and the female *qua* passive and being set in

> movement, we see that the one thing which is formed *from them* only in the sense in which a bedstead is formed from the carpenter and the wood, or a bull from the wax and the form.[31]

Aristotle explicitly states that he was "taking the widest formulation of the two opposites." His methodology, in this case, had unfortunate consequences for the concept of woman and man. Those who followed in the wake of the Aristotelian Revolution did not retain the subtle distinction that Aristotle had initiated. They did not recognize that Aristotle was formulating the difference between male and female by taking the greatest point of difference between them. Aristotle, however, was himself in great part to blame for this development.

In the passage referred to above, Aristotle continued his analysis by offering two examples of relationship. The female was compared to wood and wax, the male to carpenter and form. In both examples, the property of passivity in the female is emphasized. Wood and wax, as examples of specific matter, waited for the carpenter or the form to give them shape; the male was the activating and shaping agent. In subsequent thought, this sense of female *qua* female, or of the male *qua* male, retained its prominence over and against any subtleties Aristotle may have had in mind.

In another passage, Aristotle further delineated the ways in which the female was associated with passivity and the male with activity:

> When a pair of factors, the one active and the other passive, come into contact in the way in which one is active and the other passive (by "way" I mean the manner, the place, and the time of contact), then immediately both are brought into play, the one acting, the other being acted upon. In this case, it is the female which provides the matter, and the male which provides the principle of movement.[32]

Aristotle here developed the limits of interaction between female and male well beyond the initial description of manner of contact, to include the place and time of contact as well. The male functioned as actively initiating not only the interaction with the female, but also the dynamics of the interaction itself. The female was correspondingly described as passive in nearly every aspect of her identity.

The above passages demonstrate that even though Aristotle initiated an interpretation of matter as dynamic potential, he nonetheless connected the female to matter, with a static concept of passivity. This connection was adopted by the Aristotelian Revolution and was repeated for centuries to come.

The Earth (and Female) at the Bottom of the Universe

Aristotle believed that there were two pairs of primary opposites: hot and cold, moist and dry. From the interaction of these opposites were formed the four primary elements:

fire	= hot	+ dry	
air	= hot	+ moist	
water	= cold	+ moist	
earth	= cold	+ dry[33]	

Since cold was the privation of hot, it is not suprising that in Aristotle's cosmology the two lower elements should emerge at the bottom of a hierarchical arrangement of planets within the universe:

> It so happens that the earth and the universe have the same centre, for the heavy bodies do move also towards the centre of the earth, yet only incidentally, because it has its centre at the centre of the universe.[34]

The earth was at the bottom of the universe. Aristotle developed a complicated theory of the various levels of existence of planets and elements. At the highest point, the unmoved mover, as pure act, functioned to keep the motion within the universe constant. At the bottom, the earth rested as heavy, cold centre of matter.

Prime mover as pure act Fire	Self-Thinking Activity Circular Motion of 45–57 Planets
Air, Water, Earth as heavy matter	Motion of Generation and Growth

The association of the earth with the concept of woman in Aristotelian thought occurred in various ways. Obviously, there was an initial parallel opposition between the unmoved mover and matter, fire and earth, or male and female, at least insofar as their hierarchical relationship was concerned. Aristotle also recognized the similarity of the generating functions of fire and earth with male and female:

> By "male" animal we mean one which generates in another, by "female" one which generates in itself. This is why in cosmology too they speak of the nature of the earth as something female and call it "mother," while they give to the heaven and the sun and anything else of that kind the title of "generator," and "father."[35]

The sense in which a female generates in herself was further developed by Aristotle to include the function of nourishment. In this context, he often drew an analogy between the earth, which nourishes its seeds and plants, with the mother who nourishes her child in the uterus.[36]

Therefore, by analogy, Aristotle developed an association of the female with the earth and the male with fire and sun. The Aristotelian Revolution incorporated and maintained this hierarchical association until it was overturned by the discovery that the earth was not the heavy centre of the universe; but instead, that it moves around the sun.

WHAT ARE THE RESPECTIVE FUNCTIONS OF MOTHERING AND FATHERING IN GENERATION?

Aristotle applied his metaphysical distinctions to the question of generation. Women and men were characterized by their specific relation to the opposites hot and cold. The privative opposite, cold, was more present in the female, while the superior opposite, hot, was more present in the male. As a consequence, the mother provided only material to generation, while the father provided form. The lack of heat in the female made her unable to concoct seed that contained the form of the child; Aristotle described woman as infertile, imperfect, deformed, and containing a basic inability.

The sex polarity in Aristotle's theory of generation is perfectly consistent with his previously mentioned theory of polarity of the opposites male and female. The female was inferior to the male as mother was inferior to father. The separation of the functions of the sexes in generation also reflected the general hostility of opposites. Aristotle described the procedure through which the sex of a child was determined as a kind of battle between the parents. The male seed attempted to gain mastery over the material, which resisted this process to some degree. If the father was victorious, the child was a male resembling the father. The degree of resistance of the mother was reflected in the sex of the fetus as well as in how much the child physically resembled the mother. Aristotle's answer to the question of the respective functions of mothering and fathering in generation established the basic formula for sex polarity in generation for centuries. The particular dynamics of his theory will now be examined in detail.

Woman as Cold, and Man as Hot

The two primary opposites, cold and hot, were the metaphysical bases that Aristotle applied to his theory of generation:

> Male animals are hotter than female ones, since it is on account of coldness and inability that the female is more abundant in blood in certain regions of the body.[37]

It is likely that Aristotle derived his theory of the relation of cold to the female and hot to the male from the Hippocratic writings. In the *Regimen* of the Hippocratic School it was stated that "males of all species were warmer and drier and females moister and cooler."[38] However, while the Hippocratic theory simply stated that the greater coldness of the female and the greater heat of the male developed through socialization practices and that an equality of heat and cold was necessary for conception Aristotle imbued the presence of heat in the male with a superior value to the presence of cold in the female.

Aristotle linked hot and cold to different kinds of blood found in men and women. He believed that the blood is passed through different processes of purification before being expelled. Blood was the primary source of nourishment, it was drawn from the heart and then distributed throughout the body.[39] Aristotle did not know about the circulatory system.

The more heat that came into contact with the blood, the more pure it could become. Aristotle argued that male seed was a residue of blood in its most refined form:

> Semen is a residue derived from useful nourishment, and not only that, but from useful nourishment in its final form.[40]

The presence of heat in the male seed changed its outward appearance as well as its internal composition:

> These reasons explain the behaviour of semen as well. It is coherent and white when it comes forth from within, because it contains a good deal of hot pneuma (air) owing to the internal heat of the animal. Later when it has lost its heat by evaporation and the air has cooled it, it becomes fluid and dark.[41]

The presence of heat in the male seed was the cause of its fertility:

> In all cases the semen contains within itself that which causes it to be fertile—what is known as "hot substance," which is not fire nor any similar substance, but the pneuma which is enclosed within the semen or foam-like stuff and the natural substance which is the pneuma.[42]

The pneuma, or hot substance, in males brought about a transformation of ordinary blood. It purified the blood until it became a fertile seed, white and foamy in appearance.[43]

In women, however, the absence of heat led to the presence of a large quantity of unpurified blood. The most impure blood was discharged during the monthly cycles of menstruation. Aristotle believed that during conception, the purest part of the woman's blood formed the beginning of the body of the child:

> In these species which emit semen, when the semen from the male has entered, it causes the purest portion of the residue to "set"—I say "purest portion," because the most part of the menstrual discharge is useless, being fluid, just as the most fluid portion of the male semen is.[44]

The analogy of the action of the male seed upon female blood with the action of rennet upon milk was a description of the process of conception that was frequently repeated in later thought. Just as cold milk awaited the action of the heat in rennet, the female blood awaited the heat of the male seed:

> The action of the semen in the male in "setting" the female's secretion in the uterus is similar to that of rennet upon milk. Rennet is milk which contains vital heat, as semen does, and this integrates the homogeneous substances and makes it "set".[45]

The female provided the material upon which the heat and fertility of the male seed acted. Because she was of a colder nature, she was unable to purify her blood so that it would become fertile. In this way, Aristotle destroyed all possible notions of a female seed for conception.

Significantly, in the *Generation of Animals*, Aristotle used the words *gone* (seed) and *sperma* (sperm) interchangeably.[46] *Seed* came to mean the male contribution to conception. Woman's active contribution to conception was incorrectly rejected by Aristotle.

It is important to reflect on the fact that Aristotle intentionally rejected previous theories of generation that had maintained the presence of female seed. As mentioned in Chapter I, Parmenides, Empedocles, Democritus, Anaxagoras, and the Hippocratic writings all contained reference to some sort of contribution of female seed to the process of generation. Therefore, Aristotle's theory, which rejects all contribution of seed—or of formative element—by the mother, is a radical departure from what was thought to be the case at the time he wrote. This means that Aristotle's sex-polarity theory of generation cannot be simply explained in terms of his historical context. Instead, it must be recognized as flowing from a decision to go against the general thought of the time. In this way, Aristotle established a fundamentally new ground of defence for sex polarity by concluding that the mother provided only the material, and not seed, to the process of generation. As will be seen, from this theory of generation, Aristotle drew devastating consequences for the concept of woman in relation to man.

Woman as an Infertile, Imperfect and Deformed Man

Aristotle argued that the greater coldness in woman meant that she was an inferior kind of human being as compared to man:

> A boy actually resembles a woman in physique, and a woman is as it were an infertile male; the female, in fact, is female on account of an inability of a sort, viz. it lacks the power to concoct semen out of the final state of nourishment (this is either blood, or its counterpart in bloodless animals) because of the coldness of its nature.[47]

This relation of woman to man in terms of the ability that a man had and that a woman lacked, Aristotle argued, should be the basis upon which the two sexes were differentiated from one another. Sex polarity was the explicit understructure of sex identity:

> The male and the female are distinguished by a certain ability and inability. Male is that which is able to concoct, to cause to take shape, and to discharge semen possessing the "principle" of the "form.". . . Female is that which receives the semen but is unable to cause semen to take shape or to discharge it.[48]

The woman was an imperfect man. She was unable to bring her own source of nourishment to its perfected state. The coldness of her body kept the blood in an impure state. Aristotle even went so far as to consider this characteristic of woman as a deformity:

> Just as it sometimes happens that deformed offspring are produced by deformed parents, and sometimes not, so the offspring produced by a female are sometimes female, sometimes not, but male. The reason is that the female is as it were

> a deformed male; and the menstrual discharge is semen though in an impure condition: i.e., it lacks one constituent, and one only, the principle of soul.[39]

The principle of soul, as form, was the activating centre for the matter that became organized into a person. The heat in the fetus was derived from the degree of success that the soul principle in the male seed had in bringing the matter of the female to perfection.

Aristotle believed that the deformity in women was evident not only at conception, but also during each stage of growth:

> For while still within the mother, the female takes longer to develop than the male does; though once birth has taken place everything reaches its perfection sooner in females than in males—e.g., puberty, maturity, old age—because females are weaker and colder in their nature; and we should look upon the female state as being as it were a deformity, though one which occurs in the ordinary course of nature.[50]

The argument that the deformity of woman was an ordinary part of nature lent the weight of universality to woman's inferior condition.[51] Aristotle used this principle to explain why more male children were born deformed. Because of their greater heat, male fetuses moved around more in the womb and, therefore, they were more frequently "broken."[52] This "preeminence of the male" became a universal principle capable of explaining all differences between women and men. Aristotle gave a higher value to male sutures in the brain, to the number of teeth in men, and to the quality of male parts of the body.[53] In every respect, the deformity of woman pervaded her identity and nature. Aristotle's sex polarity linked biological and metaphysical concepts in a powerful union that remained in place for over two thousand years.

Mother as Contributor of Matter (Body), and Father as Contributor of Form (Soul) to the Child

Aristotle stated explicitly that the woman did not contribute seed to the generation of the child:

> The foregoing discussion will have made it clear that the female, though it does not contribute any semen to generation, yet contributes something, viz. the substance constituting the menstrual fluid. . . . Thus, there must be that which generates, and that out of which it generates. . . . Thus, if the male is the active partner, the one which originates movement, and the female *qua* female is the passive one, surely what the female contributes to the semen of the male will be not semen but material.[54]

Aristotle was aware that his theory rejected previous ones in which the female was believed to have provided seed for conception. In addition to his direct criticisms of Anaxagoras and Empedocles, Aristotle also argued against a general belief in the presence of female seed:

> There are some who think that the female contributes semen during coition because women sometimes derive pleasure from it comparable to that of the

> male and also produce a fluid secretion. This fluid, however, is not seminal.[55]

While Aristotle was correct in his distinction between fluids secreted during intercourse and the female contribution to conception, he was wrong in his conclusion that the female contributed only matter.

The mother, according to Aristotle, brought only material to the process of generation; her contribution was a specific kind of material. Male seed could not form just any matter. It could only form matter that had the potential to become a human being.[56] This matter became the physical basis for the formation of the human body. Aristotle concluded: "Thus the physical part, the body comes from the female, and the soul from the male."[57]

While Aristotle's description of the female contribution to generation was simple, his description of the male contribution was complex. The soul, which the father provided to the child, was analyzed from several different perspectives. Aristotle believed that the human soul contained various distinguishable functions. He listed these functions as the nutritive, the sentient, and the rational.[58] The question then became which functions of soul the father contributed to the child and whether he contributed each function actually or only potentially.

Since the soul was the form of a particular body, Aristotle realized that the soul that was present in the male semen could not be present in fact or else it would change the semen itself into a child: "It is clear both that semen possesses soul, and that is soul, potentially."[59] The soul, or form of the child, was present in the semen, but it would not begin to work until it met with its proper material. Therefore, he concluded that the soul was only potentially present in the semen.

The potential soul of the child, present in the seed of the father, became actualized when it met with the matter provided by the mother. This soul, however, actualized itself at first only in its nutritive capacity. As soon as the matter in the mother received its form, it began to grow and to absorb further nutrition from the mother.[60] After the nutritive function of the soul allowed the fetus to reach a certain level of development, then the sentient function began to actualize the material.[61] Previous to this time, the sentient function had existed only potentially. Therefore, the father provided both the nutritive and sentient functions of the soul, in a state of potential, to the seed.

Aristotle was perplexed, however, about the source of the rational function of soul. He called it a "very difficult problem."[62] He argued that the sentient soul, because it was concerned with physical activities such as walking, seeing and hearing, had to have a bodily source. The seed of the male, as a "residue of nourishment undergoing change," was such a source. The function of reason, however, did not need anything physical for its operation. Therefore, it did not need a physical origin. Aristotle concluded, rather astonishingly, that it came from outside either the mother or the father:

> It remains, then, that reason alone enters in, as an additional factor, from outside and that it alone is divine, because physical activity has nothing whatever to do with the activity of reason.[63]

The surprising aspect of Aristotle's conclusion here is that since he had no concept of God as creator, it is difficult to understand how an unmoved mover might bring reason to the fetus at a certain stage of its development. Aristotle did not perceive reason as present even potentially in the male seed, and yet the sentient function of soul prepared the material in such a way that it was capable of receiving the rational function at a certain moment in its growth. In some sense, then, the particular sentient soul that the father contributed must have had a potential within it that became activated at the proper time by an outside source. The father first activated the material of the mother, and then the unmoved mover activated the necessary capacities of the fetus already formed by the nutritive and sentient soul of the father.

Two significant consequences followed from Aristotle's association of the soul with father and the body with mother. First, the father came to be considered the cause of the child. Aristotle believed that all things could be explained through the interaction of four causes. The soul was considered to be the final, formal and efficient cause of the being. The body was its material cause. Similarly, in generation, the division of the causes occurred as follows:

Man contributes soul
final cause (potentially)
formal cause (potentially)
efficient cause (actually)
↓
Woman contributes body ⟶ child
material cause

Since the form rather than the matter was more properly considered as the cause of a thing, the father became known as the primary cause of the child: "The advisor is a cause of action, and the father the cause of the child," and "Peleus is the originative principle of Achilles, and your father of you."[64]

Another important consequence of Aristotle's theory was that the father contributed nothing material to the child. If the father contributed soul, and soul was form, and form had nothing material in it, then the father brought nothing to the child. Even if the nutritive and sentient soul must have the material of the mother to act upon, in its own nature, it was immaterial:

> The semen is not a part of the fetation as it develops. In the same way, nothing passes from the carpenter into the pieces of timber which are *his* material.[65]

The metaphysical basis of this analogy between father and carpenter, mother and wood, led to a deep fissure in the history of the male and female relationship. The father was interpreted as being the single source of the formal structure, or what we might call the genetic or chromosomal structure of the fetus; the mother was interpreted as being the single source of material that this structure organized. Indeed, that the chromosomes or genes themselves have a material structure would have been denied by Aristotle, for he believed that the father's direct contribution did not enter in any way into the material of the child. Contemporary empirical evidence has positively shown this polarity of Aristotle to be false.

The Hostile Interaction of Opposites in Generation

An imbalance in the relationship between the sexes was given its most precise statement in Aristotle's description of the way in which the sex of the child was determined. His position was based upon a metaphysics of the interaction of opposites: "Contraries act upon each other reciprocally and are destructive of each other."[66] Since male and female were contraries, it followed that they attempted to destroy one another. Aristotle believed that this battle of the sexes took place at the most fundamental biological moment, when the seed of the male met the material of the female. The father attempted to control the development of the fetus, while the mother attempted to thwart this control. If the father succeeded, the child would be a son, if the mother succeeded, it would be a daughter:

> If [the male semen] gains the mastery, it brings [the material] over to itself; but if it gets mastered, it changes over either into its opposite or else into extinction. And the opposite of the male is the female.[67]

Aristotle argued that the way in which the female might gain mastery was to conquer through her lack of heat. If the proper amount of heat were present, the child would be male; if it were absent, a female would result. Woman and man played out the conflict of the original opposites, hot and cold:

> When the "principle" is failing to gain the mastery and is unable to effect concoction owing to deficiency of heat, and does not succeed in reducing the material into its proper form, but instead is worsted in the attempt, then of necessity the material must change over into its opposite condition. Now the opposite of the male is the female and it is opposite in respect of that whereby one is male and the other female.[68]

He suggested that females were born of youthful parents because there was not enough heat in them to produce a male. More fluid in the body, the presence of a south wind, or cold water could all have the same result.[69]

In addition to Aristotle's description of the determination of the sex of the child as a battle between the parents, the physical resemblance of child to parent was also considered in the same way. If the father was successful, then the child would not only be male, but he would also look like his father:

> So that if this movement gains the mastery it will make a male and not a female, and a male which takes after his father, not after his mother.[70]

Aristotle described this process, when successful, as the effect of the seed forcing the material to "take the shape after its own pattern." If the process were unsuccessful, then he called it a departure or deviation from type:

> Some of the movements (those of the male parent and those of general kinds, e.g., of human being and animal) are present (in the semen) in *actuality*, others

> (those of the female and those of ancestors) are present *potentially*. Now when it departs from type, it *changes* over into its opposite.[71]

When Aristotle's theory is charted, the various possibilities for the formulation of the sex and resemblance of the child are as follows:

		Testicles male seed		
	perfect pattern of type	boy resembling father (seed conquers menstrual fluid perfectly)		
Uterus female material	departure from type	boy resembling mother (material partially resists seed)	girl resembling father; girl resembling mother (material more fully resists seed)	
		1st departure	2nd departure	no conception (material totally resists seed)
				3rd departure

Certain consequences followed from this theory. First of all, there was only one situation in which the father achieved complete victory: when the child was male and physically resembled the father as well. In any others, he failed, to some extent, to conquer the material. It is difficult to imagine the psychological dynamics of a society in which the vast majority of children born were perceived as a departure from a perfect type, *viz.*, when the child was female or a male who resembled his mother. Aristotle's theory of sex polarity, with its inherent antagonism between the sexes, if accepted by society at large, would have a deep psychological effect on the quality of love between mother, father, and child.

Aristotle struggled with the next obvious problem, which followed from his description of the roles of the sexes in conception. Why did nature not merely generate male children who took after the father?

> The first beginning of this deviation (of straying from generic type) is when a female is formed instead of a male, though a) this indeed is a necessity required by nature, since the race of creatures which are separated into male and

> female has got to be kept in being; and b) since it is possible for the male sometimes not to gain the mastery either on account of youth or age or some other such cause, female offspring must of necessity be produced by animals.[72]

It is as if nature had arranged things so that enough females would be produced to allow for the race to continue. Aristotle also argued that in order to give man a purpose for existence, females were not allowed to generate by themselves:

> In all animals, where the male and female are separate, the female is unable by itself to generate offspring and bring it to completion; if it could the existence of the male would have no purpose, and nature does nothing which lacks purpose.[73]

Aristotle's concept of nature was derived from his observations of what already existed in the world. Since he had no concept of creation, other possibilities were not real alternatives. Unfortunately for the history of sex identity, Aristotle's theory of generation was so erroneous that it completely misinterpreted the intention and practice of nature. It misrepresented the contribution of the parents to the child, as well as the fundamental basis of their interaction. Woman and man ought not to be in a relation of hostile opposition, but rather in a relation of cooperative complementarity.

Aristotelian sex polarity developed a totally consistent rationale for the inferiority of women in relation to man. Beginning with the association of cold with the female and hot with the male, Aristotle concluded that woman was an infertile, imperfect and deformed man. He concluded further that the mother only provided material in generation because her lack of heat made it impossible to bring her blood to boil, or to purify her blood enough to generate fertile seed. Finally, Aristotle decided that the process of generation itself was best described as a hostile interaction of the opposites male and female in which one of the pairs of contraries attempted to conquer or resist the other. As will be seen, Aristotle drew consequences for the epistemological area of wisdom from his rationale of sex polarity in the areas of opposites and generation.

DO WOMEN AND MEN RELATE TO WISDOM IN THE SAME WAY?

Aristotle gave a definitive answer to the question of how men and women relate to wisdom. First, he claimed that there were three kinds of wisdom—theoretical, practical, and productive. Then he argued that theoretical wisdom is the science of causes; it involves the seeking of definitions of genus and species. Furthermore, when this science of causes is practised through the use of syllogism, all definitions must include universals. As a consequence, philosophy came to be focused on the consideration of the universal characteristics of species.

Aristotle then turned to an analysis of the rational capacities of human existents. He argued that while women have the same kind of reason as men, in the female the higher power of reason is without authority over the lower or irrational powers. As a consequence, women have an inferior reasoning capacity; they are therefore considered capable only of true opinion and not of knowledge, properly speaking. Consequently, for Aristotle, women cannot be wise in the same way as men. It obviously followed from this that women could not be philosophers.

Aristotle's attitude towards the question of woman's and man's relation to wisdom is quite consistent with the sex polarity that he had developed in his discussion of opposites and generation. He assumed a similarity between the association of the male with soul and the female with body on the one hand, and the association of the male with the higher reasoning capacities and the female with the lower on the other. This marked the first time in western philosophy that the concept of woman was directly linked with irrational thought. Therefore, Aristotle's sex polarity brought about a clear shift on the subject of woman's relation to wisdom.

The Reorientation of Philosophy Towards Definition

Aristotle continued the tendency of previous philosophers to wrest truth from the control of the deities in order to make it directly accessible to the minds of human beings. He divided wisdom into the theoretical and practical:

> It is right also that philosophy should be called knowledge of the truth. For the end of theoretical knowledge is truth, while that of practical knowledge is action. . . . Now we do not know a truth without its cause.[74]

The philosopher, by studying the causes of things, could reach theoretical wisdom.[75] Aristotle delineated four causes of things: final, formal, efficient, and material. Since the formal cause was the essence of a thing, knowledge of this particular cause became the special task of philosophers. "To know its essential nature is, as we said, the same as to know the cause of a thing's existence."[76] The essential nature of a thing, or a form, expressed what a thing was. For Aristotle, philosophers ought to orient themselves to the discovery of this "what" in all areas of life.

Aristotle separated philosophy into divisions that have persisted to the present day. He delimited the general areas of knowledge as physics, metaphysics, logic, psychology, zoology (including biology), ethics, politics, rhetoric, and aesthetics.[77] In each area, Aristotle attempted to make distinctions and to discover the specific essences of the subject under consideration. In some areas, the subject lent itself to a more rigorous delineation than in others. Logic was able to be precise, whereas ethics and biology had to be more flexible. To be wise, then, meant to be able to bring to a specific subject the rigour appropriate to it.

This theory of flexibility of definition has an important role in Aristotle's theory of the definition of human identity and of the definition of sex identity. Aristotle developed a three-phase approach to these definitions that can be summarized by the chart on the following page.

Logic

Aristotle's logic sought the formal essence of the thing being defined: "A definition is a phrase indicating the essence of something."[78] Since, for Aristotle, forms did not exist without matter, the essence of "man," or human being, always included some reference to its material identity.[79] However, the reference was simply to the presence of a kind of materiality common to its classification as animal life. Its difference from other animals was defined by the presence of reason. Individuals, as examples of primary substances, were instances of the species.

Logic	Metaphysics	Philosophy of Nature
"Man," the species, is a rational animal	Male and female are contraries within the species "man"	1) Male is active, female is passive 2) Male provides form, female provides matter 3) Male generates in another, female generates in herself

> For instance, the individual man (*anthropon*) is included in the species "man" (*anthropos*), and the genus to which the species belongs is "animal"; these therefore—that is to say, the species "man" and the genus "animal"—are termed secondary substances.[80]

Definitions themselves were examples of secondary substances. Subsequently, the logical definition of human identity for Aristotle is that "man is a rational animal." This definition included implicit reference to woman and man as members of the same species.

When logic is the dominant mode of analysis of human identity, differences between women and men play no role. It is, of course, this aspect of Aristotelian thought that became so important to academic philosophy, which later chose to focus on the nature of "man" as a species rather than on differences between the sexes. However, Aristotle himself used two other notions of "definition" in relation to human identity, as will now be discussed.

Metaphysics

As previously mentioned in the section on opposites, Aristotle raised an important question in Book X, Chapter 9, of the *Metaphysics*. He asked whether the difference between male and female was great enough to allow it to be a difference in species. That is, Aristotle asked whether men and women had a different formal nature. His question was as follows:

> One might raise the question . . . why a female and a male animal are not different species, though this difference belongs to animal in virtue of its own nature, and not as paleness or darkness does; both "female" and "male" belong to it *qua* animal.[81]

Aristotle struggled to understand the three ways in which differences can belong to two things: 1) in form; 2) in matter as contraries in virtue of its own nature; or 3) in matter as contraries not belonging to its nature. Paleness and darkness fall into the third category, while male and female fall into the second. Neither are aspects of form, and so neither falls under the definition of essence properly speaking. "Contraries which are in the definition make a difference in species, but those which are in the thing taken as including its matter do not make one."[82]

For Aristotle, accidental characteristics of a thing may be present in two ways:

> "Accident" means 1) that which attaches to something and can be truly asserted, but neither of necessity nor usually. . . . "Accident" has also 2) another meaning, i.e., all that attaches to each thing in virtue of itself but is not in its essence.[83]

These two different notions of *accident* also have application to discussions of sex identity; for the differentiation of light and dark as applied to human beings are accidents in the first category, while male and female are accidents in the second. Aristotle recognized that the connection of sexual differentiation to the definition was in virtue of the material found in the definition of the species man. It belonged to human life *qua* animal or in *virtue of itself*. *Accident* in this sense was *usually* or *necessarily* present and, therefore, it contradicted the first meaning of *accident* in which something was asserted as being neither of necessity nor usually present. Therefore, in the *Metaphysics*, sexual differentiation was considered closer to definition of species than other differences not present by virtue of the material nature; and sexual differences were accidents in a stronger sense than other differences.

Philosophy of Nature

When we move to Aristotle's third way of distinguishing male from female, we find a very clear presentation of sexual distinctions that are necessarily or usually present in woman and man. Referring back to those passages previously mentioned under the category of generation, we find the following attempts to stipulate criteria for sexual differentiation in the *Generation of Animals*:

> The female, *qua* female, is passive, and the male *qua* male, is active—it is that whence the principle of movement comes.
>
> The female always provides the material, the male that which fashions the material into shape; this, in our view, is *the specific characteristic of each sex*.
>
> By "male" animal *we mean* one which generates in another, by "female" one which generates in itself.[84]

The use of the expressions "*qua*," "specific characteristics of each sex," or "we mean," all imply a search for distinctions close to the strength of the definitions of the differentiation between the things considered. In the Philosophy of Nature, these differences between male and female are almost defining characteristics common to the two contraries within the species. The differences are more significant than simply hair or eye colour.

Therefore, from the above analysis it can be seen that in its application to sex identity, Aristotle's theory of definition follows a pattern of moving from definition strictly stated in the logic as focusing on formal differences of species, to a consideration in the metaphysics of differences in contraries that are present by virtue of the material nature of the human species, to a consideration in the philosophy of nature that focuses on specific differences in matter between the male and female.

Historically, a wedge was eventually placed between the first and the third notion of definition. When a consideration of the metaphysical category of contraries was dropped from western thought, the philosophy of definition slowly but surely became identified only with the definition of species or formal nature. Consequently, the consideration of material differences between woman and man was relegated to the same category of accident as colour of hair or skin. In contemporary language, this is described as the separation of analytic from synthetic predicates, and the preservation of only analytic predicates in definitions.

Before considering this contemporary situation further, we need to examine one more aspect of Aristotle's theory of definition. In the *Metaphysics*, Aristotle was careful to state that definitions could involve predicates that were not necessarily universal: "All science is of that which is always or for the most part."[85] Aristotle's acceptance of science as concerning that which is only "for the most part true" allowed for a flexibility in definition that could not occur if science had to concentrate only on that which was always true. For example, in the biology of sex identity it is well known that there is a grey area of sex identification, one where some human beings do not clearly fall into the usual categories of differentiation of male and female identity. Chromosomal, hormonal or anatomical abnormalities create a situation where exceptions to the general rule do occur. So it is still the case that the biological sciences function with definitions of sex identity that are only for the most part true.

The demands of logic, however, force the disappearance of the flexibility of true philosophy or metaphysics. Aristotle is himself responsible for this fact in his careful insistence on the necessity for universal and necessary propositions as the key to logical argumentation. If only one counter-example to a statement is discovered, then the universality of the proposition is destroyed.[86] In the *Topics*, Aristotle recognizes that the criterion of universality makes the science of definition difficult: "It is obvious, then that a definition is the easiest of all things to destroy but the most difficult to confirm."[87]

Aristotle developed a carefully constructed logic that involved the use of syllogisms, in which two premises generate a conclusion. In theoretical science, the conclusion was a new piece of knowledge, while in practical science the conclusion was action. In the syllogism at least one of the premises had to be universal:

> In every syllogism one of the premises must be affirmative, and the universality must be present; unless one of the premises be universal, either a syllogism will not be possible, or it will not refer to the subject proposed, or the original position will be begged.[88]

In the history of philosophy, the syllogistic form of argumentation became the model for discursive reasoning for nearly two thousand years. As Aristotle's logic gained dominance, the inflexibility of universal predication—when applied to definitions of natural existences—created a situation where artificial distinctions had to be made in areas that, for the most part, would better have remained grey to allow the inclusion of exceptions that fell outside the category of "for the most part."

Even after Aristotelian logic was superceded by more contemporary forms of logic, the insistence on the priority of universality created a difficulty for the consideration of sex identity. For example, today, when modern technology has created a situation where an individual's anatomy can be changed to conform to a psychological sexual identification with the opposite sex from the point of view of chromosomal identity, philosophers tend to conclude that there are no necessary or universal predicates of woman and man. The law, for instance, claims that the anatomy is the defining characteristic of sex, while the Olympic Committee claims that chromosomes are the defining characteristic. It is tempting to conclude from this that all sexual distinction is accidental and therefore not philosophically significant. Indeed, this is precisely the line of argument some contemporary sex-unity theorists take when they claim that all predicates of sexual distinction are synthetic and therefore not philosophically significant.[89]

Here we have a radical polarization of predicates into analytic, or necessarily present and synthetic, or accidentally present (in the weak sense) in a thing. Aristotle's middle category of accidents, or predicates *usually but not always* present, as defended both in the metaphysical writings and the books on philosophy of nature, are excluded when the focus is placed on the demands of the logic of syllogism and universal propositions. Therefore, ironically, Aristotle's logic led to the undermining of his more flexible philosophy in his other writings, and came to have a strong influence on changing the pattern of argumentation about the philosophy of the concept of woman in relation to man. Aristotle's logic, and its demands for universality, pushed the philosophy of sex identity out of the centre of philosophical consideration by the thirteenth century. However, at this point in our study, it is important to note simply that Aristotle himself had a much more flexible understanding of the demands of determining important aspects of sex identity. After this consideration of the philosophy of definition, we will now turn to a consideration of Aristotle's views on the relation of men and women to this activity of the science of definition itself.

Woman and Irrationality, Man and Rationality

Aristotle developed a theory of the relation of sex identity to the search for wisdom that identified woman with the lower functions of reason and man with the higher ones. The same hierarchical differentiation in the biological area that associated man with providing the soul to the fetus and woman with providing the body, is found in the distinction of higher and lower capacities within the soul itself:

> As soul and body are two, we see also that there are two parts to the soul, the rational, and the irrational, and two corresponding states—reason and appetite.[90]

Man's identity was tied to the higher or rational functions,. and woman's with the lower or irrational, appetitive functions of the soul. Aristotle made this connection explicit in a passage in the *Politics*, where he raised the question of what kind of excellence of mind could be found in slaves:

> A question may indeed be raised, whether there is any excellence at all in a slave beyond and higher than merely instrumental and ministerial qualities. . . . On the other hand, since they are men and share in rational principle, it seems absurd to say that they have no virtue. A similar question may be raised about women and children, whether they too have virtues.[91]

Aristotle believed that the virtue of a thing followed from its function. In the case of human identity, the function was determined by the presence of a rational faculty.

Reason distinguished human beings from other kinds of animal life. Therefore, Aristotle came to the conclusion that while all human beings had a rational faculty, it was present in a different way in men, slaves, women, and children:

> Although the parts of the soul are present in all of them, they are present in different degrees. For the slave has no deliberative faculty at all; the woman has, but it is without authority, and the child has, but it is immature.[92]

For the concept of woman, the crucial phrase in this passage is that the deliberative faculty is "without authority" in women. What Aristotle appears to mean by this is that the lower part of the soul is not able to be ordered by the higher or deliberative faculty. Therefore, the rational powers of deliberation cannot rule or have authority over the lower functions of reason in women. Consequently, women cannot practise the necessary prerequisites for philosophy, namely deliberation and the exercise of reason in the activity of definition and syllogistic argument.

Aristotle described the lower part of the soul as "naturally opposed to the rational principle, it fights and resists that principle."[93] This division of the soul reflected the basic hostility of the sexes that has already been seen in the antagonism of opposites and in the drive for conquest in generation; the rational principle had to establish order in the soul and force the irrational elements to obey its dictates:

> Now the soul of man is divided into two parts, one of which has a rational principle in itself, and the other, not having a rational principle in itself, is able to obey such a principle. . . . In the world both of nature and of art the inferior always exists for the sake of the better or superior, and the better or superior is that which has a rational principle.[94]

Aristotle's sex polarity, then, pervaded not only the interaction of opposites and the processes of generation, but also the inner dynamics of mind and soul. The male, in his identification with rationality, was inherently superior to the female, in her identification with irrationality.

Woman and True Opinion, Man and Knowledge

While Aristotle did not explicitly say so, he seems to have believed that women were capable only of true opinion rather than wisdom. Since woman's rational faculty was "without authority," it was not able to direct its activities in an ordered way. It might be possible for her, however, to have an intuitive insight into truth. In this way, she would be like many men who fell short of the goals of practical and theoretical wisdom.

> It is quite possible that many men possess the faculty of forming an opinion whether to do or not to do a thing without also having the power of forming this opinion by process of reasoning.[95]

Aristotle took pains to distinguish opinion from scientific knowledge. Science has to locate the universal and necessary definitions of things. Opinion, on the other hand, because it did not know why something was true, often fell into error:

> Opinion in fact is the grasp of a premise which is immediate but not necessary. This view also fits the observed facts, for opinion is unstable.[96]

The person possessing only true opinion lacked a certain inner authority of reason, and was also an unreliable source of truth.

Aristotle's clearest pronouncement about the kind of people who had opinion but not knowledge followed his basic view that some people were born to rule and others to obey. While this view will be discussed in some detail in the next section, it is important here to mention that Aristotle developed, in the *Politics*, a position of separate virtue in relation to the specific capacities of the mind.

> Practical wisdom only is characteristic of the ruler. . . . The virtue of the subject is certainly not wisdom, but only true opinion.[97]

This view of the essential characteristic of ruling as belonging to wisdom is repeated in the *Metaphysics*: "The wise man must not be ordered but must order, and he must not obey another, but the less wise obey him."[98]

The limitation of woman to the realm of opinion, while man is elevated to the realm of knowledge and wisdom, follows directly from the distinction that Aristotle made previously in the *Politics*, namely that the rational faculty is present to a lesser degree in women than in men. It is logical to conclude that the imperfect formation of woman in the defective matching of form with matter that produces a female fetus provides an explanation for this difference in rational faculty. In this way, Aristotle offers a perfectly consistent rationale for sex polarity that links biological with epistemological theory.

As a consequence of this lack of control over her irrational mind, woman can only hope for the lesser virtue of opinion, while man is able to strive for the higher virtue of knowledge. It is not surprising that Aristotle also concluded that a woman ought not to participate in the public life of conversation that was so central to Greek philosophical activity.

> All classes must be deemed to have their special attributes; as the poet says of women, "Silence is a woman's glory"; but this is not equally the glory of man.[99]

A philosopher had to exercise his discursive reason by searching for the premises and conclusions of syllogism, by ordering his rational and irrational soul, and by participating in public discussion with other philosophers. Aristotle provided an explanation for why this was not to be the goal for women that clearly incorporated a view of the natural inferiority of woman in relation to man. In view of the fact that Aristotle was well aware of Plato's arguments in the *Republic* for the desirability of women becoming philosophers, it is significant that he reasserted such a strong justification for the exclusion of women from this important activity. It is not surprising, then, that there is no record of female disciples in Aristotle's school of Peripatetics.[100]

It took over two thousand years for a female philosopher to actually use the syllogism as a public method for writing philosophy. Marie von Schurman, in an ironic text written in 1641, uses numerous syllogistic arguments to debate "Whether or Not a Maid Can be a Scholar."[101] Other female philosophers sprang up in the Platonic tradition, or in the Christian tradition of double monasteries. However, generally, they did not follow Aristotelian methods for their thought. Aristotle's direct arguments for sex polarity worked effectively to exclude women from his particular approach to philosophy.

DO WOMEN AND MEN HAVE THE SAME OR DIFFERENT VIRTUES?

Aristotle brought a new rigor to moral philosophy; he argued that ethics ought to be the science of practical wisdom. It involves a capacity to reason and to act on conclusions explained by practical syllogisms. As a consequence of woman's inferior rational capacities, she was not considered capable of virtuous activity in this particular sense. In fact, Aristotle only considered examples of women in areas of human activity outside the range of ethical categories following from practical wisdom.

Aristotle did not leave women without some guidelines for virtue; he argued that a woman becomes virtuous by placing herself in obedience to a virtuous man. Women were given different virtues from men. These differences were described by Aristotle in the context of the household, of friendship, and of the general order of nature.

Aristotle argued that the connection of inferior virtues with woman and of superior virtues with man followed from the basic association of the male sex with the higher capacities of reason and of the female sex with the lower ones. Therefore, the foundation for the sex-polarity theory in ethics followed from the sex polarity in epistemology, which in turn followed from the sex polarity in natural philosophy and metaphysics. Aristotle consistently justified sex polarity in his entire philosophical corpus.

Woman as Excluded from Manly Virtues

Aristotle, in the *Nicomachean Ethics*, gave a complex definition of virtue:

> Virtue, then, is a state of character concerned with choice, lying in a mean, i.e., the mean relative to us, this being determined by a rational principle, and by that principle by which the man of practical wisdom would determine.[102]

This definition was extremely important for the attempt to make ethics into a science of practical wisdom. A virtuous person had to be able to deliberate, to use practical syllogisms, to recognize how to find the mean between the extremes of excess and defect, and finally, how to apply these ethical judgements to his own situation. Aristotle believed that only a small number of men were capable of this sort of virtue.

Six different categories of character were delineated by Aristotle: 1) godliness; 2) virtue; 3) self-restraint; 4) vice; 5) unrestraint; and 6) bestiality.[103] It is important to consider where Aristotle included women in this classification. He mentioned women, as examples, in only the last two categories, those of bestiality and unrestraint. When discussing the lowest category, bestiality, which was so base as to fall entirely outside of ethical principles, Aristotle gave as an example:

> I mean the brutish states, as in the case of the female (*ten anthropon*) who, they say, rips open pregnant women and devours the infants.[104]

The cannibal, here female, was so low as to be outside the limits of ethical judgement.

In the next lowest category, unrestraint, Aristotle felt that here the individuals were not absolutely repugnant, but rather completely weak and unable to bring themselves to the level of virtuous action. He stated that this kind of man or woman was blameless because of a certain "natural incapacity."

> Now those in whom nature is the cause of such a state no one would call incontinent, any more than one would apply the epithet to women because of the passive part they play in copulation.[105]

Aristotle here implied that because woman had a naturally passive nature, she could not be judged by the same ethical criteria as man. She could not, therefore, be considered under the remaining categories of vice, self-restraint, or virtue. All of these categories implied the presence of an active reasoning or deliberative capacity. The godly person, however, fell outside these limits by being immediately good. While Aristotle did not say so, it is possible that some women could be found in this category, for the godly person did not deliberate. He or she was just naturally good in the same way that the bestial person was naturally brutish.

The exclusion of women from the three central ethical categories of virtue, self-restraint and vice did not necessarily mean that women were left to their own devices. Aristotle proceeded to develop an ethic of separate virtue that allowed women to fulfill their specific function in society to a more or less perfect degree. In a discussion about appropriate characters for theatre, Aristotle put forward a framework for this theory:

> In the characters there are four points to aim at. First and foremost, that they shall be good. . . . Such goodness is possible in every type of personage, even in a woman or slave, though one is perhaps an inferior, and the other a wholly worthless being. The second point is to make them appropriate. The character before us may be, say, manly; but it is not appropriate in a female character to be manly or clever.[106]

Women, as inferior beings, were excluded from manly virtues, but they were good by finding and choosing their specific womanly virtue. Woman's virtue was not to be clever, but to become obedient to a clever man.

Woman's Virtue is to Obey, Man's Virtue is to Rule

In the *Politics*, Aristotle asks the question whether women and men have the same or different virtues. Developing in more detail the passage previously referred to, in which Aristotle considered different capacities of soul among men, women, slaves, and children, the philosopher asks:

> A similar question may be raised about women and children, whether they too have virtues: ought a woman to be temperate and brave and just, and is a child to be called temperate, and intemperate, or not? So in general we may ask about the natural ruler, and the natural subject, whether they have the same or different virtues. For if a noble nature is equally required in both, why should one of them always rule, and the other always be ruled?[107]

Aristotle struggled with the question previously posed by Plato in the *Meno* and in the *Republic*, namely isn't virtue required of all persons, even if they have different functions in relation to one another? His discussion continues:

> Now can we say that this is a question of degree, for the difference between ruler and subject is a difference of kind, which the difference of more or less never is. Yet how strange is the supposition that the one ought, and the other ought not, to have virtue. For if the ruler is intemperate and unjust, how can he rule well? If the subject, how can he obey well? If he be licentious and cowardly, he will certainly not do his duty. It is evident therefore, that both of them must have a share of virtue, but varying as natural subjects also vary among themselves.[108]

It is at this point that Aristotle makes the explicit link between the lower and higher faculties of the mind and virtue for women and for men.

> Here the very constitution of the soul has shown us the way; in it one part naturally rules, and the other is subject, and the virtue of the ruler we maintain to be different from the subject—the one being the virtue of the rational and the other of the irrational part. Now, it is obvious that the same principle applies generally, and therefore almost all things rule and are ruled according to nature. But the kind of rule differs—the freeman rules over the slave after another manner from that in which the male rules over the female, or the man over the child.[109]

Aristotle's theory of sex polarity has provided a natural foundation for the virtue of obedience for women and the virtue of ruling for men. His theory, which depends upon a claim that the rational faculty is "without authority" in women, logically leads to the conclusion that it is a virtue for the naturally inferior subject to obey the ruling of a naturally superior man. Since woman is unable to deliberate, she ought to follow a man who is able to do so. Woman by nature should obey, and man by nature should rule. In another passage in the *Politics*, Aristotle makes the same link between the composition of the soul and the virtues of male and female:

> It is clear that the rule of the soul over the body and of the mind and the rational element over the passionate, is natural and expedient; whereas the equality of the two or the rule of the inferior is always hurtful. . . . Again, the male is by nature superior and the female inferior; and the one rules, and the other is ruled; this principle, of necessity extends to all mankind.[110]

This same analogy between parts of the soul and the virtue of male and female is repeated once again in the *Nicomachean Ethics*. Drawing upon the notion of justice as demanding a balance in relationship, Aristotle states:

> Metaphorically and in virtue of a certain resemblance there is a justice, not indeed between a man and himself, but between certain parts of him; yet not every kind of justice but that of master and servant or husband and wife. For

> these are the ratios in which the part of the soul that has a rational principle stands to the irrational part.[111]

Consequently, Aristotle explicitly rejects the Platonic arguments for sex unity in the specific areas of the virtues of obedience and ruling because he identifies the female with the lower part of the soul and the male with the higher part. He concludes with a specific reference to Plato's theory as expounded by Socrates:

> Hence the ruler ought to have moral virtue in perfection, for his function, taken absolutely, demands a master, artificer, and rational principle as such an artificer; the subjects, on the other hand, require only that measure of virtue which is proper to each of them. Clearly, then, moral virtue belongs to all of them, but the temperance of a man and of a woman, or the courage and justice of a man and of a woman, are not, as Socrates maintained, the same; the courage of a man is shown in commanding, of a woman obeying.[112]

With this articulation of a rationale for sex polarity, Aristotle has explicitly defended a more subtle theory of different virtues for women and men in specific reference to the category of ruling and obedience. He has forged a third position between that of Gorgias, as articulated in the *Meno*, and that of Plato. Meno had defended totally opposite virtue for women and men, that is, men to rule and women to obey, while Plato had defended exactly the same virtues for women and men, depending upon what class of society they were called to. Aristotle, on the other hand, argued that the general categories of virtue were the same, that is, courage, temperance or justice, but that the specific way in which these categories were lived out were different. The practical results for Aristotle and Meno were the same, although their theories differed slightly. In practice, therefore, we can safely describe Aristotle as arguing that women and men have different virtues. The basic tenet of his sex-polarity position was an appeal to an inferior natural capacity in women for the exercise of discursive reasoning.

Separate and Unequal Virtues in the Household

Aristotle's differentiation of the virtue of ruling for men and the virtue of obedience for women received an even greater clarification in his consideration of the different kinds of rule of a husband over a wife in the *Politics*. Aristotle discerned three different kinds of relation of ruling and obedience: monarchy, artistocracy, and constitutional rule.

In the model of monarchy, Aristotle emphasized the need for a single authority: "The rule of a household is a monarchy, for every house is under one head."[113] When comparing a household to an aristocracy, Aristotle emphasized the natural worth of a ruler:

> The association of man and wife seems to be aristocratic: for the man rules in accordance with his worth, and in those matters in which a man should rule, but the matters that befit a woman he hands over to her.[114]

The sex polarity inherent in the notion of the superior natural worth of the husband became the foundation for the double spheres of authority in the household. Just as in Xenophon's *Oeconomicus*, the husband gave to the wife her area of authority; she had no natural authority as a woman, but rather, a dispensed authority that always fell under the higher authority of the husband.

Aristotle, however, did not want men to rule directly in all things. He had a dislike for the abuse of power:

> If the man rules in everything the relation passes over into oligarchy; for in doing so he is not acting in accordance with their respective worth, and not ruling in virtue of his superiority. Sometimes, however, women rule, because they are heiresses; so their rule is not in virtue of excellence but due to wealth and power, as in oligarchies.[115]

In the household, then, the good husband ruled by giving to the wife a certain sphere of activity over which she, in turn, could rule. The good wife submitted to her husband's dictates because of his inherently superior worth. In situations where women ruled the entire household, the basis for her rule was not natural worth, but rather power or money.

Aristotle recognized that the household was established through legal contract. He developed this aspect of the relation of husband to wife in his consideration of constitutional rule.

> A husband and father, we saw rules over wife and children, both free, but the rule differs, the rule over his children being a royal, and over his wife a constitutional rule. For although there may be exceptions to the order of nature, the male is by nature more fitted for command than the female.[116]

In this passage, Aristotle did allow for "exceptions to the order of nature." Sometimes a woman might be more fit to rule than a man. In general, however, the husband was the more worthy ruler. Aristotle raised the extremely important question of whether this situation was conventional or natural. In society, the authority of constitutional rule was superior not naturally, but only by convention.

> In most constitutional states, the citizens rule and are ruled by turns, for the idea of a constitutional state implies that the nature of the citizens are equal, and do not differ at all. Nevertheless, when one rules and the other is ruled we endeavour to create a difference of outward forms and names and titles of respect. . . . The relation of the male to the female is of this kind, but there the inequality is permanent.[117]

Aristotle did not say here that the difference was innate or natural, but that it was, nevertheless, permanent. In a sense, then, he left open the possibility that the rule of wife by husband could be considered similar to constitutional rule. In this way, while women and men might proceed from a basis of equality, through convention they would enter into a relation of inequality. However, when other passages of the *Ethics* and *Politics* are considered, Aristotle states clearly that woman is by nature made to obey while the man by nature is made to rule.

One important consequence of the inequality between husband and wife (whether natural or conventional) is that they were not able to enter into a friendship of equality. In the *Nicomachean* and *Eudemian Ethics*, Aristotle gave the highest importance to friendship. He believed that a man must have friends in order to be happy. Friendship was a habit that could be based on utility, pleasure, or virtue. Aristotle argued that friendship between husband and wife was more primitive in its origin than friendship among men:

> The friendship between husband and wife appears to be a natural instinct; since man is by nature a pairing creature even more than he is a political creature.[118]

The friendship of husband and wife went far beyond the goal of procreation:

> For with the human race division of labour begins at the outset, and man and woman have different functions; thus they supply each other's wants, putting their special capacities into the common stock. Hence, the friendship of man and wife seems to be one of utility and pleasure combined.[119]

Aristotle did not limit friendship in the household to utility and pleasure, but also left open the possibility of a friendship based on virtue. In this case, it was based on the desire for the good of the other partner:

> It may be based on virtue, if the partners be of high moral character; for either sex has its special virtue, and this may be the ground of attraction.[120]

It is at this point that the fundamental basis of inequality in the friendship emerged. Since women and men had different virtues in relation to one another, their friendships must reflect this imbalance. Friendships of equality were limited to men, who alone were capable of reciprocal relationships:

> There is a different kind of friendship which involves superiority of one party over the other, for example . . . that between husband and wife . . . for each of these persons has a different excellence and function.[121]

Friendships between two persons, one of whom was superior to the other, were therefore considered to be friendships of inequality. Furthermore, such a friendship excluded an equal exchange between the partners in the relationship.

Aristotle described the inequality of the relation of husband to wife as similar to that of benefactor and beneficiary.[122] The wife received more benefits from the relationship than she gave; therefore, the friendship could not be based upon an equality of exchange. Aristotle concluded that this inequality had to be rebalanced by some other means. He considered this to occur through a kind of retributive justice:

> The question what rules of conduct would govern the relations between husband and wife, and generally between friend and friend, seems to be ultimately a question of justice. . . . Those who are equals must make matters equal by loving each other equally; those who are unequal by making a return proportionate to the superiority of whatever kind on one side.[123]

Justice for friendships of inequality demanded a rebalance of what was exchanged between the partners. Aristotle suggested that the inferior partner could give the superior partner more honour.[124] He also declared that the inferior partner could offer more love:

> The affection rendered in these various unequal friendships should also be proportionate: the better of the two parties, or the more useful or otherwise superior as the case may be should receive more affection than he bestows; since when the affection rendered is proportionate to desert, this produces equality in a sense between the parties.[125]

Aristotle's theory of sex polarity laid a metaphysical foundation for an imbalanced exchange of love between husband and wife. Since the husband could confer more on the relationship, he could love less. In this development of a perpetuation of an essential inequality within the household, Aristotle defended a devaluation of the gifts and person of woman to a degree not previously thought of in philosophy. His theory of sex polarity was disastrous for both men and women who have the potential to enter into relationships of true complementarity based on a fundamental acceptance of the equal worth and dignity of the two sexes. Aristotle's original defence of a natural inferiority of woman forced him to develop an elaborate theory of compensation in order to achieve a balance in the relationship. As will be shown, his theory of sex polarity was slowly but surely integrated into the very fabric of western intellectual life.

Virtue and Character in Man and Woman

Before concluding this section on virtue, it is worth mentioning one more area that Aristotle considered in relation to sex identity. In the *History of Animals*, the Greek philosopher mentioned many different ways in which male and female animals gave evidence of differing characteristics. In his analysis of the animal kingdom he included the behaviour of man and woman as having the most highly developed animal character.

Aristotle's analysis of human character is not as significant for his general theory of sex identity as is his attempt to define sex identity in the *Metaphysics* or *Generation of Animals* because he did not claim in his writings on character that he was prescribing "what it means to be male or female." Rather, he lists a wide range of characteristics that simply appear to be associated with males and females of different species. Therefore, Aristotle can be considered in the *History of Animals* as preparing the groundwork for later analysis of masculine and feminine characteristics. In this way he is describing accidents of sex identity that are usually, but not necessarily, found in either women or men. The sexually differentiated characteristics are subsequently accidents of male or female human nature.

The description of sex-linked characteristics in Book IX of the *History of Animals* appears at first sight to be consistent with Aristotle's metaphysical differentiation of the female as being more like matter and of the male as being more like form:

> Some (animals) are capable of giving or receiving instruction. . . . In all genera in which the distinction of male and female is found, Nature makes a similar differentiation in the mental characteristics of the two sexes. This differentiation is the most obvious in the case of human kind and in that of the larger

> animals and the viviparous quadrupeds. In the case of these latter, the female is softer in character, is the sooner tamed, admits more readily of caressing, is more apt in the way of learning; as, for instance, in the Laconian breed of dogs the female is cleverer than the male.[126]

A female animal can be more clever than a male animal simply because she is more receptive; that is, she is able to absorb what she learns. This kind of pliability and cleverness must not be confused with the wisdom associated with the highest exercise of discursive reason for it is fundamentally passive rather than active. Therefore, Aristotle's differentiation of male and female characteristics in this text cannot be considered as defining the virtue of wisdom for woman or man.

In a similar way, we find Aristotle considering other characteristics of the sexes when he continues his analysis in Book IX of the *History of Animals*:

> In all cases, excepting those of the bear and leopard, the female is less spirited than the male; in regard to the two exceptional cases, the superiority in courage rests with the female. With all other animals the female is softer in disposition than the male, is more mischevious, less simple, more impulsive, and more attentive to the nurture of the young; the male, on the other hand, is more spirited than the female, more savage, more simple and less cunning. The traces of these differentiated characteristics are more or less visible everywhere, but they are especially visible where character is the more developed, and most of all in man.[127]

Certainly, many of these generalizations are consistent with the other judgements Aristotle has made about the nature of the sexes. For example, it is consistent with woman's similarity to matter that she would be softer in disposition, and it is consistent with woman's lack of authority over her irrational nature that she would be more impulsive. The contrary argument is possible in respect to man's relation to form. However, here Aristotle is not trying to deduce characteristics of sexual differentiation out of *a priori* metaphysical or epistemological axioms. Rather, he is simply generalizing from his observations of animal behaviour.

In another passage, Aristotle delineates some further aspects of male and female character:

> The fact is, the nature of man is the most rounded off and complete, and consequently in man the qualities or capacities above referred to are found in their perfection. Hence woman is more compassionate than man, more easily moved to tears, at the same time is more jealous, more querulous, more apt to scold and to strike. She is, furthermore, more prone to despondency and less hopeful than the man, more void of shame or self-respect, more false of speech, more deceptive, and of more retentive memory. She is also more wakeful, more shrinking, more difficult to rouse to action, and requires a smaller quantity of nutriment.[128]

Once again we find a long list of female characteristics observed in the most highly developed female animal, woman. None of these are very surprising, although one might want to argue that being more compassionate is a greater virtue for woman. However, just as in our previous analysis, where we saw that these characteristics would be consistent with Aristotle's concept of woman as essentially passive and by nature closer to her lower rational powers, so here the identification of compassion, emotion, and deceptiveness indicate a description of the ways in which women's inferior nature operates in the world.

The question that needs to be asked is: What would Aristotle conclude about the relation of these characteristics to the respective virtues of woman and man? To answer this question we need to return to the more analytic aspects of his theory, that is, to his description of the relation of virtue to syllogistic reasoning and to the development of discernment through the exercise of discursive reasoning. Aristotle had defined virtue as "a state of character concerned with choice." The above descriptions of Aristotle in the *History of Animals* leave open the question of choice. In fact, there is a hidden presumption that male and female animals act instinctively in the specific ways mentioned. If this is the case, then choice does not enter into the issue, and there can be no question of virtue at all.

On the other hand, some of the words used in the *History of Animals* imply a positive or negative evaluation. For example, courage, compassion, jealousy, querulousness, and so on, all imply characteristics that are virtuous or vicious in a person's character. Does Aristotle wish to imply that women and men are naturally virtuous or vicious in these specific ways? It is highly unlikely. Rather, he appears simply to be describing the natural tendencies of either sex. The natural characteristics would be outside of the practice of virtue specifically because they neglect active reflection and choice.

If we return to the original consideration of the relation of woman and man to the practice of virtue, it would appear that for Aristotle, only a few people learn how to determine by a rational principle the "golden mean" relative to their own nature so that they can act virtuously out of choice and the development of good habits. Therefore, the characteristics of man and woman listed in the *History of Animals* are simply functioning as a natural starting point for the development of the capacity to make choices that lead to virtue. They are not descriptions of the virtues themselves. Therefore, the more in-depth analyses of the virtue of woman and man as described in the *Ethics* and *Politics* have demonstrated that a virtuous woman is one who has good opinions, places herself under the obedience of a good man, and refrains from public speech or activities. A good man, on the other hand, develops practical wisdom, rules himself and others, and participates in public debate and action.

SUMMARY AND EVALUATION

ARISTOTLE AS THE FOUNDER OF THE SEX-POLARITY POSITION

While impulses towards sex polarity were found in the writings of Democritus, in the Pythagorean Table of Opposites, and in the ethical writings of Xenophon, Aristotle was the first philosopher to provide a comprehensive framework for the sex-polarity position. In his thought, woman and man were significantly different from one another, and man was naturally superior to woman. This polarization of the sexes was found in all four areas of questioning where the pre-Aristotelians had considered the concept of woman in relation to man.

The most significant aspect of Aristotle's tightly argued rationale for sex polarity was the way in which he linked conclusions from one area of thought to another. In contrast to Plato, where the linking was only implicitly expressed, Aristotle explicitly argued for the logical implications of metaphysical distinctions between the sexes—for the philosophy of nature—and of epistemological arguments for ethics. To review the key passage from *Metaphysics*, Book X, Chapter 9:

> But male and female, while they are a modification peculiar to "animal," are so not in virtue of its essence but in the matter, i.e., the body. *This is why* the same seed becomes female or male by being acted on in a certain way.*qwo*

The explicit argument for the metaphysical notion of contrariety to the process of generation is found in the phrase "This is why." Similarly, the key passage from *Politics*, Book I, Chapter 13:

> Here the very constitution of the soul *has shown us the way*; in it one part naturally rules, and the other is subject, and the virtue of the ruler we maintain to be different from that of the subject; the one part being the virtue of the rational, and the other of the irrational part. No, it is obvious that the same principle applies generally, and therefore almost all things rule and are ruled according to nature . . . the male rules over the female.[130]

In this passage the explicit argument is made evident in the phrase "has shown us the way." Aristotle's drive for consistency has brought to the forefront of human knowledge the necessity of a cohesive theory of sex identity.

The other link in the Aristotelian system, namely between the kind of formation of the male and female fetus, and the subsequent degree of intelligence and wisdom, is left implicit, at least in the surviving Aristotelian corpus. However, it is an obvious link and appears to provide the rationale for the Aristotelian assertion that woman's intelligence is less effective than man's in her incapacity for deliberation. Specifically, the defective generation of the female fetus, in which the material provided by the mother resists the imprint of the form provided by the father, explains why reason in woman does not develop to its full human potential. It is even possible that the Hippocratic assertion that intelligence is associated with heat would provide a further rationale for this position. In any event, Aristotle does not offer any other explanation for the fact that to him, woman's reason appears to be without authority over her irrational soul. It would therefore be reasonable to suppose that the defective generation of the female sex would provide this important link.

If we were to summarize the Aristotelian framework for sex polarity, focusing on the areas of linkage, it would appear as on the following page.

The two fundamental aspects of sex polarity are: 1) that the differences between woman and man are philosophically significant; and 2) that one sex is fundamentally superior to the other. Aristotle's theory of the differences between women and men have been amply demonstrated above. It may be useful, then, to summarize the Aristotelian statements that claim a specific superiority for the male sex:

	Man		Woman	
Opposites	superior, contrary, hot, fertile	like form	privation, inferior, contrary cold, infertile	like matter
Generation	perfect formation from seed of father	imposing form on material of mother	imperfect formation from material of mother resisting seed of father	
Wisdom	rational soul capable of ruling irrational soul		rational soul without authority over irrational soul	
	wisdom, public speech		opinion, private silence	
Virtue	rule by nature		obey by nature	

1. The male is separated from the female, since it is something *better* and more divine in that it is the principle of movement for generated things, while the female serves as their matter.

2. A woman is as it were an infertile male.

3. The female is as it were a deformed male.

4. The male is by nature superior, and the female inferior; and the one rules, and the other is ruled.[131]

In these statements the superior valuation of man over woman is explicitly stated. However, it is also present in the theory of contraries and in other aspects of Aristotle's thought about sex identity. Aristotle stands out from his predecessors in that he gave a complete rationale for his theory of sex polarity. He developed reasons and arguments for the philosophically significant differentiation of the sexes and for the superiority of man over woman. Therefore, he is correctly identified as the founder of the sex polarity position.

SEX UNITY AND SEX NEUTRALITY COMPARED

Although Aristotle is obviously the founder of the sex-polarity position, he also laid the groundwork for another theory of sex identity in his philosophy of definition. This theory may be called sex neutrality because it is neutral towards differences between woman and man. Aristotle did not advocate this view, as has been amply demonstrated.

However, in his claim that philosophy ought to be the science of definition and that definition ought to concentrate on form, Aristotle provided a philosophical basis for the eventual adoption of sex neutrality as one theory of sex identity.

Sex neutrality ignores the differences between the sexes because it does not consider them to be proper subjects for definition. A human being is defined by the presence of a formal nature, which is shared by woman and man alike. Therefore, sex identity is excluded from the activity of definition central to philosophy. Aristotle was the first philosopher to suggest this particular approach to definition, thereby becoming, inadvertently, the founder of sex neutrality.

Today, sex neutrality is the common, unacknowledged position of most western philosophic institutions. The concept of woman in relation to man is not considered to be a proper subject for philosophy; philosophy, it is maintained, ought to concentrate on the human species without regard to sex. In this context, it is important to recognize Aristotle's role in the development of sex neutrality. Since adopted at the University of Paris in the twelfth century, logic has dominated western academic philosophy.

Since sex neutrality suggests that the differences between the sexes are not philosophically significant, it is actually a derivative form of the sex-unity position. The two positions differ in that sex-unity theorists imply the equality and non-differentiation of women and men through their decision to consider sex differences as insignificant aspects of the person. In summary form, sex unity argues about sex identity, while sex neutrality ignores it. The consequences of these two approaches, however, are the same; woman is viewed as equal and not significantly different from man.

It might be asked if the claim that Aristotle founded sex neutrality indicates that he was, after all, not consistent in his thinking about the concept of woman. Did he hold on to sex polarity and sex neutrality at the same time? The answer to this question must draw upon his metaphysical theory of the relation of the female to the male as a privation. Aristotle believed that between two opposites, the privative member could be explained or defined in terms of the superior partner. Therefore, the human being included, by definition, the reference to woman as the privation of man; it did not include a difference of kind, but of quality within the same kind. It was therefore consistent of Aristotle to ignore the differences between the sexes in his logical writings about definition, while he concentrated upon their differences in other areas of philosophy.

The clash between sex polarity and sex neutrality as theories of sex identity occurred later in western history, when different areas of philosophy became fragmented, and when institutionalized structures emerged that took one or the other orientation as the dominant mode of thought. Here, there would be an inconsistency implied in a simultaneous adherence to both theories of sex identity. However, at the point in this study where Aristotle's thought alone is being considered, there is no inconsistency; he defended sex polarity while introducing the framework for the subsequent development of sex neutrality.

THE DOUBLE PARADOX OF PLATO AND ARISTOTLE

Plato has been described as the founder of the sex-unity position, and Aristotle as the founder of the sex-polarity position in relation to the concepts of woman and man. This description is an accurate statement of the general lines of their arguments. Both of these philosophers, however, gave something important to the opposite position; paradoxically, Plato and Aristotle aided the very positions they argued against.

Plato, in his delineation of the metaphysical categories of matter and form, gave Aristotle the framework within which to develop his comprehensive sex-polarity position. In the *Timaeus*, Plato had described the mother receptacle as a concept of empty matter whose primary function was to receive the imprint of the source, father, or form. This concept as passive receiver of form was adopted by Aristotle. The latter philosopher, however, did not believe that matter as a totally passive entity could exist independent of form. For Aristotle, matter was always of a specific kind. It was, therefore, already informed in some sense. Wood, stone, or menstrual fluid contained a specific, implicit form, which awaited completion as house, statue, or fetus. Even though Aristotle modified Plato's concept of matter, he nevertheless accepted its association with the female and with receptivity in relation to the male.

Aristotle, as mentioned above, developed the metaphysical framework for sex neutrality; this theory later became the foundation for the perpetuation and renewal of the sex-unity position. In his reorientation of philosophy towards definitions of form, Aristotle made it possible for philosophers to turn away from an interest in the differences between woman and man. Philosophy was established as a discipline that sought the form of human identity. Since the differences between women and men were based on reference to their material condition, this was no longer considered to be central to philosophical enquiry. The sex-neutrality position, as a derivative form of sex unity, then became the implicit framework for philosophy. Woman and man were considered only in regard to their common nature.

The irony is evident. Plato, the first philosopher to develop serious arguments for the sex-unity position, gave Aristotle the tools with which to develop his sex polarity. Aristotle, the first philosopher to develop a comprehensive framework for the sex-polarity position, gave subsequent philosophers the tools with which to defend the sex-unity position.

ARISTOTLE'S COMPLEX COMBINATION OF ERROR AND TRUTH

It is tempting to conclude, after this study of Aristotle's concept of woman, that his theory is so erroneous that all of his philosophy is useless in the contemporary search for a correct basis for sex identity. Indeed, most feminist philosophers have come to this conclusion. However, Aristotle had some important insights that are useful, even extremely important in this contemporary context.

First, Aristotle correctly understood that any theory of sex identity must attempt to give a comprehensive account of the differences between women and men. These differences must include reference to the zoological and biological contributions that the sexes bring to generation. In other words, a comprehensive theory of sex identity must include reference to the respective material conditions of woman and man. Furthermore, such a theory must also consider the way in which the mind functions with regard to questions of identity; mind and consciousness bring a special context to the question of the identities of woman and man. Finally, the person must be considered in terms of his or her potential for decision-making, action, and virtue. What it means for woman and man to be opposite to one another will emerge in the integration of these areas of thought. Aristotle was therefore correct in the way in which he approached the question, although he was wrong in the specific conclusions he reached. He was in error in his theory of the female as privation of the male, in his belief that the female contributed nothing active to generation, in his limitation of wisdom to the male, and in his view that women are by nature born to obey. In other words, Aristotle's methodology in approaching the question of the respective natures of woman and man was correct, while his application of the methodology failed. In the future, therefore, it is important to return to the task Aristotle originally set himself, and to try, once again, to find solutions to these problems.

The second area within which Aristotle combined truth with error is found in his theory of definition. Aristotle often appeared to make distinctions without necessarily desiring that they be universal. He thought that philosophy could make a contribution by describing what was true "for the most part"; by way of methodology, an exception could be allowed in terms of a general statement. In contemporary philosophy, where the presence of universal and necessary predicates is taken as an absolute norm for definition, any discovery of an exception destroys the general statement; this means that a general statement is always considered in terms of an exception.

For questions concerning the definition of sex identity, the balance between the exception and the general rule is crucial. The presence of exceptions in the cases of chromosomes, hormones, anatomy, and life experience is taken as evidence that no single defining characteristic common to one sex or the other can be considered definitive. Contemporary philosophers conclude that there are no significant differences between women and men. They have chosen to emphasize the exceptions more than "what is true for the most part."

Therefore, even though Aristotle was responsible for the eventual limitation of definitions to universal and necessary characteristics, he nevertheless gave evidence of a significant flexibility. A contemporary theory of the definition of sex identity must, therefore, return to the original Aristotelian preference. It must seek the characteristics that are true "for the most part" and then it must place exceptions in the proper perspective.

In conclusion, then, Aristotle must be approached from two perspectives. First, all of the error in his sex-polarity position must be confronted; it must be rooted out of his metaphysics, biology, epistemology, ethics, and politics. Next, Aristotle's insights into methodology and his flexibility in seeking definitions, particularly within the realm of nature, must be incorporated into any future theory of the concept of woman in relation to the concept of man.

RATIONALITY AND MATERIALITY UNIFIED

In the summary and evaluation of the precursors to Aristotle, it was suggested that Plato fragmented the relation of rationality and materiality within the person. It was further implied that the devaluation of materiality that emerged from this fragmentation was a common feature of the sex-unity position. It is important, therefore, to consider how Aristotle's sex-polarity theory related to this philosophical issue.

At the beginning of this section, Aristotle was seen to have rejected the theory of reincarnation. He claimed that the "soul is the first grade of actuality of a natural body having life potentially in it." Aristotle's claim that the soul is the act of the body brought about a unification within the person that was absent in Plato's philosophy. For Plato, the soul and body were entirely distinct; the soul, containing human rationality, existed prior to and after the body, which expressed materiality. Indeed, life consisted in seeking after the permanent severance of the rationality from the materiality of the person.

Aristotle's philosophy brought about a unification of soul and body, of form and matter, of rationality and materiality. He argued that a person was a unified existent with both rationality and materiality. If either of these factors disappeared, then the person no longer existed. Aristotle's philosophy overcame the serious difficulty present in Plato's fragmentation of the person. He sought to defend the person as an integral, unified being.

A philosophical problem emerged, however, in Aristotle's two-fold interpretation of matter as either passivity or potential. This problem directly concerned Aristotle's concept of woman in relation to man. The following scheme summarizes the way in which his philosophy used Plato's association of the cosmic female with passivity:

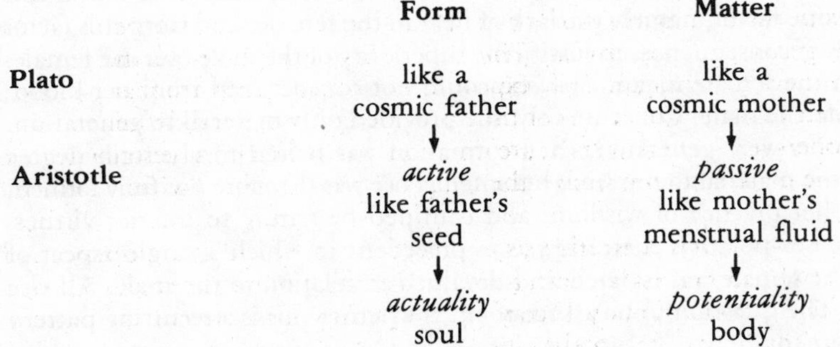

Form
Matter
Plato
like a cosmic father
like a cosmic mother
Aristotle
active
like father's seed
passive
like mother's menstrual fluid
actuality
soul
potentiality
body

Plato's association of form with father, and matter with mother was removed from the cosmic level, and incorporated into Aristotle's theory of natural generation. On this level, the male was the active sex and the female the passive one. Aristotle drew these inferences from his belief that the mother provided the matter, and the father the form to generation. At the same time, however, he also interpreted the relation of form to matter within categories that had no association with sex distinctions. Matter as potentiality was never described in a particular association with the female. Aristotle never concluded that the female related to the male as actuality to potentiality; instead, whenever he described their respective functions in generation, he invoked the relation of activity to passivity. There is, therefore, an ambivalence and tension within the two descriptions of matter as passivity, and matter as potentiality that Aristotle did not recognize and, therefore, could not resolve.

This consideration of Aristotle's thought has demonstrated that he sought to give an account of the unification of rationality and materiality within the person. This unification was achieved through the introduction of the categories of potentiality and actuality to explain the relation of matter to form. However, Aristotle did not carry out any direct consequences of this new theory for his concept of woman in relation to man.

Therefore, while Aristotle is to be commended for seeking to unify these two aspects of human existence, he was not able to provide an adequate framework for a balanced theory of sex identity.

SEX POLARITY, IMBALANCE, AND HOSTILITY

When attempting to assess exactly where Aristotle's greatest failure lay in relation to the concept of woman, it is useful to reflect once more on Plato's failure. Plato was accused of placing too much emphasis on human rationality and of devaluing human materiality. Aristotle was subsequently shown to have suggested a unification of these two factors that implied a balanced description of human life. Indeed, Aristotle sought to give a flexible and balanced account in many different areas of human activity.

It is, therefore, all the more significant that Aristotle's concept of woman reveals a definite lack of balance. More concretely, Aristotle chose to isolate what he believed was woman's contribution to generation and then, upon that idea, to develop an account of the differences between the sexes in a wide range of other aspects of human life. This pattern of isolating a single factor in woman's biological nature is common to sex-polarity arguments. In Aristotle's first development of a rationale for sex polarity, we found this tendency to choose one factor, namely the lack of heat in the female, and from this factor derive a whole series of consequences to justify the superiority of the male over the female. The lack of heat in the female meant that she could not concoct seed from her blood; she remained an infertile male. Consequently, she provided only material to generation. Further, when females were generated, their formation was halted to a certain degree by the resistance of the material to the seed; her intelligence was therefore not fully formed, she was limited in her practice of wisdom, and confined by nature to inferior virtues. Aristotle's theory of sex-polarity, therefore, set a precedent in which a single aspect of the materiality of the female was isolated and devalued in relation to the male. All else followed from this. The question to be asked, then, is whether this is a recurring pattern of sex-polarity arguments.

At this point in our historical analysis it can only be postulated that sex-unity theorists, such as Plato, devalued the material aspects of existence, whereas sex-polarity theorists, such as Aristotle, gave too much importance to an isolated aspect of human materiality. In order to ascertain whether these founders of theories of sex identity also correctly reveal the underlying errors of their respective theories, we will now turn to the next phase of the history of western philosophy to follow the slow development of arguments about sex identity.

III

THE ADOPTION OF ARISTOTELIAN AND PLATONIC CONCEPTS

Had Aristotle founded a school of disciples able to promote and defend his theory of sex polarity during the following centuries, then the Aristotelian Revolution would have been a rather straightforward affair. However, even though Aristotle did establish a school, it soon fell into decline; his theory was subsequently transmitted through indirect rather than direct means.

In the period after Aristotle's death in the fourth century BC, until the beginning of the eleventh century AD, philosophy became a battleground between Epicureanism, neo-Pythagoreanism, neo-Platonism, the religious heritage of Judaism, and early Christianity. In this time of confrontation, the previous struggle between sex unity, sex complementarity, and sex polarity was suspended. The depth and breadth of questioning of woman's relation to man that had previously been present disappeared. The philosophers of this period basically repeated conclusions reached by previous thinkers. They adopted a variety of concepts without developing them into original thought. This period in the history of the Aristotelian Revolution in the concept of woman may be characterized as the adoption of Aristotelian and Platonic concepts.

There appear to be two reasons for the continuing lack of depth in the discussion of the theories of sex unity and sex polarity in this era. The first springs from the belief of many of these philosophers that Plato and Aristotle did not propose very different philosophies. The neo-Platonists and Stoics, although they had studied the Greeks in detail, frequently ignored areas of disagreement between them. Therefore, they did not explore the philosophical issues raised by their different approaches to sex identity.

A second reason for the lack of interest in the controversy between sex polarity and sex unity resulted from the fact that the later Latin philosophers of this era were unable to read the original texts because they lacked knowledge of the Greek language. These philosophers were dependent upon second-hand knowledge of Plato and Aristotle gained through the writings of previous philosophers, who had underplayed the differences between them. The depth of thinking about the concept of woman in Plato and Aristotle remained unavailable to the Latin west.

Another perspective on sex identity entered into this period in western history through the writings of Jewish and Christian thinkers who approached sex polarity and sex complementarity through revelation. The Bible was used by Jewish philosophers to support a sex-polarity vision of the creation and fall of human nature, while it offered

Christian philosophers a conceptual basis for sex complementarity through the resurrection of the body. Subsequently, all of the theories of sex identity converged in St. Augustine, who was caught in an unresolved tension between sex unity, sex polarity, and sex complementarity.

This phase of the Aristotelian Revolution is characterized by a limited understanding of the concept of woman in relation to man. It served primarily as preparation for a later awakening of Aristotelian thought. The Stoic philosopher Galen transmitted Aristotle's sex polarity arguments about the relation of woman and man to generation. The neo-Platonist Porphyry, along with the Christian philosopher Boethius, transmitted Aristotle's logical foundation for sex neutrality. With the exception of these two, the rest of these philosophers transmitted Aristotelian concepts only. Aristotle's revolution had to wait for a further movement of thought before it could become complete.

GREEK SCHOOLS OF PHILOSOPHY

While there was considerable interest in the philosophy of sex identity in the Greek schools of philosophy, most of the remaining fragments about the concept of woman in relation to man indicate that these philosophers were basically content to apply the original ideas of their predecessors to the situation of woman rather than to push thought forward in new ways. Although the small amount of extant material makes it difficult to judge the fundamental direction of a theory, the following chart indicates the general tendency of these early philosophers. This period covers the schools of philosophy that were active from approximately the fifth to the first century BC. Each philosopher is listed under the category in which he or she considered the concept of woman in relation to man. If the theory was able to be classified at all, then the initials represent the theories of sex polarity (SP), sex unity (SU), reverse sex polarity (RSP), sex neutrality (SN), or sex complementarity (SC).

	Opposites	Generation	Wisdom	Virtue
Plato's Academy		Xenocrates (SP)	Speusippus (SU) Crates (SU) Hipparchia (SU)	
Peripatetics		Theophrastus (SU)	Theophrastus (SU)	
Epicureanism		Epicurus (SC) Lucretius (SC)	Epicurus (SU) Lucretius (SP)	
Neo-Pythagoreans			Perictione I (SU) Theano I (SU) Melissa (SU) Perictione II (SN) Aescara (SN) Theano II	Perictione I (SU, RSP) Phyntis (SU, RSP) Melissa (SP) Myia Theano II
Early and Middle Stoics		Zeno (SP) Chrysippus (SP)	Zeno (SU) Chrysippus (SP)	Cleanthes (SU)

It must be pointed out that this classification is not meant to imply that each philosopher developed a thorough rationale for one or another theory of sex identity. Rather, in these early schools of philosophy there is simply a tendency to claim that the sexes are the same (sex unity), or that they are different in philosophically significant ways, or that one sex is fundamentally superior to the other. If the male is superior, then it is classified as a theory of sex polarity; if the female is considered to be superior, then it is classified as a theory of reverse sex polarity. Technically speaking, none of these philosophers of the Greek schools can be considered as a theorist of sex identity because none of them developed the kind of in-depth arguments seen in Aristotle or Plato. However, they did serve as avenues through which the conclusions of the two original thinkers were transmitted to later western philosophers. For this reason, it is useful to classify their thought on the issue of sex identity.

PLATO'S ACADEMY

Plato founded a school of philosophy in the early part of the fourth century BC. What was the effect of his theory of sex unity on the structure of the school in which he taught for over forty years? The first significant fact is that Plato's school welcomed women as well as men. In addition to the name of Plato's mother, Perictione, which was used by neo-Pythagoreans to represent female philosophers, Diogenes Laertius, after listing the names of many male members of the Academy, stated, "And many others, among them two women, Lastheneia of Mantinea and Axiothea of Philius, who is reported by Dicaerchus to have worn men's clothes."[1]

This simple fragment is intriguing both for its confirmed inclusion of the specific names of Plato's female disciples and for its additional information that one of them wore men's clothing. It would not be inconsistent with a theory of sex unity for sexual differentiation in physical appearance to disappear. Indeed, today a "unisex" model of sexual identity leads precisely to the situation in which physical differences between the sexes are rendered invisible. The situation was slightly different in ancient Greece, for Axiothea chose to dress as a man in a context in which dress was very much a part of sexual differentiation.

After Plato's death in 347 BC, Speusippus, his sister's son, led the Academy. Diogenes Laertius also reports that the two female disciples continued to study philosophy under this new leader.

> It has been said that among those who attended his lectures were the two women who had been pupils of Plato, Lastheneia of Mantinea and Axiothea of Philius. And at the time Dionysius in a letter says derisively, "We may judge of your wisdom by the Acadian girl who is your pupil."[2]

This additional criticism by Dionysius implies that the Academy withstood some ridicule for allowing women to number in it. The openness to female philosophers was, however, completely consistent with Plato's teaching in the *Republic* and *Laws*. So Plato and Speusippus risked their reputations, out of a willingness to follow the principles of sex unity, in allowing women to study philosophy within the Academy.

Speusippus had directed the Academy for only eight years when Xenocrates assumed leadership. Both of these disciples of Plato rejected their master's belief in the existence of eternal Forms and concentrated instead on mathematical principles. The influence of Pythagoreanism increased. Xenocrates integrated some of the Pythagorean principles contained in the Table of Opposites and reasserted a kind of cosmic sex polarity in a reconsideration of the deities.

> He declared Unity and Duality . . . to be the primary causes; the former he identified with the Straight and the latter with the Crooked. He also called Unity the first or male divinity, the Father, Zeus, and Reason; Duality the female divinity, and the mother of the gods. Numbers, he said, resulted from the union of these two.[3]

The association of straight and the one with the male, and the crooked and duality with the female is also found in the Table of Opposites. The further valuation of the male as first and the female as second follows the traditional Pythagorean superior valuation of the male over the female within the relation of opposition.

At the same time as the Academy appears to have proposed a cosmic theory of sex polarity, it remained open to the actual presence of female philosophers. In a similar way, the Cynic School, which devalued the body, accepted women. Its leader Crates had a wife Hipparchia (c. 300 BC) who earned a reputation as a philosopher. Diogenes Laertius describes her life as follows:

> She fell in love with the discourses and the life of Crates, and would not pay attention to any of her suitors, their wealth, their high birth or their beauty. But to her Crates was everything. She used to even threaten her parents she would make away with herself, unless she were given in marriage to him. Crates therefore was implored by her parents to dissuade the girl, and did all he could, and at last, failing to persuade her, got up, took off his clothes before her face and said, "This is your bridegroom, here are his possessions; make your choice accordingly; for you will be no helpmeet of mine unless you share my pursuits." The girl chose, and, adopting the same dress, went about with her husband and lived with him in public.[4]

Once again we are given an indication that a female philosopher chose to wear the clothes of a man in order to belong to the Cynic School. The practice of sex unity within Greek society appears to necessitate some loss of female identity. This impression is further supported in the subsequent passage describing the interaction of Hipparchia and another philosopher:

> She appeared at the banquet given by Lysimachus, and there put down Theodorus, known as the atheist, by means of the following sophism. Any action which would not be called wrong if done by Theodorus, would not be called wrong if done by Hipparchia. Now Theodorus does no wrong when he strikes himself: therefore neither does Hipparchia do wrong when she strikes Theodorus. He had no reply wherewith to meet this argument, but tried to strip her of her cloak. But Hipparchia showed no sign of alarm or of the perturbation natural in a woman. And when he said to her: "Is this she who quit woof and warp and comb and loom?" She replied, "It is I, Theodorus, but do you suppose that I have been ill-advised about myself, if instead of wasting

> further time upon the loom I spent it in education?" These tales and countless others are told of the female philosopher.[5]

This story is interesting in several ways. First of all, Hipparchia starts her syllogism with a basic premise of sex unity, namely that the same act is virtuous for both women and men. Then she has some fun by introducing a paradoxical second premise leading to the conclusion that it would not be wrong for her to strike Theodorus. Then, Hipparchia's opponent, instead of showing the fallacy of her reasoning, leaps to an *ad hominum* attack and attempts to strip her of her cloak. In this way Theodorus tried to emphasize the difference between the male and female bodies and of the oddity of a woman shattering the public and private distinction for male and female in Greek society by attending and speaking at a banquet of male philosophers. Hipparchia, however, reveals that she has learned the Platonic dictum of choosing the soul over the body, and she wins the argument easily by an appeal to the value of education over traditional women's work. The example reveals the difficulty that existed for female philosophers even within Cynic circles, and at the same time indicates that Plato's sex-unity position did have practical consequences for the lives of individual women who sought to study philosophy.

After the second century BC, the school began to disperse into a variety of smaller schools. Platonism then associated itself in part with Stoicism, neo-Pythagoreanism, and eventually with neo-Platonism. Female philosophers played a role in all of these subsequent developments. It can be concluded, then, that Plato's theory of sex unity opened the possibility for women to study philosophy with men. Previously, women had studied philosophy primarily with other women, either in Aspasia's schools or in the sexually divided schools of the Pythagoreans. Therefore, Plato's practical contribution to the history of the concept of woman, especially in the category of the mutual search for wisdom by women and men, is significant.

ARISTOTLE'S SCHOOL: THE PERIPATETICS

Aristotle was a member of Plato's Academy from 367 to 347 BC. He founded and directed his own school, known as the Peripatetics, from 355 to 323. After Aristotle's death, Theophrastus headed the school from 322 to 286 BC. During this period, approximately two thousand students studied Aristotle and his disciples' theories. Significantly, there were no women among these students.

> It is possible to infer that since Aristotle saw no place for women in education (*Politics* I 13, 1260a ff.) there were no female members in the community in the Lyceum. No tradition connects a woman with the Peripatos.[7]

Again, it is only possible to conjecture that the theory of sex polarity had as much effect on the exclusion of women from the study of philosophy under Aristotle and his disciples as the theory of sex unity had on the inclusion of women in Plato's school. While there is no explicit proof of such an assertion, the facts are significant in themselves.

The Peripatetics focused primarily on empirical investigation:

> While holding fast by Aristotelian principles, they permitted themselves many divergences in detail. In dicussing . . . conception, for instance, Theophrastus refused to admit that all contraries belong to the same genus.[8]

In addition to writing treatises on zoology and botany, Theophrastus also wrote about friendship, love, and marriage. Unfortunately, full texts of his more than seventy works no longer exist. From remaining fragments, however, it is clear that Theophrastus argued that in order to remain self-sufficient, a philosopher ought not to marry.[9]

Theophrastus's *Characters* serves as one example of the way in which this disciple attempted to develop his master's thought. "Like other works of their author they served perhaps . . . to fill a gap in the Aristotelian corpus. They seem to have originated a Peripatetic genre."[10] The genre referred to here is satire. Theophrastus's *Characters* is one of the first examples of a collection of satirical essays that would later be prevalent in writing about the concept of woman. Theophrastus's stated purpose in writing the text was to show how people brought up in the same climate could still have different characters.[11] This attempt modified Aristotle's theory that hot and cold, wet and dry, of themselves significantly influence character.

The twenty-nine examples of different characters of negative ethical value, either from weakness or vice, all refer to men. However, in the context of many of the descriptions, reference is given to women. A few examples will suffice to indicate the tenor of Theophrastus's analysis:

> Tactlessness: Should you bid him to a wedding, he will inveigh against womankind.
>
> Superstitiousness: Set foot on a tomb he will not, nor come nigh a dead body nor a woman in childbed; he must keep himself unpolluted.
>
> Distrustfulness: When he is abed he will ask his wife if the coffer be locked and the cupboard sealed and the house-door bolted, and for all she may say Yes, he will himself rise naked and bare-foot from the blankets and light the candle and run around the house to see, and even so will hardly go to sleep.
>
> Backbiting: He will say about quite respectable women, "I know only too well what trollops they are."[12]

In all of Theophrastus's examples of women in the *Characters*, men are being criticized rather than women. Of course, it would be easy for him to produce examples of bad women if he had written this book for women rather than for men. However, Theophrastus avoids characterizing women in his satire.

As can be seen, however, Theophrastus's analysis did not begin to reach the depth of Aristotle's theory. After he passed the leadership of the Peripatos to Statos of Lampsakos in 268 BC, the school quickly declined in its philosophic influence. After this time, no work of originality was produced.[13] By the first century BC, Aristotle's school had probably disappeared. It was not until the Arabic, Hebrew, and Christian philosophers rediscovered Aristotle's writings that his specific rationale for sex polarity was incorporated once more into philosophy.

EPICUREANISM

The philosopher Epicurus, who lived from 341 to 270 BC, opened a school of philosophy in the garden of his estate around 307 BC. This school was different from those of Plato or Aristotle in that it was a closed community of persons living in obedience to Epicurus, while the Academy and the Peripatetics consisted of many students who simply came to gain intellectual knowledge from their teachers' views.

There also appears to have been both slaves and women in Epicurus's schools.[14] Gilles Ménage lists three female Epicureans: Themisto, Leontium, and Theophilia.[15] Unfortunately, no fragments remain from the early Epicureans that explicitly address the question of woman and wisdom or virtue. However, as the following critic asserts, equality was the basic tenet of Epicurus's beliefs, and he sought above all to act out his philosophical principles in his school:

> He was born into a society . . . which was also a slave-based society which reckoned men as superior to women and Greeks as superior to all other peoples. The good for man which Epicurus prescribes ignores or rejects these values and distinctions.[16]

The intriguing prospect suggested by Epicurus's acceptance of the equality of woman and man is that he sought to develop a foundation for the theory of sex unity that did not depend, as had Plato's, on a view of the identity of the person as residing in a sexless soul that was reincarnated in either a male or a female body. Epicurus rejected both the theory of reincarnation and a belief in the independent existence of an immaterial soul.

For Epicurus, human identity was completely material; the soul ceased to exist at death. In a letter to Menoeceus, Epicurus states, "a right understanding that death is nothing that to us makes the mortality of life enjoyable, not by adding to life an illimitable time, but by taking away the yearning after immortality."[17] Epicurus, influenced by Democritus and Anaximander, believed that the world was composed of the intense activity of atoms, and that the soul and body were simply a conglomeration of atoms that dispersed at death. Epicurus rejected the view that the four elements were fundamental to all generation. He therefore rejected any attribution of these elements to male and female identity. The atoms, as neutral elements, combined in different ways to form the universe.[18]

Since Epicurus rejected reincarnation and the existence of an immaterial soul, he must have developed a different sort of rationale for his belief in the equality of woman and man. One possible suggestion is that he provided a foundation for this theory in his elevation of the role of reason in human life. Epicurus continuously encouraged his disciples to live in harmony with the dictates of their higher powers of reason, which lifted them above the vicissitudes of the pleasures and pains of the body. Once again, there are no explicit passages in his writings that make this connection between reason and the equal identity of man and woman. However, this theory offers a likely basis for the inclusion of women in his school. If Epicurus had gone in this direction for a defence of sex unity, then he would have made a significant contribution to the history of sex unity. It was not until after Descartes that this kind of a rationale for sex unity explicitly evolved.[19]

Epicurus wrote about three hundred books. Of these, the following could have contained passages relevant to the concept of woman in relation to man: *On Nature* (thirty-seven books), *On Love, On Human Life, On Justice, Morals,* and *Problems*. Of the fragments that remain, most references to women concern restrictions on sexual intercourse. These passages reveal Epicurus's continual appeal to reason and order over the disorder of sexual passion. Diogenes Laertius records Epicurus's view that adultery is wrong. "As regards women he will submit to the restrictions imposed by law, as Diogenes says in his epitome of Epicurus's ethical doctrines."[20] In *Morals*, Epicurus further recommends that a man refrain from marriage.

> The wise man shall not marry, nor trouble himself with the thoughts of receiving, as it were a fresh being, in his children.[21]

Then he suggests that a man refrain from sexual pleasure altogether:

> The wise man must never yield to the charms of love; it never came from Heaven, its pleasures having nothing valuable in them, and if one is unfortunate to be overcome by it, he ought to count it a happiness, if he comes off without mischief.[22]

Therefore, Epicurus's community of men and women were encouraged to live in chastity.

Epicurus believed that pleasure was a motivating force for human behaviour, but he argued that the pleasures of the mind were better than the pleasures of the body.

> The mind, grasping in thought what the end and limit of flesh is, and banishing the terrors of futurity, procures a complete and perfect life.[23]

It is no doubt Epicurus's belief in the attraction of pleasure that led to the many attempts of others to discredit his philosophy by implying that he actually taught and lived a form of hedonism and licentiousness. These attacks usually focused on false statements about Epicurus's relations with women. Diogenes Laertius records the following examples:

> Diotimus the Stoic, who is hostile to him, has assailed him with bitter slanders, adducing fifty scandalous letters as written by Epicurus. . . . They allege that he used to go around with his mother to cottages and read charms . . .
>
> Tomicrates . . . in the book entitled *Merriment* asserts . . . that among other courtesans who consorted with him [Epicurus] and Metrodorus were Mammarion, and Hedia and Erotion and Nikidion. . . .
>
> But these people are stark mad. For our philosopher has abundance of witnesses to attest to his unsurpassed good will to all men. . . . The School itself which, while nearly all the others have died out, continues forever without interruption through numberless reigns of one scholar after another.[24]

The false view of Epicurus as a man enslaved by sexual pleasure is repeated by Athenasis in the *Deipnosophists*:

> Well, did not this same Epicurus keep Leontion as his mistress, the woman who became notorious as a strumpet? Why! Even when she began to be a philosopher, she did not cease her strumpet ways, but consorted with all the Epicureans in their gardens; wherefore, he, poor devil, was really worried about her.[25]

Epicurus, however, in a letter to Menoeceus clearly states his teachings about pleasure:

> Thus when I say that pleasure is the goal of living I do not mean the pleasures of libertines or the pleasures inherent in positive enjoyments, as is supposed by certain persons who are ignorant of our doctrine or who are not in agreement with it or who interpret it perversely. I mean on the contrary the pleasure that consists in freedom from bodily pain and mental agitation. The pleasant life is not the product of one drinking party after another or of sexual intercourse with women and boys or the sea food and other delicacies afforded by luxurious table. On the contrary, it is the result of sober thinking—namely, investigation of the reasons for every act of choice.[26]

Epicurus, therefore, clearly preferred the exercise of reason to the lower pleasures of the soul.

Epicurus's school spread its ideas and practices far beyond Greece. "Epicureanism has rightly been called 'the only missionary philosophy produced by the Greeks.' "[27] It spread to Antioch, Alexandria, Italy, and Gaul. The most famous disciple of Epicurus was the philosopher Lucretius, who lived from 98 to 55 BC.

Lucretius

Lucretius's long and detailed text entitled *The Nature of Things* carried forward many of the main tenets of Epicurus. Books IV and V of the text include writings of some importance for the concept of woman in relation to man. Lucretius considered the nature and value of sexual intercourse, the theory of generation, and a description of the evolution of human society. His view must be characterized as containing a mixture of sex complementarity and sex polarity. While Lucretius breaks new ground in his theory of conception and in his description of the dynamics of sexual arousal, in general his concept of woman in relation to man in *The Nature of Things* is a repetition of previous arguments.

The following poem begins with an invocation to the Muses and to the power of Venus, but Lucretius soon states his philosophical preference for reason and its discoveries:

> Now turn attentive ears and thoughtful mind,
> by trouble undistraught, to truth and reason; . . .
> For I shall tell you of the highest law
> of heaven and god, and show you basic substance. . . .
>
> "Matter," I call it, and "created bodies,"
> and "seeds of things."[28]

Lucretius's preference for reason over religion is given support by an appeal to Epicurus's example:

When human life lay foul before men's eyes,
crushed to the dust beneath religion's weight . . .
a man of Greece first dared to raise the eye
of mortal against her, first stood ground against her.[29]

Next, Lucretius offered his own example of an historical abuse of religion in the example of sacrifice of an innocent young woman:

Remember Aulis? How Diana's altar
was shamed by Iphianassa's blood
spilled by the Lords of Greece—great heroes, they!
They coiffed the poor girl for her wedding day; . . .
men led her to the altar, raised her up
all trembling. . . .
that her innocence at the bridal hour
fall criminal victim by a father's blow,
that ships might have clear sailing and fair winds.
So much of evil could religion prompt.[30]

Lucretius then offered reason as the alternative to emotions and religion. He constructed a science of nature that claimed that all things sprang from specific seeds and atoms. "Things are formed, now, from specific seeds, hence each at birth comes to the coasts of light from a thing possessed of its essential atoms."[31] Lucretius's materialistic concept of the world argued that everything that exists was a combination of atoms that actively moved through the universe, combining, splitting and swerving along an infinite variety of paths. The swerving phenomenon made room for freedom of the will in an otherwise deterministic universe.

The soul was not an immaterial entity capable of existence separately from the body, instead "the soul is subtly built of infinitesimal atoms."[32] As a consequence, Lucretius argued against any theory of the life of the soul after death: "For a faulty logic claims the soul immortal, . . . for all that is changed, breaks up and therefore dies."[33] In addition, Lucretius argued that the soul cannot exist before the birth of the individual; therefore, he rejected a theory of reincarnation.

> To continue: that at the sexual act or birth of animals, souls stand by, is utter nonsense—immortal souls waiting for mortal bodies in numberless numbers, or running races to see which should be first, which favoured to slip in. Or do the souls have contracts, signed and sealed: "The souls that swoop in first shall have first chance to enter: no pushing, or shoving, no argument!"[34]

With Lucretius's rejection of a theory of the separate and eternal existence of the soul, the metaphysical foundation for Plato's theory of sex unity is also removed. Lucretius instead introduced a material foundation for the equality of women and men in his description of sexual intercourse and in his double-seed theory of generation. Man and woman alike are described as capable of sexual passion, and both are characterized as contributing an equal but differentiated seed to the fetus.

Lucretius's long passage on sex identity in Book IV of *The Nature of Things* begins with a consideration of the relation between erotic images and sexual arousal:

> Then those whose semen for the first time flows into their youthful parts, now timely ripe, encounter images, sloughed off from some person, that tell of a lovely face and soft, smooth skin; these rouse and tickle that place with seed full-swollen, and often, as if the act were done, it spreads a stream, a surge, a flood, and stains the bed.[35]

Lucretius, as a scientist of nature, is determined to give purely natural explanations for the physiological dynamics of sexual arousal. He insists that it is not caused by gods, but by human nature alone and, further, that it follows the basic laws of nature. In the case of seed, Lucretius appears to be working within the Aristotelian view that seed is a more highly evolved type of blood.

> That semen, as I've just said, is stimulated in us when manhood makes our bodies strong. Many things stir and stimulate other things; man's power alone draws human seed from man. Soon as it's forced out from its starting points all over the body, it moves through limb and organ and, gathering at one special spot, at once rouses the body's genital parts themselves. The organ tickles and swells with seed; we will to eject it whither desire directs itself, straight toward the body that wounded us with love. For normally men fall toward a wound, and blood wells outward toward the blow that wounded us.[36]

Lucretius's theory of the determination of the sex of the fetus contains the Aristotelian and Democritian view that the sexes are in a battle for domination over one another. However, Lucretius differs from Aristotle in that he maintains that both woman and man provide seed to the fetus.

> Now when at mingling of seed the female force seizes, subdues, and dominates the male the children, from the mother's seed, are like their mothers; vice versa, like their fathers. But those you see like both, with features mingled of both parents, grew from the father's flesh and mother's blood when love-seed, roused and coursing through their bodies, met with equal ardor, united, lived, and neither was dominant, neither one subdued. Sometimes it happens that children may resemble grandparents, or show a great-grandfather's face. This is because our parents often carry a host of atoms combined in countless ways, passed down the family line, father to son; hence Venus at random draws resemblances, the face of an ancestor, or his voice, his hair, since these arise as much from special atoms as do complexion, body type, and size. The female, too, comes from the father's seed and males find origin in the mother's flesh, for every child is born of twofold seed, and every child resembles more that parent of whom it has more than half; this we observe whether the child's of male or female sex.[37]

In this remarkable passage, Lucretius anticipates a contemporary theory of genetic inheritance. If the theory is summarized, it would appear as in the following diagram:

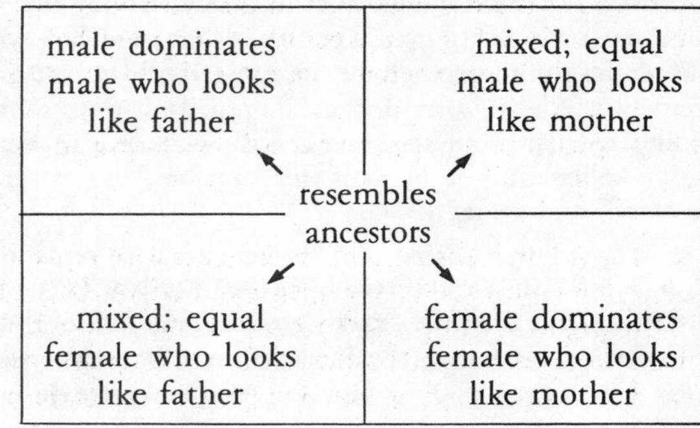

For Lucretius, the atoms, as invisible indivisible entities, carry from one generation to another complexion, body type, size, and sexual determinants through their combination into tiny seeds. All generation involves a unique combination of seeds, with each parent providing half of the total needed. Lucretius's theory clearly indicates that at least three hundred years later, Aristotle's theory of generation was not universally accepted.

Lucretius's *On the Nature of Things* was lost at the end of the fourth century AD, when the Epicurean school was closed. It was not rediscovered until 1417, long after the Aristotelian Revolution had been completed.[38] The victory of the Aristotelian Revolution meant that Lucretius's double-seed theory, with its stess on the mixing of the atom-like genes, was overturned in favour of a theory of generation that concluded that woman provided only material to the fetus and that the female fetus was an inferior or deformed male.

The next area of importance for the concept of woman in relation to man is Lucretius's very detailed analysis of the value of the pleasure and pain that accompany a sex-love relationship. Lucretius follows his master Epicurus in suggesting that it is better to rise above the vicissitudes of sexual pleasure: "Nor, lacking passion, must one lose love's joys; rather, one gains pure happiness, at no cost."[39] Lucretius then develops a series of arguments to persuade the reader to avoid falling in love. First, he argues that sexual intercourse causes pain. In the Epicurean philosophy, happiness is the absence of pain; it follows that the act of sexual intercourse ought to be avoided.

> For certainly to the healthy, pleasure's purer than to the sick. In the moment of possession impassioned lovers waver, blunder, stumble: they can't decide where first to look and touch. Whatever they seize, they crush, inflicting pain of body; sometimes they press tooth to lip and kiss like a flair, for theirs is no pure pleasure; in it are lash and goad, perforce to hurt that object, when this burgeoning madness rose.[40]

Lucretius recognizes that sexual intercourse gives a great deal of pleasure. However, he argues that this sort of intense pleasure brings with it a corresponding pain of addiction:

> But in the act, love gaily blunts these pangs, lets pleasure in, and gently curbs distress. For there is hope that in that very body that sets us afire, the flame may be put out. But nature battles against this whole idea; love's the one thing, of which the more we have the more the heart burns with insane desire.[41]

Lucretius also speaks of the pain that follows being in love when the object of the love is far away:

> For if your love is absent, still her image is with you and her name sings in your ear. But we must shun these images and carry off what feeds our love, and turn our thoughts elsewhere and jet our humours into someone's body, not keep them, and once trapped by one lone love save up sure woe and worry for ourselves. For if the cancer's fed, it lives and grows; in time, folly's a fever and pangs are millstones.[42]

In all cases, then, for the Epicurean, love ought to be avoided either because it directly brings pain, or else because the pleasure it first brings later on leads to an increase of pain.

Lucretius further argues that even the pleasure that love offers is insatiable, so that the lover always feels hungry. The union lovers seek is always illusive:

> They view bare bodies but get no fill of viewing; hands chafe but win no substance from young flesh, though they roam wildly over all the body. Besides, when two lie tasting, limb by limb, life's bloom, when flesh gives foretaste of delight, and Venus is ready to sow the female field, they hungrily seize each other, mouth to mouth the spittle flows, they pant, press tooth to lip—vainly, for they can chafe no substance off nor pierce and be gone, one body in the other. For often this seems to be their wish, their goal, so greedily do they cling in passion's bond, till pleasure loosens their limp and fainting limbs.[43]

Lucretius presents a traditional argument for sex polarity, namely that in a sexual relationship a man will lose his strength and become dominated by a woman:

> Add that they waste their strength, they strain, they die; add that the will of a woman rules their life. Fortunes go first, for Oriental robes, then honour and reputation totter and fall, . . . bitterness rises and turns bright bloom to pain, sometimes when conscience sits the tooth of guilt or a girl has tossed some doubtful word, and left it fixed in our foolish heart like a living fire. . . . And these are thrills that plague acknowledged love, when all goes well; but when love's poor and luckless, you'll pick up troubles by thousands with the eye blindfolded; better to be on watch before and avoid the pitfall, in the way I've shown; to keep from falling into the snare of love is not so hard as to escape the net once caught.[44]

From these graphic examples it is clear that for Lucretius, one ought to avoid the pain and pleasure of sexual relationships. However, the Epicurean philosopher develops his argument even further. Not content simply to devalue the experience of pleasure and pain, he takes considerable effort to devalue woman as the object of man's love. In the following passage we find a clear statement of the kind of satire against women that gained prominence in the Middle Ages and then reached new heights of articulation in the Renaissance.

> Yet, even snared and tangled, you can still get free, unless you block your own way out, and start by ignoring every fault of mind or body in her whom you desire and want. For this men often do when blind with lust, bestowing virtues where they don't exist. . . . Sallow is "honeyed," unkempt, unwashed, "informal"; she stares: "a goddess!", all bone and muscle: "a fawn." Dumpy? "She's exquisite." Tiny—"but what a mind." Huge and clumsy? "Portentous." "Pure dignity." Hare-lip? Tongue-tied? "No, lisping," "self-effacing." Shameless? A hideous bore? No, "Wisdom's lamp."[45]

Lucretius's diatribe against women argues that even women who are beautiful should be rejected because they deceive through the use of perfumes and makeup:

> Nor does this struggle escape our ladies, more than ever they struggle to hide these backstage bits of life from the men they wish to hold fast-bound in love. Vainly, for you by taking thought may draw all this to light, and analyze every smile. If hers is a pretty wit, and herself not too gross, let her go—her too; she's human: accept that fact.[46]

With Lucretius, the devaluation of woman as a means of rejection of sexual love reached a new level of expression. For the Epicurean, happiness consisted in living a life above the tensions of pleasure and pain. In this process it is clear that he envisaged man as the superior partner, capable of this kind of self-control.

Lucretius's text *On the Nature of Man* concluded with a general description of the evolution of society. In Book V he appears to accept the natural presence of generation through sexual intercourse, and he describes its evolution from a primitive to a more advanced state.

Lucretius rejected the Empedoclean stage in evolution where monsters or parts of figures combined in unusual ways:

> Just because thousands of atoms were in the world in the days when earth first brought forth living creatures this is no sign that groups could have been mixed, and limbs of one kind of lip lapped with another . . . but each has its own growth-habit, and all the kinds by nature's law maintain their differences.[47]

For Lucretius, men and women, and all other forms of plant or animal life generated from their own specific type of seed. This process, in human beings, continued itself first in a haphazard pattern of coercion, rape or struggle for survival in a state of nature:

> Whatever good luck brought their way, they took, for nature had taught them nothing but survival. In the woods, Venus linked lovers, flesh to flesh, for mutual lust would bring the two together, or else the man's raw force and wild desire, or a bribe: acorns, arbutes, or fresh-picked pears.[48]

At this early period of civilization, women and men roamed without settling in a specific place, and sexual union was not tied to any commitment beyond the sexual act itself. Then, in an analysis that sounds remarkably like Engels in *On the Origins of the Family, Private Property, and the State*, Lucretius describes the shift from a wandering society to a monogamous family:

> Then, after they got them houses, hides, and fire, and woman yielded to man and joined in one . . . and saw their own begotten children, then first the human race began to soften.[49]

As civilization became concentrated into family groups, collective labour evolved; Lucretius described men's and women's work as follows:

> As nature drove males to work with wool before the female sex (for in the arts all males are more ingenious and more skilled by far) till farmers, straight-laced men, judged this immoral and voted to pass such tasks to women's hands, while they, all men alike, endured hard toil and in hard labour toughened hand and sinew.[50]

Lucretius concludes his poem with a description of the development of civilization in all its many aspects, culminating in the Glory of Athens. Within this broader development of civilization there is no mention of the concept of woman in relation to man, which could imply that it is men alone who developed this advance in civilization. Needless to say, this description of the separation of woman's work into the indoor activity of weaving, and the men to the outdoor tasks and the more complicated aspects of civilized culture, clearly falls within the sex-polarity pattern of sex identity.

In conclusion, Lucretius is an important transition figure for the concept of woman from the early periods of Greek and Roman philosophy. He pushes thought forward in the area of the theory of conception through his descriptions of the interaction of "atomic seeds" from the ancestors in the structure of the fetus. In this aspect of his philosophy, woman is on an equal footing with man; both sexes provide seed to the fetus, and each is equally capable of sexual arousal. At this time, Lucretius's devaluation of woman, which follows from his Epicurean stress on rising above pleasure and pain, gives an indication of the sex-polarity tendency in the broader categories of wisdom and virtue. Therefore, Lucretius did not achieve the integrated concept of sex identity that has been found in Aristotle. At the same time, however, he went beyond the limitations of Aristotle's theory of generation.

NEO-PYTHAGOREANISM

The school of philosophy founded as a religious community by Pythagoras (c. 530 BC) was dissolved by the end of the fourth century BC.[51] There is considerable controversy about the dates and places of the revival of Pythagorean philosophy. However, impressive arguments are advanced by Holger Thesleff for a two-phase development: one occurred in southern Italy in the mid-third century BC; and the other originated in Alexandria or Athens at different times and arrived in Italy around the beginning of the second century BC.[52] This view of the rebirth of Pythagoreanism, either as a way of life or simply as a theory of knowledge, places the sources of neo-Pythagoreanism considerably earlier than the more generally accepted period of the first century BC to the first century AD.

For the purposes of this study, it is sufficient to note that the development of neo-Pythagoreanism brought with it some fragments and letters reportedly written by female philosophers. In addition, it also included fragments about sex identity reportedly written by men.

The difficulty in dating the writings of the neo-Pythagoreans is compounded by the fact that most of them were written by persons other than the one's whose names were attached to the texts. Scholars have puzzled over this feature of neo-Pythagoreanism and have considered reasons for it that range from forgery to the less deceitful desire to report views attributed to various previous thinkers in this tradition. The view defended by Thesleff is that the writers chose the names of previously known Pythagoreans to indicate their identification with the foundations of the school. At the same time, the ideas contained in the writings represented the thought of the person who had in fact composed the text. For the purposes of the present text, the writings of the neo-Pythagoreans are important for the history of philosophy in their own right, regardless of whether they were composed as early as the fourth century BC or as late as the first century AD, for they indicate an ongoing concern with some of the basic questions of sex identity. They also indicate the active presence of female philosophers, for it is improbable that men would choose to propose philosophical theories using the names of women if women were not respected as philosophers in their own right.[53]

The specific names of historical individuals attached to fragments with significance for the concept of woman in relation to man are: Theano, Pythagoras' wife; Myia, Pythagoras' daughter; Perictione, Plato's mother; and Phyntis, the daughter of Callicrates. In addition, texts that were written in approximately 300 BC claimed to record speeches given by Pythagoras in Croton some two hundred years previously.[54] The contents of these speeches were considered in the first chapter of this book, even though they were neo-Pythagorean in origin. As will be seen, the same themes found in the Croton speeches reappear in the writings attributed to the neo-Pythagorean women. The fundamental themes are: the separate education of women and men; the special significance of harmony; the virtue of obedience of wives to their husbands, the importance of modesty; and the need for everyone to study philosophy and to seek wisdom.

In Chapter I it was stated that the Pythagorean theory of sex identity appeared to contain aspects of sex unity, sex polarity and sex complementarity.[55] Neo-Pythagoreanism appears to lean towards sex unity and sex neutrality, with an occasional hint of reverse-sex polarity and sex complementarity. Specific fragments by various authors will now be considered in a general chronological order.

Earliest Period: c. 400–300 BC

Perictione I: Harmony of Women

Mary Ellen Waithe argues that Perictione, the author of *On the Harmony of Women*, was the mother of Plato, while Thesleff suggests that the text, while written later, was given the name of Plato's mother.[56] In either case, the author of this text ought to be kept distinct from the Perictione who wrote *On Wisdom*. This latter text will be attributed to Perictione II, from the third to second century BC.

On the Harmony of Women is very interesting for the concept of woman because it applies basic Pythagorean categories to the specific situation of women in the world. The work begins with an exhortation to obey and respect one's parents:

> We must not speak badly about our parents nor act wrongly towards them; but we must obey in small as in great things those who generated us. In any state of mind and of body, in any personal or external situation, in peace and in war, in health and in sickness, in wealth and in poverty, in fame and in obscurity, whether they are ordinary individuals or public figures, we must always stand by our parents, never abandon them, and obey them almost to madness. Such behaviour is considered good and wise by wise people.[57]

This call to obey one's parents hardly seems to follow Plato's suggestions in the *Republic*, where he wrote that children should not even be told who their parents are. Instead, it appears to flow from a different source, namely that of respecting the hierarchical structure of society. Perictione I continues by arguing that any contravention of this respect and obedience to parents will be punished by society and by the gods after death.

In contrast, a second section of *On the Harmony of Women*, which focuses on the internal qualities of the soul, could follow directly from the teachings of Plato in the *Republic*:

> It must be understood that a woman filled with moderation and circumspection is harmony. It is essential, indeed, that her soul be strongly aspiring after virtue, so that she can become just, courageous, temperate, adorned with qualities in conformity with her nature, and opposed to any vain glory. From these virtues, indeed, follow for the woman good acts for herself, for her husband, her children, her home, and sometimes too for cities, if cities and nations are governed by such a woman, as is seen under the system of monarchy.[58]

Here Perictione is encouraging women to become philosophers. Wisdom and virtue demand the internal ordering of the soul and the conformity of outward actions to this internal harmony. Significantly, woman is also able to rule over men, women and children in certain kinds of government.

The virtue of moderation is next given specific application to sexual desires:

> If then she can overcome lust and passion, woman will become harmonious and holy. This way illegitimate affairs will not follow her, but she will keep her fidelity to her husband, her children, and all her household. All those, indeed, who fall for a stranger's bed, become hostile to everyone in their own house, whether they be of a free state or servants. Such a woman plans tricks against her husband, invents all kinds of lies about him, so as to seem to be the only one who attracts attention by her kindness and the only one who runs her household, though she really only values idleness. Such misbehaviour, indeed, brings the destruction of everything that the wife and husband own together. But I have said enough on that subject.[59]

At the end of the same text, Perictione I considers the opposite situation, that of a wife faced with infidelity by her husband. In this treatment, the wife is encouraged to submit to these "disharmonious" actions in order to achieve the higher goal of the rentention of the harmonious marriage in the final analysis:

> Toward her husband the woman must act according to custom and with a heart so sincere that she must not plan anything for her own self, but work hard to save and keep her (marriage) bed. She must also be ready to endure everything that happens with her husband, whether he falls into misfortunes, or either through mistake, weakness or over-drinking he failed to do his duty, or meets with other women. Such weakness is forgiven to men, but not to women.[60]

As Perictione I develops her analysis, the apparent sex polarity of the immediate submission of the wife to the husband in spite of infidelities, becomes more of a reverse sex polarity because the woman achieves a higher degree of virtue than man by quelling and ordering her lower desires.

> It is proper then not to forget this usual custom, and not let oneself be carried away by jealousy, but to endure one's husband's anger, stinginess, complaints, jealousy, and reproaches and whatever other kind of fault he may be born with; in so doing she will order everything in conformity with her husband's will.[61]

For Perictione I, obedience is a choice for woman and not a simple consequence of her inferior nature, as it was for Aristotle. In this choice of ordering one's actions to conform to a principle outside of the self, namely the husband's will, the wife achieves a degree of wisdom and virtue that corresponds with the Pythagorean value of harmony.

> The woman, indeed, who is cherished by her husband and who handles with a loving heart her husband's goods, becomes harmony, loves her whole household and makes strangers look at her home with benevolence. But, if she does not like her husband she refuses to look after the prosperity of her house, of her children, and of her servants, or of any of the goods belonging to her home, she brings with her total ruin, wants to be considered as an adversary, asks for her husband's death as if he were an enemy, so as to be able to befriend others, and all those people her husband likes, she hates. I know that the woman who is filled with ordering and circumspection will not act in such a way. . . . In the company of her husband, she will adjust herself to the parents and friends whom her husband values, and she will consider as sweet and bitter the same things as her husband, unless she is completely lacking in harmony.[62]

The neo-Pythagorean Perictione I has therefore expressed a slightly different concept of the relation of ruling and obedience to women and men from that previously expressed in western philosophy. For Plato, there were no specific differences attributed to the two sexes, whereas for Aristotle, a belief in a difference in nature led to the view that women ought to obey and men to rule. Aristotle's sex-polarity theory, which stated that women were defective in their discursive or deliberative capacities and that they were therefore limited in their practice of virtue to obedience, is completely different from Perictione I's exhortation to a woman to conform her will to her husband's out of a harmony within the soul in which the higher powers of reason subdued and ordered the lower powers. Perictione then continues her analysis by suggesting that the wife's achievement of this virtue of harmony will lead to the harmonization of the entire household and even extend outward to strangers.

The remainder of Perictione I's text *On the Harmony of Women* is devoted to a consideration of the virtue of modesty in dress and appearance:

> As far as the body is concerned, it must be managed according to the moderation which nature shows us, whether it be about food, clothes, baths, ointments, hairdos, and everything that for the pleasure of adornment comes from gold and diamonds. . . . As for hunger and thirst, it is proper then to aim only at their appeasement, and even then by simple means. . . . In the same way to wear clothes too thin and with colours coming from the navy tint of the shell or from some other sumptuous colouration is great madness. The body, indeed, only wants not to be cold, and, by decency, not to be naked, it does not need anything else.[63]

Arguing that simple means are better than wealth, and that interior harmony and order are better than outward beauty, Perictione I consistently defends a self-controlled model of wisdom and virtue for woman. The Pythagorean emphasis on the priority of soul over body is given explicit detail in this neo-Pythgagorean text. Woman as well as man is called to an internal ordering of the soul and to live a life in conformity with this inner discipline. As will be seen, this theme is repeated in other neo-Pythagorean texts by female philosophers.

In conclusion, Perictione I's theory of sex identity appears to be in the category of sex unity for wisdom and virtue as harmony, and tending towards reverse sex polarity in the description of the superior value given to a woman who overcomes anger or jealousy in relation to a man who gives in to his sexual passions. However, Perictione I avoids drawing any absolute generalizations about the nature of man and woman, so the reverse sex polarity must be described simply as a tendency and not as a clear theory.

Theano I: Apophthegms

The name of Pythagoras's wife, Theano, was used by at least two different neo-Pythagoreans. According to Thesleff, apophthegms by Theano I were known by 300 BC.[64] These fragments differ from several letters of Theano II, which appear to have been written during a later time period.

In the first fragment, Theano I considers a misconception about Pythagoras's theory that all things come from numbers:

> I heard that a good number of Greeks thought that Pythagoras has said that everything was born from Number. But this fills us with perplexity; for how can we imagine things which do not exist but which could generate? He did not say that everything was born from Number, but that everything was formed according to Number, since in Number lies essential order, and since it is only by being a part of this order that the things themselves which can be numbered are placed first, second and so on.[65]

This fragment, which touches on generation and mathematics, simply indicates an interest in Pythagoras's theory of numbers. For the concept of woman as philosopher, it merely points out that within the Pythagorean tradition, the study of mathematics was central to all philosophical activity. This was also common to the Platonic Academy under the leadership of Speusippus and Xenocrates. Therefore, it is possible that some of the neo-Pythagorean writings, such as the one by Theano above, could have had its origin in the early Academy.[66]

The rest of the fragments attributed to Theano I involve simple pronouncements much like those of many of the pre-Socratics. One fragment significant for the concept of woman is in the category of wisdom, for it emphasizes the need for reflection: "Theano said: 'It is safer to rely on an unbridled horse than on an unreflective woman.' "[67] A woman must develop her internal ordering through reflection and the study of philosophy.

The fragments from Theano also reveal an affirmation of the immortality of the soul, the common implicit rationale for the equal access to wisdom for women and men: "Theano the Pythagorean writes: 'Life indeed would truly be a banquet for the wicked who die after badly misbehaving, if the soul were not immortal.' "[68] The immortality of the soul allows for a judgement to occur after death and, within the Pythagorean tradition, an opportunity to be reincarnated in another life as a man, woman or animal.

Following the pattern of Perictione I, Theano I also considers the virtue of modesty:

> Theano, while wrapping her cloak, showed her forearm. And, as someone said to her, "What a beautiful elbow!" she replied: "But it is not public. Besides it is fitting that not only the elbow but the words themselves of a modest woman be not for everyone, and that she fears and is careful not to appear naked in front of strangers by letting everyone hear her voice, for through the voice, indeed, is revealed the feeling, character, and the disposition of the woman who speaks."[69]

Theano I appears to argue for a reasoned sense of timing in bridging the public-private distinction. Since the Pythagorean school was a secret society, this capacity for a reasoned skill in knowing when to disclose and what to disclose, would be a virtue for both women and men who were wise. In the following fragment, Theano I clearly states this premise:

> Theano says: "There are things which it is beautiful to speak about; there are others which it is shameful to keep secret. There are also things which it is shameful to talk about; there are others which it is better to keep secret."[70]

Finally, in the area of virtue, there is one fragment attributed to Theano I that repeats the value of obedience for women, but without the development seen in Perictione I. "Theano, the Pythagorean, being asked about what duty was necessary for a married woman, answered: 'To please her own husband.' "[71]

The remaining fragments in the category of virtue that focus on chastity appear to be contradictory. In one, Theano suggests that love is the result of idleness, in another that she was famous for sharing her bed, and in a third that a woman who commits adultery is never pure, but one who has intercourse with her husband is immediately pure.[72] In general, this neo-Pythagorean would suggest that ordered sexuality was perfectly acceptable, while disordered sexuality—that which falls outside the bounds of legal marriage—was not. This would be consistent with the aspect of neo-Pythagoreanism that emphasized chastity rather than celibacy. In this context it may be that Theano's remark about her fame could have been derived from her being married to Pythagoras, rather than from the implication of a variety of sexual encounters. In this case the apparent contradiction in the different fragments would disappear.

There are not enough fragments from Theano I to assess her theory of sex identity. The demand for reflection in women may indicate a tendency to sex unity, and the demand for the obedience of a woman to her husband may indicate a tendency to sex polarity. However, as already mentioned, no conclusion is possible.

Phyntis: Temperance of Women

There is some controversy about the date of composition of the important work, *Temperance of Women*, for Thesleff suggests the third century BC, while Waithe suggests that it was written circa 425 BC.[73] The name Phyntis appears to have belonged to the daughter of an admiral from Sparta, named Callicrates, who died in 406 BC. Therefore, the selection of a date depends upon whether you believe that the original Phyntis wrote the text, or whether a later female philosopher used that name. *Temperance of Women* considers many of the themes previously found in the neo-Pythagorean writings about the concept of woman and man, particularly with reference to the categories of wisdom and virtue.

The most striking aspect of this text is its adoption of Platonic categories for the concept of virtue, while also appearing to suggest an Aristotelian sex polarity for the question of woman's and man's specific relations to these virtues. Fortunately, as a significant portion of the text remains, its arguments can be evaluated.

Phyntis begins with a consideration of the nature of virtue as the excellence of a function:

> It is proper, in short, for woman to be good and honest; but she could never become so without virtue. Each virtue, indeed, relates to something and renders perfect that thing which can receive it. The virtue proper to the eyes makes the eyes excellent; the one proper virtue to the ear makes the ears excellent; the one proper to the horse, the horse; the one proper to man, the man, and similarly the one proper to the woman, woman. Now the most important virtue of woman is temperance, because it is through temperance that she is able to praise and love her husband.[74]

This analysis of virtue as excellence or perfection of function was articulated by Plato in the *Republic*. It was also suggested, in its sex-polarity form, in Plato's *Meno*, representing the theory of the Sophist Gorgias. It was therefore a common view of the Sophists in the Hellenic world during this neo-Pythagorean period. Phyntis, however, appears to accept the argument that woman's specific virtue or excellence is different from man's. She further develops arguments to defend this position after claiming that both women and men need to study philosophy in order to discover their particular virtues.

> Many are those, perhaps, who think that it is not proper for a woman to philosophise, as it does not fit her to go horse-back riding, or give public speeches. As for me, I think that certain occupations are particular to men, others to women, and some are common to both men and women: I think that some are better adapted to activities proper to men than to women, others fit better women than men. The activities proper to man are to command armies, to govern cities, to lead the people by haranguing speech. Those which are particular to woman are to look after her house, to stay at home, to wait for and to serve her husband.[75]

Phyntis's classic statement of the public-private differentiation of spheres of activity is then continued, first by an appeal to the need for the same general categories of virtue for women and men, but then for a more specific association of women with the specific virtue of temperance:

> But I affirm that to both of them belong courage, justice, and temperance. I add too that it is proper to man as well as to woman to receive proportionately virtues which relate to the body as well as to the soul. And it is useful both for the body to be healthy, and for the soul to be healthy. The virtues of the body are: Health, strength, sensitiveness, and beauty. It is more fitting for man to exercise some (of these virtues), others are more in harmony with women. Courage and clear-sighted determination are more proper to man, as much because of the constitution of his body as because of the power of his soul. Temperance is more adapted to woman. That is why she must learn, through her education, what temperance is and by which ways and by how this good can come to woman.[76]

As can be amply seen from this argument, Phyntis uses a general appeal to both men and women to study philosophy. However, when the details of this study are revealed, Phyntis argues for a separation of the virtue of woman and of man. Her theory appears to be based on a claim that men are naturally superior in strength of body and power of soul. If this is the case, then Phyntis's arguments for temperance spring from a slightly different foundation than the arguments of Perictione I. For Phyntis, temperance, or obedience, follows from the natural weakness of women; while for Perictione, they seem to follow from a choice in women to order their passions in the face of the lack of this virtue in men.

The *Temperance of Women* continues with a list of specific ways in which woman can practise the virtue of temperance:

> I affirm there are five ways:
> First, by the sanctity and the piety she will show upon her bed;
> Second, by the modesty she will use in the clothing of her body;
> Third, by the discretion she will impose upon herself when she will go out of her own house;
> Fourth, by refraining from attending orgiastic feasts and those of the Mother of the gods;
> Fifth, by being punctual and moderate in the sacrifices she offers the gods.

> However, among all these means the most effective way to attain moderation, the one which includes them all, is to remain incorruptible as far as one's bed is concerned; and to have no intimate relations with a stranger.[77]

The above list simply states a series of customs common to the practices of women at the time, with a particular emphasis on the virtue of chastity. While there is a hidden implication that fidelity to one's husband in sexual intercourse takes an exercise of self-control, the text by Phyntis does not defend virtue as the practice of moderation of the passions, as Perictione had in ther text, *On the Harmony of Women*. Instead, Phyntis lists a series of negative consequences that will occur if a woman fails to practise chastity: she offends the gods, her parents, her family, the law, and the country. Woman is liable to the penalty of death for "falling, by lust into iniquity and excessiveness."[78]

Then Phyntis suggests that "the most beautiful adornment of a free woman and her greatest glory to be able to give proof, by the appearances of her children, of her loyalty to her husband, is if it is granted by the heavens that her children wear a sign of resemblance to the father who begot them."[79] In this final exhortation to chastity, Phyntis suggests that even the conformity of the generative material of the wife to the seed of the husband is virtuous.

The conclusion of the text, which sounds very much like Xenophon's exhortation to his wife in the *Oeconomicus*, focuses on modesty of dress:

> Concerning the ornaments which are proper to wrap the body with, it seems to me that it should be done this way. Woman must be clothed in white, with simplicity and without superfluity. She will succeed if she does not use transparent coloured silk to cover the body, but instead if she uses simple white material.[80]

Similarly, make-up and jewelery must be avoided and as a result, the woman's modesty will prove her most attractive quality.

Phyntis's concept of woman offers a peculiar combination of theories: sex unity in the general categories of wisdom and virtue; sex polarity in the practical application of virtue and in the category of generation; and sex complementarity in dress. The practical theory of sex polarity is seen in her division of specific virtues as follows:

Man's Virtue	**Woman's Virtue**
public sphere	private sphere
rule	obey
courage	temperance
strength	weakness

The tendency towards sex complementarity is seen simply in that women do not follow the same pattern of the early Platonists, who wore men's clothing, but rather, maintained a differentiation of the sexes in dress.

In conclusion, the *Temperance of Woman* by Phyntis, while offering some of the same conclusions as *On the Harmony of Woman* by Perictione I, nevertheless develops different sorts of arguments. Although Phyntis suggests that women should study philosophy, she appears to offer a rather simple set of maxims for regulating behaviour. On the other hand, Perictione I attempts to develop reasons for her theories. Both philosophers, however, indicate a real concern with the search for wisdom and virtue in women.

Middle Period: c. 300–200 BC

Melissa: Letter to Cleareta

The neo-Pythagorean letter of Melissa is a remarkable summary of the central ideas found in Perictione and Phyntis. It expresses the basic teachings of the neo-Pythagoreans on the wisdom and virtue of woman in precise language. In contrast to Phyntis's emphasis on outward appearance, Melissa places a greater emphasis on the inner quality of soul:

> You seem to be naturally full of good qualities, because the eagerness you show in wanting information about women's clothing gives good hope that you are growing pure in virtue. It is proper then that the woman who is sensible and free, approaches her husband adorned discreetly and without magnificence, clothed in white garments, clean, simple, and without sumptuousness or luxury. She must refuse indeed transparent clothes, ornated with purple and brocaded with gold. Such an attire is good for courtesans to hunt numerous prey; but for a woman who must only please her own husband, the real adornment is in her manners, not in her dress.[81]

In this passage the appeal to inner virtue, reflected in outward behaviour, is described as being taught by one woman to another. It therefore shows women as actively teaching philosophy.

Melissa develops a further philosophical rationale for internal ordering that is common to Pythagorean thought:

> She indeed who is aspiring to wisdom must not put her love of beauty in the magnificence of clothing but in the wise administration of her house, in the care she must take to please her husband by doing his will. The will of the husband, indeed, must be regarded by a wife in love with moral beauty as an unwritten law according to which she must conform her life. She must ultimately believe that she carries with her the most beautiful and the greatest dowery, if she has the sense of good order. It is important indeed to have more confidence in the beauty and richness of the soul than in the beauty of the body and the abundance of goods. Envy and sickness can deprive us of these latter advantages; the possession of the former accompany us until death.[82]

Melissa appears to be repeating Perictione I's reverse sex polarity tendency in saying that a woman achieves superior moral development when she learns how to order her soul through obedience to her husband. Melissa does not imply that woman is naturally inferior or weak or that she needs man's ruling in order to be virtuous. In addition, in her letter we find the traditional separation of body and soul so common in Pythagorean thought. The soul has a more fundamental importance and, therefore, the body must be conformed to the virtues of the soul.

While the remaining fragment from Melissa is short, it is possible to interpret her theory as containing some tendencies towards reverse sex polarity in the practical virtues, sex complementarity in dress, and sex unity in her emphasis on the quality of soul over body.

Perictione II: On Wisdom

This particular text is written by a different author from *On the Harmony of Women* discussed under Perictione I. Thesleff suggests that it was modelled on a similar text entitled *On Wisdom* by the philosopher Archytas, the head of the Italian school of neo-Pythagoreanism.[83] In both texts there is similarity to Platonic thought. The work itself, falling into the sex neutrality aspect of sex unity, does not contain any direct references to differences between women and men; instead it focuses on the common goal of wisdom for all philosophers.

> Man is born and made to contemplate the principle of universal nature, and the role of wisdom is precisely to possess and to contemplate the intelligence displayed in the (eternal) realities. . . . Wisdom seeks the principles of all real things; natural science of those which are produced by nature. Geometry, arithmetic and music discover the principles of quantity and harmony. He, then, who is able to analyze all the modalities of the real according to one and the same principle, to reorganize them and put them in good order, this one appears to be the wisest and closest to the truth.[84]

For the present study of sex identity, the important aspect of this text is that it gives a clear example of a woman using discursive reasoning in considering the nature of wisdom. Perictione II goes into further detail about the three different ways of knowing and about the relation of philosophy to the love of God. For our purposes, however, the simple extract above indicates the degree to which discursive reasoning was present in women in the neo-Pythagorean tradition. It is an example of the sex-neutrality tradition of the sex-unity theory.

Aesara of Lucania: On Human Nature

Aesara (or Aresas) is another neo-Pythagorean, reputed to have been a member of the Italian school of neo-Pythagoreanism founded by Archytas. Iamblicus describes Aesara as follows: "Aresas of the Lucanians, who had been saved by certain strangers, headed the school; to which came Diodoros the Aspendian."[85] The neo-Platonic school in Alexandria was headed by a female philosopher, Hypatia, in the fifth century AD. It would have been remarkable indeed for a female philosopher to lead a school as early as the third century BC, especially if that school included male students. Waithe includes Aesara as a philosopher in the *Project on the History of Woman in Philosophy*, and suggests that Aesara "presents a very familiar and intuitive natural law theory."[86] In addition, this neo-Pythagorean philosopher gives a clearly Platonic description of a three-part soul in the extant fragments from *On Human Nature*:

> Human nature seems to me to be the standard of law and justice both of the household and of the city-state. For one seeking and searching would find traces

> (of justice) in the same. For there is law and justice in it which is the proper ordering of the soul. For being threefold it is framed for threefold works: the reason affecting judgement and purpose, the spirited element might and power, and the desiderative element love and friendliness. And these are all so arranged with respect to one another that the best part rules and the inferior part is governed, while the intermediate part holds an intermediate position, and both rules and is ruled.[87]

The Platonic view that justice is the order and harmony of the three-part soul, composed of reason, spirit and desires, is considered in further detail:

> For if they have been given an equal share of power and rank, while being dissimilar—the inferior and the superior and the intermediate—the harmony of parts could not have been constructured throughout the soul; and if an unequal share, (supposing) the superior part had not been given the greater share, but the inferior, much folly and disorder would have arisen with respect to the soul; and if the superior (had been given) the greater, and the inferior the lesser, but each of these not according to a plan, there could have been no harmony nor love nor justice in the soul, for each one is arranged in accordance with a fitting plan, and such I affirm to be most just.[88]

Once again, this fragment indicates the use of discursive reason for understanding human nature. At the same time, within the Platonic neo-Pythagorean tradition, there is no attempt to associate one part of the soul with female and another with male identity. Women and men alike have the same three parts of soul, and the goal for them in the areas of wisdom and virtue is to achieve a right ordering within the soul.

> Such a situation justly would be said to be the good order of the soul, whichever soul, in this way, the superior part governing and the inferior being governed, would pursue the rule of virtue.[89]

Aesara, judging from the remaining fragment from *On Human Nature*, would fall under sex neutrality, or the theory in which differentiation between the sexes is not directly discussed, but in which women and men are presumed to be equal.

Later Period: c. 200–100 BC

Myia: Letter to Phyllis

Although Myia is the name of Pythagoras's daughter, Thesleff dates the letter from Myia to Phyllis at approximately 200 BC.[90] In addition, it appears to have originated in southern Italy. Most of the letter contains simple advice on the feeding and care of an infant. At one point in the letter, however, there is an attempt to focus on the character of the nurse:

> Since you just became a mother, I am sending you this advice. Choose first an excellent nurse, who is clean, and not rude nor prone to laziness or drunkenness. It is then according to such qualities that she must be judged capable of raising your children with perfection. . . . The most important part of her function, the one which tops all the others and whose consequences are felt

> during all the child's life, is that the nurse know how to feed opportunely, because she will then do at the right time everything that needs to be done; . . . she will give the breast and food not thoughtlessly but with some premeditation. . . . This nurse must not be short tempered, nor too talkative, nor indifferent in her choice of foods, but she must have a fixed diet, be temperate.[91]

The practical aspects of child care involve the capacity to judge a situation, to find the "Aristotelian" mean between extremes in time and quantity of food. The capacity for practical wisdom, to put the general principles into practice in specific situations, is the general quality of character demanded of the nurse. That is, Myia suggests that the excellent nurse is the person who knows how to do the right thing, in the right way, with the right instrument, at the right time. It especially involves the virtue of temperance—the quelling and ordering of her own desires—so that her will conforms itself to the needs of the infant rather than to her own needs. Myia suggests that the nurse forego sexual relations with her husband during her period of nursing and that she sleep only when the child has already fallen asleep. The nurse, therefore, has to practise the virtue of self-control or temperance.

While the fragment from Myia does not generalize about the specific association of temperance with the concept of woman, in Plato's thought temperance was the virtue of the lower class, or workers. In addition, in Phyntis's sex-polarity differentiation of virtues, temperance was particularly associated with women and courage with men. However, it is not possible to draw any conclusions about Myia's theory of sex identity.

Theano II: Letters

The letters of Theano II, written quite late in the neo-Pythagorean tradition, must be distinguished from the writings of Theano I, which had their origin some two hundred years earlier. The name Theano belonged to Pythagoras's wife, so its use by later neo-Pythagoreans lent some credibility to their texts. Among Theano's letters, several are thought to have different authors as well, so there is a kind of spurious authorship of spurious authors occurring. For our purposes in the present text, it is important once again simply to recognize that the letters had their origin within the neo-Pythagorean school and that they attempted to apply some basic Pythagorean concepts to the particular situation of woman. Some extracts from the letters will be examined below.

The letter to Eubule concentrates on the demands of child-rearing:

> I heard that you are raising your children in a lax way. A good mother, however, must not bring up her children for pleasure, but teach them moderation. . . . Education distorts nature when it gives their souls a taste for pleasure, their bodies an inclination for indolence, and makes them finally idle in their soul and too soft in their body. Children who are being educated must also be inured to cowardliness, even if it is necessary to distress and overstrain them, so as not to become the slaves of fear—excited when it is a question of giving into pleasures or frightened when it is a matter of submitting to hardships—but instead, to value, above all else, good behaviour, refraining from some things and clinging to others.[92]

The good parent then teaches the child how to become virtuous and, specifically, how to develop the virtues of courage, temperance, and practical wisdom. The parent must learn how to help the child discern which things to do and which to avoid.

> Let it be known to you, my dear friend, that children who live in softness will become slaves when they become adults. Deprive them of such refinements; allow them to have an austere education and not a dissipating one like you give them, and allow them to experience hunger and thirst, cold and heat, as well as the shame they may endure from their playmates and their supervisors. This way your children will acquire their excellent strength of character which will allow their soul to be flexible or rigid. Hardships, dear friend, are indeed for children, like the challenges which prepare them for the full development of their strength; when they have been immersed in that they will take on the quality of virtue.[93]

In this particular letter from Theano II, virtue becomes associated with the capacity to rise above the vicissitudes of immediate needs; it is the ordering of the passions through an appeal to a rational principle. Since there is no differentiation between boys and girls, it falls in the sex-neutrality tradition.

In the remarkable letter to Nicostrate, Theano II develops the theme that we previously encountered in Perictione, namely that a woman ought to choose to develop the virtue of self-control and obedience in the situation of a husband who is unfaithful.

> I heard about your husband's foolish actions. It is said that he maintains a courtesan, and that you suffer from jealousy. As for me, dear, I have known many men affected by the same madness. They are, it seems, enraptured by these women, and captured by them, they (the men) do not possess them (the women).[94]

The man is presented as the person who is unable to control his desires and who ends up being enslaved to the woman who is the object of these desires. The free person is the one who achieves the capacity to live according to a higher principle than pure sexual pleasure. Theano II continues her analysis by challenging Nicostrate to achieve a similar freedom by overcoming her jealousy and its resultant vindictive actions:

> But you despair night and day, you live in anxiety and you plot against your husband. Take care, dear, not to act like that. The virtue of a spouse does not consist in spying upon her husband, but in being his forebearing companion, and, being forebearing, in tolerating his madness. If he visits a courtesan, it is out of pleasure; but if he lives with a wife it is out of interest, and interest requires not mixing evil with evil nor adding madness to madness. There are some disorders, my dear, which become more exacerbated if one disapproves of them, but which calm down if we do not mention them, just as fire goes out if it is left alone. By showering your reproaches, indeed, on him who tries to hide from you, you remove all discretion to his passion and you force him to act openly.[95]

Theano's goal is to develop the foundation of marriage on the virtue of the two persons involved. This virtue, however, should be self-originated, it should not be dependent upon the character of the other person:

> As for you, don't build the friendship you owe your husband on his perfect virtue, because it is the good of the relationship which is its root. Consider then that your husband visits a courtesan only out of vice, but that he is present beside you to live a common life with you; that he loves you by a thoughtful intention, but that he is attracted to this other woman only by passion. The duration of passion is very short indeed. As soon as it has reached the highest point of its intensity, it comes simultaneously to satiety, and then it cools down. Therefore the love of a man who is not fundamentally bad for a courtesan does not last long.[96]

Theano suggests that a good man who has given into his passions will eventually discover the limitations of this path:

> What is, indeed, more futile than the desire which is filled only to its own harm? He will soon understand then that his means of living are diminishing, and that his reputation is ruined. No sensible man would persist of his own will to want to bring criticism upon himself.[97]

The letter ends with an exhortation to Nicostrate to overcome the effects that jealousy and vindictiveness have produced in her. Theano II argues that virtue is its own reward, and that it will succeed in bringing order into the disordered marriage.

> Do you decide to neglect your home and lose your husband? You will carry to the end the disapproval which follows an unhappy life. Do you want to fight this courtesan? Being careful, she will know how to avoid you, and if she wants to defend herself, a woman who has no shame can be quarrelsome. Does it seem good to be fighting every day with your husband? What more will you win? Disputes and insults do not put an end to licentiousness, but it aggravates, by its violence, the disagreement. What then? Will you plot something against him? Abandon that idea, my dear. Tragedy teaches us to keep jealousy under control, by showing us the chain of events through which Medea became a criminal. But just as one must keep our hands away from infected eyes, in the same way too do not try to hide the sorrow of your soul. Because in enduring it with nobility, you will extinguish this evil faster.[98]

Theano II's arguments for the effort to practise virtue clearly involve an appeal to the nature of woman that is capable of internal self-ordering. This model of woman's identity is remarkably different from that proposed by Aristotle, in which female nature was considered incapable of deliberative activity. In fact, Theano appears to imply that it is man, rather than woman, who lives more in relation to his lower appetites. The man, by choosing to follow his desires, becomes enslaved to his lower nature and to the woman who excites this response in him. One could argue from this that Theano II is suggesting a reverse sex-polarity position, namely that women and men are significantly different and that women are naturally superior. However, she does not go that far in her analysis.

It is much more likely that she is suggesting a sex-unity theory because of the Pythagorean tendency to place greater value on the soul than on the body. The soul is the seat of the rational principle that brings about the ordering so necessary to virtue. In this capacity and in virtue, women and men are alike.

Another letter from Theano II, to Eurydice, develops a musical analogy for the goal of moderating the passion of jealousy:

> What sorrow invades your soul? You are desperate for no other reason than that the one to whom you are married visits a courtesan and fills his body up there with voluptuousness. But it is not fitting, O wonderful woman, to be so upset. Do you not know indeed, that the ear, too, is sometimes filled with the pleasure given by a lyre or a musical song; but that sometimes when it gets saturated with them, it hears with pleasure the flute or pipe? And yet what resemblance is there between the flute and the musical chords and wonderful sound of a lyre of the highest quality? Consider it to be the same way for you and the courtesan your husband is visiting. Your husband, indeed, because of personal pride, through natural inclinations, and through reason cares about you. But when by accident he gets to the point of saturation, he goes occasionally to a courtesan, so true it is that those whose taste is corrupted keep some love for foods which are not good. Live with strength![99]

Once again, woman is exhorted to develop a prespective on the situation that interprets incident sexual passion as significantly inferior to a relationship between a woman and a man in the context of marriage. Also, the letter tends to favour the reverse sex-polarity theory in its appeal to woman to overcome her passions while the man indulges in his.

In a second letter to Eurydice, Theano II challenges her listener to consider the value of old age and to reject the temptation to imitate youth.

> Your natural radiance is done, and now is approaching the proper nobility of wrinkles. But you, you try to falsify the truth, using the artifices of make-up to deceive those who love you. You must learn, little old Lady, to surrender to time. Meadows, indeed, are not the right place for flowers at the end of fall. Think also of death, because you are not far from it, and you must apply yourself to practise the temperance required by necessity. You offend, indeed, at the same time old age and youth, because you lie by promising what you don't have anymore, and you depreciate what is really your own.[100]

The call to virtue for an elderly woman is the appeal to temper one's activities to be in harmony with one's proper age. Virtue required the conformity of the inner and outer nature, through concerted effort of self-control and temperance. Nothing about sex identity can be concluded from this letter.

In an interesting letter to Callisto, Theano II considers the question of the virtues needed to rule the household. At the outset, there is a different emphasis from the one found in Xenophon's *Oeconomicus*; Theano suggests that the virtue of ruling a household is learned not from the husband but from older women:

> To you, younger women, power has been given by law, as soon as you get married, to command your household like a master; but the training required for

> this task you must obtain from older women, who are constant advisers as far as managing a household is concerned. It is good, indeed, to inquire first about what one does not know, and to value as most profitable, the opinion of older women, because it is proper that for such a task an inexperienced soul should be educated like a young girl.[101]

The main area of skill that the young ruler of the household must learn is how to relate effectively with those who are under her authority.

> The first authority that women have in their home is authority over their servants. But kindness towards servants is, my dear, also the essential virtue. You cannot buy ownership of this virtue at the same time as you buy the body of your slaves, but the wise housewife will give birth to it within herself with the aid of time.[102]

Theano is again exhorting her listener to develop an internal ordering that will manifest itself in outward relations with others.

The letter gives explicit directions for avoiding the extreme use of force to back up one's authority:

> It is the consequence of wise actions in the manner of using servants that will ensure that they be neither worn out by weariness nor exhausted by deprivations. By nature, indeed, your servants are human beings. Some housewives have hoped to extract a most trivial gain from their slaves by subjecting them to bad treatment. They overcharged them with work and restricted them in the necessities (of life). . . . Cruelty does not bring about good will in the soul, and reasoning dispenses just as well (the) hatred of evil.[103]

The appeal to the use of discursive reason by the woman who is in authority in the household, as well as by the slave, is a significant attitude in view of Aristotle's dictum that women have no authority over their discursive reason and that slaves do not even have this faculty.

Theano II continues by arguing that if slaves do not respond to the use of reason they must be sold:

> If, though, the perversity of your slaves is invincible, you must get rid of them and sell them. What is foreign indeed to the utility of the household must be foreign to the mistress of the house. Reflection must be your judge in that situation; through it you will confront the reality of the fault with the justice of the punishment, the extent of the infractions with the estimation of the punishment. The mercy and the clemency of the mistress of the house must also remain underneath the punishments of faults. Doing so will maintain the prestige and the decency which fit your own mission.[104]

Next, an example is given of a woman who is unable to control her passions and who, consequently, is a very poor authority in the household:

> One can find, indeed, my dear, some mistresses of the house who, by dint of cruelty, turned into ferocious beasts because of jealousy or anger, and let themselves go by covering the body of their servants with whipping, as if they wanted to memorize the excesses to which their ferocity pushed them. Among their servants, some, exhausted from hardships, died in a short time; others found their salvation by escaping; and others still stopped living by killing themselves by their own hands. And afterwards, the housewife was forced to remain alone, to lament her thoughtlessness and to live in useless repentence.[105]

Theano concludes her study of the effective management of a household by appealing to a musical metaphor:

> As for you, dear, act in a way that imitates those musical instruments which, when they are too loose, get out of tune, and then break when they are too tight. it is the same thing for your servants—too much looseness gets obedience out of tune, and a tension greater than necessary disjoins and breaks what is natural. And it is in this connection that one must remember that moderation is best in everything.[106]

This letter is very interesting for the concept of woman in relation to man because it gives detailed suggestions about the virtues required for a woman in order to rule her household. It is clear that a man who rules would need the same sort of virtuous qualities, namely the capacity to be moderate and to judge each situation according to its own demands. It would be tempting here to conclude that Theano II is defending a sex-unity theory of wisdom and virtue. However, this theory is probably countered by the further supposition that the husband rules over his wife, and that the public sphere of activity for the man, or the city-state, is superior to the private sphere of activity for the woman. However, since Theano II did not consider this issue further, it is not possible to reach any further conclusions about her theory of sex identity.

As we complete this analysis of the writings of the female neo-Pythagorean philosophers, certain interesting conclusions emerge. First of all, the theories themselves contain all sorts of conflicting views about the concept of woman in relation to man. They incorporate aspects of sex unity, sex neutrality, sex polarity, reverse sex polarity, and sex complementarity. There does not appear to be any systematic attempt to develop a consistent theory of sex identity in the neo-Pythagorean school. Second, it is also clear that the question of woman's relation to wisdom and virtue was given a great deal of attention, and that women were expected to develop both their rational powers of judgement and their capacities for perfection in action. Women as well as men were exhorted to use their capacities to the fullest of their human potential. For this reason, the neo-Pythagorean philosophers stand much more clearly in the Platonic tradition than in the Aristotelian one in their theory of sex identity.

There is, of course, a common metaphysical foundation for sex unity in Plato and in the neo-Pythagoreans, namely a belief in the identity of the soul as a sexless entity capable of being born in either a male or a female body. There is no record of the Pythagoreans making any explicit reference to this theory in their conclusions for sex identity. However, the neo-Pythagoreans and Plato both influenced the development of neo-Platonism, in which such an explicit articulation is made by Porphyry in his letter to Marcella. In this way, the neo-Pythagorean female philosophers serve as an important transition point, more for the witness of their lives and the simple writings they left than for any systematic breakthrough in the analysis of the concept of woman in relation to man.

EARLY AND MIDDLE STOICISM

The Greek founder of the school of philosophy known as Stoicism was Zeno of Cittium (c. 333–261 BC). Arriving in Athens some ten years after Aristotle's death, Zeno studied under the Platonist Crates and under Xenophon. He founded his own school circa 301 BC, on a porch called "Stoa," from which the name of the school was derived.[107]

The early and middle Stoa were significant for the concept of woman in two contradictory ways: 1) from Plato's *Republic*, they appeared to derive a theory of sex unity in relation to the practice of wisdom and virtue; while 2) they adopted a theory of sex polarity in human generation from Aristotle, and of sex polarity in cosmic generation from Plato's *Timaeus*. This internal tension between sex polarity and sex unity was a constant aspect of Stoic philosophy up to the emphasis on sex unity in later Roman Stoics, such as Seneca and Musonious Rufus, and the emphasis on sex polarity in the later Stoic Galen.

Diogenes Laertius states that Zeno wrote a book modelled on Plato, also entitled the *Republic*:

> It is also their doctrine that amongst the wise there should be a community of wives with free choice of partners, as Zeno says in his *Republic* and Chrysippus in his treatise *On Government* (and not only they, but also Diogenes the Cynic and Plato). Under such circumstances we shall feel paternal affection for all the children alike, and there will be an end of the jealousies arising from adultery.[108]

There is some question among scholars whether Zeno accepted Plato's directives for the regulation of sexual relations in this utopian city. For example, Margaret Reesor suggests "that while the principle of the community of women in Plato was highly regulated towards the goal of reproducing perfect citizens, that Zeno's community of women was based on the anarchic principle of desiring the least amount of regulation of sexual relations as possible."[109] However, Diogenes Laertius states that Zeno supports marriage: "Also (they maintain) the wise man will marry, as Zeno says in his *Republic*, and beget children."[110]

From the perspective of the concept of woman, Zeno appears to suggest a unisex model of dress, with a community of men and women:

> It is objected, in the *Republic* he lays down community of wives . . . further, he bids men and women to wear the same dress and keep no part of the body entirely covered. That the *Republic* is the work of Zeno is attested by Chrysippus in his *De Republica*.[111]

For Zeno, the basis for a sex-unity position followed from the common presence of reason in wise men and women. Reason, as will be seen in a consideration of his cosmic theory of generation, is a masculine factor in human identity. Therefore, it is likely that the common dress referred to above would be predominantly a masculine dress, so Zeno's sex-unity theory would involve a loss of female identity and a subsuming of this identity under that of the male, just as it did for Plato's female disciples who "wore men's clothes."

Gilles Ménage lists the names of three female Stoics: Porcia, Arria, and Theophilia.[112] However, there does not seem to have been any strong female presence in Zeno's school. In addition, there is an implication in Athenaeus that the early Stoics were primarily interested in homosexual teacher-student relations:

> Oglers of boys you are, and in that alone emulating the founder of your philosophy, Zeno the Phoenician, who never resorted to a woman, but always to boy-favourites, as Antigonis of Carystus records in his *Biography* of him.[113]

The following passage in Diogenes Laertius suggests that Zeno did not have women in his school:

> He rarely employed men-servants; once or twice indeed he might have a young girl to wait on him in order not to seem a misogynist.
>
> He shared the same house with Persaeus, and when the latter brought in a little flute-player he lost no time in leading her straight to Persaeus.[114]

Perhaps most significant is the evidence that Zeno, like Plato before him, preferred chastity in sexual relationships as a way of subordinating the lower desires to the higher order of reason:

> To a lover of boys he remarked: "Just as schoolmasters lose their common sense by spending all their time with boys, so it is with people like you."[115]

Diogenes relates of the Stoics:

> Their definition of love is an effort towards friendliness due to visible beauty appearing, its sole end being friendship, not bodily enjoyment.[116]

In a similar vein, Zeno argued that philosophy ought to be founded on logic. Diogenes Laertius reports:

> Such, then, is the logic of the Stoics, by which they seek to establish their point that the wise man is the true dialectician. For all things, they say, are discerned by means of logical study, including whatever falls within the province of Physics and again whatever belongs to that of Ethics.[117]

The Aristotelian use of definition and syllogism was taken as a basic method for Stoic philosophy. In all situations, the higher functions of reason were to be used to rule over the passions and desires of the soul. Anger, grief and pleasure were all classified as irrational responses of the soul.[118] For Zeno and subsequent Stoics, the defence of sex unity would follow from the higher value given to reason in human life and to the concommitant claim that women and men both have a soul capable of reason.

In contrast to this tendency towards a sex-unity position, in the category of wisdom, Zeno also adopted Aristotle's theory of generation, which provided a rationale for sex polarity on the material level of human existence. Diogenes Laertius states:

> Semen is by them defined as that which is capable of generating offspring like the parent. And the human semen which is emitted by a human parent in a moist vehicle is mingled with parts of the soul, blended in the same ratio in which they are present in the parent. . . . That of the female according to them sterile, being, as Sphaerus says, without tension, scanty, and watery.[119]

In another fragment we find the same view directly attributed to the founder of Stoicism:

> Zeno indeed says that (the females) bring forth wet (or moist) matter as if from sweat from the exercise of copulation, not from seed.[120]

For Zeno, as for Aristotle, only the father contributed seed to generation, the mother was limited to providing the material that the seed of the father would shape or form. Consequently, Zeno humourously described a "defective" student as having been conceived when his father was drunk.[121]

In an interesting development, Zeno did not apply the consequences of the sex-polarity theory of generation to the sex identity of individual men and women, as Aristotle had done. Instead, he used the theory to develop an elaborate description of cosmic generation. God, the Father of the world, generated the cosmos like male seed forming the passive female material into its likeness.

> They hold that there are two principles in the universe, the active principle and the passive. The passive principle, then is a substance without quality, i.e., matter, whereas the active is the reason inherent in this substance, that is God.[122]

Zeno's cosmology was a radical departure from that of Hesiod, in which Mother Earth first generated all things. Instead, the Stoics provided a cosmology that fused Plato's metaphysical concept of the Forms as like a Father and of the receptacle as like a Mother, with Aristotle's theory that the Father shaped and formed the material of the mother in human generation:

> God is one and the same with Reason, Fate, and Zeus; he is also called by many other names. In the beginning he was by himself; he transformed the whole of the substance through air into water, and just as in animal generation the seed has a moist vehicle, so in cosmic moisture God, who is the seminal reason of the universe, remains behind in the moisture as such an agent, adapting matter to himself with a view to the next stage of creation. Thereupon he created first of all the four elements, fire, water, air, earth. They are discussed by Zeno in his treatise *On the Whole*, and by Chrysippus in the first book of his *Physics*.[123]

Here God, as father, transforms his own "seminal fluid" into the four elements.

In another example, Zeno gives a further description of the relation of cosmic father and cosmic mother:

> The deity, they say, is a living being, immortal, rational, perfect, or intelligent in happiness, admitting nothing (into him), taking providential care of the world and all that therein is, but he is not of human shape. He is, however, the artificer of the universe, and, as it were, the father of all, both in general and in that particular part of him which is all-pervading, and which is called many names according to its various powers. . . . Zeus in so far as he is the cause of life or pervades all life, so the name Athena is given, because the ruling part of the divinity extends to the mother; the name Hera marks its extension to the air.[124]

This example of allegorization of the nature of the Divine reveals an interesting aspect of Zeno's cosmic theory of generation. God, as father or cause of life, is represented by the name of Zeus, while god as air, or that in which the generation takes place, is represented by the name Hera. This cosmic mother is more like Plato's receptacle than Aristotle's material. Zeno, in fact, continues his litany of allegorized deities by claiming that earth is represented by Demeter. In the writing of later Stoics, however, Hera is used to represent the material of cosmic generation rather than the receptacle.

After Zeno's death in 261 BC, the leadership of the Stoa was passed on to Cleanthes (331–232 BC). Most scholars support the claim that Cleanthes carried on the doctrines of Zeno, who had been his teacher for nineteen years.[125] Very few fragments remain from this philosopher, so it is difficult to assess whether he changed any of Zeno's arguments about sex identity. However, Diogenes Laertius lists the names of several of Cleanthes' works. From this we can conclude that he did concentrate on the concept of woman in two specific texts: "On Marriage" and "On the Thesis That Virtue is the Same in Man and in Woman."[126]

From 232 to 208 BC, the leadership of the Stoic school was held by Chrysippus (c. 282–206 BC). As with previous Stoic philosophers, Chrysippus wrote a version of the *Republic*. Diogenes Laertius reports: "In his *Republic*, he permits marriage with mothers and daughters and sons."[127] The legalization of incest would, of course, be one logical consequence of the Platonic dictum that parents ought not to know the identity of their own children. More interesting, however, is Chrysippus's theory that women and men have the same wisdom:

> If the nature of man is capable of wisdom, it was necessary for workers, rustics, women, and finally all who bear human form to be taught, so that they may be wise; (it is necessary) for wise people to be united from every language, condition, sex, and age—The Stoics believe this very much, who said that both slaves and women must be philosophers.[128]

In addition to claiming that both women and men ought to pursue wisdom, in *De Virtute*, Chrysippus argued that women and men have the same nature and therefore the same virtue:

> It is agreed among us that the human race has the same nature and the same virtue. A woman does not have another nature than that of humanity; on the one hand, the male appears different, but it has the same nature, therefore also it has the same virtue.[129]

Chrysippus, then, follows the Stoic tradition of a sex-unity theory for the categories of wisdom and virtue.

In addition, he also appears to have followed the opposite tradition of sex polarity in the category of a cosmic theory of generation. He believed that the universe was an animate being. The organizing principle of the universe, its soul, was called Zeus, while the matter of the universe was called Hera. To live virtuously was to live in relation to the cosmic masculine principle of the universe.

> Living virtuously is equivalent to living in accordance with experience of the actual course of nature, as Chrysippus says in the first book of his *De finibus*; for our individual natures are part of the nature of the whole universe. And this is why the end may be defined as life in accordance with nature, or, in other words, in accordance with our own human nature as well as that of the universe, a life in which we refrain from every action forbidden by the law common to all things, that is to say, the right reason which pervades all things, and is identical with this Zeus, Lord and ruler of all that is.[130]

Women as well as men become wise and virtuous by living in accordance with the masculine principle of reason.

Chrysippus described the generation of the cosmos in graphic terms akin to sexual intercourse. Diogenes Laertius suggests that this shocked some of the public:

> There are people who run Chrysippus down as having much in a tone that is gross and indecent. For in his work on the ancient Natural Philosophers at line 690 or thereabouts he interprets the story of Hera and Zeus coarsely, with details which no one would soil his lips by repeating. Indeed his interpretation of the story is condemned as most indecent. He may be commending physical doctrine; but the language used is more appropriate to street-walkers than to deities.[131]

In a recent work tracing the history of Stoic cosmology, David Hahm describes the difference between Chrysippus and Zeno's concepts of the role of the cosmic mother:

> Chrysippus claims that Zeus represents god, and Hera, matter. . . . This is obviously a variation of the theory of the cosmogony, where Zeus is the *spermatikos logos* left behind in the wet matter. . . . Hera received an inconsistent interpretation by the Stoics. In the cosmogonal testimonies Hera's position is determined more by the assumed etymology (of Plato's association of Hera with air or receptacle) than by biological theory, but Chrysippus' interpretation of the Zeus-Hera myths in non-cosmogonal context manifests the Aristotelian theory that the female supplies the matter.[132]

The Stoics' tendency to take some of their concepts from Plato and others from Aristotle continued through such middle Stoa as Panaetius (185–109 BC), who led the school in 129 BC, and Posidonius (c. 135–50 BC), who led the Stoic school in Rhodes when Cicero visited there in 79 to 77 BC. According to Phillip Merlan, Posidonius and Panaetius "opened themselves to Platonic influence, particularly to the *Timaeus* and *Phaedrus*."[113] For the history of the concept of woman, this would mean that the theory of natural inferiority of woman, rather than Plato's defence of sex unity, would have been more influential on these middle Stoa.

As will be seen in the next section, Roman Stoicism picks up the same tension between the sex-unity theories of wisdom and virtue derived from Plato's *Republic* and the sex-polarity theory of generation derived from Aristotle. So the first phase of the battle for dominance of the western mind by Aristotelian or Platonic thought about the concept of woman has not led to any clear resolution. By the end of the four centuries of Greek schools of philosophy after Aristotle, no one theory of sex identity dominated. In addition, for the most part there was no further development of a theory of sex identity than had already occurred in Plato or Aristotle. The only exceptions to this general rule were the analysis of sexuality in Lucretius and the application of virtue and wisdom to particular situations of women in the neo-Pythagoreans. For the rest, the Greek schools of philosophy simply repeated some of the conclusions of the preceding thinkers, without appearing to question the reasoning of their predecessors on the issue of sex identity.

ROMAN STOICISM DISCOVERS ARISTOTLE AND PLATO

The Roman Stoics did not make any significantly new contributions to the concept of woman in relation to man with the exception of considering the need to differentiate the sexes on the level of physical appearance. For the most part they repeated the previous arguments of Plato or Aristotle.

The early Roman Stoic Cicero sought for the most part to blur the distinction between Plato and Aristotle. This proved to be somewhat awkward in relation to the concept of woman because the two Greek philosophers had entirely opposite theories about sex identity. Consequently, Cicero chose to ignore the topic, and in this way he appeared to advocate a sex neutrality position.

Seneca, on the other hand, offered several arguments in favour of the study of wisdom and virtue by women. The later Stoic Musonius Rufus continued this line of reasoning by writing a series of works to prove that the wisdom and virtue and education of women ought to be the same as men. These two philosophers, therefore, can be considered as supporting the sex-unity position as first expressed in Plato's *Republic.* At the same time, however, there is a residue of sex polarity in these Stoics' writings that comes from the tendency to associate "womanish" with an uncontrolled and unrefined nature, while "mannish" was associated with the Stoic ideal of self-control.

The later philosophers within the Stoic tradition, Pliny the Elder, Epictetus, Juvenal, Marcus Aurelius and Galen, all followed the sex-polarity theory. They tended to devalue woman in relation to man in the areas of wisdom, virtue, and generation. Once again, woman was made to represent the opposite of the Stoic ideal of virtue and wisdom, and she was caught in the vice of lack of self-control.

Aristotle's arguments were directly infused into Roman Stoicism through the writings of Galen, who accepted the claim that women were inferior to men because females were colder than males. The slow but steady progress of the Aristotelian Revolution entered into western European thought through the doorway of the Roman Stoic Galen. Therefore, even though Roman Stoicism appeared to be more open to Plato's arguments for sex unity at the beginning of its development, by the end it had become more identified with an Aristotelian defence of sex polarity.

The following listing indicates the different areas in which the later Stoics considered the question of sex identity. The initials represent the theories proposed as sex neutrality (SN), sex unity (SU), sex complementarity (SC), or sex polarity (SP). Where initials are lacking, the theory is difficult to classify. Each of the later Stoics will then be considered in turn.

Opposites	Generation	Wisdom	Virtue
			Cicero (SN)
		Seneca (SU)	Seneca (SU)
Musonius Rufus	Musonius Rufus (SC)	Musonius Rufus (SU)	Musonius Rufus (SU)
Epictetus		Epictetus (SP)	Epictetus (SP)
		Juvenal (SP)	Juvenal (SP)
	Marcus Aurelius	Marcus Aurelius (SP)	Marcus Aurelius (SP)
Galen (SP)	Galen (SP)	Galen (SP)	Galen (SP)

CICERO (106–43 BC)

The Aristotelian distinctions between matter and form, knowledge and opinion, and the importance of friendship were brought into Latin consciousness by the Roman philosopher Cicero. Cicero expressed his admiration for Aristotle several times. He described the Greek as "pouring forth a golden stream of eloquence," as "almost the outstanding figure in philosophy," and as being so thorough in his analyses that "no region in the sky or sea or land . . . has been passed over." [134] Cicero, however, also admired Plato and he attempted to blur the distinctions between the two schools of thought: "For there was no difference between the Peripatetics and the Old Academy of those days." [135] Since Plato and Aristotle had entirely different concepts of woman, Cicero's decision to ignore these differences meant that he did not consider the concept of woman of much significance. He seemed simultaneously to lean towards sex polarity, sex unity and sex neutrality.

Cicero shared Aristotle's view that the family ought to be the foundation of the state:

> The first bond of union is that of husband and wife; the next, that between parents and children; then we find one home, with everything in common. And this is the foundation of civil government, the nursery, as it were, of the state. [136]

He also rejected Plato's suggestion of a public governance of woman, and suggested the sex-polarity model of the family structure:

> Nor indeed should there be a governor placed over women, as is usually done among the Greeks, but there should be a censor to teach men to rule their wives. [137]

Cicero, however, spoke out for the rights of women in other ways. He described the passage of a Vocenian law that interfered with women's rights to own property and to receive inheritances:

> In fact that law, passed for men's advantage, is full of injustice to women. For why should a woman not have money of her own?[138]

More interesting, perhaps, is Cicero's discussion of friendship in *De Amicitia*. This work, which is modelled on Aristotle's theory of friendship, suggests that in any relation of inequality the superior partner should place himself on a level with the inferior one in order to bring about the requisite balance in the relationship. However, Cicero did not suggest that the female party was naturally inferior to the male. In one passage he considers a theory from another philosopher who describes women in a negative way:

> There are others, I am told, who, with even less of human feeling, maintain . . . that friendships must be sought for the sake of the defence and aid they give and not out of goodwill and affection; therefore, that those least endowed with firmness of character and strength of body have the greatest longing for friendship; and consequently, that helpless women, more than men, seek its shelter.[139]

Cicero rejects this argument, for he concludes that it would deprive men of the great value of friendship. It is not possible to conclude anything about his concept of woman from this example. However, it is significant that given Aristotle's specific differentiation of women and men into unequal relations of friendship, Cicero suggested instead a theory of friendship within sex unity rather than sex polarity.

Another area in which Cicero's concept of woman clearly differed from Aristotle's is found in his female personifications of philosophy, wisdom, nature, and virtue. Each of these concepts was represented by a Latin word of the feminine gender (*philosophia, sapientia, natura,* and *virtus*). Although Cicero may only have been playing with this aspect of language, he did develop the feminine dimension of these concepts in a description of philosophy as a woman:

> Philosophy herself must advance by argument—how will she find her way out?[140]

> For in virtue is complete harmony, in her is permanence, in her is fidelity; and when she has raised her head and shown her own light and has seen and recognized the same light in another, she moves towards it and in turn receives its beams; as a result love or friendship leaps into flame.[141]

Cicero's use of female personification for these concepts did not mean that he believed women were more philosophical or virtuous. Although he did refer to old wise women as *sagae*, he did not present any arguments in favour of female philosophers.[142] In fact, he stated that the same reason and nature that he had personified as female ought to "do nothing in an improper or unmanly fashion and in every thought and deed to do or think nothing unmanly."[143]

It is difficult to evaluate the use of female personification by Cicero for such terms as *wisdom, philosophy* or *virtue*. It can be claimed that this device is really a form of isolation and objectification of women, a device that ultimately contributes to woman's devaluation. This argument suggests that the higher woman is idealized, the lower her real position in society. However, there is a sense in which the use of female personification for central concepts in philosophy can be seen as having a positive connection with woman's identity. When Aristotle simply barred both women and the concept of woman from any association with the highest philosophical pursuits, a reappearance of the device of feminine personification of wisdom or virtue could be seen as a step forward. There is a kind of side effect of associating the concept of woman with these other concepts that implies that it is not contradictory to the nature of woman to be identified with the highest goals of philosophy. Therefore, the question of the eventual effect of such association on woman's identity should remain open.

There is another passage in Cicero, however, that raises some questions about the devaluation of woman. In *De Officiis*, Cicero considers two kinds of beauty:

> There are two orders of beauty: in the one, loveliness predominates; in the other, dignity; of these, we ought to regard loveliness as the attribute of woman, and dignity as the attribute of man.[144]

If Cicero is implying that a woman's beauty is found in her outward appearance, while a man's is found in the inner dignity of his soul, then he is separating the two sexes. This particular approach is not unknown in philosophy, for Immanuel Kant makes a similar distinction in his *Observations on the Feelings of the Beautiful and Sublime.*[145] This view would also make Cicero very different from the neo-Pythagoreans, who placed so much importance on trying to educate women away from a concern with outer beauty towards an inner beauty.

In conclusion, Cicero appears not to have given the concept of woman much careful thought. His views are scattered and fall into different categories of sex identity. His separation of ruling and obedience, and of appearance and dignity for women and men indicates a tendency towards sex polarity. At the same time, his support for women and men to own property is an indication of a sex-unity tendency. By neglecting to differentiate women and men in his theory of friendship, he tends towards sex neutrality. After Plato and Aristotle, Cicero's philosophy indicates a decrease in intensity concerning the concept of woman.

SENECA (AD 4–65)

This Stoic philosopher accepted and transmitted the Aristotelian division of philosophy into theoretical and practical wisdom.[146] In addition, Seneca mentioned the Peripatetic distinction between moral, natural, rational and civil philosophy; the last area included economics or the science of household management.[147] He also used the Aristotelian concepts of cause, genus, and species.[148]

Although Seneca employed various concepts from Aristotle, he emerged with a concept of woman clearly within the sex-unity tradition. Seneca believed that women had the same capacities for virtue and wisdom as had men. There are some isolated passages in Seneca's writings that, when taken out of context, could appear to defend sex polarity. For example, in the following passage from *On Anger*, Seneca seems to imply that a woman ought to be judged by a different ethical standard than a man:

> Many have pardoned their enemies; shall I not pardon the lazy, the careless, and the babbler? Let a child be excused by his age, a woman by her sex, a stranger by his independence, a servant by the bond of intercourse.[149]

However, as will be seen in the essays to Helvia and Marcia, *On Consolation*, Seneca argues forcefully that a woman ought never to try to excuse herself from the search for wisdom and virtue because of her sex.

In a second example, from *On Firmness*, we find the appearance of sex polarity overturned by a subsequent qualification:

> Some men are mad enough to suppose that even a woman can offer them an insult. What matters it how they regard her, how many lackeys she has for her litter, how heavily weighted her ears, how roomy her sedan? She is just the same unthinking creature—wild, and unrestrained in her passions—unless she has gained knowledge and had much instruction.[150]

The qualification so important in this passage is the phrase "unless she has gained knowledge and had much instruction." For Seneca, a Stoic, the key to all wisdom and virtue is the careful education and discipline of the passions. Therefore, in this context, anyone without knowledge would be wild and unrestrained.

The two works in which Seneca states that women ought to be wise and virtuous in the same way as men were both written to women. The occasion for the texts was the presence of excessive grief—of Marcia for the death of a son, and of Helvia for the separation from her son. In *On Consolation to Marcia*, Seneca offers clear arguments for the sex-unity position in the context in which women are generally considered inferior to men. Seneca begins his letter as follows:

> If I did not know, Marcia, that you were as far removed from womanish weakness of mind as from all other vices, and that your character was looked upon as a model of ancient virtue, I should not dare assail your grief—the grief that even men are prone to nurse and brood upon.[151]

To be certain that Marcia recognizes that she is being challenged to live by Stoic values, just as a man would be challenged, Seneca states:

> This evidence of the greatness of your mind forbade me to pay heed to your sex, forbade me to pay heed to your face, which, since sorrow once clouded it, unbroken sadness holds for all these years. . . . Let others deal with you gently and ply soft words. I myself have determined to battle with your grief.[152]

Seneca then offers Marcia all the rational means at his disposal to persuade her to come to an inner decision to overcome her grief. He begins by giving her examples of famous women who also had to face difficult situations of grief:

> I shall place before your eyes but two examples—the greatest of your sex and century—one, of a woman who allowed herself to be swept away by grief, the other, of a woman who, though she suffered a like misfortune and even greater

> loss, yet did not permit her ills to have the mastery long, but quickly restored her mind to its accustomed order.[153]

Seneca gives these examples with sufficient detail to enable Marcia to come to a decision to imitate the woman who chose to overcome her grief.

Next, Seneca criticizes Marcia for allowing herself to indulge in extreme reactions:

> You have tended wholly to the other extreme, and, forgetting the better aspects of your fortune, you gaze only upon its worst side . . . Do not, I pray you, covet the most perverse distinction—that of being considered the most unhappy of women. Reflect, too, that it is no great thing to show one's self brave in the midst of prosperity . . . some hardship must be encountered that will test the soul.[154]

He expects Marcia to use her reflection or discursive reasoning and to respond to the difficult challenges that life offers to her. Seneca next considers the argument that excessive grief is natural:

> "But," you say, "Nature bids us grieve for our dead ones." Who denies it, so long as grief is tempered? . . . Moreoever, in order that you may know that it is not by the will of Nature that we are crushed by sorrow, observe, in the first place, that, though they suffer the same bereavement, women are wounded more deeply than men, savage peoples more deeply than the peaceful and civilized, the uneducated, than the educated. But the passions that derive their power from Nature maintain the same hold upon all; therefore it is clear that a passion of variable power is not ordered by Nature. Fire will burn alike people of all ages and of all nationalities, men as well as women; . . . And why? Because each derives its power from Nature, which makes no distinction of persons.[155]

In this important passage, Seneca admits that women grieve more deeply than men, but he clearly denies that this intensity of passion is a consequence of the nature of woman or of man. The obvious conclusion is that women have not been educated as men to moderate their passions, particularly the passion of grief. For Seneca, this is a social problem than can be changed by a decision on the part of a woman to educate herself.

The argument does not end yet, for Seneca offers even further inducements to Marcia to overcome her grief. He states that it is an obvious fact of life that there will be disappointments and loss:

> What need is there to weep over parts of life? The whole of it calls for tears. New ills will press on before you have done with the old. Therefore you women especially must observe moderation, you who are immoderate in your grief, and against your many sorrows the power of the human breast must be arrayed.[156]

Women have the capacity and power to overcome the intensity of their passions, just as men do, if they decide to exercise this power within themselves. Seneca proceeds to give examples of men who overcame grief in extremely difficult circumstances. Then he continues:

> I know what you are saying: "You forget that you are giving comfort to a woman; the examples you cite are of men." But who has asserted that Nature had dealt grudgingly with women's natures and has narrowly restricted their virtues? Believe me they have just as much force, just as much capacity, if they like, for virtuous action; they are just as able to endure suffering and toil when they are accustomed to them.[157]

Seneca is clearly refuting any attempt to devalue woman in relation to man in her capacity for wisdom or virtue. Instead, he is arguing forcefully for a sex-unity position. In the remainder of Seneca's *On Consolation to Marcia*, many other arguments are given to convince her to live by Stoic doctrine in the concrete situation she finds herself in. It stands as a powerful essay in the sex-unity position.

Seneca incorporates a Platonic theory of the priority of an immortal soul in human life. This theory is the implicit basis for his belief in the quality and differentiation of woman and man in the history of philosophy.

In a second essay, *To Helvia on Consolation*, Seneca states that happiness is an individual human choice: "Nature intended that we should need no great equipment for living happily; each one of us is able to make his own happiness. External things are of slight importance."[158] He then tries to convince his mother that the mind is the key to human existence:

> It is the mind that makes us rich; this goes with us into exile, and in the wildest wilderness, having found there all that the body needs for its sustenance, it itself overflows in the enjoyment of its own goods. Meanwhile, hampered by mortal limbs and encompassed by the heavy burden of flesh, it surveys, as best it can, the things of heaven in swift and winged thought. . . . Its thought ranges over all heaven and projects itself into all past and future time. This poor body, the prison and fetter of the soul, is tossed hither and thither. . . . But the soul itself is sacred and eternal, and upon it no hand can be laid.[159]

Therefore, as with Plato's sex-unity theory, we find in Seneca a similar tendency to consider the body as a prison for the soul. The seat of common identity of woman and man is found in the presence of an eternal mind or soul that transcends the devalued body.

After this general introduction, Seneca next focuses more directly on the specific situation of his mother's grief for his exile.

> It is not for you to avail yourself of the excuse of being a woman, who, in a way, has been granted the right to inordinate, yet not unlimited tears. . . . The best course is the mean between affection and reason—both to have a sense of loss and to crush it. . . . The excuse of being a woman can be of no avail to one who has always lacked all the weaknesses of a woman. . . . You can not, therefore, allege your womanhood as an excuse for persistent grief, for your very virtues set you apart; you must be as far removed from woman's tears as from her vices.[160]

Once again, Seneca asks his listener to decide to rise above the general practice of women in the society and to live by Stoic doctrine. Just in case Helvia did not understand what he was saying, Seneca explicitly states that she should follow the same paths to wisdom as a man:

> And so I guide you to take that in which all who fly from Fortune must take refuge—to philosophic studies. They will heal your wound, they will uproot all your sadness. Even if you had not been acquainted with them before, you would need to use them now; but, so far as the old-fashioned strictness of my father permitted you, though you have not indeed fully grasped all the liberal arts, still you have had some dealings with them. Would that my father, truly the best of men, had surrendered less to the practice of his forefathers, and had been willing to have you acquire a thorough knowledge of the teachings of philosophy instead of a mere smattering! . . . But he did not suffer you to pursue your studies because of those women who do not employ learning as a means to wisdom, but equip themselves with it for the purpose of display. Yet thanks to your acquiring mind, you imbibed more than might have been expected in the time you had; the foundations of all systematic knowledge have been laid. Do you return now to these studies; they will render you safe. . . . If in earnest they gain entrance to your mind, nevermore will sorrow enter there, nevermore anxiety, nevermore the useless distress of futile suffering. . . . Philosophy is your most unfailing safeguard, and she alone can rescue you from the power of Fortune.[161]

In this remarkable passage, Seneca exhorts his mother to exercise her reason and will and to begin to live as a Stoic in the midst of her grief. It is a powerful example of a belief in the fundamental equality and non-differentiation of women and men, a belief that stands upon an implicit acceptance of a common human nature, of human reason.

In his other writings, Seneca occasionally considers other aspects of an equal standard of virtue for women and men. In the following passage from the essay *On Anger*, Seneca chastizes a man for holding a double standard:

> You are indignant because your slave, your freedman, your wife, or your client answered you back; and then you complain that the state has deprived you of that liberty of which you have deprived your own household.[162]

Next, in a letter, Seneca argues against a double standard of sexual morality:

> You know that a man does wrong in requiring chastity of his wife while he himself is intriguing with the wives of other men.[163]

Finally, in an even more surprising consideration of the separate spheres of activity that were common to men and women, in *On Benefits*, Seneca argues that women's work and men's work have equal value:

> Every obligation that involves two people makes an equal demand upon both. . . . It is true that the husband has certain duties, yet, those of the wife are not less great.[164]

Seneca appears to have tried, in several areas of his thought, to defend a theory of sex unity.

In conclusion, then, Seneca did not develop any new metaphysical arguments to defend sex unity; that is, he did not go beyond the arguments that Plato had advanced in the *Republic*. However, Seneca did offer a new application of a theory of sex unity to the specific practice of wisdom and virtue. As was demonstrated, Seneca chose the example of the passion of grief as a context for developing a Stoic analysis of virtue for Marcia and Helvia. These two examples of the concrete application of philosophical principles in women's lives are similar to the letters of advice of the neo-Pythagoreans. In both cases women were being challenged to develop their skills of discursive reasoning, to apply the general philosophical principles to their own situation, and to make a decision of the will to move towards a life of wisdom and virtue. Seneca's two essays are among the earliest examples of philosophical works addressed by a male philosopher specifically to women. For that reason, in addition to their significant content, they hold a place of some importance in the history of the philosophy of man and woman.

PLINY THE ELDER (AD 23–79)

While Pliny is not particularly known as a Stoic philosopher, he was nonetheless within the Stoic tradition as a scientist and writer. His thirty-seven volume work, entitled *The Natural History*, was a source book for medieval science and medicine. This work is interesting for the present study because it gives evidence of the slowly developing influence of Aristotle on western thought. Pliny combined many Aristotelian concepts with popular beliefs and superstitions. In this way, he shared and perpetuated some of Aristotle's sex-polarity claims.

In the area of generation, Pliny shared the Aristotelian view that woman provides the material and man the seed:

> It is of this substance (the menstrual discharge) that the infant is formed. The seed of the male, acting as a sort of leaven, causes it to unite and assume a form, and in due time it acquires life, and assumes a bodily shape.[165]

In addition, Pliny devalues the female in relation to the male in his description of the process of pregnancy and labour:

> If it is a male that is conceived, the colour of the pregnant woman is more healthy, and the birth less painful: the child moves in the womb upon the fortieth day. In the conception of a child of the other sex, all the symptoms are totally different: the mother experiences an almost unsupportable weight, there is a slight swelling of the legs and the groin, and the first movement of the child is not felt until the ninetieth day.[166]

The association of a poor complexion with females is probably Hippocratic in origin. The extent to which Pliny gave pronouncements within the sex-polarity tradition is seen in his statement that it was a "favourable auspice" to have one's birth result in the death of the mother.[167]

Pliny also perpetuated the ideas of other early Greek thinkers. In one passage he repeated the Pythagorean association of male with right and female with left:

> Of the two, male children most frequently are known to move in the womb; they mostly lie on the right side of the body, females on the left.[168]

In this text the Aristotelian view of the male as active and female as passive was also implied in describing the male fetus as more active. Pliny did not repeat the Aristotelian theory of the determination of the sex of the fetus, but suggested instead that the mind of either parent could have a role in determining the physical appearance of the child:

> A thought, even momentarily passing through the mind of either of the parents, may be supposed to produce a resemblance to one of them separately, or else to the two combined.[169]

This respect for the powers of the mind would be consistent with a Stoic tendency to value the mind above the body. The view that the mind could affect the shape of the developing fetus is found later on in such thinkers as Porphyry and Malbranche.[170]

Pliny is significant to the concept of woman as a transition figure, as a thinker who began to transmit some of the Aristotelian rationale for sex polarity and, in this way, he made a small contribution to the development of the Aristotelian Revolution.

MUSONIUS RUFUS (c. AD 30-101)

The most important Roman Stoic for the study of the concept of woman in relation to man was Musonius Rufus, who devoted a significant part of his *Predications* to questions of sex identity. Musonius Rufus followed in the tradition previously established by the Stoic Chrysippus, who had written a text on marriage and one on the thesis that women and men have the same virtue. In addition, Musonius's work shows the clear influence of Plato's *Republic* in its defence of an equal education for women and men. Finally, Xenophon's *Oeconomicus* appears to have been influential in Musonius's description of separate spheres of activity for women and men and in his defence of the obedience of women to the rule of men.[171]

The Stoic did not achieve consistency in his philosophy of sex identity. He defended sex unity in the category of wisdom, sex polarity in the categories of virtue and sexual differentiation, and sex complementarity in the context of marriage. Rufus Musonious is significant for the concept of woman because of the thoroughness of his arguments for women studying philosophy. The three aspects of his thought will now be considered.

Marriage and Generation

In the context in which Plato had argued for the abolition of monogamous marriage, Zeno for a community of wives, and Aristotle for the devaluation of woman in a monogamous marriage, Musonius Rufus presented a series of arguments for the community of life of a woman and a man within a monogamous marriage. His description of the union of woman and man in marriage appeared to suggest an equality of worth along with a differentiation of the sexes. In this sense it can be seen as containing a tendency towards sex complementarity.

> The main purpose of marriage is community of life and the protection of children. It is proper that the husband and wife come together in such a way

> that they live and beget children together and that they hold all things in common, and that nothing be private, not even the body. The procreation of a human being, through this union, is undoubtedly a great thing. But it is not yet enough for the married couple, for, as with animals, it can occur outside of wedlock just as it is in other kinds of sexual relationships. In marriage, community of life and mutual love must be present in all circumstances of health or sickness. For, in addition to procreation, this is the very wish of man and woman when they get married. When this love is perfect, when both spouses show it perfectly to one another, each one trying to outdo the other, then the marriage is as it should be.[172]

Particularly significant in this passage is the tremendous respect that Musonius is proposing for women as well as for the marriage relationship itself. In a context where woman had often been viewed simply as property to be owned or used in marriage, the Stoic is offering an ideal of marriage in which the woman and man own everything in common, including each other's bodies. Even more important, marriage is being presented as an opportunity to practise the virtue of love for both woman and man. In short, it is the opportunity to live the common life. In this general description, woman and man are equally dignified and worthy, and the sexes are differentiated through their complementary relation to generation and to the broader expression of mutual love.

Musonius Rufus is adament that society needs the interaction of woman and man, as differentiated, in order to remain viable:

> If marriage is destroyed, then the family, the city, and the whole human race is destroyed. For the race could not survive without reproduction; and legitimate reproduction, which is just and in conformity with law, would not exist without marriage. It is obvious that a family or city must be constituted not solely by women, nor solely by men, but by an association of both sexes. Now no association more necessary and more pleasant than that of men and women can be found. . . . In which situation is praised the community of everything, bodies, souls, and goods, if not in the union of husband and wife? This is why conjugal love is considered by all as the highest form of love.[173]

In this description of the value of the complementary association of women and men, Musonius Rufus has completely overturned Aristotle's theory that the highest form of love or friendship is found among men. In addition, he has rejected Plato's arguments in favour of a communal marriage where the individuality of the person is subsumed by the needs of the state. Instead, this Stoic argues that it is between a particular woman and a particular man, bound together in marriage through law, that love can find its fullest expression.

Underneath Musonius's theory is an appeal to the laws of nature. In the following sequence of arguments defending marriage for philosophers, the Stoic suggests that philosophers, above all persons, ought to follow the fundamental laws of nature, and that the union of male and female is one such law.

> As someone said that marriage and life with a woman was likely an obstacle to the philosopher's state, Musonius answered: "This was not an impediment

> for Pythagoras, nor for Socrates, nor for Crates, who all lived with a woman; yet no one philosophized better than they did. Crates got married even though he was deprived of material possessions. As he was homeless, he lived for days and nights with his wife under the public porches in Athens. And we, who are endowed with homes and even servants, we dare to say that marriage is an obstacle to philosophy!
>
> Assuredly the philosopher is the master, I think, the guide of men in all that is proper to man according to nature. And if there is ever a thing according to nature, it is marriage. For why did the demiurge first divide our species into two? Why did he make two kinds of sexual parts for humanity, one for the female and the other for the male? Why did he implant in both sexes a strong desire for union and community of life with the opposite sex? Why did he mix in both hearts a powerful passion for one another, the male for the female and the female for the male? Is it not obvious that he wanted the two of them to unite, to live together, to build up a common life, to procreate and to feed children in order that our race be eternal?[174]

Musonius is suggesting that sex complementarity has its roots in the order and relation of male and female in nature. The woman and man need one another for the activity of generation. Even further, however, they need one another to build up a common life and to allow for the development of love and virtue in their "mutual support of one another."

As stated previously, however, Musonius is not consistent in his theory of sex identity. He also argues strongly for a theory of sex unity in the category of wisdom, and sex polarity in the category of virtue.

Wisdom and Education

Musonius Rufus directly addressed the question of whether women ought to study philosophy:

> As he was asked whether women also ought to study Philosophy, he began to teach in approximately these words: "Women," he said, "have received from the gods the same reason as men—a reason which serves us in our mutual relationships and through which we distinguish between the bad and the good, and the right and wrong. In addition, woman has the same senses as man: sight, hearing, smell, and the rest. Both sexes have the same bodily limbs, neither one more than the other. Moreover, the inclinations towards and close natural link with virtue belong not only to men but also to women. For they are, as naturally as men, disposed to enjoy right and just actions and to reject their contraries. If so, then why would it be suitable only for men to seek and to examine how they ought to live, that is, to lead a philosophical life? Why would it be improper for women?[175]

The argument here is derived from a description of women and men as having the same capacities for wisdom—the same reason, the same senses, and the same inclination towards virtue. For Musonius, there is no difference between the sexes in terms of the capacity to think. In contrast to Aristotle, the Stoic follows a more Platonic line of reasoning. Men and women are alike in soul, therefore they have an equal capacity for the study of philosophy.

As Plato had previously argued, if women and men have the same capacity for thought and wisdom, then they ought to receive the same education.

> One day he was asked if the same education was to be given to daughters and to sons. He said: "The stable owners and the hunters do not make any difference between female and male in training their horses and their dogs. The female dog learns how to chase after an animal as well as the male, and the mare does the same work as the stallion."[176]

The Stoic argues that, in general, women and men have the same virtues of practical wisdom or prudence, of courage, temperance, and justice. He concludes with a further appeal to an argument from nature:

> If man's and woman's virtues are naturally the same it necessarily presupposes that their training and education be the same. For all animals and plants must be properly looked after in order to produce the animal's and plant's proper virtue. If men and women must necessarily know how to play the flute or cithara, we would teach them equally to be a good instrumentalist. And if they both must become good, in the proper human virtues of prudence, courage, and justice, then why would we not educate them equally? We must act in no other way than this.[177]

Since women and men have the same nature from the perspective of their reason and senses, they are therefore both capable of practical wisdom and must consequently receive the same education.

Musonius goes out of his way to reject arguments that attempt to bar women from the study of philosophy out of a fear that it will make them arrogant:

> But, by Zeus, say certain individuals, that women who join the philosophers are necessarily arrogant and bold, when disregarding housekeeping, they usually live among men, where they engage in discussions and sophistic arguments and solve syllogisms, while they should be staying at home, spinning wool.
>
> As far as I am concerned, I will never claim that a philosopher, whether woman or man, should disregard their duty of state in order to take part in discussion. I declare that whatever arguments they consider, they should argue with action in mind.[178]

Musonius holds up the same standard for female philosophers as he does for male philosophers. Philosophical activity must not take place in abstraction, nor ought it to be used as an excuse for leaving one's responsibilities. Instead, it should be the way in which a person moves from wisdom to virtues of action.

> If I was now asked which science presides over this education I would answer that neither man nor woman can be correctly raised without philosophy. I do not intend to say that women, when they philosophize become shrewd in their

> discussions and have superfluous qualities. In any event, I do not praise these qualities in men either. However, I do say that women must acquire goodness of character and the perfect honesty of morals, for philsophy is nothing but the practice of these virtues.[179]

For Musonius, then, the arguments for sex unity in the category of wisdom are limited to arguments for practical wisdom, or prudence. He is not interested in theoretical wisdom, or the logic of syllogism and demonstrative science. Both women and men ought to study philosophy in order to become virtuous persons. When we turn now to the category of virtue, Musonius will commence with what appears to be a theory of sex unity, that is, of the same virtues for women and men. However, when the practical application of the virtues is considered, it will be seen that he promotes a rationale for sex polarity, that is, for the superiority of man over woman.

Virtue and the Physical Appearance of Sex Identity

Musonius Rufus's theory of virtue in relation to sex identity begins by describing the same broad categories of virtue for women and men, then it develops a careful separation of spheres of activity for the sexes. In this way, the Stoic proposes a sex-unity theory of the virtues in general, but a sex-polarity theory of the virtues in application. This same division was previously found in the writings of the neo-Pythagorean philosopher Phyntis, as well as in Aristotle.

> It is easy to demonstrate that there are no differences between men's and women's virtues. For example, men and women must equally be prudent, for of what use is an imprudent person. They must both live justly; for without justice a man could not be a good citizen, and without justice a woman could not soundly administer the household. . . . Moreover, it is good that a woman be temperate as well as a man, for it is certain that the law chastizes the seduced as heavily as the seducer. Gluttony, drunkenness, and other similar vices are all licentious actions which greatly dishonour those who are addicted to them. They demonstrate that temperance is a necessary virtue for all human beings, whether men or women.[180]

The Platonic virtues of wisdom (in the form of practical wisdom or prudence), justice and temperance are described as being equally necessary for men and women. The only hint of differentiation of the virtues in the above passage is in the distinction between the practice of justice for men in the public state as citizens, and the practice of justice for women in the private sphere of the household.

In an interesting continuation of this argument, Musonius Rufus considers the virtue of courage, which had for Plato been primarily associated with soldiers in the midst of battle.

> It could be said that courage is proper only to men, but I disagree. For woman also must act in a virile way, and if, at least, she is perfect, she must be purified from cowardice in order not to be overcome by fear of hardships. . . . By Zeus, women must be ready to defend themselves, if they do not want to appear worse than hens or other female birds, which nevertheless defend themselves against

> bigger animals. How would women not need to be courageous? Women can even take part in armed battle. This was proven by the Amazons, who overthrew many nations by the means of arms. So, if in other women, there is a weakness in this area, it implies a lack of exercise and not a lack of natural courage.[181]

For Musonius Rufus, woman's specific sphere of virtue is the household, while man's specific sphere of virtue is the public life. At first sight, it could appear that he is suggesting a complementarity rather than a polarity of functions.

> In a detailed examination (we will find that) all the virtues required in a good woman are found in a woman who studies philosophy. For example, a woman must know household administration, the good provision of family needs, the command of servants. Now I declare that these qualities will belong above all to a woman shaped by philosophy, if it is true that everyone of these qualities is a part of life, that the source of life is nothing else but philosophy, and that the philosopher, as Socrates said, devotes his whole life to the examination of what is bad and what is good in a household.[182]

In this passage, which appears to be derived in part from Xenophon's *Oeconomicus*, the woman is described as being completely responsibile for the management of the household. She does not appear to be devalued in relation to man. As the passage continues, other aspects of woman's function in the household are delineated:

> Woman must be temperate, she must preserve her purity from illicit loves and from the relative incontinence of other pleasures. She must not be a slave of her desires, neither be the friend of the quarrel, nor fond of spending, nor be coquettish: there, then are the temperate woman's virtues.[183]

Purity is also associated with the virtue of courage for both women and men when they have to defend themselves against an outside attack on their modesty.

> Modesty must be imprinted on the soul, considering all the shameful things (that happen). When this virtue is acquired, man and woman are necessarily temperate. Moreover, the well-educated disciple, whether boy or girl, must be accustomed to stand hardships, not to fear death, nor to be discouraged by any misfortunes; by all this one could be courageous, and we have shown that women also must participate in courage.[184]

Although the Stoic argues forcefully that men as well as women must practise the virtue of temperance, he reveals a deeper belief that men are superior to women:

> If it appears unblameful and honest for a master to sleep with his slave, or even more his widowed slave, he must think about the impression he would have if a mistress slept with her slave. Would not this appear unbearable not only if she is married, but also if she is not?. . .

> Nevertheless I think that no one will consider a man worse or less able than a woman to bring his desires under control. For it is proper that men be superior to women, if it is true that they rule over women. So if they are intemperate they will be more immoral. Now everyone knows that a master who sleeps with his slave is intemperate![185]

The above passage could simply be interpreted as stating that if men rule over women they ought to be more virtuous. However, the Stoic does not suggest that the reverse could occur, or even that men ought not to rule over women. He appears to accept this order of things as an obvious starting point for his argument. He is simply arguing that men ought to be more worthy of the power of ruling that they have. Their worthiness will come through the practice of virtues and, in this situation, in the specific virtue of tempering sexual desires.

In another passage, Musonius Rufus describes the different kinds of work related to the sexes in terms of strength and weakness:

> What then, someone might say, you would like men to learn to spin wool as women do and women to devote themselves to gymnastics as the men do? This, I would not ask for. Instead, I declare, that as in the human race, male nature is stronger than female nature, we must give heavier work to the stronger and lighter to the weaker. This is why spinning and housekeeping are more proper to women than to men and in truth gymnastics and camping are more suitable to men than to women. Sometimes, however, there could be good reasons why some men undertake some lighter tasks, that seem reserved for women, and inversely, for some women to undertake some more difficult tasks ordinarily reserved for men. It depends on the conditions of the body, or the needs, or the opportunity which demands particular action.[186]

Sexual differentiation is presented in the description of the greater strength of men and of specific tasks associated with this strength. However, the Stoic allows for specific circumstances to qualify this response. In the following passage, he appears once again to move towards a sex-unity theory of function:

> Maybe all human tasks are, in fact, a common field of actions and are common to men and women, and none of them are reserved necessarily for one or the other. But certain tasks are more appropriate to one or the other sex. That is why certain tasks are said to be man's work and others woman's. However, all these works are related to virtue. We could say correctly that by nature they are all proper to both sexes, if at least we say that virtue is equally proper to both sexes. From this normally comes the conclusion that everything which leads to virtue must be taught to women as well as to men, and that the education must begin in early childhood and must equally teach what is good and what is bad. From this will come the practical wisdom of those who are learning, boys or girls alike. And there is no difference between the sexes.[187]

It may be that Musonius is following Plato's general tendency to state that in society, the female is weaker or inferior to the male, but that in the ideal world these inequalities, which function as a starting point for the two sexes, ought to be transcended through education. It is difficult to know whether he is simply asserting as a given fact the superiority and greater strength of the male with the corresponding inferiority and weakness of the female, or whether he thought it could be changed to better conform to a sex-unity theory.

Perhaps a clue to evaluating Musonius's reflections on sex polarity is found in his description of the need to differentiate the sexes in physical appearance. If the Stoic had really followed Plato's line of argument, he might also have thought that differences in the physical appearance of the sexes should be abolished. However, as the following fragments indicate, Musonius was most concerned with having men appear differently from women. In addition, he devalues the feminine when it appears to interfere with male identity.

> The beard is the male symbol, as the comb of the rooster and the mane of the lion, then if you must remove the hampering hairs, you must not touch the beard.

> Hair cutting seems to be a very indecent ornament which in no way differs from woman's concern for finery.

> Those who cut their hair and shave themselves stand to be considered as androgynous and effeminate persons.[188]

Therefore, Musonius Rufus sought to differentiate man from woman on the physical level. Furthermore, in this differentiation, he considered a man who shaved as indicating a desire to be like women and therefore as blurring the important distinction between the sexes.

In conclusion, Musonius Rufus stands out as being the one Stoic who devoted considerable time and reflection to questions of sex identity. While he did not offer any fundamentally new arguments beyond those already found in Plato and Aristotle, he nonetheless rephrased the key issues and sought particularly to defend the importance of women studying philosophy. He also argued that women and men ought to study philosophy in order to become more virtuous and that, in general, both sexes had the same virtues of prudence, temperance, justice, and courage. While the application of these virtues may differ for women and men in their specific applications, the fundamental qualities of the virtues were the same for both sexes. Therefore, Musonius argued, in contrast to Aristotle, that women were capable of the highest level of philosophy. In contrast to Plato, he argued that women and men ought to practise their respective virtues in the context of monogamous marriage. Another way to express this is to say that he argued against Aristotle that women and men were equal, and that he argued against Plato that women and men were significantly different. Finally, there appears to be a hint of sex complementarity in Musonius's focus on the value of marriage. However, he did not develop the theory that would underlie such a development. Consequently, Musonius Rufus's theory of sex identity remained caught among three partially developed theories without ever breaking through to a new level of thought on the subject.

EPICTETUS (AD 50–?)

An ex-slave who learned Stoic principles through the instruction of Musonius Rufus, Epictetus's few fragments, *Discourses* and *Manual* (as written by his student Arrian), reveal a simple repetition of Musonius's philosophy of sex identity, with a slight shift in emphasis towards sex polarity.

First of all, we find a clear attempt maintain the distinction between the physical appearance of women and men.

> Are you man or woman? "Man," Adorn man then, not woman. . . . I will show you a man who prefers to be a woman. What a shocking exhibition! [189]

Next, he argued that women should not try to be like men:

> Again, in women nature took the hair from their face, even as she mingled in their voice a softer note. What! You say the creature ought to have been left undistinguished and each of us to have proclaimed, "I am a man"? Nay; . . . we ought not to confound the sexes which have been distinguished. [190]

Epictetus supported this philosophical position with the religious claim that Hermes had sent the following message: "Not to pervert what is good and right, and not to interfere with it, but leave man man and woman woman." [191] In these pronouncements, Epictetus attempted to undermine a tendency towards a sex-unity position.

Next, Epictetus argued that women ought to be more interested in the practice of the virtue of modesty than in physical appearance.

> Women from fourteen years upwards are called "madam" by men. Wherefore, when they see that the only advantage they have got is to be marriageable, they begin to make themselves smart and to set all their hopes on this. We must take pains then to make them understand that they are really honoured for nothing but a modest and decorous life. [192]

Instead of following Musonius's example of strenuously arguing for the equal capabilities of women for virtue and wisdom, Epictetus appears to criticize women's capacity for understanding Plato's *Republic*:

> In Rome women make a study of Plato's *Republic*, because he enacts community of wives; for they only attend to the man's words and not to his spirit, not noticing that he does not first enact the marriage of one man and one woman and then wish wives to be common, but removes the first kind of marriage and introduces another kind in its place. [193]

Woman, it is implied, is more interested in moving into extramarital affairs than in living in a Platonic community of women formed before an entry into a monogamous marriage.

Epictetus is equally hard on men who seek to break the marriage bond. However, the example he uses to prove this point is one in which woman is devalued. Epictetus compares woman to a suckling pig at a banquet. While the pig is the common property of all men present at the beginning of the banquet, once it has been cut, each man should be content with his own portion.[194] The use of such an analogy appears to consider women as a piece of property to be used. Perhaps this analogy was attractive to Epictetus because of his background as a slave. In any event, it indicates a certain devaluation of woman in marriage from the rather strong defence of the value of the common life found in Musonius's description of marriage.

In fact, in other passages, Epictetus appears to advocate a detachment from woman even within the marriage relationship. He suggested that a philosopher seek to become detached from all things, beginning with simple material possessions.

> From this go on to a tunic, a dog, a horse, a field; and from that to yourself, your body and its members, your children, your wife, your brothers. Look carefully on all sides and fling them away from you.[195]

Epictetus frequently referred to the opposite of this attitude of detachment in terms derogatory to the female. He likened it to "the sickly craving of a woman with child," or to "sitting and crying like young girls," or to being a "slave to a paltry girl."[196]

The use of derogatory remarks about women was used by Epictetus to refer to the lack of temperance and courage. In this way, the Stoic attitude towards woman became associated with a sex polarity in which the female stood for the uneducated, uncontrolled passionate nature, while the male was associated with self control and detachment. These few examples indicate the rather large difference in emphasis that is found between Epictetus and his teacher, Musonius. The issue concerned whether to emphasize the capacity in women for wisdom and virtue, and whether one sex was less capable of a Stoic life of virtue than the other.

JUVENAL (AD 60–140)

While Juvenal was not a Stoic philosopher in the manner of those already studied, that is, while he did not develop arguments in favour of wisdom and virtue, he nonetheless is often classified with the Stoics because of his strong criticism of people who do not learn detachment from material possession or from the lower passions of the soul. As a satirist, writing in the tradition established by Lucilius and Lucretius, Juvenal sought to teach by exaggeration of vices rather than by holding up an ideal of virtue. If the opposite of virtue—vice—can be shown to be repulsive, then a person might be persuaded to avoid the vice and to seek instead the corresponding virtue.

Juvenal's technique has specific application to the concept of woman because he wrote one of the earliest satires, "Against Women." This piece, also called the "Sixth Satire," had a powerful influence on later thought about the concept of woman. In particular, Juvenal appears to have directly influenced Walter Map's *De Nugis Curialium* and Jean de Meun's *Roman de la Rose*. Both of these writers of the twelfth and thirteenth centuries played an important role in the development of later arguments for sex polarity.[197] Ironically, Juvenal's satire "Against Women" was written in the form of advising a man named Postumus not to marry. The irony flows from the fact that the Stoics, for the most part, recommended marriage. Therefore, in this basic aspect of his thought, Juvenal does not fit into the usual Stoic pattern of argument.

Juvenal's method of rejecting marriage is to devalue woman in nearly every aspect of her being. It is through this technique that Juvenal articulates an extremely sarcastic expression of sex polarity. His basis for sex polarity does not appear to be derived from Aristotle, although there is some theorizing among scholars that Theophrastus, the leader of the Peripatetic school after Aristotle, may have been influential.[198]

"Against Women" begins with an attack on the temperance of women. Juvenal argues that female chastity has disappeared from the face of the earth. Offering several examples of unfaithful wives, he concludes: "They do worse things, these lust-ridden women; at the bidding of sex, the least of their sins are committed."[199] The full weight of Juvenal's criticism of woman's persistent unfaithfulness implies that woman is totally driven by lust to seek out sexual partners in all sorts of degenerate circumstances. "Their appetites all are the same, no matter what class they have come from; high or low, their lusts are alike."[120] Juvenal suggests that it is impossible to find a virtuous woman to marry:

> You go seeking a virtuous old-fashioned wife? its time to summon the doctors. . . .
> Will she be satisfied with one man, this piece of perfection? Sooner I think
> with one eye. But you keep insisting you've heard of
> one who lives at home on the farm, with a great reputation.
> Well—let her live in some one-horse town as she lives in the country. . . .
> But did you never hear about things that happen in mountains, in caves?[201]

Comparing a faithful wife to the philosophical non-entity of a black swan, Juvenal concludes that if such an impossibility did exist, Postumus would not be able to stand her.

> Let her be well-behaved, good-looking, wealthy, and fertile. . . .
> Let her be a rare bird, the rarest on earth, a black swan—
> Who could endure a wife endowed with every perfection?[202]

For Juvenal, the virtues of chastity, modesty or temperance simply did not exist in man or woman. He asked Postumus, "If you're not going to love your lawfully wedded wife, Why get married at all?"[203]

The second method of attack on woman uses the inversion of the usual view that man's virtue is to rule, woman's to obey. Juvenal argued that a man who married would instead be ruled by his wife.

> Postumus, are you taking a wife?
> Tell me what Fury, what snakes, have driven you on to this madness?
> Can you be under her thumb . . .
>
> If you are simply devoted to one alone, bend your neck,
> Bow to the yoke; . . .
>
> She will regulate even your friendships,
> Slam the door in the face of a lifelong boon companion.[204]

The difficulties are compounded when the mother-in-law joins with the wife to control the husband's decisions. In all these situations, the man is forced to obey and his wife usurps the prerogative of ruling. Juvenal's analysis here is similar to the attack on woman's rule over man that was found in Lucretius's *On the Nature of Things.*

Juvenal's third attack on women focused on woman's identity itself. Juvenal suggested that women actually seek to become masculine, both with their bodies and with their minds, until their feminine identity is completely lost. The first example he considered was women who model themselves after athletes and soldiers:

> Who does not know of the blankets that women drape over their shoulders
> After athletic workouts the pastes they use for their rubdowns?
>
> Who has not seen the dummies of wood they slash at and batter
> Whether with swords or with spears, going through the manoeuvres?
>
> How can a woman be decent
> Sticking her head in a helmet, denying the sex she was born with?
> Manly feats they adore, but they wouldn't want to be men,
> Poor weak things (they think), how little they really enjoy it! . . .
>
> Ah, degenerate girls from the line of our praetors and consuls,
> Tell us, whom have you seen got up in any such fashion,
> Panting and sweating like this?[205]

It may be that Juvenal had the female soldiers of Plato's *Republic* in mind, as well as the women of Rome who engaged in athletic and mock warrior activity. The undercutting of his criticism concerns the hypocrisy of their masculine modelling, for he argued that it was simply for show.

The satire on women who imitate the minds of men followed a similar line of reasoning. Juvenal criticized their pseudo-intellectualism. In the first example he criticized women who liked to use the Greek language:

> What stinks worse than the fact that none of them trust their good looks
> till they have made themselves Greeks and jabber away in that language?
> (Though its a bigger disgrace to speak ungrammatically in Latin.)
> All their gossip, their fears, their anger, their joys and their worries,
> Their intimate secrets of soul, they pour out in Greek.[206]

In the following passage, Juvenal focuses on the hypocrisy of women who use philosophy and rhetoric for all the wrong reasons:

> Even worse is the one who has scarcely sat down at the table
> When she starts in on books, with praise for Virgil and Pardon
> For the way Dido died; she makes comparisons, placing
> Virgil on one side of the scales, and counterweights him with Homer.
> Critics surrender, professors are lost; the whole crowd is silent.
> No one can get in a word edgewise, not even a lawyer,
> No, nor an auctioneer, not even another woman,
> such is the force of her words, the syllables pouring in torrents
> Making a din like that when pots and kettles are rattled

In an eclipse of the moon. No need of trumpets or cymbals,
All by herself she can make all of the noise that is needed.
What a philosopher, too, with her definitions of morals! . . .

Postumus, my good friend, don't let the wife of your bosom
Ever acquire the style of an orator, whirling the sentence,
Hearing the enthymeme, or the undistributed middle.
Don't let her know too much about historical matters,
Let there be some things in books she does not understand.
How I hate them,
Women who always go back to the pages of Palaemon's grammar,
Keeping all the rules, and are pedants enough to be quoting
Verses I never heard.[207]

For Juvenal, woman was not capable of using wisdom for the right purposes. Instead, she uses it to show off or to correct others. In this way her knowledge is detached from its proper aim. She seeks to have the appearance of the wisdom of men, but she does not desire its true goal. Therefore, just as women were satirized for imitating the minds of men without wanting to be men, so now are they satirized for imitating the minds of men without wanting to be wise men. In this way, women, according to Juvenal, lost both their own feminine identity and the pseudo-masculine identity they imitated.

The final area in which Juvenal satirized woman's identity is in the virtue of justice. He described women who whip their servants arbitrarily, who cheat the members of their household of wages they have earned, and who are completely preoccupied with their own selfish needs for attention and the fulfillment of their sexual desires. Juvenal concluded: "No Sicilian court is more unjust than her household if she has made a decision."[208] Juvenal completed his satire with numerous descriptions of women who killed their children or other members of their family to attain their unjust goals. The murders are described as occurring by abortion, exposure, and poison.

In conclusion, then, Juvenal chose the traditional virtues that previous writers had held out as a positive value for women, namely temperance, obedience, wisdom, and justice. Then he developed graphic descriptions of women practising all the corresponding vices of sexual lust, tyranny, stupidity, and injustice. By giving such a thoroughly devalued image of woman's identity he inadvertently offered a completely articulate rationale for sex polarity. Juvenal also left vicious satires on men, particularly those from the upper classes. However, it was his "Against Women," later incorporated into literature, that developed new bases for the devaluation of women in general and that became a fundamental aspect of the sex-polarity tradition. For that reason, although Juvenal stood somewhat outside the Stoic tradition at the time he wrote his satires, his position in the history of the concept of woman in relation to man needs to be recognized as central to the tendency to devalue woman, a tendency that reaches as far as Schopenhauer and Sartre.

MARCUS AURELIUS (AD 121–180)

The Stoic school of philosophy received a new legitimacy when Marcus Aurelius, one of its foremost proponents, became emperor of Rome. The few thoughts in the *Meditations* on the concept of woman included a reflection on mothering:

> A man deposits a seed in a womb and goes away, and then another cause takes it, and labours on it and makes a child. What a thing from such a material![209]

Marcus Aurelius compared the process of birth with that of immortality at death:

> As thou now waitest for the time when the child shall come out of thy wife's womb, so be ready for the time when the soul shall fall out of this envelope.[210]

Most interesting, however, was the reappearance of the female personification of philosophy. This time she was a mother:

> If thou hadst a step-mother and a mother at the same time, thou wouldst be dutiful to thy step-mother, but still thou wouldst constantly return to thy mother. Let the court and philosophy now be to thee step-mother and mother; return to philosophy frequently and repose in her.[211]

In this description of philosophy, Marcus Aurelius conveyed a positive image of woman as mother. In contrast to this, the concept of woman in Stoicism was often trivialized through a consideration of the respective characters of Xanthippe and Socrates. While Xanthippe exemplified a kind of erratic shrewishness, Socrates exemplified stoic patience. Seneca had referred to an "endurance we commend" in describing Socrates' good humour when Xanthippe threw foul water at his head.[212] Epictetus had also reflected on the underlying philosophical attitude that allowed Socrates to act this way:

> For what did her shrewishness mean? Pouring water at will over his head, and trampling on his cake. What is that to me, if I make up my mind that it is nothing to me?[213]

Marcus Aurelius, however, admired the man himself: "Consider what a man Socrates was when he dressed himself in a skin, after Xanthippe had taken his cloak and gone out."[214]

The stoic behaviour of men was symbolized in the person of Socrates. By comparison, these legends of Xanthippe left a legacy to women of unethical and erratic behaviour in the tradition of Juvenal's satire. The perpetuation of these negative images of woman and poetic images of man created a kind of background for sex polarity in regard to concepts of woman and man.

Marcus Aurelius also used the word *womanish* in a derogatory way, which further indicates a tendency among some Stoics to associate woman with a lack of control over the passions and man with the control that is so associated with the Stoic practice of virtue. In the following passage Marcus Aurelius offers this description:

> A black character, a womanish character, a stubborn character, bestial, childish, animal, stupid, counterfeit, scurrilous, fraudulent, tyrannical.[215]

Once again, we find the association of devaluation of sex and race together, just as it had been expressed in Aristotle. Given the influential position of Marcus Aurelius as emperor, this polarization of sex and race had greater significance than if it were found simply in the writings of an obscure philosopher.

GALEN (AD 131–201)

Galen, who served as court physician to Marcus Aurelius, was a thorough advocate of sex-polarity. In an autobiographical work in which he reflected on his parents' influence, the values of Stoicism were embodied in his father:

> I did enjoy the good fortune of having the least irascible, the most just, the most devoted, the kindest of fathers. My mother, however, was so very prone to anger that sometimes she bit her handmaids; she constantly shrieked at my father and fought with him—more than Xanthippe did with Socrates. When I compared my father's noble deeds with the disgraceful passions of my mother, I decided to embrace and love his deeds and to hate her passion.[216]

While Galen did not directly associate reason and control with the concept of man or passions with the concept of woman, he did associate them with his father and mother. Also, Xanthippe and the concept of woman were linked to the lower parts of the soul. In another passage, Galen referred to women as lacking self-control in their pursuit of precious jewels.[217] Finally, he mentioned Medea as the perfect example of a person in whom anger was stronger than reason. She was led to terrible deeds because of the "immoderate movement in the desiderative part of her soul."[218]

Galen's significance to the history of the concept of woman does not come from his ethical writings. Rather, since he was the most important medical writer for early medieval thought, his theories of generation became the avenue through which Aristotelian thought continued to affect western philsophy. Although Galen changed some of Aristotle's views slightly, he nonetheless fell solidly within the tradition of sex polarity. This is demonstrated in his acceptance of the relation of hot and cold to male and female identity:

> Well, then, Aristotle was right in thinking the female less perfect than the male; . . . I shall now attempt to add, making the demonstrations correctly given by Aristotle and still earlier by Hippocrates the basis of my discussion and working out myself whatever is lacking to complete it.
>
> The female is less perfect than the male for one principal reason—because she is colder; for if among animals the warm one is the more active, a colder animal would be a less perfect than the warmer.[219]

Galen argued, then, that the degree of imperfection in woman followed directly from her lack of heat.

> The female is less perfect than the male by as much as she is colder than he.[220]

Because of this lack of heat, woman's generative organs could not escape to the outside of her body. Woman's body had an excess of nutriment (blood), her seed was imperfect, and she had only a "hollow instrument" with which to receive male seed.[211] In other words, according to Galen, the presence of greater heat in the male led to a perfection of the body that included external sexual organs, purified nutriment (seed), and the capacity to emit this seed. Galen described the relation of the male and female contribution to generation in Aristotelian terms:

> And what is the semen? Clearly the active principle of the animal, the material principle being the menstrual blood.[222]

He frequently said that the need for the seed to unite with the menstrual fluid indicated "one as the principle of motion, and the other as the material for the generation of vessels."[223] The semen was also called the "efficient principle of the animal."[224]

The male seed served as the force that set the material into motion as well as giving it shape. The seed attracted the material "as a lodestone attracted iron."[225] The seed determined how much material it needed; the material remained totally passive in relation to the male seed:

> Now it is not for the wax to discover for itself how much of it is required. This is the business of Phidias. Accordingly the artificer will draw to itself as much blood as it needs.[226]

The Aristotelian notion of the active contribution of the male and the passive contribution of the female was accepted by Galen as the heart of his theory of generation.

Galen stated that the female contribution to generation was not fertile:

> Because the female is colder than the male, the liquid in her parastatai adeneoideis is unconcocted . . . so that it is of no assistance in the generation of the animals.[227]

However, he did believe that the female provided a kind of seed to generation; in this view he adopted the Hippocratic rather than Aristotelian position. However, the female seed did not contribute actively to generation:

> The female semen is exceedingly weak and unable to advance to that state of motion in which it could impress an artistic form upon the fetus.[228]

This explanation for the inability of the female seed to contribute form to conception was based upon the Aristotelian opposites of hot and cold. Galen compared female seed to "wind eggs," which appear to be fertile but are not.[229] Similarly, he compared female anatomy to the eyes of a mole, which are present, but in an unusable form.[230] Aristotle argued that the female seed did not even exist. Galen merely reported its existence, but then undermined its effectiveness. He implied, at times, that the female seed played the same role as secretions during intercourse.[231] He believed that the female seed was retained in the uterus as part of the material that was used for generation; it did not provide form.

The main argument Galen used against the early theory of fertile female contribution to generation followed Aristotle's basic thesis that nature did nothing in vain. If the female was able to contribute fertile seed to generation, there would be no reason for the existence of the male.

> To those who think that the female too emits a fertile semen, it does not seem surprising that whenever the motions generated in it are stronger than those in the male, the fetus that is engendered is female. . . . If it does not need to

> be mixed, what prevents the female alone from emitting semen into herself and thus bringing the fetus to perfection?[232]

The development of a sex-polarity position for generation raised the problem of justifying the existence of the female. Galen shared Aristotle's contention that the female was a deformed or imperfect male and, like Aristotle, attempted to justify this lack.

> Through making the animal itself that is being formed less perfect than one that is complete in all respects, provided no small advantage for the race; for there needs to be a female. Indeed, you ought not to think that our Creator would purposely make half the whole race imperfect, and, as it were, *mutilated*, unless there was to be some great advantage in such a mutilation.[233]

Galen has been shown to be a transmitter of Aristotelian sex polarity. While he qualified Aristotle's view in order to defend the existence of female seed, he nonetheless devalued the significance of this seed to the extent that it played no active role in generation. Galen repeated Aristotle's arguments for the inferiority of the female in relation to the male. In this way, he played a more important role in the Aristotelian Revolution than any other Stoic. The thought of the Stoic philosophers Cicero, Seneca, and Musonius Rufus contained attitudes of sex neutrality or sex unity along with a residue of sex polarity. Pliny, Epictetus and Marcus Aurelius fell more clearly within the sex-polarity tradition. Galen was the only Stoic to promote sex polarity by specifically invoking Aristotle's biological theories about woman's inferiority in relation to man. He must therefore be recognized as the most important Stoic in the development of the Aristotelian Revolution.

SEX POLARITY DEVELOPED IN JEWISH PHILOSOPHY

PHILO (13 BC–AD 54)

Pythagoras and Plato were the two Greek philosophers who most influenced Philo. It might seem to follow from this that Philo would have tended towards sex unity; however, he developed a thorough defence of sex polarity. Since there were aspects of sex polarity in Plato's cosmic identification of the passive receptacle (or matter) with the female, and since Pythagoras had argued for sex polarity in the area of philosophy concerned with virtue, it is possible that Philo inherited some sex-polarity arguments from these two philosophers.

There is no clear evidence of a direct connection between Aristotle and Philo, who did not refer to the Greek philosopher in his writings. As will be seen, however, Philo's sex-polarity theory closely parallels Aristotle's in the specific areas of generation, wisdom, and virtue. This similarity may have been derived from Philo's use of early Stoic material that had been influenced by Aristotelian thought.

Another factor must be mentioned. Philo, as a Jewish philosopher, was deeply imbued with knowledge of the first five books of the Bible, the Torah. Most of his philosophical arguments for sex polarity probably emerged in his particular interpretation of these texts. In the following discussion of Philo's theory, an attempt will be made to isolate philosophical from theological arguments. When Philo defended sex polarity through an appeal to revelation, then the argument will be considered theological. When he rested his conclusions on the combined evidence of reason and the senses, even though he may have been discussing a passage in the Bible, the rationale will be considered philosophical. In this way, it is hoped that the similarity between Philo and Aristotle will be made clear. Furthermore, Philo and Aristotle will merge as influences on the sex polarity in the writings of Maimonides and St. Thomas. Therefore, even though the relationship of Philo to Aristotle may be uncertain, Philo's writings were eventually used to support the Aristotelian concept of woman. They may also have influenced the sex polarity of the later Roman Stoics in their particular association of woman with the passions, and man with the higher powers of mind.

The following chart summarizes the main conclusions of Philo's rationale for sex polarity.

	Man	**Woman**
Opposites	Active, akin to rational	Passive, akin to senses
Generation	Provides form	Provides matter
Wisdom	Symbol of mind	Symbol of senses
	masculine thought = wisdom	feminine thought = ruled by passion
	Good judgment	Deceived
Virtue	Rule	Obey
	active in affairs of state	active in affairs of home

Philo stated that in generation, the female provided the matter, and the man the form. In the context of a discussion about why men need to be circumcised and not women, Philo stated:

> The matter of the female in the remains of the menstrual fluids produces the fetus. But the male (provides) the skill and the cause. And so, since the male provides the greater and more necessary (part) in the process of generation, it is proper that his pride should be checked by the sign of circumcision, but the material element, being inanimate, does not admit of arrogance.[234]

The woman provided merely inanimate material, while the man provided the formal cause of the child. Philo drew conclusions from the male and female contributions to generation for the meaning of *male* and *female* in themselves. In a passage considering why a sheep was chosen for the Passover meal, Philo developed this argument:

> Why is a sheep chosen? Symbolically, as I have said, it indicates perfect progress, and at the same time, the male, for progress is nothing else than the giving up of the female gender by changing into the male, since the female gender is material, passive, corporal and sense-perceptible, while the male is active, rational, incorporeal and more akin to mind and thought.[235]

The respective functions in generation provided a rationale for the distinctions in sex identity. For Philo, as for Aristotle before him, the female was identified with passivity and the male with activity.

Philo identified activity with the higher part of the soul and passivity with the lower part. It is not surprising, then, that he developed an analogy between these two parts of the soul and the nature of man and woman. Using a method of allegorical interpretation derived from the early Stoics' interpretations of Greek myths, Philo stated: "In the allegorical sense, . . . woman is a symbol of sense, and man, of mind."[236] In addition to woman and man acting as symbols for differing functions of soul, Philo also argued that within each person's soul there were masculine and feminine thoughts.

> But as for the deeper meaning, in the soul of progressive man there are some thoughts that are masculine, and some offspring that are feminine. . . . Which then are the masculine thoughts?
>
> Those which are emulous of wisdom and of all virtue in general and of that which is truly good and alone is good. But the feminine kind, having position of daughters, are under service to bodily needs and are under the dominion of the passions.[237]

The feminine thoughts were passive in relation to the passions, or to the external stimulation of the senses. They responded to a situation rather than ordered it.

Philo borrowed a metaphor from Plato's *Phaedrus* that compared women's and men's living quarters to the parts of the mind, but he went further than Plato and applied it specifically to woman's reasoning capacity:

> And the woman's quarters are a place where womenly opinions go about and dwell, being followers of the female sex. And the female sex is irrational and akin to bestial passions, fear, sorrow, pleasure and desire.[238]

Philo, extending Plato's metaphor, mirrored Aristotle's theory that woman was limited by her relation to the irrational part of the mind. Philo also drew an analogy between the theory of conception and the proper relation between the masculine and feminine parts of the mind:

> It is fitting and proper for it to bring together these (parts) which have been divided and separated, not that the masculine thoughts may be made womanish and relaxed by softness, but that the female element, the senses, may be made manly by following masculine thoughts and by receiving from them seed for procreation.[239]

Just as the woman played a passive role in conception, so feminine thoughts passively received the active ordering of masculine thoughts.[240]

One of the consequences, in relation to wisdom, of Philo's sex-polarity theory was that woman was more likely to be deceived than man. Her passivity made her unable to discern error:

> Woman is more accustomed to being deceived than man. For his judgement, like his body, is masculine and is capable of dissolving or destroying the designs of deception but the judgement of woman is more feminine, and because of softness she easily gives way and is taken in by plausible falsehoods which resemble the truth.[241]

In another passage on the same subject, he identified woman with sense perception. The senses, which themselves were easily deceived, in turn were able to deceive the mind.[242]

Philo concluded that virtue was more properly thought of as male than as female. Virtue demanded that the activity of the soul be realized:

> If anyone is willing to divest facts of the terms which obscure them, and observe them in their nakedness in a clear light he will understand that virtue is male, since it causes movement and affects conditions and suggests noble conceptions of noble deeds and words, while thought is female, being moved and trained and helped, and in general belonging to the passive category, which passivity is its sole means of preservation.[243]

The link between this theory of virtue and a theory of the passive contribution of the female to generation was also made explicit by Philo:

> Giving birth is wholly peculiar to woman, just as begetting is to man. Scripture therefore wishes the soul of the virtuous man to be likened to the male sex rather than the female, considering that activity rather than passivity is congenial to him.[224]

It is difficult to overestimate the similarity between Aristotelian concepts and Philo's thought about woman. Before Philo, Aristotle was the only major philosopher to argue for a total passivity in woman's contribution to conception. Both philosophers also drew analogies from this theory of generation to woman's and man's relation to wisdom and virtue. Philo, along with Aristotle, argued for separate spheres of activity for woman and man:

> For to man are entrusted the public affairs of state; while to a woman the affairs of the home are proper.[245]

However, woman's virtue was not equal to the full virtue of man, and Philo finally concluded that virtue had "no part in the female sex."[246] In Philo, Aristotelian sex polarity found a perfect mirror.

Philo was not only a significant philosopher, but also a major theologian. Two important areas of his theological framework for the concept of woman were the conquest of the feminine personification of wisdom (Sophia) by the masculine personification of divine intellect (Logos), and his introduction of a theory of creation of woman and man. Some thorough studies of the first area have already been made.[247] It is significant, however, that while Philo had inherited a feminine personification of wisdom through his philosophical roots in Plato and through his Jewish roots in the book of Wisdom in the Bible, he nonetheless chose to devalue the feminine and to assert the ultimate victory of *Nous* and *Logos* as masculine sources of wisdom. Sex polarity permeated both his philosophy and his theology.

For Philo, creation followed the division in Genesis of two separate phases. In the first creation, God made a human genus, but without division into male or female. To some extent, Philo's interpretation followed the Platonic belief in a soul that was neither male nor female:

> But the man who came into existence after the image of God in what one might call an idea, or a genus, or a seal, an object of thought, incorporeal, neither male nor female, by nature incorruptible . . .[248]

Next, God divided this creation into two equal parts, male and female:

> "God made man," he says, "made him after the image of God. Male and female he made"—not now "him" but "them" (Gen. 1. 27). He concludes with the plural, thus connecting with the genus mankind the species which had been divided, as I said, but equally.[249]

Finally, God created individual women and men. This creation was of mortal and sensible beings. Adam was created as the first man, before Eve, the first woman. Philo argued that her creation from the side of man, instead of from the earth, was because the "woman is not equal in honour with the man."[250]

The decision to interpret this biblical account of the creation of woman from the side of man within a sex-polarity framework completed Philo's general adoption of this theory of sex identity. This particular interpretation is not necessarily implied by the account. For example, it has been used to prove that woman must be superior to man because she came later in the order of creation.[251] It has also been used to suggest the complementary equality of woman and man.[252] Philo, however, interpreted all biblical references within a framework of sex polarity. Without directly discussing the philosophy of Aristotle, Philo's concept of woman nevertheless strongly reinforced the basic direction of the Aristotelian Revolution. He particularly influenced the development of the neo-Platonic Jewish and Christian philosophies of the concept of woman in relation to man.

SEX UNITY AS DEVELOPED IN NEO-PLATONISM

Neo-Platonism made explicit the metaphysical foundation for sex unity that had been implicit in Plato's thought. Specifically, the theory of reincarnation was used by the neo-Platonists to justify the equality of woman in relation to man in the categories of wisdom and virtue. At the same time, the neo-Platonists were very respectful of Aristotle and they adopted many of his concepts, particularly in the areas of logic and generation. Therefore, their writings gave evidence of a minor conflict between sex unity and sex polarity when their theory crossed over several categories of the concept of woman in relation to man.

In its earliest form, in Plutarch, the conflict between sex unity and sex polarity expressed itself in a variety of thoughts about women. For example, Plutarch appeared to maintain a sex-polarity argument about woman's lack of contribution of seed to generation. On the other hand, on the cosmic level, he argued for a generative feminine principle posited in the goddess Isis. In addition, he believed in reincarnation, and concluded from this that women as well as men ought to strive for the full development of wisdom and virtue. For Plutarch, the conflict between these theories was solved by a devaluation of materiality. The sex polarity on the human generative level was not significant in relation to sex unity on the level of soul.

Plotinus carried on the tradition established by Plutarch. While he argued that mothering contained an active formal nature not explained through pure passivity, he nonetheless frequently associated the concept of mother with passive matter. With matter devalued as evil, woman was by association connected with the negative characterization of "lack." At the same time, Plotinus believed that the material aspect of the person—the body—was insignificant in relation to soul. This attitude left women free to become philosophers. Once again, the metaphysical foundation for this premise of non-differentiation was reincarnation as the basis of sex unity.

It was Porphyry who developed the central neo-Platonic defence for sex unity. In a work on embryology, he stated that both mother and father made a formal contribution to generation. First the father, and then the mother provided the vegetative soul to the fetus. The rational soul was given from outside either parent. He defended reincarnation, as well as the equal contribution of the parents to generation. Porphyry's argument that both women and men ought to strive for the fullest development in wisdom and virtue followed from this belief in reincarnation. In a letter to his wife, Marcella, Porphyry gave an explicit restatement of this Platonic foundation for sex unity. He therefore stands as an extremely important witness to the strength of Platonic sex unity at this stage of the Aristotelian Revolution.

Porphyry was also important for the Aristotelian Revolution because he wrote an extensive summary of Aristotle's logical works entitled *Isagoge*. This text, the first transmission of Aristotle's arguments for the definition of philosophy, was the means through which the Aristotelian rationale for sex neutrality was forwarded in western thought.

Hypatia was the last neo-Platonic philosopher significant for the concept of woman. Her contribution is not related to anything she wrote about women; indeed, Hypatia appears not to have been concerned about this subject. Since her main interest was the application of mathematics to philosophy, she can be considered as promoting the sex neutrality framework. Hypatia is important for the present study because she was the embodiment of the neo-Platonic ideal of a woman. Not only was she a philosopher in her own right, but she also directed the neo-Platonic school of philosophy in Alexandria. Therefore, it is significant that she emerged from a tradition that defended the equality and non-differentiation of woman and man.

Plato's sex-unity theory received its fullest expression within neo-Platonism. Although these philosophers did not add anything original to Plato's previous consideration of the issue, they did seek to apply his framework to the actual situation of woman and man. A common belief in reincarnation provided the metaphysical basis for a theory of the equality of woman and man, while it made apparent differences between the sexes seem insignificant. Woman or man, as human, was in reality a sexless soul enclosed in a particular material body. The goal of life was to escape this bodily prison. The study of mathematics, logic and philosophy could aid women and men in this process of escape from the material world. The later rejection of this metaphysical view of the relation of soul and body by Christian philosophy was the end of the central place of reincarnation in the sex-unity theory. The end of neo-Platonism also marked the end of the first formulation of the sex-unity theory as developed by Plato.

The following chart indicates in a general way the development of a pattern of consistency within neo-Platonic theories of sex identity. In addition, it shows the slow movement away from a sex-polarity theory and towards sex neutrality, and second, within that framework, towards a sex unity. Porphyry stands out as having provided the turning point for the neo-Platonists in his arguments both in the area of generation and in his claim that women and men ought to study philosophy in order to live in union with their souls rather than with their bodies. In this way, neo-Platonism follows the Platonic tendency to achieving an equality of the sexes through a devaluation of the body.

	Opposites	**Generation**	**Wisdom**	**Virtue**
Plutarch	sex polarity	sex polarity	sex unity	sex unity
Plotinus	sex polarity	sex polarity	sex unity	sex unity
Porphyry	sex unity	sex unity	sex unity	sex unity
Hypatia	sex neutrality	sex neutrality	sex neutrality	sex neutrality

PLUTARCH (AD 46–125)

At approximately the same time that Seneca developed sex unity in Stoicism, and Philo developed sex polarity in Judaism, Plutarch began a revival of Platonism. He was trained in philosophy at the academy in Athens; he spent the rest of his life teaching in Rome. Plutarch thus served as an important link between Greek and Latin thought.

Plutarch's philosophy fell within a sex-unity framework in the areas of wisdom and virtue. However, in his theory of generation, as well as in his view of woman's natural identity, he used a sex-polarity framework. The following chart summarizes his view, which will be studied in more detail below.

	Man	**Woman**
Opposites	hot, active	cold, passive
Generation	fertile seed	material only
Wisdom	begins stronger	begins weaker
	same wisdom	
Virtue	rule	obey
	same bravery or courage	

Plutarch accepted Aristotle's account of the respective contributions of male and female to generation: "Some think the seed of woman is not a power or origin, but only material and nurture of generation. To this thought we should cling fast."[253] He also accepted Aristotle's defence of this position through the operation of the opposites hot and cold:

> It seems that woman's seed has never had an active part at all in generation—the female's coldness is responsible—but merely offers matter and nourishment to the seed from the male.[254]

Plutarch believed, as did Aristotle, that the male seed was a purified form of blood, and that blood was the residue of nourishment in the animal. He also stated that the milk in the mother's breast was a highly purified form of blood.[255]

Plutarch thought that a certain imperfection was found in the female body. Echoing with some restraint the taboos of Pliny, Plutarch rejected Plato's suggestion that men should strip along with women: "There are certain effluences that proceed from the female body and its excretions with which it is a kind of defilement for men to be infected."[256] Using the Pythagorean Table of Opposites, Plutarch discussed the imperfection of the female body. Seeking a rationale for naming female children on the eighth day and males on the ninth, he asked:

> Or did they, like the adherents of Pythagoras, regard the even number as female and the odd number as male? For the odd number is generative, and, when it is added to the even number, it prevails over it. And also, when they are divided into units, the even number, like the female, yields a vacant space between, while of the odd number an integral part always remains.[257]

On the level of human generation, for Plutarch, the concept of woman contained an association of sex polarity, with the woman remaining passive like matter, and the man active like form.

On the cosmic level, Plutarch often seemed to repeat this association; he continued Plato's cosmic connection of matter with the concept of woman. In *Table Talk II* it was stated:

> For matter has the relation of mother or nurse to things which exist, as Plato says; and matter is all from which whatever is created has its substance.[258]

Plutarch believed that the mothering analogy functioned because matter existed first, before individual things were formed in the world. He also distinguished between the concepts of mother and father, linking them to the differences between matter and form:

> The better and more divine nature consists of three parts: the conceptual, the material, and that which is formed from these, which the Greeks call the world. Plato is wont to give to the conceptual the name of idea, example, or father, and to the material the name of mother or nurse, or seat and place of generation, and to that which results from both the name of offspring or generation.[259]

Plutarch stated that the relation of mother to father was like that of the base of a right triangle to its vertical side. The child was like the hypotenuse. In *Isis and Osiris*, written for the Delphic priestess Clea, Plutarch identified the Egyptian goddess Isis with the metaphysical concept of matter:

> The upright, therefore, may be likened to the male, the base to the female, and the hypotenuse to the child of both, and so Osiris may be regarded as the origin, Isis as the recipient and Horus as perfected result.[260]

Isis was also compared to Plato's totally passive receptacle in the *Timaeus*. She received all things without changing her identity:

> Isis, is, in fact, the female principle of Nature, and is receptive of every form of generation, in accord with which she is called by Plato the gentle nurse and the all-receptive, and by most people has been called countless names, since, because of the force of Reason, she turns herself to this thing or that and is receptive of all manner of shapes and forms.[261]

Plutarch defeated Isis with metaphysical categories in exactly the same way as Plato had defeated the earth mother. Prime matter became the cosmic mother, devoid of all life, merely waiting the activity of the Forms or Reason as cosmic father. Plutarch praised the goddess and god as being the combined source of everything that existed: "Inasmuch as Osiris contributes the origin, Isis receives them and distributes them."[262] The female principle was receptive, while the male principle was originative.

Plutarch identified a feminine principle with total receptivity on both the human and the cosmic levels. In this, he was more consistent than Plato, who had made the feminine principle passive on the cosmic level, but appeared to allow for an active feminine contribution to human generation. Plutarch joined Aristotle's theory of human generation with Plato's theory of cosmic generation to form a complete connection between the concept of woman and passivity. Correspondingly, the masculine was characterized as the active principle.

Interestingly, however, Plutarch allowed for an entity to contain both masculine and feminine principles. He did not, therefore, argue that woman and the concept of woman was defined by containing only a feminine principle, or man and the concept of man by a masculine principle. In the following passage, he described the union of masculine and feminine principles within a single entity:

> They also call the Moon the mother of the world, and they think that she has a nature both male and female, as she is receptive and made pregnant by the Sun, but she herself in term emits and disseminates into the air generative principles.[263]

This passage, then, characterized the mother as containing both male and female principles. In a similar way, Plutarch sometimes described the goddess Isis as active in relation to the world; she was called an "animate and intelligent movement," similar to the goddess Athena as being a centre of "self-propelled motion."[264] Within this characterization, Isis revealed both masculine and feminine principles.

Isis not only existed as a generative principle, she also embodied the highest wisdom. In a passage encouraging the priestess Clea to emulate Isis, Plutarch described her as:

> That goddess whom you worship, a goddess exceptionally wise and a lover of wisdom, to whom as her name at least seems to indicate, knowledge and understanding are in the highest degree appropriate.[265]

For Plutarch, wisdom and virtue resided in the soul, not in the body. It therefore followed that these characteristics transcended sex differentiation. Although Plutarch used goddesses common to Roman worship, he infused them with philosophical import, as seen in his invocation of the goddess Fortuna.[266] Plutarch believed that virtue and fortune were in conflict with one another. He described this conflict as the clash between two athletes or warriors: "I can descry Fortune and Virtue advancing to be judged and tried one against the other."[267] Although he struggled with virtue against fortune, Plutarch believed that fortune was often the stronger force, "outstripping virtue."[268]

Plutarch's complicated theory of sex identity can be seen in his claim that women are both weak and strong. The weakness of women was found in their tendency to give in to their emotions:

> With the weakest souls the inclination is to inflict hurt, producing a flaming up of the temper as great as the soul's infinity is great. That is also the reason why women are more prone to anger than men.[269]

As a consequence of woman's natural weakness, she is placed under obedience to man in marriage:

> Whenever two notes are sounded in accord the tune is carried by the bass; and in like manner every activity in a virtuous household is carried on by both parties in agreement, but discloses the husband's leadership preferences.[270]

For Plutarch, man has a natural relation to ruling and woman a natural relation to obedience.

The one situation in which this relation is reversed is found in the mother-son relationship. In *Sayings of Spartan Women*, Plutarch describes several situations in which cowardly sons were corrected and led by brave mothers. In the same work he playfully adds the reflection:

> Being asked by a woman from Attica, "Why is it that you Spartan women are the only women that lord it over your men," she said, "Because we are the only women that are mothers of men."[271]

For the ancient Greeks, Spartan women represented the reverse sex-polarity situation in which women ruled and men obeyed. Through the several examples in *Sayings of Spartan Women*, Plutarch appears to be accepting this situation positively in the specific framework of mother and son.

The most interesting text for this question, however, is Plutarch's *Bravery of Women*, which stands as one of the first biographies of women in western thought. In this text Plutarch offers examples of women who have given evidence of greater courage than their husbands. The underlying premise of *Bravery of Women* is that women and men have the same virtues. Writing to the priestess Clea, Plutarch states:

> I have also written out for you the remainder of what I would have said on the topic that man's virtues and woman's virtues are one and the same. This includes a good deal of historical exposition. . . .
>
> If, conceivably, we asserted that painting on the part of men and women is the same, . . . or if we should declare that the poetic or the prophetic art is not one art when practised by men and another when practised by women, but the same. . . .
>
> And actually it is not possible to learn better the similarity and the difference between the virtues of men and of women from any other source than by putting the lives beside lives and actions beside actions, like great works of art. . . . But, with all this, let us not postulate many different kinds of bravery, wisdom, and justice—if only the individual dissimilarities exclude no one of these from receiving its appropriate rate.[272]

Plutarch then proceeds to describe twenty-seven situations in which women worked together courageously, or in which a single woman gave evidence of the virtue of courage. In all of these situations women practised the same qualities of courage that men had done in the traditional role of a soldier on the battlefield. Some of Plutarch's examples will now be considered.

> Of all the deeds performed by women for the community none is more famous than the struggle against Cleomenes for Argos, which the women carried out at the instigation of Telesilla the poetess. . . . Under the lead of Telesilla they took up arms and, taking their stand by the battlements, manned the walls all round, so that the enemy were amazed. The result was that Cleomenes they repulsed with great loss, and the other King, Demaratus . . . they drove out. . . . Some say that the battle took place . . . the first day of that month, on the anniversary of which they celebrate even to this day the "Festival of Impudence," at which they clothe the women in men's shirts and cloaks, and the men in women's robes and veils.[273]

Plutarch gives several other examples of women who engaged in armed battle or who supported men in direct engagements with the enemy for military victories.

In an example of a different sort of courage, Plutarch describes women who risk their lives to be peacemakers:

> Before the Celts crossed over the Alps, and settled in that part of Italy which is now their home, a dire and persistent factional discord broke out among them which went on and on to the point of civil war. The women, however, put themselves between the armed forces, and taking up the controversies, arbitrated and decided them with such irreproachable fairness that a wondrous friendship of all towards all was brought about between both States and families. As the result of this they continued to consult with the women in regard to war and peace, and to decide through them any disputed matters in their relations with their allies.[274]

Therefore, for Plutarch, courage as a virtue goes beyond the usual military model. In addition, it indicated a cooperative interaction of women and men in civic life.

Significantly, Plutarch did not accept the Greek tradition of separate spheres of activity for woman and man. Instead of designating the household as the private sphere of women and the civis as the public sphere of men, he argued that women and men should work together:

> As the mixing of liquids, . . . extends throughout their entire content, so also in the case of married people there ought to be a mutual amalgamation of their bodies, property, friends, and relations.[275]

The union of woman and man was considered symbolically when the bride and groom touched the two elements of water and fire during the wedding ceremony. Plutarch offered an explanation for the choice of these two elements. He stated that they might symbolize that "Male and female apart from each other are inert, but their union in marriage produces the perfection of their life together."[276]

Plutarch's enormous respect for woman was seen in his elevation of her position within marriage. Even though she was still expected to follow her husband's leadership, due to her natural weakness, she was nonetheless a partner with human worth. In one passage, Plutarch stressed the importance of the interaction of the marriage partners:

> Can a man enter without censure the fellowship of a household, a city, a marriage, a way of life, a magistry, if they have not learned how they should get along with a fellow being?[277]

To get along with one's wife was as important as the interaction of citizens within the greater society. In order to aid this interaction, Plutarch encouraged the serious study of philosophy:

> Of the many admirable themes contained in philosophy, that which deals with marriage deserves no less serious attention than any other, for by means of it philosophy weaves a spell over those who are entering together into a lifelong partnership, and renders them gentle and amiable towards each other.[278]

Both husband and wife ought to engage in these studies. In "Advice to Bride and Groom," he appealed to the bride:

> As for you, Eurydice, I beg that you will try to be conversant with the sayings of the wise and good. . . . For you cannot acquire and put upon you this rich woman's pearls or that foreign woman's silks without buying them at a high price, but the ornaments of Theano, Cleobulian (Eumetis), Gorgo, the wife of Leonidas, Timocleia, the sister of Theogenes, Claudia of old, Cornelia, daughter of Scipio, and all other women who have been admired and renowned, you may wear about you without a price, and adorning yourself with these, you may live a life of distinction and happiness.[279]

Plutarch encouraged the woman to "admire education and philosophy." He encouraged the man to be "guide, philosopher, and teacher" to the bride. He gave a practical argument for women to pursue philosophy: it would keep them from falling into vice.

> Studies of this sort divert women from all untoward conduct; for a woman studying geometry will be ashamed to be a dancer, and she will not swallow any beliefs in magic charms while she is under the charm of Plato's or Xenophon's words.[280]

The study of philosophy was aimed at bringing a balance of harmony into life. It allowed a person to achieve an equilibrium in the face of an uncertain world.

Plutarch also accepted a woman who, aside from marriage, followed philosophy. In an essay entitled "Dinner of Seven Wise Men," the female philosopher Eumetis entertained herself by asking riddles of the other guests. Later, the specific role of her riddle-making was considered:

> She uses these [riddles] like dice as a means of occasional amusement; and risks an encounter with all comers. But she is also possessed of a wonderful sense, a statesman's mind, and an admirable character, and she has influence with her father so that his government of the citizens has become milder and more popular.[281]

Plutarch's consideration of female philosophers has revealed his admiration for the Pythagorean Theano, his belief that women ought to study mathematics, and his recognition that a philosophical mind can lead to the development of a good character. He wanted women to learn from Plato so that they could achieve a full human development. Plutarch never developed the metaphysical foundation for this theory, namely that reincarnation demanded equality of woman and man on the level of the soul. However, his philosophy appeared to be in accord with this framework for sex unity, as an implicit assumption.

Plutarch's use of sex polarity for the theory of generation, which appears to be taken directly from Aristotle, did not interfere with his basic sex unity. The probable explanation for this lack of conflict rests in the devaluation of materiality which is common to theories of reincarnation. The passivity and weakness of woman's identity as a material existent was an unimportant aspect of her identity. The material world was something that ought to be conquered; sex polarity, as evidenced in the material condition of woman's incarnation, therefore, was also something to be overcome. For Plutarch, Platonic sex unity was the correct theory of the concept of woman in relation to man. Plutarch's role in the Aristotelian Revolution was to provide a simultaneous transmission and devaluation of Aristotelian sex polarity.

PLOTINUS (AD 205–270)

Educated in the Greek philosophical tradition in Alexandria, Plotinus incorporated much of Plato's thought into his philosophy. He made extensive use of the dialogues of Plato that were related to the concept of woman, namely the *Republic, Laws, Timaeus,* and *Symposium.*[282] While Plotinus is most often associated with the revival of Platonic philosophy, Aristotle also deeply influenced his system of thought. This fact was noted by Porphyry, his most important disciple:

> His writings, however, are full of concealed Stoic and Peripatetic doctrines. Aristotle's *Metaphysics* in particular is concentrated in them.[283]

Plotinus opened a school of philosophy in Rome in 244. Since he significantly influenced later philosophic thought, it is important to consider his views on the concept of woman.

Plotinus qualified Plato's metaphor of the receptacle as a totally passive cosmic mother and instead followed an Aristotelian line of argument that the mother contributed informed matter to the child. Therefore, the metaphysical category of matter could not be compared to a mother in all of her functions. Plotinus criticized Plato's passive characterization of cosmic mothering when, in the *Enneads*, he stated:

> But those people seem to call it "mother" who claim that the mother holds the position of matter in respect to her children, in that she only receives (the seed) and contributes nothing to the children. . . . But if the mother does contribute something to the child, it is not insofar as she is matter, but because she is also form, for only form can produce offspring, but the other nature is sterile.[284]

Plotinus saved Plato's cosmic association of the concept of woman with matter by arguing that this analogy was correct in some, but not all respects:

> For when they make matter the mother of all things, they apply this title to it taking it in the sense of the principle which has the function of substrate; they give it this name in order to declare what they wish, not wishing to make matter in every way exactly like the mother; . . . they show . . . that matter is sterile and not in every way female but only female as far as receiving goes, but no longer when it comes to generator.[285]

For Plotinus, as for Plutarch before him, the female principle was one of passive receptivity, while the mothering principle contained both this female principle and an active generating principle. However, even though Plotinus argued that the Platonic metaphor of mother as cosmic receptacle was limited in its application, he frequently used the association of mother with matter. In a passage that referred to Plato's description of the mother of love as poverty, Plotinus stated:

> But his Mother is Poverty, because aspiration belongs to that which is in need; and Poverty is matter; because matter too is in every way in need.[286]

In another passage, Plotinus reflected on the birth of Athena from Zeus's head: "She is a separate reality and a substance without part in matter—for which they spoke of her . . . that she was "motherless."[287]

The lack of a mother for Athena was reflected in her lack of matter. Even when Plotinus attempted to describe the philosophical relation of form and matter, he drew upon the connection between mother and matter: "The forms which enter into matter as their 'mother' do it no wrong, nor again do they do it any good."[288]

This double movement of Plotinus's acceptance and rejection of Plato's cosmic identification of mother with passive matter makes it difficult to assess his concept of woman. Is it to be limited to passive receptivity or to be expanded to include an active dimension as well? It appears that Plotinus used the passive aspect of woman to refer primarily to her reception of the male sexual organ and of male seed. These aspects of her identity were anatomical in nature. At the same time, he implied that woman's contribution to generation—her material contribution—had an animated quality. The material that women provided was a specific kind of material, having a nature that allowed it to be developed into a child. Woman's menstrual fluid could not then be identified with passive matter that had no identity at all; it had a formal nature.

While Plotinus did not leave any writings on the respective contributions of mother and father to generation, it appears that he gave the father a more active role.

> And the cause of the child is the father, and perhaps some external influences coming from various sources which cooperate towards the production of the child.[289]

This passage indicates that Plotinus accepted Plutarch's and Aristotle's theory of human generation. The father was the active cause of generation, the female the passive contributor, although the female provided a specific, or animated material. If this interpretation is correct, the father, but not the mother, provided seed to the fetus.

Aristotle had argued that woman was unable to provide seed to generation because she lacked something that was present in the male. In the following passage, Plotinus connected this concept of lack to matter, woman, and evil. Woman was compared to a field sown by the seed of man:

> It keeps it in being; for it brings what it naturally is to actuality and perfection, like the unsown field when it is sown, and as when the female conceives by the male, and does not lose its femaleness but becomes still more female, and that is, becomes more what it is. Is matter, then, also evil because it participates in good? Rather, because it lacks it; for this means that it does not have it.[290]

Matter, woman and evil were characterized as privation. Aristotle had previously linked matter to the concept of woman. Plotinus was the first philosopher to emphasize the connection of matter with evil. He repeated this view frequently in the *Enneads*: "When something is absolutely deficient—and this is matter—this is essential evil without any share of good."[291] This evil in matter became the inheritance of the body in relation to the soul: "The nature of the body, insofar as it participates in matter, will be an evil."[292]

How did Plotinus's devaluation of matter affect his concept of woman? There is, of course, an effect by association. The female was related to matter in a specific way, in her anatomical nature as recipient of the male anatomy and seed. Plotinus probably believed, along with Aristotle, that the woman's contribution to generation contained no seed, even though her material had some formal nature. Since seed, like form, was an activating entity, woman's lack of seed further associated her with matter. Since Plotinus also maintained that matter was evil in relation to form, by association, the concept of woman became related to evil. In this way, neo-Platonism, with its devaluation of materiality, also included a devaluation of woman.

At the same time, however, Plotinus believed, along with Plato and Plutarch, that the person was primarily characterized as a soul:

> Man (*anthropos*), and especially the good man, is not the composite of soul and body; separation from the body and despising of its so-called goods make this plain.[293]

The person was defined by a relation to soul:

> The beast is the body which has been given life. But the true man (*anthropos*) is different, clear of these affections; he has the virtues which belong to the sphere of intellect and have their seat actually in the separate soul, separate and separable even while it is still here below.[294]

It would follow, then, that the difference between woman and man, as a difference in body, was not part of the true identity of the person.

Did Plotinus accept Plato's theory in the *Timaeus* that woman was an inferior kind of incarnation to man? In one passage, he argued that the position of persons in this life was a direct consequence of the quality of their previous lives:

> The inferior became inferior from its beginning, and is what it became, inferior by its nature, and, if it suffers the consequences of its inferiority, it suffers what it deserves. And one must carry back the reckoning to what happened in previous lives, because what happens afterwards depends on that too.[295]

It would appear from this passage that Plotinus maintained that incarnation as a woman was the result of some imperfection in a past life. However, he made no specific mention of women in this context.[296] Therefore, it is not certain that he viewed the female incarnation as inferior to that of the male.

In any event, Plotinus believed that women ought to strive for full personal development as philosophers. While Plotinus left no specific arguments to defend this view, Porphyry attested to the presence of female Plotinian disciples:

> There were women, too, who were greatly devoted to him: Gemina, in whose house he lived, and her daughter, Gemina, who had the same name as her mother, and Amphicle, who became the wife of Aiston, son of Iamblichus, all of whom had a great devotion to Philosophy.[297]

The sex-unity framework, which argued that there were no significant differences between the sexes, contained a consistent openness to female philosophers.

Plotinus developed the conclusions of sex unity even further than Plato. His devaluation of the material world allowed him to reject any polarity of female and male that might emerge through a consideration of the relation of matter to form. On the level of soul, all sex identity disappeared. Plotinus believed that in the intellectual world, souls that had been differentiated through their relation to matter were eventually united with the One.[298] Here, all individuality ceased; not only did male and female identity vanish, but also the difference between one soul and another. All differentiation was thought to be the result of matter; and matter was evil. Therefore, all differentiation had to disappear in the union with the One, as the Good. The equality of persons, which was a positive aspect of sex unity, was then joined by a complete loss of differentiation. Plotinus is important to the concept of woman because he so clearly developed the ultimate consequences of the sex-unity position.

PORPHYRY AND MARCELLA (AD 233–305)

Porphyry followed the pattern of many of the neo-Platonists; he studied philosophy in Athens and later went to Rome, when he was about thirty. During this period he studied for six years with Plotinus.[299] After Plotinus's death, Porphyry took over leadership of the neo-Platonic school in Rome; he edited his master's *Enneads* and wrote an introduction to Plotinus's life. In this context it is significant that Porphyry went far beyond his teacher in developing a consistent theory about the concept of woman in relation to man. In fact, Porphyry is the first philosopher to develop a completely consistent philosophy of sex unity. He understood the logical consequences of the basic premises of neo-Platonism for sex identity.

Porphyry left writings that covered all four categories of the concept of woman in relation to man. The following chart summarizes his theory of sex unity:

	Man		**Woman**
Opposites	true identity is soul		true identity is soul
		Same	
Generation	provides vegetative power in seed		provides vegetative power in blood
		Same	
Wisdom	become a philosopher		become a philosopher
		Same	
Virtue	become good		become good
		Same	

Porphyry wrote a complete text on embryology entitled *Pros Gauron*.[300] In this work, the neo-Platonist developed a theory of the equal contribution of mother and father to generation. This shift in neo-Platonism is significant in view of the fact that Plutarch had earlier supported Aristotle's theory that the female did not provide any active contribution to generation and Plotinus's theory that woman provided only an informed material to generation.

In *Pros Gauron*, Porphyry argued that the mother and father both brought a formal cause to the embryo:

> As long as the sperm is in the father, it is governed by the vegetative power of the father and by his superior soul, which combines with the vegetative power for the production of the result. When, leaving the father, the sperm has been injected into the mother, the creative natural principle associates itself with the vegetative power of the mother and her soul.[301]

Porphyry did not mention the presence of the female seed as such. He appeared to think that the mother's formal contribution came through the blood. However, he was clear in his view that the mother was not simply a passive contributor to the process.

> Even without the aid of Plato, it is necessary to examine the phenomenon in its same reality, and to demand, in a nonsuperficial way, if it is true that all generation of embryos resemble, as much as it is possible, that of plants, the father letting fall the seed, the mother receiving it to make it grow, not only like the earth, to give nourishment, nor in the same manner that new borns simply procure milk, but in a manner somewhat analogous to that which happens to grafted . . . plants: for there is in the womb a power united to the sperm.[302]

The mother, like the trunk of a living tree, provided the living force to the fetus.

Porphyry also believed, as Pliny the Elder had previously claimed, that the mother was able, through the force of her mind, to influence the physical nature of the fetus.

> The embryo forms images and opinions in communion with the mother as it participates in the imaginative and opinioning soul. For it is universally recognized that numerous animals and certainly also some women give birth to products exactly resembling models of the same kind which, during a sudden fit, they have welcomed the figures in their imagination.[303]

The contribution of the mother, then, was as active as the initial contribution of the father.

Porphyry's primary goal in the *Pros Gauron* was to consider the origin and moment of entry of the rational soul into the fetus. Porphyry differentiated between the vegetative soul that originally came from the father, the vegetative soul of the mother, and the rational soul that came from outside either parent. He argued that while the vegetative soul of the fetus was in the father's sperm, it was piloted by the father's soul; while it was in the uterus of the mother it was piloted by the mother's soul; when it issued forth from the mother, it functioned with its own pilot.

> When finally the sperm is no longer dependent on maternal governance, the mother no longer protects the being which, at its separation, breaks the mixture (of souls of the mother and fetus), and the natural creative principle also, by a decree of nature, passes from darkness to light, from a milieu of water and blood where it remained in an envelope (the body) which rests in the air. Then, at this new moment, it receives suddenly from outside its pilot, which

> finds itself there by the providence of the regulating cause of the universe, which would never permit the vegetative soul to be deprived of a pilot in the case of living beings.[304]

Despite the indication in the above passage that the moment of reception of the rational soul was at the birth of the child, Porphyry stated several times that it is not possible to know when it actually occurs:

> Let us admit, yes, the incertitude of the precise moment in time, that moreover it is neither the father nor the mother who delivers the soul. . . . For evidently, if the soul does not come from the parents, it comes from outside. Is it then at the injection of the sperm, or at the configuration of the embryo, or at the first instant of local movement in the embryo, or when at the issue of pain, the child presents itself? All of this, as you see, rests subject to doubt.[305]

Although Porphyry left open the question of when the rational soul was infused into the fetus, he stated that once the child was born, this rational soul took over the function of directing the vegetative soul.

The mother and father were equal contributors to the fetus. They both provided the guiding principle of the vegetative soul while the fetus developed; the father first, and then the mother. The imbalance that had been present in Aristotle's theory, and that had been perpetuated by the neo-Platonists Plutarch and Plotinus, as well as by the Stoic Galen, was corrected by Porphyry. Man and woman equally provided the guidance of the vegetative soul; the rational soul came through reincarnation, that is, from outside either parent.

> For, just as physical resemblances reveal that the child has taken from his parents something of their bodies, so also is it necessary that spiritual resemblances also indicate the original source from which the soul has been taken.[306]

The rational soul, as an incorporeal entity, had to have something incorporeal as its source. Porphyry concluded:

> We will show that it is not possible that the animation had taken place from a part of the father or a part of the mother, but that it was made only from outside, in a way that, even in this case, the Platonic doctrine of the entry of the soul, is not rejected as false.[307]

The reincarnated soul also survived bodily death.[308]

Porphyry recognized that a theory of sex identity based on a metaphysics of reincarnation of the soul as neither male nor female had consequences for a theory of embryology. Porphyry ridiculed earlier theories that described a different time of entry of the soul for females or males.

> If one places the entry of the soul at the moment of the first formation of the embryo, the boy was differentiated at the end of thirty days, the girl at the end of forty-two days, according to Hippocrates. If one assigns the entry at the

> moment when the embryo has begun to move; at the exact time, Hippocrates says, 'When the extremities of the little body are divided exteriorly and the fingernails and hair have taken root, then the infant begins to move: the time at this point is for the boy, three months, for the girl four.'
>
> But these are pure fables.[309]

Porphyry did not differentiate between the moment of entry of the rational soul for females or males. Since, for him, the soul had no sex, it followed that the sex of the fetus was a development of the vegetative rather than of the rational soul.

Porphyry argued that women and men ought to seek full personal development. To be good parents demanded the training of the soul as well as the body, of women as well as of men.

> Those who are destined to create the best, men and women ought to exercise themselves towards virtue, and not, as is done ordinarily to leave themselves to exercises of the body.[310]

Therefore, even though Porphyry believed in the equality of woman's and man's contribution to generation, he nonetheless emphasized the importance of their relationship to soul. The person was more properly thought of as a soul entrapped in a body.

In a letter discovered in Milan in 1816, and subsequently published under the title *The Philosopher to His Wife Marcella*, Porphyry developed the specific connection between his theory of reincarnation and the concept of woman as equal to man.[311] Porphyry described the relation of soul to body:

> What was it then that we learnt from those men who possess the clearest knowledge to be found among mortals? Was it not this—that I am in reality not this person who can be touched or perceived by any of the senses, but that which is farthest removed from the body, the colorless and formless essence which can by no means be touched by the hands, but is grasped by the mind alone.[312]

The soul, existing prior to the body, fell into an earthly existence:

> As the outer covering grows with the child, and the stalk with the corn, yet, when they come to maturity, both are cast away, thus to the body which is fastened to the soul at birth is not part of the man. But as the outer covering was formed along with the child that it may come to being in the womb, so likewise the body was yoked to the man that he may come to being on earth.[313]

The soul's descent to earth was then used as a justification for a subsequent struggle for its being released from the body once again.

In this letter to Marcella, Porphyry counselled his wife to reflect on the theory of reincarnation in terms of her own identity as a woman:

> For we are bound in the chains that nature has cast around us, by the belly, the throat and the other parts of the body, and by the use of these and the pleasant sensations that arise therefrom and the fears they occasion. But if we

> rise superior to their witchcraft, and avoid the snares laid by them, we have led our captor captive. Neither trouble thyself much whether thou be male or female in body, nor look on thyself as a woman, for I did not approach thee as such.[314]

Porphyry asked Marcella to achieve a freedom from her body by ignoring her female sex, and to concentrate instead on the power of her soul to rule over the material dimension of her existence. In this way, the captor, body, would become the captive of the soul.

Porphyry's letter continued with a statement implying that even with the equal nature of woman and man as persons, there was a kind of inferiority of woman on the material level: "Flee all that is womanish in thy soul, as though thou hadst a man's body about thee."[315] Porphyry may have been using *womanish* to imply a kind of weakness in relation to a manly strength of soul in this passage. He frequently stated that the struggle for wisdom is a difficult task that demands great strength of character:

> It has seemed to men of wisdom that labors conduce to virtue more than do pleasures. And to toil is better for man, aye, and for woman too, than to let the soul be puffed up by pleasure.[316]

Porphyry believed that Marcella was equal to the task:

> Now seeing thou art beset in a contest, attended with much wrestling and labor, I earnestly beg thee to keep firm hold upon philosophy, the only sure refuge, and not to yield more than is fitting to the perplexities caused by my absence.[317]

He considered philosophy to be Marcella's "proper mode of life": "I recalled thee also to thy proper mode of life, and gave thee a share in philosophy, pointing out to thee a doctrine that should guide thy life."[318] It would follow from these passages that even though Porphyry may have held to a residue of the theory that woman was a weaker existent than man, she ought to strive to overcome this deficiency by the careful study and practice of philosophy.

Porphyry's relation to Marcella developed into marriage after she had been widowed. In this letter, Porphyry stated that in addition to wanting to marry Marcella to protect her and to propitiate the gods of generation, he wanted a partnership with her as a philosopher: "Another worthier reason, in no wise resembling that commonplace one, was that I admired thee because thy disposition was suited to true philosophy."[319] Porphyry's openness with Marcella, and desire for an honest and profound relationship was quite extraordinary.

> I should deem it a shame to equivocate to thee, or conceal aught of mine from thee, or to withhold from thee (who honorest truth above all things, and therefore didst deem our marriage a gift from Heaven) a truthful relation from beginning to end of all I have done with respect to and during our union.[320]

Porphyry's respect for his wife and for her philosophical abilities was the ultimate fulfillment of his sex-unity theory. Woman and man, as equal partners in the world, would work together to release their souls from the material world.

Porphyry served as the meeting point for many different aspects of the sex-unity theory. In addition to developing a sex-unity explanation for generation and the consequences of this theory for woman and man's relation to wisdom and virtue, he was the first philosopher to give evidence of the specific connection between sex unity and the sex-neutrality dimension of Aristotle's theory of logic. Porphyry wrote a major commentary on Aristotle's categories entitled the *Isagoge*. This text was later joined to the Latin translations of Aristotle's original text and became an integral part of Aristotle's *Organon* in medieval philosophy.[321] The *Isagoge* gave a summarized introduction to the concepts of genus, species, differentia, property, and accident. For the definition of human being, Porphyry adopted Aristotle's view that *man* was a species, *animal* a genus, and *rational* a property.[322] The species man could then be defined as a rational animal.

One of the consequences of Porphyry's promotion of Aristotelian logic was that the search for definitions in philosophy became focused entirely upon species and genus. Since women and men were members of the same species and genus, the question of the distinctions between woman and man were pushed outside the arena of philosophical enquiry. Porphyry considered three general ways in which things could differ from one another. Common difference was exemplified by the way in which Socrates differed from Plato, or a man from himself as a child. Here the difference focused on two diverse things of the same nature. Things might also differ properly, as between color or degree of crookedness. He called this difference an "inseparable accident." Finally, things might also differ most properly:

> Moreover, one is most properly said to differ from another, when it varies by specific difference, as man differs from horse by specific difference, i.e., by the quality of the rational.[323]

Porphyry did not ask in which way woman differed from man; clearly the difference could not be "most properly," as they shared the same form. It seems unlikely that he considered their difference as a common one, since this seems to imply a sameness of type between two members of the same sex, although perhaps at different ages. A difference in matter distinguished individuals of the same type. The alternative would be a difference through "inseparable accident," by which a woman would differ from a man through an accident of birth. However, Porphyry did not mention women and men in this context; so it is difficult to know whether he would classify their differences in this way.

It is likely that Porphyry did not consider the distinction between woman and man to be very important, since he inherited his teacher Plotinus's, metaphysical framework for personal identity. The true nature of the person was found in the life of the highest part of the soul. The soul was neither male nor female; it passed through cycles of rebirth. The goal of life was to escape the state and nature of the body. It would follow from this that women and men should disregard their differences as much as possible. The sex-unity theory, with its metaphysical roots in reincarnation, received, through Porphyry, the support of Aristotelian logic.

HYPATIA (AD 370–415)

The Alexandrian school of philosophy first formed for the study of the work of Ptolemy (first century AD), later became one of the centres for the study of neo-Platonism.

One historian has claimed that the school reached the height of its development under the direction of the female philosopher Hypatia.[324] Although all of Hypatia's writings have been lost, it is known that she helped in a revision of the works of Ptolemy, wrote a commentary on Apollonius's *Conics II*, and wrote another commentary on Diophantus's *Arithmetica*.[325] Her learning was described by Socrates, the ecclesiastical historian: "She arrived at such a pitch of learning, as very far to exceed all the philosophers of her time."[326] Her learning covered not only mathematics, but "all other parts of philosophy."[327]

Most significantly, Hypatia not only studied and understood philosophy, she also taught it publicly.

> Hypatia was by way of excellence named *The Philosopher*, altogether as much on account of her profound knowledge, as for her public profession of teaching. Nor was any Professor more admired by the world, or more dear to his own scholars. Hers were as remarkable as numerous.[328]

The only female philosophers who had assumed a public teaching role prior to Hypatia were the Pythagoreans and Aspasia; they primarily taught women. Hypatia was the first female philosopher to become a renowned teacher of men. She taught not only young students, but also the leading men of Alexandria.

> She was held an oracle for her wisdom, which made her be consulted by the magistrates in all important cases; and this frequently drew her among the greatest concourse of men, without the least censure of her manners.[329]

Hypatia not only gave advice as an oracle; she was given a chair of philosophy at the Alexandrian school, indicating that she understood philosophy well enough to teach its method and content. She became the supreme example of a female philosopher within the Platonic tradition of sex unity.

Hypatia's life ended abruptly with her murder. The circumstances surrounding her death were complex. She was killed in a cycle of retributory conflicts between Christians and non-Christians. Orestes, the governor of Alexandria, respected and regularly consulted Hypatia. A group of Christian monks attacked Orestes, claiming that he was not really a Christian. In retaliation, Orestes arranged for some citizens to capture, torture, and put a monk to death. The Christian Bishop, Cyril, secretly arranged for Hypatia to be murdered as retaliation against Orestes. The events leading to her death were described as follows:

> Watching their opportunity when she was returning home from some place, they dragged her out of her chair; hurried her to the church called Caesar's, and stripping her naked, they killed her with tiles. Then they tore her to pieces, and carrying her limbs to a place called Cinaron, there they burnt them to ashes.[330]

It is possible to understand Hypatia's death as one event in a series of arbitrary tortures and murders. There is also some evidence that Hypatia was killed because she was a brilliant and powerful pagan philosopher. To find these extraordinary gifts in a woman may have caused certain men to want her destruction. She may have been killed out of envy.

> Damascius, who is the other contemporary witness of her murder, I meant besides Socrates, positively affirms that Cyril vowed Hypatia's destruction, whom he bitterly envied; and Suidas, who writes the same thing, says, that this envy was caused by her extraordinary wisdom and skill in astronomy: as Hesychius, when he mentions her limbs being carried all over the city in triumph writes that this befell her on the score of her extraordinary wisdom and especially her skill in astronomy.[331]

The death of Socrates attests to a tradition of the killing of philosophers. What is particularly significant about Hypatia's murder was the brutality with which it was committed. The severing of her body and the subsequent display of the limbs, implied a more destructive intent than simple death. It is possible that this derived in part from envy of her identity as a woman teaching philosophy to men.

It is important to consider the relation of Hypatia to Aristotle. It has been mentioned that the neo-Platonist Porphyry wrote a summary of Aristotle's *Categories*. There is some further indication that the Alexandrian school studied Aristotle's logic through Porphyry's *Isagoge*; Proclus (AD 410–485) is reputed to have studied this subject at Alexandria in the period immediately following Hypatia's death, before moving to the Athenian school.[332] The neo-Platonists' interest in Aristotle's logic would further confirm the suggestion that there is a natural connection between the sex-unity position and sex neutrality. In both theories, the equality and non-differentiation of the sexes was accepted. Certainly the extant titles of Hypatia's works indicate a total position of sex neutrality; they contain no reference to the philosophy of woman and man.

After Hypatia's death, the Alexandrian school of neo-Platonism slowly declined, while the Athenian school continued to flourish. Then, in AD 529, Emperor Justinian closed all the non-Christian schools of philosophy. At this time, the neo-Platonists moved to Syria, taking copies of some of Aristotle's and Plato's writings. Continuing the practice of writing commentaries on Aristotle's works, these exiles kept alive the seeds of Aristotle's thought. Neo-Platonism prepared the ground that in later centuries would flower into a reawakening of Aristotelianism. Finally, the Syrian commentaries, translated first into Arabic and then into Latin, brought the whole corpus of Aristotelian thought into western Europe in the thirteenth century.

For the Christian west, Hypatia's reputation faded, until a French translation of a commentary on the work of Ptolemy by her father, Theano, was made in the early nineteenth century.[333] Soon after, there was a study of Hypatia by Wolfgang Meyer, and an historical novel about her life by Charles Kingsley.[334] By the early twentieth century, Hypatia was once more a symbol of the wise woman.[335] (Recently, interest in women's history has led to the founding of a journal of philosophy and women's studies entitled *Hypatia*.)[336]

In conclusion, the neo-Platonists have given evidence of a slow progression in the development of a theory of sex identity. Beginning with Plutarch and Plotinus, we found an inconsistency with an adoption of sex-polarity theory in the categories of opposites and, at the same time, an adoption of a sex-unity theory in the categories of wisdom and virtue. Porphyry next brought about a total consistency when he defended sex unity across all four categories of the concept of woman in relation to man. Finally, Hypatia moved to a sex-neutrality theory in her lack of consideration of the question of sex identity.

Given the neo-Platonic devaluation of the body and fundamental identification of personal identity with the sexless, independently existing soul, it is not surprising that differences between the sexes would be considered philosophically insignificant and eventually ignored altogether.

SEX UNITY, SEX POLARITY, AND SEX COMPLEMENTARITY COMBINED IN EARLY CHRISTIAN PHILOSOPHY

When Christian philosophy is compared with Stoicism or neo-Platonism, one striking difference immediately appears. A third theory of sex identity or sex complementarity appears in western thought through the philosophy of St. Augustine. The re-entry of this theory of the equality and differentiation of the sexes occurred through the Christian belief in the resurrection of the body. Woman and man were thought to be eternally differentiated through the revelation by Christ that not only the soul, but the body in union with the soul constituted the essential identity of the person. This article of faith, in the specific areas of the concept of woman in relation to man, had serious consequences for philosophy.

At the same time that sex complementarity received a new justification through a belief in resurrection, early Christian thought was also formed by the theories of sex unity and sex polarity as previously articulated by Greek and Roman philosophers. This diversity of sources for the concept of *person* resulted in a period of tremendous tension in the concept of woman. None of the early Christian philosophers satisfactorily resolved this tension.

St. Augustine more fully represents the difficulties presented by the intersection of conflicting premises for sex unity, sex polarity, and sex complementarity. In fact, he is fascinating precisely because he attempts simultaneously to hold on to all three theories of sex identity. Augustine therefore stands as a meeting point of the different traditions, supporting sex polarity and sex unity while he begins a new impulse towards a theory of sex complementarity. His inconsistency, therefore, marks a step forward in the history of the concept of woman in relation to man, although he was unable to carry sex complementarity through to its inevitable consequence. Augustine's arguments in support of sex complementarity occurred primarily in the areas of opposites and generation, although in general his philosophy supports this view in limited ways in other categories as well.

This early period of Christian philosophy also gave evidence of a new form of the complementarity of women and men in the category of wisdom. This occurred in the development of the cult around St. Catherine of Alexandria as patron saint for philosophers, and in the female personification of Lady Philosophy in Boethius's *The Consolation of Philosophy*. In both these examples, the height of wisdom was expressed by a woman in dialogue with men.

At the same time, Aristotelian philosophy began its influx into Europe through the translation of his logical writings by Boethius. The logic of Aristotle suggested a sex-neutrality theory of sex identity in that it ignored sexual differentiation through its preoccupation with universal categories of species and genus. The sex-polarity arguments of Aristotle, which were found in other areas of his philosophy, were not translated and therefore did not influence the development of the concept of woman in relation to man for this period of philosophy (up to thirteen hundred years after his death).

Instead, Platonic influences were stronger, and the tendency towards a sex-unity theory therefore continued to reappear. John Scotus Erigena stands as a witness to this development in his work at the end of this early period of Christian philosophy. His affirmation of the sex-unity theory of the concept of woman in relation to man indicates that the Aristotelian Revolution had not yet occurred.

The particular theories of sex identity suggested by the early Christian philosophers is recorded in the following chart.

	Opposites	Generation	Wisdom	Virtue
Catherine of Alexandria			sex complementarity	
Augustine	sex complementarity sex unity sex polarity	sex complementarity sex unity sex polarity	sex complementarity sex unity sex polarity	sex complementarity sex unity sex polarity
Boethius			sex complementarity sex neutrality	
John Scotus Erigena	sex unity	sex unity	sex unity sex polarity	sex unity

As is evident from this chart, this period of early Christian philosophy did not achieve any consistency on the question of sex identity. Although there were some impulses towards a new philosophy of sex complementarity, the influences supporting sex unity and sex polarity continued to resurface.

ST. CATHERINE OF ALEXANDRIA (AD ?–307)

The city of Alexandria is believed to have produced two female martyrs within a period of one hundred years. According to tradition, a young Christian female philosopher named Catherine was killed by Emperor Maximillian sixty-three years before the birth of Hypatia. This story is difficult to verify and therefore has frequently been doubted. Consequently, the figure of St. Catherine serves primarily as a symbolic reference to medieval Catholic thought. St. Catherine of Alexandria came to represent the ideal wise woman, she was the female personification of a Christian philosopher. After the ninth century, Catherine of Alexandria became one of the most popular saints of medieval Europe; she became known as the patroness of female scholars and of all Christian philosophers. It is therefore important to examine the purported accounts of her life.

The first of these was recorded by Emperor Basil the First in the *Monologium Basilianum* in 866, over five hundred years after her death. Basil's account stated:

> The martyr Aikaterina was the daughter of a rich and noble chieftain of Alexandria. She was very beautiful, and highly talented, she devoted herself to Grecian literature, and to the study of the languages of all nations, and so became wise and learned.[337]

Basil's simple description was embellished by many writers in later centuries. One such development was recorded in an anonymous manuscript that describes her choice of the wisdom of Christ over the wisdom of the Greek philosophers.

> Such is all that you think today to strive against me with: Homer's reasonings, and Aristotle's tricks; Esculapius' crafts, and Galen's grips (= art); Philistio's arguments, and Plato's books; and all these writer's writings that you lean upon. Though I am well instructed in all these from such (an) early (age), that I never found many equal to me, yet, because they are full of vain-glory, and void of that blessed and life-giving doctrine, I now utterly forsake them, and give them all up, and say that I neither comprehend nor know any power but of one alone, who is the true understanding and wisdom and the eternal salvation to those that rightly believe in him, that is Jesus Christ.[338]

St. Catherine was depicted as knowing all the riches of Greek philosophical wisdom. However, instead of finding fulfillment in philosophy alone, she chose to reject it for the wisdom of faith.

The death of St. Catherine came about as a result of political events in Alexandria. Basil described these as follows:

> It happened that the Greeks held a festival in honor of their idols; and seeing the slaughter of the animals, she was so greatly moved that she went to the King Maximinus and expostulated with him in these words: 'Why have you left the living God to worship lifeless idols?' But the emperor caused her to be thrown in prison, and to be punished severely. He then ordered fifty orators to be brought, and bade them to reason with Aikaterina, and confute her. The orators, however, when they saw themselves vanquished, received baptism, and were burnt immediately. She, on the contrary, was beheaded.[339]

In St. Catherine's persecution, the pagans killed a Christian female philosopher; whereas in Hypatia's persecution, the Christians killed a pagan female philosopher. Furthermore, just as Hypatia had taught philosophy to Alexandrian men, so St. Catherine was reputed to have been wiser than the fifty best male philosophers in Alexandria. In the following embellished account, one of the philosophers described Catherine's abilities to the emperor:

> One thing I would like you to know, that we have the testimony of all the wise that are in the East, that never, until this day, have we anywhere found anyone so deep learned that he dared to dispute with us; . . . but of this maiden's reasoning there is nothing to be despised; for I shall speak the truth, in her reasons no (mere) man [*animalis homos loquitur*].[340]

The emperor, according to the accounts, was not impressed. He at first tried to torture and kill her on a wheel with spikes, but a flash of lightning broke the wheel. Finally, St. Catherine was beheaded with a sword.

Again, as with Hypatia, the death of St. Catherine could be explained as the result of political struggles between Christians and non-Christians. In addition, the legends surrounding her life indicate that she converted fifty male philosophers to her views. This

Catherine of Alexandria, patron saint of Christian philosophers.

information suggests that one of her greatest crimes may have been to teach men philosophy. If so, then St. Catherine was not merely one of many Christians caught in persecutions by Maximinus. Her violent death could have been a further indication that it was dangerous to be a female philosopher.

The life and death of St. Catherine brings out an interesting aspect to the developing concept of woman; as a feminine personification of wisdom, she influenced the history of Europe for over a thousand years. Iconography pictured St. Catherine with the wheel, the symbol of her martyrdom; it presented a powerful image of the learned woman who died defending Christian philosophy. Christian philosophers prayed to her for guidance in their search for the truth, and young girls placed themselves under her protection as their patroness. St. Catherine was classified as one of the fourteen most helpful saints in heaven, and her feast day was celebrated with great festivity. She was credited with having helped shape the history of France by appearing to Joan of Arc several times during her efforts to lead France to a military victory over England.[341]

Devotion to St. Catherine began to fade in the eighteenth century, when the authenticity of sources describing her life were questioned. The influence of Hypatia and St. Catherine have followed intertwining patterns; during early medieval history, Hypatia was eclipsed by St. Catherine, as patron of Christian philosophy, while, in the last two centuries, St. Catherine has been eclipsed by Hypatia as a non-Christian philosopher.

There is one other important way in which Hypatia and St. Catherine can be compared. It has been stated that for the concept of woman, Hypatia fell within the sex-neutrality tradition. The cult of St. Catherine may be interpreted as a preparation for a sex-complementarity position. The legends of her life gave evidence of an emerging awareness of a simultaneous differentiation and equality of the sexes.

The most important element that Christianity brought to the consideration of the concept of woman and man was a belief in the resurrection of the body. This concept of an eternal existence in which women and men were differentiated by a glorified body would provide one of the strongest bases for the theory of sex complementarity. The belief in the resurrection of the body was the central mystery of Christ's life and death; it formed the core of Christian faith. While resurrection had its origin in faith and not reason, it had to influence subsequent Christian philosophy of the person. The philosopher had to interpret, through reason and the senses, the central concepts that this mystery of faith contained.

There is no record of statements by St. Catherine applying the concept of resurrection to the concept of woman in relation to man. However, there is one statement that indicates that St. Catherine consciously differentiated herself from man: "I thank you, Lord, that you have permitted me, and wanted me to be in the number of your women."[342] Here St. Catherine is identified as affirming herself as a woman. In popular tradition, she was represented as the bride of Christ. This corresponds to the image of wisdom as the bride of Solomon. In both cases, the male and female were differentiated and then joined in nuptual union in the search for truth. The Jewish and Christian philosophers here did not seek to overthrow the body, or to escape from its prison. Instead, they welcomed the material expression of personal identity and awaited its transformation and glorification. It would follow, then, that St. Catherine can be interpreted as rejecting the sex-unity theory of human identity.

The question of whether she also stood as an example of the rejection of sex polarity is equally speculative. However, there are certain clues to be considered. First, St. Catherine appeared not to have considered obedience to man as her specific virtue; she did not obey her emperor, or the male philosophers who were sent to convince her to give up her faith in Christ. She formulated her own philosophical and religious opinions and acted on them. St. Catherine was also willing to die for her beliefs; in this she gave evidence of a strength of character that rejected the weakness associated with being female. This capacity to rule and strength to act imply that she did not, as a woman, consider herself as inferior to man. Therefore, her legends reject sex polarity. It would follow that St. Catherine can be suggested as the first symbolic representative of the theory of sex complementarity in Christian philosophy.

ST. AUGUSTINE (AD 354–430)

St. Augustine stands as a watershed in the history of the concept of woman in relation to man, for he was caught between three different theories of sex identity. For this reason, he is an extremely fascinating contributor to the philosophy of woman and man. The theory of sex unity came to him through the Stoics, the neo-Platonists, and through one aspect of the writings of St. Paul. Augustine referred to the Platonists as those "whom we rightly prefer above all others."[343]

The theory of sex polarity came to this early Christian philosopher primarily through the writings of the Jewish philosopher Philo and through some of the early Church Fathers. St. Augustine had read Aristotle's *Categories*, but he was not impressed with Aristotelian logic. In the *Confessions*, he remarked, "What profit did this study bring me? None. In fact it made difficulties for me, because I thought that everything could be reduced to these ten categories."[344] While a philosophy of sex neutrality was suggested by the *Categories*, Aristotle's arguments for sex polarity probably did not reach Augustine, for he had difficulty reading Greek. After his conversion to Christianity, Augustine immersed himself in the writings of Jewish and Christian thinkers. As will be seen, the sex-polarity framework already contained in this tradition, as well as its conflicting unity tendencies, flowed directly into the philosopher's concept of woman.

More significant, however, is the fact that Augustine was also an original thinker, and his concept of woman gives evidence of a breakthrough in one area of thought. He recognized some of the new possibilities for a theory of sex complementarity derived from a religious belief in the resurrection of the body, as well as in the belief that woman and man were created as separate and equal before the Fall. From these two theological beliefs, Augustine derived the conclusion that women and men are eternally distinguished by sex and that neither sex is naturally superior to the other. He also realized that the theological foundation for sex complementarity had philosophical consequences for the concept of woman and man, and he argued directly against those who sought to defend a sex polarity or sex unity theory in a few specific areas of thought.

At the same time, however, St. Augustine was not able to take this religious belief in sex complementarity as a starting point for a complete philosophy of sex identity. Instead, he developed a fragmented view of human identity that led to a three-leveled concept of woman in relation to man. Generally speaking, St. Augustine divided sex identity in the following way:

1. A sex-complementarity theory of women and men in heaven in a spiritual existence.
2. A sex-unity theory for women and men in the world, when oriented in the highest part of the mind towards a spiritual existence.
3. A sex-polarity theory for men and women in the world, when oriented in body and mind towards a temporal existence.

If the philosopher's complex theory of sex identity is summarized in the chart covering the four categories of the concept of woman in relation to man, we would find the general outline given on the following page:

Opposites

The key to Augustine's theory of sex complementarity is his belief in the resurrection of the body. In the *City of God* he stated explicitly: "The saints will possess at resurrection those very bodies in which they toiled in this life."[345] This view of human identity as necessarily involving reference to the body led to a two-fold rejection of previous theories of sex identity. Against the sex-polarity theorists, Augustine argued that woman's body is just as perfect as man's, and women will therefore retain their bodies after the resurrection:

> There are some who think that in the resurrection all will be men, and that women will lose their sex. . . . For myself, I think that those others are more sensible who have no doubt that both sexes will remain in the resurrection.[346]

The basic claim of sex polarity, that man is naturally superior to woman, led to the logical conclusion that if in heaven all imperfections would cease, woman would be changed into a more perfect kind of human being, that is, into man. St. Augustine, in the *City of God*, clearly rejected this thesis:

> In the resurrection, the blemishes of the body will be gone, but the nature of the body will remain. And certainly, a woman's sex is her nature and no blemish; only in the resurrection there will be no conception or child-bearing associated with her nature.[347]

Therefore, women and men both are perfect in body, and through the body the two sexes are eternally differentiated. Sex complementarity is a necessary theological conclusion from a belief in the resurrection of male and female bodies.

The second line of argument springing from the belief in the resurrection was a rejection of the theory of reincarnation as held by the sex-unity theorists. In his early writings, such as the *Free Choice of the Will*, Augustine seemed undecided about reincarnation.[348] However, by the *City of God*, he clearly rejected the theory: "The fact is that souls do not pay the penalty in this way by returning once again to life."[349] For Augustine, human identity did not consist in the soul alone, it had to include reference to the body.

> The soul is not the entire man; it is the better part of him. Nor is the body the entire man; it is the lower part of him. Rather, it is the union of both parts to which the noun "man" (*hominis nomen*) is applied.[350]

Sex Complementarity
In heaven, in spiritual existence

	Man / Woman
Opposites	Equal and different in resurrection
Generation	Equal and different in first creation of potential
Wisdom	Equal and different in self-knowledge
Virtue	Male saints equal to and different from female saints

Sex Unity
Oriented towards spritual existence in world

	Man / Woman
Opposites	Both in image of God (no male or female)
Generation	Soul equal, created by God
Wisdom	Same = love of God
Virtue	Same = freedom of will; celibacy

Sex Polarity
Oriented towards temporal existence in world

	Man	**Woman**
Opposites	created in image of God	not created in image of God
Generation	woman inferior to man in second creation of actuality	helpmate to man
Wisdom	higher orientation of mind	lower orientation of mind
Virtue	rule	obey

For the sex-unity theorists, such as Plato or Porphyry, the belief that human identity consisted of a sexless soul, which could be born again in either a male or a female body, allowed for the defence of the fundamental equality of women and men. However, for Augustine, who insisted on the centrality of the body for sex identity, equality had to be based on a different foundation. The only other theorists who had insisted on the centrality of the body to sex identity, namely the Aristotelians, had slid into sex polarity. Therefore, the challenge for Augustine was to hold onto the differentiation of the sexes through an affirmation of the body while at the same time avoiding the devaluation of woman in relation to man. Augustine was successful only in his description of heaven. When he focused on the relation of woman and man on earth, he ended up fracturing the relation of the sexes as well as the internal dynamics of human identity itself. He accomplished this through his consideration of the meaning of woman and man as "created in the image of God."

Augustine, borrowing a phrase from St. Paul, concluded in *The Trinity* that in the highest part of the mind, when a woman or a man was contemplating God, sex became irrelevant:

> Who is it then, that would exclude women from this fellowship, since they are with us co-heirs of grace, and since the same Apostle says in another place: . . . There is neither male nor female. For you are all one in Christ Jesus. Have they believing women, therefore, lost their bodily sex? But because they are renewed there to the image of God, where there is no sex, man is made there in the image of God, where there is no sex, namely, in the spirit of his mind.[351]

For Augustine, sex unity was the appropriate theory for describing the identities of woman and man in the world when their minds are focused on the spiritual realm. He repeated this claim in the *Confessions*:

> You created man male and female, but in your spiritual grace, they are as one. Your grace no more discriminates between them according to their sex than it draws distinction between Jew and Greek or slave and freeman.[352]

The movement here is important, for Augustine could have argued against a sex-polarity background that had excluded women from public worship within the Jewish tradition, that women and men better reflect the image of God as distinct complements. Instead, he insists at this point that they equally reflect the image of God by transcending their sexual identity. In this way, Augustine moves towards a neo-Platonic understanding of human identity, or towards a theory of sex unity.

It is at this point that St. Augustine makes a further move in his argument, a move that initiates a theory of sex polarity for woman in relation to man in the temporal order. In *The Trinity*, the argument is set up by the claim that human nature is only in the image of God when it is contemplating God.

> As we said of the nature of the human mind that if as a whole it contemplates the truth, it is in the image of God; and when its functions are divided and something of it is diverted to the handling of temporal things, nevertheless that part which consults the truth is the image of God, but the other part, which is directed to the handling of inferior things, is not the image of God.[353]

The above passage would imply that both women and men, when engaged in temporal things, would not be, properly speaking, in the image of God. However, Augustine continues his argument, by using a technique popularized by Philo of Alexandria, namely the symbolic representation of a theory by the different sexes. He argues that woman may be used to symbolize the orientation towards temporal things and man the orientation towards spiritual things:

> Because she differs from man by her bodily sex, that part of the reason which is turned aside to regulate temporal things could be properly symbolized by her corporeal veil, so that the image of God does not remain except in that part of the mind of man in which it clings to the contemplation and consideration of the eternal reasons, which, as is evident, not only men but also women possess.[354]

This use of woman to symbolize the lower orientation of the mind led to some far-reaching consequences in Augustine's expressions of sex identity. He concluded that only man can properly speaking be described as being "in the image of God." This conclusion is expressed in *De Genesis ad Litteram*:

> Indeed, in the same way women are not excluded from this grace of renewal and of the resurrection, after the image of God—although, in their corporeal sex, it is figured otherwise, in the sense that it is said that man only is the image and glory of God.[355]

It is also repeated in *The Trinity*:

> The woman together with her husband is the image of God, so that the whole substance is one image. But when she is assigned as a helpmate, a function which pertains to her alone, then she is not the image of God, just as fully and completely as when he and the woman are joined together in one.[356]

The now infamous dictum of St. Augustine that "woman is not made in the image of God" must be understood as flowing from this rather peculiar fragmentation of human identity that he used to symbolize the different orientations of humanity towards spiritual or temporal life. As a consequence of his symbolic use of woman to represent the temporal orientation of human existence, Augustine fell into a sex polarity in which man was superior to woman because man could represent the image of God by himself while woman could not. In conclusion, then, from this consideration of his theory of opposites, we find Augustine caught between three conflicting theories of sex identity: sex complementarity in heaven; sex unity in the highest functions of the mind on earth; and sex polarity in the lower functions of the mind in relation to the body on earth. This pattern of conflict follows his theory of sex identity throughout the remaining three categories of the concept of woman in relation to man.

Generation

Following the pattern established in the analysis of the pre-Aristotelian philosophers, we will examine Augustine's theory of generation in three areas: cosmic generation, generation of the first parents, and continuity of generation.

On the level of cosmic generation, we have already seen a shift from the dynamic Earth Mother and Father Sky in Hesiod to the passive mother receptacle and active father-like Forms in the Platonic tradition. With Augustine, who carries from the Hebrew tradition the belief in God the Father Creator of earth, we find a further shift in the concept of cosmic generation. This shift occurs in two important ways: God is understood for the first time as being totally transcendent and immaterial, and God is understood as One.[357]

In the *Confessions*, Augustine describes his struggle to move from a belief in a pagan material god to an immaterial God: "I thought it outrageous to believe that you had the shape of a human body and were limited within the dimensions of limbs like our own."[358] Augustine also moved beyond the god of the pagan philosophers:

> But what is my God? I put my question to the earth. It answered, "I am not God,". . . I asked the sea and the chasms of the deep, . . . but they answered, "We are not your God.". . . I spoke to the winds that blow, and the whole air and all that lives, it replied, "Anaximenes is wrong I am not God." I asked the sky, the sun, the moon, the stars, but they told me, "Neither are we the God whom you seek,". . . and I said, "Since you are not my God, tell me about him. Tell me something of my God." Clear and loud they answered, "God is he who made us."[359]

St. Augustine came to an understanding of God as a wholly immaterial and transcendent creator of the universe. Finally, he understood this God to be best characterized as a Trinity: "Here, then, is the Trinity, my God, Father, Son, and Holy Ghost, the Creator of all creation."[360]

The Trinity that Augustine believed in, Father, Son, and Holy Spirit, raised certain questions for the philosopher concerning sex identity. In *The Trinity* he struggled with the question of whether God had any feminine nature; his questioning focused on whether the Holy Spirit could be female:

> For I omit such a thing as to regard the Holy Spirit as the Mother of the Son and the Spouse of the Father; for it will perhaps be answered that these things offend us in carnal matters by arousing thoughts of corporeal conception and birth.[361]

Once again, woman is associated with the corporeal orientation of life, for in this discussion Augustine feared that if he considered the Holy Spirit as female it would imply that sexual intercourse occurred within an immaterial God. It is likely that Augustine chose to reject all feminine association with the Divine precisely because of his determination to differentiate the Christian God from pagan gods, a differentiation that demanded a complete rejection of the materiality of God or of the immanence of God. Suggesting that the Trinity might include reference to female identity, and thereby implying the possibility of sexual intercourse, was for Augustine a danger that had plagued the pagans whose material deities were frequently involved in intercourse with both immortals and mortals. Consequently, he rejected the presence of all feminine aspects for the nature of the Divine. In addition, Augustine was also concerned with clarifying that the trinitarian notion of God did not fall into a polytheism, which was also common in pagan religions. Consequently, the exclusion of a female dimension of the Divine made it simpler to maintain that God is One, and male.

It should be noted in passing that Augustine did not develop a theology of Mary as a cosmic force in relation to God the Father. He simply referred to her as a model for the celibate life and for Christian virtue. It was not until St. Albert the Great that Mary began to emerge in her full role as a cosmic force.[362] Instead, Augustine developed the concept of Mother Church as a cosmic feminine complement to God; it was the development of the Jewish characterization of Israel as the Bride of Jahweh. In a letter to Laetus he wrote:

> Mother Church is also the mother of your mother. She begot you both in Christ, she formed you in her womb of the blood of martyrs, she brought you forth to everlasting light, she nourished you with the milk of faith.[363]

In addition, Augustine developed a theory of the earth as being like a mother, pregnant with the *"rationes seminales"* that was the first fruit of the primary act of creation. "For as mothers are pregnant with unborn offspring, so the world itself is pregnant with the causes of unborn things."[364] Augustine rejected the Manichean and neo-Platonic theses that matter was sterile or evil. Instead, he argued that matter was always informed and that it was good precisely because it had been created by God.

Out of this material of the original creation, Augustine described the generation of the first parents. He developed a two-phased process of creation. In the first phase, woman is created as inferior to man. Following the Eloist account in Genesis, in which God is described as having created man, as male and female, Augustine states in *De Genesis ad Litteram*:

> One could not say, indeed, that the male was made on the sixth day, the woman in the course of the following days, since it was said expressly that in this same sixth day God made them male and female and blessed them.[365]

Here we find a defence of sex complementarity in the first order of creation, that is, of a separation and equality of woman and man.

However, Augustine qualifies this view in his description of a second phase of generation of the first parents. In a continuation of the interpretation of Genesis, he argues that the first creation was merely a generation of potentiality, like the *rationes seminales*. In the second creation, taken from the Jewish account in Genesis, woman is described as being secondary in the order of creation to man:

> Formerly they were created in potency by the word of God, as a sort of germinative force buried in the world. . . . Next, they were created according to the operation proper to the time, through which God operated until now and through which it was suitable that, at the appropriate time Adam had been made out of the clay of the earth and his wife from the side of her husband.[366]

Augustine gives a further description of the process:

> They were not created differently later on, but the man was created always like himself, only in one way at first and another later on. One might ask: How were they made later on? I will answer: visibly, under the form that we know,

> even if they were not born of parents and Adam was taken from clay, Eve from his side. One might ask: And how were they made in the first creation? I will answer: invisibly, potentially, in their causes, just as are made things in the future which do not yet exist.[367]

Augustine's separation of the double-process of creation that exists first in a concrete potentiality, and second in actuality, sounds something like Philo's argument that in the first creation only the genus of the human species was produced, while actual women and men were produced in the second creation. The main difference between the two theories is found in the fact that while the first creation for Philo represented a sex-unity theory, that is, there was no distinction between male and female in the species, it represented a sex complementarity for St. Augustine because male and female were distinguished and the sexes considered as equal. For both Augustine and Philo, the second creation of actual woman and man, represented by the first parents—Adam and Eve—entailed a sex polarity.

Augustine draws out the implication of Eve's creation from the side of Adam when, in *The Trinity*, he asks:

> If the woman according to her own person completes the image of the Trinity why is the man called that image when she has been taken from his side?[368]

We return to the view that since woman was taken from man's side, she is not complete in her own identity, she cannot represent the image of God by herself; while man, the complete being, perfectly represents the image of God. Augustine concludes his interpretation of Genesis by arguing that woman's generation from the side of man explains her primary function in relation to man, namely, to be his helpmate in the generative process.

> If it is not to generate children that the woman was given to the man as a helpmate, in what could she be a help for him? Is it to work the earth with him? But there was no work yet that needed the help of somebody else, and if the need was there the help of another man would have been preferable. We can say the same of the good of the presence of another person is solitude weighted on him. To live and to talk to each other, how preferable is the companionship of two (male friends) than that of a man and a woman! . . . I do not see for what goal woman would have been given to man as a helpmate if not for generating children.[369]

Therefore, Augustine has returned to his symbolic association of woman with activity on the temporal order and, in particular, with generative activity. While man by himself represents the image of God, woman, as helpmate to man, does not represent that image, particularly in the generative activity of temporal life. Augustine has completely cut out the possibility of a theory of sex complementarity between woman and man on the level of companionship or of marital generation. Instead, he has offered a theory of the polarization of the sexes in the temporal world.

It is unfortunate that Augustine did not carry forward the implications of the sex complementarity that he had recognized in the theory of resurrection and in the description of the generation of the first parents in potentiality. In the *City of God*, he appeared to realize the necessary link between these theological concepts when he said, "God, then, who made us man and woman will raise us up as man and woman."[370] In this pronouncement, Augustine held the key to the theory of sex complementarity. However, as has been demonstrated, St. Augustine pulled back from the implications of this possibility when he described the function of woman and man in the world. His failure came from not understanding the body and the generative process, as well as from his fragmentation of the person into spiritual, rational, and temporal activities.

Finally, in a consideration of Augustine's theory of the continuity of generation, we find very little evidence that he was interested in the medical details of this process. In one intriguing passage from the *City of God*, Augustine suggests that in Paradise before the Fall, generation would have occurred through choice rather than lustful impulse. His description appears to imply that the father provided the seed and the mother the place for generation:

> In Paradise, then, generative seed would have been sown by the husband and the wife would have conceived as need required, and all would have been achieved by deliberate choice and not by uncontrolled lust.[371]

After the Fall, however, conception occurred through uncontrolled sexual attraction and intercourse. In a letter to Opatus, Augustine puzzles over the exact moment when the fetus receives the soul:

> But when anyone begins to consider and examine into what is here said, it is a wonder that any human perception can understand in what manner a soul is produced in the offspring from the soul of the parent, . . . whether the incorporeal seed of the soul flows up by its own secret and invisible way from the father to the mother when conception takes place in a woman, or, which is still harder to believe, whether it is latent in the bodily seed.[372]

In another text, *De Genesis ad Litteram*, Augustine is not yet decided whether the soul is given to the fetus through the father or whether it comes directly from God.

> As regards the origin of other souls, are they coming from the parents or from above, let whoever will be able to show this do it. For my part, I still waver between the two hypotheses, bending sometimes toward one side, sometimes toward the other.[373]

However, when Augustine wrote *The City of God*, he had concluded that the nature of the child, as determined by the soul, was given by God.

> Whatever bodily or seminal causes may play a part in reproduction, whether by the influence of angels or of men or other animals, or by the intermingling of the two sexes, and whatever longings or emotions of the mother may affect the feature or the colour while the fetus is still soft and pliable, nevertheless, every nature as such, however affected by circumstances, is created wholly by the Supreme God.[374]

Significantly, this passage appears to leave open the possibility of a female contribution in the phrase "the intermingling of sexes." In addition, it leaves open the possibility, suggested by Pliny and Porphyry, that a woman may, by her mind, affect the physical features of the fetus while it is being formed. However, he clearly states that it is God, and not the mother or father who determines the identity of the child. In this way the foundation for sex polarity, which had been posited by Aristotle's insistence on the father's role in providing the soul to the child, was not accepted by Augustine. There is also no indication that the formation of a female fetus would be in any degree imperfect in relation to the formation of a male fetus. For Augustine, the male soul and the female soul were equal in worth and dignity. Both were directly given to the fetus by God.

Wisdom

In the *Confessions*, Augustine tells us that he was converted to philosophy by the study of Cicero's *Hortensius:*

> For yours is the wisdom. In Greek the word *philosophy* means "love of wisdom," and it was with this love that the *Hortensius* inflamed me.[375]

For the early Greek philosophers, as well as for the Stoics and neo-Platonists, wisdom was acquired simply through the efforts of human reason. For Jewish philosophy and the early Church Fathers, wisdom was a gift from God. St. Augustine chose to accept both of these historical roots, and he argued that God can be approached through both faith and reason: "Since divine truth and scripture clearly teach that God, the Creator of all things, is Wisdom, a true philosopher will be a lover of God."[376]

The philosopher who loves Wisdom has two different but related tasks to perform: the first involves learning about the nature of God and the second about the nature of the self. In the *De Ordine,* Augustine clearly states this double task:

> To philosophers pertains a twofold question: the first treats of the soul; the second of God. The first makes us know ourselves; the second, to know our origin.[377]

The question of the relation of wisdom to sex identity concerns precisely the second of the two tasks—self-knowledge. If self-knowledge involves full understanding of the self as male or female, then clearly, the knowledge of a man and woman would be significantly different but equal. That is, a wise woman would know some different things than a wise man simply because her bodily source of knowledge would be different. Certainly, a reading of the *Confessions* as the first example of a philosophical autobiography in the west reveals that Augustine's search for wisdom led him to a specific understanding of his own nature as man in relation to woman. If he followed his own example from the *Confessions* in developing a theory of the relation of sex identity to wisdom, then he would have argued that women and men would have an equal, but sexually differentiated content of wisdom when they focused on self-knowledge. Wisdom, within a sex-complementarity theory, would imply a difference for women and men in some aspects of the content of their respective self-knowledge.

However, when some of Augustine's other writings are examined, a shift in emphasis is found towards a sex-unity theory of the relation of wisdom to men and women. The most revealing texts are two dialogues he wrote in which he gave his mother, Monica, a central role as philosopher. In the *De Ordine*, Augustine describes himself as encouraging his mother to engage in philosophical discourse when she enters the room in the midst of a discussion of the relation between God and the problem of evil:

> (Augustine): In the meantime, mother also came in and inquired what progress we had made; for the problem was known to her as well. But when I had ordered that, in accordance with our custom, record be made of her entrance and her question, she said:
>
> (Monica): What are you doing? In those books which you have read, have I ever heard that women were introduced into this kind of disputation?
>
> (Augustine): To her I reply: I care but little about the judgements of proud and ignorant men. . . . Believe me, then, there will not be lacking a class of men to whom the fact that you converse with men on the subject of philosophy will be more pleasing, than if they were to find here something else of pleasantry or seriousness. Moreover, in olden time, women, too, have worked on the problems of philosophy. And your philosophy is very pleasing to me.[379]

St. Augustine continued the dialogue by attempting to convince his mother that she already was a philosopher, a lover of wisdom:

> Then, mother, so that you may not be uninformed, the Greek word from which the term, philosophy, is derived is in the Latin tongue, called *love of wisdom*. . . . Now if you had no love whatever for wisdom, I should utterly disregard you; and much less if you were to love wisdom as I love it. And now, seeing that you love it even more than you love me—in view of all this, shall I not gladly entrust myself to you even as a disciple?[380]

Augustine directly faced the question of whether women and men ought to search for wisdom in the same way. He described the subjects necessary for philosophy: grammar, rhetoric, dialectic, numbers, and music. Then he turned to Monica and said:

> But I pray you, mother, let not this immense seeming forest of things deter you just because we have need of some of them for what we are investigating. . . . For many persons, to be sure they are difficult to learn. But for you, whose talents are brought home to me anew every day—and I know your mind, far removed from all frivolity, both by reason of your age and by means of your remarkable moderation, and now rising above the abject misery of the body, has already risen to great heights within itself—for you, those matters will be as easy as they are difficult for duller souls who live most wretchedly.[381]

For Augustine, Monica could become a philosopher because she rose above her body, not because she entered into it to understand its operations. He ends the dialogue with an exhortation to Monica to continue to pursue philosophy: "And, Mother, . . . we enjoin the charge on you, . . . to prize nothing more highly than the finding of truth, to wish for, to think of, to love nothing else."[382]

In the *De Ordine,* Augustine mentioned another dialogue in which Monica played a crucial role. In the *De Beata Vita,* Monica does not simply function as a student of philosophy, but she teaches others the fine points of argumentation. Augustine introduces Monica as follows:

> Our mother, too, was with us. By long intimacy and diligent attention I had by this time discerned her acumen and burning desire for things divine. It was particularly on the occasion of a rather important disputation which I once held on my birthday with my companions, and which I have compiled into a little book (*De Beata Vita*) that her mind had been revealed to me as so rare that nothing seemed more adapted for true philosophy.[383]

In the dialogue *De Beata Vita*, Monica presented the main arguments. She asked the important questions, forced the necessary distinctions and presented the conclusions. St. Augustine referred to her in the dialogue as presenting the "judgement I was defending."[384] Monica proved that the soul was nourished by knowledge, that happiness concerned the correct use of the will, that unhappiness implied a lack of some sort, that skepticisim was self-defeating, and that the happy life demanded the wisdom of God.[385]

It is in the midst of the argument that Augustine reveals his sex-unity theory. He described Monica as losing her sex identity when she achieved the high degree of wisdom:

> (Augustine): What, then—is everyone, who has what he wants, contented?
>
> (Monica): Then Mother replies, "If he wills to have things right and has them he is contented; but if he wills things wrong, even though he may have them, he is unhappy."
>
> (Augustine): Mother, you have taken completely the very stronghold of philosophy. . . .

The philosopher then described a passage from Cicero and added:

> Upon which words, she so spoke out, that, unmindful of her sex, we might think that some great man was seated with us, I, in the meantime, understanding from what source, and from how divine a source these things flowed.[386]

The female philosopher, when exercising her highest reason, led others to be unmindful of her sex, or to think of her as a man. In this revealing description we see that the sex complementarity that might have been expected from a union of philosophy and self-knowledge, in the existential sense of the term, slides into sex unity. The differentiation between the sexes disappears and only a neutralized masculinity remains.

Augustine's theory of the relation of sex identity to wisdom has one further development. He also appears to introduce a polarity in his description of the relation of male and female identity to higher and lower functions of mind or soul. This tendency, which had been so clearly found in Aristotle and Philo, is repeated in various places throughout Augustine's writings. One of the most pronounced is found in the *Confessions*:

> And just as in man's soul there are two forces, one which is dominant because it deliberates and one which obeys because it is subject to such guidance, in the same way, in the physical sense, woman has been made for man. In her mind and in her rational intelligence she has a nature the equal of man's, but in sex she is physically subject to him in the same way as our natural impulses need to be subjected to the reasoning power of the mind.[387]

This fragmented view of woman and man as being in a sex-unity dynamic when the highest function of the mind is considered alone, but in a sex-polarity dynamic when the body enters into their respective identities is repeated by Augustine in *De Genesis ad Litteram*:

> So, although the diversity of sexes in two different persons figure, exteriorly and corporeally, a duality that we can find interiorly in the soul of one single person, nevertheless the woman, for she is woman by her body, is also renewed in her spiritual soul in the acquaintance of God after the image of the one who created her, . . . there where there is no more man nor woman.[388]

Therefore, Augustine makes a similar distinction to the one previously made by Aristotle, namely that a woman has a special relation to the lower functions of reason and man to the higher. However, Augustine does not conclude that woman is incapable of the higher use of reason; rather, he employs the relation as a symbolic interpretation of the polarity within the mind itself. In *The Trinity* we find this view repeated:

> And just as in man and woman there is one flesh of two, so the one nature of the mind embraces an intellect and action, or our council and execution, or our reason and reasonable appetite. . . .
>
> Therefore, in their minds a common nature is recognized, but in their bodies the division of this one mind itself is symbolized.[389]

When the mind is oriented towards the temporal world, woman represents the lower functions of reason and man the higher. In this aspect of existence, sex polarity is the proper theory for describing the concept of woman in relation to man.

In conclusion, then, we have seen Augustine develop the same three-levelled interpretation of sex identity in relation to wisdom that he had previously indicated in the areas of generation and opposites. The possibility for a theory of sex complementarity that was present in his claim that wisdom includes self-knowledge, faded into a sex unity when he interpreted wisdom as primarily involving the highest part of the mind in separation from the body. Finally, when Augustine considered the higher and lower functions of the mind he decided to symbolize these through man's and woman's relation to one another and, in particular, by woman's duty to subordinate herself to man, just as the lower functions of reason should be subordinated to the higher functions of reason.

Virtue

For Augustine, perfectly virtuous women and men were simply known as saints. St. Augustine, as Bishop of Hippo, was one of the first to state that it was a good thing to honour women and men who had lived perfect lives. In the history of the Church, the martyrs were the first "virtuous" women and men to be officially venerated; by the fourth century confessors who had lived virtuous lives were also honoured.[390] It was not until the twelfth century that the Church began to develop strict criteria for the canonization of saints. Therefore, during this early period of Christianity, saints were informally recognized and venerated. From the perspective of sex identity, it is important to note that both men and women were considered saints. Neither man nor woman was taken to be more important than the other, or less or more of a saint than the other by virtue of their sex. At the same time, saints were sexually differentiated in iconography and in the ceremonies that were used for their veneration. In this way, a theology of sanctity included from its beginnings a philosophy of sex complementarity.

Augustine followed the traditional Platonic and Stoic concepts of virtue as involving wisdom, courage, temperance, and justice. He did not associate one or another virtue with a specific sex. In fact, in the *Confessions*, Augustine avoided stating that temperance or chastity were specific virtues of woman, probably precisely because he himself was struggling for these virtues. In addition, Augustine mentions the importance of the "theological" virtues of faith, hope, and charity.[391] Once again there was no attempt to imply that one sex or the other had a favoured relationship to one or another virtue. Men and women alike were to strive for a life of perfect virtue, and their achievement of this would be fulfilled through the resurrection of the body and life in heaven as saints.

In addition, Augustine hints that in Paradise, before the Fall of Adam and Eve, women and men lived in a relationship of complementarity; neither one held a place of superiority in the specific context of ruling and obedience. In *De Genesis ad Litteram* he states: "It is not the nature, but the fault of the woman which brought her to get a master in her husband."[392] This suggestion appears to imply that, ideally, women and men would be in a relationship of differentiated equality, or complementarity. However, after the Fall, a readjustment was necessitated in which the woman had to be placed under the man.

In another passage, from the *City of God*, Augustine considers woman and man after creation, but before the Fall. In this ideal context he repeats the view that by nature there ought not to be a differentiation in the category of ruling and obedience:

> It makes no sense to say that "male" and "female" are allegories of two qualities in a single person, for example that "male" stands for the part that rules and "female" for the part that is ruled.[393]

This passage is in distinct contrast to the several others where Augustine insists upon the validity of this allegory when woman and man are considered in the temporal world. We have already seen some of these symbolic interpretations of male and female in the section on wisdom; others will be discussed further on in the consideration of Augustine's sex-polarity theory in relation to the category of virtue.

The first part of this analysis of Augustine's theory of sex identity and virtue, then, has indicated that in heaven after death, and in Paradise before the Fall, Augustine appears to be aiming towards a theory of sex complementarity. That is, in these perfect situations before the Fall of Adam or after the new redemption of life, woman and man are equal and sexually differentiated. However, when we turn to a consideration of the interim phase of life on earth, a tension between sex unity and sex polarity will once again arise.

In the preceding sections it was recognized that Augustine promoted a sex-unity theory when he considered woman and man in terms of the orientation of the highest part of their mind towards God. One of the great contributions of Augustine to the history of philosophy was his discovery of the significance of the freedom of will. Since the seat of the will was in the reason, it follows that when women and men alike exercised their will, they were acting in the image of God.

In an historical context in which women had often been considered simply as the property of their fathers or brothers, Augustine repeatedly encouraged women to exercise their freedom. In a letter to nuns who had developed a rule for one of the earliest religious communities of women, he wrote: "May the Lord grant you to observe all these regulations with love . . . not as bondwomen under the law, but as free women established under grace."[394] Women, just as men, must seek to be virtuous through the correct use of their freedom of will.

In a second example, Augustine defended a woman's choice of religion against her father's wishes. In a letter he wrote:

> Her father wanted to bring her back to the Catholic communion by severe measures, but I would not allow her to be received—a woman whose mind had been deceived—unless she willingly and freely chose the better course on her own accord. There upon, the father began to insist with blows that his daughter obey him, which I at once forbade absolutely.[395]

This example is particularly revealing because Augustine is holding up the higher value of the freedom of will in the daughter rather than the goal of increasing the number of Church members.

In this situation the equality of the virtue of the exercise of the will in freedom for both women and men was a leap forward for women in the context of a patriarchy in which woman's freedom had been given little value. In the following example from the *City of God*, Augustine defended a woman who had been raped, precisely because she had exercised the freedom of her will in the correct way.

> I affirm, therefore, that in the case of violent rape and of an unshakable intention not to yield unchaste consent, the crime is attributed only to the ravisher and not at all to the ravished. To my cogent argument to this effect, some may venture to take exception. Against them I maintain the truth that not only the souls of Christian women, but also their bodies, remain holy.[396]

The woman, just like a man, who had been violated in the body, was nonetheless perfectly virtuous if her will had been oriented in the correct way. In an historical context in which woman had been considered as ruined by rape, Augustine's defence of this higher aspect of rationality was an important step in developing an equality of virtue for the two sexes.

By itself, the equality of importance of freedom of the will for women and men does not constitute a defence of sex unity, for men and women could exercise their will differently depending upon the situations that faced them because of their sexual identity. Therefore, freedom of will could be a virtue found in sex complementarity as well as in sex unity.

However, in a more general way, the particular goal that Augustine set for both himself and for religious women involved the acceptance of an interpretation of the virtue of celibacy, which demanded a denial of body, rather than an integration and consecration of the body. In the *Confessions*, Augustine shares his own struggle against his lower nature:

> I had prayed to you for chastity and said 'Give me chastity and continency, but not yet.' For I was afraid that you would answer my prayer at once and cure me too soon of the disease of lust, which I wanted satisfied, not quelled.[397]

Augustine concluded that he had not been successful in overcoming his desires because he was willing with "half a will":

> The reason, then, why the command was not obeyed is that it is not given with the full will. For if the will were full, it would not command itself to be full, since it would be so already. . . . It is a disease of the mind, which does not wholly rise to the heights where it is lifted by the truth, because it is weighed down by habit.[398]

Eventually, Augustine, through prayer and reasoning, reaches a point where he makes a full decision to live a life of celibacy. He sends away his concubine of several years, decides not to marry another woman, and moves towards a consecrated life in which he interprets all bodily desires as enemies to be overcome.

Woman was interpreted by Augustine in this context as representing a temptation to turn away from a life oriented towards God. In the *Soliloquies* he wrote the following dialogue with Reason:

> REASON: What about a wife? Would you not be delighted by a fair, modest, obedient wife, one who is educated or whom you could easily touch, one who would bring along just enough dowry so that she would be no burden to your leisure?
>
> AUGUSTINE: No matter how much you choose to portray and endow her with all good qualities, I have decided that there is nothing I should avoid so much as marriage. I know nothing which brings a manly mind down from the heights more than a woman's caresses and that joining of bodies without which one cannot have a wife.[399]

Marriage, he believed, drew man away from a spiritually oriented existence towards a temporally oriented existence. Woman, simply by the attractiveness of her body, drew man away from the exercise of the highest parts of the mind.

In *De Libero Arbitrio*, Augustine explains that women do not lead men away from the orientation of the mind through an evil intention or through guile; rather, they inadvertently achieved this reorientation simply through the beauty of their bodies.

> The women were loved . . . for the beauty of their bodies. . . . Thus the sons of God disturbed the due ordering of this affection, that is, of attachment and love, when they became detached from God and attached to the daughters of men.[400]

Two related consequences followed from this identification of woman as the unconscious tempter of man. The first is that woman must remain under the direct control of man if she chooses to live in the world and marry; the second is that if she chooses to cover her body and to live as a consecrated nun, then she can be released from the obligation of being in obedience to a man and can, instead, live in obedience to the authority of a female superior within her own religious community.

In a *Homily on the Gospel of St. John*, Augustine explicitly states that a wife must obey her husband:

> Flesh therefore stands for the wife, similarly spirit sometimes stands for the husband. Why? Because one governs and the other is governed, one ought to command and the other to serve.[401]

The "ought"is a clear indication of the virtue associated with the act. For Augustine, virtue involves a correct ordering within the soul. The higher and lower functions of the soul ought to be reflected in the ordering of the authority within the family:

> What is worse than a household in which the woman commands the man? But the house is in order when the man commands and the woman obeys. Consequently, the man himself is in order when, in him the spirit commands and the flesh obeys.[402]

In the *Confessions*, Augustine states that even a situation in which the wife is more virtuous than the husband, obedience is the woman's specific virtue. He reflects on the relation of his own mother, Monica, to his father: "Thou didst aid her to prevail over her husband, whom she, the better obeyed, therein also obeying Thee, who hast so commanded."[403]

The key aspects of these passages, when combined with the previously mentioned reference to Augustine's claim that before the Fall women and men were equal in relation to obedience indicates that he does not believe that women, by nature must obey, but rather that women, in order to aid humanity to return to a correct ordering, were called to obedience after a fallen condition entered into the world. By analogy, in Paradise before the Fall, the sexual desires were ordered naturally under reason. After the Fall, however, sexual desires moved out of the ordering process and created precisely the kind of difficulties that Augustine struggled with in the *Confessions*. The point is subtle, but it is important in the context of Aristotelian philosophy, which states that woman by nature is inferior to man and that she therefore ought to obey his rule because her mind is not capable of finding the discursive principles of ordering within its own functioning.

In the *Confessions*, Augustine reflects on this redemptive movement of God:

> Next you formed the living soul of the faithful, the soul that lives because it has learnt to control its passions by unremitting continence. Then you took man's mind, which is subject to none but you and needs to imitate no human authority, and renewed it in your own image and likeness. You made rational action subject to the rule of the intellect, as woman is subject to man.[404]

Women in marriage, Augustine thought, ought to practise the virtue of obedience in relation to their husbands because they represent both the subjection of the lower powers of the mind in relation to the higher powers and the bodily orientation of human action in temporal life in relation to the intellectual process of thought alone. In *De Genesis ad Litteram*, this analogy is explicitly expressed:

> There is in her [the spiritual soul] almost a marriage of the man and the woman, one part ordering and other part obeying. . . .
>
> She [Providence] submitted the corporeal creature to the spiritual, the irrational to the rational, the earthly to the heavenly, the female to the male.[405]

For Augustine, woman ought to obey because of a divine ordering of relationships after the Fall. Her obedience was not a consequence of an inferior nature. The sex-polarity theory is the result of the Fall and is the temporary situation of woman in relation to man until the resurrection, during which sex complementarity becomes the pattern of relationship. Therefore, for Augustine, sex polarity is not an absolute theory of sex identity, rather it is a relative theory in specific reference to women and men who are oriented towards the temporal work of generation and family life.

Significantly, there is an example in Augustine's writings that indicates that women and men who choose a life of celibacy move out of a relationship of sex polarity and into one of either sex unity or sex complementarity. If women always had to obey men, then all nuns would be placed under obedience to priests. However, in the following letter to some sisters of a religious community who wanted to follow the obedience of the priest who was serving as their confessor rather than of the nun who was their mother superior; Augustine, as Bishop of Hippo, criticizes this request:

> Stand firm in your good purpose and you will not want to change your Superior, who had presided in that monastery for so many years, during which you have inceased in numbers and age, and who has borne you as a mother—not in her womb, but in her heart. . . . You have not received any new Superior except your spiritual director, if it is because of him that you are seeking a change, through envy for him that you have thus rebelled against your Mother, why have you not rather demanded that he should be changed for you?[406]

Augustine argues that it is not the mother superior, but rather the priest who should be removed from the situation. In this way, the simple obedience of female to male is transcended by the celibate life.

In conclusion, then, we have seen in Augustine's consideration of virtue the same tendencies that were found in other areas of his thought, namely the tendency to fragment the person and the relation of woman and man so that in certain areas sex complementarity, in others sex unity, and in still others sex polarity, becomes the rule. As stated previously, Augustine was a watershed for early theories of sex identity. He appeared to be caught between the theory of sex polarity as inherited from Philo and other Hebrew or early Christian writers, and the theory of sex unity as proposed by the Stoics and neo-Platonists, while at the same time he was the first to recognize the possibilities for sex complementarity following from the Christian belief in the resurrection of the body. Grasping the significance of this belief, which comes from a theological perspective, Augustine argued that women were not imperfect simply by virtue of their sex. For the resurrection would maintain a sexual differentiation and that meant that woman in her body was equal to and significantly different from man.

At the same time, Augustine was not able to carry forward the important philosophical consequences of this theological belief in the resurrection. Instead, he isolated the mind from the body, and a spiritually oriented existence from a temporally oriented one. By fragmenting the person and the different orientations of human life, Augustine established a fragmented set of theories of sex identity that remained in place for the next several centuries. This lack of willingness to complete the philosophical consequences of sex complementarity left Christian philosophy with a fragmented heritage until Hildegard of Bingen continued thinking about the philosophical foundations for sex complementarity in the twelfth century. Therefore, while St. Augustine began the process of defining a philosophy of sex complementarity, he was not able to carry it forward into completion.

BOETHIUS (AD 480–524)

Fifty years after the death of St. Augustine, Boethius emerged as another Christian philosopher of importance for medieval Europe. Boethius, however, did not try to integrate philosophy and theology as had his predecessor. Instead, he made a sharp differentiation between philosophy and theology. Consequently in Boethius there was no attempt to draw philosophical consequences for the concept of woman in relation to man from the Christian religious belief in the resurrection of the body or of the equal creation of woman and man.

In one significant area, Boethius's theological reflections did have an important consequence for philosophy. In struggling to understand the way in which the Trinity could function as three distinct persons in one Divine nature, Boethius became the first western thinker to offer a specific definition of person as "the individual substance of a rational nature."[407] Previous to this time, only man as species had been defined. The discovery of the unique individuality of persons was an important breakthrough for western thought. Boethius develops this insight further:

> But in all these things Person cannot in any case be applied to universals, but only to particulars and individuals; for there is no person of man if animal or general; only the single persons of Cicero, Plato, or other single individuals are termed persons.[408]

It was not until the development of humanism in the fourteenth and fifteenth centuries that an attempt was made to uncover the interior dynamic of the meaning of person as individual in such a way that sex identity would become an essential aspect of personal identity. Boethius planted the seed for this important later development in the history of the concept of woman in relation to man, but it took centuries for the seed to grow into a new direction for the philosophy of sex identity.

In general, Boethius's theory of sex identity can be classified as containing two different tendencies under the category of wisdom: sex complementarity and sex neutrality. The sex complementarity sprang from his development of the activity of philosophy as a dialogue between a male and a female personification of wisdom, while his theory of sex neutrality sprang from his relation to the transmission of Aristotle's logic. Each of these tendencies will now be studied in turn.

A sex-complementarity attitude was suggested by Boethius in *The Consolation of Philosophy* through the feminine personification of wisdom in the figure of Lady Philosophy. The search for truth is presented as necessarily including the cooperative efforts of man and woman. Lady Philosophy functions as a woman, separate and distinct from Boethius, the man who sought to learn about wisdom.

> When I silently pondered these things, and decided to write down my wretched complaint, there appeared standing above me a woman of majestic countenance whose flashing eyes seemed wise beyond the ordinary wisdom of men. . . . Her height seemed to vary; sometimes she seemed of ordinary human stature, then again her head seemed to touch the top of the heavens. And when she raised herself to her full height she penetrated heaven itself, beyond the vision of the human eyes.[409]

Lady Philosophy is perhaps modelled on Socrates' invocation of Diotima as wise teacher in the *Symposium*, or she may simply be Boethius's image of the form of the word *philosophia*, which is feminine in Latin.

Boethius began the dialogue by complaining that he had been wrongly imprisoned by corrupt rulers. Lady Philosophy explained to Boethius that this treatment was not unknown to her followers:

> Do you suppose that this is the first time wisdom has been attacked and endangered by wicked men? We fought against such rashness and folly long ago, even before the time of our disciple Plato. And in Plato's own time, his master Socrates, with my help, merited the victory of an unjust death.[410]

The Consolation of Philosophy then unfolded as a dialogue between Lady Philosophy and Boethius, in which the man was taught about the basic truths of wisdom by the woman. Lady Philosophy presented herself first in the female image of a nursemaid:

> "But," she said, "it is time for medicine rather than complaint." Fixing me with her eyes she said: "Are you not he who once was nourished by my milk and brought up on my food; who emerged from weakness to the strength of a virile soul? I gave you weapons that would have protected you with invincible power, if you had not thrown them away."[411]

The nursemaid, however, was also a physician, and Lady Philosophy soon proceeded to diagnose Boethius's illness. At the beginning of the dialogue, she tells Boethius that he was weakened by giving in to the turbulence of his emotions:

> Because you are so upset by sorrow and anger, and so blown about by the tumult of your feelings, you are not now in the right frame of mind to take strong medicine.[412]

In this situation Lady Philosophy is portrayed as being calm due to the higher powers of reason and the man, as being controlled by his lower rational nature. This is an inversion of the usual association of the female with the lower and the male with the higher powers of reason.

Lady Philosophy moved to cure Boethius's disease. In the following passage, she put forth the central question of the dialogue:

> "First," Philosophy said, "will you let me test your present attitude with a few questions, so that I can decide on a way to cure you?"
>
> "Ask whatever you like," I replied, "and I will try to answer."
>
> "Do you think," she began, "that this world is subject to random chance, or do you believe that it is governed by some rational principle?"[413]

The question of the relation between fate, chance, fortune, and a rational plan—which can be called Providence—becomes the focus of the next four books of the dialogue.

Boethius described Fortune as a goddess, in keeping with the Roman custom of his time. Lady Philosophy led her student to the slow realization that the careful exercise of reason can allow one to conquer this goddess, by the recognition that philosophy is more powerful than Fortune. "If you possess yourself, you have something you will never want to give up and something which fortune cannot take from you."[414] Reason, when properly ordered, brings about this virtue of self possession: "You can never impose upon a free spirit, nor can you deprive a rationally self-possessed mind of its equanimity."[415]

Boethius's appeal to the importance of reason can certainly be traced to his admiration of Stoicism and neo-Platonism. However, he was also a Christian, and so philosophy could not rest merely upon an adoration of reason in order to rise above the turbulence caused by the emotions in the soul. Lady Philosophy accordingly argued that reason was a pathway to understanding the nature of God who could bring an ordering in spite of the presence of disorder:

> Then if He, whom we have agreed to be the good, rules all things by himself, He must dispose everything according to the good. He is, in a manner of speaking, the wheel and rudder by which the vessel of the world is kept stable and undamaged.[416]

It follows that the philosopher must seek to comprehend the world from the perspective of this divine ordering: "Divine wisdom does what the ignorant cannot understand."[417]

Boethius then asked how this divine wisdom could be comparable with human freedom:

> "Now I am confused by an even greater difficulty," I said.
>
> "What is it?" Philosophy answered, "though I think I know what is bothering you."
>
> "There seems to be a hopeless conflict between divine foreknowledge of all things and freedom of human will."[418]

Lady Philosophy distinguished God's knowledge, as occurring in an eternal present, from human knowledge that unfolded within temporality. God knew all things "before they happened" because, in Him, everything happens, simultaneously, in the eternal present. Therefore, God's knowledge cannot interfere with human freedom:

> In this way, the problem you raised a moment ago is settled. . . . Now you see that this power of divine knowledge, comprehending all things as present before it, itself constitutes the measure of all things and is in no way dependent on things that happen later.[419]

In this way, Lady Philosophy diagnosed Boethius's disease, treated it with increasingly potent medicines and ended her physician's work with a perfect cure.

It might be argued that Boethius is actually suggesting a reverse-polarity theory, because Lady Philosophy is obviously superior to the philosopher Boethius in wisdom. However, Boethius nowhere suggests that the female, by virtue of her sex, is superior to the male, or that man should accept the insights of Lady Philosophy simply because they were posited by a woman. Instead, Lady Philosophy insists that Boethius himself come to an understanding of the reasons for her views so that he can reach the same conclusions by the same process of reasoning. Lady Philosophy's superiority lies simply in the fact that she has already achieved wisdom, not because she, by her female nature, knows more than man. By analogy, Boethius could lead a female philosopher through the same process just as Seneca had previously attempted to do with Marcia or Helvia, or Porphyry with Marcella. Therefore, *The Consolation of Philosophy* is more an example of the cooperative and complementary search for wisdom between a woman and a man, rather than of the superiority of one sex over the other.

The Consolation of Philosophy came to be one of the most popular texts in medieval Europe, so Boethius is important for the concept of woman in relation to man precisely because he gave philosophy a female personification.[420] It created the image in the reader's mind of the possibility of the highest degree of wisdom being associated with female identity. In fact, it is possible that this model of Lady Philosophy had an important role to play in the development, in the ninth century, of the veneration for St. Catherine of Alexandria as the patron of Christian philosophers. For, in iconography, St. Catherine functioned precisely as Lady Philosophy had functioned for the philosopher Boethius. The figure of St. Catherine as philosopher is in stark contrast to the image of woman as limited to the lower functions of reason, as found in Philo, Aristotle, or to some extent, in St. Augustine.

At the same time as Boethius transmitted this image of sex complementarity, he was also inadvertently responsible for the transmission of a new foundation for sex neutrality via his translations from Greek into Latin of several works of Aristotle's logic. He translated the *Categories, De Interpretatione, Prior Analytics, Posterior Analytics,* and *Topics*. In addition, Boethius's translation of Porphyry's *Isagoge*, which had summarized Aristotelian logic, focused on definitions of universals and totally ignored questions of sex identity. The underlying presupposition of Aristotle's logic is that philosophy is neutral towards sex identity. Therefore, through Boethius's translations of Aristotle's logic, philosophy slowly became reoriented towards the study of logic, and sex identity was pushed outside its perimeters.

Ironically, Boethius had hoped to translate all of Aristotle's works. Lady Philosophy refers to the Greek philosopher in *The Consolation of Philosophy* as "My true follower, Aristotle."[421] If Boethius had been successful in his plan, much more would have been transmitted to the Latin world than a rationale for sex neutrality. Instead, Aristotle's complex and consistent arguments for sex polarity would have flooded medieval Europe as early as the fifth century. However, Boethius was not successful in this plan, and it was not until the eleventh century that this Aristotelian Revolution occurred. Therefore, Boethius represents an early transition figure from Greek to medieval thought about the concept of woman. In his own work he suggested a kind of complementarity of man and woman in the search for wisdom, while in his relation to Aristotle's logic he made a sex-neutrality orientation possible.

JOHN SCOTUS ERIGENA (AD 800–875)

The four hundred years between the fifth-century Christian philosophers Augustine and Boethius, and the ninth-century Christian philosopher John the Scot are often referred to as the Dark Ages. There is no record during this time of any new developments in philosophy. The remarkable work of John Scotus Erigena, the Irish-born philosopher, gives evidence of the strong influence of neo-Platonic ideas of sex identity at this time in history. In fact, in the *Periphyseon* (The Division of Nature), Erigena completely rejected the movements towards sex complementarity that had been found in earlier Christian philosophers. Instead, he reverted to a theory of a combination of sex unity and sex polarity. He argued that God created a unisex kind of humanity first, that the Fall resulted in a division into sexes in which the male was superior to the female, and finally that redemption called for a return to a sexless identity after the resurrection. So John Scotus Erigena moved from sex unity, to a "fall" into sex polarity, and finally back into sex unity.

The Scot recognized the need to argue against the theory proposed by St. Augustine, that creation and resurrection implied a kind of sex complementarity. He specifically defended the view that God first created human beings that were neither male nor female: "According to divine intention, there would be simply man, not to be divided by the names of male and female."[422] Human beings did not generate through the division of the sexes; rather they reproduced like angels: "For he would be 'simply man' created in the simplicity of his nature, multiplied in the intelligible numbers, as the holy angels are multiplied."[423] John Scotus Erigena believed that this kind of person, devoid of sex, was the ideal result of God's creation.

Then, for Scotus, sex identity entered the world as a consequence of the Fall:

> If the first man had not sinned he would not be suffering the division of his nature into two sexes, but would be remaining without change in this primordial reason in which he was created in the image of God.[424]

This conclusion is frequently repeated: "Oppressed by the guilt of his disobedience, he suffered the division of his nature into male and female."[425] Sin, then, caused the change from a perfect, sexless human identity into an identity in the world as woman and man: "And if he were not in a state of sin there would not be in him a division of the sexes."[426]

When John Scotus Erigena defended this view, he argued that it followed from reason, rather than from revelation. He drew upon a vision of the world as flowing from an original one into multiplicity; this view had previously been articulated by the neo-Platonist Plotinus.

> For as our reason teaches us, the world would not have burst forth into a variety of both sensible species and the divers multiplicities of parts if God had not foreseen the fall and ruin of the first man when he abandoned the unity of his nature; after his fall from spiritual to corporeal things, . . . from a simple nature to the division of the sexes.[427]

Division of any sort was a negative feature of existence.

It followed, as a direct consequence of this view of multiplicity as an imperfection in the world, that the goal of life ought to consist in bringing about a new unification. For John Scotus Erigena, the best kind of unity involved the complete disappearance of differentiation:

> Since the division of substances, which took its beginning from God, and descending by degrees, reached its end in the division of man into male and female (and) again the reunification of the same substances ought to begin from man and ascend through the same degrees to God Himself.[428]

The disappearance of male and female was carried to its logical conclusions by his theory of resurrection. Instead of this event working to preserve differentiation, or sex complementarity, John the Scot argued that it would lead to a new kind of sex unity:

> In the future life after resurrection the nature of mankind will wholly lack sex, i.e., masculine and feminine form, since it will return to the very form made in God's image; God's image, moreover, is not male and female, for that division of nature was made because of sin.[429]

In this way, then, Christian philosophy was robbed of its possibilities for becoming a new foundation for sex complementarity.

John Scotus Erigena went even further in his redefinition of Christianity by claiming that in Christ's resurrection his identity as a male person was lost:

> The Lord Jesus united in himself the division of (our) nature, that is, male and female, for it was not in the bodily sex but simply in man that he rose from the dead.[430]

It is not surprising that, in 1225, the philosopher's theories were condemned by the Council of Paris. They went against the basic emphasis on the materiality of the human condition in resurrection.

In Scotus's rather ingenious argument, he went one step beyond the sex unity of the Platonists and neo-Platonists, who had considered the soul in separation from the body to be the highest and most true identity of the person. For John Scotus Erigena, the body was important, for something material was resurrected within the framework of Christian religious belief. However, he decided, out of a belief in the higher value of sex unity, that the body was devoid of any sexual differentiation. In this way, Christ, as well as all resurrected Christians, would receive a sex neutral body after the resurrection.

It might have been possible for Scotus to argue for a complementarity of sex identity after the fall from sex unity, for he simply stated that the sexes were divided into two, not that the female was derived from the male. In fact, he says little about the relation of the sexes after the division. His orientation seems to be for the most part one of sex neutrality, that is, sex is irrelevant for philosophy. Once again, Aristotelian logic may have been influential in this position of sex neutrality.

However, in one passage he appeared to identify the female with the lower functions of the soul and the male with the higher ones. This suggests a hidden polarity of the sexes in the category of wisdom. In the passage in question he states:

> The spiritual sexes are understood to exist in the soul—four *nous*, that is intellect, is a kind of male in the soul, while *aistheais*, that is sense is a kind of female.[431]

Therefore, there is a valuation of male identity as being superior to female identity in its association with the higher powers of soul.

John Scotus Erigena, in conclusion, stands as a fascinating witness to the perennial attraction of Platonism for the concept of woman in relation to man. In this theory of sex unity, sex identity is perceived as something negative in relation to personal identity. For the Platonists, sexual differentiation is irrelevant for philosophy, and the goal of women and men ought to be to escape this aspect of their respective identities as quickly as possible. Erigena attempted to describe how such a transcendence might occur at the same time as bodily existence is maintained. In this way, he developed a slightly different direction of thought from that of the Platonists, in which the body itself was devalued and rejected in favour of an immaterial soul.

Scotus stands at the end of this first phase of the development of the concept of woman in relation to man after the original development of arguments about sex identity in Plato and Aristotle. Soon, with the influx of all of Aristotle's arguments about sex identity, a shift in balance would occur and sex polarity would eventually be instituted as the dominant framework for theories of sex identity in western thought.

SUMMARY AND EVALUATION

THE SLUMBERING ARISTOTELIAN REVOLUTION

The philosophers considered in this chapter have covered a period in western history from Aristotle's death in 377 BC to John Scotus Erigena's death in AD 877. During this period of thirteen hundred years, although Aristotle's thought remained alive in the minds of western philosophers, it was not, for the most part, considered in detail. Therefore, while some Aristotelian concepts were adopted by subsequent philosophers, many of his central arguments about sex identity remained unnoticed.

A cursory glance at the philosophers in the traditions of Stoicism, neo-Platonism, Jewish and early Christian thought reveals a scattered adoption of a variety of Aristotelian concepts. The view that philosophy was a science of causes, that it ought to be oriented towards definitions, and that among its central concepts were genus, species, differentia, and so on, were all taken from Aristotle. Certain premises from Aristotle's theory of generation appeared in subsequent discussions on the same topic. His description of the concept of woman as particularly associated with the lower faculties of reason also appeared from time to time. Finally, by the end of this period of western thought, the basic corpus of Aristotle's logical works had been summarized and translated into Latin.

This rather limited transmission of Aristotelian thought was accompanied by the strong presence of Platonic theory. The Platonic emphasis on the priority of rationality in human existence led to an assertion of the sex unity theory of sex identity. Aristotle's theory slumbered, while Plato's dominated discussions about the concept of woman. This conflict between the two philosophers was seen most vividly in Stoicism and neo-Platonism.

By the end of this early period in western thought, a new element had entered into the discussion. Christianity brought forward a theory of the resurrection of the body and of the originally equal creation of man and woman. Aristotle's and Plato's thoughts were then mixed with this new challenge to the human mind. The conflicting demands of what has been interpreted as sex unity, sex polarity, and sex complementarity were found in all of the early Christian philosophers. Aristotle's philosophy of sex identity remained in the background, slumbering, until after the year 1000.

THE NEW RELATION OF SEX UNITY AND SEX NEUTRALITY

At the end of the second chapter of this book, it was observed that two theories of sex identity, with similar premises, had emerged in Greek philosophy. The sex-unity theory, which involved the explicit defence of the equality and non-differentiation of woman and man, had been developed by Plato. The sex-neutrality theory, which assumed the equality and non-differentiation of woman and man, but ignored arguments to prove it, had been given a foundation in Aristotle's logic. Since Aristotle was a staunch supporter of the sex-polarity theory, which argued for the differentiation and inequality of women and men, no direct link between sex unity and sex neutrality was established.

In the next phase of the development of western philosophy, an explicit link was made between the two theories of sex unity and sex neutrality. Porphyry, who argued directly for sex unity, also wrote an extensive summary of Aristotle's foundation for sex neutrality. The Stoic tradition had also shown a tendency towards sex unity. With their admiration for the rationality of human existence, and of its power to overcome the changing vicissitudes of human materiality, it is not surprising that the Stoics would eventually be attracted to Aristotle's logic. While the early Stoics did not manifest this development, the philosopher Boethius, who was deeply influenced by Stoicism, did do so when he translated Aristotle's logical corpus into Latin. Significantly, Boethius also translated Porphyry's commentary on the same texts, thereby providing a link between neo-Platonic sex-unity and sex-neutrality traditions and his own thought.

At the end of this period in western history a new factor entered that led to the eventual rejection of the Platonic basis for sex unity. The Christian belief in the resurrection of the body rejected the theory of reincarnation, as well as the view of the person as consisting of a sexless soul. Therefore, reincarnation, as a metaphysical basis for sex unity, received its final development in neo-Platonism. The end of this period of philosophy also marked the end of this formulation of sex unity.

As sex unity waned, sex neutrality waxed. While the basic theory that women and men are equal and not significantly different lost its support through a rejection of reincarnation, it gained new support through the slow emergence of Aristotelian logic. Sex unity did not reappear again in western philosophy until the modern period, when Descartes provided a new argument for the equality of woman and man based upon the common presence of reason in their identity. While this new pattern of sex unity is described later in this book, it is useful at this point to note simply that arguments for sex unity always seem to depend upon a philosophy that values rationality over the materiality of human existence.

THE QUESTION OF FEMALE SEED

In the second chapter of this book, Aristotle's complete rejection of the existence of a female seed in generation was seen as a foundation for this sex-polarity theory. Historians of the subject of embryology frequently imply that the issue of contention is simply whether female seed exists. However, an examination of arguments about generation after Aristotle reveals that the subject is much more complicated than may at first appear.

The question is not simply whether a philosopher believed in the existence of a female seed. The questions must be: What is the nature and function of female seed? Is it equal to the man's seed? Is it different? If different, what does it do? When these further questions are asked, a wide variety of possibilities emerge; all the answers have implications for the concept of woman.

The only philosopher who supported a fertile double-seed theory of generation in this next period in western history was Lucretius. While he did not leave a detailed analysis of this theory, he did suggest the presence of both female and male seed. Galen, who is sometimes cited as also having supported a double-seed theory of generation, appears, on further analysis, to have a rather different concept of the nature of female seed than this description might imply. While Galen did mention the presence of female seed, he believed that it was infertile, or impotent. In fact, "female seed" appears to be merely confused with female glandular secretions during intercourse. Therefore, Galen's double-seed theory collapses into a modified Aristotelian single-seed theory.

The only other philosopher to give serious attention to the question of female seed was Porphyry. It is difficult to determine what he believed about female seed. On the other hand, he did give to woman an active and formative power over the fetus during generation. Man provided the primary formative power in his seed, while woman provided a secondary formative power through her contribution of nourishment and shaping of the fetus in her uterus. It may be that Porphyry believed that woman's seed also aided this process or, once again, her seed may have been confused with glandular secretions. In any event, Porphyry did give to the woman some active role, in contrast to Aristotle and Galen, who limited her to being the passive partner in generation.

The question of the existence and nature of female seed is central to a theory of sex identity. It is known today that women and men both provide one half of the necessary structure of the fetus through their contribution of seed. A careful understanding of the dynamics of this process is necessary for the contemporary foundation of a theory of sex complementarity. While some classical and early medieval philosophers understood that the issue was central to sex identity, they did not yet have an adequate understanding of how ovulation in women occurred and how the seed provided by woman to the process of generation compared with the seed provided by man.

FEMALE PERSONIFICATIONS OF WISDOM AND FEMALE PHILOSOPHERS

The Greek tendency to personify wisdom as female was seen, in the first section of this book, to have been developed particularly by Plato in the figure of Diotima. The fullest philosophical development of the female personification of wisdom in early medieval thought occurred in Boethius's development of Lady Philosophy as a physician. In *The Consolation of Philosophy*, she diagnosed, treated, and cured Boethius's illness of soul. In this way, Lady Philosophy appeared as a variant upon Socrates' description of the philosopher as midwife.

Another influential female symbol of wisdom emerged in the legends surrounding St. Catherine of Alexandria. She was depicted as a rhetorician, a defender of Christian philosophy, and as a martyr. In the subsequent history of western Europe, St. Catherine served as patroness of Christian philosophy and inspirational helper to all who sought personal wisdom.

Once again, it must be asked whether this powerful attestation to the central role of female personifications of wisdom in western thought suggests the underlying truth that wisdom must finally be understood as demanding the cooperative search for truth by women and men. This example of the female personification of philosophy attests to the need for a complementary male and female contribution to philosophy; nonetheless, it is not an ultimate goal. Philosophy needs to be approached by the two sexes, not so much by symbols, as by the cooperative interaction of living women and men.

In this context it is important to consider the question of the existence of female philosophers in this period in western history. Among the early Greeks, women were disciples of Pythagoras, Anaxagoras, Plato, and Epicurus; Aristotle, on the other hand, accepted no female students. The Stoic Seneca taught philosophy to Marcia and Helvia. The neo-Platonist Plutarch encouraged women to study philosophy and mentioned one specific female philosopher, Eumetis. In this tradition, Porphyry stood out most prominently in his support of his wife Marcella's philosophical abilities. Similarly, St. Augustine showed his admiration for his mother Monica's philosophical insights; he wrote two dialogues in which she was a prominent figure. These examples point to a tradition of female family members being exposed to philosophical discussion.

In addition to these records of female students of philosophy, there is also considerable evidence that several women wrote and taught philosophy within the neo-Pythagorean tradition. The examples of Perictione I and II, Theano I and II, Phyntis, Melissa, Aesara, and Myia attest to the vitality and variety of writings that female philosophers contributed to the history of western thought. At the same time, it is evident that female philosophers were not original thinkers in the sense that Plato, Aristotle, or Augustine developed new theories. Nonetheless, they began to provide a context from which original female philosophers would later emerge.

The most outstanding example of a female philosopher in this period was Hypatia. Although she was the daughter of a well-known philosopher, Hypatia moved beyond being a mere disciple to becoming a philosopher in her own right. In her capacity as head of the Alexandrian school of neo-Platonism, she serves as the first example of a major female philosopher in western history. Hypatia may have agreed that women and men ought to cooperate in the search for truth and that they are equal partners in this process. However, she was a philosopher firmly planted in the neo-Platonic tradition; therefore, it is unlikely that she believed that there were significant differences between men and women.

The life and writings of Hypatia indicate that women were originally considered quite capable of comprehending the basic truths of mathematics. This fact is important because of frequent contemporary suggestions that women's minds may not be as good as men's for abstract or discursive thought. Contrary to this suggestion, the earliest examples of female philosophers were of women who also excelled in mathematics. The female Pythagoreans and Hypatia bear witness to the fact that the disassociation of women from mathematics was a later development in western history.

One interesting question was raised about the presence of female philosophers in these early schools of philosophy. It concerned the frequent discovery that women who participated in philosophy lost their female identity. Plato's and Epicurus's disciples, as well as Hipparchia, wore men's clothes. Other female philosophers were described as being "like men" when they contributed important insights to argumentation. See for example, the story of Eumetis, or Augustine's description of Monica. Other women were encouraged to disregard their sex when doing philosophy. Seneca's essays to Marcia and Helvia, or Porphyry's letter to Marcella give evidence of this situation. The pattern then begins to emerge in which many women who practised philosophy did so at peril of losing their identity as women. This was the ironic result of the influence of a sex-unity tendency so appealing to female philosophers.

At the same time, however, the neo-Pythagorean female philosophers appeared to keep a differentiation between the sexes along with their practice of philosophy. In addition, the two female personifications of philosophy in Boethius and St. Catherine were both strongly female in their articulation. It would seem, then, that the challenge to the next phase of the development of the philosophy of woman in relation to man would be whether or not women would be able to emerge as philosophers in a complementary relation to men without losing their specific female identity.

THE RELIGIOUS AND PHILOSOPHICAL ORIGINS OF SEX POLARITY

It was previously claimed that sex polarity received its first formulation in Aristotle's theory of generation. Not surprisingly, defences for sex polarity in this period immediately after Aristotle's death drew upon this philosophical origin of sex polarity. Aristotle's theory of generation reappeared, with some modifications, in the writings of Philo and the Stoics, especially Galen; these philosophers advocated sex polarity and claimed that woman had a passive role in generation.

A second philosophical source for sex polarity in the early Greek philosophers was attributed to Plato's description of prime matter as a passive mother receptacle. This description of a cosmic feminine principle of passivity reappeared in the writings of the Stoics and of Plutarch and Plotinus. While the neo-Platonists attempted to defend an active role for mothering, they nonetheless continued to associate the passive nature of matter with a feminine principle. Correspondingly, form, as the active principle, was associated with the male.

A third philosophical source for sex polarity was derived from Aristotle's claim that the lower functions of the mind were associated with women, and the higher with men. This theory was also stated in Philo and in John Scotus Erigena. In addition, St. Augustine introduced this theory in a qualified form when he associated women with the temporal orientation of the mind, and man with the eternal orientation. None of these philosophers gave evidence of having derived this view directly from Aristotle. However, it appears to have been Aristotelian in origin and may have led to a misinterpretation of Plato's description in the *Timaeus* of the lower part of the mind being similar to women's living quarters, and the higher part of the mind to the men's living quarters. In any event, regardless of the origin of this view of sex polarity, the pattern that was originally found in Aristotle reappeared in this period of late classical and early medieval thought.

In addition, sex polarity was given a new foundation through the influx of Jewish and, later, Christian religious theory. The Jewish tradition, as interpreted by its first major philosopher, Philo, was used to justify a thorough defence for sex polarity. The differentiation of the sexes, with the superiority of man over woman was viewed as divinely ordained. God, it argued, created woman as different from and unequal to man. The rationale for sex polarity included specific reference to the need for woman to obey man. In this way, the philosophical justification of the virtue of obedience as being particular to women was reinforced by a religious belief that this obedience was divinely ordained.

Early Christian philosophy, particularly as interpreted by St. Augustine, argued that woman was inferior to man because she represented the temporal orientation of existence. God, as transcendent creator of the world, created woman as a helpmate to man for the temporal activity of generation. As a consequence, St. Augustine argued, woman by herself was not properly thought of as being in the image of God. She was only in that image when joined to man in his spiritual orientation. On the other hand, man, by himself, was fully in the image of God. Through this argument, sex polarity received a new religious framework beyond the philosophical bases previously provided by the Greek philosophers.

THE RELIGIOUS AND PHILOSOPHICAL ORIGINS OF SEX COMPLEMENTARITY

In early Greek thought, sex complementarity was described as having been suggested, in an initial way, in a variety of philosophical fragments. No one philosopher, however, presented a thorough defence for this theory of sex identity. In the next phase of the history of philosophy, no new philosophical justifications for sex complementarity occurred.

However, a radically new religious foundation for sex complementarity was brought into philosophical consideration through the Christian theory of the resurrection of the body. In this doctrine, the equality and significant differentiation of woman and man was confirmed. In the philosophy of St. Augustine, the philosophical implications of the theory of resurrection for sex complementarity were first recognized.

St. Augustine also concluded that woman and man were created, in some sense, within the sex complementarity model. However, as previously mentioned, this complementarity fell into a sex polarity when woman was considered from the perspective of her temporal role as helpmate in generation, and into a sex unity when woman and man were considered from the perspective of the highest part of their minds alone.

Even though Augustine initially saw the implications of the religious theory of resurrection for a philosophy of sex complementarity, he was not able to carry this theory forward in a consistent way. This can be called "St. Augustine's missed opportunity." If this early Christian philosopher had been able to shake off the shadows of neo-Platonist sex unity and of Jewish philosophy's sex polarity, he might have been able to push thought forward in a totally new and dynamic way.

When considering why St. Augustine failed to break through to a new understanding of woman and man, several possibilities suggest themselves. In addition to the above-mentioned intellectual heritage, this Christian philosopher also had a very complex personality. His history of relations with women is varied and intense. In his struggle to extricate himself from a sexual relationship in order to become a priest, St. Augustine interpreted woman as a danger to his desire to reorient his life in a spiritual direction. This view of woman as a risk, as symbolizing the temporal life in its genital, sexual and generative aspects was reinforced by the fact that the women he related to in the search for wisdom and the practice of virtue were celibate. His mother, Monica, and the nuns he directed, therefore did not pose the same risk as his concubine. They did not awaken in him the intense response of his lower passions. Augustine, then, perceived women as having two alternative identities, a sexual nature held within a sex-polarity model, and a rational, non-sexual identity held within a sex-unity model.

St. Augustine hoped, and perhaps believed, that after death, in the state of resurrection of the body, women and men at last would achieve an integrated rational and material identity. With the passing away of the temporal world and the union of body with soul, the sex-polarity and sex-unity frameworks would disappear and sex complementarity would be achieved. Unfortunately, St. Augustine's missed opportunity occurred through his conclusion that this model of sex complementarity could not be worked for and achieved in the temporal world. He failed to recognize that the religious belief in the resurrection of the body has the potential for activating a philosophical theory of sex complementarity for woman and man in the temporal world.

THE DISCOVERY OF SPIRITUALITY AND INDIVIDUALITY

Early Greek philosophy has been characterized as having discovered the significance of the materiality and rationality of human existence. While Plato fragmented materiality and rationality, Aristotle sought to integrate these two in the person. In the next phase of western philosophy the Stoics and neo-Platonists struggled with this same issue within the framework posited by Plato and Aristotle. Both schools of philosophy gave a priority to rationality over materiality. The Stoics argued that with the exercise of reason a person could rise above the passions and the whims of fortune. The neo-Platonists followed a similar line of argument and further suggested that the soul was able to escape its bodily prison. In both of these views, rationality was considered once again to be fundamentally superior to the materiality of human existence.

To this two-fold analysis of human identity was added a third factor, the discovery of a spiritual dimension of existence. This discovery of spirituality did not occur through reason or the observation of the senses, but rather through faith. It was articulated through the traditions of Jewish and Christian philosophy that proclaimed a belief in a transcendent and totally immaterial God, as well as in an immaterial soul created directly by this God. Human beings were believed to have been created in some respects in the image of this God. Therefore, part of their identity necessarily included reference to spirituality. As a consequence of this new development in western thought of the spirituality of human existence, religious belief, which came through faith, had implications for philosophy that uses reason and the observations of the senses to understand the rationality and materiality of the same human existence.

Just as the discovery of the significance of rationality for Plato led to a devaluation of the materiality of human existence, so Augustine's discovery of spirituality led to a devaluation of the non-spiritual or temporal orientation of human life. Somehow the breakthrough of thought that opened human consciousness to an awareness initiated by a wholly transcendent, immaterial, and eternal God led to a devaluation of the immanent, material and temporal life of humanity.

The whole question of woman's and man's identity took on a new dynamic in this context, for woman was selected to represent, in a symbolic way, the devalued temporal orientation of human existence. Man, in contrast, was used to symbolically represent the orientation of the mind towards this newly discovered spiritual existence. In this way, sex polarity entered into western thought in a slightly newer way than had been previously expressed. For Aristotle, sex polarity was a theory that was discoverable through reason and the observations of the senses; for later Jewish and Christian philosophers, sex polarity appears to follow from discoveries of faith.

Sometimes, these later philosophers interpreted spirituality simply as rationality. When this happened, all sexual identity disappeared, and the theory fell into the same sort of sex unity that had been present in previously rationalist theories. Therefore, at this point in history, the spirituality of human existence had been discovered, but its relationship to rationality and materiality had not yet been correctly articulated. The integration and differentiation of the true factors of spirituality, rationality and materiality had not yet occurred.

In addition, during this same period in history, the factor of individuality in human life was also discovered. Boethius put forward a definition of person as "an individual substance of a rational nature." He argued that persons were different from other animals that could be simply understood as being one of a group of things of the same nature. Persons had to be recognized as being individuals; they had the capacity to organize themselves and to individuate themselves through self-consciousness.

When the philosophical significance of individuality was eventually developed, it would reveal a necessary incorporation of sex identity. Hildegard of Bingen, the philosopher who later developed a complete theory of sex identity, would begin to explore this aspect of personal identity. However, in this early phase of medieval philosophy, the centrality of the individuality of the person was simply recognized without being amplified. The person had been defined as including the four factors of rationality, materiality, spirituality, and individuality.

While theology focuses on the aspect of human spirituality, philosophy studies the interaction of materiality, rationality, and individuality. As was seen in the works of Augustine, philosophy and theology also influence one another so that discoveries in one area of thought can have implications for other areas. Therefore, in this early period of medieval thought, while the concept of person had made a substantial leap in complexity by including the additional factors of spirituality and individuality in personal identity, the concept of woman in relation to man had not moved very far from its previous articulation in Greek philosophy. Aside from the religious impulse towards sex complementarity, the basic lines of argument put forward by Plato and Aristotle continued without major change. In the next stage of the Aristotelian Revolution, however, considerable advancement would be made in the philosophy of sex identity as well.

IV

THE ADOPTION OF ARISTOTELIAN ARGUMENTS

The period of western history from the tenth through the thirteenth centuries saw a renewed interest in arguments about sex identity. On the one hand, a whole new foundation for sex complementarity emerged within the context of the Christian monastic education. On the other hand, sex polarity gained an entirely new rationale through the influx of Aristotelian arguments into the Latin west. While there was still some residue of interest in sex-unity arguments, for the most part this particular approach to sex identity lost the prominence it had held in previous centuries. For Islamic, Jewish, and Christian philosophy, the options appeared to be either sex complementarity or sex polarity.

The progress of the Aristotelian Revolution at its height can be seen in the following theories of sex identity proposed by philosophers between 800 and 1250:

1. Christian philosophy, pre-Aristotelian Revolution: sex neutrality, sex complementarity or sex polarity.
2. Islamic philosophy: sex unity and sex polarity.
3. Jewish philosophy: sex neutrality and sex polarity.
4. Christian philosophy, post-Aristotelian Revolution: sex polarity.

The final phase of the Aristotelian Revolution occurred through the cooperative interaction of Islamic, Jewish, and Christian philosophy. St. Albert the Great was influenced by Averroes and Maimonides, who had discovered Aristotle. He brought into the Latin world a new awareness of the Aristotelian theory of natural philosophy and, with it, the entire rationale for sex polarity.

St. Thomas Aquinas, a student of St. Albert, then carried this phase of the Aristotelian Revolution to completion. He developed a fundamentally new Christian philosophy built upon the foundation of Aristotelian theory. St. Thomas's combination of originality and dependence on Aristotle gave a deeper rationale for sex polarity than had previously existed. His theological claim that sex polarity was entirely consistent with Christian religious teaching made sex polarity invulnerable to criticism within the Christian world for centuries to come.

Christian philosophy was not always oriented towards sex polarity. Beginning with Augustine, there was a certain tendency to recognize that one philosophical consequence of the belief in the resurrection of the body was the necessary equality and significant differentiation of the sexes. In the early medieval experience of women and men studying and working together within the double monasteries of the Benedictine tradition, a new foundation of sex complementarity began to emerge. Here the theory sprang from a real experience of complementarity, rather than simply from the theoretical consequence of a theological belief. In the early writings of women and men who had this experience during the ninth through twelfth centuries, Christian philosophy slowly but surely edged towards a theory of sex complementarity.

At the end of the twelfth century, Hildegard of Bingen emerged as the first philosopher to articulate a thorough rationale for sex complementarity. Her philosophy is extremely significant for this study because she stands immediately prior to the full explosion of the Aristotelian Revolution. The far-reaching consequence of the victory of the Aristotelian Revolution was that Christian philosophy turned away from a theory of sex complementarity.

SEX COMPLEMENTARITY IN WOMEN'S AND MEN'S MONASTERIES

During the seventh through eleventh centuries, nearly all of the higher education of Christians took place within Benedictine monasteries. This "Benedictine Age" resulted in the first major effort by a philosopher to develop a consistent theory of sex complementarity. Hildegard of Bingen, by the end of the eleventh century, emerged with a complete theory of the concept of woman in relation to man, covering all four categories of opposites, generation, wisdom, and virtue. Drawing upon the medieval framework of science that described human nature in terms of the interaction of the elements and humours, Hildegard developed a complicated view of the interaction of four basic types of men and four basic types of women. Her arguments presupposed equality and a significant differentiation of the sexes. Therefore, she is rightly called the founder of the sex-complementarity theory.

It is interesting to note that historically, women did not participate in the development of the traditional theory of sex polarity. There were no women in the Peripatetic school, neither have any female philosophers left a record of actually arguing for Aristotle's theory, nor for any other theory that attempted to prove that women were significantly different but inferior to men.

Female philosophers primarily defended the sex-unity tradition, that is, they were Platonists, neo-Pythagoreans, Stoics, and neo-Platonists. In these traditions, female philosophers often appeared to lose their specific identity as women in order to follow the basic precepts of the male philosophers who led their schools. Only in the neo-Pythagorean female philosophers did we find a sense of a significant differentiation between women and men. Not surprisingly, many of the female neo-Pythagoreans studied philosophy together; they were not isolated as single women studying primarily with men.

The historical situation of women studying philosophy together, but in complement with men, also occurred in the double monasteries of the Benedictine tradition. Within that context, many women rose up who were on an equal level with men, particularly in the category of wisdom. At the same time, they maintained a significant differentiation between the sexes. The following examples indicate the developing presence of women who were capable of using their fullest intelligence in relation to man: 1) Hilda of Whitby—counsellor for men; 2) Roswitha—playwright; 3) Heloise—philospher of letters; 4) Herrad of Landsberg—author of an encyclopedia; and 5) Hildegard of Bingen—scientist, philosopher and theologian. The first three of these women provided a model of sex complementarity through their lives and writings. Hildegard of Bingen later developed a theoretical framework within which sex complementarity could be articulated as a philosophy of sex identity. The specific contributions of the women and men within the monastic tradition will now be considered in detail.

Hilda of Whitby (614–680)

Just two hundred years after Augustine and Boethius, the Abbess Hilda of Whitby stands out as the first example of a woman who lived in a relationship of complementarity with men in relation to wisdom and virtue. The grand-niece of King Edwin of Northumbria, Hilda became the Abbess of a monastery at Hartlepool. Later, in 637, she founded one of the first double monasteries of monks and nuns at Whitby.[1] One critic describes the situation in the monastery as follows:

> Some of the most famous names in early Frankish and English monastic history are names of nuns of royal descent—Hilda at Whitby, Etheldreda at Ely, Radegunde at Pointers, Bathilda at Chelles, and very many others. They were masterful and formidable ladies and they did not forget that they belonged to a ruling caste. Communities of monks were commonly attached to their nunneries in order to provide the necessary services of sacraments and temporal administration, and the great lady abbess ruled the whole organization in the spirit of one accustomed to command. These ladies of the Dark Ages have some remarkable religious and literary achievements to their credit, but their period of splendid independence did not last long.[2]

In the double monasteries, the rule was placed in the hands of either the abbot or the abbess. There was always a single authority; gender did not determine who would receive this appointment. For this reason, the double monastery stands as a clear rejection of sex polarity in the traditional category of virtue where man was considered by nature more able to rule than the woman.

Hilda of Whitby is also interesting because of her role as a teacher of men.[3] Five of those who studied under her direction later became bishops.[4] The Church historian Bede recorded that "Her prudence was so great that not only did ordinary persons, but even sometimes kings and princes, seek and receive council of her in their necessities."[5]

There is no record what Hilda taught her students. There is some evidence that Aristotle's logic played a role in monastic education, especially since these works were available in summary from Porphyry and in translation by Boethius. One historian of European education reflected: "The most stimulating and interesting morsel which the monastic teacher could place before the hungry intellect of the inquiring student was a morsel of logic."[6] Without a doubt, the general philosophy presented by the works of Boethius and St. Augustine would also be studied. Therefore, it can be surmised that a mixture of sex complementarity, sex unity and sex polarity was transmitted at first through the monastic educational tradition.

The significance of Hilda and the early abbesses who participated fully in the educational process is that the equality of woman and man was practised on a daily basis. Sometimes a woman ruled, at other times a man ruled; sometimes a woman taught and at other times a man taught. In this concrete, practical way, the underlying context of a living sex complementarity would become the soil out of which a philosophy of sex complementarity could one day emerge.

Roswitha of Gandersheim (c. 935–1002)

The first Benedictine nun to leave a written legacy was Roswitha, or Hrotsvit. While she is better known as a dramatist and poet, Roswitha also incorporated philosophical argumentation into her literary works. For this reason, she is of interest to the present study. Roswitha's philosophy of sex identity can best be summarized as arguing for an equality of woman and man in the categories of wisdom and virtue. Since Roswitha, as a dramatist, appears to keep careful lines of differentiation between the sexes, it would appear that she supported the equality of women and men within the framework of a philosophically significant sexual differentiation. Therefore, her concept of woman in relation to man can be considered as preparing the background for the eventual emergence of a philosophy of sex complementarity.

Roswitha's writings were discovered in 1494 by the humanist Conrad Celtes; John Trithemius, the Abbot of Spannheim, published them in 1501.[7] Celtes arranged them in the following three books: 1) *Hrosvithae Liber Primus* (eight legends); 2) *Hrosvithae Liber Secundus* (six plays); and 3) *Hrosvithae Liber Tertius* (two historical epics). Her writings contain one of the earliest examples of medieval drama and are therefore of significant historical value even before their content is analyzed. One modern biographer even suggested:

> There is no reason why Shakespeare should not have seen a printed collection of her works. . . . It should not be forgotten what a sensation was caused by Celtes' printing in 1501 of Roswitha's MS.[8]

Roswitha was a nun in the Benedictine monastery at Gandersheim, founded in 852 by Count Liudulf. The Abbess, Gerberga, was a close relative of Emperor Otto.

> The authority of the abbess was supreme; she had her own court; she sent her own men-at-arms into the field; she coined her own money. In such an institution culture was at its best. . . . It was in this intellectual paradise that the lot of Hrosvitha was cast.[9]

In one of the historical epics, Roswitha described "The Establishment of the Monastery at Gandersheim"; and in the other she wrote about "The Achievements of Otto."[10] Roswitha's presentation of her work to Otto is depicted in an unsigned woodcut, attributed to the artist Dürer. In her preface to this work, Roswitha offers a humble appraisal of her abilities:

> If a person of good judgement, who knows how to appraise things fairly, examines my work, he will pardon me the more readily because of the weakness

The Abbess of Gandersheim in complement with the Emperor Otto I receives Roswitha's manuscript in this woodcut by Dürer, 1501.

> of my sex and the inferiority of my knowledge, especially since I undertook this little work not of my own presumption, but at thy bidding.[11]

She also suggested that her situation as a nun precluded her from being able to write a proper military history:

> I do not boast that I am of such great wisdom . . . more than is seemly . . . as to hope to be able to express fully in words with what great strength of heavenly grace Christ, again and again, arranged it that this very King deservedly blessed passed unharmed through manifold snares and plots by a hostile faction. But I do not think it fitting for a frail woman abiding in the enclosure of a peaceful monastery to speak of war with which she ought not even to be acquainted.[12]

Then, Roswitha, with wonderful irony, proceeded to recount all of Otto's victories!

In the above two passages where Roswitha described herself in terms of the "weakness of my sex" and as a "frail woman," we find a self-depreciation common to the sex-polarity tradition. The deliberate devaluation of woman may also be compounded by the high value given to humility within the Benedictine tradition. In this context, the monks and nuns were expected always to consider themselves as the poorest of creatures in comparison with others. For this reason, the actual descriptions of women in Roswitha's writings probably serve as a more accurate indicator of her concept of woman than the remarks she uses to describe herself.

There is one fact about Roswitha's personal life that does reveal something of the concept of woman in the tenth century. Roswitha wrote all her plays in secret for fear that she would be asked to stop. Women were just beginning to become educated within the monastic tradition, but in comparison with the classical scholarly tradition, female dramatists and poets were relatively unknown. In the preface to the legends, Roswitha gives the following information:

> For as I was both young in years and not much advanced in learning, I did not have the courage to make known my intention by consulting any of the learned, for fear that they would put a stop to my work because of its crudeness of style.
>
> Unknown to others and secretly, so to speak, I worked alone. Sometimes I composed with great effort, again I destroyed what I had poorly written; and thus I strove according to my ability, scarcely adequate though that was, nonetheless to complete a composition from the thoughts in the writings with which I had become acquainted within the confines of our monastery at Gandersheim.[13]

One difficulty arose from this decision to keep her writing secret: Roswitha ended up drawing extensively upon an apocryphal source. Although this certainly lessened the authenticity of the stories she described, it did not preclude the eventual acceptance of her text. Roswitha then offered the following explanation in her preface to the legends:

> If the objection is made that, according to the judgement of some, portions of this book have been borrowed from apocryphal sources; to this I would answer that I have erred through ignorance and not through reprehensible presumption.

> For when I started to weave the thread of this collection, I was not aware of the fact that the authenticity of the material which I planned to work was questionable.[14]

Writing in Latin, Roswitha described the following legends: "The Maria," "The Ascension of Our Lord," "The Martyrdom of Blessed Gondolf," "The Sufferings of Pelegius, the Most Precious Martyr," "The Fall and Conversion of Theophilius," "The Life of Basilius," "The Passion of Saint Dionysius, the Illustrious Martyr," and "The Martyrdom of Agnes." Most of these stories consist in demonstrating the superiority of basic Christian virtues, especially chastity. The hero or heroine of each legend withstands an incredible variety of tortures and escapes various attempted murders to survive, still defending the faith in Christ. The purpose of the legends is to incite the reader to greater fidelity and personal strength.[15]

It is primarily in the plays of Roswitha that philosophical argument is used. Before the content of some of the plays is examined, however, it is useful to consider the prefaces she used to introduce her work. Here, Roswitha demonstrates a mature grasp of the significance of her work:

> There are many Catholics, and we cannot entirely acquit ourselves of the charge, who, attracted by the polished elegance of the style of pagan writers, prefer their works to the holy scriptures. There are others who, although they are deeply attached to the sacred writings and have no liking for pagan productions, make an exception in favour of the works of Terence, and fascinated by the charm of their manner, risk being corrupted by the wickedness of the matter. Wherefore I, the strong voice of Gandersheim, have not hesitated to imitate in my writings a poet whose works are so widely read, my object being to glorify, within the limits of my poor talent the laudable chastity of Christian virgins in that selfsame form of composition which has been used to describe the shameless acts of licentious women.[16]

In the context in which male poets used their gifts to describe non-virtuous women, Roswitha, now calling herself "the strong voice of Gandersheim," became the first woman in western history to use her talent to describe virtuous women.

Roswitha declared that she had received this gift of writing from God; at the same time, she indicated her skill at incorporating whatever knowledge was available to her in the tenth century:

> (God) has given me a perspicacious mind, but one that lies fallow and idle when it is not cultivated. That my natural gifts might not be made void by negligence I have been at pains, whenever I have been able to pick up some threads and scraps torn from the old mantle of philosophy, to weave them into the stuff of my own book, in the hope that my lowly ignorant effort may gain more acceptance through the introduction of something of a nobler strain, and that the Creator of genius may be honoured since it is generally believed that a woman's intelligence is slower.[17]

The image of the torn old mantle of philosophy could easily have been taken from Boethius's *Consolation of Philosophy*, which by now had become the most widely read philosophy text of the medieval period. Lady Philosophy described her torn mantle at the beginning of the work, when she referred to the way that philosophers such as Socrates had been treated by others. In this situation, Roswitha is placing herself among the philosophers who seek to wear that torn mantle. Therefore, a shift in identification has occurred from the simple female personification of philosophy in Boethius's figure of Lady Philosophy, to the real female philosopher, Roswitha.[18]

Roswitha learned philosophy from her Abbess, Gerberga, and her teacher, Rikkardis. She also shared her writings with some unnamed men, most likely Benedictine monks in relation to the sisters' monastery. In the following passage, the complementary interaction of women and men is clearly seen:

> To you, learned and virtuous men, who do not envy the success of others, but on the contrary rejoice in it as becomes the truly great, Hrotswitha, poor humble sinner, sends wishes for your health in this life and your joy in eternity. . . .
>
> To think that you, who have been nurtured in the most profound philosophical studies and have attained knowledge in perfection, should have deigned to approve the humble work of an obscure woman! . . .
>
> Until I showed my work to you I had not dared to let anyone see it except my intimate companions. I came near abandoning this form of writing altogether, for if there were so few to whom I could submit my compositions at all there were fewer still who could point out what needed correction and encourage me to go on. But now, reassured by your verdict (is it not said that the testimony of three witness is "equivalent to the truth"?), I feel that I have enough confidence to apply myself to writing, if God grants me the power, and that I need not fear the criticism of the learned whoever they may be.[19]

The plays that Roswitha had given the learned men included "Gallicanus," "Dulcitius," "Callimachus," "Abraham," "Paphnutius," and "Sapientia." The latter two plays contain dialogue of particular interest to philosophers. In both, Roswitha displays her knowledge of current philosophical issues, and her skill in using this knowledge in a wider story about the struggle between virtue and vice. Once again, in this passage we find the movement from a proclaimed devaluation of sex identity to confidence as a female writer. At first, Roswitha describes herself as a "humble sinner" and an "obscure woman." However, by the end of the passage she declares that she has confidence and does "not fear the criticism of the learned whoever they may be." Roswitha was well aware of her talents as a thinker and a writer. When she was able to have these capacities recognized by a few men she valued, she became free to realize her potential as a female philosopher and playwright. Some of her more philosophical works will now be considered in detail.

In the play "Paphnutius," the main character is a hermit philosopher who disguises himself as a lover in order to convert the prostitute Thais to Christianity. At the beginning of the play Paphnutius is engaged in the following dialogue with his disciples:

PAPHNUTIUS: You know that the greater world is composed of four elements which are contraries, yet by the will of the creator these contraries are adjusted in harmonious arrangement. Now, man is composed of even more contrary parts.
DISCIPLES: What can be more contrary than the elements?
PAPHNUTIUS: The body and the soul. The soul is not mortal like the body, nor the body spiritual as is the soul.[20]

The discussion continues with a consideration of the meaning of harmony, of substance, and of music.

DISCIPLES: What is music, master?
PAPHNUTIUS One of the branches of the "quadrivium" of philosophy, my son. Arithmetic, geometry, music, and philosophy form the quadrivium.
DISCIPLES: I should like to know why they are given that name.
PAPHNUTIUS Because just as paths branch out from the quadrivium, the place where four roads meet, so do these subjects lead like roads from one principle of philosophy.
DISCIPLES: We had best not question you about the other three, for our slow wits can scarcely follow what you have told us about the first.[21]

Paphnutius continues, nonetheless, to give the lecture on the relations between harmony, music, mathematics, and the rotation of the planets. Eventually his disciples protest:

DISCIPLES: True it may be, but I am weary of this disputation. We are all weary, because we cannot follow the reasoning of such a philosopher!
PAPHNUTIUS Why do you laugh at me, children? I am no philosopher, but an ignorant man.
DISCIPLES: Where did you get all this learning with which you have puzzled our heads?
PAPHNUTIUS: It is but a little drop from the full deep wells of learning—wells at which I, a chance passerby, have lapped, but never sat down to drain.[22]

This dialogue between Paphnutius and his disciples reveals the knowledge that Roswitha had of philosophy in the tenth century. As one of the four parts of the quadrivium in classical education, philosophy integrated the other disciplines related to mathematics and music.[23] While the history of institutionalized education will be considered more thoroughly in Chapter V, it is important at this point to recognize that Roswitha was well aware of its structures, even though she perhaps identifies herself with Paphnutius, who has been limited to "lapping" little drops from the deep wells of learning.

While Roswitha characterizes the philosopher in the above play as a man, in "Sapientia" the philosopher is a woman. Sapientia is the mother of three virgin martyrs who were tortured and put to death by Emperor Hadrian. At the beginning of the play, Antiochus reports to Hadrian that Sapientia has been leading all the women of the country to abandon the worship of pagan gods in order to embrace Christianity. Hadrian suggest that they attempt first to ask Sapientia, as a favour, to worship the pagan gods.

ANTIOCHUS: That may be best. This frail sex is easily moved by flattery.
HADRIAN: Noble matron, if you desire to enjoy our friendship, I ask you in

all gentleness to join me in an act of worship of the gods.
SAPIENTIA: We have no desire for your friendship, and we refuse to worship your gods. . . .
HADRIAN: The splendour of your ancestry is blazoned on your face, and the wisdom of your name sparkles on your lips.
SAPIENTIA: You need not waste your breath in flattering us. We are not to be conquered by fair speeches.[24]

Dispensing with the use of flattery, Hadrian seeks to discover more about Sapientia and her family. He asks the ages of her three daughters, who are named Faith, Hope, and Charity. Displaying a rather thorough knowledge of elementary mathematics, Roswitha constructs the following dialogue:

SAPIENTIA: What do you say, children? Shall I puzzle his dull brain with some problems in arithmetic?
FAITH: Do, mother. It will give us joy to hear you.
SAPIENTIA: As you wish to know the ages of my children, O Emperor, Charity has lived a diminished evenly even number of years; Hope a number also diminished, but evenly uneven; and Faith an augmented number, unevenly even.
HADRIAN: Your answer leaves me in ignorance.
SAPIENTIA: That is not surprising, since not one number, but many, come under this definition.[25]

Hadrian asks his guest several more questions until Sapientia offers the following explanation:

SAPIENTIA: Every number is said to be "diminished" the parts of which when added together give a sum which is less than the number of which they are parts. Such a number is 8. For the half of 8 is 4, the quarter of 8 is 2, and the eighth of 8 is 1; and these added together give 7. It is the same with 10. Its half is 5, its fifth part 2, its tenth part 1, and these together give 8. On the other hand, a number is said to be "augmented" when its parts added together exceed it. Such for instance, is 12. Its half is 6, its third is 4, its fourth is 3, its sixth 2, its twelfth 1, and the sum of these figures is 16. And in accordance with the principle which decrees that between all excesses shall rule the exquisite proportion of the mean, that number is called "perfect," the sum of the parts of which is equal to its whole. Such a number is 6, whose parts—a third, a half, and a sixth, added together, come to 6. For the same reason 28, 496, and 8000 are called "perfect."[26]

After considerable further dialogue, Hadrian responds:

HADRIAN: Little did I think that a simple question as to the age of these children could give rise to such an intricate and unprofitable dissertation.
SAPIENTIA: It would be unprofitable if it did not lead us to appreciate the wisdom of our Creator, and the wonderous knowledge of the Author of the world, Who in the beginning set everything in number, measure, and weight,

> and then, in time and the age of man, formulated a science which reveals fresh wonders the more we study it.[27]

Needless to say, Hadrian could not convince Sapientia and her daughters to worship pagan gods. He therefore contrived a series of ingenious methods of torture for them. Faith survived a whipping, the mutilation of her breasts, roasting over a fire, and being dropped into a brazier of pitch and wax until Hadrian finally beheaded her. Hope survived whipping, laceration with nails, broken bones, disembowelment, and being thrown into a fire before she also was beheaded. Even Charity managed to defy the emperor:

> CHARITY: Although I am small, my reason is big enough to put you to shame.
> HADRIAN: Take her away, Antiochus, and have her stretched on the rack and whipped.
> ANTIOCHUS: I fear that stripes will be of no use.
> HADRIAN: Then order the furnace to be heated for three days and three nights, and let her be cast into the flames.
> CHARITY: A mighty man! He cannot conquer a child of eight without calling in the fire to help him![28]

Once again, Hadrian had finally to resort to the sword to behead his victim. Surprisingly, Sapientia was left to bury her children and continue her work of conversion.

There are several aspects of the play "Sapientia" that are interesting for the concept of woman in relation to man. In the first place, the sex-polarity concept of woman is represented by the man Antiochus when he states that "the frail sex is easily moved by flattery." The play serves to reverse this concept by proving that woman is the opposite of frail. The second inversion occurs in the interactions with Hadrian, who thought he could out-think the woman and her children. Instead, we find Sapientia referring to Hadrian as having a "dull brain" before she completely confuses him with mathematical puzzles. The young girl Charity finally concludes the inversion of wisdom when she says, "although I am small my reason is big . . ." Finally, the use of sheer force by men is shown to be insufficient to bend the will of the woman or her daughters. In all of these ways, the concept of woman is revealed as containing wisdom, virtue, and strength.

The description of Sapientia is noticeably like the image of St. Catherine of Alexandria, which had, since the ninth century, become popular in Europe. The image of a female Christian philosopher standing up to a male pagan philosopher and being able to match or even better his intelligence in argument is a theme that fascinated the medieval mind. Although Sapientia was represented as a married woman, while St. Catherine was a virgin, the female personification of wisdom was common to both images. Sapientia simply carries the Christian dynamic of the image further in giving birth to the three theological virtues of Faith, Hope, and Charity. The implication of the two examples is that reason alone, when represented by pagan philosophers, is not equal to reason when combined with faith. The latter overturns the former and Christian philosophy vanquishes pagan philosophy.

It is interesting to note as well that the kind of philosophy Roswitha discusses appears to flow from the Pythagorean and neo-Platonic schools, with their emphasis on harmony in mathematics and music. There appears to be no influence of Aristotelianism except perhaps in the logic of argumentation. However, there is too little of that to draw any conclusions one way or another. Therefore, Roswitha's contribution to the history of the concept of woman in relation to man appears to occur just before the influx of Aristotelian theory. It represents an example of the developing complementarity of women and men through the active interaction of both kinds of philosophers within the context of the Benedictine double monasteries.

St. Anselm (1033–1109)

This important eleventh-century philosopher was called "Augustinus Redivivus" because he was so deeply influenced by the fifth-century Christian philosopher Augustine.[29] It is interesting to discover that Anselm also had a three-tiered theory of sex-identity. However, Anselm held an unresolved tension among sex neutrality, sex polarity and sex complementarity that differed significantly from St. Augustine. The following list compares the two theorists:

St. Augustine	Levels of Existence	St. Anselm
sex complementarity	highest	sex neutrality
sex unity	middle	sex polarity
sex polarity	lowest	sex complementarity

Therefore, while for St. Augustine sex complementarity represented the highest theory of sex identity, for Anselm sex neutrality held this position. The justification for this significant difference lies in St. Anselm's rationalism and his claim that reason was a more accurate method of approach to the truth than faith. Therefore, he sought to elaborate many fundamental concepts of theory using arguments that appealed to reason. As has been seen in previous writers, sex neutrality is the consequence of the exclusive use of reason in arguments about sex identity.

At the same time, when Anselm turned the use of discursive reason towards concepts that spring up from the world, he represented a sex-polarity theory of the relation of the concept of woman and man. This is seen in his analysis of God as Father. Finally, when Anselm writes from the perspective of his intuitive reason, a surprising revelation of sex complementarity is articulated. This is seen in his development of a theology of Mary, of a notion of Christ as Mother, and in his correspondence with numerous women. In addition, Anselm gives evidence of the concrete basis for sex complementarity that was evolving through the frequent interaction of women and men within the Benedictine tradition of education and religious life.

The philosophical foundation for St. Anselm's sex neutrality was the logic of Aristotle, as summarized in Porphyry's *Isagoge* and Boethius's translation of the *Organon*.[30] Anselm sought to use Aristotelian categories and methods in an attempt to found religion on a more rational ground. In the most famous "ontological" arguments for the proof of the existence of God, Anselm defines God simply as "that than which no greater can be conceived."[31] This definition of God represented the highest knowledge of God. It is clearly a definition without any reference to sex identity, therefore it is a definition within the sex-neutrality tradition.

Anselm differentiates the highest level of knowledge of God, in which there is no sexual differentiation, from the lower, more popular level in which God is sexually differentiated as Father:

> Now if anyone wants to know why, although there is no sexual distinction in the Supreme Being, the parent in the Supreme Being is called father rather than mother, if the offspring is called son rather than daughter . . . then he should find (the answer) clearly stated in this small book of mine.[32]

Drawing upon the traditional medieval female personification of wisdom, Anselm asks in the *Monologium* why the Divine Nature would not more appropriately be interpreted as feminine rather than masculine:

> I think I ought not to by-pass the question of which set of terms is more suitable for them—"father and son" or "mother and daughter"—for there is no sexual distinction in the Supreme Spirit and the word. For if the Supreme Spirit is appropriately father and its offspring appropriately son because each is spirit, then by parity of reasoning why is it not appropriate for one to be mother and the other to be daughter because each is truth and wisdom.[33]

Anselm's use of discursive reason, and his love of logic, makes this question of the female identity of the Divine a necessity. His decision to face this question squarely is significant in the history of philosophy. St. Augustine also raised it in his consideration of the nature of the Trinity, but as previously demonstrated, he rejected all possibility of the inclusion of a feminine dimension to God because of the danger it held for images of sexual intercourse. Augustine was so concerned about supporting the immateriality and transcendence of a single God in the context of a pagan polytheism that believed in material, immanent, and plural gods and goddesses, that he rejected any concept that might confuse this new shift in thought about the Divine Nature.[34] However, Anselm is not faced with the same context some six hundred years later, and he is able to raise the question again. Anselm's context is one in which the female personification of wisdom has achieved a heightened expression through the popularity of Boethius's *Consolation of Philosophy* and the common belief in St. Catherine of Alexandria as the epitome of wisdom. Therefore, it is appropriate for him to consider whether the feminine is associated with the source of all wisdom, which is contained in the third member of the Trinity, or the Holy Spirit.

Anselm's analysis in the *Monologium* continues by rejecting the simple sex-polarity argument in favour of the masculine interpretation of God, namely that the male is by nature superior to the female, and therefore that God would have to be male rather than female:

> Is it (preferable to call them father and son) because among those natures which have a difference of sex it is characteristic of the better sex to be father and son and of the inferior sex to be mother and daughter. Now, although such is naturally the case for many beings, for others the reverse holds true. For example, in some species of birds the female sex is always the larger and stronger, the male sex smaller and weaker.[35]

By using an appeal to the senses and to discursive reason, Anselm rejects the arguments that males are always superior to females and that, therefore, maleness in itself is a perfection, or femaleness an imperfection. Therefore, God is not called Father for Anselm because of a natural superiority of the male.

Anselm concludes in the *Monologium* that God is called Father because He is first in the order of generation. Reasoning from an incorrect theory of generation, Anselm states:

> But surely, the Supreme Spirit is more suitably called father than mother because the first and principal cause of offspring is always in the father. For, if the paternal cause always in some way precedes the maternal cause, then it is exceedingly inappropriate for the name "mother" to be applied to that parent whom no other cause either joins or precedes for the begetting of offspring.[36]

The belief that the process of generation is initiated by the seed of the father and that the mother's contribution follows later, misled Anselm in his efforts to find a reason for calling the first person of the Trinity Father. Since this view of generation originally received its articulation in Aristotle, and was later amplified in Galen and Porphyry, we find that Anselm has probably inadvertantly accepted an Aristotelian rationale for sexual differentiation within the Divine Nature.

Anselm concluded that the Divine Parent who generated Christ had to be Father and not Mother. Then he argued that the one generated, or Christ, had to be Son rather than Daughter because of the demands of resemblance:

> But if a son is always more like a father than is a daughter, and if no one thing is more like another than this offspring is like the Supreme Father, it is most true that this offspring is a son, not a daughter.[37]

Anselm's argument is perfectly logical, given the false premise with which he began.

Anselm's completely masculine interpretation of the Deity is developed even further in a discursive text entitled *De Processione Spiritus Sancti.* In this work Anselm developed the view that the Holy Spirit proceeds both from the Father and the Son.[38] Both this text and the *Monologium* are examples of the use of discursive reasoning to consider the nature of God. Anselm is explicit in stating his methodology in the preface of the *Monologium*:

> Now, whatever I have stated in this treatise I have stated in the role of one who by reflection alone investigates, and disputes with himself about points which he had not previously considered.[39]

As the evidence demonstrates, when Anselm uses his reflection alone he reaches first a view of God as beyond all sexual distinction; and when he incorporates available theories of the philosophy of science into his reflection, he draws conclusions about the nature of God that imply a completely masculine identity.

The fascinating aspect of Anselm's writings for the concept of woman in relation to man do not end here, however. For when Anselm expresses his own intimate relation with God through the use of intuition, passion and the emotions, the Divine Nature is experienced as strongly feminine. In this remarkable shift, Anselm has moved from a sex-unity theory, through a sex-polarity theory, to a sex-complementarity theory for the Divine Nature.

The key to Anselm's initiation of a new interpretation of the feminine nature of God is not through a female Holy Spirit or through a Mother Creator, but rather, through the feminine dynamics of Christ's interaction with the world. In a prayer to St. Paul, Anselm exclaims:

> And you, Jesus, are you not also a mother?
> Are you not the mother who, like a hen,
> gathers her children under her wings?
> Truly Lord, you are a mother;
> for both they who are in labour
> and they who are brought forth
> are accepted by you.
> You have died more than they, that they may labour to bear.
> It is by your death that they have been born,
> for if you had not been in labour
> you could not have borne death;
> and if you had not died, you would not have brought forth.
>
> For, longing to bear sons into life,
> you tasted of death,
> and by dying you begot them.
> You did this in your own self . . .
> So you, Lord God, are the great mother.[40]

Thus the first aspect of Christ's motherhood involves his labouring to bring forth new life. St. Anselm, playing with images of fathering and mothering concludes that God and St. Paul are both fathers and mothers:

> Then both of you are mothers.
> Even if you are fathers, you are also mothers.
>
> For you have brought it about that those born to death
> should be reborn to life—
> you by your own act, you by his power.
> Therefore, you are fathers by your effect
> and mothers by your affection.
>
> Fathers by your authority, mothers by your kindness.
> Fathers by your teaching, mothers by your mercy.
> Then you, Lord, are a mother,
> and you, Paul, are a mother too.[41]

Anselm is aware of the originality of this idea in an historical context in Christianity in which God has been exclusively referred to by philosophers and theologians as Father. He continues his prayer:

> Why should I be silent about what you have said?
> Why should I conceal what you have revealed?
> Why should I hide what you have done?
> You have revealed yourselves as mothers;
> I know myself to be a son. . .
> Paul, my mother, Christ bore you also;
> so place your dead son at the feet of Christ, your mother,
> because he also is Christ's son.
> Rather, throw him into the heart of Christ's goodness,
> for Christ is even more his mother . .
> St. Paul, pray for your son, because you are his mother,
> that the Lord, who is his mother too,
> may give life to his son.
> Do, mother of my soul,
> what the mother of my flesh would do.[42]

The view that St. Paul and Jesus are mothers through their role in giving birth to the soul is the key point in Anselm's analysis. However, he develops the mothering of God even further to include the dynamics of nourishing, comforting, and protecting that are part of child-rearing:

> Christ, my mother,
> you gather your chickens under your wings;
> this dead chicken of yours puts himself under those wings.
> For by your gentleness the badly frightened are comforted,
> by your sweet smell the despairing are revived,
> your warmth gives life to the dead,
> your touch justifies sinners.
> Mother, know again your dead son,
> both by the sign of your cross and the voice of his confession. . . .
> For from you flows consolation for sinners;
> to you be blessing for ages and ages. Amen.[43]

The astonishing aspect of this prayer is the extent to which Anselm goes to develop and defend his interpretation of Jesus and St. Paul as mothers. Having already argued for the particularly masculine nature of the Trinity when considered from the internal dynamics of its own identity, and given the generally accepted view of the masculinity of St. Paul, Anselm's explicit appeal to the motherhood of God and of the Apostle is significant. When attempting to come to terms with how such a different attitude towards the nature of God emerges in a prayer than the one which is suggested in the discursive writings, a possible explanation surfaces. When Anselm is using his discursive reason to argue about the nature of God, he depends upon common philosophical concepts available to him. In this case, the theory of generation provides the basis for the fatherhood interpretation. This use of reason differs first from the highest application of logic in the ontological argument from God's existence in which no sex identity enters into the topic. It also differs from the intuitive reasoning that springs forth naturally in a personal prayer. In this latter situation, images surface about the Divine Nature that do not come about on the conscious discursive level, and the Divine Nature is revealed as being experienced as both father and mother. Therefore, Anselm appears to open up, through intuition, access to a complementary feminine aspect of the Divine.[44]

The assertion of the importance of the feminine is also expressed in Anselm's prayer to Mary. As mentioned previously, for St. Augustine, Mary's importance was relatively undeveloped compared with her later significance. Anselm stands as an important intermediate figure between the role of Mary in Augustine's thought and her role in St. Albert the Great's. By the end of the thirteenth century, Mary had emerged as a powerful complement to God as Father, Son and Holy Spirit. Anselm begins his prayer to Mary by asserting her secondary status in relation to God:

> A thing to be wondered at—
> at what height do I behold the place of Mary!
> Nothing equals Mary,
> nothing but God is greater than Mary. . . .
>
> All nature is created by God and God is born of Mary.
> God created all things, and Mary gave birth to God. . . .
>
> So God is the Father of all created things,
> and Mary is the mother of all re-created things.
>
> God is the Father of all that is established,
> and Mary is the mother of all that is re-established.
>
> For God gave birth to him by whom all things were made
> and Mary brought forth him by whom all are saved. . . .[45]

The complementarity of God the Father of Christ, and Mary the mother of Christ is slowly but surely developed.

In the next image, Anselm states that Mary, who is the mother of Christ, is also his own mother. Therefore, Anselm concludes that he and Jesus are brothers:

> Blessed assurance, safe refuge,
> the mother of God is our mother.
> The mother of him in whom alone we have hope,
> whom alone we fear,
> is our mother.
> The mother of him who alone saves and condemns
> is our mother. . . .
>
> Seeing it I rejoice, and hardly dare to speak of it.

For if you, Lady, are his mother,
surely then your sons are his brothers? . . .
With what affection should we love
this brother and this mother. . . . [46]

As Anselm allows the images of Mary and Jesus to unfold further, a new complementarity of the regal Lord and Lady emerges:

Lord, son of my Lady,
Lady, mother of my Lord,
If I am not worthy of the bliss of your love,
certainly you are not unworthy of being so greatly loved. . . .

Lord and Lady, surely it is much better for you to give grace
to those who do not deserve it
than for you to exact what is owing to you in justice? [47]

Finally, Anselm concludes his prayer with a veneration of Mary and Jesus:

So I venerate you both,
as far as my mind is worthy to do so;
I love you both,
as far as my heart is equal to it;
and I serve you both,
as far as my flesh may. [48]

In this final description, Anselm has brought together mind, heart, soul, and flesh in a unified affirmation of the complementarity of Jesus, who is the masculine incarnation of God, and of Mary, who is the feminine mother of God.

The above "Prayer to St. Mary" therefore gives evidence of the same movements towards a sex complementarity as was previously found in the "Prayer to St. Paul." Once again, the hypothesis presents itself that Anselm's theory of sex complementarity emerged through his intuitive reason, or through the emotional and intellectual outpouring that occurred spontaneously in prayer.

To summarize St. Anselm's complex example of thought about the relation of sex identity to the Divine Nature, it would appear as though his theory followed from three kinds of reasoning:

Logical reasoning	God's essential nature	sex neutrality
Discursive reasoning in relation to the science of nature	God's internal nature as a Trinity	sex polarity
Intuitive reasoning in prayer	God's nature in relation to the world	sex complementarity

It is interesting to consider how Anselm came to a theory of sex complementarity. St. Augustine appeared to reach this theory through an intellectual apprehension of the logical consequences of the theory of resurrection. In addition, Augustine's personal experience of women tended to support primarily a theory of sex polarity, although he occasionally appeared to have an experiential basis for his defence of sex unity in the category of wisdom. In contrast to this previous example, Anselm appears to derive his defence for sex complementarity from experience, while sex neutrality and sex polarity are defended from intellectual grounds. This lends support to the hypothesis suggested in this chapter that the concrete experience of men and women within the double monasteries of the Benedictine tradition led to the situation in which sex complementarity naturally arose.

Anselm was a Benedictine monk who later became Archbishop of Canterbury. He was in frequent correspondence with women throughout his life, as teacher, spiritual director, and friend. Therefore, it is not surprising that the above prayers, which articulated a move towards sex complementarity, were organized and sent to the countess Matilda of Tuscany:

> It has seemed good to our Highness that I should lend you these prayers, which I edited at the request of several brothers. Some of them are not appropriate to you, but I want to send them all, so that if you like them you may be able to compose others after their example.[49]

Anselm encouraged his female friends to develop their literary skills within the context of Christian life.

Of the several hundred letters extant from Anselm, several are addressed to women. When Anselm was Prior at the Benedictine monastery in Bec (1063–1078), he wrote to conclude a spiritual alliance with a woman named Frodeline:

> The good odor of your reputation, which carried everywhere spreading itself far like a sweet balm, has reached me. Since then I have always wished a favorable opportunity to allow me to enter into a relation with you. By knowing you, I hope to be able to advance a little into your friendship, for I see myself very poor of personal goods, and I would be able in this way to add your merits to mine by a communion full of love.[50]

It is clear that Anselm respects women and seeks to share in the mutual search for wisdom and virtue with them.

During the period that Anselm was Abbot (1078–1093), one letter encourages the Countess Ida to greater perfection: "In truth, I always hold on to the hope that your prudence grows more full of a clear-sighted vigilance . . ."[51] The exhortation to greater prudence is an example of Anselm's recognition that women are capable of the highest exercise of practical wisdom. In a second letter during this same period, Anselm attempts to persuade Ermengarde to allow her husband to enter monastic life. In this letter he argues: "That your prudent strength and your courageous prudence will give him then to God."[52]

It is important not to conclude from this letter that Anselm supported celibacy *per se* over and against marriage. For Anselm clearly supported the decision to marry, even though he considered virginity to be a higher form of life. In the *Cur Deus Homo* he states:

> Although the state of virginity is better than the marital state, neither of them is definitely required of man. Instead, we say both of him who prefers to marry and of him who prefers to keep his virginity that he ought to do what he does. For no one claims that virginity ought not to be chosen or that marriage ought not to be chosen. Rather, we say that before a man has decided on either of them, he ought to do the one which he prefers.[53]

In the *Facere*, St. Anselm considers several arguments for and against marriage. Using Aristotelian logic he concludes:

> Accordingly, since to marry or not to marry ought to be in accordance with his wishes, we say that if he wants to he ought to marry, and if he does not want to he ought not to marry.[54]

The view of St. Anselm, that the wish of the man or woman should determine whether marriage or celibacy ought to be the proper choice in life, had implications in concrete situations. In the above-mentioned letter to Ermengarde, the husband wanted to enter into a celibate life after having been married. Anselm was attempting to persuade the wife to the same desire, for he would not allow the husband to enter a monastery without his wife's permission. In another example, Anselm allowed a young nun who had not yet taken her vows of celibacy to leave the monastery to marry, because this was what she wanted to do.[55]

It was during Anselm's tenure as Archbishop of Canterbury (1093–1109) that we have the most examples of his letters to women. He wrote letters of spiritual direction to the Countess Ida, to the Countess Clemence, and to the Countess Mathilde; he wrote letters of counsel and advice to the Abbess Mathilde, the Abbess Adelize, and the Abbess Eulalie; he wrote letters of request and thanks to Queen Mathilde.[56] In one letter to the queen, Anselm returned to the theme of the value of maternity:

> With all possible affection and as much as I dare to allow myself to address your Highness, I ask and beg your piety, I supplicate it and give it, as a faithful friend, the counsel to employ all its zeal to maintain the Church in England in peace and tranquillity. Let it come particularly to the aid of its weakest and least powerful children, to those who are plunged into tribulation and desolation; to regard them as orphans of Christ. Resembling the mother hen of which the gospel speaks, deign in your mercy, to guard them under your eyes, console them and comfort them by your protection.[57]

From these few examples it can be seen that Anselm lived in frequent communication with women who were educated and powerful, and who appeared to enjoy a kind of relationship of sex complementarity in every-day situations. Anselm's experience of interaction with women went far beyond the confines of a monastic life when he was promoted to Archbishop. Anselm showed a disposition towards viewing women as equal and significantly different from men that was carried forward into his apostolic work. In this way, Anselm continued to prepare the ground for further developments in the philosophy of sex complementarity.[58]

Abelard (1079–1142) and Heloise (1101–1164)

The Christian philosopher and theologian Abelard developed a slightly different theory of sex identity from those considered up to this point in the history of western thought. In a certain sense, Abelard developed a contradictory theory of extremes, for he supported a philosophy of sex polarity on the level of nature and, simultaneously, a theology of reverse sex polarity on the level of response to grace. By nature, men were the "stronger sex" and women the "weaker sex" in soul, mind, and body. However, Abelard claimed that women were superior to men in their response to grace and in their capacity for religious life. Abelard also sought to temper these extreme statements of the superiority of one sex over the other by a defence of an equality of women and men in two areas. First, supporting a sex-unity theory, he argued that through reason and the opportunity to participate in the life of grace, there should be no differentiation of male and female. Secondly, moving towards a theory of sex complementarity, Abelard developed a relationship with Heloise and with her religious community at the Paraclete that bespoke sexual differentiation within the context of the equality of woman and man.

Abelard's rather contradictory theory of sex identity can be summarized as follows:

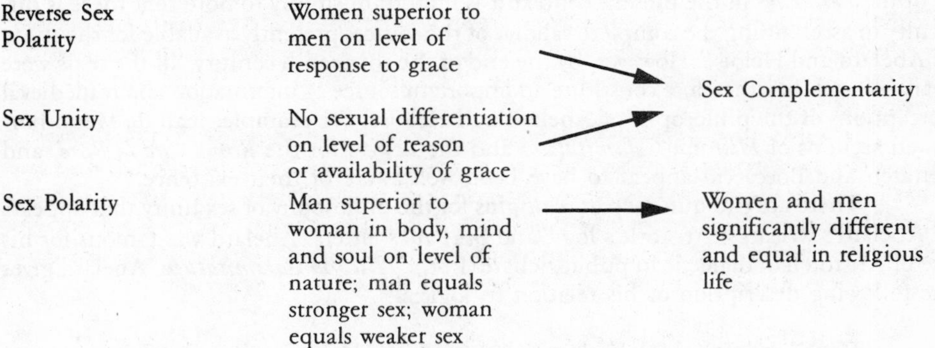

Heloise, in contrast to Abelard, appears to have maintained only two of the four theories of sex identity: sex polarity and sex complementarity. For the most part, Heloise postulated a theory of sex polarity in which she continually described woman as the weaker sex, inferior to man. At the same time, however, Heloise's actual interaction with Abelard appears to move towards the evolution of a more practical sex complementarity. Therefore, Heloise's theory of sex identity can be summarized as follows:

Sex Polarity	Man superior to woman in body, mind and soul; man equals stronger sex; woman equals weaker sex	Sex Complementarity Women and men significantly different and equal in religious life

While Heloise's strongest arguments are for sex polarity, Abelard's arguments support the combination of sex polarity and reverse sex polarity. However, as mentioned previously, they also fall to some extent within the tradition of sex complementarity as it evolved through the concrete situation of the double monasteries.

There is considerable debate associated with the authenticity of the main texts for Abelard's and Heloise's theories of sex identity, namely their *Letters*, the *Historia Calamitatum, Touching the Origin of Nuns, An Institute or Rule of Nuns,* and the *Problematica Heloissae*. John Benton suggests that some of the works were in part forged by a monk from a later century:

> My hypothesis is that Abelard established the Paraclete as a double monastery similar to Fontevrault for its use not only an *Exhortatio ad Fratres et Commonachos* but also an *Exhortatio ad Sorores*. Some time in the thirteenth century, perhaps at the time of the electoral crises in the later 1280's, one of the monks attempted to overthrow the authority of the nuns who ruled the double monastery. To this end he (or someone working for him) created a forged rule by inserting some institutional changes into this hypothetical tripartite *Exhortatio ad Sorores*.[59]

Benton also offers arguments concerning the varied sources of the other texts referred to above. However, other scholars, such as Etienne Gilson, affirm the authenticity of the *Letters*.[60] In the present context it is important simply to note that there is difficulty in ascertaining the complete validity of the sources presently available for the study of Abelard and Heloise. However, by the end of the thirteenth century, all the texts were available and they therefore constitute an important source of information about medieval perceptions of the philosophy of Abelard and Heloise. For example, Jean de Meun borrowed sections of *Historia Calamitatum* and the *Letters* for the *Roman de la Rose*, and Petrarch and Boccaccio appear to have been well aware of their existence.[61]

There are two quite separate origins for the philosophy of sex unity that appears in Abelard's writings: Aristotle's logic and St. Paul's letters. Abelard was famous for his use of Aristotelian dialectic in public debate. In the *Historia Calamitatum*, Abelard gives the following description of his relation to logic:

> I found the armory of logical reasoning more to my liking than the other forms of philosophy, I exchanged all other weapons for these, and to the prizes of victory in war I preferred the battle of minds in disputation. Thenceforth, journeying through many provinces, and debating as I went, going withersoever I heard that the study of my chosen art most flourished, I became such as one of the Peripatetics.[62]

Abelard learned Aristotle's logic through the *Isagoge* of Porphyry and through Boethius's translation of the *Organon*.[63] The adoption of Aristotle's dialectic method of argument was developed by Abelard into what became known as the scholastic method; Abelard was consequently called "Doctor Scholasticus."[64] Abelard described his self-perception at the height of his early career, when he served as head of the Cathedral School in Paris between 1108 and 1118:

> I returned to Paris, and there for several years I peacefully directed the school. . . . Thus I, who by this time had come to regard myself as the only philosopher remaining in the whole world, and who had ceased to fear any disturbance of my peace, began to loosen the rein of my desires, although I had always lived

> in the utmost continence. And the greater progress I made in my lecturing on philosophy or theology, the more I departed alike from the practice of the philosophers.[65]

Abelard's texts *Ethics* and *Dialectics*, which spring from the logical writings, refer to sexual differentiation. They focus on the problem of universals and of judgements that refer to humanity without sexual distinction.[66] Therefore, these fundamental contributions of Abelard to philosophy suggest a sex neutrality derivation of sex unity.

The theological foundation for Abelard's arguments of sex unity came from his belief that Christ, on the level of justice, sought to make no distinction between woman and man:

> And so Christ, the end of justice, and the consumation of all good; . . . as He had come to call either sex and to redeem them, so thought fit to unite both sexes in the true monkhead of His congregation, that thereafter authority for this profession might be given both to men and to women, and the perfect way of life might be given both to men and to women, which they should imitate.[67]

In the same essay, *Touching on the Origin of Nuns*, Abelard sought to prove that from the beginning of Jesus' ministry "It appears that the religion of woman was not disjoined from the order of clerics. Which women also were clearly joined with the men in name, since we speak both of deaconesses and of deacons."[68] The equality of women and men does not necessarily imply a sex-unity theory, but, in a sermon, Abelard develops this interpretation by appealing to the theory of the Apostle Paul:

> Who . . . is so singular in dignity as Christ, in whom the Apostle says there is "neither male nor female"? In the body of Christ, which is the church, difference of sex, therefore, confers no dignity; for Christ looks not at the condition of sex, but the quality of merits.[69]

The theory of St. Paul, also transmitted through St. Augustine, stated that "In Christ there is no male nor female." Abelard accepted this interpretation in discussions of the gift of grace and the possibility of living a perfect life. He argued simply, that Christ offers this to both men and women without any sexual distinction. Therefore, the perfection of wisdom and virtue are accessible to either woman or man without sexual distinction.

However, Abelard combines this sex-unity description of the accessibility of grace and the perfect life with another very different approach to the capacities and actual responses of women and men in the world. It is this aspect of human nature that captures his most careful argumentation. His philosophical justification for sex polarity will now be examined.

Abelard developed a rationale for the natural superiority of man over woman in *Touching on the Origin of Nuns*:

> And men are naturally, both in mind and in body, stronger than women. Wherefore rightly is the manly nature indicated by the flesh, which is nearer to the bone; womanly weakness by the skin.[70]

This division of nature leads to the conclusion that men naturally rule over women. In *Historia Calamitatum*, Abelard derives the following conclusions:

> The weaker sex needs the help of the stronger one to such an extent that the apostle proclaimed that the head of the woman is ever the man (1 Cor, xi, 3), and in sign thereof he bade her ever wear her head covered (ibid., 5). For this reason I marvel greatly at the customs which have crept into monasteries, whereby, even as abbots are placed in charge of the men, abbesses now are given authority over the women, and the women bind themselves in their vows to accept the same rules as men.[71]

Abelard continues his analysis of the digression from the natural rule of the stronger over the weaker with the following reflection on double monasteries in which the abbess rules over both women and men:

> In many places we may even behold an inversion of the natural order of things, whereby the abbesses and nuns have authority over the clergy, and even over those who are themselves in charge of the people. The more power such women exercise over men, the more easily can they lead them into iniquitous desires, and in this way can lay a very heavy yoke upon their shoulders. It was with such things in mind that the satirist said: "There is nothing more intolerable than a rich woman." (Juvenal, *Sat.* IV, v, 459).[72]

The use of Juvenal to support a sex-polarity theory is an obvious appeal to philosophical authority. In this passage, Abelard is very clear about the superiority of man over woman in the natural order.

Abelard describes the situation in which a woman overturns the natural order by ruling men as being corrupted by the devil. In *An Institute or Rule of Nuns* he states:

> What will the weaker sex be able to avail against him? By whom is his seduction so greatly to be feared as by woman? For her he first of all seduced, and through her her husband likewise, and led all their posterity captive. Greed of a greater deprived woman of a lesser good. By this art also will he now easily seduce a woman, when she desires rather to govern than to serve, driven thereto by ambition of wealth or honour.[73]

The greater weakness of woman is seen, according to Abelard, in the nature of the first woman, Eve. In his *Hymns*, Abelard developed a differentiation of the sexes so that while Adam was created in the image of God, Eve was only created in God's likeness.[74] The lesser degree of resemblance of the Divine for woman is similar to Augustine's claim that woman by herself is "not in the image of God" when she is considered from the perspective of her orientation towards the temporal world. The consequences of this lower degree of resemblance to God is that woman, by nature, is more prone to sin. Abelard develops the consequences of this analysis of woman's nature in specific reference to Eve's role in the Fall.

In *Ethics*, Eve is described as carrying the greater blame. Abelard divides the process of sinning into three phases, and he argues that in all three stages the woman is the first to give in. In the first phase, the person is persuaded to act in the wrong way:

> When we say that sin or temptation occurs in three ways, namely in suggestion, pleasure, and consent, it should be understood in this sense, that we are often led through these three to the doing of sin. This was the case with our first parents. Persuasion by the devil came first, when he promised immortality for tasting the forbidden tree.[75]

After agreeing in mind to the negative suggestion, woman then allowed the influx of pleasure to increase:

> Pleasure followed, when the woman, seeing the beautiful fruit and understanding it to be sweet to eat, was seized with what she believed would be the pleasure of the food and kindled with longing for it. Since she ought to have checked her longing in order to keep the command, in consenting she was drawn into sin.[76]

Finally, the woman made the error of actually carrying forward the negative desire into an act:

> And although she ought to have corrected the sin through repentance in order to deserve pardon, she finally completed it in deed. And so she proceeded to carry through the sin in three stages.[77]

Abelard applied this analysis of the relation of Adam and Eve to his own situation of the seduction of Heloise when he had been hired to be her tutor. In *Historia Calamitatum*, Abelard described his meeting with Heloise's uncle, Canon Fulbert:

> I pointed out that what had happened could not seem incredible to any one who had ever felt the power of love, or who remembered how, from the very beginning of the human race, women had cast down even the noblest men to utter ruin. And in order to make amends even beyond his extremist hope, I offered to marry her whom I had seduced, provided only the thing could be kept secret, so that I might suffer no loss of reputation thereby.[78]

However, after the wedding, Heloise gave birth to a son, named Astrolobe. Heloise gave the son over to Abelard's sister to raise and pretended to enter a convent in order to escape her uncle's fury. Canon Fulbert, fearing that Abelard had simply rid himself of Heloise by sending her to a convent, organized some men to castrate Abelard. The public nature of this event completely exploded the secrecy of the situation, and Abelard retired to the monastery of St. Denis, while Heloise officially entered the Convent of Argentueil where she was staying.

In an exchange of letters, Heloise wrote to Abelard lamenting that she was unable to share the punishment for their act even though, as a daughter of Eve, she was more to blame for the situation:

> Alone wert thou in the punishment, two were we in the fault; and thou who were the less guilty was borne all. . . . Unhappy that I am, born to be the cause

> of so great a crime! O constant bane of women, greatest against the greatest of men! . . . For the first woman drove the man from Paradise, and she who had been created for him by the Lord as a helpmeet was turned to his supreme destruction.[79]

Abelard's response, however, shifts to a different level of analysis, for he suggested that he bore the greater responsibility and therefore deserved the greater punishment.

> Two were in the fault, one in the punishment. This also is granted by the divine commiseration to the infirmity of thy nature, and in a measure justly. For inasmuch as naturally thou wert the weaker in sex and the stronger in continence, thou wert less liable to punishment.[80]

Abelard's responsibility rested in the active initiation of the situation, Heloise's in being the object that stirred this movement in Abelard. In *Historia Calamitatum*, Abelard clearly admits his method in "determining to unite" himself with Heloise.[81] In a letter to Heloise, he is even more specific about her responses to his initiatives during periods in which the Church had practised abstinence:

> And thee so unwilling and to the utmost of thy power resisting and dissuading me, being weaker by nature, often with threats and blows I drew to consent.[82]

Therefore, even though Abelard sought to escape the blame in his discussion with Heloise's uncle while he was still hoping to keep his situation secret, after the public castration he appeared to change his perspective on the events, and no longer blamed Heloise or her "weaker" sex for the situation.

Abelard slowly began to evolve another theory of the nature of woman in relation to man that completely reversed the sex polarity he had accepted in the order of nature: in the order of grace the weak moved ahead of the strong. In *Touching the Origin of Nuns*, Abelard summarized his theory as follows:

> But who would say that there was so complete a fulfillment by the dispensation of the divine grace in any as in the very infirmity of the womanly sex, which both sin and nature had made contemptible? Examine the different states in this sex, not only virgins and widows, or wives, but also the abominations of harlots, and thou wilt see the grace of Christ to be fuller in them, so that according to the words of the Lord and the Apostle: "The last shall be first, and the first last."[83]

For Abelard, woman's nature in the order of grace "transcends even men."[84] He argues that this possibility was present from the beginning, through the different ways of generation of the first parents:

> The benefits of divine grace, or the honours shown to women, if we seek for them from the first beginning of the world, we shall straightway find that the creation of woman excelled by a certain dignity, inasmuch as she indeed was created in Paradise, but man without.[85]

Significantly, Abelard is the first to argue for a theology of reverse sex polarity. McLaughlin claims that Abelard was the first to specifically defend the dignity of woman in the historical context of the twelfth century, which frequently referred to the dignity of man.[86] In this way, Abelard's philosophy of sex polarity on the level of nature was overturned by the theology of reverse sex polarity in the order of response to grace.

Abelard defends his theory of the dignity of woman by producing numerous examples from the Old Testament, the New Testament, and the lives of the saints that indicate the greater response of women to grace. The most forceful example focuses on the life of Mary Magdalene:

> Perpend therefore the dignity of woman, from whom when He was alive Christ, being twice anointed, to wit both on the head and on the feet, received the sacraments of Kingship and Priesthood. . . . But the former anointings by the woman shew forth His special dignity both as King and as Priest. The anointing of the head the higher, that of the feet the lower dignity. And lo, He receives the sacrament of Kingship also from a woman.[87]

Abelard connects the significance of this anointing with the fact that woman is, in the order of nature, the weaker sex:

> For behold, a woman anoints the Most Holy, and by her deed proclaims Him at once to be Him to Whom she believes, and Whom the Prophet had foretold in words. What, I ask, is this bounty of the Lord, or what the dignity of women, that he should allow both His head and His feet to be anointed by women only? What, I demand, is this prerogative of the weaker sex . . . that a woman should also anoint and, as though with bodily sacraments consecrating Him to be King and Priest, make him in body the Christ, that is to say the anointed?[88]

Abelard considers the Hebrew tradition in which only men anoint, and the present experience in Christianity in which only male bishops anoint. While he does not draw any conclusions from this about the desirability of women entering the sacramental priesthood, he suggests that these examples show that in Christ's own life women held the more important place.

Abelard produces two other examples from the life of Mary Magdalene to support his reverse sex polarity. In the first he suggests that women were more faithful and constant in their loyalty to Christ then were men.

> Wherefore Matthew, when he had related of himself and the rest: "Then all the disciples forsook him, and fled," added to the perseverance of the women, who remained by the Crucified as long as it was permitted them.[89]

In the second example, women's greater constancy led to their selection by Christ to be the first to proclaim his resurrection:

> The Lord Himself also, appearing first to Mary Magdalene, says to her: "Go to my brethren, and say unto them, I ascend unto my father." From which we

> gather that these holy women were constituted as it were female Apostles over the Apostles.[90]

It is interesting to note in passing that the figure of Mary Magdalene may have been particularly attractive to Abelard because of his own situation. His great respect for her was further recognized in the selection of the name Sainte-Madeleine-de-Trainel for the first priory founded from the monastery, the Paraclete, of which Heloise was the Abbess and Abelard the Director.[91]

From the Old Testament, Abelard produced more examples of women who were stronger than men;

> And if, after Eve, we consider the virtue of Deborah, of Judith, of Esther, surely we shall blush not a little for the strength of the male sex. For Deborah, a Judge of the Lord's people, when the men failed, gave battle, and, their enemies overthrow and the Lord's people set free, powerfully triumphed. Judith, unarmed, with her Abra, approached the terrible host, and with his own sword cut off the head of one Holofernes. . . . Esther by her word alone set her people free. . . . The memory of which famous deed has earned yearly among the Jews the tribute of solemn rejoicing. Which no deeds of men, however splendid, have obtained.[92]

In a further example of a comparison of women and men who suffered martyrdom, Abelard returns to his theory of sex identity:

> Because, as we have said, inasmuch as the female sex is naturally weaker, so is its virtue more acceptable to God and more worthy of honour; that martyrdom has not deserved any memory in our feasts, in which a woman bore no part, as though it were not held a great matter if the stronger sex should endure such things.[93]

The view that God prefers women's virtue precisely because it springs from a weaker nature is a central theme of Abelard's argument:

> And just as the sex of women is feebler, so is their virtue more pleasing to God and more perfect, according to the testimony of the Lord Himself, wherein exhorting the weakness of the Apostles to the crown of strife he says: "My grace is sufficient for these; my strength is made perfect in weakness."[94]

In this way, Abelard has based his reverse sex polarity on the foundation of sex polarity. The greater superiority of women in the order of response to grace is a direct consequence of the inferiority of women in the order of nature. Stated in another way, for Abelard the theology of reverse sex polarity was established on the premises of a philosophy of sex polarity.

In trying to understand how Abelard could have developed a theory of sex identity with such radically opposite poles, it is worthwhile recalling that Abelard is known as the founder of the scholastic method of argumentation. This method proceeds to answer a philosophical question by first listing all the arguments *pro* a certain position, then all the arguments *contra* the position, and finally to develop a resolution that favours one of the posited positions or else a new position developed through the synthesis of the *pro* and *contra*. It may be that this scholastic method underlies Abelard's approach to sex identity. The *pro* position would argue that men are superior to women, while the *contra* position argues that women are superior to men. The synthesis would be that neither is superior to the other.

In addition, Abelard was prone to extreme reactions. He was constantly embroiled in arguments with his secular and religious peers, and he would flip from a positive evaluation of his time of sexual union with Heloise as "burning with the happiness of love" to a negative evaluation of the same time as the "shameful pollutions which preceded our marriage."[95] Therefore, Abelard tended to state his positions in the most extreme way.

It is within this context that his evolving practice of a relationship of sex complementarity with Heloise could be interpreted as a kind of synthesis of the *pro* and *contra*. The best area within which to see this movement is in his comments on the relations of men and women within a double monastery. Heloise had requested Abelard to write a rule for her nuns at the Paraclete after they had to leave the monastery at Argenteuil. While living as Abbot of St. Gildas, Abelard offered the Paraclete, which he had built with the help of his students and benefactors some years previously. As a result of Heloise's request, Abelard wrote the first rule specifically directed to a women's religious community. All previous rules used by women had been written originally for men and simply adapted to women's situations. In *An Institute or Rule of Nuns*, Abelard described sex complementarity in the following areas: authority; work; privileges; and study. Each area will be examined in turn.

Abelard began his statements about authority by drawing upon a military analogy:

> As in the camp of the world, so in the Camp of the Lord, that is in monastic congregations, certain persons are to be set up who shall preside over the rest. Just as there a single commander, at whose nod all things shall be done, is over them all. . . . So also must it be done in monasteries, that there one matron shall preside over all.[96]

Within a women's community, a single female authority directs all the other women:

> In a ship there is one steersman. In a house there is one master. In an army however great they look to the orders of one man. . . . That concord therefore may be preserved in all things it is proper that one woman be over all, whom all may obey in all things. Under her also certain other persons, as she herself shall decide, ought to be set up, as they were so many magistrates.[97]

Abelard prefers the authority to be called Deaconess rather than Abbess, because the former term signifies the responsibility of the leader to serve her subordinates rather than assume an unnecessary air of superiority. In a similar way Abelard states that the authority must be careful not to live a more privileged life than her community.[98]

Next, Abelard stipulates that wherever there are women's monasteries, men's monasteries must be close by:

> It is fitting . . . that monasteries of men should not be wanting from the monasteries of women, and that by men of similar religion all things without be administered to the women.[99]

The active function of the double monasteries raises the question of the authority structure in relation to male and female identity. Abelard continues by outrightly suggesting a theory of sex polarity:

> We believe that monasteries of women more firmly observe their calling if they are governed by the rule of spiritual men . . . and always, according to the Apostolic institution, the head of the woman is the man. . . . And so we, . . . wish monasteries of women to be so ever subject to monasteries of men that the brethren may take care of the sisters, and one man preside as a father over both, to whose dispositions either monastery shall look.[100]

In this way, the *Rule*, at first sight, overturned the precedent in many double monasteries where the abbess was the single authority.

However, when Abelard continues to develop his description of the way in which the rule of the abbot occurs, an interesting qualification emerges:

> Nor without consulting her (the Deaconess) shall he decide aught touching the handmaids of Christ, of these things that pertain to them, nor shall he order aught of any of them save through her, nor presume to speak to them. But whensoever the Deaconess shall have summoned him, let him not delay to come, and whatsoever she shall have advised him touching those things whereof she or her subordinates have need, let him not delay to carry out, as far as he is able.[101]

In practice, then, the male authority gives way to the female authority in all areas which pertain to the women's monastery. Abelard reinforces this by an appeal to the theory of sexual differentiation on grounds of strength and weakness:

> Lest however the men, being stronger than the women, presume to burden them in aught, we order that they also shall presume nothing against the will of the Deaconess, but shall do all things at her nod, and all alike, men as well as women, make profession to her, and promise obedience, that the peace may be so much the more lasting, and concord better preserved, the less licence allowed to the stronger, and that the strong be so much less burdened by obedience to the weak, the less they have to fear their violence.[102]

Therefore, Abelard has developed a theory of sex complementarity within the setting of double monasteries, in which the head of the women's community obeys the head of the men's community, while all the men and women give to her their promise of obedience.

This close cooperation between men's and women's monasteries results in an increase of love:

> And that both monasteries may be joined together by so much the greater mutual affection, and be the more solicitous one for the other, the more closely the persons that are in them are united by some propinquity of affinity.[103]

Abelard divided the monastic work into two realms: the outside work was done by men, and the inside work by the women, who remained cloistered. This may appear to imply a devaluation of the female in relation to the male by the traditional differentiation in which the public realm held more esteem than the private. However, in the inversion that occurred in religious life, the contemplative vocation to the cloister held a higher position of respect than the external vocation. In addition, in actual practice, the work that the women did in the enclosure involved a very wide range of skills. The wardrober, for example, had to raise and shear sheep as well as know how to make and care for linens, the cellaress was in charge of the mill, bakehouse, gardens, orchards, bees, herds and flocks, as well as of the refectory, and the portress had complete responsibility for the reception and sorting out of male and female guests.[104] The men, in complement with the women, were in charge of missions for the monastery to distant locations, of the erection of buildings, and management of lands away from the enclosure. In addition, the women made clothes for the men, while the men agreed to protect the women's monastery if necessary.[105] It is not surprising that within this context of mutual work and support, a relationship of sex complementarity would emerge.

Although Abelard did not live in the double monastery attached to the Paraclete, his frequent visits to the women's monastery allowed for an extremely different basis for interacting with women than did his early situation in Paris, in which he was a distinguished professor of philosophy teaching in a predominantly male environment. The women with whom he interacted at that time were simply students eager to learn from a teacher who was their superior. Therefore, the double monastery appears to function as a background for developing the philosophy of an equality and significant differentiation of woman and man.

Abelard sought to defend women's access to certain privileges that had been exclusively limited to men's monasteries in the past. Speaking as a philosopher, Abelard claimed that reason, not custom, should determine practice:

> For we utterly forbid that custom ever be set above reason, that anything be ever defended because it is the custom, but because it is of reason; or because it is in use, but because it is good, and so much the more readily received the better it shall appear.[106]

Abelard proceeds to argue that if men in monasteries are allowed to drink wine, then so should women. It is ironic that this is the one context in which Aristotle is invoked to defend a theory of sex identity. Abelard is referring to a derived Aristotelian theory:

> Macrobius Theodosius in the fourth book of the *Saturnalia* says thus: Aristotle says that women are rarely inebriated, old women often. The woman is of an extremely humid body. This we learn from the lightness and brilliance of her skin. We learn it especially from the regular purgations, relieving the body of its superfluous humour. . . . The woman's body is pierced with many holes.

> ... By these holes the vapour of the wine is speedily released. On what ground then is that allowed to monks which to the weaker sex is denied?[107]

The irony here is that Aristotle is being used to support a theory of the equality of the sexes, when in fact his own theory led to very different conclusions. For Abelard, however, Aristotle is associated primarily with logic, and this association leads to the sex-neutrality derivative of sex unity.

Abelard also uses reason over custom to argue that women ought to be allowed to eat meat:

> If to the Pontiffs themselves and to the Rulers of Holy Church, if moreover to monasteries of clerks it is allowed without offence to eat even flesh . . . who can blame the allowing of these things to women, especially if in the rest they endure a greater strictness? For it is enough for the disciple that he be as his master. And it seems great foolishness if what is allowed to monasteries of clerks be forbidden to monasteries of women.[108]

It can be seen, then, that for Abelard the communities of men and of women ought not to be distinguished by the categories of superior or inferior, but rather be equal in responsibilities and privileges. The final area in which we find a complementarity emerging is in the category of wisdom. In the *Rule*, in a discussion of the dangers of being attracted to luxury, Abelard does describe women as having weak minds:

> And rightly did he [St. Peter] consider that women rather than men ought to be warned from this vanity, whose weak mind more strongly desires it, that by them and in them luxury may have a firmer hold.[109]

Therefore, once again, Abelard's starting point is the natural inferiority of women to men in mind and body.

In an interesting play on the traditional view that women ought to be silent while men participate in speech, Abelard develops a distinction between simply remaining silent, which is a passive response, to studying silence, which is the active response of contemplatives: "And evidently to study silence is more than to keep silence. For study is the vehement application of the mind to the doing of something . . ."[110] Abelard enjoins the women to be active in the study of silence during specified times in the monastic horarium. At other times, he encourages learning and speech.

In a letter to the nuns of the Paraclete, Abelard encourages the study of Latin, Hebrew, and Greek:

> In the person of your reverend mother you have a pattern which can suffice for you in all matters, in the exemplification of virtue, of course, as much as in the study of literature she is familiar not only with Latin literature, but with Greek and Hebrew as well—she appears to be the only woman at the present time who has acquired that skill in the three languages which is proclaimed by all as a special grace in the blessed Jerome, and which is highly praised by Jerome himself in the afore-mentioned venerable women. . . . What we have lost in men, let us recover in women: and, to serve as a condemnation of men

> and a judgement on the stronger sex, let the queen of the south [the Queen of Sheba] search once more for the wisdom of a true Solomon—in you.[111]

In the *Rule* it is predominantly the role of the abbess or deaconess to teach; Abelard considers the situation in which an uneducated woman is elected to this post:

> And if she be not lettered, let her know that she is to accustom herself not to philosophical studies, or dialectical disputations, but to the doctrine of life and the display of works. As it is written of the Lord: "Begin both to do and teach," to wit first to do, and afterwards to teach.[112]

Even with the above qualifications of the study of logic, Abelard insists that the abbess should seek to learn:

> And if to gain a better knowledge of anything, she consider that she ought to turn to the Scripture, let her not be ashamed to ask and to learn this of the lettered, nor in these matters let her despise the teaching of letters.[113]

Heloise, who was "lettered," functioned precisely in this manner when she served as Abbess of the Paraclete. She asked questions, made distinctions, and then taught her community both philosophy and theology.

Abelard's theory of wisdom was not limited to theoretical studies. In fact, when he describes, in the *Rule*, the specific functions of different members of the monastic community, a surprisingly wide range of knowlege in the area of practical wisdom emerges. The sacristan, for example, "ought to be learned especially in the computation of the moon, that according to the order of the seasons she may provide for the oratory." The chantress has charge of writing; the infirmarian "must not be lacking in knowledge of medicine" or the arts of the mortician; and the portress must be "discrete in mind" and able to edify by "giving a fitting reason."[114] Abelard concludes his description of the different offices in the monastery by suggesting that those sisters who are suited for the "study of letters" be exempted from the necessity of meeting guests whenever they arrive:

> Let all the office-bearers save the Chantress be attached to these duties, who study not letters, if such may be found as are suited for this, that they may more freely devote themselves to letters.[115]

It is clear, then, that Abelard considers the search for wisdom through practical or theoretical knowledge very important to women in monastic life.

> What could be more absurd than to give time to reading and not to take pains to understand? . . . To such a reader is that saying of the philosopher rightly applied: "An ass before a lyre." For as an ass is before a lyre so is a reader holding a book and unable to do that for which the book was made.[116]

In conclusion, then, as far as Abelard's philosophy of sex complementarity is concerned, the above analysis has revealed that even though he stated this theory in the extreme categories of "men are superior to women on the natural order" and "women are superior to men in the order of response to grace," in the practical daily living of women and men within the double monasteries, or in the situation in which Abelard frequently visited the Paraclete as Abbot of St. Gildas, the actual philosophy that governed the situation in the categories of wisdom and virtue involved a strong movement towards sex complementarity.

A similar result is discovered by analysing the writings of Heloise, for she began within the sex-polarity tradition of sex identity, and appeared to end with a movement towards a concrete sex complementarity. Heloise's theory differed from Abelard's in the lack of any reverse sex polarity in her thought. In fact, in her arguments she actively sought to deny any possibility of the superiority of woman over man.

Heloise's letters are the main source of information we have about her thought, for she left no other texts for posterity. However, the letters are very revealing of her most intimate thoughts and feelings, and they consitute sufficient information to be able to reconstruct her theory of sex identity. Heloise's acceptance of a sex-polarity theory is seen in her application of the categories: superior/inferior, stronger/weaker, and less blameworthy/more blameworthy, to men and women.

The attribution of superiority to the male is seen first in the various forms of salutation Heloise used in her letters to Abelard. In the first letter, after she officially entered the monastery at Argenteuil, she wrote, "To her master, nay father, to her husband, nay brother; his handmaid, nay daughter, his spouse, nay sister: To Abelard, Heloise."[117] When Abelard addressed his answer "To Heloise his dearly beloved sister in Christ, Abelard her brother in the same," Heloise responded with an argument for sex polarity:

> I marvel, my all, that against the custom of writing letters, nay against the natural order of things, at the head of the greeting in thy letter thou has made bold to set my name before thine, to wit the woman before the man, the wife before the husband, the handmaid before the master, the nun before the monk and priest, the deaconess before the Abbot. Right indeed is the order and honourable that they who write to their superiors or to their equals place the names of those to whom they are writing before their own. But if they write to their inferiors, those take precedence in the order of writing who take precedence in rank.[118]

Abelard then responds with his theory of reverse sex polarity, namely that in the order of grace, woman is superior to man:

> Of the unnatural (as thou sayest) order of our greeting, that was done, if thou examine it closely, according to thine opinion also. For it is common knowledge, as thyself has shown, that when anyone writes to his superiors their names are put first. And thou must understand that thou didst become my superior from that day on which thou becamest to me my lady, becoming the bride of my Lord.[119]

Heloise, however, thought of herself as more wedded to Abelard than to Christ:

> In the whole period of my life (God wot) I have ever feared to offend thee rather than God, I seek to please thee more than Him. Thy command brought me,

> not the love of God, to the habit of religion. Do not, I beseech thee, presume so highly of me.[120]

She rejected Abelard's arguments for a reverse sex polarity in its specific application to her own life. Directly attacking Abelard's tendency to support the superiority of women in the level of response to grace, Heloise states:

> Cease, I beseech thee, from praise of me, lest thou incur the base mark of adulation and the charge of falsehood. . . .
>
> I wish not that, exhorting me to virtue, and provoking me to fight, thou say: "Strength is made perfect in weakness."[121]

Heloise insists that her weakness is the most she can associate with her nature and that the reverse sex polarity that Abelard suggests is false in its application to her.

In a remarkably frank discussion of her own sexuality, Heloise describes herself as not capable of the life of celibacy that is part of the identity of the Bride of Christ. Once again appealing to a sex-polarity differentiation of the stronger and weaker sexes, Heloise compares Abelard's and her responses to the life of celibacy:

> That grace, beloved, came to thee unsought, and by healing thee from these goads a single injury to thy body has cured many in thy soul. . . . But in me these goads of the flesh, these incentives to lust, the very fervour of my youth and my experience of the sweetest pleasures greatly stimulate, and all the more oppress me with their assaults the weaker the nature is that they are assaulting. They preach that I am chaste who have not discovered the hypocrite in me.[122]

Heloise's assumption of woman's weakness in the order of nature is never overturned into a superiority of woman on the level of response to grace. She therefore remains within the theoretical confines of sex polarity that had been present in Abelard.

Heloise frequently refers to women's weakness. In a passage in which she reflects on the needs of the newly formed women's community at the Paraclete, she says:

> Frail enough, from the weakness of the feminine nature, is this plantation; it is infirm, even were it not new. Wherefore it demands more diligent cultivation and more frequent.[123]

In another letter Heloise questions the wisdom of excluding male guests from the monastery:

> If excluding men from our hospitality we admit only women, is it not evident that we must offend and exasperate the men whose services monasteries of the weaker sex require . . . ?[124]

Therefore, she appears simply to accept the natural weakness of women and the natural strength of men.

Heloise totally accepted Abelard's leadership. Idolizing him, she asks, "For what excellence of mind or body did not adorn thy youth?"[125] Heloise's complete efforts went towards conforming herself to Abelard's will:

> I have at once performed all things that you didst order, till that when I could not offend thee in anything I had the strength to lose myself at thy behest. And what is more, and strange it is to relate, to such madness did my love turn that what alone it sought it cast from itself without hope of recovery when, straightway obeying thy command, I changed both my habit and my heart, that I might shew thee to be the one possessor both of my body and of my mind.[126]

Heloise's absolute conformity to the "mind and body" of Abelard occurred in the following key moments of her life: 1) in her acquiescence to his sexual advances while she was his student in Paris; 2) in her agreement to the secret marriage and the sacrifice of her son; 3) in her acceptance of the false entry into the convent at Argenteuil; 4) in her willingness to make a full commitment to religious life; and 5) in her acceptance of the position of Deaconess of the religious community of the Paraclete.

From the correspondence, it is clear that Heloise did not always submit easily to Abelard's directives.[127] In addition to the resistance that has previously been mentioned towards her acceptance of the religious life, Heloise is best known for her arguments against marriage. In a letter written after becoming a nun she wrote:

> And if the name of wife appears more sacred and more valid, sweeter to me is ever the word friend, or, if thou be not ashamed, concubine or whore. . . . I preferred love to wedlock, freedom to a bond. I call God to witness, if Augustus, ruling over the whole world, were to deem me worthy of the honour of marriage, and to confirm the whole world to me, to be ruled by me forever, dearer to me and a greater dignity would it seem to be called thy strumpet than his empress.[128]

Then, in an attack on the use of marriage by women for monetary gain, Heloise compares marriage to prostitution:

> Nor should she seem herself other than venal who marries a rich man rather than a poor, and desires more things in her husband than himself. Assuredly, whomsoever this concupiscence leads into marriage deserves payment rather than affection; for it is evident that she goes after his wealth and not the man, and is willing to prostitute herself, if she can, to a richer one.[129]

Heloise believed that the purity of love was better retained outside marriage than from within.

The most extensive discussion of Heloise's objections to marriage were repeated by Abelard in *Historia Calamitatum*. In this text he focuses totally on those arguments that she produced to defend the position that it would be harmful to Abelard to marry. Abelard states:

> Forthwith I repaired to my own country, and brought back thence my mistress, that I might make her my wife. She, however, most violently disapproved of this, and for two chief reasons: the danger thereof, and the disgrace which it bring upon me. . . . What penalties, she said, would the world rightly demand of her if she should rob it of so shining a light. What curses would follow such a loss to the Church, what tears among the philosophers would result from such a marriage! . . . She vehemently rejected this marriage, which she felt would be in every way ignominious and burdensome to me.[130]

On the practical side, if Abelard publicly married, he would lose his position in the Cathedral School of Paris, for that school had as faculty only men who either were priests or who were studying for the consecrated life. Heloise's arguments, however, went far beyond concern for Abelard losing his job.

Invoking the example of several historical philosophers, Heloise argued that marriage and the life of philosopher were incompatible. She mentioned the Stoic philosopher Cicero, who stated that he "could not devote himself to a wife and to philosophy at the same time."[131] Seneca, whose lost work, *On Matrimony*, was not available, was invoked to support the claim that everything must be given up for the study of philosophy.[132] Through an example in St. Augustine's *The City of God*, Heloise brings forward the name of Pythagoras to support a life of celibacy for philosophers.[133] Heloise also reminds Abelard of a purported incident in which Xanthippe harangued Socrates before showering him with a bucket of waste. She concluded: "Remember that Socrates was chained to a wife, and by what a filthy accident he himself paid for this blot on philosophy in order that others thereafter might be made more cautious by his example."[134] Even Theophrastus, Aristotle's disciple, was included in this battery of arguments against marriage. "Theophrastus set forth in great detail the intolerable annoyances and the endless disturbances of married life, demonstrating with the most convincing arguments that no wise man should have a wife."[135]

The wide range of arguments that Heloise used against Abelard's proposal of marriage indicates that she was well-read in both philosophy and theology. She was no doubt familiar with the Stoic writers at first hand. Many of her arguments, however, come second-hand through the writings of St. Jerome. It is interesting to note in passing, that Jerome is credited with having written the "greatest slander of women since Juvenal's sixth satire" in his letter of *Advice to Eustochium* and in his work *Against Jovinianus*.[136] The pattern of argument in Juvenal, Jerome, and now Heloise, is to reject marriage by introducing a devaluation of woman.

Heloise continues her argument with the claim that philosophers are poor and, therefore, not being able to hire servants, they would be so personally involved in domestic work that they could not continue their philosophical calling:

> Then, turning from the consideration of such hinderances to the study of philosophy, Heloise bade me observe what were the conditions of honourable wedlock. What possible concord could there be between scholars and domestics, between authors and cradles, between books or tablets and distaffs, between the stylus or the pen and the spindle? What man, intent on his religious or philosophical meditations, can possibly endure the whining of children, the lullabies of the nurse seeking to quiet them, or the noisy confusion of family

> life? Who can endure the continual untidiness of children? The rich, you may reply, can do this . . . But to this the answer is that the condition of philosophers is by no means that of the wealthy.[137]

The pull of family life away from philosophy may have been a real concern for Heloise because of the pattern Abelard followed when he first became involved with her in Paris. Abelard revealed, in *Historia Calamitatum*, that his teaching and research simply fell apart during this period:

> In the measure as this passionate rapture absorbed me more and more, I devoted ever less time to philosophy and to the work of the school. . . . My lecturing became utterly careless and lukewarm; I did nothing because of inspiration, but everything of habit.[138]

However, Heloise was convinced that the romantic ties of love would not survive within marriage. Abelard reports:

> Her final argument was that it would be dangerous for me to take her back to Paris, and that it would be far sweeter for her to be called my mistress than to be known as my wife; nay, too, that this would be more honourable for me as well. In such case, she said, love alone would hold her to me, and the strength of the marriage chain would not constrain us.[139]

In spite of the impressive range of Heloise's arguments against marriage, Abelard held firm to his plan until she simply "made an end of her resistance."[140] In this complicated interaction, several facets of Heloise's concept of woman emerge. She did not consider that woman and man could help one another in the search for wisdom through a bonded commitment in marriage, such as was proposed by Porphyry to Marcella. Neither did she even consider that marriage could offer any positive framework for a development of a real complementarity between women and men. Instead, Heloise considered marriage strictly as a union within the model of sex polarity and, consequently, that a man would be better to avoid it.

At the same time that Heloise was vigorously defending a theory of sex polarity, she inadvertently revealed the power of her intellect and the extent of her learning. Her frequent references to the Stoics or to other philosophers and theologians reveal that she easily entered into arguments and discussions on an equal basis with men. The first person to recognize Heloise's unusual intellectual gifts was her uncle, the Canon Fulbert. In *Historia Calamitatum* Abelard states:

> Now there dwelt in that same city of Paris a certain young girl named Heloise, the niece of a canon who was called Fulbert. Her uncle's love for her was equalled only by his desire that she should have the best education which he could possibly procure for her. Of no mean beauty, she stood out above all by reason of her abundant knowledge of letters. Now this virtue is rare among women, and for that very reason it doubly graced the maiden, and made her the most worthy of renown in the entire kingdom.[141]

The early fame of Heloise's learning was also affirmed in a letter written to her by Peter the Venerable:

> I had not quite passed the bounds of youth and reached early manhood when I knew your name and your reputation, not yet for religion but for your virtuous and praiseworthy studies. I used to hear at that time of the woman who . . . devoted all her application to knowledge of letters. . . . At a time when nearly the whole world is indifferent and deplorably apathetic towards such occupations, and wisdom can scarcely find a foothold not only, I may say, among women who have banished her completely, but even in the minds of men, you have surpassed all women in carrying out your purpose, and have gone further than most men.[142]

This example of Heloise's learning is significant in the history of the concept of woman in relation to man because it signals the beginning of a movement in which women outside of the monastic life were actively learning philosophy. That Heloise was not the only woman in Paris studying with the faculty of the Cathedral School from Notre Dame is attested to by Abelard's reflection that before his affair with Heloise, he had "diligently kept myself from all excesses and from association with the women of noble birth who attended the school."[143]

The contrast between learning in the secular world and in the monastery was developed in the letter from Peter the Venerable to Heloise:

> You turned your zeal to learning in a far better direction, and as a woman wholly dedicated to philosophy in the true sense, you left logic for the Gospel, Plato for Christ, and the academy for the cloister.[144]

However, as the letters indicate, Heloise did not lose these secular philosophical skills; rather, she integrated them into a new dynamic of learning and teaching. The most effective example of Heloise's new approach to wisdom is found in her final letter to Abelard, in which she raised numerous questions about how the rule for women's monasteries ought to be different from the rule for men's monasteries.

On the surface, Heloise uses the same phrases about stronger sex and weaker sex to refer to man and woman, but from the way in which the questions are asked it is clear that Heloise is referring to sexual differentiation beyond a simple polarity. Heloise begins by asking Abelard:

> That thou wilt instruct us by what origin the order of nuns began and what is the authority for our profession. And the other is that thou wilt institute some rule for us and set it forth in writing, which shall be proper for women and shall definitely describe that state and habit for our conversation which we do not find to have been at any time done by the Holy Fathers. Through the default and indigence whereof it now arises that to the profession of the same Rule men and women alike are received into monasteries, and the same yoke of monastic institution is imposed on the feeble sex equally with the strong.[145]

Heloise proceeds to critically analyse the rule of St. Benedict, which she claims "was written for men alone, so by men alone can be obeyed in full." [146] Heloise produces dozens of examples of the way in which the rule cannot be applied to women:

1. How does the clothing of monks relate to women during times of menstruation?
2. Should the Abbess (like the Abbot) eat with all the guests?
3. Should the Abbess (like the Abbot) read the Gospel?
4. Should the Abbess (like the Abbot) eat with men?
5. Should wine be allowed?
6. Should the nuns go outside the monastery to gather the harvest?

For each question Heloise offers arguments for the difficulties that the situation creates for women. In the following example she reflects on the problems of accepting a nun into the community after only one year of probation:

> Nay, what could be more foolish than to enter upon an unknown path, not yet explored? What more presumptuous than to choose and profess a life of which thou knowest nothing, or to make a vow thou canst not fulfill? And inasmuch as discretion is the mother of all virtues, and reason is the mediator of all good, who will consider that to be either a virtue or good which is seen to disagree with both reason and discretion? [147]

Heloise once again invokes the differentiation of weak and strong:

> But who does not see it to be disjoined from all reason and discretion if, in imposing burdens, the strength of those on whom they are to be imposed be not first considered, that human industry may follow the natural constitution? Who lays such burdens upon an ass she seems fitted for an elephant? . . . That is, the same for the weak as for the strong, for the sick as for the whole, for women as for men? For the weaker sex, forsooth, as for the stronger? [148]

Playing with the logical argument, Heloise carries out the full implications of an admonition of St. Benedict that the abbot should adjust himself to all sorts of different persons within the monastery when she argues:

> For if in certain things he is obliged to temper the rigour of the Rule of the young, the old and the infirm according to the weakness or infirmity of their nature, what would he provide for the weaker sex whose feeble and infirm nature is known to all? Perpend therefore how far it departs from all discretion of reason that women and men alike should be bound by the profession of a common Rule, and the weak laden with the same burden as the strong. [149]

The Abbess continues by bringing forward even more arguments that appear to reverse the order of custom and to introduce benefits for women. Drawing upon the authority of Aristotle, she requests that women should be able to drink wine because "nature has furnished our sex with a greater virtue of sobriety." [150] Finally, Heloise asks why the "Canons, considering our weakness, have decreed that deaconesses ought not to be ordained before forty years, and then after diligent probation, whereas deacons may be promoted after twenty?"[151]

The significant aspect of Heloise's analysis here is that it offers the distinct impression that while she uses the old categories of polarity in her constant references to woman's weakness and man's strength, underneath this mode of speech she believes in a differentiation of the sexes within a context of equality. Towards the end of the letter she concludes:

> From these words it is clearly gathered that virtues alone acquire merit before God; and who so are equal in virtue, howsoever they may differ in works, deserve equally of Him.[152]

There is some evidence, in addition, that Heloise did not in practice accept the strict suggestions in Abelard's rule for the regulation of her nuns at Paraclete. Luscombe observes:

> The earliest manuscript (Troyes 802) also contains details of customs observed at the Paraclete, perhaps in Heloise's lifetime. These are known as the *Instructiones*. . . . They indicate that there were probably considerable differences between the principles laid down by Abelard following Heloise's request and the way of life that was apparently followed by the nuns. One example is the eating of meat; . . . another is the place of the Abbess over whom Abelard put a male superior. It has been suggested that the Rule and the rest of the correspondence were forged in the course of an election dispute in the 1280's. It is simpler to believe that Heloise or her order by no means felt obliged to follow Abelard's *Rule.*[153]

The view that Heloise and Abelard developed a progressively more complementary relationship after the foundation of the Paraclete is suggested by the text *Problemata Heloissae*, a dialogue of questions and responses about the interpretation of Scripture by Heloise and Abelard. McLaughlin reflects:

> How seriously she took her tasks as a teacher and exegete she showed in her *Problemata*, in which the "silence of Heloise" was broken, and on a subject that may reflect her own view of the priorities, and the practicable, in Abelard's program for her community.[154]

Heloise served as Abbess for her community for thirty-six years, until her death. After her initial adjustment to religious life, Heloise is believed to have had a conversion to her new situation and to have developed as a confident and mature leader of the women in her monastery.

The philosophy of sex identity contained in the thought of Heloise therefore leaves a certain puzzle. While she gave evidence of progressively moving towards sex complementarity in her own life, her writings for the most part defend sex polarity. This fact is most vividly reinforced by the use to which Heloise's letters were put in later centuries. Jean de Meun, in the second part of the *Roman de la Rose*, presented her arguments against marriage. In addition, he was the first to translate the letters from Latin into French.[155] Jean de Meun's *Roman de la Rose* gave extraordinary popularity to arguments for sex polarity that reinforced the negative aspect of Heloise's arguments against marriage. The arguments were always grounded in the devaluation of woman. At the same time, Jean de Meun also used the name "la saige Heloys," or "the wise Heloise."[156] Thus the "wise Heloise" inadvertently becomes the first woman to argue for the devaluation of woman in western thought.

The story of Abelard and Heloise continued to fascinate European scholars and writers for centuries. Walter Map appears to have referred to them, and Petrarch, who owned one of the first copies of the correspondence, wrote an annotated commentary directed to both Abelard and Heloise.[157] A forgery in the fourteenth or fifteenth century of a 1,500-page illuminated manuscript entitled *The Letters of the Abbess Heloise of the Paraclete* contained "Heloise's" instructions to Gaultier on love.[158] In these developments, the arguments of the philosophers in support of sex polarity became less important for the popular imagination than the actual models of their lives. Heloise and Abelard came to represent the height of complementarity in a fated romantic love. From their deaths in the twelfth century until the French Revolution in 1792, Heloise and Abelard were buried side by side at the Paraclete. Even though the monastery was destroyed, their remains were carefully guarded and moved in a public procession. The plaque placed over their new grave read as follows:

> The first year of the French Republic, November 9, 1792, the remains of Heloise and Abelard, which had rested at the Paraclete more than 800 years (sic), were transferred from that church and left in the crypt of this chapel by order of the Administration of this district and the care of Dominique Antoine Mesnard, priest of this place, and in the presence of the same administrators, the mayor, the president, judges and some national commissioners from the civil tribunal, and finally the Justices of peace (interior and exterior). . . . Happy this community to possess the remains of these unfortunate spouses! . . . As much as they loved each other during their lives, their mortal remains are intermingled in the same tomb after their death.[159]

The union and differentiation of Heloise and Abelard had entered firmly into the popular imagination, where it remained as an example of a romantic complementarity of woman and man lived out in love and sacrifice.

Hildegard of Bingen (1098–1179)

The experience of sex complementarity that had been progressively expanding through the number of double monasteries within the Benedictine tradition from the ninth to the twelfth centuries, created an environment in which a philosophy of sex identity began to challenge the previously stated premises of sex polarity and sex unity. It is within this context that Hildegard of Bingen emerged as the first philosopher to articulate a complete theory of sex complementarity. Although some previous Christian philosophers, such as Augustine, Boethius and Anselm, had defended sex complementarity in certain isolated categories of thought about woman and man, Hildegard was the first to develop a rationale for this theory across all four categories of the concept of woman in relation to man. For this reason, Hildegard is rightly considered as the foundress of the sex complementarity position.

Hildegard was not completely consistent in her theory of sex identity. On the theological level, she gave evidence at times of the same paradoxical combination of sex polarity and reverse sex polarity that was found in Abelard. Namely, she refers to woman as the weaker sex who is made superior to man by God's grace. However, Hildegard balances her intermittent references to this paradox with a thorough and far-reaching defence of the equality and significant differentiation of woman and man. Hildegard's theory of sex complementarity can be summarized as follows:

Sex Complementarity in Heaven

	Man		Woman
Opposites		equal and different in resurrection	
Generation		first parents, Adam and Eve, equal and different	
Wisdom		equal and different in knowledge	
Virtue		male saints equal to and different from female saints	

Sex Complementarity in the World

	Man		Woman
Opposites	more like fire and earth		more like air and water
		equally in image of God	
Generation	deposits cold seed		warms and strengthens seed
		God provides soul	
Wisdom	practical knowledge of man in relation to woman		practical knowledge of woman in relation to man
Virtue	follow Christ; stronger though less self-control; rule by love		follow Christ; weaker though more self-control; obey by choice
		equal access to public and private spheres of activity	

Hildegard was given over to the care of the Abbess Jutta at the double monastery of Mount St. Disibode at the age of eight. At fifteen she entered the monastery as a novice and, at the death of Jutta in 1126, Hildegard became Abbess, at the age of twenty-eight.[160] In the context of the double monastery, Hildegard was exposed to the main Christian writers of the time, including Augustine, Boethius, and Anselm. Joseph Singer also suggests that Hildegard's writings give evidence of familiarity with Aristotle's *De Caelo et Mondo* and *Meteorologica*, Isidore's *De Rerum Natura*, Bernard Sylvester's *De Mundi Universitate Sive Megacosmos et Microcosmos,* Constantine of Africa's *On the Nature of Man,* and Hugh St. Viktor's *On the Members and Parts of Man.*[161] If Singer is correct, it would indicate that Hildegard was a very learned woman.

However, Hildegard rarely refers to scholars in her writings, and she implies that all her knowledge was infused directly by God. She describes this process in the old paradox of sex polarity and reverse sex polarity. Woman, who is inferior since Eve, will be made superior to man, by the direct infusion of Divine knowledge. In a vision, she records being told by God:

> Therefore write it large from a fountain of abundance, and so overflow in mystical erudition, so that they may tremble at the profusion of your irrigation, who wished you to be considered contemptible on account of Eve's transgression. But thou dost not get this knowledge from men, for thou receivest it from above.[162]

In the *Scivias*, Hildegard reports that the result of mystical illumination was the increase in understanding of the meaning of texts with which she was already familiar:

> It happened in the year 1141 of the Incarnation of God's Son Jesus Christ, when I was forty-two years and seven months old, that the heavens opened and a fiery light of great brilliance came and suffused my whole brain. . . . And suddenly I came to understand the meaning of the book of the Psalms, the Gospel and the other canonical books of both the Old and New Testaments—although I could not interpret the words of their text, nor divide the syllables, and I had no knowledge of cases or tenses.[163]

In another description from the *Vita*, Hildegard includes philosophy in the category of things whose meanings were revealed through visions:

> I understood the writings of the prophets, the Gospels, and the other saints, and of certain philosophers, without any human instruction. And I expounded some of then, although I had scarcely any knowledge of literature, as an uneducated woman had taught me.[164]

It would follow from these obervations, that Hildegard had most likely already studied the texts of some philosophical writings whose meaning was clarified for her in the experience of infused knowledge.

For Hildegard, however, the most obvious source of knowledge about sex identity and the concept of woman in relation to man was her own observation of human nature in her years of work in the infirmary of the monastery. Benedictine monasteries often had a hospice for pilgrims and for the sick. Hildegard worked as a nurse-physician in the hospice connected to her monastery. As a result of her acute powers of observation and organization of information, she wrote a scientific treatise classifying the curative powers of herbs. More germane to the question of sex identity, Hildegard also wrote a text in which she analysed the biological composition of men and women and the effects of these factors on personality and human interaction. In *Causae et Curae*, one of the earliest books on the psychology of personality written in the west, Hildegard produced numerous personal observations on human nature. In this way, she functions as a philosopher who supports her views with empirical evidence. Therefore, although Hildegard claims to have received her knowledge directly from God, when the texts she wrote are examined in some detail, they reveal a sophisticated philosophical mind generating fresh and original hypotheses in new areas of thought.

Hildegard of Bingen is accessible to the contemporary public in a way that far exceeds any female philsopher who preceded her in the west. All of her major works are available.[165] The titles of the texts with philosophical and theological significance are as follows:

Latin	German	English equivalent
Scivias	*Wisse die Wege*	*Know the Way*
Liber Simplicis Medicinae (Physica)	*Naturkunde*	*Natural Arts*
Liber Compositae Medicinae (Causae et Curae)	*Heilkunde*	*Healing Arts*
Liber Vitae Meritorium	*Der Mensch in der Varantwortung*	*Man in Responsibility*
Liber Divinorum Operum (De Operatione Dei)	*Welt und Mensch*	*World and Man*

Hildegard's other writings include:

> Lives of St. Disibode and St. Rupert, . . . hymns and canticles of which she wrote both words and music; 50 allegorical homilies; a morality play; for diversion a language of her own composed of 900 words and an alphabet of 23 letters, and also letters to popes, cardinals, bishops, abbots, kings, emperor, monks, and nuns, men and women of varies levels of society, both in Germany and abroad.[166]

No woman previous to Hildegard revealed such a wide range of knowledge and creative thought. The extraordinary breadth of her writing skills, which ranged from music to drama, to scientific texts on the classification of stones and herbs, to theological speculation, to language games, to the philosophy of psychology, reveal a genius unparalleled by a woman and matched by very few men up to the twelfth century. The additional discovery that Hildegard was the first person to develop an original theory in support of the philosophy of sex complementarity makes her contribution to the history of the concept of woman in relation to man all the more significant. Hildegard's theory of sex identity will now be examined in each of the four categories of opposites, generation, wisdom and virtue.

Opposites

Hildegard believed that women and men were opposite in much the same way as the elements were opposite. The elements, and the humours derived from them, worked together to bring about all change in the world:

> Mankind lives out of the four elements. Namely, God has put the world together out of these four elements such that one cannot be separated from another; the world would no longer be, could one exist without the other. On the contrary: they are inextricably linked with one another.[167]

Aristotle had also given a central importance to the elements. However, in his theory woman was described as being more like the two lowest elements (earth and water) and man as being more like the two highest elements (air and fire). Hildegard took a different view. She argued that man was more like the highest element, fire, and the lowest element, earth, while woman was more like the two middle elements, air and water. In this way, the two sexes balanced each other out, so that neither one was fully superior or inferior to the other.

The differences between Aristotle's and Hildegard's theories of relation of sex identity to the elements is summarized in the following two charts:

Aristotle's Sex Polarity in Relation to the Elements

fire air	man	higher	active	lighter	superior
water earth	woman	lower	passive	heavier	inferior

Hildegard's Sex Complementarity in Relation to the Elements

fire	man	
air	woman	interconnection of elements, neither
water	woman	sex is superior or inferior
earth	man	

Hildegard offered a theological defence of her association of the elements with sex identity. She stated that the association of man with the earth arose from his direct creation by God from the earth, while woman's lack of association with this element sprang from her direct creation from the body of man:

> Adam, who was created out of the earth, was awakened with the elements and thereby transformed. Eve, however, having emerged from Adam's rib was not transformed. So through the vital powers of earth, Adam was manly and through the elements he was potent. Eve, however, remained soft in her marrow and

> she had more of an airy character, a very artistic talent and a precious vitality for the burden of the earth did not press upon her.[168]

It is important to note that in the above passage Hildegard did not value one sex above the other. The man had more power or strength because of his creation from the earth, but the woman had more refinement and creativity because of her creation from bone. The artistic and vital character of woman was connected with the greater presence of air in her body.

> The woman, however, did not experience such a transformation; taken from flesh, she remained flesh. That is why . . . she is so to speak an airy being, for it is her task to bear the child to maturity and to give it birth. She also has a cloven skull and thinner skin so that child she carries in her womb may get air.[169]

In the above passage Hildegard shows how freely she integrates religious faith with empirical observation. A belief in the story of the creation of Adam and Eve is supplemented by Hildegard's observations of the interaction between mother and child during pregnancy. She observed further that the greater presence of earth in the male reflected itself in physical appearance. More earth meant more hair, and men, in general, had more hair than women.[170]

Hildegard also believed that the balance of the various elements in a person had important consequences for character. The interaction of the elements and the humours provided a basic personality pattern for individual men and women. As will be seen in the subsequent sections of this chapter, Hildegard developed a complicated psychology of female and male development. She considered it to be a central task of philosophy to make explicit the different ways in which woman and man interact with one another. In all her theories of interaction, however, there is a decided effort to guard the equality and significant differentiation of the sexes.

Hildegard also described both woman and man as being created "in the image of God." Although writing very clearly within the Christian tradition of God as Father, Son and Holy Spirit, Hildegard frequently refers to the feminine aspect of the Divine Nature. Barbara Newman describes a vision from the *Scivias*:

> In Hildegard's first vision of the feminine Divine, she beholds a radiant woman adorned by suppliant angels. A voice from heaven identifies her as *Scientia Dei*, the knowledge of God: "She is awesome in terror as the Thunderer's lightning, and gentle in goodness as the sunshine. In her terror and her gentleness, she is incomprehensible to men, because of the dread radiance of divinity in her face and the brightness which dwells in her as the robe of her beauty. . . . For she is with all and in all, and of beauty so great in her mystery that none could comprehend how sweetly she bears with men, and how she spares them with inscrutable mercy."[171]

Since God is both feminine and masculine, Hildegard concludes that woman and man reflect this bisexual divine nature in their sex identities. In addition, she argues that both sexes contain in their souls a masculine and feminine nature. Newman continues:

> For when God created male and female in His image, Hildegard remarks, he extended this dual likeness to the soul as well as the body. The male designates strength, courage, and justice in the inward man, while the female denotes mercy, penance, and grace.[172]

The division of the soul into masculine and feminine aspects is not new to philosophy. Aristotle and Philo had developed a similar division along sexual lines. However, once again we find a difference in the evaluation of the qualities associated with male and female identity. For Aristotle and Philo, the division of souls was within a framework of sex polarity, while for Hildegard it was within a framework of sex complementarity.

Aristotle and Philo's Sex-Polarity Division of the Soul

masculine	rational, discursive reason, with authority	superior
feminine	irrational, sense, without authority	inferior

Hildegard's Sex-Complementarity of Soul

masculine	strength, courage justice	equally important
feminine	mercy, penance grace	

Hildegard frequently argued that men ought to develop the feminine qualities of mercy and grace, while women ought to develop the corresponding masculine qualities of courage and strength.[173] In this way, even though she designated particular qualities as masculine or feminine, a wholly integrated woman or man would have both aspects of their nature developed. The main difference between the sexes would be that a man's natural starting point was the masculine qualities, so that he needed to develop feminine qualities, while a woman's natural starting point was the feminine qualities, so that she needed to develop her masculine side. Therefore, in her consideration of woman and man as created in the image of God, Hildegard has maintained the balance so central to sex complementarity.

Generation

Hildegard's analysis of generation proposes two different theories, one before and one after the Fall. In her description of paradise, Hildegard states that woman generated by herself, without the help of man:

> The first mother of mankind was equipped according to the model of ether; the way ether carries the stars undamaged within it, thus she carried unharmed and undamaged and without pain mankind (within her) for she had been told: Go ye forth and multiply.[174]

Hildegard then suggests that man's testicles descended after the Fall and that man, for the first time, produced seed:

> Had man remained in paradise, he would have perpetually existed in an immutable and perfect state. But after his sin all of this was changed into another, quite bitter condition. For now the blood of he who is excited in the fiery heat of passion, ejects an effervescent humor, which we call seed.[175]

After the Fall, the continuity of generation demanded the sexual interaction of woman and man, whereas before it demanded only the cosmic parenting of woman.

Hildegard's analysis of human generation followed Aristotelian lines as qualified by Porphyry and Galen. She believed that woman did not contribute seed to generation. Drawing upon the theory that woman was naturally weaker than man, Hildegard states that woman contributes only blood and a kind of foam:

> The blood of the woman, who is weak and fragile, has no such seed: rather, she emits a thin and scanty foam, for she unlike man is not composed of two different types, namely earth and flesh, but is only of man's flesh.[176]

Therefore, after the Fall, woman lost not only the full power of generation, but also an equal role in the provision of seed for the child.

However, even with this sex-polarity description of the continuity of generation, Hildegard does not conclude that woman is inferior to man. She suggests that the woman heats up the man's seed and allows it to develop:

> [The man's] blood pours into the woman a cold foam which then congeals in the warmth of the motherly tissue taking on that blood-mixed state. In the beginning this foam remains in the warmth and later is maintained by the dry humors of the motherly nourishment growing into a dry, miniature like form of the human being until finally the script of the Creator, who formed man, penetrates under expansion of human formation as a whole, much the way a craftsman shapes his superior vessel.[177]

Within the sex-polarity tradition, which envisions heat as superior to cold, Hildegard once again seeks to bring about a balance between the sexes that would not allow either one to be essentially superior to the other. The man deposited the seed, the woman "warmed it up and strengthened it," and God brought it to life, by implanting the soul.[178] The suggestion of a different, but equal contribution by woman and man indicates Hildegard's movement towards a sex-complementarity theory of generation.

Hildegard gave a very detailed account of the complete process of generation. During the first month the seed slowly formed into a blood-like mixture that took on the shape of the child. The humours of the mother brought about the congealing, the development of shape, and the growth. Hildegard stated, however, that at this point the fetus was not properly described as alive, but rather as merely surviving. After one month, God infused life into the child.

The most striking aspect of Hildegard's description of the development of human life is her insistence on the complete integration of soul and body. This fact shows an

In this representation of a vision of Hildegard, God contributes the soul to the fetus already growing inside the mother's uterus.

important contrast between her theory and previous theories of sex unity that tended to devalue the body. As will be seen, sex complementarity, in its first complete articulation by Hildegard of Bingen, appears to maintain a balanced approach to the body and soul.

Hildegard drew upon a number of natural metaphors to explain how the soul and body were integrated. In *Causae et Curae*, the soul was compared to a great wind:

> The spirit of life draws near according to God's will and touches yonder form without the mother noticing, touches it like a strong, warm wind, that sweeps across the plains with a rage; it pours into the foam and intertwines into all its limbs.[179]

In the *Liber Divinorum Operum*, the relation of soul and body was compared to the intimate interaction of water in the earth: "For as water pours through all the earth, so the soul passes through the whole body."[180] The same metaphor was also used in the *Liber Compositae Medicinae*: "And the way the waters dash to particular spots, so the soul infuses our body over which it is all the same superior."[181] Finally, the soul, according to Hildegard, "wanders everywhere through this form like a caterpillar spinning silk."[182]

In all of the above natural metaphors, Hildegard emphasized the complete integration of soul and body. In this way, she rejected the Platonic tradition in which a soul was considered separate and distinct from the body. At the same time, although Hildegard's theory paralleled the Aristotelian integration of human rationality and materiality, it avoided the devaluation of the female that is so central to Aristotelian thought. In this way, Hildegard offered a new synthesis of body and soul that led to a complementarity, rather than a polarity of the sexes.

In Chapter III, Augustine's affirmation of the resurrection of the body was cited as offering the potential for a philosophy of sex complementarity by its recognition of the centrality of the body in the definition of personal identity. Hildegard, significantly, states that in the resurrection, the sexual aspect of man's and woman's natures will be maintained:

> Thus all men in the twinkling of an eye shall rise again in body and in soul without any contradiction of cutting off their members, but in the integrity of their bodies and their sex.[183]

The specific argument against the "cutting off of their members" implies that in the context of Hildegard's discussion, some suggestion had been made that the anatomical aspect of sexual differentiation would be destroyed in the resurrection. This view would have followed from a sex-unity tendency such as that suggested in the writings of John Scotus Erigena. In this theory the more perfect human state would be a unisex model. Hildegard's argument against the sex-unity theory of resurrection is, therefore, different from Augustine's argument against the sex-polarity interpretation of resurrection in which women would be changed into men. However, both Hildegard and Augustine insisted on the ultimate equality and differentiation of woman and man in the resurrected state. They understood this theory of sex complementarity to be the logical consequence of

In another vision, Hildegard sees the sexually differentiated soul leave the body of a dying woman.

the Christian theological belief in the resurrection of the body. In this view, human perfection necessarily involves reference to sex complementarity.

Wisdom

Hildegard believed that wisdom demanded self-knowledge. Since women and men had a sexually differentiated relationship in reference to the elements, wisdom demanded reflection on the relations between this material difference. Close association with the elements earth and fire gave man more natural power and greater passion. Woman's association with the elements of air and water gave her a more refined and gentle disposition. For Hildegard, the search for wisdom led woman to a certain recognition of her weaker status:

> The fear of God dwells in the sanctity of the chosen woman, for God has formed the woman so that she shall have awe for Him, and awe also for her husband. Therefore, it is only just if the woman displays a demure nature. By that she is, so to speak, the house of wisdom, for in her nature both worldy and spiritual matter comes to be realized.[184]

The above passage reads like a simple support for sex polarity in its emphasis upon woman's awe for man and her demure nature. However, Hildegard did not consider natural passion and strength to be superior qualities in a human being. She gave an equal evaluation to the more refined natural character of woman.

Hildegard's theory of the complementarity of the two sexes is nowhere more clearly expressed than in her analysis of sexual intercourse. In the following passage; she explains the differing elemental sources for man's and woman's sexual desires:

> For as soon as the storm of passion arises with a man, he is thrown about in it like a mill. His sexual organs then are so to speak the forge to which the marrow delivers its fire. That forge then transmits the blaze to the male genitals and makes them flame up mightily. If however, the wind of lust arises from the female marrow, it comes into the uterus that hangs at the navel and stirs the woman's blood with excitement. But the uterus possesses a wide and so to speak open space around the navel region so that wind can spread around the woman's womb; therefore, it lets her flow with passion less vehemently.[185]

Hildegard appears not to give a superior value to either the fire-like sexuality of the man or the air-like sexuality of the woman. She perceives them as equal and complementary. In yet another passage, Hildegard describes woman's sexual desires as similar to the gentle heat of the sun penetrating the earth:

> Such is the woman's sexual pleasure, gentle and silent and yet of a steady firey desire to receive and bear children. . . . It is of a lighter nature than that of man.[186]

In addition to the above general differentiation of the two sexes, Hildegard also developed a complicated psychology of different kinds of persons within either sex. She described four kinds of women and four kinds of men. Her analysis included reference to the humours, a common category in medieval thought that focused on the quality of blood, phlegm, yellow and black bile present in a person. The humours were thought to effect both health and personality.

Hildegard's Four Types of women

	Type I	Type II	Type III	Type IV
muscular structure	very heavy	moderately heavy	delicate	meagre
blood	clean, red	whiter	drier	slimy
colour of skin	clear and white	sullen	pale	dark
fertility	moderate	very	partial	rare
menstruation	light	moderate	heavy	very heavy
character	artistic, content	efficient, manly, strict	intellectual, benevolent, loyal, chaste	unstable, ill-humoured
possible diseases after early menopause	depression, melancholy, pains in side, unhealthy glandular secretions	insanity, problems with spleen, dropsy tumors	paralysis, imbalanced, liver problems, cancer	abdominal pains, spinal pains, early death

Hildegard's theory of the intricate connection between body and soul is clearly seen in the above chart. She understands personality as having a clear connection with quality of blood and muscles; in addition, she sees the relationship between personality and color of skin, intensity of menstruation, and disease. Her analysis is astonishingly modern in its emphasis on the interaction of psychological and biological factors, while it is at the same time medieval in its consideration of elements and humours.

In the following summary of Hildegard's theory of the four kinds of men, we find a somewhat less detailed, but similar kind of analysis.

Hildegard's Four Types of Men

	Type I	Type II	Type III	Type IV
blood	fiery	fiery and windy	windy and black bile	weak in all respects
colour of skin	red hue	mixed red and white hue	sombre	unclean and pale
fertility	very	moderate	partial	infertile
character	hearty and hale	balanced	very dangerous, no moderation	weak, effeminate
children	tend to be unrestrained, coarse-mannered children	balanced, happy, well-mannered children	mean or evil children	

It is interesting to note that Hildegard included reference to fertility as well as to the quality of progeny in her analysis of types of women and men.

Hildegard's analysis of the kinds of women and men had as one of its purposes the goal of leading people to a heightened self-knowledge. Wisdom consisted, in part, in learning about one's own basic material constitution, and about how this kind of personality might affect other people. If Hildegard had merely completed her analysis with the above general descriptions, it would have been significant for the history of a philosophy of sex identity. However, she went much further, giving detailed assessments of the ways in which each type of man related to each type of woman in both sexual and chaste relationships. It is in these passages that Hildegard's frankness, combined with her gift of poetic description, makes her one of the most important philosophers in the history of the concept of woman.

> [The first type of men] love coition with women and are anxious to get out of other men's way and to avoid them, for they are more inclined to women than to men. . . . As soon as they get sight of a woman, hear of one or simply fancy one in thought, their blood is burning with a blaze. Their eyes are kept fixed on the object of their love like arrows as soon as they catch sight of it.[188]

The strong presence of the element fire in this kind of man made him a persistent companion. The second type of man, however, had a stronger presence of the element wind:

> The addition of wind in their genitals moderates and tames the fiery power within themselves. . . . That is why one refers to them as a golden edifice of sexual embrace. . . . With women they can have an honorable and fruitful relationship. The eyes of such men can meet squarely with those of the women, much in contrast to those other men's eyes that were fixed on them like arrows.[189]

Hildegard understood perfectly well the difference between a man who sought to relate to a woman as a sex object to be possessed, and a man who sought to be joined to the whole woman as a person.

Hildegard's description of the remaining two kinds of men developed other kinds of male character in equally vivid detail. The third kind of man suffered from an overabundance of black bile in his blood. This turned him into an evil sort of companion.

> The wind in their genitals has three characteristic features: for one, it is fiery, then also windy and finally intermixed with the smoke of the black bile; therefore, they are incapable of having a genuine loving relationship with any being. Through that they become bitter, avaricious and full of foolishness and abundant passion. In intercourse with women they know no moderation and act like donkeys.[190]

Hildegard used the animal metaphors of wolves of prey, lion, and bear to describe this kind of man. She argued that some of these men "retained an instinctive hatred towards [women's] sex." This hatred caused their genital organs to become violently twisted away from their original purpose. Hildegard ended her analysis with a warning:

> If they were permitted, these men would kill a woman during their intercourse, for there is nothing of the tenderness of loving desire nor of sincerity in their embrace.[191]

Hildegard's distinction between the first kind of passionate lover and the third kind of violent misogynist was important. While the first kind of man at least offered some possibility of relationship, the third should be avoided altogether. The fourth kind of man turned out to be indifferent to women. He suffered from a general weakness in possession of all the elements:

> The wind in their genitals has little fiery force, for it is lukewarm like water that has hardly been heated. His two spheres, meant to serve him like bellows to mend the fire, are stunted, underdeveloped and too feeble to erect the trunk, for they do not hold within them the riches of the fiery power. Such men can be loved in sexual embrace, whereby they desire to cohabit with women as well as with men. . . . They are not tormented by envy so more out of good will love women who are weak as well, for the woman is weak and in her weakness appears more like a boy.[192]

Hildegard concluded that a relationship with this kind of man was rarely productive.

Hildegard's description of the four kinds of women did not go into as much detail about lovemaking. However, just as she had described which kind of man was most attractive to women, she also considered which kind of woman was most attractive to men. The first kind, or artistic women, are "charming and lovely in their embrace."[193] The second, or manly kind of women, "are very attractive to men and understand how to captivate them; therefore, men are very fond of such women."[194] Hildegard seems to be using "manly" here to refer to a woman similar to the contemporary earth mother image. The third kind, or the intellectual woman, had a more difficult time. "Although men like their way of living, they shun them a bit, for such women attract them, is true, but don't know how to captivate them."[195] The fourth kind, or unstable women, appeared to discourage men altogether. "Men likewise have a disinclination for such women and also love them very little. And should they really at one point reach a sexual pleasure, it will not last but shortly."[196]

Hildegard was not only interested in describing sexual relations between women and men. As a nun in close relation to a man's monastery, she was equally interested in how men and women interacted on the personal level when genital sexuality was not a factor in the relationship. Hildegard was as insightful in this dimension of male-female relationships as she had been previously. She argued that the second type of man and the second type of woman were best able to live with the opposite sex in chastity. Significantly, these two types of women and men were also best able to sustain a marriage. In other words, it was precisely the same characteristics that enable a person to have a balanced relationship with a member of the opposite sex that also gave them the necessary character for a productive spiritual life.

In more detail, Hildegard outlined the ways in which each man dealt with chastity. The first kind of man, with the fiery nature, had a very difficult time with women:

> They wither away and drag about as if dying, unless they can let loose the foam of their seed in another way by means of lustful dreams or thoughts or perverse acts.[197]

Hildegard reflected that they would even be aroused by inanimate objects and subsequently exhausted by the struggles of their sexual drives. As a consequence they had to avoid women at all costs:

> Should these types wish to shun women voluntarily, may it be out of necessity, shame, fear or love for God, then they have to shun them like poison and have to flee from them, because they find it too hard not to embrace women.[198]

In this way, Hildegard explained the multitude of writers—such as Jerome, Lucretius or Juvenal—who counselled men to avoid women.[199]

The second kind of man, or the person with a balanced nature, was quite able to live in chastity: "They are also capable of abstaining from them (women) and to look at them in a friendly and moderate way."[200] However, Hildegard observed that this kind of man needed to have female friends:

> If the above mentioned men remain without women, they are inglorious like a day without sunshine. . . . In company with women their joy is like a clear day when the sun is shining brightly.[201]

Consequently, Hildegard's description of the most perfect kind of man included a clear statement of the need for that man to be in a complementary relation with women. It could be a sexual relationship, as within marriage, or it could be a celibate bond. The second kind of man was capable of developing either creatively.

The third kind of man, or the person with an abundance of black bile, was frequently able to avoid women without much difficulty: "Some of these men can avoid the female sex, for they feel no love and dislike women."[202] They appear to be quite unable to form any meaningful kind of relationships with either women or men:

> They neither receive any love from their fellow men, nor have any inclination to a social life of their own, all the more since they exhaust themselves with continuous figments of their imagination. Then when they meet people they already are full of hate, malevolence and the wrong attitude so they can't enjoy company anymore.[203]

Therefore, this kind of man would tend to be as erratic and violent in chastity as he was in a sexual encounter. Finally, the fourth kind of man, or the weak man, could live in chastity without too much effort:

> Obviously, they do not have to suffer much from lust in their emotional life, except for having to grapple with it at times in their imagination or in their ideal life. Because they demonstrate such deficiencies in their bodily condition, they are also awkward in drafting their spiritual world.[204]

It is clear that this kind of man would not have a very intense or creative relationship of complementarity with a woman.

Hildegard's discussion of the effect of celibacy on women did not focus as much on their subsequent relation with men as on the effects of this situation on their health. She argued that the first kind of woman, the artistic woman, needed a sexual relationship with a man.

> If they have to remain without men and can't give birth to children, they suffer from quite a number of bodily conditions. If they have men, they are healthy.[205]

The second kind of woman, the earthy woman, however, was able to live without men.

> They can abstain from intercourse, if they want to, without suffering particular damage. However, often when they do avoid the company of men, they are quite difficult and unbearable in their manners.[206]

Hildegard believed that the second kind of woman did not adjust well to abstinence in many cases. However, they were the only kind who were able to retain their good health. The third kind of woman, or the intellectual woman, appeared to suffer from the lack of a relationship with a man:

> In sexual union, they act chaste, are loyal to their men and healthy with them, but suffering if without them. Then they are ailing, both because they don't know in which particular man to trust or because they have not got a man at all.[207]

Hildegard did not consider it a negative quality of woman to need the company of men. On the contrary, she argued that the fourth kind of woman, the unstable woman, was the only one who quite happily lived without men.

> Thus they are healthier, stronger and merrier without men, all the more since they often feel very weak after having had intercourse with men.[208]

To be happy without contact with members of the opposite sex seemed to point to a lack of personal development for Hildegard. Only those women and men who responded to one another in a whole and balanced way were considered examples of ideal women and men. This meant that abstinence would bring about some initial suffering until the relationship was transformed into another dimension of complementarity. Women and men who had achieved this balanced transformation were able to have deep personal bonds with one another. Indeed, their happiness in some way depended upon the development of such complementarity bonds.

Hildegard's theory of the interaction of the four types of women and four types of men, as developed in *Causae et Curae*, is summarized in the chart on the following page.

The second types of man and woman turn out to be the ideal or most perfect examples of human development. It is significant that this particular combination of elements and humours involves a balance particularly of the male and female elements of fire and air. In fact, Hildegard explicitly draws out this implication in the following passage:

Hildegard's Theory of the Interaction of the Sexes

Four Types of Men: Generally More Earth and Fire

Type I	Type II	Type III	Type IV
too much fire	balanced air and fire	too much water in form of bile	weak in all elements
passionately interested in sexual relations with women	honourable and fruitful relationship with women (sexual and celibate)	hates women, masochistic	indifferent to women, effeminate

Four Types of Women: Generally More Air and Water

Type I	Type II	Type III	Type IV
more earth through heavy muscular structure, more fire through red blood	balanced earth through moderate muscular structure, more air through white blood	less earth through delicate muscular structure, less water with drier blood	weak in all elements through meagre muscular structure, slimy blood
needs to be with men	likes to be with men, but does not need to	remains loyal to men, but suffers because cannot keep their interest	not interested in men

Generative Relationship

moderately fertile	very fertile	partially fertile	rarely fertile

> Often they too (the second kind of men) must bear some pain when they try with all their strength to abstain; but they are so adroit, a wisdom that takes its beautiful self-control out of the female element: for they are in possession of a sensible understanding.[209]

Therefore, the ideal man has developed the feminine side of his nature—which is naturally masculine—in much the same way as an ideal woman develops the masculine side of her nature—which is naturally feminine. In this way, Hildegard developed a unique theory of the complementarity of woman and man both within the internal structure of their personal identity as well as in the external dynamics of their interaction in either married or celibate relationships.

Wisdom, in conclusion, demands of both sexes an astute understanding of their own specific natures both as woman or man and as individuals within the broader category of sexual identity. Because women and men differ in their sexual identity, the specific kind of self-knowledge they would have would also differ in detail of content. However, the general goal of self-knowledge as the path to wisdom would be the same for both sexes.

Virtue

Hildegard developed a sex complementarity in connection with her theory of virtue in three different areas: the nature of virtue; the relation of woman and man to ruling and obedience; and the relation of the sexes to the public and private spheres of activity. Each of these areas will now be studied in turn.

Hildegard considered the broad category of virtue from the theological perspective in the *Scivias, Liber Vitae Meritorium*, and *Liber Divinorum Operum*. In these texts she described the ways in which all Christians ought to struggle towards the good and away from evil. Virtue followed from the personal transformation that a love of Christ could bring in a person's life. While Hildegard often spoke of virtue in broad categories, without specific reference to sexual differentiation, she always recognized the individual context of actions for any person. To know what ought to be done in any particular situation demanded a knowledge of the people involved. Virtue followed from wisdom. Therefore, the same sort of sexual differentiation that had been discovered in the category of wisdom, was carried forward into the concrete actions demanded by the practice of virtue.

Hildegard also considered virtue in her morality play *Ordo Virtutum*. In a recent study of this play by Bruce Hozeski, it is revealed once again that Hildegard was an original thinker and writer:

> In the twelfth century *Ordo Virtutum*, revealing Hildegard's freedom of dramatic invention through her sense of personifications and figurations, is, then, important since it pre-dates by approximately two centuries any other known liturgical morality play.[210]

The complementarity of the play is established at the outset by a movement back and forth between the male patriarchs and prophets and the female virtues:

> PATRIARCHS AND PROPHETS: Who are those who look like a cloud?
> VIRTUES: O holy ancients, what makes you wonder at us? The Word of God becomes clear in the form of man, and therefore we shine with Him, edifying the members of His glorious body.
> PATRIARCHS AND PROPHETS: We are the roots and ye the branches, the fruit of the living bud, and we were the shadow in Him.[211]

The complementarity of male and female, represented as a relationship of root and branches, as shadow and light, is carried forward throughout the play.

The *Ordo Virtutum* describes the struggle of a soul moving from a state of vice to a state of virtue. The soul desires to become "a daughter of the king":

> VIRTUES: We ought to serve as soldiers with thee, O daughter of the king.
> BUT A TROUBLED SOUL COMPLAINED: Such hard labour, and such a heavy weight I have in the garment of this life, because it is so hard for me to fight against the body.
> THE VIRTUES TO THE SOUL: O soul, created by the will of God, and most fortunate instrument, why dost thou trouble thyself so much against that which God in the virgin nature destroyed? Thou oughtest to overcome the devil by our aid.
> THE SOUL: Hasten and help me to stand.[212]

In the play, the separation and struggle between the soul and body is seen as a false view of the self. The Virtues are convinced that integration and ordering of the body is possible in life. Drawing upon a metaphor of virtues as warriors, which springs from the

Crusades, the personification of Victory indicates that even the source of evil can be conquered by Virtue:

> VICTORY TO THE VIRTUES: Ye most brave and glorious knights, come and help me to conquer that deceitful one.
> VIRTUES: O most sweet warrior, who swallowed the greedy wolf in the torrent! O glorious crowned one, we willingly fight with thee against this deceiver.
> HUMILITY: Therefore bind Satan, O very bright virtues!
> VIRTUES: O our queen, we will be obedient to thee and we will fulfill thy precepts in all things.[213]

The female personification of the Virtues, with the corresponding description of them as knights in combat with the vices or the devil as the source of evil, is an interesting fusion of male and female identity. For Hildegard and for Herrad of Landsberg—who will be studied in the next section—this fusion of male and female identity did not imply a sex-unity development. For the knights are dressed as women rather than men. In this way, female identity is depicted as developing the male qualities of strength, courage, and fortitude without losing the natural female relationship to grace, mercy, and prophetic insight. Therefore, a complementarity, rather than a polarity of the sexes is preserved.

In the second area of virtue to be considered, Hildegard begins her analysis by appearing to repeat the traditional sex-polarity differentiation that men, by nature, ought to rule, and women to obey. In describing woman, Hildegard states, "She was formed from the flesh of man; therefore she is subject to him, it is true, but she is in a much greater position of quiescence."[214] On closer examination, however, the above passage marks a radical departure from the sex-polarity theory as articulated by Aristotle. The Greek philosopher had argued that woman ought to obey because she was not in control of her emotions, while Hildegard asserts that she is more in control of her emotions than man out of her "greater position of quiescence."

In another passage, Hildegard also begins with an apparent sex polarity but adds a qualification that moves towards an equality of the sexes. Hildegard starts with the claim that woman ought to be in "awe" of man:

> Did she not know this awe, she could never cherish the reserve of chastity, but rather would bite everything she could like a den of adders. The awe-sruck woman, however, gathers all riches of good works and holy virtue in her womb, and she does not stop until she has accomplished everything good.[215]

The important aspect of this awe is that it comes from within the woman herself. She "gathers" her virtuous acts, and she "accomplishes everything good." Her control is not imposed from outside, but springs up within herself, as a method of practising human perfection.

It is important to note that Hildegard is writing about subjection in the context of a Benedictine monastic tradition in which obedience is understood as a valuable method for learning to overcome the limitations of selfishness, egotism, and personal will. In this context, obedience towards the Abbot or Abbess of the monastery, as the representative of Christ, constituted an important element in the development of virtue. Here it made little difference whether one obeyed a woman or a man. Hildegard could argue, then, that within marriage, it would be useful for a woman to practise awe of her husband in order to develop further her natural tendency towards self-control.

At the same time, obedience was not considered to be an absolute for Hildegard. While it ought to be practised for the most part, there may be times when it should be abandoned for a higher goal. In two incidents of Hildegard's life, she asserted her own will over and against her Abbot and the Bishop, both of whom, generally speaking, she should obey. In the first incident, soon after she had been elected Abbess of the woman's community at Mount Disibode, she decided to take the nuns from this double monastery and to found a new monastery for women at Rupertsberg because Disibode was dominated by a much larger and more powerful community of men. The Abbot disapproved of her plan and did everything in his power to block it. Hildegard went over the Abbot's head and tried to persuade the Archbishop of Mainz to support her. After a great deal of manoeuvring she won.[216]

In a second incident, Hildegard buried in the tombs of her monastery at St. Rupertsberg a young man who had been excommunicated from the Church. The Archbishop of Mainz placed her monastery under interdict, and ordered her to exhume the body. Hildegard refused.[217] These two incidents indicate that in Hildegard's personal life, the practice of obedience could also be overturned in the specific practice of virtue. Obedience was not forced by nature, but practised by choice.

Therefore, Hildegard's theory of the relation of woman and man to obedience and ruling followed in the tradition of the neo-Pythagorean philosopher Perictione rather than that of Aristotle; for obedience when adopted as a choice became virtue. Since obedience was the virtue of choice for a woman and ruling for a man, it would happen that in certain circumstances the virtuous choice would be the opposite, namely that the woman would rule and the man obey. In the above two examples, this inversion of virtue occurred.

In the third area of virtue to be considered, Hildegard broke through the traditional separation of the activities of women and man into private and public spheres. She understood her call to be that of a prophet in an age that had grown weak or effeminate. Hildegard claimed that "Society had been plunged into feminine levity; so that to the scandal of men, women prophesy."[218] The view that women had been called to prophesy because men were weak or immoral was further repeated in the writings of Elizabeth of Schönau, who was deeply influenced by Hildegard. In a passage from her *Visions*, Elizabeth states:

> People are scandalized that in these days the Lord deigns to magnify His great mercy in the frail sex. But why doesn't it cross their minds that a similar thing happened in the days of our fathers when, while men were given to indolence, holy women were filled with the Spirit of God so that they could prophesy, energetically govern the people of God, and even win glorious victories over Israel's enemies? I speak of women like Hilda, Deborah, Judith, Jael, and the like.[219]

In the call of women to prophesy, the traditional limitation of the virtue of silence for women and speech for men is shattered. Woman is virtuous by speaking, just as is man. The difference between the sexes, however, is also present and it is significant precisely because a woman is called to speak rather than a man. A sex-unity theory would have ignored the differences between the sexes, but Hildegard is aware that the power of prophesy is due in part to the fact that a woman, the weaker vessel, is chosen to confound the strong.

As Barbara Newman states, Hildegard took her prophetic speeches far and wide:

> Between 1158 and 1159 Hildegard travelled along the Main, preaching at monastic communities in Mainz, Wertheim, Wurzburg, Kitzingen, Ebrach, and Bamberg. Her second trip in 1160 took her to Metz, Krauftal, Trier, where she preached publicly. Within the next three years she visited Boppart, Andernach, Siegburg, and Werden, addressing clergy and people together at Cologne. After 1170 she undertook her fourth and final journey in Swabia, preaching at Rodenkirchan, Maulbronn, Hirsau, Kircheim, and Zwiefalten.[220]

This extensive travel and public speaking reveals that Hildegard believed women ought not to be limited to the private sphere of activity or, inversely, that the public sphere ought not to be limited to men. During the twelfth century, the concept of the cloister for Benedictine nuns did not imply that the nuns were unable to go out into the world. Rather, it primarily indicated that there was an enclosure within the monastery that excluded the entry of people from outside. It was not until later in western history that the cloister restricted the movement of women into the public spheres of activity.

In addition to Hildegard's public speaking, her communication beyond the monastery also occurred through writing. From the beginning, Hildegard submitted her writings to the scrutiny of men:

> When the visions experienced since childhood increased in later life, she confided in her confessor Godfrey and authorized him to submit the matter to the abbot, and, later to the Archbishop of Mainz. A committee of theologians gave a favorable verdict on the authenticity of her visions and assigned the monk Volmar to act as her secretary. Eugene III appointed a committee to review her writings, and again a favorable report followed.[221]

Working in complement with Volmar within the context of the double monastery of St. Disibode, Hildegard dictated her works in Latin. In addition to the numerous books she wrote, Hildegard's correspondents include St. Bernard of Clairvaux, Gilbert of Gemblous, and a master of the Cathedral School of Paris, Odo of Soissons.[222] Through this extensive correspondence Hildegard entered into an intimate exchange of ideas with some of the leading men of her day, even after she had moved—by her own choice—out of the context of the double monastery into an exclusively women's monastery at Rupertsberg. Her fame, therefore, enabled an exchange between women and men to continue without any changes to the basic context of complementarity that the double monasteries offered.

> Hildegard's influence extended beyond her monastery through her extensive correspondence and because of her travels throughout Germany and parts of Gaul. She spoke to people of all classes and walks of life exhorting them to reform and to heed the prophesies and divine warnings entrusted to her. During her last years she was so ill that she had to be carried from place to place and

The Abbess Hildegard of Bingen works in complement with the monk Volmar within the context of a double monastery.

> was unable to stand upright. Nevertheless, she remained available to all who sought her, discussing perplexing questions, encouraging and exhorting her nuns, admonishing sinners, and writing continuously.[223]

There is some controversy about whether or not Hildegard took a further important trip to Paris in 1174. It is argued by some scholars that Hildegard, at the age of 76, made this arduous trip of several hundred miles—in a cart—to submit copies of *Scivias, Liber Divinorum Operum* and *Liber Vitae Meritorum* to the Bishop of Paris for consideration.[224] Abelard had died thirty years previously, the Cathedral School of Notre Dame had a reputation for its excellence in philosophy and theology, and the masters guilds had been slowly formed in Paris since 1140. Hildegard would have been aware of this shift in the centre of higher education from the Benedictine monastries to the Bishop's schools in Paris. One goal of this reputed trip was to seek to have her texts integrated into the developing curriculum of academic theology. Hildegard is reported to have requested the Bishop to ask all the masters of theology in Paris to study her writings. The process is described as having taken three months for one single master of theology, who gave the works back and simply affirmed them as "divinely inspired."[225] The works, however, were not integrated into the curriculum.

The belief in Hildegard's Parisian trip is contested by other scholars, who argue that it was carried out by Hildegard's literary executor, the Canon Bruno of Strassbourg, several years after her death.[226] However, both versions of the story point to the growing importance of the educational situation in Paris, since it was deemed necessary to take Hildegard's writings to the centre of intellectual study. As will be demonstrated in Chapter V, the concept of woman in relation to man was significantly altered by the developments in thirteenth-century Paris. Hildegard is particularly significant to this study because she wrote just before the explosion of the Aristotelian Revolution. That her philosophy of sex complementarity was original and complete within her medieval context, is witness to the effects of the concrete practical interaction of women and men springing from the double monasteries and reaching far beyond into broader society. As there was a true complementarity in a long-term living situation, it was inevitable that a philosophy of sex complementarity would eventually evolve.

The situation in Paris, however, was radically different from the double monasteries, for by the time the masters guilds and small schools evolved into the University of Paris, women were excluded from formal study. At the same time, the total influx of translations of Aristotle's works, containing a devaluation of women, became integrated into the academic curriculum. In this way, the slowly developing foundation for a philosophy of sex complementarity, as articulated by Hildegard, was pushed into the background of philosophy and theology, where it stayed for several centuries until a new philosophical foundation for the equality and significant differentiation of the sexes would re-emerge. Therefore, Hildegard stands as an important transition figure, just at the end of the period in western thought before the Aristotelian Revolution in sex identity occurred.

Herrad of Landesberg (1130–1195)

The *Hortus Deliciarum*, or *Garden of Delights*, is the first extensive encyclopedia written for women in the west. It was composed primarily during the years 1170 to 1196, just towards the end of Hildegard of Bingen's most productive years. The Abbess Hildegard and the Abbess Herrad are presumed to have been aware of one another's existence, although there is no record of direct correspondence. Both women, however, represent the heights of achievement under the category of wisdom.

The Monastery of Hohenburg was founded in the eighth century by Aldaric, the Duke of Alsace, for his daughter Odile. In the twelfth century it was restored under the direction of the Abbess Rilinda. In *Hortus Deliciarum*, Rilinda is described as follows:

> The venerable Rilinda of the church of Hohenburg, abbess in her time of the same church, who diligently restored the ruined parts and in her wisdom revived the divine religion that had almost been destroyed in it.[227]

While Rilinda is also cited in the development of the encyclopedia, Herrad proceeded to bring the *Hortus* to its full development when she was elected Abbess on Rilinda's death in 1176. According to Eckenstein, Herrad attempted to write an encyclopedia that would "embody in pictures and words, the knowledge of her age."[228] The size and scope of the project were extraordinary:

> [The *Garden of Delights*] consisted of 324 parchment leaves of folio size, which contained an account of the history of the world founded on the biblical narrative, with many digressions into the realm of philosophy, moral speculation and contemporary knowledge.[229]

Another scholar describes the content of the encyclopedia in which Herrad brought together the important sources already available to her through other writers:

> Incorporating a wide range of contemporary knowledge, it was a compendium of 12th-century thought. Herrad's personal authorship included only a preface and a few short verses, but selections comprising about 45,000 lines represented sources ranging from the fathers to her contemporaries. Its miniatures, numbering at least 344, were its chief claim to distinction.[230]

The most frequently mentioned sources with philosophical significance for Herrad were Boethius, Augustine, Anselm, and Anselm's student Honorius Augustodunensis, who had written an encyclopedia some time between 1108 and 1120.[231] She also appears to have been aware of the Stoics and neo-Platonists. In addition, Herrad included references to the theologians Hugh of St. Viktor, St. Bernard, Clement, Gregory, Jerome, and John Chrysostom, and church historians Bede, de Césarée, and de Lisieux. Unlike Hildegard, Herrad admits she was influenced by the actual texts of philosophers. In the introduction to the *Hortus*, she states that her sources of knowledge were both human and divine:

> This book titled *Garden of Delights* I myself, the little bee composed inspired by God, from the sap of diverse flowers from Holy Scripture and from philosophical works.[232]

Herrad also knew of Socrates, Plato and Aristotle, although only through secondary sources. However, as will be seen in the consideration of the category of wisdom, she correctly recognized their significance to the history of philosophy.

The folios in the *Hortus Deliciarum* were divided into the following subject categories: The Life of Christ; St. Anselm on the Sacraments; the Virtues and Vices; the Church and Society; Eschatological Texts; the *Sentences* of Peter Lombard; Clement; the Spiritual Rule; list of Popes; Church Calendar; and the Monastery at Hohenburg.[233] The text itself was written in Latin and German, in only three different scripts. "All the emphasis on writing gives a strong impression of a book used for teaching."[234]

In 1178, Herrad asked the Premonstratensians from the Abbey at Loraine d'Estival for some land to construct a priory and chapel. The monks from the Abbey lived and worked in close relationship with the nuns. In 1180, Herrad bought and founded a second monastery, larger than the first. It included—in addition to the church and convent—a farm, a hospital for the poor, and a hospice for pilgrims. Consequently, Herrad reveals herself to have been a creative businesswoman as well as a scholar and artist. Like her contemporary Hildegard, Herrad reached a high degree of personal development that poured forth in a variety of concrete achievements for others.

The history of the *Hortus Deliciarum* unfortunately includes a severe fire in 1870, which completely destroyed the original manuscript that had been stored in the library of Strassbourg. However, after extensive research, a reconstruction of the manuscript has recently been published. By a careful study of this text it is possible to glean some concrete information about the theory of sex identity that Herrad suggested in her massive work.

The title of the *Hortus Deliciarum* contains an obvious, playful reference to the garden of Eden as containing the tree of knowledge. Clearly, for Herrad, Eve is not given the negative interpretation that was so often found in other medieval writers. In addition, in the miniatures, Eve is represented as the same size as Adam, which symbolically suggests a complementarity of functions. This equality and differentiation of woman and man is found both in the drawings of the Creation and of the Fall.[235]

In a poem about Adam and Eve at the moment of the Fall, Herrad gave some indication of the complementarity of their interaction:

> One day
> While Adam stood
> In his delightful domain,
> There came the black
> Father of death
> With his terrible face:
> And to Eve,
> Standing on her left,
> He spoke in a whisper:
> Hear me, woman, do what I shall say:
> Eat of the fruit that is forbidden to you,
> So you will be like a lord, do not doubt it.
>
> You will be a lord
> If you enjoy
> The fruit of this tree;
> You will know everything;

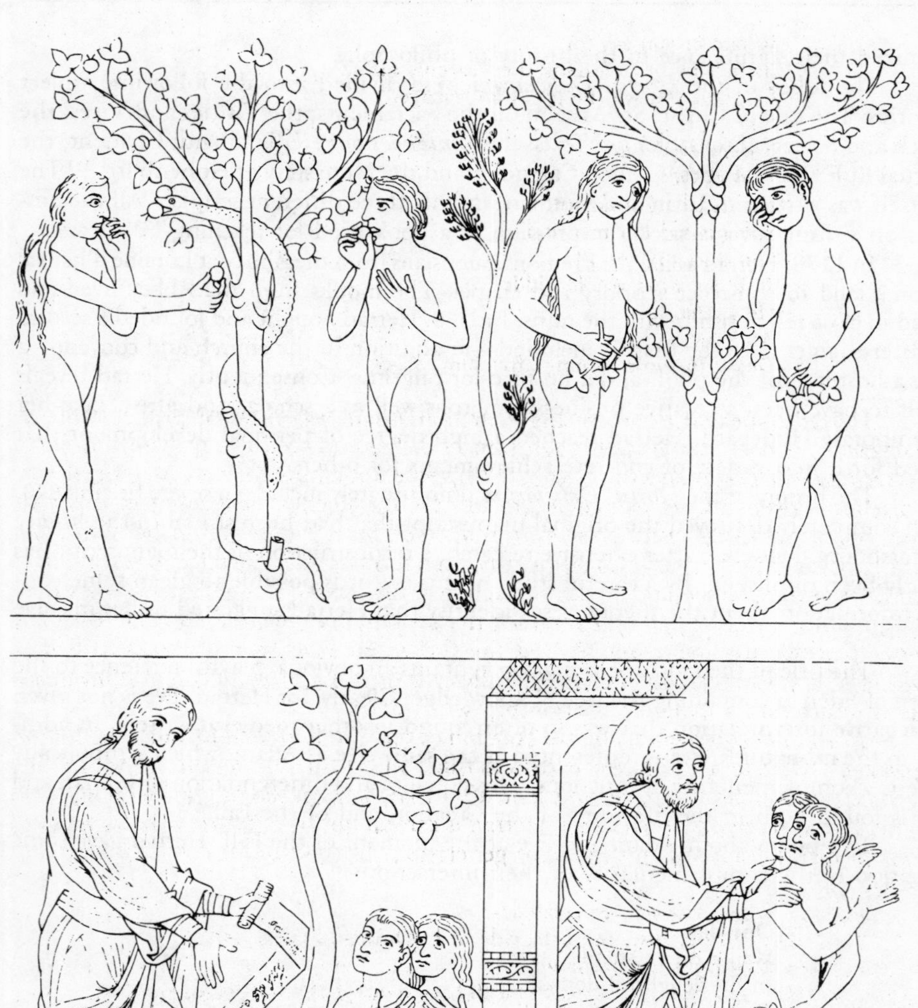

In Herrad's encyclopedia, the *Garden of Delights,* Adam and Eve are portrayed as equal and differentiated.

Whatever you ask for,
It shall be done among the heavenly ones . . .
Eat, and you will be given knowledge.

Eve believed him
And obeyed
His treacherous advice.
She advised her husband
(An amazing thing)
To enjoy what was forbidden.
He agreed
And gave
Death to those coming after him.[236]

Herrad appeared to accept the view that Adam was the first principle of the human race and that primarily through him both life and death were transmitted. In a catechism on the first man a pupil asks, "Why were not all the elect created together?" The teacher answers, "God wanted Adam to have the likeness of himself in this also, so that, just as all things were born from him, God, so all men should be born from him, Adam, including Eve."[237] Consequently, even though Herrad's selections contained a semblance of complementarity in the interaction of Adam and Eve after they were created, the origin of the two first parents contained the sex-polarity preference for the first male as better representing the image of God the Father. However, Eve is also described as "advising" her husband, and Herrad playfully calls this "an amazing thing." Obviously, Eve is entering into a dynamic relationship with Adam.

In another commentary on the creation of the world, Herrad includes the following passage: "On the sixth day the earth was filled with its living creatures, and the first man was created in God's image; and soon after that, woman was made, by taking a rib from his side as he slept."[238] However, Herrad is careful not to conclude that woman was inferior to man because of this mode of generation. In the catechisms she continued:

PUPIL: Where was woman created?
TEACHER: In paradise, from the side of her husband as he slept.
PUPIL: Why from her husband?
TEACHER: So that, just as she was with him in one flesh, so through love she should be with him in one mind.
PUPIL: What kind of sleep was that?
TEACHER: Ecstasy.[239]

Herrad borrowed extensively from the *Sentences* of Peter Lombard to develop her catechism on the microcosm. In this passage she summarizes Lombard's theory that human life reflects the same elements as found in the world at large, that is the microcosm and macrocosm have the same material structure:

PUPIL: Of what does man consist?
TEACHER: Of two substances, a spiritual and a corporeal.
PUPIL: From where does the corporeal substance come from?
TEACHER: From the four elements. That is why he is called a microcosm, that

> is a miniature universe, because from the earth he gets flesh and bones, from water blood, from the air breath, and from fire heat.[240]

The element fire also appears to be nearly divine, or at least analogous to the Divine Nature. For as the catechism continues, Herrad, again applying the thought of Lombard, considers the nature of the second aspect of human existence, or its spirituality:

> PUPIL: Where does his spiritual substance come from?
> TEACHER: From the spiritual fire, as we believe, in which the image and likeness of God is expressed.
> PUPIL: What image of likeness?
> TEACHER: The image of his appearance. The likeness is conceived in quality and quantity. The divine nature consists of a trinity, and the soul holds a reflection of this, having memory, through which it recalls the past and anticipates the future, understanding, through which it comprehends what is present and what is invisible, and will through which it rejects evil and chooses the good.[241]

The relation of fire to the divine is also developed in Herrad's description of the book of *Revelation*. One of the central figures in this image is "the woman, that is the Church, who is clothed with the sun and has the moon under her feet."[242] The complementarity of God the Father, as the sun, and the feminine church wearing this masculine power as her cloak, is vividly represented by a drawing in the *Hortus Deliciarum*. On this cosmic level there is no sense of female identity being passive or weak in relation to male identity.

The above section of the Catechism is also significant because it indicates the level of sophistication that Herrad used to teach her nuns philosophy. The division of the soul into the three parts—memory, understanding, and will—implies that the women are expected to develop an ability to discern the internal operations of the soul. In short, they are being asked to use their discursive reason. In the following passage, extracted from St. Augustine, Herrad further develops an understanding of the nature of the soul:

> The soul, then, is a substance created invisible, incorporeal, immortal, very like God, bearing no likeness except that of its creator, and no colour; it is contained in no place, it is circumscribed by no body, it is bounded by no place, it is how the soul is to be thought of and understood, like wisdom, justice and other virtues.[243]

In an inscription to the Nine Muses, Herrad stipulates even more clearly the steps of discursive reasoning that she expects her nuns to follow:

> The first thing is to gather learning.
> The second is to desire knowledge.
> The third is to persist in meditation.
> The fourth is to grasp the subject of your meditation.
> The fifth is to retain what you have grasped.
> The sixth is to find something else like it.
> The seventh is to pass judgement on what you have found.
> The eighth is to choose the good.
> The ninth is to express well what you have chosen.[244]

This exposition of the steps of wisdom and action significantly develops the use of the Nine Muses beyond simple sources of inspiration. If Herrad thought of wisdom for women as simply passive response to inspiration or intuition using a lower level of the mind, she would not have gone to the trouble of delineating, step by step, the discursive process.

In another passage, Herrad explicitly considers the nature of philosophy. It is interesting to note that Herrad was well aware of Aristotle's function as the source of dialectics and logic at this point in history, just before the full explosion of the Aristotelian Revolution.

> Philosophy is defined as the love of wisdom, and has three departments. *Physics*, that is, natural science, which deals with the nature of things. Pythagoras divided this into arithmetic, geometry, astronomy and music. *Logic*, that is, the science of speech, in which truth is distinguished from falsehood. This was divided by Aristotle into dialectic, rhetoric, and grammar. *Ethics*, that is, moral philosophy, which either repels vices or induces virtues. Socrates divided this into justice, fortitude, temperance and prudence.[245]

Perhaps the most famous of the portrayals of wisdom in Herrad's *Hortus Deliciarum* are her depictions of Philosophy, The Liberal Arts, and The Poets. Philosophy, personified as a woman with the crown of the three divisions of the field, is seated on a throne. From her breast flow seven streams of water, symbolic of the seven liberal arts. At her feet sit Socrates and Plato, taking down dictation from her inspiration. In the following inscriptions on the text, Herrad clearly suggests that the Holy Spirit is the feminine "philosophia":

> Philosophy: ethics, physics.
> All wisdom is from the Lord God; only the wise can accomplish what they desire.
> Seven streams of wisdom flow from philosophy: they are called the Liberal Arts.
> The Holy Spirit is the inventor of the Seven Liberal Arts, which are grammar, rhetoric, logic, music, arithmetic, geometry and astronomy.
> Philosophy taught men to explore the nature of the universe.
> Socrates; Plato: philosophers.[246]

The rather disjointed prose of the above inscription follows from the fact that the phrases were placed around the miniatures in appropriate places, to explain the meaning of the artistic representtion to the pupils who were studying from the encyclopedia.

The inscriptions on the above figure continue with descriptions of the specific gifts of each of the seven Liberal Arts:

> Controlling by art thoughts that are inspired, I, philosophy, divide the subject arts into seven parts:
>
> Grammar: a birch-rod. Through me a person learns what speech, letters and syllables are.
>
> Rhetoric: a pen, tablets. If you are an orator, you will look for support for your case from me.

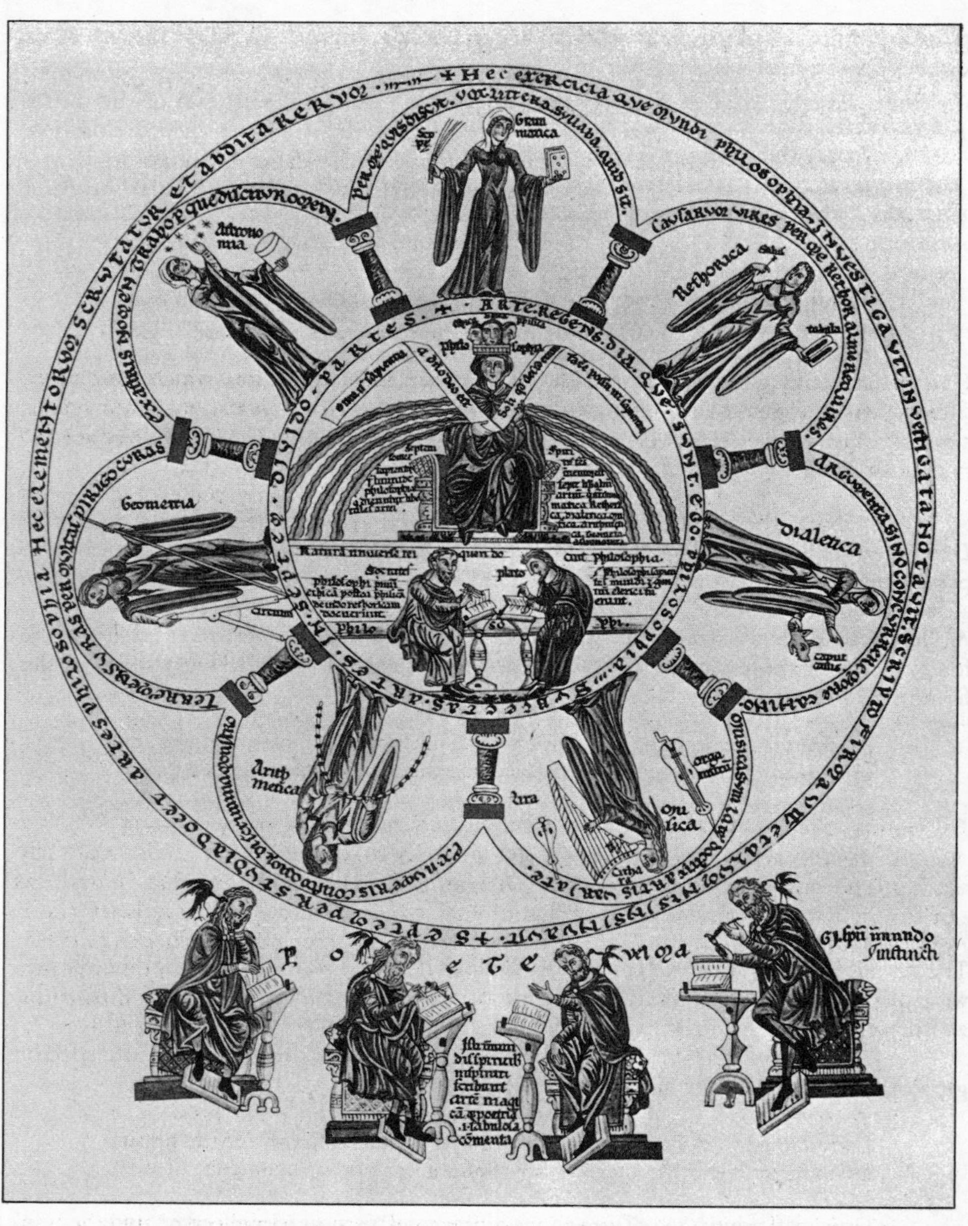

Herrad depicts philosophy as a woman seated on a throne pouring forth seven streams of wisdom to Socrates and Plato. The circle is completed by female personifications of the seven liberal arts, with the poets excluded below.

> Dialectic: the head of a dog. I let arguments run up against each other, like dogs.
>
> Music: a lyre, a harp, an organistrum (cello). I, music, am the teacher of my art far and wide, in many different forms.
>
> Arithmetic: a counting rod. I consist of numbers, whose differences I demonstrate.
>
> Geometry: a pair of compasses. I direct the measurement of land with great care.
>
> Astronomy. I take my name from the stars (*astra*), through which omens for the future are learned.[247]

Herrad has outlined here the curriculum of classical Roman education, which was divided into the trivium (grammar, rhetoric and dialectic) and the quadrivium (music, arithmetic, geometry and astronomy). Again this illustrates the degree to which classical education had been incorporated into the heart of the monastic situation.

Next, in the same illustration, Herrad follows the Platonic refutation of poets by placing them outside the circle of the philosophers and the liberal arts. Contrasting the knowledge of philosophers with the inspiration of poets, she states:

> These are the activities which the philosophy of the pagans investigated, and having investigated, noted them down in writing and passed them on to the minds of their pupils. Philosophy teaches the arts through seven fields of study; she delves into the hidden aspects of the world.
>
> Poets or magicians: they are imbued with an unclear spirit. These men, inspired by unclear spirits, write magic and poetry, that is imaginary fictions.[248]

For Herrad, then, knowledge demanded the rigorous thinking of philosophy. When it was also inspired by the Holy Spirit it led straight to the throne of wisdom. In her elaborate description of the method and subject matter of philosophy, it is clear that Herrad was not simply reserving the study of philosophy for men within pagan or Christian traditions. Instead, she was encouraging her nuns to make the same efforts in search of truth.

In a similar way, the *Hortus Deliciarum* also describes the application of virtues to woman's and man's situation in the world. Herrad made an interesting distinction in a consideration of the knowledge of good and evil before and after the Fall:

> PUPIL: Was the knowledge of good and evil in the apple?
> TEACHER: Not in the apple, but in the transgression. For before his sin man knew good and evil: good by experience, evil by knowledge of it. After his sin, however, he knew evil and experience and good only by knowledge of it.[249]

The existential differentiation of experience of the good, versus an intellectual apprehension of the good, provides the background for Herrad's complicated depiction of life as a struggle up a ladder to regain direct experience of the good. "The ladder of virtue signifies the ascent through which the virtues and the religious practice of holiness by which the crown of eternal life is won."[250] Applying the "science" of numerology, Herrad states:

> There are fifteen steps, and people reach for the heavenly region by fifteen branches of love (i.e., virtues, which hang from love like branches from a tree). Fifteen is three times five, because it is our duty, through faith in the Holy Trinity, to perform the works of love with our five senses.[251]

Herrad lists the steps as including the following virtues: patience, kindness, piety, simplicity, humility, contempt of the world, poverty, peace, goodness, spiritual joy, sufferance, faith, hope, long suffering, and perseverance.[252] Herrad then describes in vivid detail examples of men and women who "fall off the ladder of virtue." Her descriptions lay no blame on one or the other sex, but rather they place the responsibility for the situation squarely on the shoulders of the person involved. In this Herrad avoided all tendency to blame men, to satirize men, or to devalue men in relation to women's fall from virtue into vice. Both women and men, in whatever station they live, are challenged to practise virtue. Herrad describes a nun who falls from this ladder of virtue:

> This nun, who denotes all false nuns, seduced by the blandishments and gifts of the priest and lured by the display of the world and the riches of her parents, falls back and does not grasp the crown of life.[253]

Then a hermit is evaluated:

> This hermit has the face of false hermits. Cultivating his own garden and minding his own plants with excessive care, he is drawn away from preaching and taken away from the sweetness of divine contemplation for which he ought to be free to concentrate.[254]

Next, a monk is criticized:

> This monk is a representative of false monks. Gloating over his property and money, he lets his heart stray from his religious duties and keeps it fixed immovably in the place where his treasure is.[255]

Even secular clerics fall off the ladder of virtue:

> This cleric, who denotes all false clerics, is given over to drunkenness, lechery, simony and other vices, and he falls back and makes very little progress towards winning the crown of life on high.[256]

Finally, a lay woman and a soldier are also depicted as failing together to achieve perfect virtue:

> That soldier and that lay woman represent all unfaithful lay people who, loving various outward shows of the world and spending their time in fornication, avarice and pride, are brought down to the earth and are rarely lifted up to the contemplation of the crown of life.[257]

Men and women fall off the ladder of virtue in a variety of ways. Herrad depicted both sexes as equally responsible for the quality of their lives.

Prudentia interficit
vanam gloriam
Vana gloria
Fraus
Rapina
Violentia
Fallacia

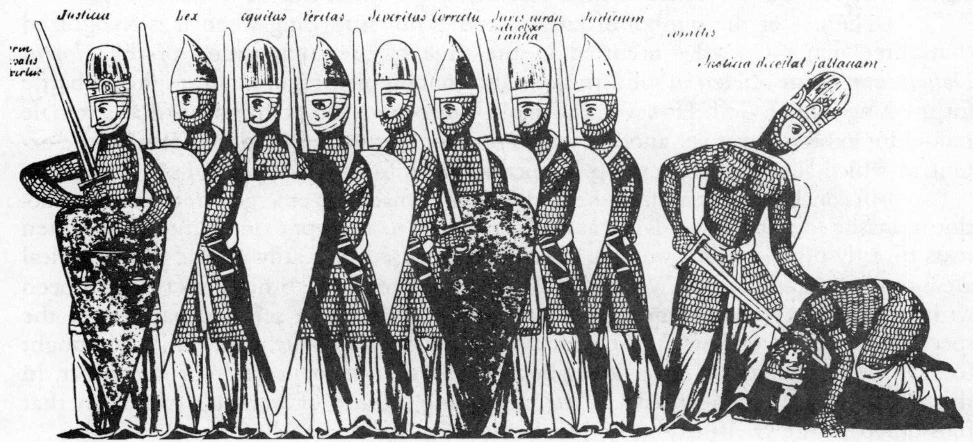

Herrad depicted the virtues and vices as female knights locked in deadly battle. The sexual differentiation is clearly evident in comparison with images of male knights also found in the *Garden of Delights.*

While Herrad's above depictions imply that most virtues are what would be called "theological" virtues, she also developed an extensive classification of the natural virtues more common to traditional philosophy. Prudence, or practical wisdom, is described as the principal virtue, which works in complement with judgement, memory, understanding, foresight, reason, and their companions.[258] In a fascinating series of illustrations, Herrad depicts the natural virtues as women dressed up in the manner of knights. In one illustration Prudence kills Vainglory while the female knights called Deceit, Violence, Robbery, and Fraud engage in a battle with Justice, Law, Fairness, Severity, Correction, and Fidelity to Oaths. Justice is shown as the victor when she beheads Deceit.[259]

The use of the symbol of knighthood is not surprising when it is recognized that three major Crusades occurred in the time of the composition of the *Hortus Deliciarum*. Many of Herrad's illustrations also contain pictures of male knights in battle for the kingdom of God. However, the explicit incorporation of knighthood as a female model for existence was yet another innovation for Herrad, especially in view of the extent to which she went to develop its pictorial significance.

In conclusion, Herrad, in the tradition of women who emerged from the Benedictine monastic education, stands out as the first woman to attempt to institutionalize written texts directly organized for women. These texts focused primarily on the philosophical areas of wisdom and virtue. While she used, for the most part, other texts that had been written by men, Herrad nonetheless continually adapted the selected passages to the specific situation of women. At the same time, she did not devalue men, but rather sought to describe challenges in life as facing both sexes either in cooperation or in conflict. In this way, Herrad added greatly to the expanding culture of women's education that blossomed in the twelfth century, just before the Aristotelian Revolution.

The example and philosophy of sex complementarity that had begun to be articulated by women and men within the Benedictine Age was about to be challenged by an Aristotelian rationale for sex polarity. For the Islamic philosopher Averroes and the Jewish philosopher Maimonides were working on integrating Aristotelian philosophy into their thought at the same time that Hildegard was writing her philosophy of sex complementarity and Herrad was assembling her encyclopedia. Therefore, at precisely the same moment in history—the twelfth century—when sex complementarity reached a new height in its development, the groundwork for the Aristotelian explosion of sex polarity was being prepared. This period stands as a crossroads in the history of the philosophy of sex identity. Before this study turns to these Islamic and Jewish discoveries of Aristotle, some attention will be given to another phenomena that was also occurring at the same time. In popular literature a striking move towards a satirical sex polarity also occurred, alongside a slight move towards a sex complementarity in the poems of courtly love.

SEX POLARITY IN POPULAR LITERATURE

Outside of the monastic context in which women and men were developing relationships of complementarity, a different sort of sexual identity was emerging. The advent of the Crusades brought about a different kind of balance between the sexes. While within the monastery many female and male monastics achieved a kind of equal status, in the world outside, the absence of upper-class knights—who were seeking to recapture Jerusalem—created a situation in which aristocratic women were interacting with lower-class men. The result of this imbalance was the outburst of a new kind of poetic exchange in the person of the troubadour poets. In this situation the woman, because of her superior class, often assumed a position of superiority to the man, and a romantic reverse sex polarity was articulated.

At the same time, a different sort of renewed genre of popular writing sprang up, written by men who had been attached to the courts. Disillusioned by the corruption of courtly life, Walter Map and Andreas Capellanus both launched into satirical treatises against women, much along the lines of Juvenal or Lucretius. Their texts, which received considerable attention, articulated a sex-polarity theory of sex identity. It would seem that the simultaneous presence of reverse sex polarity and sex polarity outside of the double-monastic tradition gives further strength to the argument that the philosophy of sex complementarity sprang up in the eleveth and twelfth centuries because of women and men working and studying together within the more protected environment of double monasteries.

The Crusades and Courtly Love

In the study of Hildegard's morality play *Ordo Virtutum,* we encountered the female personification of the virtues being described as "glorious knights," and in Herrad's *Hortus Deliciarum* the struggle of the virtues against the vices was frequently depicted as a battle between different forces of knights, which included both male and female warriors.[260] The Crusades, instituted by Christians for the purpose of retaking the city of Jerusalem, officially began in 1095.[261] During Hildegard's and Herrad's lifetimes, three minor crusades occurred during the years 1096 to 1099, 1146 to 1148, and 1189 to 1192.[262] Therefore, they would have been very familiar with the concept of knighthood.

Women were able to join the Crusades if they were accompanied by their husbands, brothers, or military guardians.[263] For centuries, the question of permission from one's spouse caused much disagreement within the Church. Canon Law, as written by Gratian in 1151, stated:

> First, neither party to a marriage might licitly make a vow without the consent of the other party. Second, a vow made by one party without the other's consent was not binding and might, at the insistence of either party, be broken. Third, a vow made with the consent of the other party was binding and must be kept.[264]

This law meant that a husband could not decide to join the Crusades unless his wife agreed, and vice versa. Later, in 1209, Pietro Colliuaccina, under the direction of Pope Innocent III, changed this situation in the *Compilatio III*:

> The principle that wives might follow their husbands on crusade was also enunciated in *Ex multa*, a further canon of this title in *Compilatio III*; but if this permission might be considered a concession to the wives of crusaders, *Ex multa* further provided that men might take the crusade vow and fulfill it without seeking their wives' consent. This provision radically altered the status of the crusader's wife, and also, incidentally, marked a notable innovation in canonistic attitudes concerning the vows of married persons.[265]

While women had the right to travel with their crusading husbands, they lost the power over his decision-making.

Later in the same century, this position was challenged by St. Thomas. He argued that a husband ought not to be able to go on a Crusade without his wife's permission because he was responsible for guarding her chastity. If she did not want him to leave, and if he went anyway, then he was responsible for any infidelity on her part. "He was free to go only if his wife could remain chaste of her own volition during his absence or if he were to take her with him." Thus St. Thomas rejected the legal right guaranteed to husbands by the decretal *Magne* by invoking the higher moral obligation of husband to wife.[266] In any event, although wives were given permission to travel on the Crusades, most did not go. This situation then established a context for the development of new social interactions between the noblewomen and the men who remained in Europe while the Crusaders were attempting to win back Jerusalem. Wives were put in charge of fiefdoms during their husbands' absences. In this way, they acquired a position of authority over a large number of men.

A tradition began to emerge of an aristocratic woman entering into a love bond with one of the knights who attended her while her husband was away. The relationship was often bounded by the precepts of chastity, but each person involved sought to return the affection of the beloved. The first two records of women who engaged in and wrote about this courtly love interaction reveal that women were quite comfortable initiating an aspect of the relationship.

In the record of the earliest female troubadour, Tibors (c. 1130–1182), we find the following verse:

> Sweet handsome friend, I can tell you truly that
> I've never been without desire since it pleased
> you that I have you as my courtly lover.[267]

The best known female troubadour is the Countess of Cia (born c. 1140). In the following two excerpts, first her affection for a man is expressed, and then her sorrow at being rejected:

> The Lady who knows about valor
> should place her affection
> in a courteous and worthy knight
> as soon as she has seen his worth,
> and she should dare to love him face to face . . .
>
> My worth and noble birth should have some weight,
> my beauty and especially my noble thoughts;
> So I send you, there on your estate,
> this song as messenger and delegate.
> I want to know, my handsome noble friend,
> why I serve so savage and so cruel a fate.[268]

That a woman might take the initiative in the courtly love relationship is explicitly stated in the following poem by Castelloza (born c. 1200):

Knights there are I know who harm themselves
in courting ladies
more than ladies them,
when they are neither
higher born nor richer;
for when a lady's mind
is set on love, she ought
to court the man, if he shows strength and chivalry.[269]

In these clearly pre-Aristotelian images of woman as the active and man as the passive recipient of affection, we see an inversion of the Greek philosopher's categories of sex identity. That the woman is from a higher class than the man overturns the traditional sex distinctions in the tradition of sex polarity.

In the next poem, a fascinating discussion about the relation of woman and man, and of superior to inferior, is described. The poem, written by Maria de Bentadorn (born c. 1165) and Gui d'Ussel, incorporates a view of reverse sex polarity presented by the woman, and a position of sex unity presented by the man:

Gui d'Ussel, because of you I'm quite distraught,
for you've given up your song,
and since I wish you'd take it up again,
and since you know about such things,
I'll ask you this: when a lady
freely loves a man, should she do
as much for him as he for her,
according to the rules of courtly love?

Lady Maria, *tensons*
and all manner of song
I thought I'd given up
but when you summon, how can I refuse to sing?
My reply is that the lady
ought to do exactly for her lover
as he does for her, without regard for rank;
for between two friends neither one should rule.

Gui d'Ussel, suitors when they're new
are not at all like that,
for when they seek a lady's grace
they get down on their knees, hands joined, and say:
"Grant that I may freely serve you, lady,
as your man," and she receives them;
thus to me it's nothing short of treason
if a man says he's her equal *and* her servant.

Lady, it's embarassing
to argue that a lady should
be higher than the man with whom
she's made one heart of two.

Either you'll say (and this won't flatter you)
that the man should love the lady more,
or else you'll say that they're the same,
because the lover doesn't owe her anything
that doesn't bear love's name.[270]

Gui d'Ussel suggests that courtly love destroys rank and introduced an equality between the woman and man, while Maria de Bentadorn argues that the woman maintains her superiority in the relationship. The poem, however, reveals a complementarity between the two who are writing it, for the woman elicits the poem from the man by her question, and while the man answers her, she challenges him to go further in his thinking. Therefore, paradoxically, the creative intellectual result of courtly love was often a kind of sex complementarity. The sexes were considered as significantly different and yet the inequality of sex was balanced by the inequality of class.

The troubador poets were located in southern France, in the same areas as the Cathari, a small group of dissident Christians who were against the authority of the Roman Church. In 1209, Pope Innocent III proclaimed a crusade against the Cathari, called the Albigensian Crusade. This crusade lasted until 1243, during which time "more than 300 towns and 200 castles were stormed or burned and all their inhabitants massacred."[271] The troubadour poets were accordingly repressed. In the thirteenth century, four more large crusades to recapture Jerusalem took place from approximately 1218 to 1231, 1228 to 1229, 1244 to 1254, and 1267 to 1270.

For the concept of woman in relation to man, the conjoined history of the Crusades and the poets of courtly love left, by and large, a legacy of a short period of positive evaluation of female identity, with perhaps a tendency to idealize woman. At the same time, it also contained a devaluation of woman. It is this underside of the concept of woman in the popular literature that will be studied in the writings of Andreas Capellanus and Walter Map.

Andreas Capellanus (c. 12th century)

The Art of Courtly Love is a lengthy treatise of three books by Capellanus addressed to a young man named Walter (Gaultier). It was an extremely popular text that set forth three different aspects of its subject: how to win love; how to keep love once it was won; and why love ought to be rejected. As can be seen by these subject headings, the third section refuted the premises of the first two. From the perspective of the concept of woman in relation to man, the first two sections struggle with the issues of equality that occur in the courtly love tradition, while the third section is an outright defence of sex polarity.

Although courtly love was known for its limitations of chastity, Capellanus's text implies that its goal was sexual consummation. In the first chapter love is defined:

> Love is a certain inborn suffering derived from the sight of and excessive meditation upon the beauty of the opposite sex, which causes each one to wish above all things the embraces of the other and by common desire to carry out all of love's precepts in the other's embrace.[272]

Capellanus describes this movement from meditation to action in explicit detail:

> For when a man sees some woman fit for love and shaped according to his taste, he begins at once to lust after her in his heart; then the more he thinks about her the more he burns with love, until he comes to a fuller meditation. Presently he begins to think about the fashioning of the woman and to differentiate her limbs, to think about what she does and to pry into the secrets of her body, and he desires to put each part of it to the fullest use. Then after he has come to this complete meditation, love cannot hold the reins, but he proceeds at once to action.[273]

Capellanus explicitly differentiates the sexes in the category of courtly love:

> Now, in love you should note first of all that love cannot exist except between two persons of opposite sexes. Between two men or two women love can find no place, for we see that persons of the same sex are not at all fitted for giving each other the exchanges of love or for practising the acts natural to it.[274]

Therefore, he does not propose a sex-unity model of love, such as was common to the Platonic and neo-Platonic traditions. Instead, for Capellanus, the sexual differentiation of two persons in a relationship was central to the activity of courtly love.

At the same time, however, in the first book of his treatise Capellanus suggests that the advent of courtly love brought about a new equality between the sexes. This was the view propounded by troubadour-poet Gui d'Ussel.[275] In the new equality, character, and not sex or rank, will provide the key to differentiation:

> Since all of us human beings are derived originally from the same stock and all naturally claim the same ancestor, it was not beauty or care of the body or even abundance of possession, but excellence of character alone which first made a distinction of nobility among men and led to the difference of class.[276]

Capellanus develops various hypothetical dialogues among men and women of different classes to indicate how love might be won by a suitor. In the context of these dialogues, the question of equality is continually raised by the man, although it is rejected by the woman. In the first example, a man of the middle class speaks with a woman of the same class:

> THE MAN SAYS: In the beginning the same nature created all men, and to this day they would have remained equal had not greatness of soul and worth of character commenced to set men apart from each other by the inequality of the nobility."
>
> THE WOMAN SAYS: If I am as noble as you are trying to make me, you, being a man of the middle class, should seek the love of some woman of the same class, while I look for a noble lover to match my noble status; for nobility and commonality do not go well together or dwell in the same abode.[277]

The equality sought for by the man is rejected by the woman. In the second example, a man of the middle class speaks with a noblewoman:

> THE MAN SAYS: Love is a thing that copies Nature herself, and so lovers ought to make no more distinction between classes of men than Love himself does. . . .
> THE WOMAN SAYS: Who are you that ask for such great gifts? I know well enough what you look like, and the family you come from is obvious. . . . It is not without cause or reason that this distinction of rank has been found among men from the very beginning; it is so that every man will stay within the bounds of his own class and be content with all things therein and never presume to arrogate to himself the things that were naturally set aside as belonging to a higher class, but will leave them severely alone.[278]

The rank that gave the woman superiority over the man was a privilege that she was not eager to lose. Therefore, for her, love was not the equalizer that man of the middle class took it to be.

Andreas Capellanus develops a rather witty complementarity between the women and men in his hypothetical dialogues. In fact, judging from the quality of responses he gives to both the women and men, he appears to be suggesting an actual complementarity of the sexes. In the third example, he continues the conversation between a man of the middle class and a woman of the nobility:

> THE MAN SAYS: I see that you are thoroughly instructed in the art of love, I ask you to give me a lesson.
> THE WOMAN SAYS: You seem to be upsetting the natural order and course of things, since first you ask for love and then you show yourself in every way unworthy of it by asking like a raw recruit to be trained in the science of love.[279]

That woman is capable of discursive reasoning is continuously presented in *The Art of Courtly Love.* While in the above example the woman came from a higher class than the man, in the next example the man is from a higher rank. However, it is the woman who presents not only the best logical argument, but also the most moral position:

> THE MAN SAYS: Everybody knows that love can have no place between husband and wife. They may be bound to each other by a great and immoderate affection, but their feeling cannot take the place of love, because it cannot fit under the true definition of love. For what is love but an inordinate desire to receive passionately a furtive and hidden embrace?
> THE WOMAN SAYS: If you understood the definition correctly it could not interfere with love between husband and wife, for the expression "hidden embraces" is simply an explanation in different words of the preceding one, and there seems to be no impossibility in husband and wife giving each other hidden embraces and, . . . what is more, can be practised every day without sin. I ought therefore to choose a man to enjoy my embraces who can be to me both husband and lover.[280]

Capellanus's description of woman in this first book of *The Art of Courtly Love* presents her as man's equal in reasoning and virtue, as well as man's opposite in sexual identity. Therefore, he appears to be suggesting a kind of sexual complementarity underneath the general description of courtly love.

Book Two of the text simply considers ways of keeping love alive. It suggests such general principles as: "Love is always increasing or decreasing. . . . It is not proper to love any woman whom one should be ashamed to seek to marry. . . . When made public love rarely endures," and "A man in love is always apprehensive."[281] There is, however, no consideration of sex identity as such.

It is in Book Three that Andreas Capellanus develops his far-reaching defence of sex polarity. In the introduction to this book, Capellanus describes his purpose in a seeming contradiction:

> Now, friend Walter, . . . you can lack nothing in the art of love since in this little book we gave you the theory of the subject fully and completely, being willing to accede to your request because of the great love we have for you. You should know that we did not do this because we consider it advisable for you or any other man to fall in love, but for fear you might think us stupid; we believe, though, that any man who devotes his efforts to love loses all his usefulness.[282]

In order to convince Walter of the uselessness of love, Capellanus states that the devil is the source of sexual love, that the sexual act weakens a man in body, destroys the wisdom of his mind, and shortens his life.

However, Capellanus's most thorough argument against love involves a complicated and far-reaching devaluation of the object of love, which, in Walter's case, is woman. The striking aspect of Capellanus's analysis is that he generalizes about woman's nature instead of suggesting that his descriptions would be more accurate for a few women. Some examples will indicate the direction of his analysis:

> No woman ever loved a man or could bind herself to a lover in the mutual bonds of love. For a woman's desire is to get rich through love. . . . Woman is also a miser, because there isn't a wickedness in the world that men can think of that she will not boldy indulge in for the sake of money. . . . That every woman is envious is also found to be a general rule. . . . And so it naturally follows that a woman is a slanderer, because only slander can spring from envy and hate.[283]

Appealing to theology to justify the gluttony in woman's nature, Capellanus argues:

> We can detect all these qualities in Eve, the first woman, who although she was created by the hand of God without man's agency was not afraid to eat the forbidden fruit and for her gluttony was deservedly driven from her home in Paradise.[284]

Eve is also invoked to explain woman's role in the loss of immortality:

> Wasn't Eve, the first woman, who, although she was formed by the hand of God, destroyed herself by the sin of disobedience and lost the glory of immortality and by her offence brought all her descendents to the destruction of death? Therefore if you want a woman to do anything, you can get her to do it by ordering her to do the opposite.[285]

As the treatise continues, Capellanus employs a metaphor that sounds very much like the Aristotelian theory of woman's resemblance to matter and man's to form:

> No woman ever makes up her mind so firmly on any subject that she will not quickly change it on a little persuading from anyone. A woman is just like melting wax, which is always ready to take a new form and to receive the impress of anybody's seal.[286]

The devaluation of woman then reaches a degree thus far not articulated in the history of philosophy. Capellanus continues:

> Everything a woman says is said with the intention of deceiving. . . . Therefore never rely upon a woman's promise or upon her oath, because there is no honesty in her. . . . Every woman is a liar, because there isn't a woman living who doesn't make things up that are untrue and who doesn't boldly declare what is false.[287]

The ridicule of woman then degenerates even further:

> Again, every woman is a drunkard. . . . Every woman is also loud-mouthed, since no one of them can keep her tongue from abuses. . . . Indeed, a woman does not love a man with her whole heart, because there is not one of them who keeps faith with her husband or lover.[288]

The Art of Courtly Love then reaches the obvious conclusion:

> It doesn't seem proper, therefore, for any prudent man to fall in love with any woman, because she never keeps faith with any man; everybody knows that she ought to be spurned for the innumerably weighty reasons that have already been given.[289]

Capellanus develops his conclusion by urging Walter to choose the path set forward in the second part of the book rather than that described in the first part. From the perspective of the theory of sex identity, Capellanus urges the acceptance of sex polarity rather than sex complementarity.

> In the latter part of the book we are more concerned with what might be useful to you. . . . Therefore, Walter, accept this health-giving teaching we offer you and pass by all the vanities of the world.[290]

The popularity of Capellanus's text is attested to, for example, by the spurious manuscript of 1,500 pages called *The Letters of Abbess Heloise of the Paraclete*, which was written during the fourteenth to fifteenth centuries. In this text "Heloise" instructs Walter (Gaultier) on love.[291]

The study will turn now to a second example of a popular text that falls directly into the sex-polarity tradition by depending upon a devaluation of woman. Since Walter Map was a contemporary of Andreas Capellanus, it is safe to assume that the trend towards tracts incorporating a sex polarity was broader than an isolated example. While Capellanus's analysis sought to undermine the traditions of courtly love, Walter Map directly attacked the institution of marriage.

Walter Map (c. 1140–1209)

Born in Wales, Walter Map served as a clerk in the royal household of England for several years. In addition, he travelled to France in 1160 and 1199, and to Rome in 1179, where he had ample opportunities to observe the decadence of court behaviour. Walter Map is credited with having written the popular *Advice of Valerius to Ruffinus the Philosopher Not to Marry* (c. 1181).[291] That this text was written in Latin and published under the pseudonym "Valerius" led to much confusion. When Walter Map attached the text to the fourth part of his *De Nugis Curialium* (*Courtiers' Trifles*) he added the following observations about this ironic situation:

> We know that this discourse hath delighted many; it is eagerly seized, carefully copied, read with huge enjoyment. Yet there are some, but of the baser sort, who deny it is mine. For they envy the epistle and rob it, by force, both of its honour and its author.[292]

Walter Map's treatise achieves the same end as that of Capellanus, that is, men are discouraged from relations with women because women are viewed as devalued objects of their affections. However, it reaches the end by a different road, for while Capellanus criticized courtly love, Map criticizes marriage itself. Both popular writers, however, fall squarely in the sex-polarity tradition. Map begins, as did Capellanus, with the claim that the goal of love is an illusive one:

> Thou art all aflame with thy desires, and, being ensnared by the beauty of the lovely person, thou knowest not, poor wretch, that what thou seekest is a chimera. But thou art doomed to know that this triform monster, although it is beautified with the face of a noble lion, yet it is blemished with the belly of a reeking kind and is beweaponed with the virulent tail of a viper.[293]

Walter Map also brings in the theological claim that woman's nature has been defective since Eve:

> The first wife of the first man (Adam) after the first creation of man, by the first sin, relieved her first hunger against God's direct command. Great hath been the spawn of disobedience, which until the end of the world will never cease from assailing women and rendering them ever unwearied in carrying the full consequences of their chief inheritance of their mother. O friend, a man's highest reproach is a disobedient wife. Beware![294]

Therefore, Map's sex polarity had the theological foundation that woman is by nature inferior to man.

Walter Map is insistant that this affliction of woman extends across all members of the female sex:

> Even the very good woman, who is rarer than the phoenix, cannot be loved without the loathsome bitterness of fear and worry and constant unhappiness. But bad women, of whom the swarm is so large that no spot is without their malice, punish bitterly the bestowal of love, and devote themselves utterly in dealing distress, "to the division of soul and body." . . . Fear all the sex.[295]

The key point in Map's argument is that women seek to divide the body from the soul of man by eliciting masculine sexual responses that take men away from their proper duties. Associating the sexual desires with the lower part of the soul-body relationship, Map describes Jupiter as being undermined by a woman: "My friend, lo, him who is worth lifting above the heavens, a woman hath lowered to the level of brutes!"[296]

Walter Map's advice to the philosopher Ruffinus then continues by producing examples of philosophers who did not marry, following a similar line of argument as found in Heloise's advice to Abelard, or St. Jerome's *Adversus Jovinianum.*[297]

> Cicero, after the divorce of Terentia, was unwilling to marry, professing himself unable to give his attention at once to a wife and to philosophy.
>
> Cato of Utica said, "If the world would exist without women, our intercourse would not be without gods.[298]

Then, in a play on Aristotle's logic and the relation of subject to predicate, Map records the following dialogue:

> Metelus answered to Marius, whose daughter he would not marry, though she was of large dowry, great beauty, high birth, and fair fame: "I prefer to be mine own than hers." Marius replied to him: "Nay, she will be thine." Then said Metellus: "Not so, a man must needs belong to his wife, for it is true to logic that the *predicates* will be such as the *subjects* will permit."[299]

The argument that a man loses his freedom when in a relationship with a woman is found in Juvenal's "Satire Against Women" and in Lucretius's *The Nature of Things.*[300] Map simply puts this claim in the playful language of Aristotelian logic. He identifies the woman as the subject and the man as her predicate.

In a poem entitled *Golias de Conjuge non Ducenda*, which is attributed to Map, we find the same view:

> He who marries a wife burdens himself too much,
> from which burden death alone frees him;
> the husband serves the wife, and the wife rules
> and he has been made a slave who had been free.[301]

The inversion of the order of nature in which man is the ruler and woman the ruled, is frequently the subject of satire. The poem continues, as does the treatise, by a devaluation of woman.

Walter Map concludes his advice to Ruffinus by an attack on women similar to Capellanus's claim that woman is evil:

> Women journey by widely different ways, but by whatever windings they may wander, and through however many trackless regions they may travel, there is only one outlet, one goal of all their trails, one crown and common ground of all their differences—wickedness.[302]

The treatise is concluded with the following observation:

> But, to support belief in my words by the testimony of the ancients, read *Aureolus* [*Little Golden Book*] of Theophrastus and the story of Jason's Medea, and thou wilt find almost nothing impossible to woman. My friend, may the omnipotent God grant thee power not to be deceived by the deceit of the omnipotent female.[303]

The Advice of Valerius to Ruffinus the Philosopher Not to Marry thus contains a significant differentiation of the sexes, and the devaluation of woman in relation to man. Therefore, it is a clear example of a text within the sex-polarity tradition. Its tremendous popularity simply adds to the impression that only in the protected confines of the double monasteries was a new theory of sex identity able to emerge. In society at large, sex polarity was the more generally accepted theory of the concept of woman in relation to man.

The remainder of the *Courtiers' Trifles* contained several different stories of women and men of the Middle Ages. It also often contained references to pagan deities and pagan heroes rather than focus on particular Christian models of virtue or vice. In this way, Walter Map began to prepare a way for the development of humanism in the fourteenth century. Map is also often mentioned as the author of the Lancelot stories and the tales of King Arthur.[304] In these stories, woman is often presented in a romanticized way, even though she is frequently portrayed as leading men away from higher ideals. However, Walter Map's primary essay on sex identity is found in his advice to Ruffinus, and this text is clear in its support of sex polarity.

This study will now turn to the development of the philosophy of sex identity in Islamic and Jewish writing before it reaches the articulation of the Aristotelian Revolution in later Christian philosophy. As will be seen, the slowly developing rationale for sex complementarity, which had achieved a heightened expression in Hildegard of Bingen, was overtaken by new support for sex polarity. This support will go far beyond the simple popular base found in Capellanus and Map; it will enter into a phase of sophistication through the writings of academics and scholars, and through the addition of arguments directly articulated by a rediscovered Aristotle.

SEX UNITY AND SEX POLARITY INCORPORATED INTO ISLAMIC PHILOSOPHY

The two important Islamic philosophers, Avicenna and Averroes, both thought a great deal about the concept of woman. Their philosophy was influenced by Plato and Aristotle, as well as by the Koran. However, the Arabs believed that philosophy was higher than religion (in direct contrast to Christian philosophers). Therefore, their arguments for sex unity or sex polarity developed along philosophical, rather than theological lines.

The Arabs are most significant to the Aristotelian Revolution because they conveyed such respect for Aristotle's thought. Avicenna wrote an encyclopedic summary of Aristotle's main arguments, while Averroes wrote nearly forty commentaries on Aristotle's writings. Through these paraphrases of the philosopher's fundamental arguments, Aristotle's thought moved beyond its Greek origins.

The particular relationship that these philosophers had to the controversy between the different theories of sex identity is more difficult to assess. Avicenna is best known for his criticism of Aristotle's theory of generation. He argued that the female did make a formal contribution to generation and that man's seed was a formal and material contribution. He therefore rejected Aristotle's single-seed theory of generation. However, when Avicenna described in detail the particular formal contributions of male and female, it turned out that the female contribution was inferior and secondary to the male's. Therefore, Avicenna proposed a modified sex polarity.

Averroes then proceeded to reject Avicenna's qualification of Aristotle's theory of generation. He reasserted Aristotle's argument that the female provided matter and the male form, and that this difference was the result of the greater heat in the male. In other areas as well, Averroes repeated Aristotle's arguments for sex polarity. Women ought to obey men and they are not capable of friendships of equality with men. However, in a commentary on Plato, Averroes argued that women and men have the same end and that women are capable of philosophy. It seems that Averroes repeated the pattern that first emerged in the early Christian philosophers, namely, a simultaneous assertion of sex unity and sex polarity. For the Islamic philosophers, however, justification of the sex-unity theory did not follow from a theory of equality before God, as claimed by the Christians, or from a theory of reincarnation as claimed by the Platonists. Instead, Avicenna maintained that the active intellect was the same in all persons, and Averroes argued that both the active and passive intellects were the same in all persons. Therefore, at the highest level of existence all distinctions between the sexes disappear.

The two Islamic philosophers can be classified as supporting the various theories of sex identity in the following ways:

	Avicenna	**Averroes**
Opposites	sex polarity	sex unity sex polarity
Generation	modified sex polarity	sex unity sex polarity
Wisdom	sex polarity	sex unity sex polarity
Virtue	sex polarity	sex unity sex polarity

AVICENNA (980–1037)

Even though Avicenna was greatly influenced by the "Divine" Plato, he accepted Aristotle as an important philosopher. Avicenna referred to him, in *The Metaphysics*, as "He who is the leader of the wise and the guide and teacher of philosophers."[305] In his autobiography Avicenna described his meeting with Aristotle:

> I read the *Metaphysics* but I could not comprehend its contents, and its author's object remained obscure to me, even when I had gone back and read it forty times and had to go to the point where I had memorized it.[306]

Later on, Avicenna was reluctantly pressed to buy a book from a local bookseller.

> So I bought it and, lo and behold, it was Abu Nasn Al-Farabi's book on the objects of the *Metaphysics*. I returned home and was quick to read it, and in no time the objects of the book became clear to me because I had got to the point of having memorized it by heart.[307]

Al-Farabi was the first to transmit Aristotle and Plato to the Arab world. He wrote a significant amount about the concept of woman in the context of a discussion of human generation. Al-Farabi also led Avicenna back into the original Aristotelian corpus in which women and men were differentiated.[308] This movement constituted an important turning point in western philosophy.

Avicenna was requested to write a commentary on Aristotle. He agreed to do so only if his commentary could be a summary of his points of agreement with Aristotle rather than a critique of the philosopher. These first commentaries, called the *Kitab al-shifa,* came to be considered as an encyclopedia of Aristotelianism. They included commentaries on the *Organon, Physics, Metaphysics,* and later, on the books on *Animals, Ethics, Politics,* and *Poetics.*[309] The metaphysics was translated into Latin in the mid-twelfth century. Therefore, some of Avicenna's writings about Aristotle became known in the west before Aristotle's own texts other than his logic. In other words, summaries of the structure of Aristotle's arguments passed into western thought through the hands of the Arabs.

For the most part, Avicenna gave an accurate rendering of Aristotle's arguments. However, he was misled by the false attribution to Aristotle of fragments from Plotinus's *Enneads.* These fragments were included in a spurious work called *The Theology of Aristotle.* As a result, Avicenna believed that Aristotle had developed a theology consistent with the neo-Platonic tradition. This error, however, did not affect Avicenna's concept of woman because he argued against the neo-Platonic belief in reincarnation. He stated that it is not possible for separate souls to exist before their birth in a human body. Without matter it would not be possible for souls to be individuated. When individual women and men were created, a new soul for each person came into existence. He concluded:

> It is then proved that the soul comes into existence whenever a body does so fit to be used by it.[310]

When a person's life was over, however, the soul continued to exist separately from the body. Therefore, even though Avicenna rejected reincarnation, he accepted a belief in eternal life. Once women and men had been differentiated, the differentiation continued:

> But after this separation from their bodies the souls remain individual owing to the different matters in which they had been.[311]

Therefore, Avicenna's concept of person included a concept of soul that was necessarily differentiated as male or female.

In trying to assess whether Avicenna's concept of woman fell into the sex-neutrality or sex-polarity tradition, it is important to recognize the effect of Aristotelian logic. As stated previously, in Aristotle's logical writings, the species man, rather than women or men, was the subject under investigation. Avicenna, in his commentaries on the *Organon*, continued that tradition.[312] Therefore, Avicenna continued to perpetuate the framework that would eventually be used to develop the sex-unity position. However, the development of his own concept of woman followed Aristotelian lines of sex polarity. In the category of opposites, generation, wisdom, and virtue. Avicenna defended the following modified Aristotelian arguments for sex polarity.

	Man	Woman
Opposites	like fire and air	like water and earth, privation of man
Generation	provides primary formative power, fertile seed	provides secondary formative power, weak seed
Wisdom	more rational	less rational
Virtue	public sphere owns woman	private sphere property of man

In the *Metaphysics,* Avicenna accepted Aristotle's description of the female as the privation of the male. Opposites, according to Aristotle, included two poles, of which one was a negative form of the other. The negative form was called privation. For Avicenna, the female was opposite to the male, not as an equal but rather as an inferior member of the same genus. In his metaphysics of opposites, then, Avicenna followed the two bases for sex polarity: differentiation and inequality. Avicenna's *Metaphysics* gives evidence of sex polarity in other categories as well. In one passage he states that: ". . . in reality [woman] is not very rational and is quick to follow passion and anger"; and in another "[man] must own her, but not she him."[313]

This framework of sex polarity was also reflected in Avicenna's theory of generation. In the *Canon of Medicine,* a link is made between the theory of elements and male and female contributions to generations:

> The human being takes its origin from two things—1) the male sperm, which plays the part of "factor"; 2) the female sperm, . . . which provides the matter.

> Each of these is fluid and moist, but there is more wateriness and terrene substance in the female blood and the female sperm, whereas air and igneity are predominant in the male sperm.[314]

The male had more presence of the lighter elements, fire and air, while the female had more of the heavier elements, water and earth.[315] The symbolic expression of the sex-polarity position in terms of the relation of elements and heavenly bodies then became identified with the situation of the earth at the bottom of the universe:

> The Earth is an "element" normally situated at the centre of all existence. In its nature it is at rest, and all others naturally tend towards it, at however great distance away they might be. This is because of its intrinsic weight.[316]

All that was female became valued as heavier and inferior to all that was male.

In two very important aspects, Avicenna disagreed with Aristotle's theory of generation. He argued that the female and male both provided seed and matter to the fetus. As a consequence, he softened the radical sex polarity of Aristotle, in which the female made a totally passive contribution to the process of generation. Probably following Hippocrates, as well as the neo-Platonic tradition established by Plotinus and Porphyry, Avicenna argued that both female and male seed existed:

> Some members take their origin *from the semen*: namely members composed of like parts, except the flesh and fat. Other members come *from the blood*: namely the flesh, and the fat. Other members come from *both the male and female "sperm."*[317]

Avicenna made a distinction between a primary formative power and a secondary formative power in seed. The male seed had the primary formative power of ordering or separating the different faculties in the fetus, while the female seed had a secondary formative power of shaping each member through its specific development. This view followed the same process Porphyry had described in his treatise on embryology. The father directed the primary stage of development, and the mother the secondary one. This direction demanded the contribution of form as well as matter.

> The formative power (i.e., the male element) which separates from one another the various faculties in the sperm and rearranges them in such a way that each member (and tissue) receives the temperament appropriate to it—thus to nerve, its distinctive temperament; to bone, its distinctive temperament. The one "sperm" apparently homogeneous, opens out in all these directions. This is called the *primary* formative faculty.
>
> The informative or plastic faculty . . . is that (in the female element) whereby, subject to the decree of Allah, the delineation and configuration of the members is produced, with all their cavities, form, positions, and relations to one another, their smoothness or roughness, and so on . . .[318]

Avicenna's development of primary and secondary formative functions of seed, and his association of the primary function with male seed and the secondary with female seed, can be seen as a redevelopment of sex polarity at a more sophisticated level than was present in Aristotle. The male still had the superior role in the formation of the fetus. Therefore, even though Avicenna believed in the existence of female seed, it turned out that on the level of human generation, the inequality between male and female persisted. He was therefore firmly within the sex-polarity tradition.

Avicenna argued against Aristotle's view that the father's seed did not enter into the matter of the embryo. He used Aristotle's analogy with cheese-making to develop this point:

> According to the teaching of philosophy, the process of generation may be compared with the process which takes place in the manufacture of cheese. Thus the male "sperm" is equivalent to the coagulum of the milk. The starting point of the clot "man" is in the male semen. . . . Just as the beginning of the clotting is in the milk, so the beginning of the clotting of the form of man lies in the female "sperm." Then, just as each of the two—rennet and the milk—enter into the "substance" of the cheese which results, so each of the two—male and female sperm—enters into the "substance" of the "embryo."[319]

Avicenna was correct in that the male seed entered into the substance of the fetus. He was also correct in that the presence of the male seed near the female seed brought about a process of setting, or consolidation. However, he did not yet understand the specific nature of male and female seed as equal bonding units with similar structures. His efforts to correct Aristotle's mistaken views were important. However, they did not go far enough to break the increasing strength of the Aristotelian Revolution. Averroes, St. Albert the Great, St. Thomas, and Giles of Rome reasserted the Aristotelian theory of the radical differentiation of a male seed that contributed only form, and a female seed that contributed only matter to generation.

The Canon of Medicine, by Avicenna, became an extremely important text in the study of medicine. In it, Avicenna discussed the nature of pregnancy,[320] as well as the important distinction between the primary and secondary sexual characteristics of women and men.[321] More importantly, however, even though Avicenna attested to the existence of female seed in this work, the fact that the male seed had a primary formative function while the female had a secondary formative function meant that sex polarity was accepted.

Furthermore, Avicenna's criticism of Aristotle did more to introduce the western world to Aristotle than to lead to the acceptance of his own views. Therefore, in a paradoxical way, Avicenna helped the Aristotelian Revolution in sex identity even though he rejected some of Aristotle's ideas. By taking Aristotle seriously, he paved the way for his eventual, nearly complete domination of western thought.

AVERROES (1126–1198)

This philosopher, a contemporary of Hildegard of Bingen and Herrad of Landsberg, stands as a fascinating witness to the tension between sex unity and sex polarity at this point in Islamic western history. Averroes was open to sex-unity arguments through

Platonic influences that placed a high value on human rationality and on the sex neutrality present in Aristotelian logic. At the same time, Averroes adopted a sex-polarity theory about human identity that was derived from a study of Aristotelian arguments in the *Metaphysics, Ethics, Politics*, and *Generation of Animals*. Averroes appears never to have resolved this conflict; he allowed sex polarity to function as the general theory of religion for the people of the world, while sex unity was suggested for those who sought to follow the philosophical life of higher reason. A summary of Averroes's theory of sex identity is found in the following chart:

	Man	**Sex-Unity Orientation of Philosophy**	**Woman**
Opposites		same active and passive intellect	
Generation		same in relation to soul	
Wisdom		same way to be philosophers	
Virtue	rule		rule
		same end	

	Man	**Sex-Polarity Orientation of Reglion**	**Woman**
Opposites	hot		cold
		woman privation of man	
Generation	provides fertile seed		provides infertile seed, matter
Wisdom	strong deliberative powers, speech		feeble deliberative powers, silence
Virtue	rule		obey
		woman unequal friend of man	

Averroes's relation to the arguments of Aristotle and Plato on sex identity will now be considered. While Avicenna certainly made Aristotle's theories accessible to the Islamic world through his summaries, Averroes brought philosophers even more directly to the Greek philosopher's arguments. While Avicenna's encyclopedia served as a simple summary of Aristotle's arguments, Averroes developed systematic commentaries that, instead, led the reader back into the intricate subtleties of Aristotle's thought.[322] At the suggestion of Abu Ya Gub Yusuf, Averroes wrote thirty-eight commentaries on Aristotle.[323]

These commentaries were divided into three different lengths: paraphrase (minor commentary); brief exposition (middle commentary); and complete exposition (major commentary). Because of Averroes's extensive use of Aristotelian commentaries, he became known simply as "the commentator," just as Aristotle became known as "the philosopher."

In addition to the extensive set of commentaries Averroes made on Aristotelian texts, he also wrote a work entitled *Colliget*, which contained references to many Aristotelian theories.[324] Of specific relevance to the concept of woman is a section of this work devoted to the respective functions of woman and man in generation. Averroes rejected Avicenna's view that the female seed continued in a lesser fashion the function of the male seed. He argued that female seed and male seed *had* to be different, for if they had the same nature, then woman might be able to impregnate herself:

> But it is known by a natural argument that if the seed of the woman was able to do the operation which the seed of the man does, then the woman would generate by herself and the man would not be necessary.[325]

Averroes believed that women did at times generate a kind of seed. However, after reading Aristotle, who rejected all reference to female seed, Averroes decided that female seed had no role in generation. He described his reasoning as follows:

> If you ask: "How does it appear that the seed of the woman does not give any aid in generation," then it must be said that it is manifest to sense and it is known through an argument based upon sense because a man sees that a woman is impregnated without making seed. And after I read the books of Aristotle I asked many women about this; and they responded that many were impregnated without making seed even when intercourse was displeasing to them. And I even saw that many of them were pregnant after having been raped by men.[326]

Averroes equated female seed with the secretion that occurred when intercourse was desired by the woman. He used a similar argument to prove that female seed could not be identified with matter.

> This attests that the seed of the woman is not the material of the embryo because many women are impregnated without making seed as has been said. And repeatedly the womb of the woman throws out its own seed while it drags into itself the seed of man. And all these things show that the seed of woman is superfluous, running down because of pleasure, just as saliva runs down from the mouth of one who is famished when he sees something for eating.[327]

Averroes allowed only one function to the female seed. He argued that it might add some heat to the mixture of male seed and female menstrual fluid to aid in the process of generation.[328] The use of heat as a principle was often referred to by Averroes. He argued that menstrual blood was expelled because it lacked sufficient heat for generation. In addition, refined blood became both seed in the male as well as milk in lactating women. All of these views were Aristotelian in origin, and Averroes referred frequently to the philosopher in his discussion.

Most striking was Averroes's reassertion of the Aristotelian position that the female contributed matter and the male contributed form to the fetus. He argued that the mother and father each contributed a specific part to the process of generation:

> Therefore, whatever is given as part to the embryo, through it the embryo is. And the matter and form are these two parts, and one of them is the donor of matter and the other is the donor of form. And it is impossible that the woman should give form and the man matter. Therefore, because the donor of the nutriment must necessarily be the donor of the matter, and the woman is the donor of the nutriment therefore, she has to be the donor of the material and the man the donor of the form, and so said Aristotle.[329]

Through the *Colliget*, Averroes transmitted not only Aristotle's association of the female with matter and the male with form, but also Aristotle's arguments for this association. Furthermore, because the Arab philosopher and the Greek philosopher both appeared to be using the scientific evidence of the senses to support this association, their theory became even more strongly believed. It did not matter that they were both incorrect in their assessments of the existence and function of the female seed. The Aristotelian Revolution resulted in the perpetuation of this incorrect biological theory for many centuries.

Averroes's thirty-eight commentaries on Aristotle were written after he completed the *Colliget*. They were based on translations twice removed from the original Greek. Averroes used an Arabic translation of a Syriac text of Aristotle. Even with this disadvantage, Averroes achieved a remarkable similarity to the original Aristotelian corpus. By isolating certain key passages on the concept of woman from commentaries on the *Metaphysics*, *Ethics*, and *Politics*, and by comparing the original Aristotelian text with Averroes's commentary, it is possible to demonstrate his crucial role in this phase of the Aristotelian Revolution.

In the commentary on the *Metaphysics*, Averroes raised the central question originally posed by Aristotle:

> It must be asked whether the woman does not differ from the man in the order of form since the man is contrary to the woman and diversity is contrariety.[330]

The commentator then summarized Aristotle's discussion of the issue by arguing that the distinctions of male and female were not distinctions of form but of matter. However, the distinction of male and female was not completely accidental to animals as is, for example, the distinction of colour. It was an essential distinction of animal.

> That division is essential since the division of animals into male and female is with respect to what it is to be animal but it is not so in respect to white and black.[331]

Averroes concluded that sexual differentiation is an essential accident of animal. He referred to Aristotle's argument that the male and female were formed from a different action on the same kind of seed.

> And then he [Aristotle] says: therefore, the same seed, etc. And therefore, the matter of the male and the female universally is one. For the same seed when it suffers one thing becomes male and when it suffers the contrary thing becomes female. . . . And he maintains that accidently I become one thing through heat and cold in the way which has been stated in the *Generation of Animals*.[332]

Aristotle had argued that when the seed met with the proper amount of heat a male was produced, when it met with more cold a female was produced. In this commentary, then, Averroes merely repeated the Aristotelian theory.

In Averroes's commentary on the *Ethics* a similar process occurred. The significant passage to be isolated in connection with the concept of woman concerned the relation of unequal friendship between husband and wife. Aristotle had argued that since the man was superior to the woman, there would be a certain imbalance in their relationship. Averroes reiterated this argument:

> He [Aristotle] says: even in the kinds of love one is above the other. And this comes from addition and superfluity just as a father to a son, old man to young man, husband to wife, and ruler to ruled.[333]

Aristotle claimed that since friendship demanded a certain equality, women had to pay back this imbalance by giving more honour and love to the man. Averroes repeated this argument in his commentary. In this way, not only were Aristotle's concepts brought into the Islamic world, but also his arguments. When Averroes's works were translated into Latin by Michael Scot (between 1230 and 1240), Aristotle's arguments made their way directly into Latin philosophy.[334]

Nowhere is the transmission of Aristotle's arguments more evident than in Averroes's commentary on the *Politics*. Here, the basic Aristotelian theory that women by nature ought to obey and men by nature to rule was repeated.

> Since truly there are three parts of domestic life, one of ruling (master and slave) about which we have spoken above, another of fatherhood, and a third of the marriage relationship. For he rules over the wife and sons . . . but not in the same way, but over the wife as a free citizen and over the sons as an emperor. For the man is by nature superior to the woman.[335]

Averroes recounted Aristotle's philosophical arguments for separate virtues for woman and man. He drew the parallel between the virtues of the separate parts of the soul and the respective virtues of women and men. The highest part of the soul should rule, and the lower part of the soul should obey, just as men should rule and women should obey.

> Why are the state of ruling and obeying most natural? For in different ways is a child superior to a slave, a male to a female, and a father to son. These parts of the soul are in all of them, but they are in them differently. For a slave altogether does not have the capacity of deliberating, the wife has it but feebly, and the son has it but in an undeveloped way.

Aristotle's claim that the deliberative faculty was present in women but without authority was transmitted by Averroes as a feeble presence of the rational powers. Consequently, woman became good by obeying man. Her virtues differed from those of men. Averroes mentioned that this claim rejected Socrates' view that women and men had the same virtue, and he concluded with Aristotle's example of silence as a particular virtue of woman.

> Therefore it is fitting just as the poet said about women, that a disinclination to talk is a glory for woman but not for man.[337]

It would be easy to conclude from the above study of the *Colliget* and Averroes's commentaries on Aristotle that he accepted Aristotle's sex-polarity theory in its entirety. However, another text by Averroes offers a clue to the more complex thought of this Islamic philosopher on the subject of woman's identity. Averroes wrote a detailed commentary on Plato's *Republic* before he read Aristotle's *Politics*.[338] In this commentary, Averroes offered some theories that fell within the sex-unity tradition. While it is difficult to ascertain when Averroes was merely repeating Plato or when he was developing his own philosophy, it is generally accepted that when the commentator used the expression "we say," he was developing his own position. Most striking, then, is the following passage in which Averroes argued that women have the same end as men:

> And we say that women, insofar as they are of one kind with men, necessarily share in the end of man.[339]

Averroes had summarized Socrates' question that opened the discussion of the nature of woman. If woman had a different nature from man, then she would follow different pursuits. Specifically, she would remain in a capacity of full-time housekeeper and educator of children. If, on the other hand, woman had the same nature as man, then she would follow the same pursuits as men. Socrates concluded that they had the same nature, and Averroes appeared to agree. He felt that, generally, women were weaker than men, but that women nonetheless had the capacity to become philosophers.

> Since some women are formed with eminence and a praiseworthy disposition, it is not impossible that there be philosophers and rulers among them.[340]

Averroes, then, appeared to believe that women were capable of the highest intellectual and virtuous development. How does this view relate to the previous theories repeated from Aristotle? It is possible to claim that Averroes changed his mind after reading Aristotle's *Politics*, and that he switched from a sex-unity to a sex-polarity theory. It is equally possible, however, that he maintained a consistent sex-unity theory and merely brought forward Aristotle's arguments for consideration. It is not possible to determine this here. However, there are some additional factors that lend weight to the second possibility. Averroes's Islamic background may have contributed to an interest in the formation of a utopian society, a republic based on the principles of Islam. Many of Plato's arguments worked in such an ideal.

Averroes was concerned that women be able to develop in several ways. He criticized certain societies that limited women's capabilities:

> The competence of women is unknown, however, in these cities since they are taken (in them) for procreation and hence are placed at the service of their husbands and confined to procreation, upbringing, and suckling. This nullifies their (other) activities. Since women in these cities are not prepared with respect to any of the human virtues, they frequently resemble plants in these cities.[341]

The *Commentary on the Republic* continued by describing Plato's theories about the regulation of generation, the community of wives and children, and the abolition of private property.[342] In all of these areas, Averroes accurately summarized Plato's views.

It might be asked whether Averroes's Islamic religion, based on the Koran, would naturally predispose him towards adopting a sex-polarity interpretation of the relation of female to male, rather than the sex-unity theory proposed by Plato. In answering this it is important to mention that Averroes believed that religion was an inferior source of knowledge compared to philosophy; that while the masses might believe religious theories, the few who reached the high level of philosophy would know the truth. In this framework, Plato's view could transcend the sex polarity of Islam.

There is a further argument needed to explain why Averroes might have preferred Plato over Aristotle on the question of woman's identity, since both were philosophers and since in most other matters Averroes preferred Aristotle. This argument can be found in Averroes's theory about the nature of the soul. He believed that the active and passive intellect were the same in everyone.[343] In the *Incoherence of the Incoherence*, Averroes described this view as follows:

> The necessary conclusion therefore is that the soul of Zaid and the soul of Amr are identical in their form. An identical form inheres in a numerical, i.e., a divisible, multiplicity, only through the multiplicity of matter. If then the soul does not die when the body dies, or if it possesses an immortal element, it must, when it has left the bodies, form a numerical unity.[344]

The soul was separable and universally present in all persons. It was therefore the same in women as in men. Since philosophy and virtue were the result of the correct use of this soul, it followed that people who used their intellect well could become wise and virtuous. In this way Averroes's metaphysical structure of the person resembled Plato's belief in the soul as undifferentiated with respect to sex. Therefore, it is quite possible that Averroes believed that the sex-unity position was the correct philosophical theory of woman and man's identity. At the same time, the sex-polarity position would hold in a general way for the masses.

Therefore, even though Averroes himself may have preferred Plato's sex-unity theory, the ultimate consequence of his philosophy led to the adoption of Aristotelian sex polarity. Since St. Thomas and other Christian philosophers rejected Averroes's belief in the unity of the intellect, they rejected a possible metaphysical structure for the sex-unity theory. Furthermore, Averroes's extensive commentaries on Aristotle's works brought forward the whole collection of Aristotelian arguments in support of sex neutrality. Averroes therefore functioned as an important link in the slow but progressive domination of Aristotelian thought about women.

SEX UNITY AND SEX POLARITY INCORPORATED INTO JEWISH PHILOSOPHY

Maimonides, who discovered Aristotle through the Islamic philosophers, was the next significant philosopher to further the second stage of the Aristotelian Revolution. Just as the Arabic philosophers had attempted to make Aristotle the foundation of Islamic philosophy, so Maimonides decided to integrate Aristotle into Jewish philosophy. Maimonides was so consistent in this pursuit that his work became a principal source for the transmission of Aristotle's arguments for sex polarity.[345]

The earlier Jewish philosopher Avicebron appeared only to transmit the sex neutrality of Aristotle's logic. However, some aspects of Avicebron's thought were used by the *Qabbalah* to support sex polarity. Maimonides, on the other hand, directly brought forward Aristotelian arguments for sex polarity in all of the four basic philosophic areas delineated in this text. On the subject of opposites, he argued that woman resembles the properties of matter, and man the properties of form. He also argued that woman contributes no seed to generation because she is colder than men. Then he limited woman's access to wisdom to a kind of practical art. Finally, he argued that women ought to obey and man to rule. In all these areas, Maimonides appealed to Aristotle for a philosophical justification for the sex polarity he already accepted through religious theory. By the end of the twelfth century, Jewish philosophy was firmly grounded in Aristotelian arguments. The following chart summarizes the general directions of medieval Jewish philosophy about sex identity:

	Avicebron	**Derivative Qabbalah**	**Maimonides**
Opposites	sex neutrality	sex polarity	sex polarity
Generation	sex neutrality		sex polarity
Wisdom	sex neutrality	sex polarity	sex polarity
Virtue	sex polarity	sex polarity	sex polarity

Avicebron (1021–1058)

Solomon ibn Gabirol, later known as Avicebron, was the first major Jewish philosopher after Philo, who had lived nearly one thousand years previously. Avicebron lived in Spain and wrote in Arabic, which caused so much confusion about his religious background that many later writers considered him to be Islamic or even Christian. It was not until 1845 that Avicebron was positively identified as a Jewish philosopher.

Avicebron was influenced by a spurious work attributed to Empedocles. In addition, he was also influenced by the spurious *Theology of Aristotle*. Since these two sources were primarily neo-Platonic in orientation, it might be expected that Avicebron would adopt a sex-unity position towards the concept of woman. From the neo-Platonists, Avicebron inherited central concepts that had been found in Plato. Particularly, he employed a distinction between form and matter and promoted a theory of the universal presence of matter in all things. This theory, which became a source of considerable debate in subsequent medieval Christian philosophy, was later rejected by St. Thomas as un-

Aristotelian. Avicebron was well acquainted with the Platonic analogy between the sun and the Form of Good, and he used this to emphasize the higher value of forms over matter.[346] In addition Avicebron mentioned and employed many of his concepts and arguments from the logical works.[347]

Avicebron was also known as a great poet. In his poetry, the soul was frequently given a female personification in relation to a male God.

> My soul shall declare to Thee Thou are her former.
> . . .
> She serves Thee as handmaid while yet in the body.[348]

However, Avicebron also expressed some flexibility about the masculine nature of God when he described God as a mother:

> O my God!
> . . .
> As a suckling child didst Thou nurse me, and at my mother's breasts didst Thou set me securely.
>
> With Thy sweet delights Thou didst sate me, and when I came to stand Thou didst strengthen me, and set me upright.[349]

As a poet, Avicebron used female personification rather frequently. For example, wisdom was described as a mother with whom Avicebron had a covenant.[350]

As a philosopher, however, all personification was eliminated. In his most central philosophical work, entitled *The Fountain of Life*, there was no mention of male or female in any context at all. God was referred to merely as the primary creator. Most striking of all, in his numerous discussions of generation, the specific functions of woman and man were not even mentioned.

> TEACHER: What is growth and what is reproduction?
> PUPIL: Reproduction is to engender a thing from its similar.[351]

Even in the context in which Avicebron considered the relation between nutrition and reproduction, no mention of male or female was made.[352]

There is a possible reason why Avicebron developed a philosophical work that specifically deleted mention of male and female. This work abounded with categories taken from Aristotle's logic. In addition to form and matter, Avicebron referred to genus, differentia, substance, species, actuality, and potentiality. Therefore, it is possible that Avicebron believed that philosophy should consider the human without regard to the significant distinctions between woman and man. If this suggestion is correct, then *The Fountain of Life* became one of the first metaphysical texts in the sex-neutrality tradition that based itself upon Aristotelian logic.

However, *The Fountain of Life* also contained a principle of the relation between superior and inferior things. This principle claimed that "if the inferior derives from the superior, then the totality existing in the inferior must exist in the superior."[353] Avicebron believed that the intellectual soul was superior to the material in the person.

> Since physical substantiality is placed at the inferior extreme and is made of material and structure it is in contrast (*oppositum*) to reason which is at the superior extreme.[354]

Similarly, the lower principles of the soul existed in the higher, but not vice versa:

> Growth and reproduction exist in the animal principle, but sense-perception and motion do not exist in the vegetable.[355]

These basic Aristotelian principles provided a framework from which sex polarity could develop. Bearing in mind the Aristotelian association of the concept of woman with the properties of matter and the concept of man with properties of form, it is not surprising that Avicebron's philosophy was used by others to justify sex polarity, even though he himself, as far as is known, did not directly do so.

The first application of Avicebron to sex polarity can be found in later uses of his philosophy in the study of the *Qabbalah*. The mystical side of his philosophy made it naturally compatible with Qabbalist theology. Avicebron's belief that superior and inferior principles interacted in the world became applied to the relation between the Holy Spirit and the Church. According to one source:

> The Qabbalists called the Holy Spirit, the Mother; and the Church of Israel Daughter. Solomon engraved on the walls of his temple, likeness of the male and female principles to adumbrate this mystery; . . . This was, however, not in obedience to the Torah. They were symbolical of the Upper, the spiritual, the former or maker, positive or male, and the Lower, the passive, the negative or female, formed or made by the first.[356]

Following, perhaps, Philo's theory of the creation of the neutral species man before male or female, the *Qabbalah* states:

> The terrestrial Adam, like its predecessors, the perfect paradigm of celestial man, was yet an androgene. . . . Then Yhvh Elohim creates, from Adam's side, woman. The latter however existed in Adam, in potentiality, from the first.[357]

Then polarity enters in the description of the symbolic reference to Adam and Eve:

> Adam is the rational soul, Eve, as the Hebrew name indicates, the animal soul, and the serpent is the vegetative or appetitive soul.[358]

Avicebron himself did not draw these parallels in this philosophical work. However, his philosophical categories allowed for such a religious application.

It is difficult to know whether Avicebron, as a philosopher, would have agreed with the sex-polarity position. In another book, which merely reports second-hand some of his ethical teachings, there is only one statement that would imply that women ought to be controlled by men: "The best of animals needs the whip, the purest of women a husband, and the cleverest of men to ask advice."[359] According to these "sayings of the wise man Avicebron," men should avoid a bad wife, attempt to find a good wife, and remain faithful to her.[360] In addition, Xanthippe was described as being rebuked by Socrates for her tears at his impending death.[361] These sayings, however, are more like maxims than an ethical theory. They do not constitute any basis for the claim that Avicebron promoted sex polarity. In conclusion, therefore, Avicebron has to be understood as a transitional philosopher. He gave Aristotle's arguments and concepts further credibility by incorporating them in his major work, *The Fountain of Life*. He did not appear to promote Aristotle's sex polarity, even though others later on may have used some of his philosophical arguments in the context of sex polarity. Avicebron, therefore, represented a sex-neutrality orientation of Jewish philosophy just before the Aristotelian Revolution occurred.

Maimonides (1135–1204)

This medieval Jewish philosopher, a contemporary of Averroes, Hildegard and Herrad, was known by several names. For the Hebrews, his name was Moses Ben Maimon, for islamic philosophers it was Abu Imran Musa ibn Maimun ibn Ubayd-Allah, and to Christians he was known as Rabbi Moysus (Aegyptius).[362] Maimonides was the key to the Aristotelian Revolution in Jewish thought, for he found in Aristotle a philosophical foundation for the sex polarity he already adhered to through his religious beliefs. Educated in the rabbinic schools in Egypt and trained as a physician, Maimonides had access to arguments for sex polarity through the writings of Philo, Hippocrates, and Galen. In addition, he discovered Aristotle through the commentator Alexander of Aphrodisias (c. 191–211) and through the Islamic philosophers Al-Farabi, Avicenna, and Averroes. Maimonides did not appear to know about the philosophical writings of his predecessor Avicebron. In one revealing comment to his translator, Maimonides stated:

> The only books worth studying are those of Aristotle and his true commentators Alexander of Aphrodisias, Themistius, Averroes. Al-Farabi and Avicenna are also important, but other writings such as those of Empedocles, Pythagoras, Hermes, Porphyry, represent a pre-Aristotelian philosophy which is obsolete, and are a waste of time.[363]

This general rejection of non-Aristotelian material had the consequence that arguments for sex complementarity or sex unity, which had been formulated by these authors, were dismissed as "obsolete." Instead, Maimonides gave a strong affirmation for philosophical arguments for sex polarity as articulated within the Aristotelian framework. Although Maimonides wrote in Arabic, his works were soon translated into Hebrew and Latin, and thus had a direct influence on Albert the Great and St. Thomas. Therefore, Maimonides is an extremely important transition figure in the middle of the Aristotelian Revolution.

The chart on the following page summarizes the way in which Maimonides incorporated Aristotelian arguments in each of the four categories of the concept of woman in relation to man.

In the first area of consideration, opposites, Maimonides associated the female with properties of matter and the male with properties of form. He referred, in *The Guide for the Perplexed*, to the Platonic origins of this association, presumably in the consideration of the relation between the mother receptacle and the Forms: "Thus Plato and his predecessors designated Matter as the female and Form as the male."[364] Maimonides,

	Man	Woman
Opposites	hot, like form	cold, like matter
Generation	contributes fertile seed, pure blood	contributes infertile matter, impure blood
Wisdom	demonstrative argumenation, strong souls	practical art, weak souls
Virtue	rule	obey

however, adopted the association for his own purposes. Using Philo's method of symbolic interpretation of the Scriptures, he compared matter to an unfaithful married woman:

> The nature and the true reality of matter are such that it never ceases to be joined to privation; hence no form remains constantly in it, for it perpetually puts off one form and puts on another. How extraordinary is what *Solomon* said in his wisdom when likening matter to *a married harlot*, for matter is in no way found without form and is consequently always like *a married woman* who is never separated from *a man* and is never *free*.[365]

In another passage in *The Guide for the Perplexed*, he drew out this association for everything female:

> *Man* (*'ish*) and *woman* (*'ishshah*) are terms that at first were given the meaning of a human male and a human female. Afterwards they were used figuratively to designate any male or female among the other species of living beings. Thus it says: *Of every clean beast thou shalt take to thee seven and seven, the man and his woman*. It is as if it said *male* and *female*. Thereupon the term woman was used figuratively to designate any object apt for, and fashioned with a view to being in, conjunction with some other object.[366]

Woman had no identity alone, just as matter could not be alone. Woman had to be in union with man, just as matter had to be in union with form. In this way, Maimonides' association of the female with matter and the male with form was perfectly consistent with Aristotle's sex-polarity theory.

Maimonides also accepted the Aristotelian theory that the male was hotter than the female. Appealing to a later restatement of this view, Maimonides claimed, "In many places he [Galen] asserts that the male is warmer than the female. It is upon this (assertion) that he bases the fundamental of all medicine."[367] However, in a text in which he criticized Galen, Maimonides argued that the Stoic philosopher did not draw the necessary consequences of the greater heat in the male body and the purity of the male blood:

> It is also possible that he [Galen] did not finish (reading and studying) the words of *Aristotle*, or that he didn't see or know of them, and therefore didn't mention them when he commented on this book. One may hear the statement

of *Aristotle* and his words in this matter (in the original) in the eighteenth treatise of his book "animalia" where he asserts: "The warmth that is found in the female is weak, although occasionally some people claim the opposite of this, namely that the blood in the female is more abundant than the male. . . . They further think that blood in general has this same form, and it is sufficient for them that it is moist and has the appearance of blood. They do not know, however, that (women) have very little pure blood containing good chymes and that menstrual blood is not at all pure." This is the statement of *Aristotle* and it is the truth.[368]

The belief that most of the woman's blood was impure was used to explain Jewish laws of uncleanliness associated with menstruation. Women were considered unclean during menstruation and for seven days afterwards, until they performed a ritual bath.[369] Menstruation was considered to be an illness in women.[370] For example, too much menstruation, or loss of blood, could change the moist quality of a woman's skin, rendering it dry like a man's.[371] During pregnancy, the fetus would attract the purest blood, leaving the impure.[372] However, everyone was tainted by an association with the impurity and uncleanliness of woman:

> Philosophers tell us that it is most difficult and rare to find a man who, by his nature, is endowed with every perfection, moral as well as mental. . . . "How can man be justified with God? How can be pure one that is born of woman?"[373]

Maimonides accepted Aristotle's claim that seed was a more highly purified form of blood. It was formed by a process of transformation of nutrition.

> The sperm is a residue from the aliments left over and above what has been required for the organs during the third digestion.[374]

Similarly, the milk of mothers was also a purified form of nutrition:

> Milk of the mother is the proper nutrition for the newborn infant, because its composition is the same as the blood from which he was created.[375]

Maimonides appears to have left open the question of whether female seed existed. Certainly he was acquainted with Hippocrates' double-seed theory, and he also knew of Aristotle's rejection of female seed. Apparently following Galen, Maimonides seemed to allow for the possibility of the existence of female seed, but argued that it was infertile and not important. In a passage from his commentaries on the Commandments, he argued that women did not have to make an offering for an involuntary influx of seed, whereas men did. Her significant contribution to generation was limited to menstrual fluid:

> It is the emission of semen that makes a man liable for an offering, but if a woman has a sort of emission of semen, she is not a *zavah*, and it is only a flux of blood that makes a woman liable for an offering, whereas a flux of blood does not make a man liable. The world "flux" means only "flowing out," and

> what flows out is not always the same thing. The Sages say explicitly: "a man conveys uncleanness through semen, a woman through blood."[376]

In addition, there is a section of *The Guide for the Perplexed* where Maimonides described male and female organs of reproduction, but no location for the production of female seed is mentioned.[377] Finally, a further reflection of a view that the female contribution to generation is not considered to be significant could be seen in Maimonides' statement in *The Book of Women*, that women are not bound to reproduce: "The obligation to be fruitful and multiply is incumbent upon the man, but not on the woman."[378]

Rather astonishingly, Maimonides also brought forward some Pythagorean doctrines, which had perhaps been transmitted through Hippocrates, that associated the determination of the sex of the fetus with the opposites right and left. In the *Medical Aphorisms* he stated:

> One should examine a male at the time he reaches puberty. If his right testicle is larger, he will give rise to male offspring; if it is the left, he will give rise to females. The same situation applies for the breasts of a girl at the time of puberty.[379]

This explanation implies that the seed of the male, along with some aspect of the female body, determines the sex of the fetus. Although the breast is listed above, in another passage Maimonides focuses more on the location of the fetus in the uterus:

> Male (fetuses), in the majority of instances, are conceived by the women on the right side (of the uterus) whereas the female (fetus) is conceived on the left side. The reverse of this situation only happens exceptionally.[380]

In both of the above considerations of the Pythagorean association of male with the right and female with the left, Maimonides offers no suggestion that female seed might play a role in the determination of the sex of the fetus. Instead, for the most part he repeats the Aristotelian theory that the mother simply provides the matter and the place of development for the child.

Maimonides wrote a great deal about the proper attitude towards sexual intercourse. He believed that men should be careful not to release seed too frequently:

> Semen is the strength of the body and its life, and is the light of the eyes. Whenever too much is ejaculated, the body decays, its strength is spent, and its life destroyed. As Solomon said in his wisdom: "do not give your strength to women, and your years to that which destroys kings."[381]

Indeed, since women were "impure" for at least twelve days of their monthly cycle, and since Maimonides believed that intercourse should take place only during the night of the Sabbath, it appears that couples would meet only twice each month.[382] Maimonides described this process in terms that clearly indicated a masculine initiation of the activity:

> The act itself that brings about generation has no name at all, the following expressions signifying it: *yishkab* (he lies), *yib al* (he marries), *yiqah* (he takes), *yegalleh ervah* (he uncovers the nakedness), and no others.[383]

However, the female was not simply used by the male. Maimonides made it clear that the satisfaction of both partners was the goal:

> She should not be asleep and he should not force her if she is unwilling, but (intercourse should take place) when both wish it and in a state of mutual joy. He shall converse and play with her a little so that their souls become tranquil.[384]

In this way the male was the active partner and the female the passive partner, both in the initiation of the sexual act and in conception. Therefore, Maimonides' views on generation reflected his metaphysical understanding of the way in which male and female related as opposites.

In the question of the relation of woman and man to wisdom, Maimonides did at times personify wisdom as female, following the tradition of the Book of Wisdom. However, he made it clear that this feminine wisdom had as her ultimate goal the leading of philosophers to God the Father.[385] Maimonides delineated four common ways in which people were considered to be wise: 1) the possession of rational virtues; 2) the possession of moral virtues; 3) the possession of practical arts; and 4) the possession of cunning. He mentioned women as wise only in respect to the practical arts: "The term is applied to acquiring arts, whatever the art might be . . . and [to] all the women that were wisehearted."[386] By implication, women were wise through a practical knowledge of particulars, rather than through a reasoned knowledge of principles. According to Maimonides, both the rational and moral virtues demanded a three-step process. In the first step, knowledge of the Torah was learned through tradition. In the second state, wisdom was learned through demonstrative philosophical arguments. In the third stage, a particular action was determined as following from the first two sources. Maimonides developed Aristotle's practical syllogism and attached it to the first premises found in the Torah. Women, however, were not taught the Torah:

> These two commandments are not obligatory upon women, for in explanation of their obligatory character He has said (exalted be He) that the law of the Lord may be in their mouth, and women are not under obligation to study the Torah.[387]

Therefore, women, did not have access to the first step of the search for wisdom. By Maimonides' statements, women remain limited to the third level of wisdom, to practical arts without the benefit of either the philosophical demonstration or the religious traditions of the Torah.

Aristotle had argued that women were unable to achieve wisdom because the irrational faculties of their soul dominated the rational ones. Maimonides made a similar suggestion in an essay entitled "On the Management of Health." He considered why certain people seemed to be the victims of their emotions to the extent that they fell into depression:

> Therefore you find these passions have a very great influence only on those individuals having no knowledge of philosophic ethics or the disciplines and admonitions of the Law—such as youths, women, and foolish men. For due to the excessive tenderness of their souls, these people become anxious and despair.[388]

He further argued that the intrusion of external goods also led these souls to undue happiness:

> Similarly, if these individuals obtain one of the goods of this world, their joy thereby increases. Due to their souls being poorly disciplined, such individuals suppose that they have obtained a very great good, and their wonder and exultation greatly magnify what they have obtained. . . . The cause of all this is the soul's excessive tenderness and its ignorance of the truth of things.[389]

By implication, then, the woman's soul was unable to be in the correct balance because it was led to extremes by its lower faculties. Therefore, similar to Aristotle, woman's reason was "without authority."

Maimonides frequently wrote about the need for a wise person to achieve a balance and a rational control of the emotions. He referred to the lower tendencies of the soul as the "matter" of the person. In the following passage from *The Guide for the Perplexed*, the lack of authority in the lower part of the soul was connected to the concept of woman:

> As for Solomon's dictum, a woman of virtue who can find, . . . For if it so happens that the matter of man is excellent and suitable, neither dominating him nor corrupting his constitution, that matter is a divine gift. To sum up: it is easy, as we have mentioned, to control suitable matter. If it is unsuitable, it is not impossible for someone trained to quell it. For this reason Solomon—both he and others—inculcated all these exhortations. Also the commandments and prohibitions of the law are only intended to quell all the impulses of matter.[390]

Again, by implication, woman was identified with the person who was not able to achieve control. Her irrational faculties dominated rather than subjected themselves to the rational soul. Maimonides, therefore, proposed an Aristotelian structure of the concept of woman in its relation to wisdom.

Maimonides did not conclude that women should not be taught any knowledge. On the contrary, he argued that they should be encouraged to develop as best they could. In the Talmud, he stated:

> A third reason the Sages composed their Drachos in the form they did, is that the instruction of the nation's masses must be through such allusions and parables, so that the women, youth and children, will also benefit from it until it will eventually develop and perfect their intellects; and then they will comprehend and be enlightened to the actual meanings behind those allusions.[391]

It is not clear from this passage whether Maimonides believed that women could achieve this deeper understanding or whether he was referring merely to children and youths, some of whom would one day reach manhood. It would seem likely that he believed women always had a more restricted relation to wisdom than did men.

Maimonides drew a consequence for women's and men's relation to virtue from his view that women's souls were different from men's. In *The Guide for the Perplexed* he argued that since women's souls were without the authority of their own reason, it was best to place them under the authority and control of a man.

> As women are prone to anger, being easily affected and having weak souls, there would have been grave troubles, quarrels, and disorder in the house, if their oaths had been under their control. . . . Therefore, the matter, with everything pertaining to it, is given into the charge of the master of the house.[392]

While the above passage concentrated on the distribution of food in the household, Maimonides also considered the general situation of the relation of ruling and obedience between men and women. Maimonides preferred an Aristotelian ethic that placed virtue as a mean between two extremes. He cited as example a society, mentioned by Aristotle, in which vice prevailed. Here women ruled men:

> Accordingly they have no thought and no perception except in relation to eating and copulating, as has been stated, clearly with regard to these wretched people wholly given over to eating, drinking, and copulating. . . . It also says: *And women rule over him*; this being contrary to what was required of them in the beginning of creation: *And thy desire shall be to thy husband and he shall rule over thee.*[393]

Thus, Maimonides' method of combining Aristotle with the study of the Talmud demonstrated perfectly the introduction into Jewish philosophy of a philosophical basis for sex polarity. Maimonides brought about the intimate interconnection of Aristotelian sex polarity with the most basic religious texts in Judaism. As a consequence, the view that it was woman's virtue to obey and man's to rule became further justified in western thought. Women and men were virtuous in different ways.

Maimonides wrote a great deal more about women. A book on the Code, entitled *The Book of Women*, is divided into four subjects: marriage; divorce; the rape of virgins; and wayward women. These issues are similarly discussed in *The Commandments*, both positive and negative, as well as in Book III, Chapter 49, of *The Guide for the Perplexed*. In this latter work, Maimonides explicitly connected Aristotle's philosophy with Jewish teaching on the above subjects.

Ironically, Maimonides even misquoted Aristotle to support the claim that sexual desire should be avoided. He counselled a young student to concentrate on studying until sexual desire faded: "I have already made you know the text of Aristotle's saying that this sense is a disgrace to us."[394] The misuse of Aristotle began to emerge as a significant historical force in western Europe, where all sorts of spurious texts emerged. (These works will be considered in some detail in the final chapter of this book.) They indicated the power of the Aristotelian Revolution; a situation emerged in which the name Aristotle was used as an authority for all sorts of theories of sex identity.

At this point it is important simply to note that Islamic and Jewish philosophy acted as a vanguard for the Aristotelian Revolution, which would find its full development in the works of St. Albert and St. Thomas. Specifically, these two Christian philosophers studied the writings of Maimonides and were struck by his use of Aristotle as a philosophical framework for a religious view of human nature. The development of the influence of Aristotle on Christian philosophy will now be traced during the period of 800 to 1250.

THE REASSERTION OF SEX POLARITY IN LATER MEDIEVAL CHRISTIAN PHILOSOPHY

After centuries of movement back and forth between theories of sex unity, sex complementarity, and sex polarity, without any one theory dominating western thought, suddenly a whole new situation arose when Aristotle's arguments in defence of sex polarity were made available to Latin scholars. St. Albert the Great discovered the wealth of Aristotelian thought through Maimonides, and he transmitted this rationale for sex polarity to his student St. Thomas. In this way all the previous association of female identity with the qualities of matter, and male with the qualities of form, gained new prominence. The medieval Christian philosophers concluded, with Aristotle, that the female was a defective or deformed male in body and in mind.

COMMENTARIES AND TRANSLATIONS OF ARISTOTLE'S CORPUS

The practice of writing commentaries on Aristotle's texts has a long history.[395] The first phase of the commentaries, from the third and fourth centuries BC, began with the Peripatetic school in Athens under the direction of Theophrastus. Another well-known commentator in this school was Alexander of Aphrodisias (in 200 BC).

The second phase of Aristotelian commentaries is found from the third to the sixth centuries AD, in the neo-Platonic schools. As previously mentioned, the neo-Platonic Porphyry wrote a commentary on Aristotle's logic entitled the *Isagoge*.

In the fifth and sixth centuries Aristotle's works began to be translated into other languages. The *Categories* were translated into Syriac. Boethius translated the *Categories, De Interpretatione, Prior Analytics, Posterior Analytics*, and *Topics* into Latin. By the ninth century, most of Aristotle's works were translated into Arabic, with the exception of the *Politics* and the *Eudemian Ethics*. It was the existence of these Arabic texts that made Aristotle's arguments about sex identity available to Avicenna, Averroes, Avicebron, and Maimonides. As previously mentioned, Averroes, who wrote over thirty-eight commentaries on Aristotle, became known simply as "the commentator."

By the twelfth century, partial texts of Aristotle's writings, other than the logic, began to be translated into Latin. James of Venice translated the *Physics, De Anima, Metaphysics,* and *Parva Anima*. Hermicus Aristippus translated the *Meteorologica* and possibly *De Generatione et Corruptione*. There were also anonymous translations of *Nichomachean Ethics* (Books I and II), *Posterior Analytics*, and *Physics*. In this way, some of Aristotle's arguments for sex polarity began to surface alongside the sex neutrality suggested by logic.

Then, in the thirteenth century, the explosion of interest in Aristotle occurred. Michael Scot translated all of the works of Aristotle from Arabic into Latin. However, St. Albert the Great was apparently dissatisfied with the quality of the texts, which had passed from Greek to Syriac Arabic and then to Latin. He asked fellow Dominican William of Moerbeke to make direct translations from Greek to Latin of the complete works of Aristotle.[396] These new translations included for the first time the *Poetics, Rhetoric, Politics*, and the missing books of the *Metaphysics* and the *Generation of Animals*. Therefore, all of the Aristotelian rationale for sex polarity was now available to the Latin west.

St. Albert soon became convinced that Aristotle provided a much needed foundation for Christian philosophy. He therefore resolved "to make Aristotle intelligible to the Latins."[397] This resolution led St. Albert to write commentaries on the following Aristotelian texts: the *Organon, Physics, Generation of Animals;* and four additional works in natural philosophy, *De Anima, Metaphysics, Nichomachean Ethics,* and *Politics.*[398]

When the impact of Aristotle's philosophy on Latin Europe is compared with the impact of Plato's philosophy, an interesting consequence occurs for the history of sex identity. Only three of Plato's dialogues were translated into Latin by this time—*Timaeus, Meno*, and *Phaedo*. Therefore, the only theory of Plato concerning the concept of woman in relation to man that would be known to Latin readers of the twelfth and thirteenth centuries was the sex polarity presented in the *Timaeus*. Neither the *Republic* nor the *Laws*, which contained Plato's extensive arguments for sex unity, were available in Latin until the Renaissance. Consequently, all interest in Greek philosophy at this time in the development of western philosophy pointed to a rationale for sex polarity.

ST. ALBERT THE GREAT (1193–1280)

St. Albert (also known as Albertus Magnus) was not an original thinker in the field of speculative philosophy; he merely transmitted ideas previously developed in the field. Albert the Great's originality emerged primarily in the area of science or natural philosophy, where he made significant discoveries in the classification of fish, mammals, birds, insects, plants, and minerals. In addition, he argued that the world was a sphere during a time when most thinkers still believed it was flat, and he correctly understood the composition of the Milky Way. One critic states:

> He treated among other things, of astronomy, meteorology, climatology, mineralogy, alchemy, chemistry, physics, mechanics, anthropology, zoology, psychology, weaving, navigation, architecture, botany. In almost every subject he anticipated by several centuries some of the major discoveries of modern times.[399]

It was the ironic effect of Albert's genius in the field of science that led to the credibility of his philosophy of sex identity, although he had no formal training in philosophy. The irony, however, is that St. Albert's concept of woman in relation to man was based on the same erroneous foundation as was Aristotle's theory.

St. Albert's theory of sex identity is nearly a complete blueprint of the Greek philosopher's theory of sex polarity. There is, however, an interesting addition, for St. Albert developed a theory of Mariology in which he reversed many of the views he had proposed for women in general. Therefore, he continues in the tradition of Augustine,

Anselm and Abelard in holding a multi-level theory of sex identity that never appears to resolve its internal contradictions. The following chart summarizes the general lines of his arguments.

Reverse Sex Polarity

	Mary	**Men**
Opposites		
Generation		
Wisdom	perfect knowledge	imperfect knowledge
Virtue		

Sex Polarity

	Man	**Woman**
Opposites	hot, dry, active	cold, moist, passive
Generation	more perfectly ordered, greater strength, provides fertile seed, form	less perfectly ordered, weaker strength, provides infertile seed, matter
Wisdom	strong intelligence, constant ideas, understanding	weak intelligence inconstant ideas, affections
Virtue	intellect moves towards the good, rule by nature, stronger in cardinal virtues	appetite moves towards evil, obey by nature, weaker in cardinal virtues

Opposites

The question of how woman and man relate to one another as common members of a species was described by St. Albert in his commentary on Aristotle's *Metaphysics*. In this work Aristotle's arguments were simply restated. At the beginning of the commentary the central question was asked:

> Some will wonder from what has been said why woman does not differ from man in species, since male and female seem to be contraries of the same genus, and are different as opposites. For male and female are not different in species, although male and female seem to be contrary differences of animal not accidentally but in itself, insofar as it is animal.[401]

Then, after a lengthy discussion about other kinds of differences, Albert repeated Aristotle's conclusion:

> The solution to the question brought forward earlier is easy, because it is true that male and female are proper qualities of animal but not differences (of form). . . . They are caused by accidents of matter, which are related to generation. . . . And this is clear from the fact that the same seed becomes female and male, if there are contraries according to heat and cold, as we have shown in the *Generation of Animals*.[402]

Woman and man were members of the same species. Therefore, their differences could not be formal but had to be merely material.

St. Albert moved the discussion of whether male and female could form a different species from his commentary on Aristotle's *Metaphysics* into *De Quaestiones Animalibus*. After repeating Aristotle's basic thesis that the differences between male and female were differences in matter and not in form, Albert nevertheless began to associate woman with the properties of matter and man with the properties of form.

> Male and female are not different in the essence of the species. And when it is said that they possess, as it were, acting principle and material, it ought to be recognized that this is not because of essential form or material, but because of accidental arrangement, as hot water turns into cold water by means of an arrangement accidentally acquired. And therefore from this it does not follow, that they differ in essence but in respect of accidental characteristics. And thus the male possesses the nature of acting because of the strength of principle and warmth, and the female has the nature of receiving by reason of cold and moisture.[403]

Although Albert was careful to state that the association of the female with passivity and the male with activity was accidental, he nevertheless developed a theory about this association that implied that this difference was central to the identity of the sexes. Albert the Great argued that in the process of generation, woman contributed material and man form. As a consequence, woman became identified with properties of matter and man with properties of form. In St. Albert's creative work, *Summa de Creaturis*, this theory of Aristotle's was explicitly cited:

> Aristotle says in *De Animalibus 16* that "the female gives the matter and the male gives that which creates.". . . And again in the same place, "it is clear that matter is from the female and the principle of movement is from the male."[404]

The basic association of the male with hot, dry and active, and the female with cold, wet and passive or receptive is taken by St. Albert directly from Aristotle. In the next section, on generation, the thirteenth-century scientist derived a wide range of conclusions about the implications of this difference for reproduction.

Generation

The category of hot and cold was applied to the differentiation of male and female birds:

> Males are naturally warmer than females. From the same seed from which a female is produced a male could be produced if warmth were more powerful. Eggs are oblong because of the strength of the warmth and round because of its weakness; and in males there is greater warmth than in females; therefore males are generated from oblong eggs and females from round ones.[405]

St. Albert frequently involved the opposites hot and cold to describe human generation. He believed that the male fetus formed more quickly than the female: "The quick formation comes from the strength of the warmth and in the male warmth is stronger, therefore he is formed more quickly in the uterus."[406] Albert also used the categories of wet and dry to explain the different speeds of development of male and female fetuses:

> Although the seed may be formed according to the material, nevertheless the form of the animal can not be shaped quickly. From which it follows that evil moisture is bounded by the appropriate limit, and therefore the seed of the female, because it is moister, acquires its own final shape more slowly.[407]

Finally, he concluded that the male was born more easily than the female:

> The male is produced from stronger warmth than the female, and therefore is formed and takes shape more quickly in the uterus than the female, and a swifter emergence follows the swift formation.[408]

St. Albert had some difficulty explaining why women matured more quickly than men after birth, since he had linked speed of maturing with the respective amounts of heat. He used Aristotle's theory that puberty resulted from the presence of refined nutrition in the body:

> The woman also is colder and wetter, and, therefore, because of the weakness of warmth, more quickly overflows with menstrual blood or produces seed, which is superfluity of food. But warmth in a man is more powerful and uses more food by converting it into the substance of the limbs; thus, there is less left over, and consequently, for seed; and, therefore, a woman is ready more quickly to conceive than a man to beget.[409]

St. Albert argued that men naturally ought to live longer because of their greater amount of heat, but that women in fact lived longer because they worked less and had coition less. Even though women had less natural heat, they conserved what they had and therefore lived longer.[410]

Finally, Albert applied the opposites hot and cold to an analysis of the intensity of sexual desire in women and men. He argued that women were more interested in intercourse in the summer and men in the winter:

> In the male, coitus is more vigorous in the winter in respect of his nature at other times, and in the female in summer. And this is the reason, because generally a man is of a warmer nature than a woman, and therefore the inner heat is dulled in summer because the surrounding outside heat makes the natural interior warmth exhale and disperse. . . . But it is the opposite in a woman.[411]

More germane to the question of generation, St. Albert, in *Quaestiones Super de Animalibus*, asked directly whether females produce seed:

> Properly speaking the female does not produce seed. And the reason for this is, because seed is the superfluity of the most recent food completely digested, but the completeness of digestion comes from strong warmth; moreover females have weak warmth, and therefore in the female there is not sufficient strength for the generation of seed. But rather, just as steadfast warmth produces seed in the male, so weak warmth produces menstrual blood in the female, because menstrual fluid is crude and undigested blood.[412]

At first view, it appears as though St. Albert merely repeated Aristotle's theory that the female did not contribute any seed to generation. However, the scientist had studied Galen and Avicenna, both of whom argued for the presence of female seed. St. Albert then introduced a kind of compromise theory, which claimed that seed occurred in some women. In the following passage from the *Quaestiones Super de Animalibus*, we find St. Albert invoking an example of racial polarity to support his theory of sex polarity:

> In another way, seed can exist in the female, and this is possible when great warmth is kindled in them. And such seed is found more in black females, who subject themselves more compared with all others, i.e., than white; because black females are warmer, and especially dark ones, who are very pleasant for lying under, as writers say, because they have a nice opening of the vulva, that sweetly surrounds the shoot. And this occurs in lean individuals more than in fat ones, because in fat people the excess of seed is converted into fat and lessens warmth; in lean ones the reverse occurs.[413]

St. Albert, along with Galen and Avicenna, mistook glandular secretions at the time of intercourse for female seed, which actually occurs during ovulation. He also concluded, with his predecessors, that this seed was not a fertile contribution to generation:

> Nevertheless, it ought to be stated, that seed has not been found in females capable for producing according to the proper method of seed, because in appropriate seed there is an active force, both formative of members and directive of life, and such a force exists only in the seed of the male.[414]

Therefore, Albert reasserted Aristotle's modified theory of generation by limiting the presence of seed to only a few women, and then concluding that even in these cases it played no fertile role in generation.

St. Albert did go beyond Aristotle in another way when he borrowed from Galen a theory that the material contribution of the female was divided into two parts: material for the body of the fetus and material for the nutrition of the fetus:

> There are many parts of menstrual blood: for one part is transformed into the body of the seed, and another part is changed into things which fill the empty spaces of the body, as into fat and meat; and a third part is transformed into nourishment of the fetus, and still another part is excess.[415]

St. Albert compared woman's material contribution to the divided nature of an egg:

> The menstrual blood of the female is proportionate or corresponds both to the white and yellow of an egg, because from one part of the menstrual fluid the fetus is formed materially and from another it is nourished.[416]

Albert also qualified Aristotle's description of the male contribution. Aristotle had argued that the seed of the father did not enter materially into the fetus. It merely provided the form of the material presented by the mother. St. Albert, however, claimed that some of the moisture of the father's contribution could enter the fetus:

> The philosopher says properly, that seed is not part of the material of the conceived, except insofar as it has active and moving force, and the moving and acting of this kind is not part of generating. Therefore, properly speaking, seed is not part of the conception. Nevertheless, nothing prevents some material part of this from joining the body of the conceived, from which it is mingled with menstrual fluid, and the physicians understand it in this way.[417]

St. Albert maintained Aristotle's main thesis that the formal activating force of the seed did not enter materially into conception, but he allowed the material aspect of the seed to blend with the mother's material contribution. "If it is mixed, this is only true for the material moisture and not for the moving and acting spirit."[418]

The father provided the life force of the child, the mother the material that was shaped by this force:

> Therefore, principle, which arranges seed and form or directs the life force, flows from the life force of the father in the seed; it is not from the life force of the mother, because she is not ordering the arrangement of nature, but only is holding the material for the reception of form.[419]

St. Albert borrowed Aristotle's distinction between actuality and potentiality to explain the way in which the father's seed communicated this form to the fetus:

> In the seed there is no soul in actuality but in potentiality. Nevertheless, there is in the seed the strength of life in action, because just as in the movement of hurled objects the first mover acts by imparting a certain force to the second mover, because of which the second can move when the first one stops, in this way a certain principle can be removed from the father with the seed, whose strength moves and works when the father is resting. . . . In *Metaphysics* VII the philosopher says, that "seed acts just as craftsmen, because just as in the mind of the doer there is no swelling in action, so in the seed there is no soul in action, only in potentiality. And in Book II *De anima* the philosopher says that soul is the motion of the body possessing life in potentiality.[420]

The father, therefore, transmitted the potential form of the child. Once the seed made contact with the material of the mother, however, the soul became the act of the fetus.

Aristotle distinguished the vegetative, sentient and rational faculties of the human soul. He argued that the soul was a unity and, therefore, that it could not be infused into a fetus in parts. However, Aristotle left open the possibility that the rational soul came from outside the father. He never resolved this apparent contradiction. St. Albert, on the other hand, argued that the entire soul had to be infused at the same time:

> Therefore, we cannot say that the rational powers are created by God, while sensible and life-giving powers are brought forth from the substance of the seed. Rather we say that the whole soul is created by God and infused into the body.[421]

St. Albert appeared to describe the work of God and the father as a simultaneous meeting of formative powers. In *On the Nature and Origin of the Soul* he stated:

> All those who spring from a union of male and female are so generated because a drop from the man is dissolved wholly or almost wholly into spirit and penetrates into the drop from the woman by pulsing through her and distinguishing and forming her through the formative power that is in it. And because the power of the soul of the father and the heavenly intellect is in that spirit, a sentient soul is produced from its matter.[422]

Albert brought Aristotle's theory of the association of woman with matter and of man with form into the core of natural philosophy in the Latin world. Even with the slight qualifications that he made, St. Albert primarily served as a pathway for Aristotle's central arguments. This is all the more significant when it is recognized that St. Albert had studied Galen and Avicenna, who at least modified Aristotle's theory to some extent. However, Albert generally weakened these modifications and reverted to a more basic identification of woman with the properties of matter and man with the properties of form. This identification is seen in his subsequent characterizations of woman as passive and man as active. In the preceding passages, woman's contribution to generation was described as being penetrated, shaped and formed by man's contribution. In the *Summa de Creaturis*, Albert explicitly stated that the female was passive in relation to generation:

> A bodily organism is defined in comparing it with soul, and the soul is defined in comparing it with body. So also is defined passive in comparison with active and active in comparison with passive. And in like manner female in comparison with male, and male with female. They work towards the same end, the one effectively, the other materially.[423]

The passivity of the female and the activity of the male, as found in their respective contributions to generation, became integrated into the basic concepts of their respective identities. As a consequence, the female was devalued in relation to the male.

The key to St. Albert's theory of determination of the sex of the fetus is in the phrase that he used several times, namely that the male possesses "strength of principle and warmth." The presence of strength and warmth in the male seed would produce a male child. In one passage St. Albert considers aiding this process:

> By means of skill and medicine warmth can be induced into the seed and strengthened: therefore, the seed, if it has been dispersed towards the female, through medicine it can be arranged towards the male, and vice versa.[424]

St. Albert also echoed Aristotle's belief that the wind, through affecting the heat of the body, might also affect the sex of the child.[425] However, Albert is careful to set clear limits on the efficacy of the opposites hot and cold within the female body:

> Others say, that warmth is the chief source of generation of the male and cold of the female; but that still cannot be true, because according to this, if a male embryo were projected into a cold matrix, it would change into the nature of a female, and the reverse would occur if the female were projected into a warm matrix.[426]

Therefore, while hot and cold appeared to play a certain role at the moment of conception, as soon as the fetus formed it was no longer possible to change its sex. St. Albert qualified this conclusion in another passage, in which he argued that after birth, a male could be changed into a female but not vice versa.

> Important members can be destroyed, but those destroyed cannot be restored. But the female in the first moments of generation has been deprived of the principal members of generation, of course, the testicles, at least exteriorly, but they are inside in the base of the matrix. On account of that, the male can lose the principal member, but the female herself cannot recover that which she was deprived of in generation, and therefore the male can be made female because when the members have been cut off in which warmth and principle flourish, he returns to the arrangement of the female, and after that becomes cold and wet in the manner of the female. But those members cannot be grown in the female after her completed production, and therefore she cannot be made into a man.[427]

The presence of hot or cold affected the initial determination of sex of the fetus and accompanied the adult man or woman. However, these opposites merely served as a sign of the deeper differences between the sexes.

Therefore, the generation of males and females was due to the relative strength of the contributions of the parents. If the strength of the father's contribution prevailed, then the child was male; if it did not, then the child was female. Albert appealed to Aristotle to support this theory:

> Therefore, it ought to be said according to the thought of the philosopher, that strength of principle [virtus] is the chief cause of the male and weakness is the cause of the female. . . . From the seed well ordered the male is generated, and therefore strength of principle is the cause of the male. The positions of all others can be reduced to this cause. . . . Powerful warmth accompanies strength of principle, and it is characteristic of warmth or order, and therefore it is said by some, that warmth is the cause of the generation of the male.[428]

For St. Albert, greater strength is the determining factor of sex, and greater strength is a result of greater heat, so man is identified with the principle of strength, while woman is identified with a weakness in principle. St. Albert concludes that youths and old men tend to produce females because their principle is weaker than men in their prime. The superiority of the stronger principle of the male led to the repetition of Aristotle's claim that nature intended to produce males:

> Concerning the first purpose of nature, it is to produce the better so far as she can. But concerning the second purpose, it is that, if she is deficient in the better, to produce what is close to herself. And therefore when natural principle is powerful, she produces a male; when however she is hindered from the production of a male on account of the resistance of the material, if the dispositions of the material excel or simply overcome, she produces something similar to that from which the material is removed, that is, she produces a female.[429]

While St. Albert accepted Aristotle's basic theory that in each particular conception nature intended to produce a male, he nonetheless qualified Aristotle's view by introducing a distinction between nature in particular and nature in general. In this way, St. Albert defended the view that women were created for an important purpose, that is, God intended to produce women in some way:

> Nature is two-fold: universal and particular. Universal nature intends to preserve the entire universe and its parts, . . . therefore universal nature chiefly intends to conserve the species. But a species of animals cannot be preserved without production of individuals, and for that production of female as well as male is required. Therefore, universal nature intends the female, as that without which the species cannot be saved.
>
> Particular nature moreover intends to produce like itself, and because in the generation of animals the characteristic of a male is acting, and the characteristic of a female is not, therefore the active element principally intends to produce the male.[430]

Albert's argument depended upon a subtle distinction between the basic direction of nature as a whole and the individual nature of the seed of a man. The contribution of the father aimed towards producing its likeness, or a son. However, this intention became thwarted in order to allow the general intention of the forces of nature at large to be fulfilled.

This distinction between the particular and the general intentions of nature has a potential for modifying the radical sex polarity of Aristotle, and even for suggesting sex complementarity. That is, the view that nature intends to differentiate women and men in general, and that the specific division of humanity into two sexes is a more perfect arrangement than if there were simply one sex, implies that it is better to have women and men in the world rather than to have only men. However, Albert does not draw out the implications for sex complementarity in this distinction between universal and particular nature. His complete immersion in an Aristotelian rationale for sex polarity simply leads him to produce an explanation for why women exist at all, if in fact on the particular level nature always intends a male. For Albert, nature in general produces the female in order to preserve the species. However, as will be seen in the next section, Albert's disciple Thomas Aquinas will take this distinction between universal and particular nature further, and he will begin to uncover some of its implications for sex complementarity.

St. Albert described in some detail the different ways in which the interference with the impetus of particular nature could produce a male resembling the father. One description referred to the previously discussed opposites, hot and cold:

> If nevertheless there is a defect in the material or the warmth, which it uses as an instrument, and it cannot generate appropriately according to plan, then it (nature) directs that which it can, and thus particular nature chiefly intends the masculine; nevertheless secondarily and occasionally it intends the feminine.[431]

If the material is defective, then it cannot be shaped into a male by the form of the father's seed; or if the material is too cold, the seed cannot achieve its impetus towards the generation of the male. St. Albert, following Aristotle, also described this interaction of the parents' contributions as a kind of battle of the sexes:

> Although the seed of a man unites itself to the contribution of the woman as an acting force towards material, nevertheless whenever the "seed" of the female is disobedient and too much resistant to the active force, then the principle of the male does not totally conquer, and therefore it cannot perfectly make the fetus like itself, but acts according to the demands of the material, and a female is produced.[432]

The claim that the female fetus resulted from "disobedience" or rebellion by the material contributed by the mother was a clear biological explanation within the sex-polarity tradition.

The description of the activity of generation as a kind of hostile interaction of opposites was carried further than the mere sex of the fetus. The question of physical resemblance of one or the other parent was also considered:

> Insofar as the principle of an animal is in the seed, it produces an animal; and insofar as it is the principle of a human being, it produces a human being; and insofar as it dominates according to "maleness," it produces a male, and insofar as it dominates according to accidental and individual arrangements, it produces a son similar to himself in conditions of this type.[433]

St. Albert repeated Aristotle's theory that the degree of resemblance to a parent indicated the degree of success in domination:

> From which (it follows that) complete victory of the seed of the male over the material of the female is the cause for the fetus being made like the father. If moreover the strength of the seed dominates according to the requirements of the species, and does not dominate or surpass according to the requirements of the individual male, then its warmth is weak, and the cold moisture of the female overflows. If the material resisting the active force simply dominates, . . . then a female like the mother is produced.[434]

In addition to the "ideal situation," in which a male child resembling the father is conceived, and the "worse situation," in which a female resembling the mother is produced,

Albert also offers a description of the way in which a weak male is produced:

> Wise men apply their minds to imagination and reason, and they pour forth their thoughts and meditations. From this, for the most part, natural strength is weakened, and therefore their seed is undistributed and bad, and because of this weak sons are produced, because he who is good in study is poor in business and reproduction of the sex act.[435]

The implication here is that a lesser degree of strength on the part of the male seed will lead to the middle situation in which a male resembling the mother or a female resembling the father is produced. If St. Albert's theory is summarized, using the charts developed in the first two chapters to describe the different theories of conception, it would appear as follows:

	Male Seed	
	Hot and Strong	Less Heat and Strength
Female Material Cold and Moist	boy resembling father (seed fully dominates material)	boy resembling mother (seed partially dominates material)
	girl resembling father (material partially overpowers seed)	girl resembling mother (material fully overpowers seed)

The sex polarity of St. Albert's analysis was frequently repeated. In the following passage he reflects on the fact that the male production of seed is superior to the capacities of the female body:

> Because nature always intends that which is better, and separates that which is better and more noble from the more ignoble in enduring things, and the active one is more noble than the passive one just as form is more noble than matter, therefore in generation of animals nature separates male as if more noble from the female because animals produce by means of the separation of seed, in which division the male is, as it were, acting, and the female, as it were, receiving.[436]

The natural superiority of the male over the female, which has been described in the categories of opposites and generation, is now carried forward by St. Albert into the category of wisdom.

Wisdom

In Book V, Quest, 6, of *Quaestiones Super de Animalibus*, St. Albert raises the question of whether woman or man is more driven by the appetites. He places the question in the scholarly framework of *pro, contra* and *resolution*:

> PRO: The natural and living faculties are weaker in women, and more pressed down than in men, and may be called inferior; therefore the procreative instinct is more intense in them and consequently their desire. . . .
> CONTRA: Desire comes from the source of warmth; but the male is warmer than the female; therefore . . .
> RESOLUTION: From this it follows that desire in accordance with indirect judgement is greater in women, and reasoned arguments show this, but desire in accordance with direct judgement is greater in man.[437]

The interesting aspect of this argument from the perspective of the concept of woman in relation to man is the assumption that the natural and living faculties are inferior in women. This consequence directly follows from the fact that the female is generated from a weaker seed than the male, therefore, in the female fetus the ordering principle is weaker from conception. St. Albert continues his argument using these assumptions:

> The apparent appetite and love in women is greater because of the weakness in her judgement, because as matter seeks to be under every form . . . so it is with woman, she seeks to be under what she does not have, because on account of the weakness of her reason she judges what she does not have is better than what she has. And therefore she seeks intercourse more frequently than man.[438]

The "weakness of woman's reason" is further explained in the context of her closeness to the affections and man's greater closeness to the understanding. In the following passage, the polarized Aristotelian interpretation of wisdom is repeated:

> Discipline is two-fold: for a certain discipline is given concerning matters of affection, and another concerning the understanding, and this consists in learning and contemplating. The female is more amenable to the first than the male, because she is more easily moved by desires to which she is attracted. But she is resistant to the second. Because of the coldness of the constitution of woman, the refined strengths are weakened because her principle has been badly affected, and consequently her intellect is weaker.[439]

The defective generation of woman is directly used as an explanation of her weaker intelligence. In addition, in this passage, the greater presence of coldness provides the rationale for her intellectual limitations. St. Albert, then, has forcefully repeated Aristotle's framework for sex polarity in the category of wisdom.

St. Albert also argues, from the greater presence of the element water in woman, that female intelligence is defective. In the following passage from his commentary on Aristotle's *Politics*, St. Albert expands on the Greek philosopher's ideas (which are italicized) :

> *For the male by nature*, that is naturally, *is more dominant than the female.* And because someone could object, that a certain woman is wiser and more vigorous than a man, and because of this he makes an exception, saying: *Unless it remains constant in some way* it happened *against nature*, to wit that a man is lacking and a woman excels; and this is against the order of nature. For it is according to the nature of woman to have inconstant ideas, because of moisture; moreover men because of the opposite composition, have unchanging ideas.[440]

This discussion of the natural aspects of woman's intelligence as inconstant and inferior to man's intelligence is particularly interesting with respect to St. Albert's development of a theology of Mary as the ultimate example of human wisdom. It would appear from the above that Mary's wisdom would have to be considered "against nature" in view of her female identity. However, before St. Albert's arguments about Mary are examined, it is necessary to complete the consideration of his philosophy of sex polarity in relation to men and women in general.

Virtue

Aristotle had argued that reason was "without authority" over the passions in women. In St. Albert's commentary on the *Politics*, this argument is accepted and amplified:

> *As a free man rules a slave, so the masculine dominates the feminine*, in another way, and as the man, that is, the father, *the boy. All* the slave, the woman, and the boy *have the parts of the soul*, rational and irrational in appetites and anger, *but they exist in the soul differently. A slave*, one who is by nature a slave, *has no power of decision*, and therefore can never plan; *a woman has, but it is weak*, and therefore, she does not complete her planning properly; *a boy has, but it is not developed* because he does not have settled ideas.[441]

Woman's inconstancy made it impossible to carry out acts based on moral principles. St. Albert concluded that since capacities for reasoning differed among women, men, slaves, and boys, that their respective capacities for virtue also differed. "Women, boys, and slaves lack or are weak in the cardinal virtues."[442] The cardinal virtues of temperance, courage, justice, and wisdom or prudence demanded the capacity to reason well, or to deliberate. If woman's intelligence is weak from her conception as a female, then she would not be able to live out the demands of the cardinal virtues.

St. Albert continues his analysis of woman's weaker capacity for virtue in the *Quaestiones de Animalibus*, where he considers women's inferior capacity for following the order of laws:

> The female is less fit for laws than the male. For the constitution of a female is more moist than a male, but it is characteristic of moisture to relapse easily and to hold firm poorly. For moisture is easily moved, and therefore women are inconstant and always seeking new things.[443]

The argument is also made that because of woman's basic inconstancy, she ought not to be allowed to speak publicly in law courts. Referring to Aristotle's phrase "silence is a woman's glory," St. Albert concludes:

> Because of this it is secured in laws, or civil code "let women not be brought into cases." The opinions of women are uncertain and inconstant, and enticing the minds of judges.[444]

When the traditional separation of the virtues of ruling and obeying for woman and man is considered, St. Albert suggests that the natural inferiority of woman leads to her desire for subjection to man:

> Matter is said to seek form and woman man, because woman seeks intercourse with man, but this is understandable because everything imperfect naturally seeks to be perfected; and woman is an imperfect human being compared with man. Therefore, every woman seeks to be subject to man. For there is no woman who does not want to take off the female "ratio" and put on the male naturally. And in the same way matter seeks to put on form.[445]

However, the inconstancy in woman conflicts with her desire to be subject to man, and St. Albert concludes that woman ends up being unfaithful to a single authority: "When she is in the act under one man, if it were possible, at the same time she would wish to be under another. Therefore there is no faithfulness in a woman."[446] When these observations of St. Albert are compared with the views of Hildegard about woman's nature, it is difficult not to be struck by their total antithesis. For Hildegard, woman was more naturally restrained and prone to virtue, while for the Dominican, woman was exactly the opposite. The extent to which St. Albert went to defend his interpretation of woman's inferior relation to virtue is found in the following passage from the *Quaestiones de Animalibus*:

> A female is more skilled in evil and wrong deeds, that is, more cunning, than a male, because by however much nature takes away from one operation, she directs the same amount to another one. A woman lacks in the intellectual faculties, which consists in the apphrension of good, the understanding of truth, and the avoidance of evil. Therefore she directs more to the appetites, which tend toward evil, unless it is ruled by reason, as was apparent in *Ethics* VII. From which it follows that appetites move woman to every evil, just as intellect moves man to every good.[447]

This argument that woman is a negative presence in the world is repeated in the *Politicorum*:

> Wise men reveal their plans and deeds least of all to their wives. For a woman is a man that has been ruined, and has a nature of failure and lack of relation to the male, therefore naturally she lacks confidence in herself, and therefore that which she cannot acquire by herself she strives to acquire by means of lies and diabolical deceptions. Therefore, in brief, everyone ought to be warned away from every woman as if from a poisonous serpent and a horned devil, and if

> it were right to say what I know about women, the whole world would be stunned.[448]

With this vehement attack on woman, St. Albert has joined the more popular satirical tradition previously encountered in Juvenal, Capellanus, or Walter Map.[449]

From the above analysis it has been demonstrated that St. Albert's philosophy of sex polarity was grounded in the works of Aristotle. In summary, the line of reasoning was as follows:

man	**hot, dry, strong principle**	}	**perfect conception**	→	**strong mind**	→	**good acts**
woman	**cold wet, weak principle**	}	**imperfect conception**	→	**weak mind**	→	**weak or evil acts**

At the same time, St. Albert went even further than Aristotle in linking the arguments from opposites to generation, to wisdom, and to virtue. He recognized the implicit structure of Aristotle's thought and amplified it wherever possible to make the meaning of the differentiation of the sexes perfectly clear.

In his philosophy of sex identity, St. Albert differentiated woman from man across all four categories of sex identity. At the same time, he clearly interpreted man as superior and woman as inferior in all aspects of existence. In this way, Albert the Great stands at the floodgates of the Aristotelian Revolution. However, in an ironic development to his thought, as much as woman in general was devalued in relation to man, so much was Mary, as Mother of God, valued as superior to men. In St. Albert's radically new interpretation of Mary, grace overturned nature, and a member of the "inferior" sex became greater than all men. This study will examine just one aspect of St. Albert's Mariology, namely his analysis of Mary as the "Throne of Wisdom."

Mariology

In the writings of St. Anselm, Mary began to emerge as a forceful person in relation to men. Then Abelard developed the theory that the sex polarity inherent in the natural inferiority of woman as the weaker sex was overturned at the level of response to grace, where the "weaker became the stronger." St. Albert takes this line of thought one step further in his extraordinary description of Mary as containing perfect knowledge of all things, even while she lived on earth.

St. Albert wrote about Mary in a number of contexts. He described her in *De Annuntiatione, De Incarnatione, De Resurrectione, De Temperantia, De Natura Bona* and in his commentary on Peter Lombard's *Sentences.*[450] However, the most important text for the present study is called *Mariale sive Quaestiones super Evangelium.* While the attribution of the authorship of the *Mariale* to Albert the Great is contested, it has not been disproved.[451] In this text, Albert raised fourteen different questions about the nature and extent of Mary's knowledge of the world. Mary, in the line of iconography associated with St. Catherine of Alexandria, Boethius's Lady Philosophy, Hildegard's Divine

Sapientia, or Herrad's Philosophia and Woman with the Sun, represented the epitome of knowledge, which far exceeded that of any living man.

In the development of the *Mariale*, Mary is described as knowing the following areas to perfection:

> The seven liberal arts including the trivium of grammar, rhetoric, and logic (dialectic) and the quadrivium of music, astronomy, arithmetic and geometry.
>
> The four areas of study at the University of Paris including civil law, natural philosophy (physics), medicine and theology.
>
> All mechanical arts useful to women.[452]

In this way, Mary's wisdom bridged the classical system of education, which focused on the liberal arts, and the radically new system of education developing in Paris in the twelfth and thirteenth centuries. In addition, she combined both theoretical and practical wisdom. Therefore, Mary was described as having more knowledge than all the learned men or women who ever existed. St. Albert's arguments for this extraordinary depiction of the relation of one woman to the category of wisdom will now be considered in detail.

Question 96: Whether the Blessed Virgin knew all the mechanical arts. St. Albert usually invoked several reasons for his answer to each question. He first argued that Mary had to know everything because she lacked no good: "All knowledge is from the number of goods; but she lacked no good; therefore, she had all knowledge."[453] He then qualified this answer by arguing that she knew only those mechanical arts necessary for women.

> Likewise, Nature is not lacking in necessary matters, and does not overflow in superfluous ones; therefore grace is much stronger; but certain mechanical arts were necessary to the Blessed Virgin, those relating to women; certain were superfluous, as relating to men; therefore she had the former and not the latter.[454]

In this question St. Albert divided practical knowledge into areas useful to women and areas useful to men. In the next question, St. Albert considered the degree of expertise of Mary's knowledge in the area of women's practical arts.

Question 97: Whether she knew the more subtle and more noble arts relating to women, as those which involve the fashioning of gold, working with silks, and fine seams and textures and things of this type. St. Albert invoked the seamless garment worn by Christ at the crucifixion as an example of something made by Mary. He then appealed to a philosophical relation of cause and effect:

> Just as effect to effect, so cause to cause; but the effect having been caused by the mechanical art of the Blessed Virgin disproportionately excelled the effect caused by the mechanical arts of others; therefore mechanical knowledge in the most Blessed Virgin excelled practical knowledge in everyone.[455]

Mary was the best artisan in natural crafts among all women. Therefore, she had the most knowledge of the mechanical arts. From practical knowledge, St. Albert moved to theoretical knowledge.

Question 98: Whether the Blessed Virgin knew the liberal arts in the highest degree. St. Albert first drew upon scriptural analogies to explain Mary's knowledge in this area:

> Proverbs 9:1: Wisdom has built a house for herself, she has made seven pillars; that house is the Blessed Virgin, the seven pillars are the seven liberal arts; therefore the Blessed Virgin had knowledge of the seven liberal arts.[456]

Then he argued that Mary ought not to be denied praise that other human beings received for their knowledge of the liberal arts:

> Also, some holy men are praised because of such knowledge. . . . (Also) the sainted Catherine, and many others; therefore the Blessed Virgin ought not to lack that material for praise.[457]

The liberal arts in medieval times comprised what were known as the trivium and the quadrivium. After proving that Mary had a general knowledge of the seven areas of knowledge, St. Albert turned to each area in detail. He asked first whether Mary knew the trivium (grammar, rhetoric and dialectic).

Question 99: Whether she knew grammar. For the first answer, St. Albert appealed to a passage in the Gospel of Luke in which Mary was described as preserving all her knowledge in her heart: "Therefore she knew how to read. And it follows, that she understood because to read and not to understand is to be negligent therefore she knew grammar."[458] Furthermore, St. Albert argued that not only did Mary read and understand, but she also expressed her knowledge verbally: "Also, she never made a mistake in speaking, therefore she knew grammar."[459]

Question 100: Whether she knew rhetoric. Mary appeared to know this aspect of the trivium through her more basic acquaintance with scripture. St. Albert offered no other rationale for this knowledge. More interestingly, Albert argued that Mary knew the foundations of civil law that had been gathered by the Romans in the classical period and brought together into a code developed through the use of Aristotle's dialectic method.

Question 101: Whether she knew civil laws, statutes, and decrees. Albert argued that Mary was the supreme example of an advocate, and therefore she must have knowledge of the law:

> The wisdom of the advocate is shown in three ways. One, that he succeeds in everything in front of a just and wise judge. Two, that he succeeds against a clever and wise adversary. Third, that he succeeds in a desperate case. But the most Blessed Virgin obtained the desired sentence in the presence of the wisest judge, God; against a very clever adversary, the devil; in our desperate cause therefore she is the wisest advocate.[460]

He further argued that Mary had the skill of a Sophist in "turning the worse to the better":

> Likewise some advocates are able to prove that the unjust is just in the manner of a Sophist, but the Blessed Virgin has acted this way concerning our unjust

> acts therefore much better than all others she best knew how to allege excuses for us all.[461]

Finally, St. Albert claimed that Mary's function as a ruler necessitated legal knowledge:

> Also, she herself was a female ruler: therefore she could establish laws, and the interpretation of law was within her, and she had all laws enclosed in the inner part of her heart: therefore the most Blessed Virgin knew all laws and rhetoric.[462]

The significant aspect of the above description of Mary's capacities in law is that she not only knew the laws themselves, but also the rationale for their defence. Therefore, her knowledge was discursive as well as intuitive. St. Albert explicitly made this point in his next question.

Question 102: Whether she knew logic. After arguing that Mary had to know logic in order to destroy heresies and understand arguments in Scripture, Albert claimed that she used logic in her struggle to overcome evil in the world.

> Likewise, it is clear by following the divisions of logic, which are proofs, the art of eloquence, demonstration, and dialectic. For she knew proofs in the fullest measure, because she never yielded to temptation. She possessed the art of eloquence to the highest degree, for she understood all the tricks of the devil and revealed all his sophisms. She possessed dialectic in the greatest manner, because fittingly she was ignorant of nothing and knew how to solve problems. She had skill in demonstration to the highest degree, because she brought to a conclusion the most noble feeling about a most noble subject through herself.[463]

It is clear that Mary did not suffer from the "lack of consistency resulting from the moist nature of women." She was able to bring all thoughts to their proper conclusion. She knew both the first principles of thought as well as the logical operations that could generate conclusions from premises. She had the best knowledge possible of syllogistic reasoning.

St. Albert did not end with the above areas of knowledge. He argued that Mary also had extensive knowledge of the world through her wisdom in the natural sciences.

Question 103: Whether she knew physics and medicine. St. Albert's first answer appealed to Aristotle:

> The philosopher says that knowledge of the soul is altogether important, especially in natural science: but the Blessed Virgin had the most complete knowledge of the soul, therefore she knew herself very completely.[464]

He also claimed that because she understood the use of minerals, plants and animals in scripture, she understood their basic nature from the perspective of natural science.

St. Albert furthermore attributed the wisdom of a physician to Mary: "Also, there is no disease still uncurable, but that she knew and could cure it; therefore she possessed knowledge of medicine in the highest degree."[465] He developed three further arguments to prove that her curative powers were unsurpassed. These views are all the more astonishing in light of the fact that all women were excluded from the Faculty of Medicine at the University of Paris.

The question of whether Mary's knowledge extended to non-Christian subjects intrigued Albert. He brought out this question in a consideration of Mary's relation to the quadrivium, the second foundation of Roman classical education. The quadrivium consisted of the study of music, astronomy, arithmetic, and geometry.

Question 104: Whether the quadrivium existed in the Blessed Virgin. In response to this question, St. Albert first listed six arguments against her having such knowledge. They included the view that the quadrivium only "tended toward grace," but Mary was already full of grace and therefore did not need this knowledge. Furthermore, none of the saints were praised for this pagan knowledge. Next, the quadrivium appeared to be knowledge merely from curiosity, and not from any real good. Finally, it was more like knowledge of creatures and not of God, and therefore Mary did not need it.

On the other hand, St. Albert listed three arguments to prove that Mary did have knowledge of the quadrivium. The first argument was as follows:

> She herself was most perfect in regard to feeling, therefore also in regard to thought; but she chose all things "able to be chosen" therefore she knew all things "able to be known."[466]

He also claimed that even something tending to the good could bring something more to what is already good, so pagan knowledge added something to Christian knowledge. Finally, he claimed that since Abraham already had such knowledge that Mary ought to have it, too.

St. Albert then turned to a consideration of each of the subjects of the quadrivium. He argued in Question 105 that Mary knew music, in Question 106 that she knew astronomy, in Question 107 that she knew arithmetic, and in Question 108 that she knew geometry.[467] His arguments nearly always referred to Mary's original knowledge of the scriptures. In order to understand harmony, the workings of the stars, computations, and measurements as measured in the Bible, Mary had to have scientific knowledge common to these fields. Therefore it turned out that the knowledge in the quadrivium was also knowledge common to the Christian tradition.

St. Albert, however, was also interested in the Queen of the Sciences, theology. He therefore asked, in Question 109, whether Mary knew theology perfectly. St. Albert produced eight arguments to prove that Mary had knowledge of metaphysics and theology. Most of these arguments drew upon a symbolic interpretation of scriptures. However, St. Albert also argued from the example of other people:

> Also, the apostles knew theology, although they had not studied it; therefore much more strongly the Blessed Virgin [knew theology].
>
> Also, she herself has a splendid circle of teachers; therefore she knew the science of theology.[468]

St. Albert implied that Mary gained this knowledge directly from the Holy Spirit:

> From this moreover it is concluded, that perfect knowledge of all the Scriptures according to the intellect of the Holy Spirit himself speaking through the Scriptures, extends to the state which is superior to the common condition of the wayfarer (on earth); this is the status of the most Blessed Virgin, and so she knew theology in much greater proportion to all others.[469]

At the University of Paris, the Faculty of Theology used as its primary text the *Sentences* of Peter Lombard. This four-volume work brought together a wide range of opinions on theological matters using Aristotle's dialectic method. Since Mary was supposed to have thorough knowledge of theology, St. Albert then had to determine whether this meant that she knew Lombard's *Sentences*.

Question 110: Whether she knew the material of the book of the Sentences. The problem for St. Albert was to determine whether Mary merely knew the topics considered by the *Sentences*, or whether she knew the actual work of Lombard. His response in the first book implied that Mary's personal experience allowed her to know the subjects considered.

> For the material of the first book is reduced to two topics, to material about the Trinity and to material about predestination and the power and will of God, but she knew most of all about this material, she who had experienced the power and goodness of God in herself.[470]

However, when St. Albert considered the second book of the *Sentences*, Mary's knowledge appeared to be more extensive:

> The second book is about Angels and the acts of the six days of creation and the status of mankind; but the Blessed Virgin knew all these matters most perfectly; therefore she knew the second book of the *Sentences* totally.[471]

The third book of the *Sentences* revealed Mary's capacity for virtue:

> In the third book is treated the Incarnation of the Word and virtues; but she knew that completely, who understood the Incarnation through experience, and knew the virtues in the highest degree in herself.[472]

Finally, St. Albert argued that Mary's personal experience after leaving the earth, gave her knowledge of the fourth book of the *Sentences*:

> In the fourth book is written about the sacramental graces and the resurrection; she possessed the sacramental graces to the fullest, . . . she even had a body after the body of God most similar to the bodies of the resurrection which are immune from guilt and punishment, . . . and so she especially understood the nature of the bodies of the resurrection.[473]

St. Albert then concluded: "From these therefore it is clear, that the most Blessed Virgin possessed (knowledge of) the Bible and *Sentences* to the fullest degree."[474]

The most obvious question that must now be asked is how did Mary know all these things? St. Albert described Mary as knowing how to read, to give speeches, to make sophisticated legal arguments, to develop and use philosophical proofs, to understand the basic principles of mathematics and natural science, to practise medicine, and to explain the basic issues of metaphysics and theology, as described in Lombard's *Sentences*. Woman had previously been characterized by St. Albert as naturally incapable of such wisdom. Why was Mary so different?

Mary did not attend university. Therefore, she could not have learned what she knew in the way ordinary men and women gained knowledge and wisdom. Mary's knowledge came through a direct infusion from God. St. Albert described the Holy Spirit as teaching Mary the truths of scripture in Question 109. In the same question he also described her as having a "splendid circle of teachers," although St. Albert was silent about who these teachers might have been. It is tempting, then, to conclude merely that St. Albert believed Mary learned everything directly from the Holy Spirit. However, there also appeared to be another source for her extraordinary knowledge. St. Albert believed that Mary learned through the effect of carrying Christ within her during pregnancy.

Robert Buschmiller, in *The Maternity of Mary in the Mariology of St. Albert the Great*, claims:

> The Divine Maternity is in truth the very fundamental dogma in all of St. Albert's consideration of Mary. Among later theologians it has become a common opinion to ascribe the supreme excellence of Mary to her sanctifying grace. They conclude that the excellency that became Mary by reason of her sanctifying grace was greater than the excellency of the Mother of God by reason of her divine maternity, absolutely considered in itself. This was not the opinion of St. Albert at all, who viewed all the eternal preparation and subsequent glories of Mary in reference to her Divine Maternity.[475]

Consequently, Mary's knowledge flowed from the transformation caused by the presence of Christ within her. Since Christ was omniscient, Mary acquired this knowledge by her intimate reception of the Second Person of the Trinity. Therefore, for Albert the Great, Mary's wisdom did not come directly from the Holy Spirit but indirectly through Christ.[476]

In trying to evaluate the significance of St. Albert's concept of woman it is important to reflect upon his description of the natural inferiority of woman as well as on his description of the superiority of Mary. It is sometimes claimed that the exaltation of Mary above the normal human condition was a compensation for the devaluation of women in general. While this may sometimes be an accurate psychological explanation for this phenomenon, there is more to be said about its philosophic basis. When viewed from a philosophical stance, St. Albert's Mariology becomes the perfectly consistent consequence of his theory of generation.

St. Albert had argued, following Aristotle, that in conception the mother provided the material that was formed by the active shaping power in the father's seed. Mary was no exception to this basic principle of natural philosophy. When Mary conceived Christ, she only provided the material for his nature. The Holy Spirit provided the formal nature that actively shaped this material. The conception was perfect because the child, Christ, perfectly resembled God as Father.

The presence of God as Christ within Mary then worked to transform her. Mary, as a fully developed human being, herself became a kind of material for the formative power of God. Her perfect identity as non-resistant material for the working of the Holy Spirit led to her complete absorption of the wisdom of God. Therefore, it followed that Mary knew everything that God knew. She was the perfect philosopher, theologian, lawyer, physician, scientist, and so on.

St. Albert's description of Mary had certain consequences for the concept of woman. It offered a rationale for the exclusion of women from academic centres of higher learning. While St. Albert recognized the importance of grace and the resulting infused knowledge that came directly from God, he also supported the efforts of men to learn philosophy, theology and science from the efforts of their own will. In fact, Albert was an important teacher at the University of Paris in its early years. He also taught in universities in Germany from 1248 to 1277. From his own example, it can be inferred that he valued men's efforts to develop the skills of discursive reason through natural means.

It is in this context, then, that it is possible to understand how Mariology could have been used to justify the exclusion of women from such dynamic learning situations. If woman's nature became limited to the description of her identity as passive contributor of material to generation, then it could be argued that woman ought to learn wisdom in the same way as she became impregnated with male seed. In other words, woman's passive nature implied that she could best learn by limiting herself to the reception of grace given from God. For woman to enter into the rigorous activity of study and learning through the effort of her will would be for her to take on the formal activities associated with being a man capable of generating fertile seed.

It is possible, therefore, to interpret St. Albert's Mariology as partially due to the logical extension of his acceptance of Aristotle's theory of generation. With woman characterized as essentially passive in generation, Mary became the most perfect woman by virtue of her complete receptivity to God. Indeed, it was her receptivity to the word of God that led to her being called the Throne of Wisdom. Mary was the ultimate woman; she served as the model for all other women. Since Mary learned everything directly through the infusion of grace, St. Albert believed that all women should limit themselves to this means of gaining wisdom.

Of course, the one-sided limitation of women's access to wisdom was a false conclusion of the Aristotelian Revolution. Men were encouraged to develop both their capacities for active human reasoning as well as receptivity to grace. It is also obvious that Mary was an active contributor to the conception and growth of Christ. To develop a model of Mary as essentially passive is to completely underestimate and misunderstand her significance. Therefore, it is far more interesting to discover a situation in which grace builds upon and transforms a nature already perfected than to follow Albert's theory of grace overturning an "imperfect" or "deformed" nature.

Therefore, while Albert's theory of Mariology appears, at first sight, to contradict the Aristotelian concept of woman, upon further investigation it turns out to be quite consistent with Aristotle's theory of generation. It also reveals the intricate way in which theological arguments in medieval Christian thought depended upon and developed from the foundation of philosophy.

Albert the Great had a significant influence on the development of the philosophy of sex identity. He had joined the Dominican order in 1223 and gained a reputation as an excellent teacher during his time at the University of Paris. After his return to Germany, Albert established a school in Cologne and was later appointed Provincial of the German province. He then preached publicly across Germany, thereby making his ideas widely known. Albert's learning was so extensive that he was called "Doctor Universalis."[477]

It is perhaps a sign of fame that forgeries or spurious works attributed to a particular author emerge. Two such texts about the concept of woman, involving theories spuriously attributed to Albert, are worth noting here. The first is a text entitled *De Secretis Mulierum.*[478] This book, which contains a combination of theories about generation, some of which were Aristotelian, other's Albert's, and still more from different sources, appeared shortly after the Dominican's death and circulated among private homes until the eighteenth century. It will be considered in some detail in the final chapter of this book. At this point it is worth noting that it contains a popularization of the sex polarity associated with Albert's theory of opposites and generation.

The second text is entitled *De laudibus B. Mariae Virginis*. This book, originally attributed to St. Albert, was later recognized as being authored by Richard St. Laurent. According to Thomas R. Heath, the author of the text made Mary nearly identical to God:

> He applies the Our Father to her: Our Mother, who art in heaven, give us your daily bread. Or again he says that Mary so loved the world that she gave her only begotten Son for the life of the world. . . . He includes her flesh in our Holy Communion.[479]

The false attribution of this work to St. Albert simply underlines the tendency in the popular imagination to associate him with two very different views: on the one hand that ordinary woman is devalued in relation to man, and on the other that Mary is exalted above mankind. Therefore, for most readers of Albert the Great, the concept of woman in relation to man contains a contradiction.

In conclusion, perhaps Albert's strongest contribution to the history of the philosophy of sex identity is his influence on the development of Aristotelian theory. By Albert's extensive commentaries and by his role in evolving Latin translations of the Greek philosopher's works, Albert stands as a central figure in the explosion of the Aristotelian Revolution. The next crucial step in this radical new development in western thought occurs through the legacy St. Albert passed on to his most famous student. St. Thomas Aquinas studied with Albert in Paris from 1245 to 1248, and then followed his master to Germany from 1248 to 1252. It was during this period of intensive study that St. Thomas began to develop an entirely new and original Christian philosophy grounded upon Aristotelian thought. The degree of closeness of thought between these two men is attested to by the fact that Albert travelled to Paris in 1277, just three years before his death, to defend Thomas Aquinas against the condemnations of Bishop Tempier. As Weisheipl states in "Thomas d'Aquinas and Albert His Teacher":

> He proceeded to praise and glorify Thomas in the highest terms, declaring that he was personally prepared to defend the writings of the aforesaid Friar Thomas as the splendor of truth and sanctity before the most competent critics.[480]

In this new allegiance, the move towards incorporating Aristotle into Christian thought had gone too far to hold back. The Aristotelian Revolution achieved a new degree of intensity through the work of Albert's student Thomas. At the same time, however, Thomas brought some modifications to Albert's radical sex polarity in terms of the concept of woman. While Thomas accepted the Aristotelian foundation for sex polarity as a descripton of the relation of woman and man on the natural level, he moved towards sex complementarity on the level of grace.

ST. THOMAS AQUINAS (1224–1274)

This giant in Christian philosophy made significant advances on the theories of sex identity found in his predecessors. Augustine had been caught in a three-tiered philosophy of sex identity that contained an unresolved tension between sex polarity, sex unity and sex complementarity. Thomas forged a new synthesis that allowed him to resolve at least the sex polarity-sex unity contradiction in Augustine. By introducing a theory of difference in perfection according to a scale of degrees of perfection, Thomas avoided the ironic Augustinian pronouncement that woman was in the image of God in the highest part of her intellect, which contained no sex identity, while she was not in the image of God when considered in her temporal existence. For Thomas, woman was always in the image of God, but she reflected this image less perfectly than man.

In relation to Anselm, who had argued that at the highest level, sex identity was irrelevant to the "reflection of the image of God," Thomas argued instead that a person necessarily included a material aspect of his or her nature. Therefore, sex identity would always be an essential part of personal identity. Accordingly, since personal identity reflected the image of God, Thomas argued that the soul was the form of the body, and that the body related to the soul as potentiality to actuality. In this description of the interaction of soul to body as "like to like," Thomas rejected the Platonic tendency to perceive the body as a prison or source of conflict in relation to the soul.

Finally, while on the one hand accepting the general Aristotelian rationale for sex polarity in describing woman in relation to man on the natural level in the world, Thomas developed a new support for a theory of sex complementarity when considering male and female identity on the level of grace and in heaven. In this way he went further than had Augustine in merely recognizing the potential Christian theology for demanding a theory of the equality and significant differentiation of woman and man.

Thomas achieved a new kind of consistency by arguing that while woman begins life as imperfect in relation to man, she may end in eternal life in a full relation of sex complementarity. With this shift, Thomas avoided the extreme contradictions found in Abelard or St. Albert, where the sex polarity of the world appeared to be overthrown by a radical sex polarity at the level of response to grace. For Thomas, grace did not overturn or destroy human nature. He believed instead that grace built on or perfected nature. Therefore, woman was able to achieve the full perfection of her "imperfect" nature. For Thomas, moving from nature to grace was not a move from sex polarity to reverse sex polarity, rather it was a move from sex polarity to sex complementarity. The following chart summarizes his view:

	Man	Woman
	Sex Complementarity on Level of Grace	
Opposites	Two sexes more perfect than one, both sexes are resurrected	
Generation	God intends to produce both males and females	
Wisdom	The sexes are equally capable of infused wisdom of contemplation	
Virtue	The sexes are equally capable of theological virtues	

	Man	Woman
	Sex Polarity on the Level of Nature	
Opposites	Most perfect reflection of image of God, first principle of human beings	Less perfect image of God, different, derivative, lack "eminence of degree"
Generation	Provides vegetative and sentient soul-power, the active sex	Provides matter, the passive sex
Wisdom	Reason, capable of intellectual virtues, natural wisdom, speech	Weak in reason, less capable of intellectual virtues, silence
Virtue	Rule, strong in cardinal virtues, public sphere of activity	Obey, weak in cardinal virtues private sphere of activity

As can be seen from the above chart, St. Thomas nearly perfectly mirrors Aristotle's arguments for sex polarity on the level of nature. Because of his explicit repetition of the Aristotelian rationale, he became one of the most important sources for defending Aristotelian sex polarity. Even though St. Thomas did attempt, on the theological level, to move beyond the natural sex polarity he had so strongly endorsed, the statements he made in favour of sex complementarity were often lost in a far larger support for sex polarity.

Opposites

For St. Thomas, the concept of woman in relation to man is analogous in some respects to the relation that exists between God and prime matter. In the *Summa Theologiae*, he describes the difference between God and matter as a difference between actuality and potentiality:

> God cannot contain matter. First, because the very existence of matter is a being potential; whilst God, as we have seen, contains no potentiality, but is sheer actuality.[481]

For St. Thomas, actuality precedes potentiality, and God as Trinity of Father, Son and Holy Spirit precedes the creation of the world and all that is in it. In the *Summa Theologiae*, the philosopher continues to develop the analogy between God as Father of the world and Adam as father of the human race:

> When all things were first formed, it was more suitable for the woman to be made from the man. . . . First, in order thus to give the first man a certain dignity consisting in this, that as God is the principle of the whole universe, so the first man, in likeness of God, was the principle of the whole human race.[482]

In Thomas's commentary on Peter Lombard's *Sentences*, the association of principle with man's identity is extended from Adam to all men:

> The male among humans has more of the principles of source with respect to the woman than among other animals. For this reason, it was more fitting that the female human being be taken from the male.[483]

The phrase "principles of source" refers to the now familiar theory that the seed of the father is the cause of the fetus. In the *Summa Theologiae*, this theory is summarized: "The relation of being the source of generation in the highest form of life is called 'fatherhood.' "[484] The philosopher developed an elaborate theory of degrees of reflection of the nature of God. The following diagram summarizes the main lines of his argument:

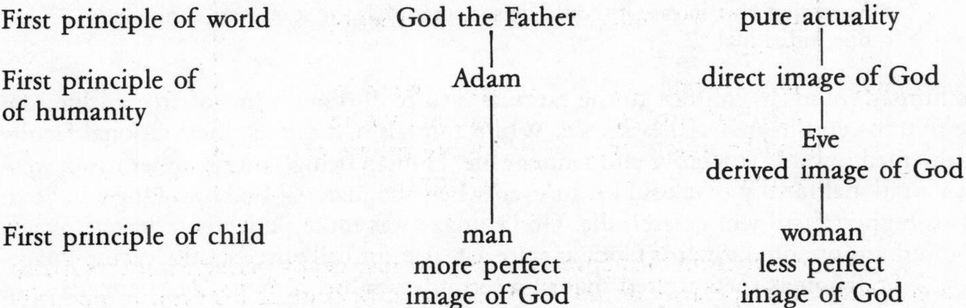

St. Thomas carefully considered the question of whether or not woman and man are both created in the image of God. He was well aware of St. Augustine's argument that woman, in her spiritually oriented existence, was in the image of God, while in her temporally oriented existence she did not properly reflect this divine image. St. Augustine had argued that woman had to be joined to man to be in the image of God. St. Thomas rejected St. Augustine's argument and claimed that woman was created in the image of God in body and in mind. For Aquinas, the crucial question focused on whether material bodily existence could be considered as "in the image of God." In the *Summa Theologiae* he emphatically stated that it was:

> Again, Genesis says: *God created man after his own image, after the image of God he created them*. But the distinction of male and female refers to the body. So God's image in man refers to the body as well as to the mind.[485]

In another passage in the same work, St. Thomas implied that the image of God was found more perfectly in the highest activities of the mind. While this activity was found in both women and men, it appeared to have no direct relation to sexual identity:

> Scripture, having stated *after God's image he created him, adds male and female He created them*, not to present the image of God in terms of sexual distinctions, but because the image of God is common to both sexes, being in the mind which has no distinction of sex. And so in *Colossians*, after the Apostle has said *according to the image of Him who created him, he adds, where there is neither male nor female*.[486]

This view, similar to Augustine's defence of sex unity, seems to negate St. Thomas's earlier insistence on the image of God being reflected in the materiality of human life. However, the problem of apparent inconsistency was solved by the introduction of a concept of degrees of presence in the image of God.[487] The more closely a person approximated the pure actuality of God, the more he or she was in the image of God. Since the mind more perfectly contained the image of God:

> Hence: God's image is found equally in both man and woman as regards that point in which the idea of "image" is principally realized, namely an intelligent nature. Thus, after saying in Genesis, *after God's image He created him*, i.e., man, it adds *male and female He created them*; and it puts *them* in the plural, as Augustine says, in case it should be supposed that the sexes were combined in one individual.[488]

The human mind, in contrast to the rational faculty of other forms of created life, was able to transcend its material existence. While animals had minds, their rational faculty was oriented towards vegetative and sentient life. Human beings, on the other hand, were given a rational faculty that could exist even when the material body no longer existed. In this highest faculty of created life, God's image was more perfectly reflected. When the mind was oriented towards God, as pure act, it most fully lived in the divine image.

St. Thomas then argued that in a secondary sense, a man more perfectly contained the image of God than a woman. Man's direct creation by God implied an immediate transfer of divine image that was absent in woman's creation as derived from man:

> But as regards a secondary point, God's image is found in man in a way in which it is not found in woman; for man is the beginning and the end of woman, just as God is the beginning and end of all creation. Thus after saying that *the man is the image and glory of God, while the woman* is the glory of man, the Apostle goes on to show why he says it, and adds: for the man was not from the *woman, but the woman from the man; and the man was not created for the woman, but the woman for man.*[489]

St. Thomas developed a theory of a hierarchy of perfection. In the *Summa Contra Gentiles* he expressed this theory as having Aristotelian origins: "The agent is superior to the patient, and the maker to the thing made (Aristotle *De Anim.* III 5 [430a 17]), as act to potential. Now the more immaterial a thing is, the higher its level of being."[490] In the broad sense, God, as pure act, is the most perfect being, next, in descending order, come angels, or spiritual beings with no matter, then human beings, with the most highly developed rationality, then animals and plants.

St. Thomas also considered the gradation of sexuality within a species as hierarchical. The male, having a closer approximation to the actuality of God through his more perfect generation and his capacity for providing principle or act to his offspring, was superior to the female. However, St. Thomas adds that the variety of two sexes within one species is a greater perfection than if there had been only one sex, even if the female is less perfect than the male. The argument in the *Summa Contra Gentiles* continues: "Just as a variety in the grading of things contributes to the perfection of the universe, so the variety of sex makes for perfection of human nature."[491]

In this extremely important statement of principle, Thomas has moved towards sex complementarity. For the argument that the "variety of sex makes for the perfection of human nature" implies that the differences between women and men are significant and that there is an overall value to this difference that surpasses the individual superiority of a single man in relation to a single woman. Had Thomas held to the absolute superiority of the male in all respects, then he would have had to conclude that a more perfect world would include only men. However, St. Thomas's claim that variety is a perfection will force him to go beyond the simple sex polarity brought forward by the Aristotelian Revolution.

St. Thomas accepted Aristotle's argument that the differences between male and female were not so great as to make the two sexes into different species. In his commentary on Aristotle's *Metaphysics*, St. Thomas repeats the Greek philosopher's conclusion and emphasizes the role of the active power of generation associated with the male:

> He accordingly says, first, that the question arises why woman does not differ specifically from man, since female and male are contraries, and diffferences in species is caused by contrariety, as has been established. [Male and female] do not pertain to animal by reason of its substance or form, but by reason of its matter or body. This is clear from the fact that the same sperm insofar as it undergoes a different kind of change can become a male or a female animal, because, when the heat at work is strong, a male is generated, but when it is weak, a female is generated. But this could not be the case or come about if male and female differed specifically; for specifically different things are not generated from one and the same kind of sperm because it is the sperm that

> contains the active power, and every natural agent acts by way of a determinate form by which it produces its like. It follows then that male and female do not differ formally, and that they do not differ specifically.[492]

For St. Thomas, the difference between things was always a matter of degree, not of absolute differences in kind. Therefore, male and female differ in degrees of actuality within the limits established by their species identity.

In another important development—derived from his Aristotelian heritage—St. Thomas argued for the absolute integration of body and soul, or of human materiality and rationality. Claiming that "the body is related to the soul as potentiality is to act," St. Thomas presents the relation of soul and body not as a struggle between two opposing and hostile entities, but rather as a closely knit association of "like to like, in the sense that potency resembles its act."[493] In the *Summa Contra Gentiles* Thomas concludes: "The soul is the form of the animated body."[494]

By rejecting the neo-Platonic claim that the definition of man contained reference only to the soul, Thomas concludes in *On the Power of God*: "Thus the definition of man which signifies his essence, includes flesh and bones."[495] The philosopher furthermore accepts Boethius's definition of a person that includes reference to individuality as well as to the other factors just mentioned. "Accordingly we reply that the person signifies nothing else but an individual substance of a rational nature."[496] So the body is a necessary aspect of personal identity both for individuals and for the species in general.

In the *Summa Theologiae*, St. Thomas describes the integration of rationality, materiality and individuality in the species man as follows:

> For as it belongs to the very conception of "this man" that he have this soul and this flesh and bone, so it belongs to the very conception of "man" that he have soul, flesh, and bone.[497]

This insistence on the necessary integration of body into personal identity has important consequences for the philosophy of sex identity. For St. Thomas, female identity or male identity cannot be lost in favour of a neutral sex identity such as was suggested by John Scotus Erigena, nor can the body of a woman, for example, be regarded as a prison to be escaped, as suggested by Plato or Porphyry.[489] The loss of female or male identity is an impossibility when the body is included in the definition of the person.

St. Thomas recognized the philosophical consequences of this view of the necessary connection of soul and body as actuality and potentiality, or like to like, in a consideration of the Christian theory of resurrection. In the *Summa Contra Gentiles* he said, "It is, then, contrary to the nature of the soul to be without the body. . . . Therefore, the immortality of souls seems to demand a further resurrection of the bodies."[499]

The intimate connection between a particular woman's body and soul, or a particular man's body and soul is so important that Thomas argued against the notion that a soul can be attached to different bodies. In short, he rejected reincarnation or the transmigration of souls: "As regards philosophy, according to which determinate matters and determinate movable things are assigned to determinate movers, . . . the soul resumes the same body that it has left."[500] This affirmation for the necessary connection between a particular soul and body in the *Summa Contra Gentiles* is further amplified in *On the Power of God*, where Thomas concluded: "The soul's nature cannot be perfect unless it be united to the body."[501]

For the theory of resurrection this means that a woman will receive her own renewed female body and a man his own renewed male body. Thomas was well aware of the arguments that if a woman's body is a kind of imperfection, then the resurrection might change this imperfect female body into a more perfect male body. He argued that the division of sex itself is more perfect than a single sex and therefore:

> The frailty of the feminine sex is not in opposition to the perfection of the risen, for this frailty is not due to a shortcoming of nature, but to an intention of nature. And this very distinction of nature among human beings will point out the perfection of nature and the divine wisdom as well, which disposes all things in a certain order.[502]

Consequently, woman and man, in the full integrity of their sexuality, will be present at the resurrection:

> One ought, nevertheless, not hold that among the bodies of the risen the feminine sex will be absent, as some have thought. For, since the resurrection is to restore the deficiencies of nature, nothing that belongs to perfection of nature will be denied to the bodies of the risen. Of course, just as other bodily members belong to the integrity of the human body, so do these which serve for generation—not only in men but also in women. Therefore, in each of the cases members of this sort will rise.[503]

In the *Summa Theologiae* the question of whether all will rise again in the male sex is specifically asked. Drawing on arguments from Aristotle, Thomas poses the negative side of the question:

> That which is produced incidentally and beside the intention of nature will not rise again, since all error will be removed at the resurrection. Now the female sex is produced beside the intention of nature, through a fault of the formative power of the seed which is unable to bring the matter of the fetus to the male form: wherefore the Philosopher says (*De Animal.* xvi, i.e., *De Generat. Animal*, ii) that *the female is a misbegotten male*. Therefore the female sex will not rise again.[504]

Using the distinction first suggested by his teacher, Albert the Great, Thomas forcefully answers this suggestion:

> Just as, considering the nature of the individual, a different quality is due to different men, so also, considering the nature of the individual, a different sex is due to different men. Moreover, this same diversity is becoming to the perfection of the species, the different degrees whereof are filled by this very difference of sex and quantity. Wherefore just as men will rise again of various stature, so will they rise again of different sex. . . . Although the begetting of a woman

> is beside the intention of a particular nature, it is in the intention of universal nature, which requires both sexes for the perfection of the human species.[505]

Thomas recognized that the logical conclusion of an Aristotelian sex polarity for the doctrine of the resurrection would be that women would be changed into men. Since the resurrection was to change all imperfections to perfections, and since woman was an imperfect generation, she would be changed into the perfect, or male, human form. However, the Christian philosopher rejected this logical conclusion by drawing a distinction between imperfection in particular nature and perfection in general nature. In this way, he opened the door to a new support for sex complementarity. That is, the general intention of nature, or God, involved the claim that two sexes were better than one, and the "imperfection" of the generation of an individual woman was balanced by the "perfection" of women's generation in general.

Generation

St. Thomas began to write his own theories on generation just after St. Albert had completed his twenty volumes of commentaries on Aristotle.[506] It is not surprising, therefore, that he based his concept of woman in relation to man in this category almost completely upon his teacher's philosophy. St. Thomas accepted and transmitted Aristotle's basic claim that the birth of an individual woman was the result of a kind of mistake in nature. In the *Disputed Questions on Truth*, St. Thomas stated:

> The active principle in the male seed always tends towards the generation of a male offspring, which is more perfect than the female. From this it follows that conception of a female offspring is something of an accident in the order of nature—insofar as it is not the result of the natural causality of the particular agent.[507]

In the *Summa Theologiae*, St. Thomas listed some of the ways this accident occurred:

> For the active power in the seed of the male tends to produce something like itself, perfect in masculinity; but the procreation of a female is the result either of the debility of the active power, or some unsuitability of the material, or of some change affected by external influences, like the south wind, for example, which is damp, as we are told by Aristotle.[508]

When a perfect instance of human generation occurred, a male was produced. The man, an example of the perfect union of the active power of seed with material suitable for human life, reflected the image of God as pure act. The sex polarity contained in this view is repeated by St. Thomas in his commentary on the *Sentences* of Peter Lombard. Drawing once again on the philosophy of Aristotle, he wrote:

> The generation of woman occurs, as is said in *De Animalibus* 18 or *De Generatione Animalum* 4.1, from that which the seed cannot overpower in the nature of woman to guide it in the final arrangement of the perfect sex.[509]

Again the view of man as the "perfect sex" and woman as the "imperfect sex" is qualified by the distinction between nature as universal and nature as particular. The analysis in the commentary on the *Sentences* states:

> Although woman is beyond the intention of a particular nature which acts in the seed, intending to produce offspring perfectly like the one generating, nevertheless it is not beyond the intention of the universal nature.[510]

In the *Summa Theologiae* this theory is repeated:

> Only as regards nature in the individual is female something defective and "manqué.". . . But with reference to nature in the species as a whole, the female is not something "manqué," but is according to the tendency of nature, and is directed to the work of creation.[511]

The Latin word represented by the French *manqué* is *occasionatum*. This word implies "missing the mark." Had the act of individual generation gone well, then the active power of the male seed would have hit the mark and a man would have been generated. Aristotle implied that this was the proper aim of all generation. St. Thomas, following St. Albert, had to explain how nature, which was created by God, allowed the mark to be missed so much of the time. He concluded that God willed this to happen so that the human race might have continuity. God intended woman to be generated and arranged for the mark to be missed approximately half the time. In this way, God created the world with a potential for the generation of both woman and man.

In direct contrast to John Scotus Erigena, who had argued that the division into male and female sexes was the result of a fall from original nature, St. Thomas, in the *Summa Theologiae*, defended the generation of women and men as being willed by God:

> Now the tendency of nature of a species as a whole derives from God, who is the general author of nature. And therefore when He established a nature, He brought into being not only male but the female too.[512]

In this distinction, Aristotle's sex polarity was modified by the view that God willed sexual differentiation in general, even though the individual generation of a woman was a defect in the order of nature. Therefore, Thomas introduces the same modification encountered in the consideration of opposites, namely that while, individually, woman is inferior to man, when considered generally it is a greater perfection to have two sexes than to have only one. Therefore, Thomas Aquinas suggests a sex polarity to explain the generation of individuals and a sex complementarity to explain the continuity of generation of the species.

St. Thomas made extensive use of St. Albert's commentary on Aristotle's *Generation of Animals* to explain the differences between the mother and father in human generation.[513] In the *Summa Theologiae* he stated:

> In the higher animals brought into being through coitus, the active power resides in the male's semen, as Aristotle says, while the material of the fetus is supplied by the female.[514]

The mother supplied the specific material that was capable of being transformed into human life.[515]

The specific contribution of the man to generation was described by St. Thomas in more detail. He argued that the seed of the father did not directly transmit the soul or form to the fetus, but rather gave what could more properly be termed "soul power." In an early work, *On the Power of God*, he explained this activity as follows:

> From the moment of its severence the semen contains not a soul but a soul power; and this power is based on the spirit contained in the semen which by nature is spumy and consequently contains corporeal spirit. Now this spirit acts by disposing matter and forming it for the reception of the soul.[516]

The seed of the father, then, acted by disposing the material of the mother in such a way that it would become a living child. This theory is repeated in the *Summa Theologiae*: "Man begets his like in that by the semen's power the matter is disposed to receive a certain kind of form."[517]

The process by which the material of the mother slowly was transformed into a fetus is described in great detail by Aquinas. First, the material was given a vegetative soul.[518] When the subsequently formed material reached a certain level of development, the sentient soul began to function.[519] After this entity reached another stage of development, the rational soul was given to it directly by God.[520] Therefore, the material was provided by the mother, the power for the vegetative and sentient soul by the father, and the rational soul by God.[521]

St. Thomas believed that the respective contributions of the parents and God did not imply that the soul was divided into parts, as Plato had argued. He also disagreed with St. Albert, who had argued that the lower soul did not disappear but merely evolved into a higher identity.[522] His own view, as stated in *On the Power of God*, was as follows:

> By the formative force that is in the semen from the beginning, the form of the semen is set aside and another form induced, and when this has been set aside yet another form induced, and when this has been set aside yet another comes on the scene, and thus the vegetal form makes its first appearance; and this being set aside, a soul both vegetal and sensitive is induced; and this being set aside a soul at once vegetal, sensitive, and rational is induced, not by the aforesaid force but by the Creator.[523]

In answer to the question of why God did not simply provide the rational soul, which included other functions, at the outset, St. Thomas argued that the fetus had to have achieved a certain level of development before the rational soul could be accepted. Therefore, the father's seed served as a way of preparing the material for the eventual contribution of God.[524]

The most significant consequence of St. Thomas's claim that woman provided only matter to generation was his conclusion that she was the "passive sex." The medieval philosopher described procreative patterns as falling along a continuum. At the bottom of the scale were those kinds of vegetative life that did not procreate by themselves, but that depended completely on outside forces, such as the heat of the sun. Next, on an ascending scale, were those kinds of living things that generated by themselves, such as plants that procreated with seed. These were described by St. Thomas as containing both active and passive powers of generation. Then, in more complicated animals, procreation was dependent upon the union of two different things: "Next up the scale are the perfect animals which have the active power of procreation in the male sex and the passive in the female."[525] St. Thomas frequently repeated this view in the *Summa Theologia*:

> In every kind of generation there is required an active and passive capacity. Since then in all living things that show a distinction of sex the active capacity is in the male and the passive in the female, the rhythm of nature demands that male and female should mate in copulation for procreating.[526]

A basic principle of St. Thomas's metaphysics was that passivity was inferior to activity. This judgement had clear consequences for the process of generation:

> The active power which is in the semen cannot be caused by the mother (although some indeed maintain this), because the woman is not an active principle but a passive one.[527]

The devaluation of woman in relation to man was expressed in the devaluation of mother in relation to father:

> The fleshy generation of animals is perfected by an active power and by a passive power; and it is from the active power that one is named "father," and from the passive power that one is named "mother."[528]

Man, as father, shared an active power with God, the Father. Woman did not share in this identity.

St. Thomas argued that the more passive something was, the better it could yield to the active power. Lack of yielding then became a sign of a defect in material. In the following passage, the way in which a male and female twin might be produced was considered:

> In the conception of twins, the matter is separated by the operation of nature; and one part of the matter yields to the active principle more than the other part does because of the latter's deficiency. Consequently, in one part a female is generated, in the other, a male.[529]

In the theory of generation, a basic relationship of superior to inferior resulted from the characterization of one sex as containing the active principle and the other the passive one.

A rather interesting complexity in Aquinas's thought becomes apparent when his two characterizations of matter as passivity and potentiality are compared. These two descriptions lead to two ways of understanding the relation of matter and form. The list on the following page makes this point clearer.

If form and matter are considered from the perspective of actuality and potentiality, then their relationship is one of cooperation of like to like; when they are considered from the perspective of activity and passivity, their relationship is one of contraries.

actuality ———————— form ———————— activity

like to like   of   contrary to contrary

potentiality———————— matter ————————passivity

How does this difference relate to the concept of woman and man? St. Thomas's theory may be summarized as follows:

like to like
potentiality to actuality

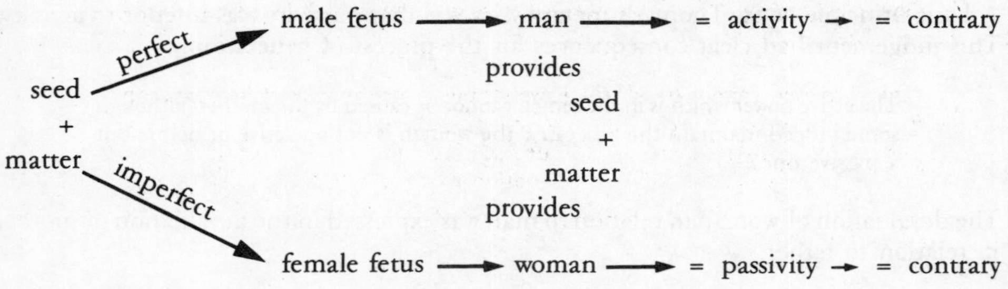

potentiality to actuality
like to like

The internal tension between the association of male and female identity with the contraries of activity and passivity, or with the similarities of actuality and potentiality indicates the general struggle this philosopher had in modifying Aristotle's rigid sex polarity. The framework of potentiality and actuality is much more consistent with the contemporary scientific understanding of the process of generation. For example, the gonads of a fetus have the potential to be actualized into male anatomy with the injection of the hormone testosterone. If this hormone is lacking, then the potential remains within the framework of female anatomy. Therefore, it is possible to say that in some sense the female anatomical nature of the fetus has the potential to be actualized into the male anatomy. This is a movement of like to like, not of a battle between contraries.

The rigid Aristotelian sex polarity, springing from Democritus, which interprets the interaction of the sexes as a battleground between two hostile forces, one actively pursuing its end, the other passively resisting its conqueror, does not as accurately explain the process of the determination of the sex of the fetus. Therefore, Thomas was misled both by his teacher Albert and by the direct inheritance of the Aristotelian rationale for sex polarity. The extent of his misunderstanding of this process is revealed in two theological examples of the application of his philosophy to generation. The first concerns the role of Mary as Mother of Christ, and the second the role of Eve in the transmission of original sin.

St. Thomas believed that the generation of Christ occurred through the union of passive material supplied by Mary and the active soul power supplied by God. In the *Summa Theologiae*, he considered the nature of these contributions:

> According to Aristotle, the male semen does not play the role of "matter" in the conception of animals; it is rather prime agent, so to speak, while the female alone supplies the matter. So even if male semen were lacking in Christ's conception it does not follow that the necessary matter was missing.[530]

The active power was not supplied by a man, because Mary was a virgin at the moment of conception. The union of God with humanity was then described as a union of the active power provided by the Holy Spirit with a passive power provided by Mary. The specific contribution of Mary was considered by St. Thomas in detail. He was determined to reject any argument that Mary's contribution could be characterized as active:

> Some say that the Blessed Virgin effected something actively in the conception of Christ, . . .
>
> This, however, cannot stand, since everything is for the sake of its operation, as it is said, nature would not for the purpose of the work of generation distinguish between male and female sex unless there were a distinction between their operations. Now in generation there are two distinct operations, that of the agent and that of the patient. It follows that the entire active part is on the male side, and the passive part on the female side. . . .
>
> Since it was not given to the Blessed Virgin to be father of Christ but mother, the consequence is that she did not receive an active power for the conception of Christ. . . .
>
> So it is to be held that in the actual conception of Christ, the Blessed Virgin did not actively effect anything in the conceiving, but ministered the matter only.[531]

Mary's only active role consisted in preparing herself to receive the Divine seed. The sex polarity of the Aristotelian theory of generation was repeated by St. Thomas in this consideration of the Blessed Virgin:

> The generative power in the female is imperfect in relation to that which is in the male. And so must as in the arts, an inferior art disposes the matter while the superior art imposes a form, as is said in the *Physics*, so female generative power prepares the matter while male active power fashions the matter which has been prepared.[532]

The second theological argument to which St. Thomas applied the philosophical concept of woman's role in generation concerned the role of Eve in the transmission of original sin. For St. Thomas, original sin was understood to be a kind of disorder in the soul that accompanied all human beings descended from Adam. Original sin was differentiated from actual sin in that the former was not the result of an act of will while the latter did imply such an act:

> So too the disorder which is in an individual man, a descendent of Adam, is not voluntary by reason of his personal will, but by reason of the will of the

> first parent, who through a generative impulse, exerts upon all who descend from him by way of origin even as the will of the soul moves bodily members to their various activities.
>
> Accordingly, the sin passing in this way from the first parent to his descendents is called "original"; as a sin passing from the soul to the body's members is called "actual."[533]

Original sin was transmitted through a "generative impulse" from the moment Adam and Eve brought about a disorder in Paradise by an act of will to disobey God. All subsequent persons, then, were born with a tendency to bring about disorder in the universe through acts of their own will.

Since the transmission of sin demanded an active impulse, St. Thomas concluded that it had to be given through the seed of the father. The mother's passive contribution of material would not be able to transmit an active impulse. He concluded, rather astonishingly, that Eve had nothing to do with the transmission of original sin:

> Now it is the teaching of philosophers that the active causality in generation is from the father, the mother merely providing the material. Therefore, original sin is not contracted from the mother but from the father.
>
> Accordingly if Eve and not Adam had sinned, their children would not have contracted original sin. And conversely, they would have contracted it if Adam alone and not Eve had sinned.[534]

While it may appear comforting for women to learn that they have nothing to do with the transmission of original sin, at closer examination St. Thomas's theory is still damaging to the concept of woman. It implied that Eve's existence had no significance beyond her generative function. She had no moral or religious role to play as "mother of life."

Therefore, the passive role of Mary in the life of Christ was a mere imitation of the passive role of Eve in the life of subsequent generations. St. Thomas recognized this parallel:

> We grant that Christ was a descendent of the first parent of the flesh. For all that, he did not incur the contamination of original sin as the fourth argument concluded. For it was only the matter of His human body which He received from the first parent.[535]

Mary, a descendent of Adam, could not herself transmit original sin because she only provided the material in generation. St. Thomas, therefore, did not believe it necessary to devote intense arguments, as had St. Albert, to the lack of original sin in Mary.[536] Instead, he concentrated on the purity of her material contribution, that is, the purity of her blood. This concept of woman, through its emphasis on passivity, reduced woman to a kind of invisible presence in generation.

This consideration of Thomas Aquinas's theory of generation has shown the extent to which he incorporated Aristotle's sex-polarity arguments. Woman was described as a passive principle in generation, man as an active one. The female fetus was considered a defective generation in relation to the male fetus because it did not perfectly receive the form transmitted through the seed of the father. At the same time, St. Thomas modified the radical sex polarity contained in this view through his insistence that the intention of nature in general was to produce females. This modification allowed for the affirmation of the "perfection of the variety of sex in nature," while at the same time accepting the inherent inferiority of the generation of the female in individual cases.

Wisdom

The sex polarity present in St. Thomas's theory of generation also emerged in the category of wisdom. The relation of woman to wisdom was different from that of man. Thomas Aquinas developed a two-fold path to wisdom: philosophy used the "natural light of reason," while theology used the "light of divine revelation."[537] Aquinas believed that these two avenues to wisdom were complementary instead of conflicting. As expressed in the *Summa Theologiae*: "Since grace does not scrap nature but brings it to perfection, so also natural reason should assist faith."[538] Maintaining that theology was the superior of the two paths to wisdom, Aquinas described the relation of theology and philosophy as analogous to queen and handmaid, statesman and soldier, or architect and worker.[539]

For Aquinas, the proper object of knowledge was not the feminine *sophia*, but rather the masculine *logos*, or Son of the Father. In the *Compendium of Theology*, Aquinas described the activity of knowing in terms of a sexual analogy:

> A being is said to be conceived in a corporeal way if it is formed in the womb of a living animal by a life-giving energy, in virtue of the active function of the male and the passive function of the female, in whom the conception takes place. . . . In a similar manner, what the intellect comprehends is formed in the intellect, the intelligible object being, as it were, the active principle, and the intellect the passive principle.[540]

The intelligence is characterized as female in relation to the object of thought that, as male, initiates the process of conception.

The question now is whether women and men had different relationships to the thinking process. The issue settled on a consideration of the different relations of the two sexes to the intellectual virtues. In the *Summa Theologiae*, St. Thomas defined this as follows: "A correct judgement made through rational investigation belongs to the wisdom which is an intellectual virtue."[541] In his commentary on Aristotle's *Politics*, St. Thomas repeated the Greek philosopher's claim that woman's natural powers of reasoning were weak:

> But since a woman is free, she has the capacity for understanding but her capacity is weak. The reason for this is on account of the changeableness of nature, her reason weakly adheres to plans, but quickly is removed from them because of emotions, for example, of desire, or anger, or fear, or something else of the kind.[542]

It would appear to follow from this that woman is held under the sway of the lower powers of her intelligence, and that it is therefore more difficult for her to sustain the constancy of the rational investigation that is necessary to intellectual virtue.

In another approach to wisdom, St. Thomas claims in the *Summa Theologiae* that "To govern and judge belongs to the wise person."[543] In the same text we find the following qualification of woman's capacity to rule made by the philosopher directly following a passage in which woman's defective generation has been considered:

> For the human group would have lacked the benefit of order had some of its members not been governed by others who were wiser. Such is the subjection in which woman is by nature subordinate to man, because the power of rational discernment is by nature stronger in man.[544]

The implication in this passage is that St. Thomas is following Aristotle's claim that since the higher powers of discursive reasoning are "without authority" in woman's mind, she ought to be ruled by a man whose rational discernment is capable of ordering both his mind and hers.

In his consideration of Aristotle's *Politics*, St. Thomas appears to favour Gorgias's attempt to distinguish virtues for different groups of people. In this case, he is leading up to making a particular separation of virtues for women and for men:

> Those who wish to speak about human actions in the universal, so much they deceive themselves, because they cannot plainly arrive at the truth. . . . Indeed how much better do they argue who enumerate the virtues in a specific way, as Gorgias did . . . because acts are individual. . . . And therefore as a certain poet wrote something particularly about a woman pertaining to her excellence, thus also it ought to be considered about them all.[545]

The particular virtue being considered is that of speech for men and silence for women. Thomas Aquinas signals his approval of the Aristotelian theory by his addition to the prescriptions of St. Paul:

> For what is appropriate for the ornament of a woman or her integrity, that she is silent, proceeds from the modesty which is owed to women; but this does not relate to the ornament of a man, instead, it is fitting that he speaks. Therefore, the Apostle warns (I Cor. 14: 34, 35) *Let woman keep silent in the churches and if they wish to learn anything, let them ask their husbands at home.*[546]

It is difficult not to think here of the implications of the view that silence is a virtue for women for a woman such as Hildegard of Bingen, who had preached throughout Germany. The development of intellectual virtue for men demands the opportunity to engage in public *disputatio*. It is precisely this vigorous exchange and debate that enabled Abelard, St. Albert, and St. Thomas to sharpen their theories and arguments in order to better approximate truth through the mutual use of the "natural light of reason." The view that it was woman's special virtue to remain silent in public was bound to lessen the possibility of women achieving any degree of intellectual virtue. Indeed, it would add to the perceived weakness of the female intellect, for it takes constant exercise of the intellect to develop the capacity for reasoned argument.

It must now be asked whether Thomas Aquinas followed in the footsteps of his master Albert in claiming that Mary reversed the general situation of woman in the category of wisdom. In the *Summa Theologiae*, St. Thomas makes the distinction between intellectual virtue and the gift of wisdom: "The gift of wisdom differs from the acquired virtue of wisdom. The latter comes through human effort, the former *comes down from above*."[547] It follows that Mary did not have the acquired virtue of wisdom, but rather the gift of wisdom:

> The Blessed Virgin unquestionably received, to an intense degree, the gift of wisdom, the grace to work miracles and even to prophesy, just as Christ. Still, she was not given them to use as Christ used them, since their use was kept consonant with her way of life. She used wisdom in contemplation. Thus Luke says, *she treasured all these things and pondered them in her heart.* But she did not use wisdom by teaching since this was not thought becoming to women; I am not giving permission for a woman to teach.[548]

St. Thomas's prescription against teaching for women brings back the recollection of Heloise teaching her nuns Latin, Greek and Hebrew, or Herrad of Landsberg teaching her nuns through the encyclopedia *Hortus Deliciarum*. The question here is whether St. Thomas believed that women ought always to be silent. Was Mary in some way superior rather than inferior through her gift of wisdom?

While it is difficult to answer this question, St. Thomas does imply that the gift of wisdom is higher than the acquired virtue of wisdom. In the *Summa Theologiae* he states: "From the fact then that the gift is higher than the virtue of wisdom it gets closer to God by a certain union of soul."[549] Thomas's own life offers a clue to this puzzle, for towards the end of his life he had a personal experience that led him to "hang up his writing instruments on the wall," and to give up all further philosophical research. The experience led Thomas to state: "All I have written seems to me like a straw compared to what has now been revealed to me."[550] The hundreds of books using discursive reasoning appeared to the philosopher and theologian of little value in comparison to the direct experience of infused wisdom. It would seem, then, that he did believe that the natural weakness of women's intellect was of little importance in the general order of things. Mary's gift of wisdom surpassed all the efforts of philosophers and theologians to discover through thought the exercise of their powers of discursive reasoning.

In this shift of emphasis away from simple temporal activities for philsophers and theologians, St. Thomas has once again modifed the theory of sex polarity in the category of wisdom. His general view of the temporal world followed Aristotelian lines of reasoning by arguing that women were inferior to men in discursive reasoning because of the weakness of their intellect, which resulted from their defective generation. In the interaction with the spiritual world, however, women as well as men were capable of infused wisdom. Therefore, depending on how much value is given to Thomas's statement that his discursive works are "like straw," the Aristotelian sex polarity in his category of wisdom is modified by a move to sex complementarity.

Virtue

St. Thomas developed a complex theory of the two different kinds of virtue: cardinal and theological. The category of cardinal virtues included the four "natural virtues" previously accepted by most philosophers: temperance; courage; justice; and wisdom (or prudence).[551] Theological virtues incorporated the three virtues of faith, hope, and charity.[552] The cardinal virtues could be achieved by the effort of the person alone, while the theological virtues needed the "power of God."[553] Aquinas concludes: "Intellectual and moral virtues can be caused in us by our own acts. . . . Therefore there is no good reason why they should be caused in us by infusion."[554]

Virtue is associated, for Thomas, with the capacity to order the self properly.[555] It must, therefore, be asked whether women and men have the same or a different relationship to the capacity for ordering. In a consideration of the cardinal virtues St. Thomas expands on a passage from Aristotle's *Politics*. Aristotle had simply stated that the passivity of women in sexual intercourse is natural and therefore should not be judged under the moral categories of temperance or intemperance (continence or incontinence).[556] St. Thomas goes far beyond the Greek philosopher in stating:

> He offers the example of women in whom, for the most part, reason flourishes very little because of the imperfect nature of their body. Because of this they do not govern the emotions. Hence wise and brave women are rarely found, and so women cannot be called continent and incontinent without qualifiction.[557]

For Thomas, women appear not to be prone to acquiring the cardinal virtues of continence, wisdom or courage because they are incapable of ordering their emotions. Aquinas concludes that women participate in the cardinal virtues, but in a lesser way than do men.

In the following commentary on Aristotle's *Politics*, this view is amplified:

> In a similar way moral virtues must be considered; for all share in them, but not in the same way; but each one participates in them as far as it is necessary for the appropriate role. From which it follows that the one who rules, whether, a state, servants, woman or sons, must possess a perfected moral excellence because his work is simply the work of an architect, that is of the principal builder. For just as the principal artist directs and orders the servants of art who work with their hands, so the leader directs his subjects; and therefore he has the capacity of reason which compares in the same way as the chief artist to the interior parts of the soul.[558]

The weakness of woman's natural intelligence led to her weak capacity for ordering, which in turn led to her being placed under the rule of a man. Aquinas continues to develop Aristotle's theory in his commentary on the *Politics*.

> And thus it is right that the one who rules has perfected reason; but each one of the others who are subject, has as much of reason and excellence as the one who rules causes in them, that is, as much as is right that they possess, which suffices to follow the direction of the leader by fulfilling his commands. And so it is clear that there is some moral excellence, that is, temperance, courage,

> and justice, nevertheless it is not the same for man and woman and other subjects, as Socrates thought; but the strength of the man is for the purpose of ruling, in order that he may not neglect what must be done out of fear; but in a woman a subordinate and supplementary strength exists, in order that she may not neglect to perform the appropriate service out of fear.[559]

It could be argued that St. Thomas was simply repeating Aristotle's theory and that he was not necessarily admitting his agreement. Therefore, it is significant that he repeated this opinion in the development of the view that a woman, who is by nature weaker in her reasoning capacity, ought to be placed under the rule of man. In the *Summa Contra Gentiles* Thomas made the following statement:

> For the female needs the male, not merely for the sake of generation, as in the case of other animals, but also for the sake of government. Since the male is both more perfect in his reasoning and stronger in his powers.[560]

In the same text, Aquinas joined Aristotle's views with the story of Eve's creation from the side of Adam to conclude that it was woman's virtue to obey and man's to rule:

> As Aristotle says, with man, male and female are not only joined together for the purposes of procreation, as with other animals, but to establish a home life, in which man and woman work together at some things, and in which the man is the head of the woman. So the woman was rightly formed from the man, as her origin and chief.[561]

St. Thomas clearly followed the sex-polarity tradition that held that woman and man had a different relation to the virtues of obedience and ruling. The primary characteristic of virtue—to govern—was associated with man, while a secondary or derived virtue—to be governed by someone else—was associated with woman.

In another passage from the *Summa Theologiae*, St. Thomas appeared to raise the possibility that woman was not necessarily subjected to the rule of man until after the Fall. However, on closer examination, the same passage pointed to his belief in an original weakness in woman's reasoning powers that would imply that her obedience was natural:

> Subjection and inferiority are a result of sin; for it was after sin that woman was told, *Thou shalt be under the power of the man*; and Gregory says that where we have done no wrong, we are all equal. Yet woman is by nature of lower capacity and quality than man; for the active cause is always more honorable than the passive, as Augustine says.[562]

Once again, the basic theory of the difference in eminence or degrees of perfection enter into St. Thomas's view of the concept of woman in relation to man. The imperfect reflection of the image of God in woman led to her weakness of mind, and to her need for the virtue of obedience.

In a significant passage from the *Summa Theologiae*, Thomas argues that the relation between women and men of ruling and obedience in the natural world has no consequences for their relationship after the resurrection. In the discussion about whether woman will be changed into man after the resurrection, the following argument is made: Woman is subject to man in the natural order. Therefore woman will rise again not in the female but in the male sex. Aquinas refutes this claim by an argument for sex complementarity:

> Woman is subject to man on account of the frailty of nature, as regards both vigor of soul and strength of body. After the resurrection, however, the difference in those points will be not on account of the difference of sex, but by reason of the difference of merits. Hence the conclusion does not follow.[563]

After the resurrection, there will be both men and women, but neither sex will be superior or inferior to the other by nature. This view supports the significant differentiation and equality of the sexes. Any variety in perfection will occur purely on the "grounds of merit," that is, on how well a person achieved perfection on the level of virtue. However, while men and women live together on earth, the man by nature rules because he is the "perfect sex" and woman by nature obeys.

There are interesting consequences from the theory of the natural virtue of ruling for man and the natural virtue of obeying for women. The first concerns Thomas's argument about the divine right of kings, and the second about the reservation of the sacrament of the priesthood for men.

In a work entitled *On Kingship*, Thomas argued that the rule of one person was always better than the rule of two. "Among bees, there is one king bee and in the whole universe there is one God, Maker and Ruler of all things. . . . It follows that it is best for a human multitude to be ruled by one person."[564] The one ruler, in reflecting the nature of God should be male: "Hence the man ruling a perfect (i.e., most self-sufficient) community (i.e., a city or a province), is automatically called the king. The ruler of a household is called a father."[565] Once again, the male is characterized as more perfectly reflecting the eminence of degree of the image of God.

In the second example, in an appendix to the *Summa Theologiae*, St. Thomas considers "Whether the Female Sex is an Impediment to Receiving Orders." His argument concludes: "Since it is not possible in the female sex to signify eminence of degree, for a woman is in the state of subjection, it follows that she cannot receive the sacrament of Orders."[566] The argument depends upon the nature of the female body as less perfectly reflecting the image of Christ that is represented by the priest. Thomas uses an analogy to make his meaning clear. Just as the sacrament of the sick demands the body of a sick person to be efficacious, so the sacrament of the priesthood demands a male body in order to be able to signify the eminence of degrees and the corresponding capacity to rule.

Thomas believed in separate spheres of activity for women and men. Drawing upon the spurious *Oeconomicus*, attributed to Aristotle, Thomas states, in his commentary on the *Sentences* of Lombard:

> As Aristotle says in *Economicus* 1:3 that male and female are joined in the human race not only for reproduction of offspring but also for the sharing of works in a common life, so that each one's works may suffice for the other. From this it seems that the works of man and woman differ. Because in the sharing of

> life and the rule of the home the man is the head of the woman, the male among humans has more of the principles of source with respect to the woman than among other animals. For this reason, it was more fitting that the female human being be taken from the male.[567]

In this fascinating passage, Thomas has linked the theory of generation in which the male is the better "principle of source" with the theory of virtue in which man rules over woman, and with the activity of virtue in which woman is limited to the private sphere and man to the active sphere. The invocation of Aristotle, even though it is a spurious work, simply reinforces this integrated ground for sex polarity. The content of the spurious *Oeconomicus* will be considered, along with other such texts attributed to Aristotle, in Chapter V of this book, where the far-reaching implications of the Aristotelian Revolution are considered.[568]

Thomas frequently invoked the more perfect way in which man served as a principle of nature to differentiate virtuous activities. For example, in the *Summa Theologiae*, under a consideration of the virtue of charity, he asked, "Whether a man ought to love his mother more than his father?" The argument concluded:

> Strictly speaking, however, the father should be loved more than the mother. For the father and mother are loved as principles of our natural origin. Now the father is principle in a more excellent way than the mother, because he is the active principle, while the mother is a passive and material principle. Consequently, strictly speaking, the father is to be loved more.[569]

Aristotle had also considered woman as inferior to man in the natural virtue of friendship. In an interesting modification of Aristotle's theory, Thomas avoided all reference to friendships of inequality. Instead, he argued that woman is an equal friend to man. In the *Summa Contra Gentiles* Aquinas states:

> The greater the friendship is, the more solid and long lasting it will be. Now, there seems to be the greatest friendship between husband and wife, for they are united not only in the act of fleshy union, which produces certain gentle association even among beasts, but also in partnership of the whole range of domestic activity.[570]

Even more specifically, St. Thomas ignored Aristotle's view that women were not capable of true friendship, and he appealed to an Aristotelian argument—that it is only possible to befriend a few people—to support the notion of friendship between man and woman:

> Furthermore, strong friendship is not possible in regard to many people, as is evident from the philosopher in *Ethics* VIII. Therefore, if a wife has one husband, but the husband has several wives, the friendship will not be equal on both sides.[571]

St. Thomas stated that women and men needed to be free in relation to one another, in order for the friendship to be equal:

> Friendship consists in equality. So, if it is not lawful for the wife to have several husbands, since this is contrary to certainty as to offspring, it would not be lawful, on the other hand, for a man to have several wives, for the friendship of a wife for her husband would not be free but somewhat servile.[572]

The equality of friendship between husband and wife is further reflected in Thomas's consideration of adultery. In the *Summa Theologiae* he argued:

> Adultery is not only a sin of lust but also a sin of injustice. From this latter point of view it can be considered as a kind of greed. . . . Adultery is worse than simple theft because a wife is more dear than earthly possessions.[573]

Thomas frequently argued against the inequality of wife in relation to husband. In the following passages from *Summa Contra Gentiles*, although the argument begins with an assumption of the difference in virtue of ruling and obeying for man and woman, the result is that neither sex has the right to divorce the other:

> It seems obviously inappropriate for a woman to be able to put away her husband, because a wife is naturally subject to her husband as governor, and it is not within the power of a person subject to another to depart from his rule. So, it would be against the natural order if a wife were able to abandon her husband.[574]

On different grounds, Aquinas argued that a man ought not to be able to divorce a woman:

> Therefore, if a husband were permitted to abandon a wife, the society of husband and wife would not be an association of equals, but instead a sort of slavery on the part of the wife.[575]

In trying to understand how Thomas was able to modify Aristotle's sex-polarity arguments about friendship, it is important to consider that for a Christian philosopher marriage was not simply a natural association between men and women, rather, it was a sacrament of the Church. In a move that went against Church tradition, which understood marriage as something to be avoided if possible, St. Thomas saw it as something good. In a similar way he also interpreted sexual pleasure within the sacrament of marriage as good. In the *Summa Theologiae* he stated: "The abundance of pleasure in a well-ordered sex act is not inimical to right reason."[576] As a result of these views, Thomas did not devalue woman as such, even though he understood her to be a less perfect result of generation. There is not in Thomas any of the ridicule of woman found in other writers such as Jerome, Juvenal, Heloise, Capellanus or Map.

In a similar way, Thomas argued against the Pythagorean association of woman with evil in *On the Power of God*:

> Pythagoras said that things were divided into two genera, good and evil; in the genus of good things he placed all perfect things, such as light, males, rest and the like, while in the genus of evil he placed darkness, females and the like. . . . Wherefore Pythagoras placed women, as being imperfect, in the genus of

> evil. . . . Now this error is utterly impossible; since all things must be traced to one first principle which is good.[577]

After a consideration of woman's relation to the natural virtues, there is also the question of her relation to the theological virtues of faith, hope and charity. In the *Summa Theologiae*, Thomas defines a theological virtue as one that is said "to be theological from having God as the object to which it adheres."[578] Since these virtues are in part due to the direct infusion of grace, it would follow that woman's nature would in no way be limited in relation to their practice. Therefore, in a similar way to that in which woman in the category of wisdom was able to receive infused wisdom, woman in the category of virtue was able to live out the theological virtues. Once again, Mary is presented as being the most perfect person. In a prayer written shortly before his death St. Thomas stated that "individual saints excelled in special virtues; Mary excelled in them all."[579]

The practice of the theological virtues over and above the natural virtues was the goal for women and men. The consequence of successfully achieving this goal was the sanctification of the persons involved. Female saints could be as perfect as male saints, for both achieved the total perfection or actualization that their natures allowed. Therefore, even though sex polarity may be the framework in which the potential for actualization of the two sexes was explained, the final result of this actualization opened to a sex complementarity.

In conclusion, then, St. Thomas, by incorporating the intellectual framework of sex polarity as first articulated by Aristotle, put forward a Christian philosophy of sex identity that presented a sex polarity on the level of nature—which moved into a sex complementarity on the level of grace. For after the resurrection, women and men, reunited with their bodies, will live in a perfection that is differentiated in value by the merit of their lives.

Thomas turned out to be the most influential philosopher in the Christian west. He taught at the University of Paris in the faculties of arts and theology, he taught at the University of Naples, and his several hundred books became the source of nearly all western Christian thought for centuries. St. Thomas was canonized in 1323, proclaimed a doctor of the Church and, in 1879, Pope Leo XIII insisted that Thomas's writings be taken as the basis for all theology. After Thomas's teacher, St. Albert, had returned from defending Thomas's views against the Bishop of Paris in 1277, he re-read all his student's works.

> At a solemn convocation convened by him, he put forward an exceedingly great and glorious commendation, concluding with the assertion that the latter's writings had put an end to the labours of all other men till the end of time, and that henceforth they would labour in vain.[580]

With this pronouncement, the stage was set for St. Thomas's thought to dominate the Christian world.

SUMMARY AND EVALUATION

HILDEGARD AS THE FOUNDRESS OF SEX COMPLEMENTARITY

One of the most striking aspects of this study of the concept of woman in relation to man in the second half of the medieval period is the slow but steady development of a philosophical foundation for sex complementarity. In western history sex complementarity had always been present in discussions of sex identity, but up to this point it appeared only in a peripheral way in comparison to the solid articulation of philosophical grounds for sex unity or sex polarity. Empedocles suggested sex complementarity in early Greek philosophy, and Augustine recognized its theological grounds in early Christian philosophy. It was not until Hildegard of Bingen, however, that sex complementarity was given a thorough defence as a theory of sex identity.

In attempting to assess why this breakthrough in the history of the philosophy of sex identity occurred in the twelfth century, several factors arise. The first one is the situation of women and men within the Benedictine tradition of education. For the first time in history, significant numbers of women and men together studied and discussed philosophy within the context of double monasteries. The example of Hilda of Whitby, Roswitha, St. Anselm, Heloise and Herrad all point to the release of creative energies and to the quality of writing that emerged within this situation in which women and men had equal access to the highest and broadest sources of knowledge. Therefore, it can be concluded that one central factor in the preparation for a philosophy of sex complementarity is the actual experience of women and men jointly participating in the practice of philosophy.

Within this context, the genius of Hildegard of Bingen had the opportunity to flower. Drawing upon the scientific knowledge available to her, Hildegard wove an intricate theory of the relations of the elements and humours to sex identity. Integrating the rational, material and spiritual aspects of human nature into a unified whole, Hildegard argued that women were equal to but significantly different from men. The individuality of human existence within this framework was limited in her analysis to four general types of women and four general types of men. However, within this limitation Hildegard revealed a sophisticated understanding of male and female interactions in both chaste and sexual relationships. Her drive for thoroughness and consistency across all four categories of opposites, generation, wisdom and virtue makes her the first western philosopher to articulate the complete concept of sex complementarity. Therefore, Hildegard rightfully holds the title of foundress of the philosophy of sex complementarity.

The legacy that Hildegard left was soon buried by the onrush of the Aristotelian Revolution. The greater sophistication of the Aristotelian method brought with it a plethora of arguments in favour of sex polarity. Hildegard's writings were left to languish inside monastic libraries for centuries. However, the tragedy of the negligence of her works at that time in history may now turn out to be of benefit to contemporary philosophers, for all her writings have been preserved and are now able to be analysed, evaluated, and developed. Therefore, the example of Hildegard can become as significant to the developing philosophy of sex complementarity as Plato was for sex unity or Aristotle for sex polarity. It is possible for contemporary philosophers to integrate and move beyond Hildegard in an attempt to articulate contemporary grounds for sex complementarity. This would mean, for example, using contemporary scientific knowledge about male and female identity as a starting point for an analysis of sex identity, which would include many of the same questions Hildegard asked. It would also imply seeking the same kind of integration of rationality, materiality and spirituality, while going further in developing a more contemporary understanding of the significance of the factor of individuality in understanding the person as such. In this way, Hildegard can finally be recognized as the foundress that she was, and she can begin to influence the direction of further considerations of sex identity that will one day go far beyond the limitations of her analysis and her age.

THE WEAKENING INFLUENCE OF PLATONIC GROUNDS FOR SEX UNITY

Another significant aspect of the philosophic age considered in this chapter is the progressive loss of Platonic or neo-Platonic arguments for sex unity. In comparison with the preceding chapter, in which there were several examples of philosophers emerging within the Platonic tradition of sex unity, in this latter period only a few remained loyal to that tradition. For example, Avicenná and Averroes within the Islamic philosophy, and Avicebron within the Jewish philosophy, appear to have argued at times for the equality of woman and man on the grounds that the body is an unimportant aspect of human identity. Anselm, in the Christian tradition, also argued that at the highest level of comprehension of the nature of God sex identity is irrelevant.

However, the devaluation of the body as a method for the introduction of equality between woman and man was less evident in philosophical arguments as the medieval period progressed. This occurred for two different reasons: in the first case, the belief in the reincarnation of the soul and of the independent existence of the soul in total isolation from the body was seriously challenged by Christian philosphers whose belief in the resurrection of the body demanded a different understanding of the relation of body and soul. Secondly, the influx of Aristotelian arguments that insisted upon the necessary integration of body and soul, like matter and form, challenged the Platonic division of matter and form or soul and body. Consequently, for Aristotelian Christians, the body was the central factor in personal identity. A consequence of this belief in the necessary integration of soul and body for the theory of sex identity, was that differences between women and men were philosophically significant.

By the end of the thirteenth century, Platonic grounds for sex unity had practically disappeared. It would not be until after the development of Cartesianism in the seventeenth century that a significantly new foundation for the philosophy of sex unity would appear in western thought. In the meantime, the sex neutrality suggested by Aristotelian logic provided a foundation for the rejection of sex differences within academic philosophy.

THE TENSION BETWEEN SEX COMPLEMENTARITY AND SEX POLARITY IN THE TWELFTH CENTURY

With the disappearance of a vital Platonic foundation for sex unity, the battle for precedence among theories of sex identity was relegated to the newly developing grounds for sex complementarity and the old grounds for sex polarity. In early medieval philosophy this battle ground was vividly seen in the internal structure of the philosophy of St. Augustine. However, in the twelfth century the conflict is seen between three different groups of writers, none of whom had direct influence on any of the others.

The traditional grounds for sex polarity were found first of all in the writings of Andreas Capellanus and Walter Map, whose popular satires on women greatly devalued one sex in relation to the other. At the same time as they were writing these satires, the Islamic philosopher Averroes was commenting on Aristotle's rationale for sex polarity, and Maimonides was attempting to integrate this Aristotelian rationale for sex polarity into Jewish philosophy. While these efforts were in some way peripheral to the rest of their philosophy, they nonetheless served, with hindsight, as a trumpet call in advance of the coming revolution.

Sex complementarity, on the other hand, was receiving its first complete development by Hildegard in the monastic environment at Bingen. The irony of all these activities occurring in the same century simply heightens the sense of urgency surrounding the struggle for a new theory of sex identity. The environment of the mutual respect of women and men in the monastic setting contrasted vividly with the satires written by men about women in the courtly environment. The careful "scientific" grounds for sex complementarity seen in the scholarly Islamic and Hebrew traditions again brought a new level of consideration to the subject not found in either the popular literature or in Hildegard's analysis. In the end, it was these scientific grounds for the new empirical method, introduced to the west by Aristotle, that gained the upper hand. The attempt to integrate Hildegard's "pre-scientific" or "pre-Aristotelian" writings into the newly formed curriculum of higher education in Paris failed.

Finally, the twelfth century is also the time of the Crusades. These intense and violent struggles between Christians and Moslems to regain control over the Holy City of Jerusalem had to be present in the minds of the writers of the philosophy of sex identity. The vivid image of the knight as a new and glorious kind of martyr dominated a great deal of thought about vigorous activity. Hildegard's morality play *Ordo Virtutum* and Herrad's *Hortus Deliciarum* applied the image of the knight to women in their monasteries. However, the knight was predominantly a male image, and when the University of Paris was founded early in the thirteenth century, the students and masters—all male—were sworn into the university like knights entering an "intellectual crusade." At this major turning point in western history, women were suddenly cut off from access to higher education, and the philosophy of sex complementarity lost the existential grounds it had enjoyed since the eighth century.

THE EXPLOSION OF ARISTOTELIAN GROUNDS FOR SEX POLARITY IN THE THIRTEENTH CENTURY

The master-student team of the two Dominicans St. Albert the Great and St. Thomas Aquinas, brought about the completion of this phase of the Aristotelian Revolution. Albert's decision "to make Aristotle intelligible to the Latins," and Thomas's decision to use Aristotle as the foundation for a new Christian philosophy resulted in the complete integration of Aristotle's arguments for sex polarity into western thought. Woman was perceived on the natural level as inferior to man in body and mind, and her inferiority was explained through an Aristotelian rationale in the categories of opposites, generation, wisdom, and virtue. Specifically, woman was considered as the passive sex because of her inability to provide seed to generation. She was then also considered to be weak in her reasoning powers and in her capacity for natural virtue.

On the level of response to grace, St. Albert suggested a slightly different theory from Thomas. Following the tradition already established in the writings of Abelard, Albert resorted to a reverse sex polarity in his radical description of Mary as the throne of wisdom. Thomas, however, somewhat qualified his teacher's extreme position when he opened a door to sex complementarity on this higher level of existence. He argued simply that male and female saints were equal but significantly different, and that the imperfection that marked woman's nature on earth had no importance in heaven.

Albert and Thomas's extensive use of Aristotle's arguments on the natural level had the consequence that their philosophies are easily identified as falling into the tradition of sex polarity. The tremendous popularity of these Dominicans in the thirteenth century led to the further result that Aristotle's arguments for sex polarity gained a new respectability. In fact, Aristotle was affirmed in a new and more intense way than he ever was in the past. All the questions about the greater value of Plato or Aristotle that had been so prominent during the sixteen hundred years since their deaths were now resolved in favour of the student over the master. For the Aristotelian Revolution achieved a definitive victory for the Christian west, which was to remain in effect, in some respects, even to the present.

While the negative effect of the Aristotelian Revolution was surely its total affirmation on the natural level of the theory of sex polarity, in quite another way it had a positive effect on the history of the philosophy of sex identity. For Aristotle, the key aspect to the concept of person was the belief that a person is a completely integrated being, in human rationality and materiality. Thomas added to these integrated factors a third factor of individuality, which had been previously recognized by Boethius, and a fourth aspect of spirituality, which had been recognized by Augustine. In this way, Thomas Aquinas forged a new synthesis—also recognized by Hildegard of Bingen—of the concept of person as necessarily containing the integration of rationality, materiality, individuality and spirituality. The first three factors are found in philosophy through the exercise of reason and the observations of the senses, while the latter factor is found in theology through faith. This view of the person is one that ought to be maintained and developed within a twentieth-century context.

Consequently, in the consideration of the effect of the Aristotelian Revolution, especially in the person of St. Thomas, we are faced with the following paradox. While Thomas was misled by Aristotle in the adoption of his rationale for philosophical differences between women and men, he was correctly led by Aristotle towards the goal of presenting a philosophy of the person as an integrated, unified existent. Therefore, in this assessment of the effect of the Aristotelian Revolution on the western mind, it is possible to conclude that only part of the concept of woman in relation to man should be rejected.

In fact, Thomas Aquinas partially opened the door to a philosophy of sex complementarity on the highest level of existence. He recognized that in heaven it was not possible to speak of man as superior to woman. At the same time, he believed that it was also necessary, through the integral relation of body and soul, to insist on the significant differentiation of woman and man. The body, in the resurrection, will keep its sexual differentiation; therefore, a specific woman and a specific man will receive sexually differentiated bodies. It is possible today to build on that theological foundation for sex complementarity and on the Thomistic concept of the person as an integrated existent, to forge a new philosophy of sex identity that would not have any reference to the false theories of Aristotle's biology and the equally false conclusions that were drawn from it.

V

THE INSTITUTIONALIZATION OF ARISTOTLE

The study of the first two phases of the Aristotelian Revolution has shown a radical growth in the power of the revolution from its early transmission of Aristotelian concepts to its later transmission of Aristotelian arguments. With the third stage of the revolution a similarly intense change occurs. Here Aristotelian arguments were institutionalized to such a degree that they were transmitted throughout all of western Europe.

Obviously, if Aristotle's arguments had merely re-emerged in the thought of a few isolated philosophers, they would not have affected the concept of woman and man for the vast majority of people in the western world. However, the Aristotelian Revolution was woven into the very fabric of the western educational system. Through this means it could claim a decisive victory over the direction of human thought.

The institutional shift in western higher education occurred when the university system was developed. The University of Paris, established by secular bishops in the early thirteenth century, wrenched Christian higher education away from the Benedictine monasteries. The University of Paris became the model for the many universities soon founded all across Europe. By the mid-thirteenth century all of Aristotle's works became required reading at the University of Paris. Through the pre-eminence of Paris, Aristotle became the most important thinker throughout university education. The Aristotelian Revolution had conquered the minds of intellectuals in Europe.

Finally, Aristotle's thought reached beyond the academic world into the homes of ordinary citizens. This process occurred first through the dissemination of knowledge by members of numerous mendicant orders. These clerics simplified concepts and arguments in order to "preach in the streets." In this way, Aristotelian sex polarity was transmitted in an organized way outside of the universities.

A sign of the widely dispersed knowledge associated with Aristotelian sex polarity is found in the large number of popular works that were falsely attributed to the Greek philosopher. A study of these "doubtful and spurious works" reveals an astonishing array of popularized sex-polarity theories about the concepts of woman and man. It is appropriate, therefore, to complete this study of the third stage of the Aristotelian Revolution with a consideration of some of these texts. The institutionalization of Aristotelianism resulted in the ultimate triumph of Aristotle's thought over all other theories of sex identity.

Nowhere is this triumph as dramatically seen as in the separation of women and men in the centres of higher learning. The monastic tradition had seen the practice of co-educational study for over three hundred years. The University of Paris excluded women from all of its faculties from the start. This example of the exclusion of women from university education was followed by a large number of other universities. Therefore, women lost access to academic skills at the same moment as the Aristotelian Revolution in sex polarity was being completed. Both sex unity and sex complementarity had evolved within a cooperative environment that included both women and men. Aristotle had argued that women were not capable of wisdom through discursive reasoning. The Aristotelian Revolution made this theory a practical reality. By being excluded from university education, women received a crippling blow to their identity that they have only overcome in the present century. Therefore, the Aristotelian Revolution, through the institutionalization of Aristotelian arguments, formed a definite framework for the contemporary consideration of woman and man.

In order to better understand the impact of the institutionalization of Aristotelianism as the philosophy of sex identity, a brief survey of the history of educational institutions and the concept of woman in relation to man follows.

EARLY INSTITUTIONS OF HIGHER LEARNING AND THE UNIVERSITY OF PARIS

Schools of philosophy had been established in Greece as early as the fourth century BC.[1] Two hundred years later the Greek system of lecturing was imported to Rome.[2] By the first century AD, several schools of grammar and rhetoric had been established.[3] Hadrian supported this educational trend by funding the Athenaeum, a public building with accompanying library that served as an informal university.[4] Here philosophy was directed primarily towards skills in argumentation and logic as an important element in the study of law.

At the same time, a school of philosophy had been established in Alexandria; the philosophy of mathematics was studied along with neo-Platonism.[5] This school functioned from the first century until all non-Christian schools of philosophy were closed in 529 by Emperor Justinian.[6] Since Aristotelian concepts were part of Plotinus's metaphysics, some Aristotelian influence was imported through this educational institution. Furthermore, by the end of the school many early Greek commentaries on Aristotle's arguments were being studied regularly.

Obviously, Aristotle's thought was central to his Lyceum in Greece. This institutional structure was gone, however, by the first century. In Rome, Aristotle's thought was institutionalized second-hand through Cicero and lecturers who had some knowledge of the Peripatetic tradition. As previously demonstrated, this resulted primarily in the incorporation of some central Aristotelian concepts.

By 425, the Byzantine world had an institutional structure that included philosophy in the State University of Constantinople.[7] Although Aristotle was studied little in the beginning, by the time the University of Cairo was founded in 970, direct translations of the philosopher's work enabled Aristotle's arguments to become a core element in Islamic institutional education. With the subsequent commentaries by Avicenna and Averroes, Aristotle's arguments became the basis for all further Islamic philosophy.[8]

Higher education for Jewish philosophers occurred primarily through private centres established within synagogues. The Talmud served as the central text.[9] Maimonides' incorporation of Aristotle's arguments in his major work, *The Guide for the Perplexed*, as well as in other commentaries on the Talmud, insured that Aristotle became integrated into the heart of institutionalized Jewish education.

Within the non-Christian educational structures, female philosophers emerged only within the neo-Platonic and early Greek schools. Hypatia, at the head of the neo-Platonic school in Alexandria, achieved the height of success as a philosopher within a formal educational system. There appear to be no records of any female philosophers in either of the early Jewish or Islamic institutional settings.

Early Christian institutionalized education took place from 800 to 1200 in Benedictine monasteries.[10] These monasteries trained both their own members as well as outsiders. In addition, since women's monasteries were frequently established alongside men's monasteries, female philosophers had access to the centre of Christian philosophical activity. This period served as a high point in women's education for many centuries to come.

> The nunnery was a refuge for female intellectuals, as the monastery was for the male. Although the majority of nuns were at best literate, most of the learned women of the Middle Ages—the literary, artistic, scientific, and philosophical stars were nuns.[11]

Aristotle influenced early Christian institutionalized education primarily through his logical works. Boethius had translated these writings, as well as Porphyry's *Isagoge*, which made Aristotle's arguments in logic directly available to the Latin world. In addition, some of Aristotle's biological theories emerged second-hand through Galen, Avicenna and Averroes's works in medicine. Finally, some of Aristotle's theories on ethics and politics came second-hand through Stoics, such as Cicero and Seneca. Therefore, in this early period, Aristotle's arguments were only partially integrated into Christian institutionalized education.

The subsequent availability of direct translations and commentaries on all of Aristotle's works, combined with the establishment of the first major university at Paris, led to Aristotle's arguments becoming a foundation for all western education by the end of the thirteenth century. The University of Paris, founded in the early thirteenth century, excluded women from its ranks of students and masters until 1868. This resulted in women being isolated from the centre of all significant philosophical activity. In addition, the new trend to founding religious orders with a specific separation of women and men meant that even within the monastic setting, women became limited in their access to information and teachers of the highest rank in philosophy. Consequently, the side-effect of the institutionalization of Aristotelian sex polarity was the exclusion of women from the philosophic endeavour. Aristotle had argued that women could not be wise in the same way as men; European society became structured in such a way that this theory inevitably became true.

The shift from monastery to university was devastating for female philosophers: "The transference of educational activity from the monks to the secular clergy constituted . . . the great educational revolution of that century."[12] This transfer of power occurred in several stages of consolidation of the educational structures. As long as this structure remained within the Benedictine monastic tradition, women were able to study with men. As previously demonstrated, Roswitha, Herrad of Landsberg and Hildegard of Bingen represented the height of development of female philosophers within this educational system. It is most significant that Hildegard's executor travelled to Paris in 1214 to bring her works to the attention of the new educational masters. As early as the end of the eleventh century, the Cathedral School of Paris had begun to open its doors.[13] Some women of the nobility were able to enroll officially as students; they were also able to receive private instruction from its tutors. It was in this context that Abelard taught Heloise from 1108 to 1118. The formation of the masters' guilds took place from 1140 to 1180.[14] Therefore, the institutional structures in Paris were being consolidated at precisely the time Hildegard was writing her philosophy of sex complementarity and Herrad developing her encyclopedia for women. However, theology at Paris was being formed instead around the *Sentences* of Peter Lombard, a work that contained no references to female philosophers or theologians.

While no precise date is known for the beginning of the University of Paris, certain privileges were being granted to the masters as early as 1200. A Bull of 1210 recognized some laws associated with the guilds, and by 1215 statutes were established.[15] Informally, four different "nations" had been slowly developing themselves at Paris from as early as 1181. They were referred to officially by Honorius II in 1227, and legally recognized by 1231 in the Bull of Gregory IX. The four nations represented the French, the English (later replaced by the Germans), the Normans and the Picards. These four groups became the constitutive basis for the Faculty of Arts and Letters.[16] By 1231, the relation between the University, or Stadium, and the Bishops had been officially settled. All students and masters had to be ecclesiastics; women, therefore, were officially excluded. Interestingly, this shift in the access of women to higher learning may not have been as much the result of the church structure attempting to rid women of an opportunity they once enjoyed within the monastic setting as of the fact that the university was modelled upon a military conception of knighthood. Masters were sworn into their positions as knights had been sworn into a brotherhood of arms. The University of Paris became, according to Rashdall, "an intellectual knighthood."[17]

There is no question that the academic power the ecclesiastics at Paris wrenched from the Abbots and Abbesses within the Benedictine tradition brought about an entirely new concept of higher education. At first this power remained primarily within the hands of secular bishops. Little by little, however, other religious orders encroached. In 1217 the Dominicans established a house in Paris, in 1219 the Franciscans followed, and then the Cistercians, Premonstrantensians, and Augustinians. By 1254, only one of five teaching positions in theology was held by a secular priest.[18] Many of these new religious orders placed an emphasis on teaching in the streets instead of within the confines of a monastery. Women's orders, however, were still cloistered. Therefore, the division between women's and men's religious education increased. The mendicant orders may have entered into strong conflicts with the seculars on many issues, but on the question of women and higher education they both agreed. Women were not to be at the centre of knowledge and learning.

The exclusion of women from the University of Paris cannot be blamed entirely on the above factors. Blanche of Castille (1182–1252), the Queen-Regent of France, also played a role. This powerful woman ruled at the time that the University of Paris was being consolidated. Conceivably, she could have had some influence on its development in relation to women, if she had chosen to. Blanche of Castille had become embroiled in a dispute at the University of Paris between some unruly students and a local innkeeper. She sent in police to quell a small riot and several students were killed. As a result, the masters closed the university in protest for a two-year period, from 1229 to 1230. By 1231, Blanche of Castille had negotiated a settlement, even though great efforts had been made to discredit her:

> Ignoring the lurid gossip, Blanche made peace overtures to the University, reconfirmed its privileges, and within two years induced masters and students to return to Paris.[19]

It is an unfortunate missed opportunity in history that Blanche of Castille did not attempt to introduce the means for women's orders to establish parallel bases in Paris in order to further their educational opportunities. When the university reconvened, it began a new period of growth and development that firmly sealed the separation of women from the development of western philosophical thought.

By 1254, the original university had developed four separate faculties. The Faculty of Arts, the Faculty of Theology, the Faculty of Medicine, and the Faculty of Law were now officially differentiated. The latter three faculties became the modern equivalent of graduate schools, while the Faculty of Arts served as an "undergraduate" school. The original intent of the division of areas of study was clearly tied to a desire for integrated knowledge. Philosophy, always the core curriculum in the Faculty of Arts, was a preparation for more specialized study in theology, medicine, and law. However, once the institutional separation of branches of knowledge was made, a slow but steady rupture in the unity of knowledge began to occur. Controversial questions began to bring the different faculties into conflict with one another. Ultimately, university education became more and more fragmented until philosophy became cut off from theology, medicine, or law. This meant that the concept of woman began to be studied from isolated perspectives within the four different faculties. Aristotelianism became integrated into each faculty, though not always in the same way. By considering the different patterns of development of the institutionalization of Aristotle's theories it will be possible to demonstrate the far-reaching consequences of this revolution in educational structures.

ARISTOTLE AND THE FOUR FACULTIES AT THE UNIVERSITY OF PARIS

Aristotle's philosophy was integrated into the various faculties at Paris in different ways. Each of the faculties—Arts, Theology, Medicine and Law—had a specific academic goal and a different set of priorities. Therefore, different Aristotelian texts were used in each.

Aristotle's logic, available for many centuries before his other works were translated, became accepted into the Faculty of Arts as the core of academic philosophy. It replaced both grammar and rhetoric and established itself as the safest method for all philosophical enquiry. As a consequence, a sex-neutrality position was established as the practical result of this central place for logic. At the University of Paris a new form of sex neutrality was based not on Plato or the neo-Platonists, but on the logical writings of Aristotle. Roger Bacon is a philosopher who developed this tendency further at Paris.

The Faculty of Arts also taught Aristotle's moral and natural philosophy. These works did contain his rationale for sex polarity. However, philosophers were soon forbidden to discuss theological issues, and an inner pressure began to develop towards sex neutrality in ethics. Natural philosophy also began to develop along sex-neutrality lines. The eventual triumph of Aristotle in the Faculty of Arts led to the establishment of a new basis for sex neutrality rather than to the perpetuation of sex polarity in philosophy.

In the Faculty of Theology, however, quite the opposite occurred. The initial subject of study for this faculty was Peter Lombard's *Sentences*. A study of the commentaries of St. Bonaventure reveals a slow but steady progression towards Aristotelian sex polarity. St. Bonaventure, following St. Augustine, argued for a theory of sex identity that divided the person into the spiritual and temporal dimensions. He carried through the tension of a theory including sex unity, sex polarity and sex complementarity. St. Thomas and St. Albert, who also taught in this faculty, argued strenuously for a modified sex polarity that permeated all dimensions of woman's and man's existence. With St. Thomas's canonization and acceptance as the authoritative teacher of theology, the Aristotelian Revolution triumphed in the complete acceptance of sex polarity in this faculty. All of the clergy studying at Paris learned this theological rationale for sex polarity and subsequently transmitted it to congregations of the faithful throughout Europe.

In the Faculty of Medicine, Aristotle's theory of sex polarity was eventually transmitted through the writings of a student of St. Thomas, Giles of Rome. He argued against previous theories of the existence of female seed. He believed that the mother provided only passive matter to generation.

Finally, in the early history of the Faculty of Law, both civil law and canon law were studied. Aristotelian logic had been used by Ireneus to establish the study of civil law, and by Gratian to establish the study of canon law. In addition, some of Aristotle's legal and political concepts were integrated into the body of the law itself. There were aspects of both sex unity and sex polarity theories in the body of the laws themselves.

The first most significant fact about the four faculties at the University of Paris is the exclusion of women from all branches of study. Prior to this active exclusion of women from the centre of higher education, women had studied and written both philosophy and theology. They had also practised and taught medicine at academic centres in Italy and Spain. The establishment of the four faculties at Paris marked a direct separation of women and men from the cooperative study of truth.

The separation of women and men was accompanied by a separation of different groups of men in a second significant way. The Faculty of Theology focused on knowledge gained through faith, while the Faculty of Arts emphasized knowledge gained through reason. Although this distinction between faith and reason at first led to cooperation between the faculties, by the end of the thirteenth century a law had been passed that prohibited philosophers from teaching any theological issues. Therefore, the approach to the concept of woman from reason was divorced from the approach to this subject through faith.

A similar separation occurred between the faculties of theology and medicine. While at the beginning, students at Paris could study in both fields, a law was soon passed prohibiting clerics from studying medicine. The distinction here related to the soul and the body. Theology studied the soul, and medicine the body.

Finally, the Faculty of Theology also became separated from the Faculty of Law. This separation referred only to civil law and not to canon law, which remained a subject for theologians. The distinction underlying this division of faculties related to the difference between secular and religious elements in society. Then, within canon law itself, a new hierarchy was developed that depended upon a legal distinction between clergy and laity; all women were defined as members of the laity. Abbesses soon lost both the jurisdictional and sacramental powers that they had enjoyed before this development of a canon of ecclesiastical laws. Sex polarity then crept into the content of the law itself.

The careful study of the relation of Aristotle to the four faculties at Paris reveals the slow but definite integration of Aristotelian thought about the concept of woman and man. In addition, a simultaneous development of a large number of significant distinctions occurred: men became separated from women, faith from reason, the soul from the body, and clergy from laity. The entire university system was fragmented into faculties; established in an original harmony, it developed into relationships of hostility. Knowledge came to be pursued by people with isolated methodologies. This process of fragmentation has continued to the present time. Universities now consist of a plethora of disciplines all vying for the central place in the determination of truth. Aristotle had correctly argued for the need to make significant distinctions in the search for truth. However, the institutionalization of Aristotle turned these distinctions into rigidly defined areas of knowledge that made a unified approach to the person nearly impossible. The shadow of the institutionalization of Aristotle haunts the corridors of the contemporary academic world like a ghost from the thirteenth-century University of Paris.

THE FACULTY OF ARTS

The first works of Aristotle to reach Paris came through the Latin paraphrases of Avicenna's commentaries on the philosopher.[20] In addition, a spurious work, containing a neo-Platonic framework, appeared as the *Theology of Aristotle.* Since these texts contained some ideas contrary to the Christian faith in 1210, all "books of Aristotle on natural philosophy and his commentators" were condemned.[21] Aristotle's logic, however, was left within the curriculum. In the statutes of 1215 this was explicitly stated:

> The works which, according to these first statutes, must be read in the ordinary lessons, were the following: 1) Aristotle's treatises on logic; 2) Priscian's grammar.[22]

Aristotle's logic eventually replaced all of the previous tradition of the study of grammar: "The change away from grammar and rhetoric to logic in philosophy was the most striking development in the arts course during the thirteenth century."[23]

The same statute, drawn up for the University of Paris by the papal legate, forbade "lectures on physical and metaphysical books of Aristotle."[24] This became known as the second condemnation of Aristotle. This condemnation was renewed in 1231 by the Bull of Gregory IX, with the addition "at least until they shall have been examined and purged."[25] It was at this time that Latin translations of works by Averroes, including several commentaries on Aristotle's philosophy, were introduced in Paris. This fact may have contributed to a change in attitude towards Aristotle at the University.[26] In addition, even though the condemnation of Aristotle had been reinforced by the threat of excommunication, in the English nation at least, Aristotle's works continued to be studied in private.[27] In any event, the bans on Aristotle appear to have been lifted by 1235.[28]

St. Albert the Great taught at the University of Paris during the years from 1243 to 1248.[29] Since the ban had been lifted on Aristotle's works, St. Albert was able to put into practice his aim to "make Aristotle intelligible to the Latins." From Paris, St. Albert went to Cologne, where St. Thomas remained as his student for several years. In 1252, St. Thomas received a teaching post at the University of Paris on St. Albert's recommendation. During the years from 1252 to 1259 and from 1269 to 1272, St. Thomas developed his new form of Christian Aristotelianism at Paris. According to Rashdall, "The Dominicans conceived and executed the idea of pressing, not merely (as of old) the Aristotelian logic but the whole Aristotelian philosophy, into the service of the Church."[30] This masterminding by the Dominicans St. Albert and St. Thomas effectively brought about the victory of the Aristotelian Revolution.

Institutional structures came to reflect the changing attitude towards Aristotle by finally, officially requiring the works of Aristotle to be read. The year 1255 was the crucial turning point in the Aristotelian Revolution.

> It was in 1255 that Aristotle's *Physics*, interdicted until then under pain of excommunication, was officially authorized at Paris, simultaneously with his metaphysics, the work *De Animalibus* and the treatise of the soul: in a word, all of the greater and lesser works of the Greek philosopher which hence forward entered, in their totality and triumphality, into the university schools, to exercise there for several centuries an intellectual domination, whose equal it would be impossible to find in the history of human thought.[31]

The turning point of 1255 when all of Aristotle's works became required reading at the University of Paris led to the decision to stop this first study of the concept of woman in relation to man at the mid-point of the thirteenth century. Something radically new happened in western civilization when the main educational institution of that culture required a thorough knowledge of Aristotle from all of its students. Rashdall explains:

> The next statute bearing on the subject belongs to the year 1255, and gives us the list of books, in order, upon which a master was required to lecture at that date. The Aristotelian treatises mentioned in this statute in addition to the "old and new logic" and the *Ethics* are the following: *Physica, Metaphysica, de Anima, de Animalibus, de Caelo et Mundo, Meteorica, de Generatione*, and other minor works.[32]

The Aristotelian Revolution worked itself into the very heart of the curriculum of the faculties at Paris. The early schools of western education had been divided into what were called the trivium (grammar, rhetoric and dialectic) and the quadrivium (arithmetic, astronomy, geometry and music).

> They (Aristotle's works) transformed the physiognomy of the arts in two primary respects. The first was to enthrone dialectic or logic as the arbiter of discussion and demonstrative validity, reducing it to the rules of the syllogism. The second was to make Aristotle's works the mainstay of the study of arts, so that whereas the *trivium* was effectively reduced to Aristotle's logic, the old divisions of the *quadrivium* became largely subsumed under his different scientific works.[33]

The Faculty of Arts contained those subjects that later broke off to become the academic disciplines of mathematics, physics, biology and astronomy, in addition to the two main philosophical areas of logic and ethics. Aristotle's theories became central to the foundation of all these areas. By examining the writings of one of the early teachers in this faculty at the University of Paris, it will be possible to assess some of the effects of this transformation of curriculum on the concept of woman.

Roger Bacon (1214–1294) first studied and lectured in Paris from approximately 1245 to 1251.[34] In contrast to both St. Albert and St. Thomas, who moved quickly from the lower Faculty of Arts to the higher Faculty of Theology, Roger Bacon always remained a philosopher. For this reason, his writings offer particularly interesting evidence about an approach to the concept of woman within the framework of philosophy alone. In his early years at Paris, Bacon wrote a series of commentaries on Aristotle called *Questiones.*[35] Bacon resisted the pattern, set by St. Albert, of accepting Aristotle's opinion on all matters. Instead, Bacon mainly adopted Aristotle's scientific approach to philosophy without accepting all of his views on particular subjects. Consequently, Bacon generally ignored the question of the significance of differences between woman and man. For example, in his *Questiones* on the *Metaphysics* of Aristotle, no mention was made of male and female as contraries.[36] This early pattern was repeated in later years when Bacon developed a mathematical foundation for a scientific approach to philosophy. The differences between women and men were no longer thought to be important when philosophy became influenced by a mathematical orientation of science.

After Bacon left Paris, he returned to England and became profoundly affected by a spurious work attributed to Aristotle entitled *Secretum Secretorum.*[37] In this book, Aristotle was described as teaching Alexander that the secrets of philosophy were revealed by God to only a few wise men in history. This revelation contained the view that the universe had a unified composition that only these enlightened philosophers could comprehend. "The essence of the whole world, low or high, near or far, is one and the same."[38] Bacon decided to find this essence and to re-establish philosophy on a new scientific ground. To this end he learned Greek and Hebrew, as well as studied medicine, optics and astronomy. In addition, he became a Franciscan friar and returned to Paris in 1267 to develop this new philosophy in a book entitled *Opus Majus*.

Even though Bacon insisted that the end of all philosophy ought to be human action, he nonetheless established the *Opus Majus* on scientific premises.[39] He believed that in this new approach to philosophy he would carry out Aristotle's original philosophical approach, although in a new way.[40]

> We must strive that the wonderful and ineffable utility and splendor of experimental science may appear and the pathway may be opened to the greatest

> secret of secrets, which Aristotle had hidden in his book on *The Regimen of Life.*[41]

Bacon would carry out Aristotle's plan, but go beyond the original philosopher:

> For of famous philosophers Aristotle alone with his followers is stamped with the approval of all wise men, since he organized the branches of philosophy as far as possible in his age; but nevertheless he did not reach the limit of wisdom, as will be clearly shown below.[42]

Bacon criticized translations of Aristotle, the ignorant rejection of Aristotle, and coaxed philosophers to learn Greek in order to return to the original texts.[43] The *Opus Majus* contained references to Aristotle on nearly every page. That Bacon's concept of woman fell into the sex-neutrality rather than the sex-polarity tradition, then, is all the more significant.

Nowhere is Bacon's scientific approach to philosophy more evident than in his consideration of the theory of generation. It has been suggested that Bacon wrote a commentary on the *Generation of Animals* during his early period in Paris.[44] Since all trace of this work has been lost, the *Opus Majus* must serve as the key to Bacon's theory of generation. In it he developed mathematical hypotheses to explain certain aspects of generation. In this shift, Bacon was a precursor to Descartes's mathematical study of the formation of the fetus.[45] In the following passage, Bacon described how twins were differentiated:

> For all points on the earth's surface are the centres of different horizons, to which the vertices of different pyramids of the celestial forces come, so that they are able to produce plants of different species on the same very small spot of the earth's surface, and to cause twins in the same womb to differ in complexion and habits.[46]

The influence of heavenly forces on generation was particularly pronounced in Bacon's philosophy. In some passages he implied that both female and male seed existed and cooperated in generation.

> The forces of the heavens and stars produce everywhere different things in their properties and natures and diversity in things generated according to propogation. And not only the multiplication of celestial force is operative, but that of father and mother, since forces are determined in the seeds, as physicians teach. Especially from the vital principle of the mother is there a continual multiplication of force and species over the fetus up to the completion of generation and birth.[47]

The mother developed the second phase of generation, as explained in Avicenna's *Canon of Medicine.*

Bacon frequently considered only the father's function in generation. In a passage in which the prolongation of life was being discussed, Bacon never referred to the mother's role in health of body and quality of soul:

> Thus by neglect of the rules of health sons weaken themselves, and thus the son's son has a doubly weakened condition. . . . For sins weaken the powers of the soul, so that it is incompetent for the natural control of the body. . . . This weakening process passes from father to son, and so on.[48]

The father was significant because he provided the efficient cause or first movement in generation, although the mother carried the second process forward.

> In the *Vegetabilia* Aristotle says in the first book on Plants that the sun is the father of plants and the earth the mother; and in the *Animalia* he maintains the same principle, because in regard to man, concerning whom the principle seems less applicable he says in the second book of the *Physics* that man and the sun generate man out of matter, and it is evident that a father does not continue nor terminate generation but only begins by letting the seed fall.[49]

Bacon clearly did not adopt Aristotle's framework for generation without qualifying it with reference to his own views on the subject. However, that he so often referred to the philosopher meant that Aristotle's arguments were transmitted through his teaching at the University of Paris.

In ethics Bacon also frequently referred to the philosopher. Sometimes, however, these references were inaccurate. For example, he used Aristotle to defend chastity.[50] He also used Aristotle to defend poverty and contempt of the world.[51] When Bacon summarized Aristotle's many contributions to ethics, his sex-polarity theory in relation to women's virtue was never mentioned. Instead, Bacon continuously referred to Seneca, whose theory of sex identity in ethics was most carefully explained in letters to Helvia and Marcia. Seneca's ethics seemed more practical to Bacon and they therefore formed the framework for his development of a moral philosophy. While Bacon did not argue directly for women's ethical equality with men, his constant reference to Seneca's letters to Helvia and Marcia implied a concept of woman as capable of full moral development.

Finally, in another section of the *Opus Majus*, Bacon described the temptation of sin in mathematical principles that applied equally to woman and man. He argued that the degree of angle of visual temptation mattered in ethical judgements.

> Most of all must we avoid letting the direct delectable species fall at equal angles into our sense, because then it is strongest, especially if the vertex of the short pyramid meets it. So Eve perceived the species of the voice of the serpent and of the visible apple and its sweet odor.[52]

This example brings to the forefront once more Bacon's primary preference for the approach of physics and mathematics to basic philosophical questions. It is not surprising, then, that his concept of woman fell into the sex-neutrality tradition. He did not, however, base this theory on Plato's acceptance of the reincarnation of a sexless soul. Instead, Bacon stands as the first significant example of a philosopher who developed a sex-unity theory from the principles of logic, especially in its concise development through mathematics. This development would have important consequences for the concept of woman in later periods of philosophy.

The movement towards sex neutrality as exemplified by Roger Bacon was not the only theory of sex identity taught in the Faculty of Arts. Both Albert the Great and St. Thomas taught within this faculty during the early years of the University of Paris. The practice explained above of commenting on Aristotle's treatises offered ample opportunity to expound a theory of sex polarity. In the Faculty of Arts, regular study of Aristotle's *Ethics, Politics, Metaphysics,* and *Generation of Animals* would have resulted in the continuous explication of an Aristotelian rationale for the philosophically significant differences between women and men to be introduced to explain the foundation for sex polarity as a philosophy of sex identity.

Therefore, at the beginning of the development of a curriculum in the Faculty of Arts at the University of Paris, there was a tension between arguments in support of the sex polarity found in moral philosophy and natural philosophy—based on the study of zoology—and the assumption of sex neutrality that was practised in the study of logic and natural philosophy when based on mathematics. Eventually the movement towards sex neutrality would carry the major force and establish the tradition of ignoring sex differences within the study of philosophy that remained, generally, in effect until the twentieth century.

The Faculty of Arts served as the "undergraduate" faculty for the University of Paris. It is important, therefore, to consider also the curricula of the "graduate" faculties in the same institution in terms of the theories of sex identity that they perpetuated.

THE FACULTY OF THEOLOGY

As *Sacra Facultas*, the Faculty of Theology at Paris attracted the most brilliant minds of thirteenth-century Europe. Even more than medicine and law, theology held the first place in creative intellectual thought in this century. As Gordon Leff observes, the Faculty of Arts simply served as a way into theology as the higher science:

> Although it would be untrue to deny an originality in the arts faculty, there was little scope for it there other than in logic; art provided the critical dialectical and speculative instruments for grappling with the questions of substance then at Paris, . . . [which] were almost entirely theological.[53]

During the first century of operation in Paris the following men taught in the Faculty of Theology: Albert the Great, from 1243 to 1248; Thomas Aquinas, from 1252 to 1259 and from 1269 to 1272; and Bonaventure, from 1253 to 1268. Together, these three theologians laid the foundation of western scholastic thought.

The studies in the Faculty of Theology were extremely rigorous and demanding. It took many years of study before someone could be recognized as a Master of Theology. The following lists the progression of St. Bonaventure's life at the University of Paris:

1236–1242	student at the Faculty of Arts
1243–1248	student at the Faculty of Theology (as a Franciscan)
1248–1250	Biblical Bachelor
1250–1252	Bachelor of *Sentences*
1253–1255	Licentiate (1254—Master in School of Minors)
1257	Master Cathedratus

The entire process took twenty years, and St. Bonaventure was forty before becoming a Master in the Faculty of Theology.[54] In the next two centuries this process ranged from fourteen to sixteen years; it usually included approximately six years' study of philosophy in the Faculty of Arts and eight years' study in the Faculty of Theology before the student could begin to teach.[55]

Within the Faculty of Theology itself, studies were divided into two phases that included three years' study of the Bible followed by at least two years' study of Peter Lombard's *Sentences.*[56] The *Sentences*, as previously mentioned, systematically incorporated the teachings of the early Church Fathers on the Bible. Using a dialectic method, Lombard brought various Christian interpretations of Scripture into one text. The *Sentences* were written between 1150 and 1157, while Lombard was a master in the Cathedral School of Notre Dame.[57] Nearly one hundred years later, they became the core curriculum of theology at the University of Paris. Since this situation did not change for several centuries, the *Sentences* became an important respository of the theological approach to the concept of woman.

Peter Lombard's *Sentences* was divided into four parts: 1) God; 2) Creation; 3) Redemption; and 4) Sacraments. The second part, views on creation, contained the most significant references to women. Since Lombard wrote before most of the works of Aristotle had been translated into Latin, he did not refer to the philosopher in his monumental work. As will be seen, however, commentators on the *Sentences* subsequent to the Aristotelian Revolution brought Aristotle back into the study of this theological text. Since there are hundreds, if not thousands, of printed commentaries on the *Sentences*, it would be possible through a comparative analysis of these texts to follow the influence of Aristotelian thought on the development of theology in this early period of its institutionalization.[58] Here, only the commentary of St. Bonaventure will be considered as an example. References have already been given to St. Albert and St. Thomas's commentaries on the *Sentences.*[59]

Lombard does not appear to have been an original thinker on the question of the concept of woman. Instead, he repeated the common interpretations of philosophers such as St. Augustine or St. Anselm, as well as early Church theologians. In the first place he affirmed the importance of the singleness of God's nature:

> We must note carefully here why He did not create man and woman at the same time like the angels, but first man, and then woman from man. "That the source of the human race might be one so that in this the pride of the devil might be confounded, and the lowliness of man be raised up through the likeness of God."[60]

As St. Augustine had done previously, monotheism was affirmed in the context of widespread polytheism. Man became the preferred representative of the image of God through his primary creation.

Lombard did not conclude from this, however, that woman was inferior to man. In fact, he went out of his way to emphasize the created equality of the two kinds of persons:

> Woman was made from man and so she was formed not from just any part of his body, but from his side, in order that it might be shown that she was created for a partnership of love. If she had been created from his head she would seem to be preferred for ruling; if from his feet, she would have to be subjected to slavery. And so because she was made neither mistress nor maidservant, but companion, she had to be produced neither from the head nor from the feet, but from the side, in order that man might learn that he must put her next to himself, having learned that she was taken from his side.[61]

In a way, Lombard raised the possibility of a complementarity of woman and man in his analysis of the creation story in Genesis. He argued that woman's soul came not from man but from God, and that it was created at the time of her conception.[62]

In a consideration of the Fall, Lombard argued that woman's sin was different from man's. Woman sinned from pride and the desire to be equal to God.

> It is often asked whether so much pride and love of independence which was in woman was also in man. To this we reply that Adam was not seduced in the same way as woman, for she did not think that what the devil suggested was true. But we can believe that he was seduced in this: that he thought that what was deadly sin was a venial sin.[63]

He argued that marriage before the Fall was merely a duty given to woman and man, that is to be fruitful and multiply. After the Fall, however, marriage became a remedy: it allowed for the control of desire. It was within this context that woman moved more clearly into a relation of forced obedience to man.

St. Bonaventure's *Commentary on the Sentences* provides a first glimpse of the development of Aristotelian thought within the Faculty of Theology. At the time he wrote the commentaries he had extensive knowledge of Aristotelian arguments.[64] However, as is well known, St. Bonaventure also chose to develop his own theories from St. Augustine and St. Anselm. As a result, a tension between sex unity and sex polarity emerged from Bonaventure's commentary.

In a discussion of the creation of man and woman in the image of God, St. Bonaventure stated:

> The image, as far as its being is concerned, consists principally in the soul and its powers, and chiefly in these insofar as they can be turned to God. In this there is no distinction between male and female, slave and free. Therefore, the image as far as its fullness or its being is concerned, is not found in man anymore than in woman. But in its well-being or clearer expression the image lives more in the soul to the extent that the body had order and disposition. Since in the body there is distinction of the sexes and according to the distinction of sexes the representation is greater to the extent that it governs or gives life. The man is the head of the woman and man is the source of the woman, and it is not man for the woman, but woman for man. Because of this the image is found in a more excellent way in the male sex than in the female.[65]

This fascinating passage argues for a sex-unity theory in the highest part of male and female identity. This view had previously been expressed by Anselm and, to a lesser degree, by Augustine. It simply stated that the highest image of god contains no reference to male or female identity. At the same time, however, when the body is considered in relation to human existence, it turns out that man is better able to order himself than is woman. Consequently, he better reflects the image of God in his temporal existence than does woman.

St. Bonaventure developed the differentiation between woman and man in this lower orientation in great detail. Woman symbolized the lower function of reason and man the higher: "Man, because he is strong and governs the woman, signifies the higher faculties of reason; woman, the lower."[66] This differentiation of woman and man was then used to explain the creation of Eve from Adam:

> This formation is also in accord with the man and woman signifying the higher and lower faculties. As man is stronger and woman is weaker, so there are higher and lower faculties. And as woman is formed from man so the lower faculties come from the turning of the spirit to them. When this happens the mind leaves the watchfulness of contemplation and in some way its efficacy is weakened and it is inclined to the softness of woman. Therefore, in this way it is said to be put to sleep and the bone is taken away and woman is formed.[67]

Using the same argument that had appeared in Albert the Great, Bonaventure refers to man as the principle of the human race. The principle is the cause of generation; active and efficacious.

> The formation of Eve from the rib of Adam was a harmony with the *dignity* of the first man who was the *principle* of all his species, men as well as women, just as God is the *principium* of the universe.[68]

For St. Bonaventure, the polarity of woman and man was best expressed as a difference in strength and weakness, a difference that no doubt arose from their more or less perfect generation. Bonaventure uses the same qualification of Aristotle's view, that woman is a defective man (*femina est aliquid deficiens et occasionatum*), as was used by Albert the Great and St. Thomas.

> To the first objection that says that woman is a defective man we must reply that Aristotle did not mean that woman is beyond the intention of nature, but that the power of nature has some defect in producing a woman compared with the production of man. But the defect is not contrary to the order of nature, but rather preserves that order. For according to the order of nature, in the same body some members are stronger and some are weaker. In the same way in the same species there are produced some individuals of one sex and others of the other.[69]

Therefore, while nature as a whole intended the female as well as the male, according to St. Bonaventure, the birth of individual females signalled a weakened and less perfect conception:

> Although the male sex is better in itself than the female, the well-being of nature does not depend solely on the male, but on male and female, and therefore nature desires both rather than one of the two.[70]

Even with the qualification of "the intention of nature," Bonaventure nonetheless transmits the fundamental Aristotelian sex polarity, as do his contemporaries Albert and Thomas. Sex polarity was clearly the foundation for the Faculty of Theology at Paris.

St. Bonaventure considers the process of sex determination in the fetus in some detail. After considering whether the right or left side of the uterus was a factor, invoking Aristotle, he concluded:

> The third reason comes from the strength of the male seed. If the male seed is very strong, from the threefold course of heat and power resting in it, then the mixture and combination becomes stronger and the stronger sex is generated, that is the male. But if its power is weak, then the mixture is softer and more frail and from it is produced the weak sex, that is the female. This third argument is the strongest of the three. For as Aristotle says, it is the male seed that is the principal mover in the generation of either male or female.[71]

There is some question about whether St. Bonaventure held a double-seed theory of generation.[72] While he did not appear to believe that both woman and man contributed a material and formal nature to the fetus, his theory can in no way be described as a theory of the equality of female and male seed. The following passage about the determination of sex demonstrates his view quite clearly:

> Properly speaking, the seed of the woman never predominates over the seed of the man. Therefore, it is said that the female seed predominates because the male seed is so weak in power that it is more suited to the generation of the female sex than the male.[73]

The female seed, then, did not complement the male seed but rather served as a contribution of the woman, who in herself was a weaker member of the human couple. In fact, in another passage in his *Commentary on the Sentences*, St. Bonaventure linked this aspect of woman's nature with the metaphysical distinction between matter and form: "The imperfect nature of woman seeks man as matter seeks its form."[74] Consequently, in the *Breviloquium,* marriage was described as a union of active and passive. "Matrimony must be the conjunction of two persons who differ as agent and patient, that is, as male and female."[75] From the above passages, then, it can be seen that St. Bonaventure incorporated many Aristotelian notions in his theological arguments.

In St. Bonaventure's consideration of the Fall, a similar pattern evolved. First, he argued that the woman was the first to be tempted because she was the weaker of the two persons. Next, he argued that original sin was passed down only through Adam. Giving a similar argument to that of St. Thomas Aquinas, Bonaventure actually claimed that original sin was transmitted through the soul and therefore only through the seed of the male.

> Since the sin of the man was the cause of the transmission of sin to posterity . . . the greater corruptions resulted from the sin of the man and in this respect the blame of the man is said to be the greater.[76]

Woman's sin was irrelevant, because of her primarily passive and weak nature. In this way Aristotle's arguments about the concept of woman were given theological application. Therefore, St. Bonaventure's position in the Faculty of Theology aided the development of the far-reaching consequences of the Aristotelian Revolution.

By far the greater influence on the promotion of Aristotle's theories of the concept of woman in relation to man occurred through the teachings of Albert the Great and Thomas Aquinas. In addition to their respective commentaries on Lombard's *Sentences*, in which woman is presented as naturally less perfect than man in all four categories of opposites, generation, wisdom and virtue, the relation of Aristotelianism to woman's identity was continually woven into the massive *Summa Theologiae*. This enormous work of nearly ninety books brought together all the major theological arguments available to the Christian west. In addition, it definitively established Aristotle as the authority in all areas of philosophy fundamental to a new Christian philosophy.

Just as in any institution of higher learning, the Faculty of Theology at the University of Paris suffered from internal political conflicts. The struggle involved differences between the neo-Augustinians who evolved from St. Bonaventure, and the Thomists, who evolved from St. Thomas. In addition, a struggle ensued between the Faculty of Theology and the radical Aristotelians within the Faculty of Arts.[77] These struggles primarily involved the question of the relation of reason to faith. Their immediate effect on the concept of woman was very small, for in both faculties, and in both the Thomists and the neo-Aristotelians, Aristotle's sex polarity was accepted whenever the concept of woman was considered. St. Thomas was canonized in 1323, and by 1325 Etienne Bourret, Bishop of Paris, revoked the sentence of excommunication and condemnation attached to the Parisian condemnation of 1277 from those propositions "insofar as they touch or seem to touch the doctrine of the aforesaid Blessed Thomas."[78] The debate between the neo-Augustinians and the Thomists was permanently resolved. The concept of woman, as studied in the Faculty of Theology, was accordingly completely grounded in Aristotelian sex polarity.

The question of the interaction of the faculties of theology and arts brought a different dimension into the historical study of the concept of woman. As mentioned previously, in the Faculty of Arts the concept of woman was studied in Aristotle's biological, ethical and logical works. Therefore, there was a certain tension within the faculty between the sex polarity in the ethical and biological works, and the sex neutrality of the logical works. The concept of woman, when considered from the biological and ethical point of view, slowly became detached from philosophy altogether and moved into the faculties of medicine and law, respectively. The Faculty of Theology also considered these issues, insofar as they related to the Bible and revelation. Eventually, philosophy was formed by logic, and the sex-neutrality theory reigned supreme. One important step in this process occurred when the Faculty of Arts decided not to discuss theological issues:

> On April 1, 1272, the conservative and apparently orthodox majority of the Arts Faculty . . . promulgated a regulation (which said that) no master or

> bachelor of arts was to determine or even to dispute a theological question. . . . Should he do so, . . . he was to be removed from the faculty forever unless he retracted within three days.[79]

Obviously, it was much safer for philosophers to adopt a basic sex-unity position and thereby consider only human identity in the most basic way, without regard to sexual distinction, than to risk losing their teaching positions. As philosophy and theology became separated from one another, the consideration of the concept of woman was eventually fragmented, and the institutionalization of this fragmentation determined the way in which the concept was studied for centuries to come.

THE FACULTY OF MEDICINE

A study of the Faculty of Medicine at Paris is important for the concept of woman in three specific ways. The first concerns the issue of female physicians; the second the question of female contribution to generation; and the third the fragmentation in knowledge brought about by the separation of medicine from philosophy and theology.

The connection between women and medicine had been very close in ancient history. Certainly in Greece and Rome women had practised medicine for centuries.[80] Subsequently, medicine was studied and practised in Benedictine monasteries from the seventh to the twelfth century.[81] Hildegard of Bingen is one example of a Benedictine nun who both practised and wrote about the cure of disease.[82] The first formal institution to develop into a medical school outside the monastic tradition was established in Salerno, Italy.

> In 1137, Roger II, King of Sicily, regulated for the first time, as it seems, the professional examinations in medicine. The doctors of the school, aided by the royal assessors, constituted the jury, and conferred the licence—not the right to teach, but the right to practise medicine (*Licentia medendi*). Any person, pretending to exercise the medical art without having obtained this licence, was punished by the confiscation of his property and a year's imprisonment.[83]

The development of institutions to determine who could practise medicine and who should be excluded was an important event in women's history. It was precisely through this avenue that women were later excluded from medicine at the University of Paris.

The medical school at Salerno appears always to have welcomed women. In its early years a woman named Sichelgaita was teacher in the area of poisons.[84] The conspicuous presence of female faculty at Salerno gave rise to the phrase *"mulieres Salernitance."* Considerable controversy surrounds the reputed existence of a woman named Trotula, or Madame Trotte, wife of the physician John Plutearius. Some sources claim that she held a chair of medicine at Salerno and wrote two medical texts entitled *De Morbis Mulierum et Eorum Cura* and *De Compositione Medicamentorum*. According to Joseph Needham:

> A not uncommon medieval manuscript *De Passionibus Mulierum* is usually ascribed to Trotula of Salerno, a matron. It recommends support of the perinaeum in childbirth and primary suture of lacerations. The text contains many references

> to Muslim and Hebrew physicians, speaks of numerous drugs from Arabic pharmacopoeias, and avoids magical formulae.[85]

However, Charles Singer claims that Trotula did not exist and that the books referred to were actually written by a male professor named Trottus.[86] In any event, it is clear that women attended and graduated from Salerno from its beginnings. The following official decree of the university upon the graduation of Francesca, wife of Metteo de Romana, with a doctorate in surgery gives ample proof:

> Whereas the laws permit women to practise medicine, and whereas, from the viewpoint of good morals, women are best adapted to the treatment of their own sex, we, after having received the oath of fidelity, permit the said Francesca to practise the said art of healing, etc.[87]

Women were also accepted in medical schools at Bologna, Padua, Pavia, Rome, and Naples.[88]

With this early background of female physicians, it is all the more significant that the Faculty of Medicine at the University of Paris excluded women.

> There was a Medical Faculty in Paris composed of male members exclusively, and these gentlemen were stubbornly opposed to a sister physician presuming to care for human ills in competition with themselves, so in the year 1220 an edict was issued which prohibited the practice of medicine by anyone who did not belong to the Faculty of Medicine, and according to its constitution and by-laws, only males were eligible for membership in the Faculty.[89]

Professors at Paris not only excluded women from their ranks of students and teachers, they also went out into the world to stop women from practising medicine. One woman, named Jacobe Felicie, was put to trial for breaking the law by practising medicine. Although all her clients testified on her behalf, she was found guilty and fined. Felicie had taken on patients who had been discharged from treatment by other physicians. She was convicted because "she had presumed to put her sickle into the harvest of others."[90] It was not until 1868 that women were allowed entry to the University of Paris medical faculty.

A difference between Paris and other universities also emerged in the issue of woman's contribution to generation. The faculty at Paris never achieved the reputation in medicine that Salerno, Bologna, or Montpelier did. In part, this was probably due to the conservatism of its approach, and to its heavy dependence upon the theoretical rather than practical or scientific approach to medicine. As early as 1072, Constantine of Africa, a Benedictine monk, had brought translations of Hippocrates' and Galen's works to Salerno. Montpelier followed the same tradition, and by the end of the twelfth century Avicenna's *Canon of Medicine* was also included as a central text.[91] All of these sources at least agreed upon the existence of female seed, although they included some disagreement about the function of this seed.

The specific question about what effect Aristotle's view of female seed had upon the study of medicine can best be examined by the situation at Bologna. Rashdall argued that Aristotle soon became central to the curriculum:

> And the study of medicine according to medieval notions was closely bound up with the study of Aristotelian physiology, and consequently with the whole of the Aristotelian philosophy. Aristotle, regarded in northern Europe chiefly as the basis of speculative philosophy and as the indispensable propaedeutic for the scholastic theologian, was in Italy studied largely as constituting the scientific basis of medicine.[92]

Aristotle had argued that female seed did not exist and that woman merely contributed passive material to generation. It seems to follow, then, that Bologna would perpetuate this erroneous view. However, another important factor emerged at Bologna that countered the Aristotelian theory in this specific area: Mondino da Luzzi (1276–1328) began to perform dissections of the human body. He wrote a text based upon his observations called *Anatomia*. This book became the primary source for all medical schools that taught surgery.[93] In it women were described as having seed. Clearly, the practical experience of dissection led to the discovery of the ovaries. Mondino da Luzzi frequently referred to both Galen and Avicenna in support of his theories.[94] It is not surprising, then, that Mondino da Luzzi claimed that women's seed did not have a generative function, rather he confused it with glandular secretions during intercourse:

> But though they are thus alike in origin they differ in the places at which they end. In women they end at the womb in the outer part where be the testicles, and they are wound and plaited about the outside of the womb. And the cavities of the testicles in women are filled with small portions of glandular flesh and so they are not as the testicles of men, but rather resemble the testicles of the hare and are to generate a saliva-like moisture which causes the libido.[95]

Therefore, the *Anatomia* perpetuated the modified Aristotelian view passed through Galen that woman did not have an equal contribution to man in generation.

In Paris, da Luzzi's theories were introduced in the fourteenth century. However, in the curriculum listed in 1270, neither Hippocrates nor Galen are mentioned.[96] It took nearly one hundred years for Paris to catch up with her southern neighbours, and by 1395 these early sources were included, as were Avicenna and Averroes.[97] However, in general, Paris remained locked into a consideration of theories of medicine that were in contrast to Bologna, which focused on surgery, and Montpelier, which focused on practice. The preoccupation with theory meant that Aristotelian sex polarity was even more entrenched in the consideration of female contribution to generation. In its extreme form it was articulated by Giles of Rome, a student of Thomas Aquinas, who taught at the University of Paris from 1285 to 1295. Although this period is a generation past the cut-off point of the mid-thirteenth century considered in this book, the text *De Formatione Corporis Humani in Utero*, which Giles wrote during the period from 1274 to 1278, summarized and criticized all major medieval theories of generation. His evaluation of the theories of Hippocrates, Galen, Avicenna and Averroes always took the perspective of the radical Aristotelian position. In this way, sex polarity was integrated into the heart of the study of medicine at Paris.

The question of the existence and nature of female seed preoccupied Giles. He associated Galen with the double-seed theory because of his knowledge of the early physician through Avicenna's *De Animalibus*.[98] He rejected "Galen's" view:

> The female seed is lacking in active virtue or formative function since it is not true seed; and the womb is only the site of generation not an agent in the process.[99]

In support of this position, Giles appealed to Aristotle:

> The female seed is like that of the male in name only, being as yet unsuitable for generation since it has only a passive virtue. Aristotle (GA 727a) remarks that if it were a seed, it would not be a menstruum; and if it were a menstruum it would not be a seed, which is more than to say that it is the matter.[100]

Female seed turned out to be merely a glandular fluid emitted by women as part of an irrigation of the uterus. Menstrual fluid remained opposite in nature from anything active. "The menstruum plays the part of prime matter, entirely passive, potential and undifferentiated, as Aristotle taught."[101]

The association of the female with passivity of matter and the male with the activity of form was made explicit in Giles: "The blood of a woman is related to the reception of form as the seed in man to the induction of form."[102] Giles argued that the male seed carried the *pneuma*, or highly refined hot substance, that transmitted the form to the fetus. This male contribution was completely formal and did not enter in any way into the material of the fetus: "The spirit emitted with the semen a) is not organic, b) forms the members, c) does not occur in the matter of the fetus."[103] The separation of male and female through their respective association with form and matter completely reaffirmed Aristotelian theory.

One important consequence of this application of the distinction between form and matter to the concept of woman was found in Giles's theory of the determination of the sex of the child. Directly following an Aristotelian line of argument, Giles argued that conflict between the form carried by the father and the matter provided by the mother explained the eventual sex of the fetus:

> That which is active is contrary to that which is passive; so if the male seed triumphs, it attracts the matter to itself, and induces in it the likeness of the father. If the menstruum resists, then the matter received from the mother is more suited to receiving the likeness of the mother.[104]

Giles followed Aristotle's claim that the passive resistance of matter produced females and the active domination of form produced males. The heart of sex polarity included an inherent hostility between male and female.

> Consequently, the principal cause of femininity is the number of ways in which the menstruum can resist the seed effectively, because of the weakness of the agent and the resistance offered by the passive element. The principal cause of masculinity is the number of ways the semen exerts dominion.[105]

Giles developed a complex theory of the interaction of ten different factors to explain the inner dynamic of this hostile process:

Factors	Male Fetus	Female Fetus
quality of seed	warm	cold
quantity of seed	more	less
age of parents	middle age	young or old
side of uterus	right	left
side of testes	right	left
weather	warm	cold
weather	dry	wet
diet	warm	cold
wind	north wind (dry)	south wind (wet)
position of stars		

In this chart, the influence of Aristotle's theory of the relation of the contraries hot and cold on Giles's theory of the determination of sex is evident. It is also obvious that the formation of the female was less perfect than the formation of the male.[106] Following Albert the Great and Thomas Aquinas, Giles concludes:

> In the case of man, the male agent is disposed to generate a male, the generation of a female in any particular case being beyond the intention of the agent. For this reason woman is called an "imperfect man," a *mas occasionatus.*[107]

The female's imperfection was also used by Giles to explain why women mature more quickly than men after birth.

> Giles reasons that, because nature accomplishes more quickly those things about which it is less careful, a woman is therefore more quickly assigned to her appointed function; for a woman is a less perfect kind of man (*mas occasionatus*).[108]

Oddly enough, Giles had argued the reverse about the development of the fetus. Males developed more quickly in the uterus because they were superior. That is, the male fetus was hot and dry, and therefore the material coagulated and began to develop more quickly. This example indicates the way in which Giles's *a priori* sex-polarity assumption about the superiority of the male and the inferiority of the female formed his "empirical" observations of the world.

Finally, Giles's devaluation of the female as an imperfect man was accompanied by a re-evaluation of the male as a divine-like being. This precept of sex polarity was completely integrated in Giles's biology:

> The non-organic spirit conveyed by the semen perfuses the menstrual matter, forming the members and initiating the spirits proper to them, and all of this as an agent of the soul of the father. Its "quasi-divine" character is apparent in the organized and apparently intelligent way in which the fetus develops.[109]

The philosophy of Giles of Rome can be seen as the perfect incarnation of the Aristotelian Revolution. As a teacher at the University of Paris he was able to transmit this view to numerous students. The institutionalization of Aristotelianism in the Faculty of Medicine involved a radical reassertion of the philosophical bases for the sex-polarity theory in the area of natural science, more commonly known as biology. In addition,

Giles wrote a political tract, *Regimen Principum*, which incorporated Aristotle's sex polarity arguments in the areas of ethics as political theory.[110] The *De Formatione Corporis Humani in Utero* became a central text in several other medical schools as well as at Paris.[111] For example, several commentaries on it were written at Bologna. Many of the commentators rejected Giles's extreme Aristotelianism, particularly on the question of female seed. However, its extensive use indicates the extent of the exposure of Aristotle's ideas in institutionalized education by the end of the thirteenth century.

The original closeness between philosophy and medicine was soon ruptured at the University of Paris. Much in the same way as philosophy and theology had begun in harmony with one another, but had, in a rather short time, polarized and entered into conflict, so medicine and philosophy soon moved apart. In the beginning of the university system, a philosopher—such as Giles of Rome—might be seriously studied by physicians and, in an opposite sense, a philosopher would seriously study medical theories written by physicians such as Hippocrates and Galen. However, almost as soon as the University of Paris had been established, another institutional decision created a deep breach between these two faculties, as well as between theology and medicine. By the end of the thirteenth century, priests were forbidden to study medicine:

> The Corpus Juris Canonici contains a decree prohibiting secular clerics and regulars from attending public lectures at the universities in medicine and law. . . . The reason adduced is, lest through such sciences, spiritual men may be again plunged into worldly cares.[112]

The separation of priestly duties from the integration of body and soul was in marked contrast to the Benedictine tradition, which treated the whole person in its monastic hospices. Just as the division between the faculties of philosophy and theology reflected a separation of reason and faith, so the division between these two faculties and the Faculty of Medicine reflected a separation of mind and soul from body.[113] The institutionalization of this separation began as early as 1215:

> As to the practice of medicine by clerics, the Fourth Council of the Lateran (1215) forbade its employment when cutting or burning was involved. In the decree (c. Sententiam 9, ne cler. vel mon.) it is said: "Let no subdeacon, deacon or priest exercise any art of medicine which involves cutting or burning."[114]

While clerics were still able to study medicine in private and even to give counsel to sick people, they were forbidden to practise surgery or to join in public discussion about medicine.

It is significant that the exclusion of women from medicine, theology and philosophy occurred at exactly the same time as institutionalized education began to fragment human knowledge. Certainly, Hildegard stood as one of the last examples of a person who incorporated philosophy, theology and medicine in an attempt to develop an integrated approach to the person. Aristotle, Avicenna, Averroes, Maimonides, St. Albert, and Giles of Rome had also written within this comprehensive framework. However, with the development of separate faculties within the university, an institutionalized framework was established that would soon render it less and less likely for anyone to be able to develop an integrated approach to the person. With the further isolation of the Faculty of Law, the study of legal patterns for human interaction was fragmented from other kinds of knowledge as well.

THE FACULTY OF LAW

It is difficult to prove a direct effect of the Aristotelian Revolution on the development of western legal theory. Unless the Greek philosopher was specifically mentioned in a rationale for a law, it is impossible to know whether Aristotle was the immediate source for the concept of woman or man. However, it is possible to describe a general relation between Aristotle and the development of the study of law. In this respect, Aristotle appears to have influenced the development of law in two specific ways. First, he gave it certain basic concepts; second, he initiated the scientific method, which was later used to develop separate laws into cohesive codes or canons.

Aristotle's first contribution to western law included the development of legal definitions of state, the distinction between distributive justice and corrective justice, and a careful consideration of the difference between voluntary and involuntary actions.[115] These crucial concepts were adopted by the Stoics, and especially by Cicero. As mentioned previously, Cicero did not perpetuate Aristotle's theory of sex polarity. Therefore, when he passed on the key legal concepts of the Greek philosopher, no significant distinctions were made between woman and man. Cicero's thought later became integrated into the heart of Roman law. Therefore, Aristotle directly affected the development of Roman legal theory in some of its central concepts, without at the same time giving a basis for the integration of sex polarity into the law.

Aristotle's second contribution to the study of law came through the adoption of his dialectic method by legal theorists. This process occurred in two different but related contexts. First, in the early twelfth century, Irnerius developed a canon of civil law (*Summa codicis*) by applying the method of reasoning that had been developed by Abelard. As previously explained, this method (known as the scholastic method) had been modeled by Abelard on Aristotle's logical treatises. Ireneus used this method to revise the separate laws of Justinian.[116] The second context for the use of Aristotle's method of legal theory came with the development of canon law. Gratian, who some historians believe was actually Ireneus's student, wrote a *Decretum* (1140) that organized the various laws of the Roman Church into a single work.[117] The *Decretum* employed the method used by Ireneus.[118] This method consisted of presenting a subject for consideration, listing arguments pro and con, and then presenting a solution. One example of this method is found in the following passage, which considered whether women could sue priests in court. Gratian stated:

> Women cannot, however, achieve the priesthood . . . and for this reason they may not raise a complaint or give testimony against the priests in court.[119]

He continued, however, by pointing out that in the Old Testament women did serve as judges and that they therefore seemed to have the right to be present and to argue in court. Finally, after appealing to an argument of St. Paul's, Gratian concluded that women should no longer have this right:

> In the Old Covenant much was permitted which today (i.e., in the New Covenant) is abolished, through the perfection of grace. So if (in the Old Covenant) women were permitted to judge the people, today because of sin, which woman brought into the world, women are admonished by the Apostle to be careful to practise a modest restraint, to be subject to men and to veil themselves as a sign of subjugation. [120]

The dialectic method, which was first established by Aristotle, was used by Abelard in theology, by Ireneus in civil law, and by Gratian in canon law. Because of its claim of being scientific, the legal codes that became established through the use of the Aristotelian method were given a place of honor in the institutionalized study of law.

The history of the study of law in Europe is as diverse as the history of the study of medicine. By the year 1000, Bologna had been established as a school for rhetoric and grammar. Then, in the early twelfth century, Countess Matilda requested Ireneus to develop an edited version of Roman law. [121] In this way, just as Blanche of Castille had played a role in the formation of the University of Paris, so another woman affected the crucial direction of the law faculty at the University of Bologna. Irnerius's *Summa codicis* became the standard text for all subsequent study of civil law.[122]

The development of the study of law at the University of Paris took a very different direction from that at Bologna. Instead of coming from a tradition of rhetoric or philosophy, the study of canon law emerged from the study of theology. After Gratian's *Decretum* was completed in 1151, and Pope Gregory had sent it to Paris for study, a separate Faculty of Decretals was established. [123] This faculty later became known as the Faculty of Canon Law. Rather quickly, the Church attempted to separate the study of civil law from the study of canon law. In 1139, the Council of Lateran forbade members of religious orders to study civil law, as did the Council of Tours in 1163. Then, in 1220, the Bull of Honorius III prohibited the teaching of any civil law at Paris. In 1254, Pope Innocent IV prohibited the study of Roman law all over France, England, Scotland, Flanders, Spain, and Hungary. [124] By the mid-fourteenth century, the study of canon law included six years for the baccalaureate followed by four years for the licentiate. This program was considered to be much easier than medicine or theology and it therefore attracted students who sought the easy way into European ecclesiastical society. Needless to say, women were not allowed to study law at Paris.

The question about the concept of woman contained in Roman and canon law still needs to be carefully examined. Although Gratian attempted to separate the two kinds of law, it is clear that there was a great deal of overlapping of theory. For example, in both civil and canon law the age for male puberty was set at fourteen and for females at twelve. [125] In addition, in both kinds of law, children born in marriage took the father's domicile, while those born outside of marriage took the mother's. [126]

It is often argued that women had a better status within Roman law than in later legal situations. Certainly, in regard to woman's rights to own property, Roman law was to be preferred to those laws that placed all of woman's property under the control of her husband at marriage. The following two laws of Justinian indicate the Roman views:

> We therefore, reducing all things to an equality, and making our disposition conformable to the laws of the twelve tables, have by our Constitution ordained,

> that all legitimate persons, that is, descendents from males, whether male or female, shall be equally called to the rights of succession *ab intestato* according to the prerogative of their degree.[127]

> No husband can alien or mortage, even with consent of his wife, any property provincial or Italian, obtained with her, as a marriage portion; lest the frailty of women should occasion the ruin of their fortunes.[128]

Of course, it is difficult to tell whether these laws were created for the good of the women themselves, or for the good of the family of the women, or for the father who did not want their sons-in-law to take away the family fortune. Justinian did argue, however, that it was wrong to deny women all inheritance:

> The ancient law, preferring descendents from males, . . . but with the Emperors Valentinian, Theodosius and Arcadius, would not continue such a violence against nature; and inasmuch as the name of a grandchild and great granchild, is common, as well to descendents by females, as by males, they granted an equal right of succession in either case.[129]

Pointing out that the tradition had, however, diminished women's inheritance by one third, Justinian concluded that the inheritance of women and men should be equal.

Interestingly, Roman law denied women the possibility for adoption except when their children had died:

> Nor can women adopt; for the law does not place even their own children under their power; but when death hath deprived them of their children, they may, by the indulgence of the prince, adopt others as a comfort for their loss.[130]

This law clearly indicates that even though women could own property they were not, if married, generally considered legally responsible for their own children.

The relation between women and men in marriage was not equal in other ways in Roman law. The punishment for a woman caught in adultery was much stronger than for a man: "If a man catches his wife in adultery, or finding her drunk, he may, with the consent of her relations punish her even with death."[131] Canon law, however, argued that adultery by either partner was grounds for separation, but not for death.[132] In this respect, canon law brought an equality into the marriage relationship that was missing in Roman law. This equality was further maintained in canon law through the theory of the mutuality of the "conjugal right." Both husband and wife had the right to sexual relations with the other partner: "Among these rights and duties the chief place is held by the right to request and the duty to render the marital or carnal relations."[133] Canon law explicitly developed a legal basis to protect women from rape or abuse of this right by a husband: "It is suspended also when it is sought immoderately or in an inappropriate place or by one who is drunk or otherwise lacks the use of reason."[134] In this way, canon law, in distinction from Roman law, placed a great deal of emphasis on the interior relationship between a woman and man in marriage. Furthermore, it declared that a woman could not be forced to marry someone against her will.[135] Therefore, canon law attempted to stop the practice of kidnapping a wife and forcing her to marry her abductor.

When Roman law and canon law are compared with respect to the concept of woman outside of marriage, one significant difference immediately emerges. In Roman law, woman was mentioned only in relation to specific activities, whereas in canon law, women were classified as a group for the first time.

In Roman law, women were considered in connection with midwifery, banking, and serving as witnesses:

> Again, where a midwife gives a drug to a woman who dies in consequence Labeo makes this distinction; if she administered the drug with her own hands, she must be held to have killed the woman; but if she gave it to the woman for her to take herself . . . the midwife furnished the cause of death rather than killed.[136]

> Women are held to be excluded from the function of banker, as that business is one for men.[137]

> Those persons are good witnesses, who can legally take by testament; but no woman . . . can be admitted as witness to a testament.[138]

It can be argued that the presence of the above laws indicate that women were commonly practising medicine and that they were seeking to be both bankers and witnesses. Otherwise there would be no need for laws to control their behaviour in relation to these activities.

Canon law classified all women as "laity," in distinction to some men who were classified as "clergy."[139] Baptism legally conferred citizenship in the Church.[140] Among citizens, a specific hierarchy was legally stipulated. Women became excluded from clergy by several different canons. First of all, tonsure, or the cutting of hair, was made a prerequisite for entry into the clergy, and then women were not allowed to receive tonsure:

> Tonsure is not an order, but rather a preparation for the reception of orders. Through its reception a baptized man leaves the lay state and enters the clerical state, thus becoming a member of the ecclesiastical hierarchy. Women are not capable of receiving it and hence are barred from entrance into the hierarchy.[141]

The legal division of members of the church into two distinct groups was a major turning point in women's history. It marked the beginning of a new phase of church history, superceding the two earlier stages that focused on charismatic and sacramental leadership.

> During this time, ecclesiastical lawyers introduced the idea of jurisdictional power, and the law began to define the power of the priesthood as divided into powers of order and jurisdiction. Not until this period did the church actually become a governmental authority.[142]

The exclusion of women from all governing functions of the church had many consequences. Probably the most dramatic was the eventual revocation of the jurisdictional powers of abbesses. Canon 118 stated: "Only clerics can obtain the power either of orders or of ecclesiastical jurisdiction." [143] It had been the practice in medieval Europe to allow many abbesses jurisdictional powers over clergy in their domain. [144] While canon law stated that only clergy had these powers, popes continued to allow selected abbesses these powers until the Council of Trent (1545–1564). [145] At this time abbesses were no longer allowed to function in direct relation to the Holy See but were forced under the jurisdiction of their local bishops. In this way canon law built in a structure that eventually excluded women from all ecclesiastical power.

In addition to the jurisdictional powers of the clergy, women were also legally barred from participation in some of the sacramental powers. They were prohibited from handling sacred objects on the altar and from carrying the Eucharist to the sick. It has been shown that Gratian based his arguments for these laws on forged texts called *Epistola Decretalis.* [146] Gratian also depended heavily on arguments produced by the early Church Fathers, and especially on Augustine's claim that woman was not in the image of God. That laws were explicitly mentioned leads to the conclusion that up to this time, women were included in some respects in the sacramental function of the priesthood.

Gratian's *Decretum* was added to, in various phases, by decretals of popes. In 1210, Pope Innocent III took a further series of sacramental functions away from women.

> It sharply condemns the practices of certain Abbesses in these dioceses of giving ecclesiastical, and thus priestly, blessings to nuns under them, of hearing their confessions, or reading the Gospel and preaching publicly. [147]

This pronouncement was reinforced by Pope Gregory IX:

> The *Decretals* of Pope Gregory IX (1234) took from Abbesses their right of public preaching and reading the Gospel and of hearing the confessions of their nuns. [148]

Women were no longer able to be teachers and counsellors in the Church. Their opportunities to preach, or to speak publicly of virtue and wisdom were eliminated; woman's virtue became as Aristotle had suggested—silence. Significantly, Hildegard, who serves as a clear example of a woman who travelled widely, preached publicly and counselled, lived just before this full incorporation of canon law into the structures of the Church.

Once this legal structure was introduced into the Church, women were eliminated from many of the areas of power and influence they had enjoyed during the Benedictine age. The University of Paris became the symbolic centre of this rigorous exclusion of women from access to all higher education, as well as to the practice of medicine and law. In its authoritative exclusion of women, Paris stood as the embodiment of the sex-polarity tradition. It is not surprising, then, that when Aristotle's works became accessible to the scholars at Paris his philosophy would be welcomed as providing the necessary foundation for the justification of sex polarity as a way of life. The establishment of the University of Paris, the development of canon law, and the influx of translations of Aristotle all occurred within a period of one century. These series of coincidences led to the ultimate completion of the Aristotelian Revolution through the institutionalization of Aristotle's thought, not only in church theory but also, eventually, throughout most of western European society.

THE INFLUENCE OF THE UNIVERSITY OF PARIS ON EUROPEAN THOUGHT

The impact of the Aristotelian Revolution was reflected in both the structure and curriculum of the University of Paris. As has been demonstrated, the concept of woman was affected in several ways by this development. First of all, the division of the university into different faculties established the basis from which the eventual fragmentation of knowledge would occur. Furthermore, while theologians adopted Aristotle's sex-polarity philosophy, philosophers adopted the polarized view present in the Aristotelian writings in natural philosophy, ethics and politics, while at the same time incorporating a new version of sex neutrality through the acceptance of the fundamental principles put forth in Aristotle's logical works. The University of Paris served as a channel for the infusion of Aristotelian thought into the profusion of new universities, as well as into the basic fabric of European society. In this way, it became the final perpetuator of the Aristotelian Revolution.

The thirteenth century stands as the most important century for the emergence of the university in European history. The following list of the founding dates of various universities bears witness to this fact: Salerno, 10??; Bologna, 1158; Paris, 1200; Oxford, 1200–1258; Cambridge, 1217; Montpelier, 1220–1298; Padua, 1222; Naples, 1224; Avignon, 1227; Toulouse, 1229; Salamanca, 1243; Curia Romana, 1244; Valencia, 1245; Seville, 1254; and Lisbon, 1288.[149] Nearly every city with the financial means to do so wanted to have its own university to compete with Paris. The end of the Benedictine age came with an explosion of secular universities aimed at providing access to higher education for the broader public.

In the fourteenth century the founding of universities spread even further than France, Italy, Spain, Portugal, and England. The following universities were founded elsewhere: Dublin, 1310; Prague, 1347; Florence, 1349; Vienna, 1365; Cologne, 1385; and Heidelberg, 1385.[150] In all of these universities, while the curriculum at Salerno was the model for medicine and the curriculum at Bologna was the model for law, the structure and curriculum of Paris was established as the model for all faculties of arts and theology. Gabriel Compayré describes the situation as follows:

> I have spoken of the Faculty of Arts at Paris only; but the programs were the same everywhere. I have before me, for example, the statutes of the Faculty of Toulouse in 1309, in which are found the same books, but with the difference that Aristotle's *Ethics* and *Physics* occupy a more important place. Thus, the ten books of the *Nicomachean Ethics* had to be read in two years, and read from one end to the other. . . . Another distribution of subjects is made, and a different order proposed for the succession of lectures; but it is always, as one may say, the same game of cards, though played in another style. Aristotle reigns as sovereign master at Oxford and Cambridge also.[151]

The University of Paris became the channel for the transmission of Aristotle to all the universities of Europe. According to Hastings Rashdall: "Whatever was read and taught in Paris was sure, sooner or later, to be read and taught in Oxford."[152] The important position of the University of Paris and the centrality of Aristotle in its curriculum led to the entrenchment of Aristotelian theory in higher education for centuries.

> At Oxford the study of Aristotle remained an integral part of the university curriculum until the middle of the seventeenth century; particular attention was given to the reading and explication of the logical, ethical, and political works.[153]

Since the concept of woman was intricately connected with these particular texts, Aristotle's views about women were incorporated into the heart of all academic study.

Even more significant, however, was the fact that academic theories did not remain solely within the ivory-tower confines of the universities. The mendicant orders took their ideas into the streets in an explosion of zeal for preaching to all Christians. The Dominicans founded houses in Bologna, Paris and Oxford so that their members could be close to the universities. In this way the intellectual framework of the Aristotelian foundation for philosophy and theology was popularized and transmitted to a vast number of people who did not themselves attend university. Consequently, Aristotle was taught all over Europe.

The University of Paris also came to have an extremely important relation to King Charles V of France. The university was called "the eldest daughter of the King."[154] "The political position of Paris gave its university a place in the political and ecclesiastical world which no other university ever occupied."[155] In this way the theories at the university were integrated into the secular political structure of Europe. Furthermore, Paris was central to the political dimension of church structure. It was called "the first school of the Church."[156] "Again and again Paris led the way and Rome followed."[157]

The Aristotelian Revolution worked its way into all the significant structures of western Europe by the end of the fourteenth century. One example of this process is reflected in the fact that the French lawyer Jean de la Terre Rouge made use of Aristotle's arguments in a case against Charles VI's attempt to disinherit the Dauphin in 1420. The lawyer argued that since the father gave the shape or form to the child through his seed, this implied a kind of identity between father and son, and, therefore, that this bond ought not to be rejected.[158]

The French court was later used to defend Aristotle in an even more direct way. In 1536, a philosopher named Peter Ramus publicly claimed that Aristotle's logical theories were false. He was prohibited by the court of Francis I from "uttering any more slanderous invectives against Aristotle."[159] A hundred years later, three other philosophers were similarly punished by a decree passed by the parliament of Paris in 1624.

> The decree followed the royal precedent, but was more severe in its terms, prohibiting all persons under pain of death, "from holding or teaching any maxim contrary to the ancient and approved authors."[160]

The support of Aristotle by the legal system of France is an indication of how deeply imbedded his philosophy had become. Certainly, European society did not accept all of Aristotle. It chose only those aspects that could be harmonized with Christianity. The canonization of St. Thomas in 1323 allowed Thomism to become the acceptable way to be Aristotelian. As far as the concept of woman was concerned, however, Aristotelianism and Thomism were clearly the same. Both theories developed a solid foundation for sex polarity.

It should be mentioned that in one respect at least, the University of Paris did not succeed in setting an acceptable model for all other universities. Women were excluded from Paris, but they were able to attend universities in southern Europe. It has already been noted that women were present at Salerno and Montpelier. There is also evidence that they studied at Salamanca. However, the exclusion of women from Paris, as well as from the two important universities in England, meant that they were not able to study at the most important universities in Europe. Since Paris held such a significant position in Europe, and Cambridge and Oxford were central to advanced English education, women were deprived of access to the necessary tools for their intellectual development. As a consequence, they were not able to study Aristotle either to learn his arguments or to develop skills for the rejection of his views where they were based on false premises or faulty reasoning. They were left with the disastrous inheritance of the view that woman is a defective man. The institutionalization of the Aristotelian Revolution accomplished the perpetuation of this philosophy in one form or another up to the present time.

Finally, another sign of the powerful effect of the Aristotelian Revolution was the explosion of forgeries or spurious texts attributed either to Aristotle or to well-known Aristotelians. A similar kind of situation arose with the plethora of texts written by neo-Pythagoreans who borrowed names of previous Pythagoreans to lend further credibility to the theories contained in the texts. The desire for an authoritative authorship also led many people to invoke the memory of Greek philosophers. With the advent of the printing press in the fifteenth century, the popularization of Aristotle reached a new level of intensity. This study of the effect of the Aristotelian Revolution on the concept of woman will end with an examination of some of the best known "doubtful and spurious" texts.

THE POPULARIZATION OF ARISTOTLE: DOUBTFUL AND SPURIOUS WORKS

The history of philosophy has often been plagued by the appearance of books falsely attributed to a particular person. In view of the intensity of the Aristotelian Revolution, it is not surprising that several books were falsely ascribed to Aristotle. It is also quite understandable that a great many of these books would have something to say about the concept of woman.

The first three examples of spurious works to be considered appeared in the ninth to the eleventh centuries. They first appeared in Arabic and were later translated into Latin. This pattern followed the path of the Revolution itself. *The Theology of Aristotle* attempted to reconcile Aristotle with neo-Platonism. *The Apple or Aristotle's Death* made Aristotle appear to believe in eternal life. The *Secretum Secretorum* described Aristotle as a Christian prophet. These three works all attempted to redefine Aristotle to conform to certain monotheistic beliefs.

The *Oeconomicus*, on the other hand, appears to have been Greek in origin. While the first three works contained only scattered thoughts about women, this work focused almost entirely on the subject of woman's relation to man. It developed a sex-polarity theory consistent with Aristotle's *Politics* and was available in Latin by the mid-thirteenth century.

A most significant spurious work was falsely attributed to St. Albert the Great. The *De Secretis Mulierum* first appeared in Latin in the fourteenth century, after the

Aristotelian Revolution had conquered Paris. In it, Aristotle's theory of generation was reasserted when it was argued that woman provided only passive matter to generation, while man provided active form. In addition, it brought forward several sex-polarity arguments to describe the development of the fetus.

Finally, the most significant of all of the spurious works for the present study, *Aristotle's Masterpiece*, emerged between the fifteenth to the sixteenth centuries as an extremely popular gynecological text. With the invention of the printing press, this spurious work entered into the homes of many people in western Europe. This collection of four short works presented a barrage of simplified Aristotelian arguments for sex polarity. While it accepted the presence of female seed, it rejected any fertile role for this contribution to generation. The Aristotelian distinction between hot and cold was employed to describe why woman and man are different. The female was considered a passive principle, the male as an active principle in generation. Finally, man was described as a superior kind of human being and woman as an inferior one. Through this work, the basic foundation for Aristotelian sex polarity was incorporated into the fundamental relationships of ordinary men and women. The institutionalization of Aristotelianism was now complete.

The chart on the following page summarizes the general tendencies towards theories of sex identity in these spurious tracts.

LIBER DE CAUSIS and THEOLOGY OF ARISTOTLE

One of the first books to reach Paris was the *Liber de Causis:*

> Of much greater historical importance than these is the *Liber de Causis* which passed in medieval times for the work of Aristotle, but is in fact (as Aquinas recognized), a translation of an Arabic work based on the *Elements of Theology.*[161]

This work is now believed to have been written in Arabic in the ninth century. This text, entitled "On the Pure Good," was translated into Latin by Gerard of Cremona in 1187.[161′] Proclus' *Elements of Theology* contained a neo-Platonic concept of soul, person and God. It did not, therefore, mention differences between woman and man. Furthermore, it accepted a doctrine of reincarnation: "Every intra-mundane soul has in its proper life periods and cyclic reinstatements."[162] As previously shown, the belief in reincarnation almost always accompanies a sex-unity theory. The claim that this work was Aristotle's made the Greek philosopher appear to have some belief in God and in the eternal existence of souls, without reference to a specific male or female body. However, a careful examination of Aristotle's philosophy shows that these assumptions were falsely attributed to him.

Since Aristotle and Plato had such different concepts of woman, a work that appeared to unify the two thinkers could only serve to confuse people about this aspect of their philosophies. Therefore, the *Liber de Causis,* by identifying Aristotle as a neo-Platonic philosopher, added to the historical complexity of tracing the concept of woman. It implied that Aristotle supported the metaphysical foundation for sex unity rather than for sex polarity.

The spurious *Theology of Aristotle,* a compilation of selections from books iv, v, and vi of Plotinus' *Enneads,* caused a similar kind of confusion by identifying Aristotle with neo-Platonism.[162′]

Text	Man	Woman	Theory
Liber de Causis	Soul separate from body through incarnation		sex unity
The Apple or Aristotle's Death	Woman and marriage an impediment to search for wisdom		sex polarity
Secretum Secretorum	Strong, like fire, air and water	Weak, like earth	sex polarity
Oeconomicus	Equal reverence in marriage		sex complementarity
	Rule, stronger, public sphere of activity	Obey, weaker, private sphere of activity	sex polarity
De Secretis Mulierum	Seed, hot, active, right	No seed, cold, passive, left	sex polarity
Aristotle's Masterpiece	Seed, hot, active, right, perfect	No seed, cold, passive, left, derived	sex polarity
The Experienced Midwife	Seed, active, hot, dry, right	No seed, passive cold, wet, left	sex polarity
Aristotle's Problems	Dry, hot, better, perfect	Cold, wet, infertile (?) seed	sex polarity, possible sex complementarity

THE APPLE or ARISTOTLE'S DEATH

This process of redefining the past is nowhere more clearly seen than in this work, which was falsely attributed to Aristotle. *The Apple* was modelled upon Plato's *Phaedo*, in which Socrates held a conversation with his disciples immediately before his death. In *The Apple*, Aristotle was shown as accepting a belief in a personal God. His last words were "I commit my spirit to the Receiver of the Spirits of the Wise."[163] Aristotle was made to appear saved, or at least consistent with some of the main beliefs of the western monotheistic tradition.

In the dialogue, Aristotle suggested that the disciples study his works:

> I have written another book, called *Metaphysics*; in it I have shown clearly that the upper firmaments and the stars are not of the elements which we see existing under the moon; they are of another nature . . . and there, from on high, the wise soul flowed into the body; it is not composed of another element, but on the contrary is simple, clean, and pure. Blessed is that soul which is not corrupted by the evil works of this world, and knows its Creator![164]

The attempt to join Aristotle's writings with a belief in personal salvation was explicitly made in the dialogue. Aristotle was also reputed to have said, "If you would follow my ways, imitate my books."[165] This spurious work, then, served a valuable function in the progression of the Aristotelian Revolution.

It is not known whether *The Apple* is Greek in origin. The first authenticated record of it is the tenth-century Arabic version. It was translated into Hebrew in Barcelona in 1235, and then into Latin in Sicily in 1255.[166] A copy was donated to the University of Paris in 1263 and from there it spread throughout Europe.

> It is evident from the manuscript tradition, then, that the *Liber de Pomo Dive de Morte Aristotilis* (*The Apple*, or *Aristotle's Death*), though not on the well-known official lists in the medieval manuals of instruction, was widely taught in universities all over Europe; in fact, we can say that it was at least informally considered part of the standard collection of Aristotelian writings. After its translation into Latin in the second half of the thirteenth century, it spread very rapidly; it was copied in increasing numbers in the fourteenth century, and maintained its popularity in the fifteenth.[167]

There was considerable controversy about the authenticity of the manuscript, and Maimonides, for example, called it spurious.[168] However, it was thought to be genuine by a great many other scholars for centuries.

The Apple contained one passage of particular significance for the concept of woman. It would appear that the influence of a preference for chastity led the author of the manuscirpt to imply that women lead men away from the proper study of philosophy. Whether this preference came from Islamic, Christian, Peripatetic or Stoical influences is difficult to determine. While Aristotle himself was married, his disciple Theophrastus, according to Juvenal, was opposed to marriage. In any event, this view in the spurious *The Apple* did contribute to the devaluation of women when Aristotle was reputed to have said:

> Do you not see that the desires and delights of the body such as women and children and wealth and eating and drinking still more impede the search after wisdom? And that when you abandon these lusts you do so in order to protect the intellect and to devote yourselves to knowledge?[169]

Consequently, this text contributed further to the impression that women were defective and inferior to men, and that they led men away from philosophy even though it falsely attributed the rejection of marriage to Aristotle himself.

SECRETUM SECRETORUM

This important book, which was also falsely attributed to Aristotle, followed a similar pattern of emergence in western thought as had the two preceding works. The earliest authenticated manuscript was written in Arabic. It was translated into Hebrew between 1190 and 1218, and into Latin by Philip of Tripoli in 1243.[170] Robert Steel claims that "Its immediate success is shown by the number of quotations made from it by Albertus Magnus and Thomas Aquinas."[171] In addition, the philosopher Roger Bacon read the *Secretum Secretorum* shortly after he had taught at the University of Paris: "His whole later life and the emotional intensity with which he pursued it can be traced to the impact of this book."[172] Through the *Secretum Secretorum*, Bacon was converted to a vision of universal science. He decided to undertake the study of science, medicine, Greek, and later, of Hebrew. Therefore, the *Secretum Secretorum* had an important role in the development of western thought even though it later turned out to be a spurious work.[173]

In the *Secretum Secretorum*, Aristotle was depicted as writing to Alexander the Great about secrets that had been revealed to him by God. In the introduction, an anonymous writer stated:

> I have seen written in several books of Grecian history that God made a revelation to him (Aristotle), saying: Verily I prefer to call thee an angel rather than a man.[174]

This attempt to describe Aristotle as an angel or prophet was another way of redefining the past in order to make the Greek philosopher conform to Islamic thought. Aristotle was also described as having been "lifted up to Heaven in a column of light" at his death.[175] Roger Bacon's notes on the *Secretum Secretorum* went even further; he claimed that Aristotle was a Christian:

> Philosophers like Plato, Aristotle, and Avicenna were not idolators, but worshipped God like the Fathers from Adam to Moses. Aristotle had the cult of the Trinity.[176]

Aristotle's secret wisdom then became acceptable to the Christian intellectual world.

In the *Secretum Secretorum*, the concept of woman received a variety of descriptions. First of all, it presented the view that sexual intercourse with women was acceptable in moderation. It recommended that a king might indulge for short periods of three to four days: "A King should participate in amusements with his family, for they warm the soul and please the senses and exhilarate the body."[177] The key to this activity was "Aristotelian" moderation:

> The things that fatten and cheer and add flesh to the body are: moderation in cohabitation. . . . And those that emaciate and weaken the body are: . . . excessive love, . . . sleeping with old women.[178]

In an interesting way, Roger Bacon chose to exaggerate this view when he paraphrased the *Secretum Secretorum* in his *Opus Majus*. The original text had merely condemned the inordinate seeking of pleasure or lust, while Bacon inferred that any intercourse was bad:

> For if love were natural, all would be in love, and always so: nor would one be deterred by shame, another by satiety. For this reason Aristotle in the *Secret of Secrets* says to Alexander, "Kind Emperor, do not yield to the desire for sexual intercourse with women, since such intercourse is a characteristic of swine. What glory it is for you if you practise a vice that is characteristic of unreasoning animals and follow the action of brutes? Believe me without question that sexual intercourse involves the destruction of our bodies, the shortening of life, the corruption of virtues, the transgressing of the law, and the adoption of effeminate manners.[179]

Bacon, who wished to defend celibacy, redefined not only Aristotle, but also the spurious *Secretum Secretorum*.

In only one place in the original text was woman portrayed as dangerous to man. Aristotle was reported as praising Greek women who had pursued knowledge. He stated: "They knew how to make predictions by stars, what house to choose for various purposes, and other sciences, such as medicine, etc."[180] Then the philosopher warned Alexander to be careful of women who know how to mix poisons:

> O Alexander, do not put thy trust in the service of women, except the woman who values her loyalty above her life and thy possessions. For thou art no more than a mere trust in their hands, and thy life is at their mercy. Beware of poisons, for many have lost their lives by them.[181]

In addition, when woman was referred to in general in the *Secretum Secretorum*, she was criticized only once: "O Alexander, never grieve for what is past, for it is the quality of women and weak persons."[182] The *Secretum Secretorum*, therefore, contained some negative attitudes towards women, although it did not develop these into any comprehensive theory about women.

The only general view about women occurred in the context of statements about the relation of woman to the earth, and of man to the sun. Woman was used, metaphorically, to describe the four different seasons of the earth. While the descriptions were poetic and appeared to be favorable to women, they nonetheless identified woman with the earth, which was the lowest of the planets.

> Spring: The earth is bedecked and ornamented, and the world becomes like a young girl adorned and resplendent before the onlookers.
>
> Summer: The strength of bodies increases, and the earth becomes like a bride laden with riches and having many lovers.
>
> Autumn: The weather changes, and the earth becomes like a matron who has passed the years of her youth.
>
> Winter: The animals grow thin, bodies grow weaker, and the world becomes like a decrepit old woman to whom death draws near.[183]

The identification of woman with the earth had further implications when the valuation of the four elements was made clear.

On the cosmic level, the *Secretum Secretorum* mirrored the Aristotelian view of the relations and valuation of the four elements:

> The earth is the centre of all the spheres and it is the coarsest of all bodies in essence and thickness or most solid of these in substance.
>
> The prepondering element in all minerals is earth. . . . The prepondering element in animals is air. Hence vegetables are superior in composition to minerals, and animals are superior to vegetables.

> Man is the noblest of all elements in construction, and the preponderating element is fire.[184]

The claim that fire was superior to earth was connected with a view of the planets as having male or female personifications.

> All things have been created from a single essence
> whose father is the sun and mother the moon.
> It has been impregnated with the air. The earth
> has sucked it from its teats.[185]

The planets were the creators of the elements: "Every planet creates that which resembles it. Saturn creates the earth, Jupiter the water, Mars air, and the Sun fire."[186] Roger Bacon, in his notes on the *Secretum Secretorum*, merely drew out the logical consequences of these views:

> Some signs are masculine, others feminine. The sun, Mars, and Jupiter are masculine, the Moon, Venus, and Saturn feminine.[187]

In the cosmic sense, then, the masculine aspect of the Sun corresponded with the superiority of fire over the other elements. Here, Aristotle's sex polarity emerged in the context of astrology in the spurious *Secretum Secretorum*. The stars were said to influence the fetus before birth:

> Everyone is born at a certain hour, and his subsequent proficiency in arts and his successes or failures in his undertaking depend upon the influence of the stars over his nativity.[188]

Astrology, for Bacon, was an important science for the prediction of human behaviour.

In this work we again find the same irony that emerged in *The Apple*, where Aristotle was invoked to reject marriage—which in fact he accepted in his own writings and life. In the *Secretum Secretorum*, Aristotle is used to support astrology, when in fact the Greek philosopher attempted to remove superstition from the study of science in order to base the philosophy of action on strictly empirical grounds and voluntary acts of will. In their desire to redefine the past, spurious works frequently distorted the philosophy of the author they seemed to invoke.

OECONOMICUS

While the concept of woman appeared only in a fleeting and peripheral manner in the above works, it is one of the central themes in the next three books to be considered. It is interesting that so many of the spurious Aristotelian texts concerned the concept of sex identity.

The *Oeconomicus* was concerned with the theme of household management. It appears to be derived, in some way, from the *Oeconomicus* of Xenophon.[189] Therefore, it probably was of Greek origin. It was translated into Latin between 1267 and 1295, and thereafter was included as a central writing of Aristotle in the *Politics*.[190] It has recently been discovered to be spurious. Therefore, the concepts of woman and man that it contains were important to the history of thought. In fact, Averroes wrote a lengthy commentary on the text, and St. Thomas frequently referred to it.

Aristotle became redefined through this text in several ways; he spoke of prayer, of the holy bond of marriage, and of the mutuality of fidelity:

> And in truth nothing is so peculiarly the property of a wife as a chaste and hallowed intercourse. And hence it would not befit a prudent man to cast his seed wherever chance might take it, lest children should be born to him from a bad and base stock, on an equality with his legitimate sons; and by this the wife is robbed of her conjugal rights, the children are injured, and above all, the husband himself is enveloped in disgrace.[191]

The text implied that Aristotle believed women and men were equal to one another and that they ought to share a mutual respect:

> And again, Ulysses thus addresses Nausicaa,
> "Lady, I do admire thee and revere."
>
> Homer accordingly considers that these are the mutual terms on which a husband and wife should stand. For no one admires and reverences his inferior; but such feelings arise only in regard to beings superior to each other in nature, and more friendly disposed; and further in the case of persons inferior to others in wisdom towards their superiors.[192]

Aristotle had argued rather forcefully in the *Ethics* that women and men were capable of only inequality in their relationships. The woman, as the inferior partner, had to redress the balance in the relationship by giving greater awe or reverence to her husband. The spurious *Oeconomicus* then contradicted this other view by proposing a direct equality of reverence between husband and wife.

The spurious *Oeconomicus* often dwelt on the mutuality of husband and wife. It was argued that whereas lower forms of animal life merely come together for the purpose of reproduction, men and women had a natural bond that aimed towards the goal of a happy life.

> But as to a man, the first object of his care should be respecting a wife; for the society which exists between the male and female is above others natural. . . . The male and female cooperate here not only for the sake of existence, but of living happily.[193]

Accordingly, husband and wife were urged to forgive one another for faults.[194] Even more, the husband was told not to beat his wife: "First of all, then certain laws are to be observed towards a wife, and especially to refrain from injuring her."[195] While Socrates, in Xenophon's *Oeconomicus*, also disliked physical methods of coercion (which he called "colt-breaking"), Aristotle did not explicitly forbid this practice in either the *Ethics* or *Politics*.

Probably the most interesting aspect of the redefinition of Aristotle can be seen in the discussion of obedience. The Greek philosopher had argued that women by nature obey and that men by nature rule. In the *Oeconomicus*, women were encouraged to obey their husbands even when their commands were not good. In a context in which fidelity to a husband, "for better or worse," was being considered, the text praised a woman who always obeyed:

> The well-ordered wife will justly consider the behaviour of her husband as a model of her own life, and a law to herself, invested with a divine sanction by means of the marriage tie and the community life. . . . So it will be seemly for her to show herself of one mind with her husband, and tractable, not only when her husband is in good luck and prosperity, but also when he is in misfortune.[196]

While the author allowed the wife to refuse any command that is "base and not worthy," she was expected to follow all other orders. Aristotle had argued that a woman ought to obey a man because he had the capacity for rational wisdom whereas in woman this rational faculty was "without authority." In the *Oeconomicus*, on the other hand, woman was encouraged to obey, even when she knew that her own judgement was more correct than her husband's. The author concluded with the forceful claim: "Observing such rules as these, the wife ought to show herself even more obedient to the rein than if she had entered the house as a purchased slave."[197]

The question of the similarity or difference between women and slaves is a perplexing one in the *Oeconomicus*. The first sentence of the second chapter implies that both women and slaves were classified as the property of man. "The component parts of a house are a man and property."[198] By implication, woman was not included in the definition of the household. However, as the work progresses, it appears as though the wife was not directly included under property. The third and fourth chapters give a description of the wife's function in the household, and the fifth chapter returns to a consideration of property: "But of property, the first and most necessary part is that which is best and chiefest; and this is man. Hence it is necessary to obtain worthy slaves."[199]

If woman was thought of as property, then she would have been discussed along with slaves. The *Oeconomicus*, however, was by no means consistent on this point. In the passage immediately after woman has been told to be more obedient than a slave, she is referred to as "bought": "For she had been bought at a high price, for the sake of sharing life and bearing children; than which no higher or holier tie can possibly exist."[200] Furthermore, in still another passage, woman is presented primarily in terms of her capacity to receive and carry man's seed. While it appears that the author was promoting women's education, in fact he was promoting his progeny:

> On this account nothing is to be omitted which tends to the fit education of a bride, so that the children may be born of the best possible mother. For the husbandman neglects nothing so as to cast his seed upon the richest and best wrought ground.[201]

Therefore, all that can be concluded from the *Oeconomicus* is that this work presented an ambiguous view of the relation between the concept of woman and property. On the one hand it seemed to argue for a mutuality and equality between woman and man that was not present in Aristotle. On the other hand it simultaneously developed a theory of obedience that went even further than Aristotle to reduce woman to a kind of property of man.

The one area in which the spurious *Oeconomicus* was consistent with Aristotle's *Ethics* and his *Politics*, as well as Xenophon's *Oeconomicus*, concerned the division of labour between woman and man within marriage. All these sources advocated separate spheres of activity for woman and man.

> Thus divinely predisposed towards such a society is the nature of both the male and the female. For the sexes are at once divided, in that neither of them have powers adequate for all purposes, nay, in some respects even opposite to each other, though they tend to the same end.[202]

This general statement of principle was developed in great detail throughout the *Oeconomicus*.

> For nature has made the one sex stronger and the other weaker, that the one by reason of fear may be more adapted to preserve property, while the other, by reason of its fortitude, may be disposed to repel assaults; and that the one may provide things abroad, while the other preserves them at home. And with respect to labour, the one is by nature capable of attending to domestic duties, but weak as to matters out of doors; the other is ill-adapted to works where repose is necessary, but able to perform those which demand exercise. And with respect to children, the bearing of them belongs to one sex, but the advantage of them is common to both; for the one has to rear them, and the other to educate them.[203]

The public sphere was described as natural and divinely ordained for man, while the private sphere became the domain of women. Physical strength, activity and passivity, and relation to fear were invoked as the basis for this separation of place of work. As a consequence, woman's virtue consisted of her acceptance of this limitation: "A good and perfect wife ought to be mistress of everything within the house, and to have the care of everything according to fixed laws."[204] This prescription of separate spheres meant that woman and man ought not to attempt any activity in the other's domain: "For it is unseemly for a man to know all that goes on in the house; in all respects indeed she ought to be obedient to her husband, and not to busy herself about public affairs."[205]

The spurious *Oeconomicus* certainly contributed to the philosophical rationale for separate spheres of activity for woman and man. The belief that it was written by Aristotle only added to its credibility. This coupling of the theories of the philosopher with religious—and particularly with Christian—emphasis on prayer, forgiveness, the holy bond of matrimony and obedience, only served to further acceptance of the ideas contained within it. Even though there was also an impulse within the work towards a mutuality of respect between husband and wife, the dominating philosophy served to reinforce the previously acceptable sex-polarity view of woman as inferior to, and even as a kind of property of man.

DE SECRETIS MULIERUM

The next spurious work to be considered was falsely attributed to St. Albert the Great, rather than to Aristotle himself. However, the *De Secretis Mulierum* became one of the major sources for another spurious work directly attributed to the Greek philosopher, entitled *Aristotle's Masterpiece*. Because the *De Secretis Mulierum* also contains numerous direct references to Aristotle, it seems appropriate to consider it within the context of consequences of the Aristotelian Revolution.

The title of *De Secretis Mulierum* is literally translated as *The Secrets of Women*. However, this work has also been referred to as *The Secrets of Albert*, as well as *The Mysteries of Human Generation.*[206] It appeared in Latin within a century of St. Albert's death in 1280 and was recognized as spurious by Peter of Prussia by the end of the fifteenth century.[207] However, it continued to be read and attributed to St. Albert by lay audiences for centuries beyond that time.

> Albert's writings were often copied and printed in the next few centuries, and even as late as 1601 *De Secretis Mulierum*, an epitome of his books on generation, was published. In some sense, it still is, as it forms the backbone of the little book *Aristotle's Masterpiece*, of which thousands of copies are sold in England every year.[208]

Even the English-language version of *De Secretis Mulierum*, published in London by John Quincy in 1725, made no mention of its spurious attribution to St. Albert.

The work itself concentrates on several different aspects of the generative processes. Aristotle's philosophy was directly incorporated into its theory about the nature of the male and female contributions to conception:

> Every man, naturally begotten, is generated from the seed of the father and the menstrual blood of the mother; and this is agreeable to the opinions of all philosophers and physicians. I mention physicians, because Aristotle, who was a philosopher, asserts that the seed of the father does not constitute in any respect the substance of the foetus, but says that the foetus is produced by the menstrual blood of the mother only.[209]

While the author of this spurious work was not decided about whether the male contribution entered substantially into the fetus, he did conclude that the female contribution was limited to the menstrual fluid. In addition, the Aristotelian association of the male with hot and the female with cold was reasserted: "A woman is naturally cold and moist, but a man is hot and dry. . . . The heat that is in a woman, is always weak in respect to the heat that is in man."[210] As a consequence, the man produced seed through his greater heat. It was the blood concocted into a pure form.[211]

The *De Secretis Mulierum* repeated Aristotle's claim that the soul of the fetus became functional at the three stages represented by the vegetative, sensitive and intellectual levels, respectively.[212] The intellectual soul came from outside the mother or father, while the sensitive and vegetative souls were provided by the father's seed. In this way the child was secured, while the female menstruum served as its matter.

The sex polarity, or more positive valuation of male over female, of the Aristotelian philosopher entered into *De Secretis Mulierum* in various ways. First of all, the author gave advice on how to conceive a male child, although no similar directions were given for the conception of a female.[213] It was also speculated that lightning might be able to change a female fetus into a male.[214] In a discussion of hermaphrodites, the male was described as the "more noble of the two sexes":

> Avicenna says, that if the seed falls on the left side of the womb, then a female child will be begotten: if into the right side, a male child, if in the middle, an hermaphrodite; that is, one who has or participates in both natures. But it receives its shape from the man, according to nature, as being the more noble of the two, tho' they are two distinct natures.[215]

This nobility was directly associated with activity as proper to the male and passivity as proper to the female: "They can perform acts of coition as a man, or receive and suffer them as a woman, that is, to be both active and passive as to the act of generation."[216]

The differentiation between male and female in relation to the opposites right and left was not Aristotelian, but rather Pythagorean in origin, although Aristotle was the first to write down the Pythagorean Table of Opposites.[217] This valuation gave clear preference to the right over the left and therefore included a sex-polarity framework in its foundation. The following list contains some of the ways in which this distinction was used in the *De Secretis Mulierum* to determine the sex of an unborn child.[218]

Male Fetus	**Female Fetus**
Mother's face red	—
Mother moves lightly and easily	—
Belly swollen on right side	Belly swollen on left side
Breast milk well formed	Breast milk watery and dark
A drop of the mother's blood will fall to the bottom of a glass of water or urine	A drop of the mother's blood will float on top of water or urine
Right breast is larger	Left breast is larger
Salt placed on top of breast will melt	—
When walking, mother places right foot forward first	When walking, mother places left foot forward first
Pain in right side	Pain in left side

The above description shows how Aristotle's sex polarity, with its preference for the male over the female, was united to the sex polarity of the Pythagorean Table of Opposites. It mingled superstition with fact in an intricate way, thereby contributing to the devaluation of women in popular literature.

ARISTOTLE'S MASTERPIECE

A study of this spurious work demonstrates the way in which the Aristotelian Revolution reached far beyond its origins in the thirteenth-century University of Paris: "*Aristotle's Masterpiece* remained until the mid-nineteenth century America's most widely-read medical book."[219]

The spurious *Aristotle's Masterpiece* appears to have been partly based on the equally spurious *De Secretis Mulierum*, which in turn may also have been inspired by the spurious *Secretum Secretorum*:

> The exact relation between Albertus' *De Secretis Mulierum* and the innumerable compendia of popular book sets on generation which appeared in the following centuries, often under the title *Aristotle's Masterpiece*, are complicated and would fittingly provide the subject for serious historical research. This would be of great interest, since it is probably correct to say that these booklets, reprinted and modified a hundredfold, formed and still form today the main source of instruction on sexual and embryological matters for the working-class portions of Western Europe.[220]

The invention of the printing press in the mid-fifteenth century allowed the Aristotelian Revolution to scatter its concepts and arguments through the literate west. The concept of woman perpetuated by these printed works became deeply entrenched in western thought through this medium. *Aristotle's Masterpiece*, then, offers a key to understanding the progressive spread of Aristotle's concept of woman.

It is difficult to determine exactly when *Aristotle's Masterpiece* first appeared. Certainly by the beginning of the sixteenth century it was well known.[221] The book was actually a compendium of several different works, each of which probably originally appeared at a different date. Although the works are repetitive, they will be treated separately in order to extract the specific variations on the concept of woman contained in each one. The four works included in the larger manuscript are entitled: 1) *Aristotle's Masterpiece*; 2) *The Experienced Midwife*; 3) *Aristotle's Problems*; and 4) *Aristotle's Last Legacy*.

The exact claim about the relation of Aristotle to these texts is complicated. It is sometimes argued that Aristotle directly wrote them. This claim is impossible to support, even superficially, because the texts include references to Galen, Avicenna, and even Duns Scotus, who wrote considerably after Aristotle. More probably, the attribution to Aristotle implied that the author presented Aristotle's views about specific topics and compared these views to those of other philosophers. The goal of the works was to imply that Aristotle's thoughts were correct about the wide range of topics they contained. This goal then enabled the works to be called *Aristotle's Masterpiece*. The process of redefining Aristotle was stretched finally to include nearly all major aspects of what is now considered to be gynecology. In a certain sense, this "masterpiece" became the ultimate redefinition of Aristotle's concept of woman.

Aristotle's Masterpiece

This work, whose name was adopted as the title for the entire collection, contained several sections concerning the concept of woman. The following list indicates some of the subjects considered: a description of the generative organs; a description of the act of coitus; praise of marriage; a discussion of virginity; a description of signs of conception; a description of signs of the sex of the fetus; a discussion of barrenness and impotence; a description of the qualifications of a midwife; a description of labour, birth and after birth; a description of difficult deliveries; and physiognomy.[222] It is clear that one intention of the author was to provide a practical book to aid in conception and birthing. Behind this intention, however, a concept of woman in relation to man is presented. In many respects this concept mirrored the Aristotelian view. In an 1813 printing of *Aristotle's Masterpiece*, the editor began with the following observation:

> To say that Aristotle, the learned author of the following sheets, was reported to be the most learned philosopher in the world, is no more than what every intelligent person already knows. . . . Though Aristotle applied himself to the investigation of the secrets of nature, yet he was pleased to bring into a fuller and more true light those secrets with respect to the generation of man. Thus he styled his *Masterpiece*; and in this he has made so thorough a search, that he has as it were turned nature inside out.[223]

The editor chose to play with a poem that the author of the *Masterpiece* used to describe the way in which woman and man were opposite: "For those what have the strictest searchers been, find women are but men turn'd outside in; And men if they but cast their eyes about, may find they're women with their insides out."[224]

The discovery that women and men had similar generative organs was frequently reflected on in the *Masterpiece*. The author correctly described the function of the clitoris and its similarity to the male organ in its relation to sexual pleasure.[225] The presence of the testicles on the outside of the male was matched by the ovaries inside the female, and so on. However, the male testicles were not thought to make the same contribution to generation as the ovaries of the female:

> The testicles in women are very useful; for where they are defective, generation work is quite spoiled; for though these little bladders which are on their outward superficies contain nothing of seed, as the followers of Galen, etc., erroneously imagine, yet they contain several eggs (about the number of twenty in each testicle) one of which being impregnated by the most spirituous part of man's seed to the act of coition, descends through the oviducts into the womb, where it is cherished till it becomes a live child.[226]

The author of *Aristotle's Masterpiece* was well aware of the controversy about the female contribution to generation. Although the existence of female eggs was accepted, which was certainly in advance of the view that the female merely contributed menstrual fluid, the Aristotelian view was reaffirmed in the claim that the egg was merely a passive contributor to the process. The relation of opposites, hot with the male and cold with the female, was used to explain this difference:

> They [women's ovaries] differ also in their substance being much more soft than those of men, and not so well concocted; their bigness and temperature differ in that they are less and colder than those in men. Some indeed will have their use to be the same as in men, but that is for want of judgement; for Aristotle

> and Scotus both affirm that women have no seed, and that their stones differ also in their use from those of men; their use being as I already said, to contain that egg which is to be impregnated by the seed of man.[227]

The greater presence of heat in men was also used to explain why women became unable to conceive children sooner than men.[228] Heat allowed the blood in men to become concocted into a pure state that subsequently could be transformed into fertile seed.[229] Therefore, the *Masterpiece*, for the most part, merely reasserted Aristotle's theory of generation.

The polarity between woman and man was expressed in the metaphysical categories of activity and passivity:

> Now in conception, that which is first to be regarded, and without which it cannot be, is the seed of man, that being the active principle, or efficient cause of the foetus. . . . The next thing is the passive principle, to the foetus (for there must be both in order to conceive) and this is an ovum or egg, impregnated by the man's seed.[230]

The concept of woman became entirely connected with this passive function, and the concept of man became entirely connected with this active function.

> I have shown in the former section that there are two things to be regarded chiefly in conception, to wit the active and passive principle. This in part shows that differences in sexes is a prerequisite to conception. So nature has ordained there must be a proper vehicle for the active principle to be injected therein to and there must also be a passive principle to be impregnated thereby, so the woman has no active principle to impregnate, and therefore, without different sexes, there can be no conception.[231]

Therefore, *Aristotle's Masterpiece* reaffirms the passivity of woman even though it recognizes the presence of the egg during ovulation. Sex polarity, as a theory of male and female identity, reaffirmed its basic premises even when new evidence indicated that the female contribution might be much more like the male contribution than was thought by Aristotle or Galen.

In the last section of the *Masterpiece*, in which physiognomy is discussed, the negative valuation of the female in relation to the male is explicitly stated. The author stipulated that the discussion would concentrate on the male:

> Therefore the judgements we pass properly concern a man, as comprehending the whole species, and but improperly the woman, as a part thereof, and derived from the man.[232]

The view that woman was a derivative or imperfect form of man was clearly within the tradition of Aristotelian sex polarity.

In two significant respects *Aristotle's Masterpiece* differs from Aristotle about the concept of woman. The first difference concerns the description of the qualities of a midwife. Here the woman was given a very positive characterization:

> Nor are the qualifications assigned to a good surgeon improper to a midwife, viz. a lady's hand, a hawk's eye, and a lion's heart: to which may be added activity of the body, and a convenient strength, with caution and diligence, not subject to drowsiness, nor apt to be impatient. She ought to be sober and affable, not subject to passion, but bountiful and compassionate, and her temper cheerful and pleasant, that she may better comfort her patients in their sorrow.[233]

Aristotle had argued that woman was not able to achieve practical wisdom. The woman of the above description, however, appears to have spent a great deal of effort to develop a mature and reliable character. Of course, Aristotle could have argued that this woman was "naturally" good. However, it is more likely that a woman of the above description would have spent many years achieving such a balanced character.

The second topic that digresses from Aristotelian theory concerns the prediction of the sex of the fetus. The following list described the different ways to determine whether a woman was pregnant with a boy or a girl.[234]

Male Fetus	Female Fetus
Lays on right side	—
Woman rising from chair rests on right hand	Woman rising from chair rests on left hand
—	Belly rounder and higher
Complexion clear	Complexion swarthy
Right side harder	—
Right nipple redder	—
Moves more easily in pregnancy	—
Circles under right eye	Circles under left eye
A drop of the mother's milk will float on the surface of water	A drop of the mother's milk will sink to the bottom of water

This list of superstitions about the sex of the child varied only slightly from the spurious *De Secretis Mulierum*. Oddly, the last suggestion is in some ways the opposite of a similar suggestion in the *De Secretis Mulierum*. However, in some of the examples a clear preference for the male fetus is indicated. For example, it was suggested that it is easier to bear a boy than a girl, and that the mother of a boy looked better. In this way a certain aspect of sex polarity was present in this process.

The Experienced Midwife

The first printed English edition of this work appeared in 1700. The title page contained the following information:

> Aristotle's Complete and Experienced Midwife. In two parts:
> I. A guide for child-bearing women in the time of their conception, bearing and suckling their children with the best means of helping them both in natural

> and unnatural labours together with suitable remedies for the various indispositions of newborn infants.
>
> II. Proper and safe remedies for the curing of all those distempers that are incident to the female sex and more especially those that are any obstruction to their bearing of children. A work far more perfect than any yet existent and highly necessary for all surgeons, midwives, nurses, and child-bearing women. Made in English by W—— S—— M.D., London.[235]

Sir D'Arcy Power implies that William Salmon, the stated translator of the work, may have been its author.[236] Salmon wrote and lived in sixteenth-century England and North America. This book, written in English when most other medical books were available only in Latin, became extremely popular. It is therefore important to examine its concept of woman.

The structure of *The Experienced Midwife* is nearly identical to that of the *Masterpiece*. It deleted a few subjects and developed others, with particular emphasis on practical medical advice. The following are the main themes in the order in which they appear in the text: a description of the generative organs; a description of the signs of conception (including care of the woman after conception); a description of signs of the sex of the fetus; a description of the formation of the child; a description of labour, birth and after birth; a description of difficult deliveries; a description of the medical care of infants and children; descriptions of and cures for barrenness and impotence; and a description of the medical cures for women's diseases.[237] While the author shows a familiarity with medical texts by Hippocrates, Galen and Avicenna, it is clear that he designed his work on the earlier, spurious *Masterpiece*.

The most fascinating section of the text included a discussion of the now infamous question of the nature of the female contribution to generation. The author initially declared his opposition to the theory that women contributed seed:

> It is true that Galen and Hippocrates did erroneously imagine that the stones in women did both contain and elaborate seed as those do in men, but it is a great mistake; for the testicles of women are as it were no more than two clusters of eggs, which lie there to be impregnated by the most spirituous particles.[238]

The discovery that women's ovaries in some way paralleled male testicles led to the need to clarify this specific nature of the contribution of the ovaries. The author argued that the most expert opinion concluded that the female contributed no seed:

> Some authors affirm that by these women discharge seed into the bottom of the womb: but the whole current of our modern authors run quite another way, and are positive that there is no seed at all in their vessels.[239]

After this direct affirmation of the Aristotelian position, the author of *The Experienced Midwife* decided to review some of the details of the various arguments for and against female seed. He stated that the ancients argued in two ways that women had seed:

1. Woman had seed because she had seminal vessels and nothing is created in vain.
2. Women who copulate get twice as much pleasure as men because they get pleasure from the emission of their own seed as well as from the reception of male seed.[240]

Against these attempts of the ancients, the moderns argued that women did not have seed for the following reasons:

1. Women's eggs are like eggs of a fowl because if they are boiled they yield the same consistency.
2. All generation needs an active and a passive principle; therefore, the male provides the active principle in seed and the female the passive principle in the egg.[241]

There is an obviously Aristotelian influence in the second argument. It is, however, the next phase of the argument that is most interesting. The author admitted that not all moderns accepted the above arguments. Indeed, some rather strongly rejected them. The objectors included male theorists as well as women themselves:

> But, not withstanding what is here urged by our modern anatomists, there are some late writers of the opinion of the ancients, viz. that women have both and emit seed by the act of copulation, and good women themselves take it ill to be thought merely passive in those wars, in which they make such vigorous encounters, and positively affirm, they are sensible of the emission of their seed in those engagements, and that a great part of the delight they take in that act consists in it. I will not therefore go about to take any of their happiness away from them, but leave them in possession of their felicity.[242]

There is no question that the author rejected these arguments for women's seed, reducing them to "felicity." Even though women were for the first time mentioned in these discussions, the author's arguments, unfortunately, appears to contain the belief that women's seed was contained in the secretions they emitted during intercourse. The women, therefore, did not yet have an adequate understanding of their contribution. They were, however, correct in their attempt to reject the passive characterization of their contribution.

The separation of the sexes into active and passive contributors to generation was the clear result of the Aristotelian Revolution. The author of *The Experienced Midwife* frequently repeated this view:

> As the generation of mankind is produced by the coition of both sexes, it necessarily follows that the instruments of generation are of two sorts, to wit male and female; the operation of which are by action and passion, and herein the agent is the seed and the patient blood.[243]

The contrary interaction of the agent and patient were further tied to the Aristotelian theory of the interaction of the contraries hot and cold:

> The author of our being has laid an injunction upon men and women to propogate their kind, hath also so wisely fitted them for that work; and seeing that in the act of coition there must be an agent and a patient (for if they be

> of one constitution, there can be no propogation) therefore the man is hot and dry, and the woman cold and moist. It is therefore necessary that the woman should be of a cold constitution, because in her is required a redundency of matter for the nourishment of the infant depending on her.[244]

This view was reiterated in such a way that the male and female were thought to be incapable of having any similarity in their respective contributions to generation. It was also argued to be ordained by God:

> The universal course of nature being formed by the Almighty of a composition of contraries, cannot be increased by a composition of likes; and therefore if the constitution of the woman be hot and dry as well as the man there can be no conception; and if, on the contrary, the man should be of a cold and moist constitution as well as the woman, the effect would be the same, and this barrenness is purely natural.[245]

The Aristotelian framework made it impossible to uncover the correct theory of the female and male contributions to generation. It is now known that both male and female simultaneously provide similar and different contributions. The union of their nuclear contributions brings about the activation of the egg. The way in which these contributions meet is different for the two sexes, but it is not possible to correctly characterize one sex as active and the other as passive. The Aristotelian theory was clearly wrong.

In one significant area *The Experienced Midwife* improved upon *Aristotle's Masterpiece*. In the original work, the signs of the conception of a male or female were stated as definitive. In the derivative work the author suggested some caution in their application. The signs, however, were very much the same. The author listed only the signs of a male fetus, while concluding: "In all it is to be noted, that what is a sign of a male conception, the contrary holds good of a female."[246]

Male Fetus
1. a woman rising from chair rests on her right hand
2. the belly is rounder and higher
3. the child lies on the right side
4. the right nipple is harder
5. the right breast is plumper and harder
6. the woman's colour is clear
7. the woman has circles under her right eye
8. a drop of mother's milk in water will float on the surface

Interestingly, once again one of the signs was opposite to one reported in an earlier work. In the *Masterpiece* the female fetus, rather than the male, was associated with the second sign. In general, however, the Pythagorean table of right and left continued its early association with male and female.

The author of *The Experienced Midwife* also rejected one of the theories that had been prominent in medieval philosophy. He argued that there was little evidence to support the claim that the male fetus formed more quickly than the female:

> The fourth and last time assigned by physicians to the formation of the child is about the thirtieth day after conception for a male but for a female, they tell us forty-two or forty-five days are required; though for what reason I know not, nor does it appear by truth: for if the male receives its formation fifteen days sooner than the female, why should it not be born much sooner too?[247]

In conclusion, it has been shown that *The Experienced Midwife*, for the most part, merely repeated Aristotelian arguments that had originally been stated in the *Masterpiece*. Because of the tremendous popularity of these two works and of their use by the general population in Europe and North America, Aristotle's sex polarity was transmitted over and over again. It is no wonder, then, that it took so long for the basic premises of the Revolution to be challenged.

Aristotle's Problems

This little work, which is placed in the centre of *Aristotle's Masterpiece*, had a different origin from the other works being considered. It was based upon another spurious work of the same title, which probably appeared in the Peripatetic school soon after Aristotle's death.[248] The original work, written in Greek, consisted of a consideration of several questions ranging across the fields of mathematics, music, biology and zoology, as well as the study of human character. Most of the time the questions were posed but no answers were given. This collection of philosophical problems was translated into Latin by Theodore Gaza in 1438.

The version of *Aristotle's Problems* that was included in *Aristotle's Masterpiece* emerged in English by 1595, when it was printed by the Widow Orwin with the title *The Problems of Aristotle with other Philosophers and Physicians*. This version included a great deal more about women, as well as sections attributed to Marc Anthony Zimaras and Alexander Aphrodiseus.[249] The second version of *Aristotle's Problems* revealed the ability of the Aristotelian Revolution to explain nearly all differences between women and men. A comparison of the two texts is helpful here.

In the original *Problems*, the opposites dry and moist were introduced in several different contexts. For example, it was suggested that women might be more prone to miscarriage in spring because of the greater moisture during this season.[250] Or it was suggested that women and boys did not have beards because of their greater moisture.[251] The left ear was called the "female ear" because it had greater moisture.[252] Finally, it was asked whether in wet districts more females than males were produced because the greater moisture thickened the seed more slowly.[253]

The opposites hot and cold were also used to explain differences between the sexes:

> Why are men less capable of sexual intercourse in summer, but women more so? . . . Is it because the hot characteristics fail in the summer by the excess of heat, but the cold ones flourish? Now a man is dry and hot, but a woman is cold and moist. So the power of the man is diminished at that time, but that of women flourishes because it is balanced by its contrary.[254]

In spite of this passage, in the original *Aristotle's Problems*, the opposites hot and cold did not frequently appear in explanations. The *Problems* included in *Aristotle's Masterpiece*, however, continuously introduced this factor.

The sex polarity of Aristotle's philosophy was also reflected in the original *Problems* in another way. The female was clearly seen as a defective male. In one passage it was asked why some men enjoyed being passive in intercourse. The following explanation was given:

> Such persons are unnaturally constituted; for though they are male this part of them has been maimed. Such maiming produced either complete destruction or a distortion of type. This latter is impossible for it would imply their becoming female.[255]

The conception of the female as a distortion of the male was repeated in another passage: "Why is it a more terrible thing to kill a woman than a man? And yet the male sex is naturally better than the female."[256] Consequently, the original spurious *Problems* merely transmitted Aristotelian sex polarity through its questions and answers.

The *Problems* and *Aristotle's Masterpiece* were much more explicit about a wide range of female and male characteristics. While they appear to have derived a structure from the original work in that they frequently considered similar issues, they went far beyond the original method used. The original text asked more questions than it answered. The second text gave definitive answers to nearly everything asked.

The first major development in the second text related to the use of the opposites hot and cold to explain several distinctions between the sexes. The following excerpts demonstrate the point:

> Why are not women bald?
> Because they are cold and moist, which are the causes that the hair remaineth.[257]
>
> Why have men more teeth than women?
> By reason of the abundance of heat and blood, which is more in men than in women.[258]
>
> Why have females of all living creatures the shrillest voice, a crow only being excepted, and a woman shriller than a man, and smaller?
> According to Aristotle, by reason of the composition of the veins, as appears by a similitude, because a small pipe sounds shriller than a great; and also, in women, because the passage where the voice is formed is made narrow and straight, by reason of cold.[259]
>
> Why are not women ambidexter as well as men?
> Because as Galen saith, a woman in health that is most hot, is colder than the coldest man in health.[260]
>
> Why do men feel cold sooner than women?
> Because the men being hotter than women, have their pores more open, and therefore the cold doth sooner enter into them than women.[261]

> How comes women's blood to be thicker than men's?
> Their coldness thickens, binds, congeals, and joins it together.[262]
>
> Why have women narrower breasts than men?
> Because there is more heat in men, which doth naturally move to the uppermost part of them, making those parts great and large, . . . but in women cold predominates, which naturally tends downwards, and therefore women often fall on their backside, because their hinderparts are gross and heavy, by reason of cold ascending thither; but a man commonly falls on his breast by reason of its greatness and thickness.[263]

As can be seen from these passages, the *Problems* in *Aristotle's Masterpiece* took some of Aristotle's theories far beyond their original application. Once the theoretical framework of the Aristotelian Revolution was established, it was used to explain just about everything.

The *Problems* in *Aristotle's Masterpiece* also included a discussion of male and female contributions to generation. This discussion implied at first that both male and female contributed seed:

> Why is a man's seed white and a woman's red?
> This is white in man by reason of his great heat and quick digestion, because rarified in the testicles; but a woman's is red, because 'tis the superfluity of the second digestion.[264]

The text concludes that the male properly provides the seed and the female the matter, or the male is the efficient cause and the female the material cause of the fetus.

> Doth the man's seed enter into the substance of the child?
> We say, the seed does not go into the substance of the child; and it is proved thus, because the matter and the efficient cause should all be one, which is against the philosopher.[265]

Aristotle, as the philosopher, was frequently appealed to in support of a theory. In a passage where the causes for barrenness are being considered, the author stated: "It is evident in philosophy, that the agent and the patient ought to have the same proportion, else the action is hindered."[266] The Aristotelian claim that nature always intends to form a fetus into a male was used in a discussion of the generation of hermaphrodites: "Nature tends always to that which is best, therefore she does always intend to beget a male; . . . when nature cannot perfect the male, she brings forth the female too."[267] Finally, the text contained the Aristotelian view that the male offspring that resembled the father was the result of the male seed conquering the matter of the female.

> Why are some children altogether like the father, some like the mother, some like both, and some like neither?
> If the seed of the father doth wholly overcome that of the mother, the child doth wholly resemble the father; but if the mother predominate, then it is like the mother.[268]

In one interesting context it is mentioned that woman's thoughts are capable of influencing the physical features of the fetus. In this way, the phenomenon of a white mother producing a black child was explained.[269] In *Aristotle's Masterpiece* it had been suggested that the mother's imagination could affect the character of the fetus.[270] Also, in *The Experienced Midwife*, woman's imagination was used to explain the generation of monsters.[271] In this way a certain active function of the female contribution was allowed through the mind, while it was rejected in the body. The difficulty of this, however, was that it appeared only to be invoked in negative situations, as an interference with the activity of the male contribution rather than in any positive aspects of mothering. *Aristotle's Problems*, then, did little to change the direction of the Aristotelian Revolution. Woman remained devalued in relation to man in all of these descriptions of her concept.

The devaluation of women in a theory of generation had consequences in other areas as well. In the spurious *Zimaras' Problems*, which was also contained in *Aristotle's Masterpiece*, woman's intellectual and ethical capacities were discussed: "How comes [sic] most women's wits inapt in good things, and prompt in naughty? Because of a privation which seems to be coupled and joined to her nature."[272] The author argued that woman was either immediately good or not good at all. In this way the Aristotelian theory was given specific application.

> Why do men say a woman's first counsel should be chosen?
> Because (as we see in things that want reason) their actions and motions are guided to their proper ends by superior powers. . . . So a woman's understanding, though she knows not the reason of good and evil is sometimes directed by an infallible truth to take some things in hand.[273]

Aristotle had claimed that woman was not able to deliberate because of a "lack of authority" in her reason. The spurious work merely drew out the explicit consequences of this claim.

The Aristotelian Revolution had also included the direct association of women with matter. *Zimara's Problems* applied this association in a rather peculiar consideration of the loss of woman's virginity:

> Why does a woman love that man best who had her maidenhead?
> It is because that as matter doth covet a form of perfection, so doth a woman the male.[274]

The lack in the female was also used to explain her unvirtuous tendency towards greed:

> Why are clergymen and women most covetous?
> The nature of woman is imperfect, and therefore they think it impossible to fully satisfy themselves; they gather together, and keep that by which they may help their need; and by industry and art they covet to obtain that which nature did not give them.[275]

In conclusion, then, it can be said that the above spurious works merely carried on the general conclusions of Aristotle about the concept of woman in relation to man. In many respects it applied the conclusions to issues Aristotle never considered. However, this application merely revealed the general acceptance of Aristotelian sex polarity in western Europe from the fourteenth to the nineteenth century.

Aristotle's Last Legacy

The final part of *Aristotle's Masterpiece* to be studied was rather appropriately called *Aristotle's Last Legacy*. According to Sir D'Arcy Power:

> Side by side with the *Masterpiece* is *Aristotle's Last Legacy* which began life frankly as a chapbook to be sold at Fairs and by hawkers. The first edition I know of is undated but was probably printed about 1690.[276]

The title page claimed that the work was translated by a Dr. Borman and that it referred to palmistry, dreams, and other kinds of "riddles." However, the text of *Aristotle's Last Legacy* appears, rather, to be a combination of the previously discussed *Masterpiece* and *The Experienced Midwife*. It is interesting, however, because in some specific ways it gave a different emphasis to certain issues.

The general topics discussed in the *Legacy* include: a description of virginity; a description of the organs of generation; a description of the act of coitus; a description of the signs of conception; a description of the signs of the sex of the fetus; a description of and cures for barrenness; praise of marriage and coition; a description of the midwife; and the medicines prescribed for labour.[277] This work is extremely practical in its orientation and clearly aimed at giving readers concrete applications for its theories.

The first interesting subject discussed concerned the ways to tell whether a woman was a virgin. It is particularly significant that this book attempted to correct a theory previously presented in the spurious *De Secretis Mulierum*. In the earlier work, falsely attributed to Albert the Great, the absence of the hymen was considered to be the necessary and sufficient proof for loss of virginity:

> We shall now treat of, and show the signs whereby a man may know whether a woman has been debauched. Here we must observe, that at the first time of coition some women are very much broken so that their private parts are overstretch'd and enlarged, by reason of the man's instrument being too thick and no ways fit for, or adapted to the woman's, and by that means her private parts are extended; so that a man may find an easy entrance without pain or trouble; and then he may depend upon it that some other person has ploughed up the ground before him.[278]

The *Masterpiece* was the first text to attempt to correct this view. It gave a rather technical description of the position and nature of the hymen and then concluded:

> I must do the fair sex this justice, to let the world know, that although wherever this is found, it is an undoubted token of virginity, yet it will not follow, that where this token is wanting, that virginity is deflowered.[279]

The Experienced Midwife gave a further technical statement on this topic:

> What I have said of the effusion of blood which happens in the first act of copulation, though when it happens it is an undoubted sign of virginity, showing the caruncles myrtiformes have never been pressed till then; yet when there happens no blood, it is not always a sign that virginity is lost before.[280]

Aristotle's Last Legacy went one step further. Its author made an explicit statement defending women who had been wrongly accused:

> Upon the whole, when a man marries, and finds, upon lying with his wife, the token of her virginity he has all the reason in the world to be satisfied he has married a virgin; but if on the contrary, he finds them not, he has no reason to suspect her of unchastity, as if she were not a virgin, since the hymen, or claustrum virginale may be broken so many other ways, and yet the woman be both virtuous and chaste. . . . And thus much I thought myself bound to say in defence of the female sex, who are often accused and suspected of dishonesty, when there is no occasion for it.[281]

Of course, it is significant in itself that all of these spurious works concentrated on the theme of virginity in the first place. That they all included this topic is sign enough of the importance it was given in general society. Indeed, it is merely a further indication that the woman's body was viewed as the male's property within marriage. Any violation of this property by another man ruined her usefulness. Even the metaphor of ploughing used in the *De Secretis Mulierum* drew attention to the relation of woman to the earth. Aristotle's theoretical framework, which identified the female with passivity, merely became modified so it could be used to explain the significance of female virginity to the male.

The first sentence of *Aristotle's Last Legacy* indicated the way in which Aristotle's thought was used by these theorists of sexuality:

> The great maker of the universe, that gives all creatures life and being and a power in themselves to propagate their kind, even to the end of the world, has to that end created them male and female, and these of contrary qualities; for, in this noble pair, man and woman, the man is hot and dry, the woman cold and moist; and these two differing qualities uniting, are ordained by nature for the procreation of children, the seed of man being the efficient cause, and the womb of woman the field of generation, wherein the seed is nourished, and the embryo formed, and in due time brought forth.[282]

The woman as a field in which seed had been deposited, provided the material cause of the child.

The author of *Aristotle's Last Legacy* gave almost the exact same arguments about the nature of woman's contribution to generation as had the author of *The Experienced Midwife*. The similarity in reasoning was not surprising in view of the fact that the sections on the signs of the sex of the fetus and on the qualities of a good midwife were identical in the two texts.[283] In the discussion of the question of female seed, the author mentioned that ancient writers supported the existence of female seed because nothing was created in vain, and because women experienced double pleasure in coition. Then the arguments by which the moderns proved the ancients to be erroneous were stated:

women's eggs were like fowl's eggs, and that there needed to be separate active and passive principles in generation. The next stage in the discussion, however, differed from the other text. *The Experienced Midwife* had mentioned that women themselves believed they contributed seed to generation, and it also gave a vague mention to some modern medical writers who supported this contention. The author of *Aristotle's Last Legacy*, however, omitted any reference to women's own perceptions, while referring to a specific medical writer to support this view.

> But notwithstanding all this, Culpepper, in his directory for Midwives, positively affirms, that the testicles or stones of a woman are for generation of seed, and to deny this, is both against reason and experience. I will not undertake to determine the controversy, but leave the reader to judge for himself.[284]

It is not surprising that the ultimate result of the "last legacy" of the Aristotelian Revolution would be to render invisible women's own perceptions of their nature. This is consistent with the basic sex polarity of the Aristotelian theory. Woman was associated with passivity, with material causation, with the lowest of the elements and with the earth. This association was made clear in the most complicated of philosophical texts, as well as in the most popularized pamphlets. The study of doubtful and spurious works has proven how deeply the Aristotelian framework penetrated the thought of individual women and men of western Europe, England, and North America. The Aristotelian Revolution, which was institutionally grounded in the development of the university structure in the thirteenth century, continued to function as late as the nineteenth century, as evidenced by the above texts. It is no wonder, then, that twentieth-century considerations of the concept of woman continue to dig into the bedrock of Aristotle. Until this foundation has been removed, the struggle to develop a correct philosophy of the concept of woman in relation to man will be doomed to failure. When it has been removed it will become possible, at last, to begin once more the important task that philosophy recognized from its beginnings. What is and ought to be the relation between woman and man?

SUMMARY AND EVALUATION

THE VICTORY OF THE ARISTOTELIAN REVOLUTION

This chapter has demonstrated the steady movement of the Aristotelian Revolution from slumbering, to explosion, to popular victory, Within these stages, the concept of woman was caught and defined for centuries. The ultimate victory of the Aristotelian Revolution is confirmed by the fact that Aristotle's philosophy has so permeated western Europe that it has become an unnoticed element in the contemporary debate about the relationship of woman and man. In other words. Aristotle is the invisible foundation of western thought about woman and man.

The final stage of the Revolution, the accomplishment of its decisive victory, moved the impact of Aristotle beyond concepts or structured arguments to the institutionalization of his thought. The Greek philosopher's rationale for the respective identities of woman and man was disseminated in a complex academic form throughout most European educational structures, in a simplified form through formal and informal preaching in the churches and streets, and in an exaggerated and superstitious form in popular pamphlets on gynecology.

When it is recalled that the first efforts to think about the concept of woman in relation to man were recorded in a variety of fragments by early Greek philosophers, Aristotle's victory is even more impressive. Among the theories proposed in the beginning of western philosophy, only two remained at the end of the Aristotelian Revolution: sex polarity and sex neutrality. Both of these theories were founded on the philosophy of Aristotle. Among the many original thinkers on this question, only one prevailed. By the end of the thirteenth century, Aristotle's victory was complete.

THE INSTITUTIONALIZATION OF SEX NEUTRALITY

The first result of the Aristotelian victory was the adoption of his logical texts as the central curriculum of the Faculty of Arts at Paris. These works emphasized the definition of persons in terms of forms or universals. Differentiation of persons through sex or other material aspects was not thought to be relevant to logical enquiry. As a consequence, philosophy, as developed within the Faculty of Arts, established itself within a tradition of sex neutrality.

Sex neutrality is described as a derivative form of the sex-unity theory. It accepts, without argument, that women and men are equal and that their differences are not significant, at least for the study of philosophy. Historically, the sex-unity tradition—as developed by the Pythagoreans, Plato, and the neo-Platonists—was always acccompanied by the study of mathematics, as well as by a theory of the reincarnation of the soul. The association with mathematics appears to be no more coincidental to sex unity than does logic, as a derivative form of mathematics, to sex neutrality.

This linking of theorists, who viewed philosophy as essentially related to logic and mathematics, to an affirmation of sex unity or sex neutrality was found from the first moments of the foundation of the University of Paris, as seen in Roger Bacon, who gave evidence of this trend in his writings at that time. Sex neutrality is a theory that essentially ignores the materiality of human existence and instead focuses its formal structure on rationality. Aristotle provided a convenient rationale for this preference in thinking and the victory of the Aristotelian Revolution ensured that it would become the respectable way to do philosophy for centuries to come.

THE POPULARITY OF ARISTOTELIAN SEX POLARITY

Beyond the domain of academic philosophy, it was sex polarity, not sex neutrality, that resulted from the Aristotelian Revolution. At first the Revolution moved through the study of biology into the study of the theory of medicine. Giles of Rome was seen to have been an exemplary figure in this process. Having based his theory of the inferiority of woman on Aristotle's biological writings, he became one of the main theorists for the medical faculty at Paris. These theories were incorporated into the most important faculty at Paris, theology, where they were used to defend a total superiority of man as more perfectly resembling the nature of God. Through the commentaries on Lombard's *Sentences*, by St. Bonaventure and St. Thomas, the Aristotelian rationale for sex polarity was fully integrated into the study of theology.

Sex polarity even emerged in the study of civil and canon law. While specific laws did not mention Aristotle, they proved to be quite consistent with his thought about woman and therefore reflected the general trend of institutionalizing the rationale for the inferiority of woman in relation to man. The establishment of academic centres for the study of law, as well as for the canons of law, merely deepened the ground for sex polarity within the broader structure of society.

The impact of Aristotle can be seen through the numerous popular and spurious texts that appeared throughout Europe after the Greek philosopher's technical works were made required reading at Paris in 1255. Aristotle's association of the male with active, hot, dry and superiority, and the female with passive, cold, moist and inferiority, worked its way into thousands of popular tracts purporting to help women deliver and care for infants in the home. Aristotle seemed to reach everywhere and into everything, even into the most intimate, personal, sexual dimensions of life.

In a way, this explosion of the popular tracts falsely attributed to Aristotle can be interpreted as one of the first effects of media saturation in the history of the west. The invention of the printing press in the fifteenth century made it possible for numerous authors to disperse their thoughts. Whereas in the past, texts resided for the most part in the libraries of monasteries or universities, now everyone could purchase, inexpensively, the latest "home philosophy" of sex identity. Given the usual interest in literature about sexuality, it is not surprising that "Aristotle's" gynecological texts were very popular. As the above analysis has shown, these texts usually offered a watered down version of the basic Aristotelian rationale for sex polarity. In this way, the Greek philosopher, albeit through spurious works, continued to support sex-polarity opinions about the concept of woman in relation to man. Unfortunately, these opinions almost always devalued woman in relation to man.

THE DISAPPEARANCE OF SEX COMPLEMENTARITY

One of the most striking consequences of this pervasive victory of Aristotelian thought was the total loss of the existential and theoretical foundation of sex complementarity, which had been so prevalent in the preceding period. The energy and drive associated with the efforts of Roswitha, Heloise, Hildegard or Herrad to participate in and to lead other women into the heart of the intellectual activity of the age had nowhere to go in the thirteenth century. With women cut off from sharing an intellectual life with men, which had been so possible within the double monasteries of the Benedictine age, they lost the ground they had gained in those years of moving towards a philosophical foundation for the theory of sex complementarity.

At the same time, the philosophical foundation for sex unity had been undermined by the rejection of the theory of reincarnation. Consquently, sex polarity appeared to be the most attractive of the theories of sex identity for such writers as Albert the Great, Thomas Aquinas, Bonaventure or Giles of Rome. Consequently, woman was more and more widely perceived as being born through a defective meeting of form and matter. She was an "imperfect" man with an "imperfect" mind. With this philosophical devaluation of the woman in relation to man, any possibility for a philosophical foundation for sex complementarity that demanded the fundamental acceptance of the equality and significant differentiation of the sexes was effectively destroyed.

The disappearance of the theory of sex complementarity occurred also through the rejection of all previous forms of philosophy that were not scientifically based. The pre-Socratics, Stoics, and neo-Platonists, along with Plato—in those few tracts of his that were available—depended upon an intuitive approach to philosophy. These philosophers recorded what they thought without having to defend a theory through empirical testing and verification. Hildegard of Bingen occupied a prominent position within this tradition of personal observation and assessment. Such works became suspect in contrast to those that were supported by the extensive empirical research to which Aristotle, St. Albert, or Roger Bacon had recourse. The consequence of this rejection of non-scientific philosophy was that all previously articulated suggestions in favor of sex complementarity, found in such thinkers as Empedocles or Hildegard, as well as the premises supporting the basic equality of women and men found in the neo-Platonists or Stoics, were dismissed without consideration.

A further factor in the disappearance of sex complementarity might be connected with the struggle between the Augustinians and the Thomists at this period in the history of the University of Paris. St. Augustine had recognized the implications of creation and resurrection for sex complementarity, even though he was unsuccessful in developing a theory consistent enough to incorporate this insight. The Thomists, however, while allowing St. Augustine an important position in the development of Catholic thought, often posited St. Augustine as someone to argue against. Since St. Thomas, thanks to Aristotle and Albert the Great, developed a thorough defence for the theory of sex polarity, it is not surprising that St. Augustine's sex complementarity was lost, along with other of his "questionable" assumptions.

The disappearance of a theoretical interest in sex complementarity was accompanied by the end of a practical interest in sex complementarity. This occurred in many areas of human activity; the most significant of which, at first sight, was the refusal to accept women into the University of Paris. The cooperative search for truth of women and men within the traditions of Pythagoreanism, Stoicism, neo-Platonism, and early Christian monastic education came to an end. Men took this task upon themselves, alone; women were excluded from the academic study of philosophy and theology, as well as from the study and practice of medicine and law. In addition, women were excluded from the hierarchical, jurisdictional, and sacramental structures of the church. Sex complementarity, within the heart of the Catholic life of the west, as praxis and as teaching, had disappeared.

The victory of the Aristotelian Revolution, then, not only developed the strength of sex polarity and sex neutrality, it also contributed to the complete disappearance of a theory of sex complementarity. Christian thought was infused with sex polarity, and the academic study of philosophy with sex neutrality. Women were excluded from both areas of research. Consequently, any new foundation for a theory of sex complementarity had to await a time that would make it possible to find a way back into the centre of creative thought about woman and man.

THE UNIVERSITIES AND THE FRAGMENTATION OF KNOWLEDGE ABOUT THE PERSON

A final consequence of the Aristotelian Revolution concerns the evolution of the structures of higher education. Aristotle had made certain distinctions in his thought that led to the division of knowledge into different areas, dependent both upon the object and the methodology used in the search for truth. His distinctions have been adopted and refined throughout western history. By the time that the University of Paris was established, some clear distinctions had been made. The Faculty of Arts was established upon the general science of cause, the Faculty of Theology upon the science of God as first cause, the Faculty of Medicine upon the science of the health and disease of the body, and the Faculty of Law upon the science of the political and social relations of persons in law. Each field of study was given a separate curriculum, physical location, faculty, and student body. At first, some of the personnel and texts overlapped. Students who studied in the Faculty of Arts often moved up to the graduate Faculty of Theology. However, slowly but steadily, the distinctions sharpened until, by the end of the thirteenth century, faculty members in arts were forbidden under threat of dismissal to discuss any subject properly studied in theology, and students were forbidden to study either medicine or law.

The different areas of knowledge, institutionally separated from one another having become the basis for the fragmentation of the university structure, also had far-reaching ramifications for the concept of woman in relation to man. In fact, this poses one of the most difficult problems for the contemporary search for the truth about a theory of sex identity.

The problem can be brought into focus, somewhat, by considering which aspects of the person are emphasized within each area of study. The following summary suggests a pattern:

Faculty of Arts	Faculty of Theology	Faculty of Medicine	Faculty of Law
rationality	spirituality	materiality of human body	materiality of society

The Faculty of Arts at Paris, through its identification with philosophy, chose to concentrate on what can be known about the person by reason. It concentrated on the rationality of the person by a consideration of formal, rather than material aspects. The Faculty of Theology, on the other hand, gave priority to the spirituality of the person, concentrating on what could be known by faith, revelation, and a study of the scriptures. It also perceived the person as an essentially spiritual existent. The Faculty of Medicine, on the other hand, turned to a consideration of the materiality of human existence, of its proper functioning in a healthy body, and of the defects of the diseased or injured body. At this early stage in the development of the academic study of medicine, the rationality or spirituality of human existence was not studied with the same attention. A further analysis of the materiality of existence was developed in the Faculty of Law. Here, the material structures of human relationships and institutions were the focus of attention. The person was perceived primarily as a legally defined existent with duties and rights. This was characteristic both of the study of civil law and of canon law within the broader framework of theology. Overall, the factor of individuality was reflected upon when it appeared appropriate, as in ethics, in disease, or the particular circumstances of a legal case.

The unfortunate consequences of this differentiation of rationality from spirituality and materiality in human existence, was the institutionalized fragmentation of thought about the person. The tendency for scholars and theoreticians to specialize in one area, to the exclusion of other forms has led to the fragmentation within knowledge itself. The person is an existent with the four factors of spirituality, rationality, materiality, and individuality. Any theory that purports to explain personal identity must distinguish, as well as integrate, all four areas. The pressing task now becomes: How can what has been divided be united?

CONCLUSION

This long and arduous journey tracing the concept of woman in relation to man through twenty centuries of western philosophy has come to an end. Three questions can now be asked: What has been achieved? What are the limits of the work? What further research flows from its conclusions?

This book is the first systematic attempt to study the history of the philosophy of sex identity. While there are a great many excellent texts that focus on the philosophy of sex identity of a single author, and others that attempt comparisons among one or two thinkers across different time frames, up to the present time, no one has analysed the structures of the concept of woman in relation to man. Therefore, this book opens a new field of contemporary study. In fact, it could be the vanguard of a field of study called simply "The Philosophy of Woman and Man."

Another achievement of this text is to have given definitive proof that the philosophy of sex identity was a central aspect of philosophy since its inception in Greece in the sixth century BC. As soon as a philosopher considered the nature of man, a consideration of the nature of woman also occurred. Fundamental questions about sex identity were found in nearly every philosopher up to the thirteenth century. This fact must astonish those readers who thought that the philosophy of sex identity was of contemporary interest only.

In addition, a careful analysis of the kinds of questions asked by philosophers about the concept of woman in relation to man revealed four broad areas of concern: in metaphysics the question arose about how, or if, man and woman are opposite; in the philosophy of science, questions focused on the relation between the contribution of mother or father to generation and sex identity itself; in epistemology, the issue focused on whether women and men had the same or different faculties of reasoning and whether they were wise by knowing the same or different things; in ethics, the question was whether women and men were virtuous by performing the same or different acts.

The repetition of these questions over nearly two thousand years established an historical pattern of argument that delineates a specific field of study. In addition, this study has revealed a repetition of answers to these questions, which has been specified as falling loosely into three different theories of sex identity: sex unity; sex polarity; and sex complementarity, with the derivative theories of sex neutrality and reverse sex polarity. The astonishing regularity of the repetition of similar arguments over thousands of years indicates that even with widely different cultural and historical situations, certain ideas assume a life and stability of their own.

It was in this context, then, that the special effect of Platonic arguments for sex unity, and Aristotelian arguments for sex polarity were examined. The conclusion of this work indicated that in spite of the strong attraction for a Platonic justification for sex unity in western history, in the long run, the Aristotelian rationale for sex polarity was victorious. This ultimate victory of the early Greek philosopher's views was called "The Aristotelian Revolution in the Concept of Woman."

In the effort to understand the ways in which the philosophy of sex identity first sprang up in western thought and then to follow up these significant insights through their elaborate historical developments, I have tried always to present a truthful and balanced account of the philosopher under consideration. Therefore, it would appear that a value of this book is its effort to bring into the light all that a philosopher thought about the philosophy of sex identity, without exaggerating or distorting the passages to support a single interpretation. In this way, it could open the field to further evaluation and scrutiny without prejudicing the results that this broader scope of evaluation will inevitably bring.

What are the limitations of this work? Due to the large scope of the philosophers considered, it is inevitable that some descriptive errors will arise. The responsibility for the selection of texts and interpretations of the passages is completely my own. While this book can be considered as opening a new field of systematic study, the limitations in its account of particular philosophers will be overcome by the future research of experts in historical periods of individual philosophers.

In the area of interpretation, it is obvious that the use of the concepts "equality" and "philosophically significant differences" is extremely crude in some respects. Therefore, the classification of theories under the categories of sex unity, sex polarity or sex complementarity will need to be rendered more precise in coming years. At the same time, however, in spite of the limitations of the simplicity of the concepts, they do aid this preliminary study by indicating the general direction the thought of a philosopher took about the concept of woman in relation to man. The crudeness of the concepts, then, makes it possible to perceive the patterns in the broad sweep of arguments across two millenia.

Another limitation of the text is its perhaps seemingly arbitrary cut-off point in the mid-thirteenth century. It was noted that 1250 seemed to be a good symbol for the ultimate victory of the Aristotelian Revolution because all of Aristotle's texts became required reading at the University of Paris in 1255. Therefore, there is a certain justification for the choice of date. At the same time, however, there are some important writers of the thirteenth century who have not been included in this study. Religious writers such as Beatrix, Mechtild of Hagdeburg, or more popular writers such as Jean de Meun, Guillaume de Lorris, or Raimon Lull have not been considered. The reason for their exclusion is that their writing is more connected with what happened after the Aristotelian Revolution in subsequent centuries than it is in the period leading up to this moment in history.

In a similar way, the example of Giles of Rome was used to indicate some of the effects of the Aristotelian Revolution on later thirteenth-century thought in medicine, even though he lived after the cut-off date of 1250. In addition, only one aspect of Giles's thought was considered, rather than the thorough analysis that was given to most persons considered in the text. This limitation serves as a linking point, much as tongue-and-groove interconnect pieces of lumber. Giles links Aristotle to the after-effects of the Aristotelian Revolution.

When the question of future research flowing from this text is raised, the most immediate answer is that the effort of tracing the history of the concept of woman in relation to man needs to be continued beyond the mid-thirteenth century in order to further develop knowledge about this important area in the history of philosophy. In a further project, funded by the Social Sciences and Humanities Research Council of Canada from 1983 to 1986, I am undertaking to continue this research from 1250 to approximately 1800.

Some of the questions asked in this new project are: What kind of arguments are presented for theories of sex identity as a result of the Renaissance, the advent of modern philosophy, or other significant historical revolutions in thought? A preliminary study has thus far indicated that sex complementarity received a new formulation through the development of fourteenth-century humanism, sex unity through the development of seventeenth-century Cartesianism, and sex neutrality through the integration of the mathematical method into academic philosophy. In addition, reverse sex polarity received its first systematic articulation in the work of Agrippa in the sixteenth century, while sex polarity received a whole new range of arguments beginning, especially with Rousseau, in the eighteenth century.

In addition, in these later development of theories of sex identity in modern philosophy, the basic concepts of "equality" and "significant differentiation" received a much more sophisticated analysis. Philosophers began to qualify considerations of equality as "equal in what respect" and considerations of the differentiation of woman and man as "different in what specific respects." Therefore, as in so many other fields of philosophy, the consideration of the concept of woman and man reached new levels of expression that were more consistent with modern concepts of the person.

One other interesting question that also rises from this study is how the four categories— of opposites, generation, wisdom, and virtue—are ultimately related to the concept of woman in relation to man. The present study has indicated that the categories take a certain historical precedence. They appeared century after century in discussions of sex identity. However, it has not yet been demonstrated that they are ontologically connected with the philosophy of sex identity. However, it is my belief that they are ontologically connected, and that any thorough analysis of the concept of woman in relation to man would need to consider these four areas of thought. However, as just stated, this thesis remains to be proven.

In a similar way, this study has revealed a progressive understanding of the person as containing four different factors: rationality; materiality; individuality; and spirituality. The first three factors appear to be discovered through the use of reason and the observations of the senses, while the fourth needs the pathway of faith. Again, while certain philosophers have stood out historically as being the first ones to recognize the significance of a particular factor, no attempt has been made to prove the necessity of the four factors in any analysis of the person. Once again, while I believe that this can be proven, the study itself only indicates the historical precedence of the use of these factors in analysing human existence.

Next, the three theories of sex identity, loosely described as sex unity, sex polarity and sex complementarity, have been characterized as containing different approaches to the concept of woman in relation to man. Sex unity was judged as always containing a devaluation of the body, sex polarity as always choosing some limited and isolated aspect of the body and valuing this factor as superior in either woman or man, while sex complementarity was described as presenting a balanced view of the integration of the body into personal identity. Further research will need to verify whether this is a consistent pattern in later theories of sex identity.

It is important to note that two different interpretations of sex complementarity are often confused. One interpretation suggests that a man and a woman are incomplete in themselves without the other. This implies that both are "half a person" unless joined with the other. This view usually places a heavy emphasis upon "masculine" and "feminine" aspects of consciousness. It also often holds up a model of an androgynous individual as the ideal who combines the masculine and feminine within a single identity. For example, when Hildegard of Bingen described an individual as having a balanced nature of the masculine element fire and the feminine element air, she was considering this kind of complementarity.

The second interpretation of complementarity is even more important for the development of the history of philosophy. In this view, sex complementarity involves the relationship between two complete individuals one of whom is a man and the other a woman. Both are whole persons, and neither is incomplete without the other. However, sex complementarity arises when these two complete individuals come into relationship with one another. That the two are equal and yet significantly different here allows for the development of a third entity that goes beyond either of them. This generated third party could be a biological child, or it could be something of an entirely different order. Hildegard of Bingen also considered this kind of sex complementarity when she studied the fertility of the interaction of four types of men with four types of women. In the next phase of the history of the concept of woman, it will be important to follow the development of the sharpening of the differences between these two interpretations of sex complementarity.

The last chapter of the book has left the consideration of the concept of woman in relation to man with a serious problem of the fragmentation of knowledge within the university structure as established in Paris in the thirteenth century. It is well known that this fragmentation of knowledge is a contemporary inheritance of the ordinary academic situation, and that some efforts have been made to forge a new synthesis in research through various interdisciplinary approaches to the person. Therefore, another important path for future research is the question of how concretely can a new organic synthesis of knowledge, which considers the person as a unified existent in the midst of intricate and creative human relationships, be achieved.

It is my hope that the present book has opened a new field of study. Further, I hope that this field, which is the obvious extension of philosophy into the philosophy of man and woman, will finally regain the place it once held in the history of philosophy. That nearly every philosopher during the first two thousand years of its western heritage thought about the concept of woman in relation to man should be enough to bring this subject into the consciousness of every contemporary philosopher. The movement from consciousness to curriculum is, of course, the key movement from idea to institutionalization. Just as the Aristotelian Revolution gained its dominance through precisely this move into institutionalism in the thirteenth century, so today the wider and more creative opening of a field of study must become institutionalized in contemporary university curricula. Then various theories of sex identity can be considered within the context of the most up-to-date scientific knowledge about the person as well as with the widest and deepest range of evaluative considerations. It is only when the philosophy of man and woman takes its rightful place once again in the heart of academic philosophy that the closest approximation to truth, with its widest possible dispersion, will be able to occur. Philosopy may at times appear to be an abstract and isolated discipline. However, I believe that it also has the potential to transform the world. If this book has contributed even a little towards achieving that goal, it will have a accomplished a purpose beyond its purely scholarly merit.

NOTES

Introduction

1. It should be mentioned that the word *concept* which is common in philosophy today, derived from the Latin *conceptus*, which includes the meanings of "conceiving as a pregnancy," a "catching on fire" or a "collecting or gathering together." This sense of a structured thought as vital, or alive, is what I wanted to convey by the use of the word *concept*.

2. See, *The Sexism of Social and Political Theory*, eds. Lorenne M.G. Clark and Lynda Lange (Toronto, Buffalo, London: University of Toronto Press, 1979); and *Discovering Reality*, eds. Sandra Harding and Merrill B. Hintikka (Dordrecht: Holland/Boston; U.S.A./London, England: D. Reidel Publishing Company, 1983).

3. See, *History of Ideas on Woman*, ed. Rosemary Agonito (New York, N.Y.: G.P. Putnam's Sons, 1977; and *Visions of Women*, ed. Linda A. Bell (Clifton, New Jersey: Humana Press, 1983).

4. See, Jean Bethke Elsthain, *Public Man, Private Woman: Women in Social and Political Thought* (Princeton, New Jersey: Princeton University Press, 1981); Carol McMillan, *Women, Reason and Nature* (Princeton, New Jersey; Princeton University Press, 1982); Carolyn Merchant, *The Death of Nature: Women, Ecology, and the Scientific Revolution* (San Francisco: Harper and Row, Publishers, 1980); and Susan Moller Okin, *Women in Western Political Thought* (Princeton, New Jersey: Princeton University Press, 1979).

5. For a good description of the history of philosophical anthropology, see Mieczytaw A. Kropiec, O.P., *I-Man: An Outline of Philosophical Anthropology* (New Britain, Conn.: Marial Publications, 1983); and Cardinal Karol Wojtyla, *The Acting Person* (Dordrecht, Holland/Boston, U.S.A./London, England: D. Reidel Publishing Company, 1979).

6. The philosopher Boethius was the first to offer a definition of "person" as an individual substance of a rational nature. See, *The Theological Tractates* (Cambridge, Mass. and London: Harvard University Press and William Heinemann, 1918), III, 5, p. 85.

7. While other frameworks may be developed for a concept of woman, the framework that sprang from the original questions of the earliest Greek philosophers appear to have a kind of fundamental priority in that they established the way in which the concept of woman has been thought about for over two thousand years in the west. At this point all that can be claimed is that the priority is not logical but rather historical. It may turn out with further study that there is a logical priority for these categories as well.

8. See Shulamith Firestone, *The Dialectic of Sex* (New York: Bantam, 1971).

9. See Christine Allen, "Sex Unity, Polarity or Complementarity?", *International Journal of Women's Studies*, Vol. 6, No. 4 (September/October 1983), p. 315; Sigmund Freud, "Femininity," *New Introductory Lectures on Psychoanalysis* (Middlesex, England: Penguin Books, 1973); Jean Paul Sartre, *Being and Nothingness* (New York: Philosophical Library, 1956); and Stephen Goldberg, *The New Inevitability of Patriarchy* (New York: Macmillan, 1953).

10. Heinrich Cornelius Agrippa von Nettesheim, *On the Superiority of Woman Over Man* (New York: American News Company, 1873); Ashley Montagu, *The Natural Superiority of Woman* (New York: Macmillan, 1953); Valerie Solanis, "The Scum Manifesto," *Sisterhood Is Powerful* (New York: Random House, 1974); and Jill Johnson, "Woman Prime," *Lesbian Nation* (New York: Simon and Schuster, 1973).

11. The possibility of sex complementarity has been suggested by various theorists, but it has never been fully developed in a way to avoid falling back into a hidden sex polarity.

See, John Stuart Mill, *The Subjection of Women* (Cambridge, Mass., and London, England: The M.I.T. Press, 1970); Virginia Wolfe, *A Room of One's Own* (New York and London: Harcourt Brace Jovanovich, 1957).

12. Allen, *op. cit.*

13. Carole Gilligan, *In a Different Voice* (Cambridge, Mass., and London, England: Harvard University Press, 1982); Jean Bethke Elsthain, *op. cit.*; Rosemary Ruether, *New Woman, New Earth: Sexist Ideologies, and Human Liberation* (New York: The Seabury Press, 1951); Jessie Bernard, *The Future of Motherhood* (New York and Baltimore: Penguin Books, Inc., 1975); Jessie Bernard, *The Female World* (New York: The Free Press, 1981); and Betty Friedan, *The Second Stage* (New York: Summit Books, 1981).

14. See, John Paul II, *The Original Unity of Man and Woman* (Boston: St. Paul Editions, 1981).

15. St. Augustine is particularly fascinating in this respect. See, Chapter III, "St. Augustine."

Chapter I

1. See, Martin Heidegger, *The Question Concerning Technology and Other Essays* (New York: Harper and Row Publishers, 1977); *What Is Called Thinking* (New York: Harper and Row Publishers, 1972); and *The End of Philosophy* (New York: Harper and Row Publishers, 1973).

2. See, Aristotle, *Metaphysics* in *The Basic Works of Aristotle* (New York: Random House, 1941), X 9, 1058a, pp. 29-31.

3. Karl Jaspers, *Way to Wisdom: An Introduction to Philosophy* (New Haven and London: Yale University Press, 1969).

4. P.T. Geach, *The Virtues* (London, New York, Melbourne: Cambridge University Press, 1979).

5. Hesiod, *Theogony* (Indianapolis, Indiana: Bobbs-Merrill Company, Inc., 1953), I, 1-115, p. 54.

6. *Ibid.*, II, 116-153, p. 56

7. *Ibid.*

8. *Ibid.*, 154-210, p. 57.

9. *Ibid.*

10. See, Erich Neumann, *The Great Mother* (Princeton: Princeton University Press, 1974); Merlin Stone, *When God Was A Woman* (New York: Dial Press, 1976); and Robert Graves, *The White Goddess* (New York: The Noonday Press, 1969).

11. Hesiod, *op. cit.*, XII, 820-1022, p. 78.

12. *Ibid.*

13. *Ibid.*, p. 79.

14. *Ibid.*

15. Robert Graves, *The Greek Myths* (Great Britain: Penguin Books, 1060); see, Philip Slater, *The Glory of Hera: Greek Mythology and the Greek Family* (Boston: Beacon Press, 1968).

16. Hesiod, *op. cit.*, X, 507-616, pp. 69-70.

17. Hesiod, "Works and Days" in *Hesiod* (Cambridge, Mass.: Harvard University Press, 1967), 49-50, 60-63, 68, 80, pp. 5-9.

18. *Ibid.*, 90-97, p. 9.

19. *Ibid.*, 376, p. 31.

20. *Ibid.*, 755-757, p. 59.

21. Hesiod, "The Catalogues of Women and the Eoiae" in *Hesiod*, *op. cit.*, pp. 154-220, 256-266.

22. *The Love Songs of Sappho*, trans. and Introduction by Paul Roche (Toronto: Mentor Books, 1966), Fragments 73, 74 and 143, pp. 80-125.

23. *Ibid.*, pp. xx-xxi.

24. *Ibid.*, Fragment 71, p. 79. The verse structure has been consolidated in this passage.

25. *Ibid.*, Fragment 55, p. 67. See, Richard Jenkyns, *Three Classical Poets: Sappho, Catullus and Juvenal* (London: Unwin Brothers Limited, 1982), pp. 1-84.

26. *Ibid.*, Fragment 38, p. 53. The verse structure has been consolidated in this passage.

27. Kathleen Freeman, *The Pre-Socratic Philosophers: A Companion to Diels, Fragmente der Vorsokratiker* (Oxford: Basil Blackwell, 1966), pp. 55-64.

28. *Ibid.*, p. 62.

29. Charles Kahn, *Anaximander and the Origins of Greek Cosmology* (New York: Columbia University Press, 1960), p. 110.

30. Freeman, *op. cit.*, p. 125.

31. Aristotle, *De Mundo* in *The Basic Works of Aristotle, op. cit.*, 5, 396b7.

32. Heraclitus, *Heraclitus of Ephesus* (Chicago: Argonaut, 1969), p. 98. See, Heraclitus, *The Cosmic Fragments* (Cambridge: The University Press, 1954), pp. 166-179.

33. Aristotle, *The Athenian Constitution, The Eudemian Ethics, and On Virtues and Vices* (Cambridge, Mass. and London: The Loeb Classical Library, 1935), VII, 1, 1235a26.

34. Aristotle, *Metaphysics, The Basic Works, op. cit.*, 986a22-25.

35. The specific selection of the ten pairs may have remained fluid until Aristotle recorded them. However, "the theory of opposites in its dualistic form probably goes back to him [Pythagoras]." Freeman, *op. cit.*, p. 82.

36. Aristotle, *Nicomachean Ethics, The Basic Works, op. cit.*, I, 6, 1096b29-34.

37. Diogenes Laertius, *Lives of Eminent Philosophers* (Cambridge, Mass. and London: Harvard University Press and William Heinemann, Ltd., 1941), VIII, 14, Vol. II, p. 33.

38. *Ibid.*, VIII, 30, Vol. II, p. 347.

39. Freeman, *op. cit.*, p. 83.

40. Mario Meunier, *Femmes Pythagoriciennes* (Paris: L'Artisan du livre, 1932), Prolégomènes, p. 9. Translated by Christiane Teasdale.

41. Cornelia J. de Vogel, *Pythagoras and Early Pythagoreanism: An Interpretation of Neglected Evidence on the Philosopher Pythagoras* (Assen: Van Gorcum, 1966), p. 90.

42. J.A. Philip, *Pythagoras and Early Pythagoreans* (Toronto: University of Toronto Press, 1966), p. 139, 144. See, Vogel, *ibid.* p. 124.

43. Philip, *ibid.*, pp. 139-140.

44. Diogenes Laertius, *op. cit.*, VII, 42, Vol. II, p. 359.

45. See, Chapter III, "Neo-Pythagoreanism."

46. Diogenes Laertius, *op. cit.*, VIII, 8, Vol. II, p. 327.

47. *Ibid.*, VIII, 32, Vol. II, p. 347.

48. Vogel, *op. cit.*, pp. 110-111.

49. *Ibid.*, pp. 100-101.

50. *Ibid.*, p. 62.

51. *Ibid.*, pp. 83-84.

52. *Ibid.*, pp. 130-131.

53. Kathleen Freeman, *Ancilla to the Pre-Socratic Philosophers: A Complete Translation of the Fragments in Diels, Fragmente der Vorsokratiker* (Cambridge, Mass.: Harvard University Press, 1956), Fragment 1, p. 42.

54. *Ibid.*, Fragment 8, p. 44.

55. *Ibid.*

56. *Ibid.*

57. For a more thorough discussion of this controversy see Freeman, *The Pre-Socratic Philosophers, op. cit.*, pp. 140-146. Freeman concludes: "To sum up: on the one hand, the Way of Opinion is utterly false, not the views of Parmenides; but on the other hand, it was such that had he accommodated himself to phenomena, he would have to believe," pp. 145-146.

58. Freeman, *Ancilla, op. cit.*, Fragment 12, p. 45. See, Kahn, *op. cit.*, p. 160.

59. *Ibid.*, Fragment 17, p. 46.

60. Freeman, *The Pre-Socratic Philosophers, op. cit.*, "There were passages. . . on sex determination which seem to refer to Alcmaeon and his school," p. 143; "Lastly come explanations of organic life—the origins of man (from the sun or from slime?), sex determination; the difference between the sexes, due to admixture of hot and cold, and subject to variations according to the direction taken by the spermatozoön. This was in contradiction to the view expressed by Alcmaeon, that the ovum was the essential factor," p. 151.

61. Freeman, *Ancilla, op. cit.*, Fragment 18, p. 46.

62. Leonardo Taran, *Parmenides: Eleates* (Princeton: Princeton University Press, 1965), pp. 264-265.

63. Freeman, *The Pre-Socratic Philosophers, op. cit.*, p. 270.

64. Freeman, *Ancilla, op. cit.*, Fragment 4, p. 83.

65. *Ibid.*, Fragment 12, p. 84.

66. Felix Cleve, *The Philosophy of Anaxagoras: An Attempt at Reconstruction* (New York: King's Crown Press, 1949), p. 42. See, Daniel Gershenson and David A. Greenberg, *Anaxagoras and The Birth of Physics* (New York: Blaisdell Publishing Co., 1964), Fragment 115, p. 102.

67. Aristotle, *Generation of Animals* (Cambridge, Mass. and London: Harvard University Press and William Heinemann, Ltd., 1943), 763b27.

68. Gershenson, *op. cit.*, Fragment 274, p. 152.

69. *Ibid.*, Fragment 274, p. 152.

70. *Ibid.*, p. 196.

71. See, Taylor Caldwell, *The Glory and the Lightening* (Garden City, N.Y.: Doubleday, 1974), for a fictional reconstruction of the life of Aspasia.

72. Plato, *Menexenus* in *The Collected Dialogues of Plato* (New York: Pantheon Books, 1961), 336c.

73. *Ibid.*, 237e-238a.

74. *Ibid.*, 249d.

75. "Aspasia" in *Encyclopedia Britannica, Micropedia*, 1968, Vol. 1; Xenophon, *Memorabilia and Oeconomicus* (New York and London: G.P. Putnam's Sons and William Heinemann, 1923), III, 14-16, p. 389.

76. Freeman, *Ancilla, op. cit.*, Fragment 17, p. 53. See also, Fragments 6 and 7, p. 52. Empedocles sometimes uses the names of Dieties for the elements: Zeus for fire, Hera for earth, Aidoneus for air, and Nestis for water.

77. *Ibid.*, Fragment 134, p. 67. See also, Fragments 27-29, p. 56.

78. *Ibid.*, Fragment 17, pp. 53-54. See also, Fragments 87, p. 61 and 151, p. 68.

79. This chart is an adaptation of one found in Dennis O'Brien, *Enpedocles' Cosmic Cycle* (Cambridge: The University Press, 1969), pp. 196-200.

80. Freeman, *Ancilla, op. cit.*, Fragment 17, p. 53.

81. *Ibid.*, Fragment 57, p. 58. See also, Fragment 58, p. 58.

82. *Ibid.*, Fragment 61, pp. 58-59. See also, Fragment 60, p. 58.

83. *Ibid.*, Fragment 21, p. 55. See also, Fragment 23, p. 55.

84. *Ibid.*, Fragment 26, pp. 55-56.

85. Herman Diels, *Die Fragmente der Vorsokratiker* (Zurich: Weidmann, 1966), Fragment 72, Vol. I, p. 297. Translated by Annette Dale.

86. Freeman, *Ancilla, op. cit.*, Fragment 62, p. 59.

87. See, O'Brien, *op. cit.*, pp. 196-200. "*Oulophué* we shall argue, are the creatures which best exemplify Love's unity and perfection," p. 199.

88. Freeman, *Ancilla, op. cit.*, Fragment 117, p. 65.

89. *Ibid.*, Fragment 62, p. 59.

90. *Ibid.*, Fragments 65-67, p. 59.

91. Freeman, *The Pre-Socratic Philosophers, op. cit.*, pp. 193-194.

92. Aristotle, *Generation of Animals, op. cit.*, 722b15.

93. Freeman, *Ancilla, op. cit.*, Fragment 112, p. 64.

94. *Ibid.*, Fragment 17, p. 53.

95. *Ibid.*, Fragment 4, p. 52.

96. *Ibid.*, Fragment 80, p. 30.

97. Karl Marx, *Doktor dissertation (1841): Differenz der democratischen und epikurischen Naturphilosophie* (Jena: Friedrich-Schiller Universität, 1964).

98. Freeman, *The Pre-Socratic Philosophers, op. cit.*, pp. 295-300.

99. Diels, *op. cit.*, Fragment 139, Vol. 11, p. 123. Translated by Annette Dale.

100. *Ibid.*, Fragment 141.

101. *Ibid.*, Fragment 143.

102. Aristotle, *Generation of Animals, op. cit.*, 764a8-12.

103. Freeman, *Ancilla, op. cit.*, Fragment 34, p. 99.

104. Aristotle, *Generation of Animals, op. cit.*, 769a15-25, 764b23-30.

105. *Ibid.*, 769b32-35.

106. Freeman, *Ancilla, op. cit.*, Fragment 31, p. 99.

107. *Ibid.*, Fragment 110, p. 103.

108. *Ibid.*, Fragment 274, p. 116.

109. *Ibid.*, Fragment 273, p. 116.

110. *Ibid.*, Fragment 267, p. 116.

111. *Ibid.*, Fragment 111, p. 103. See also, Fragment 75, p. 101.

112. *Ibid.*, Fragment 32, p. 99.

113. *Ibid.*, Fragments 276-277, p. 116.

114. W.K.C. Guthrie, *The Sophists* (Cambridge: The University Press, 1971), pp. 30-44.

115. G.B. Kerferd, *The Sophistic Movement* (Cambridge: Cambridge University Press, 1981), p. 42.

116. Plato, *Symposium* (Indianapolis: The Bobbs-Merrill Company, 1956), 208c. For a further discussion of Socrates and Diotima see, Chapter I, "Plato: Wisdom".

117. Plato, *Protagoras* in *The Collected Dialogues, op. cit.*, 349a.

118. Protagoras, *The Older Sophists*, ed. Rosamond Kent Sprague (Columbia, South Carolina: University of South Carolina Press, 1972), Fragment B1, p. 18.

119. Kerford, *op. cit.*, p. 43.

120. Plato, *Protagoras, op. cit.*, 320d.

121. *Ibid.*, 325a. While this quotation is taken from a hypothetical statement, it is consistent with Protagoras' views.

122. Aristotle, *The Art of Rhetoric* (Cambridge, Mass.: Harvard University Press, 1965), 173b18-30.

123. Aristotle, *On Sophistical Refutations* (Cambridge, Mass.: Harvard University Press, 1965), 173b18-30.

124. *Ibid.*, 174a8-9.

125. See, Robin Lakoff, *Language and Woman's Place* (San Francisco: Harper and Row, 1975); *She Said/He Said: An Annotated Bibliography of Sex Differences in Language, Speech, and Nonverbal Communication*, eds. Nancy Henley and Barrie Thorne (Pittsburgh: Know, Inc., 1975); Philip Smith, *Languages, The Sexes and Society* (Oxford: Basil Blackwell, 1984).

126. Plutarch in *The Older Sophists, op. cit.*, Fragment 22, p. 65.

127. Gorgias in *The Older Sophists, ibid.*, Fragment 11, p. 50.

128. *Ibid.*, p. 51.

129. *Ibid.*, pp. 51-54.

130. *Ibid.*, p. 54.

131. *Ibid.*

132. *Ibid.*

133. Plato, *Meno* in *The Collected Dialogues, op. cit.*, 71d-72a and 73c.

134. *Ibid.*, 72d-73a.

135. *Ibid.*, 73c-d.

136. Xenophon in *The Older Sophists, op. cit.*, Fragment 2, p. 79.

137. Kerferd, *op. cit.*, pp. 45-46; and Guthrie, *op. cit.*, p. 279.

138. *The Older Sophists, op. cit.*, Fragment 2, 21-22, p. 79.

139. *Ibid.*, 23, p. 79.

140. *Ibid.*, 27, p. 80.

141. *Ibid.*, 30-31, pp. 80-81.

142. *Ibid.*, 32, p. 81.

143. Herrad of Hohenbourg, *Hortus Deliciarum* (New Rochelle, N.Y.: Cartzas Brothers, Publishers, 1971). See, Chapter IV, "Herrad of Landsberg".

144. *The Older Sophists*, *op. cit.*, Fragments 109 and 111, p. 224.

145. *Ibid.*, Fragment 123, p. 228.

146. *Ibid.*

147. *Ibid.*

148. *Hippocrates*, W.H.S. Jones, ed. (London and New York: William Heinemann and G.P. Putnam's Sons, 1923), Vol. I, pp. xxii-x1. See, Frances Adams, *The Genuine Works of Hippocrates* (New York: William Wood and Company, n.d.), pp. 25-38.

149. *Ibid.*, Vol. IV, *Aphorisms* V, pp. 167, 171.

150. *Ibid.*, p. 169.

151. *Ibid.*, Vol. IV, *Regimen* I, xxxiv, p. 281.

152. *Ibid.*, xxvii, p. 265.

153. *Ibid.*, *Aphorisms* IV, 1xii-1xiii, pp. 175-177. See also, *Airs, Waters, Places*, Vol. I, IV, p. 79; X, p. 101.

154. *Ibid.*, *Airs, Waters, Places*, xxi, p. 125.

155. *Ibid.*, xxii, pp. 127-129. The factor of too much horseback riding was also considered.

156. *Ibid.*, xvii, pp. 117-119.

157. *Ibid.*, xxiii, p. 131.

158. *Ibid.*, Vol. I, *Ancient Medicine*, xvi, p. 43.

159. *Ibid.*, Vol. IV, *Regimen*, xxvii, pp. 265-267.

160. Hippocrates, "De la génération" in *Hippocrate*, Tome XI (Paris: Société l'édition "les belles lettres," 1970), i-iv pp. 44-47. All passages from this text are translated by Odile Hellman.

161. *Ibid.*, viii, p. 49.

162. *Ibid.*, vi, p. 48.

163. *Ibid.*, vii, p. 49.

164. *Ibid.*, xx, p. 66.

165. *Ibid.*, xxi, p. 67.

166. Hippocrates, Vol. IV, *op. cit.*, *Regimen* I, xxxv, p. 281.

167. *Ibid.*, xxviii, pp. 267-269.

168. *Ibid.*, xxix, pp. 269-271.

169. Hippocrates, Vol. I, *op. cit.*, *Aphorisms*, VII, x1ii, p. 203.

170. *Ibid.*, *Ancient Medicine*, p. 53.

171. Xenophon, *Memorabilia and Oeconomicus*, *op. cit.*, p. xxiv. "Isomachus as he appears in this book, is quite clearly Xenophon."

172. *Ibid.*, III, 10-12, p. 387.

173. *Ibid.*, III, 14-16, p. 389.

174. *Ibid.*, VII, 2, p. 413.

175. *Ibid.*, 3, p. 415.

176. *Ibid.*, 18-24, pp. 419-421.

177. *Ibid.*, 25-26, pp. 421-423.

178. *Ibid.*, 26-27, p. 423.

179. *Ibid.*, 26-27, pp. 423-425.

180. *Ibid.*, 32-43, pp. 425-429.

181. *Ibid.*, VIII, 3-10, pp. 429-431.

182. *Ibid.*, IX, 18-19, pp. 445-447.

183. *Ibid.*, X, 2-10, pp. 447-449.

184. *Ibid.*, XI, 1, p. 453.

185. See, Christine Garside, "Plato on Women," *Feminist Studies*, 2, 213 (1975), pp. 133-138.

186. Plato, *Timaeus* in *The Collected Dialogues, op. cit.*, 51a-b.

187. *Ibid.*, 50c.

188. *Ibid.*, 50e.

189. *Ibid.*, 50c-d.

190. Plato, *Republic* in *The Collected Dialogues, op. cit.*, 453a.

191. *Ibid.*, 453e-454b.

192. *Ibid.*, 454c-e.

193. Plato, *Phaedrus* in *The Collected Dialogues, op. cit.*, 246b-c.

194. Plato, *Timaeus, op. cit.*, 34c.

195. Plato, *Republic, op. cit.*, 619e-620c.

196. Plato, *Timaeus, op. cit.*, 90e-91a.

197. *Ibid.*, 91d-92b.

198. Plato, *Republic, op. cit.*, 455c-e.

199. Plato, *Phaedo* in *The Collected Dialogues, op. cit.*, 66c-e.

200. *Ibid.*, 61d.

201. See, Simone de Beauvoir, *The Second Sex* (New York: Vintage Books, 1974), p. 182.

202. Plato, *Symposium, op. cit.*, 189e-191e.

203. See, Paul Friedlander, *Plato* (New York: Pantheon Books, 1964), for a thorough discussion of Plato's different uses of myth.

204. Plato, *Timaeus, op. cit.*, 91b-c.

205. Plato, *Laws* in *The Collected Dialogues, op. cit.*, 782e-783a.

206. *Ibid.*, 636c.

207. *Ibid.*, 838e-839a.

208. *Ibid.*, 721b.

209. *Ibid.*, 785b.

210. Plato, *Symposium, op. cit.*, 211c.
211. Plato, *Phaedrus, op. cit.*, 256a-b.
212. Plato, *Republic, op. cit.*, 508d-e.
213. Plato, *Ion* in *The Collected Dialogues, op. cit.*, 536a.
214. Plato, *Republic, op. cit.*, 608d.
215. *Ibid.*, 607a.
216. Plato, *Timaeus, op. cit.*, 69e-70a.
217. Plato, *Republic, op. cit.*, 455e-456a.
218. Plato, *Laws, op. cit.*, 785b.
219. Plato, *Republic, op. cit.*, 452a.
220. Plato, *Laws, op. cit.*, 804e.
221. Plato, *Timaeus, op. cit.*, 18c.
222. Plato, *Symposium, op. cit.*, 201c.
223. *Ibid.*, 206b.
224. *Ibid.*, 202a.
225. *Ibid.*, 204b.
226. *Ibid.*, 212b.
227. *Ibid.*, 208e-209a.
228. *Ibid.*, 209c.
229. Plato, *Theatetus* in *The Collected Dialogues, op. cit.*, 149a-150b.
230. See Chapter I, "Georgias," and *Meno, op. cit.*, 71e.
231. *Ibid.*, 72a.
232. *Ibid.*, 73a-b.
233. Plato, *Republic, op. cit.*, 456b.
234. *Ibid.*, 457b.
235. *Ibid.*, 458c.
236. Plato, *Laws, op. cit.*, 780e-781a.
237. *Ibid.*, 781a-b.
238. *Ibid.*, 770d.
239. Plato, *Republic, op. cit.*, 460c-d.
240. Plato, *Phaedrus, op. cit.*, 59e.
241. *Ibid.*, 464c-d.
242. Plato, *Laws, op. cit.*, 776a. See also 930b-c.

Chapter II

1. Aristotle, *Metaphysics* in *The Basic Works of Aristotle*, Richard McKeon, ed. (New York: Random House, 1941), 985a 10-16; 933a 11-15.

2. Aristotle, *Generation of Animals*, A.L. Peck, trans. and ed. (Cambridge, Mass. and London: Harvard University Press and William Heinemann Ltd., 1943), 765a 20.

3. *Ibid.*, 764a 15-21.

4. *Ibid.*, 764a 30-35.

5. *Ibid.*, 764b 23-30; 769a 15-25.

6. Aristotle, *Politics* in *The Basic Works of Aristotle, op. cit.*, 1266a 34-36.

7. *Ibid.*, 1263b 8-13.

8. *Ibid.*, 1261a 11-16.

9. *Ibid.*, 1262b 18.

10. *Ibid.*, 1262b16-20.

11. *Ibid.*, 1261b23-1262a 3.

12. *Ibid.*, 1262a 25-30.

13. *Ibid.*, 1262a 40-1262b 3. Aristotle also argued that the development of two different types of class within a common state could lead to class conflict. See, 1264a 22-25.

14. *Ibid.*, 1262b 24-29.

15. *Ibid.*, 1262a 13-18.

16. *Ibid.*, 1264b1-8.

17. Aristotle, *De Anima* (On the Soul) in *The Basic Writings of Aristotle, op. cit.*, 412b8, 413a 3-8. In the *Nicomachean Ethics* Aristotle did leave open the possibility that the rational soul might continue in some sort of union with the unmoved mover; but the absence of matter would lead to a total loss of differentiation.

18. Aristotle, *Metaphysics, op. cit.*, X 9, 1058a 29-31.

19. *Ibid.*, 1058b 22-25.

20. While the anatomy of the embryo has this characteristic through the influence of the hormone testosterone, the chromosomal structure does not.

21. Aristotle, *Generation of Animals, op. cit.*, 768a 8-10.

22. Aristotle, *Metaphysics, op. cit.*, X 4 1055b 16.

23. Aristotle, *Physics* in *The Basic Writings of Aristotle, op. cit.*, 192a 3-10.

24. *Ibid.*, 12-15.

25. Aristotle, *Metaphysics, op. cit.*, 1055b 25-29.

26. Aristotle, *Generation of Animals, op. cit.*, 738b 20-25; see also, Aristotle, *Parts of Animals* (Cambridge, Mass. and London: Harvard University Press and William Heinemann, 1937), 641b 25-642a 2.

27. *Ibid.*, 761a 6-10.

28. Aristotle, *Physics, op. cit.*, 192a 22-24.

29. Aristotle, *Generation of Animals, op. cit.*, 732a 5-10.

30. See, Joseph Owens, *The Doctrine of Being in the Aristotelian "Metaphysics"* (Toronto: Pontifical Institute of Medieval Studies, 1978).

31. Aristotle, *Generation of Animals*, op. cit., 729b 15-20.

32. *Ibid.*, 740b 20-25.

33. Aristotle, *Meteorologica* (Cambridge, Mass. and London: Harvard University Press and William Heinemann, 1952), 378b 10-12; 382b 28-32. See also, Aristotle, *Metaphysics, op. cit.*, 1070b 10-15. The hot and cold were considered to be *active* contraries and the moist and dry to be *passive* contraries. The subsequent association of the female with cold and the male with hot is a further indication that, in Aristotle's thought, the female was not always characterized as passive. See also, *Parts of Animals, op. cit.*, 648b 4-10.

34. Aristotle, *On the Heavens* (Cambridge, Mass. and London: Harvard University Press and William Heinemann, 1939), 296b 15-26, 295b 26-29, 296b 27-29. See also, *Meteorologica, ibid.*, 339a 11-20.

35. Aristotle, *Generation of Animals, op. cit.*, 716a 9-17.

36. *Ibid.*, 739b-740a 30.

37. *Ibid.*, 765b 10-18. I am grateful to Lynda Lange for bringing this association to my attention in 1973.

38. See, Chapter I, "The Hippocratic Writings," and *Hippocrates* (London and New York: William Heinemann and G.P. Putnam's Sons, 1923), Vol. IV, xxxiv, p. 281.

39. Aristotle, *Generation of Animals, op. cit.*, 725a25-28.

40. *Ibid.*, 726a26-28; *Parts of Animals, op. cit.*, 635b 13. Aristotle presented several arguments to prove that semen was a form of nourishment: 1) When children are young and need all their nourishment for growth they procure no semen; 2) Large animals give birth to fewer offspring than small ones because they need more nourishment; 3) Fat people use more nourishment in their body and therefore produce less semen; and 4) Men are tired after the emission of semen which implies a loss of nourishment.

41. *Ibid.*, 735b 33-38; *Parts of Animals, op. cit.*, 523a 12-15.

42. *Ibid.*, 736b 35-737a 8.

43. *Ibid.*, 736a 19-22. Here Aristotle mentioned the similarity to the poetic account of the birth of Aphrodite from the foam of the sea.

44. *Ibid.*, 739a 7-13; 733b 18-21.

45. *Ibid.*, 739b 21-25.

46. *Ibid.*, note to 724b 13.

47. *Ibid.*, 728a 13-27.

48. *Ibid.*, 765b 10-18.

49. *Ibid.*, 737a 26-30.

50. *Ibid.*, 775a12-16. It is possible that Aristotle adopted the Hippocratic theory that males develop more quickly than females. For the Hippocratic writers, this view was derived from a belief that the male seed was stronger than the female seed, while for Aristotle it was derived from the belief that the male seed was hotter that the female. See, Chapter I, 'The Hippocratic Writings," and "De la génération," in *Hippocrate*, Tome XI (Paris: Société l'édition "les belles lettres," 1970), xx, p. 66 and xxi, p. 67.

51. It is not clear whether Aristotle believed that it was the intention of nature to produce females or the intention of nature to produce only males. See, *Generation of Animals, op. cit.*, 768a 12.

52. *Ibid.*, 775a 4-12.

53. Aristotle, *Parts of Animals, op. cit.*, 648a 2-14, 635b1-2; and Aristotle, *History of Animals* (Cambridge, Mass. and London: Harvard University Press and William Heinemann, Ltd., 1943), 491b 1-5, 501b 20-24, 545a 14-19.

54. Aristotle, *Generation of Animals, op. cit.*, 729a 28-32. See, 730b 11-13.

55. *Ibid.*, 736b 13-29. The quotation continues: "Speaking generally this happens in fair-skinned women who are typically feminine, and not in dark women of a masculine appearance." See also, Chapter II, "Aristotle's Rejection of Theories of Female Seed."

56. *Ibid.*, 742a 18-25.

57. *Ibid.*, 738b 20-25. See also, *Parts of Animals, op. cit.*, 641b 25-642a 2.

58. The functions within the soul are not identified with parts of the soul as Plato had maintained, because for Aristotle the soul was a unity. Sometimes, however, the functions were developed further to include reproductive and locomotive activities as well. See, *De Anima* in *The Basic Works of Aristotle, op. cit.*, 416a 18-19.

59. Aristotle, *Generation of Animals, op. cit.*, 735a 11-15, 736b 8-11, 736a 26, 726b 18, 729b 6, 731b 19, 740b 30-741b 3.

60. *Ibid.*, 736b 8-14.

61. Aristotle, *De Anima, op. cit.*, 417b 16-20.

62. Aristotle, *Generation of Animals, op. cit.*, 736b 8-14.

63. *Ibid.*, 736b13-29.

64. Aristotle, *Metaphysics, op. cit.*, 1012a 24-33; and *Nicomachean Ethics* in *The Basic Works of Aristotle, op. cit.*, 1071a 17-23.

65. Aristotle, *Generation of Animals, op. cit.*, 730b 18-24.

66. Aristotle, *On the Heavens, op. cit.*, 286a 33-35, 279a 16-18; *Physics, op. cit.*, 188b 25; Aristotle, *Categories* in *The Basic Works of Aristotle, op. cit.*, 13a 18-20. Compare, however, with other passages in which Aristotle described opposites as aiming towards a mean. *Nicomachean Ethics, op. cit.*, 1059b 20-25 and Aristotle, *Eudemian Ethics* (London and Harvard: Loeb Classical Library, 1935), 1239b 20-1240a 5.

67. Aristotle, *Generation of Animals, op. cit.*, 766b 16-20.

68. *Ibid.*, 766a18-23.

69. *Ibid.*, 766b 28-767a. See, *History of Animals, op. cit.*, 573b 30-574a.

70. *Ibid.*, 767b 20-28, 723a 28.

71. *Ibid.*, 768a12-16, 768a 8, 768b 23-25.

72. *Ibid.*, 767b 10-15.

73. *Ibid.*, 741b1-5. See, *History of Animals, op. cit.*, 538a 5.

74. Aristotle, *Metaphysics, op. cit.,*, 993b 19-23.

75. *Ibid.*, 982a 1-2. As will seen, women had a different relation than men to both the theoretical and practical wisdom.

76. *Ibid.*, 983a 24-983b 1. See also, *Posterior Analytics* (Cambridge, Mass. and London: Harvard University Press and William Heinemann Ltd., 1960), 90a 20-24.

77. Later his texts were divided as follows: Physics, First Philosophy; The Organon including: Categories, On Interpretation Prior and Posterior Analytics, Topics, On Sophistical Refutation; On the Soul, The History of Animals, The Parts of Animals, On the Generation of Animals, Nicomachean Ethics and Eudemian Ethics; Politics; Rhetoric; and Poetics, respectively.

78. Aristotle, *Posterior Analytics*, *op. cit.*, 92b 36-38; *Metaphysics*, *op. cit.*, 1078b 15-25; *Categories*, *op. cit.*, 3b 18-23; *Parts of Animals*, *op cit.*, 643a 23-26.

79. *Ibid.*, 89a36-38; *Categories*, *op. cit.*, 8a 25-9a 15; Aristotle, *Topics* (Cambridge, Mass. and London: Harvard University Press and William Heinemann, Ltd., 1936), 102a 17; *Metaphysics*, *op. cit.*, 1027a 12.

80. Aristotle, *Categories*, *op. cit.*, 2a 11-18; *Posterior Analytics*, *op. cit.*, 93a 3-4; *Topics*, *op. cit.*, 33-34. Aristotle often used "species" and "genus" interchangeably.

81. Aristotle, *Metaphysics*, *op. cit.*, 1058a 30-34.

82. *Ibid.*, 1058b 1-4.

83. *Ibid.*, 1925a 13-15.

84. Aristotle, *Generation of Animals*, *op. cit.*, 729b 15-20, 738b 20-25, 716a 9-17.

85. Aristotle, *Metaphysics*, *op. cit.*, 1065a 2-6.

86. Aristotle, *Topics*, *op. cit.*, 102b 3-6, 128b 16-20, 128b 34-129a 3, 154b 32-37.

87. *Ibid.*, 101b 37.

88. Aristotle, *Prior Analytics*, *op. cit.*, 41b 6-10.

89. Alison Jaggar, "On Sex Equality," *Ethics*, Vol. 84, No. 4 (July 1974), 275-291.

90. Aristotle, *Politics*, *op. cit.*, 1334b 13-20.

91. *Ibid.*, 1259b 20-23.

92. *Ibid.*, 1260a 10-15.

93. Aristotle, *Nicomachean Ethics*, *op. cit.*, 1102b 13-19.

94. Aristotle, *Politics*, *op. cit.*, 1333a 18-23.

95. Aristotle, *Eudemian Ethics*, *op. cit.*, 1226b 19-27.

96. Aristotle, *Posterior Analytics*, *op. cit.*, 89a 16-20; *Topics*, *op. cit.*, 100b 22-28.

97. Aristotle, *Politics*, *op. cit.*, 1277b 27-30.

98. Aristotle, *Metaphysics*, *op. cit.*, 982a 18-20.

99. Aristotle, *Politics*, *op. cit.*, 1260b 28-31.

100. John Patrick Lynch, *Aristotle's School: A Study of a Greek Educational Institution* (Berkeley: University of California Press, 1972), pp. 90-91.

101. Maria von Schurman, *The Learned Maid* (Oeingenii Muliebris ad Doctrinum et Meliores), 1641.

102. Aristotle, *Nicomachean Ethics*, *op. cit.*, 1106b 36-1107a 2.

103. *Ibid.*, see, Book VII.

104. *Ibid.*, 1148b20-21. Note that Aristotle used the feminine article with the word for man *anthropos*. This combination was a derogatory epithet for slavish women. When St. Thomas commented on this passage the bestial person was changed into a man. See, St. Thomas Aquinas, *Commentary on Nicomachean Ethics* (Chicago: Henry Regnery Co., 1964), VII, LVC 1372.

105. *Ibid.*, 1148b 31-1149a 1.

106. Aristotle, *Poetics* in *The Basic Writings of Aristotle*, *op. cit.*, 1454a 16-23.

107. Aristotle, *Politics*, *op. cit.*, 1259b 30-35.

108. *Ibid.*, 1259b 35-1260a 4.

109. *Ibid.*, 1260a 4-12.

110. *Ibid.*, 1254b 5-15; *Metaphysics*, *op. cit.*, 982a 17-19.

111. Aristotle, *Nicomachean Ethics*, *op. cit.*, 1138b 6-13.

112. Aristotle, *Politics*, *op. cit.*, 1254b 16-25.

113. *Ibid.*, 1255b 18. Aristotle compared the rule of fatherchild to king-subject, or master-slave to tyrant-subject, and of husband-wife to monarch-subject. See, 1260b 23-1262b 20.

114. *Ibid.*, 1160b 33-1161a 2.

115. *Ibid.*

116. *Ibid.*, 1259a 35-1259b 9.

117. *Ibid.*

118. Aristotle, *Nicomachean Ethics*, *op. cit.*, 1162a 12-18; *Eudemian Ethics* 1242a 30-35.

119. *Ibid.*, 1162a 21-26.

120. *Ibid.*, 1162a 21-26.

121. *Ibid.*, 1158b 15-30.

122. Aristotle, *Eudemian Ethics*, *op. cit.*, 1238b 15-30.

123. Aristotle, *Nicomachean Ethics*, *op. cit.*, 1162a 33-1162b 8; *Eudemian Ethics*, *op. cit.*, 1242b 3-22.

124. Aristotle, *Eudemian Ethics, op. cit.*, 1239a 20-35.

125. Aristotle, *Nicomachean Ethics, op. cit.*, 1158b 25-28, 1161a 25-30. 0.

126. Aristotle, *History of Animals* in *The Basic Works of Aristotle*, *op. cit.*, 608 a 18-29. I am grateful to Frances Sparshot for raising the question of the philosophical significance of these passages in an unpublished manuscript.

127. *Ibid.*, 608 a 35-608 b 5.

128. *Ibid.*, 608b 6-14.

129. Aristotle, *Metaphysics*, *op. cit.*, 1058b 22-25.

130. Aristotle, *Politics*, *op. cit.*, 1260a 4-10.

131. Aristotle, *Generation of Animals*, *op. cit.*, 732 a 5-10; 728a 13-27; 725 a 25-28; *Politics*, *op. cit.*, 1254 b 5-15.

Chapter III

1. Diogenes Laertius, *Lives of Eminent Philosophers* (Cambridge, Mass. and London: Harvard University Press, 1941), III, 46. See also, Pierre Boyance, *Le Culte des Muses chez les Philosophes Grecs: études d'histoire et de psychologie religieuses* (Paris: E. de Brocard, 1972), pp. 272-273. Lynch argues that Axiothea disguised herself as a man in order to attend the Academy after reading a copy of Plato's *Republic.* See, John Patrick Lynch, *Aristotle's School: A Study of Greek Educational Institutions* (Berkeley: University of California Press, 1972), p. 57.

2. *Ibid.*, IV, 1.

3. Eduard Zeller, *Plato and the Older Academy* (New York: Russell and Russell, Inc., 1962), pp. 584-585.

4. Diogenes Laertius, *op. cit.*, VI, 96-97.

5. *Ibid.*, 97-98.

6. Lynch, *op. cit.*, p. 140.

7. *Ibid.*, p. 92. See also, Felix Grayleff, *Aristotle and His School* (London: Duckworth, 1974, p. 51. This opinion was contradicted by Gilles Ménage's list of women Peripatetics: the daughter of Olympiodorus and Theodora. However, I have been unable to find any corroboration for his claim. See Aegidio Menagio (Gilles Ménage), *Historia Mulierum Philosophorum* (Amsterdam: Henricum Westernium, 1692). See translation by Beatrice H. Zedler, *The History of Women Philosophers* (New York: University Press of America, 1984).

8. Eduard Zeller, *Aristotle and the Earlier Peripatetics* (New York: Russell and Russell, Inc., 1962), Vol. II, p. 358.

9. *Ibid.*, pp. 405-409. See also, Diogenes Laertius, *op. cit.*, Vol. I, pp. 483-509 and *Theophrastos:* Περι Συζεβειασ (Leiden: E.J. Brill, 1964).

10. *The Characters of Theophrastos* (London and New York: William Heinemann Ltd. and G.P. Putnam's Sons, 1939), p. 6.

11. *Ibid.*, p. 37.

12. *Ibid.*, pp. 71, 81, 85-86, and 115.

13. Lynch, *op. cit.*, p. 143.

14. A.A. Long, *Hellenistic Philosophy: Stoics, Epicurians, Sceptics* (New York: Charles Scribner's Sons, 1974), p. 15. See also, "Epicurus" in *Encyclopedia Britannica* (1968), p. 638.

15. Gilles Ménage, *op. cit.,* Chapter ix, pp. 42-3.

16. Long, *op. cit.*, p. 75.

17. Diogenes Laertius, *op. cit.*, X, 125. See also, X, 139.

18. *Ibid.*, X, 40-45.

19. Karl Marx wrote his Doctoral Dissertation on Epicurus. Significantly, he developed his own foundation for a theory of sex identity. See, *Doktordissertation von Karl Marx* (1941), 'Differenz der democratischen und epikurischen Naturphilosophie' (Jena: Friedrich-Schiller Universität, 1964).

20. Diogenes Laertius, *op. cit.*, X, 118. See also *Epicurus' Morals* (New York: AMS Press, 1975), Max. vii, p. 30.

21. *Epicurus' Morals*, *ibid.*, Max. ix, p. 24.

22. *Ibid.*, Max. ix, p. 24.

23. Diogenes Laertius, *op. cit.*, X, 145.

24. *Ibid.*, X, 3-10.

25. Athenaeus, *The Deipnosophists* (Cambridge, Mass. and London: Harvard University Press and William Heinemann, Ltd., 1937), XIII, 588d, p. 173.

26. *The Philosophy of Epicurus*, ed. George F. Strodad (North-western University Press, 1963), p. 185.

27. Long, *op. cit.*, p. 17.

28. Lucretius, *The Nature of Things* (New York: W.W. Norton and Company, Inc., 1977), I, 50-56, p. 2.

29. *Ibid.*, I, 56-58, p. 2.

30. *Ibid.*, I, 84-102, p. 3.

31. *Ibid.*, I, 166-170, p. 5.

32. *Ibid.*, III, 178-180, p. 61.

33. *Ibid.*, III, 783-786, p. 74. See also, "And so when the body dies, we must admit the soul dies too, dispersed throughout the body," 798-800, p. 75.

34. *Ibid.*, 777-783, p. 76.

35. *Ibid.*, IV, 1030-1035, p. 106.

36. *Ibid.*, IV, 1035-1050, p. 106.

37. *Ibid.*, V, 1210-1233, pp. 110-111.

38. Joannes de Mondino de Luzzi Ketham, *Fasciculo di Medicina* (Venice, 1493) (reprinted, Florence: Relier and Co., 1925), Introduction by Charles Singer, p. 25. See also, George Depue Hadzsits, *Lucretius and His Influence* (New York: Longmans, Green & Co., 1935).

39. Lucretius, *op. cit.*, IV, 1078-1080, p. 107.

40. *Ibid.*, IV, 1078-1083, p. 107.

41. *Ibid.*, IV, 1083-1092, p. 107.

42. *Ibid.*, IV, 1062-1068, p. 107.

43. *Ibid.*, IV, 1102-1113, p. 108.

44. *Ibid.*, IV, 1120-1148, pp. 108-109.

45. *Ibid.*, IV, 1148-1165, p. 109.

46. *Ibid.*, IV, 1185-1192, p. 110.

47. *Ibid.*, IV, 915-925, p. 134.

48. *Ibid.*, IV, 960-965, p. 135.

49. *Ibid.*, IV, 1010-1015, p. 136. There is a line missing from the original of this passage in the poem. See also, Frederick Engels, *The Origin of the Family, Private Property, and the State* (New York: Pathfinder Press, 1972).

50. *Ibid.*, IV, 1355-1360, p. 144.

51. Holger Thesleff, *An Introduction to the Pythagorean Writings of the Hellenistic Period*, in *Acta Academiae Aboenis Humaniora* (Abo: Akademi, 1961), xxiv, 3, p. 51. I am grateful to Mary Ellen Waithe for bringing my attention to this work.

52. *Ibid.*, p. 99.

53. For a good discussion of this issue see, Mary Ellen Waithe, "Authenticating the Fragments and Letters," in *The Project on the History of Women in Philosophy* (St. Paul, Minn.: forthcoming), Vol. 1, Chapter iii.

54. Thesleff, *op. cit.*, pp. 106-107.

55. *Ibid.*, pp. 13-16. See also, Eurytos, Kallikratidos, Okkelos, and Arignote, pp. 11-24.

56. *Ibid.*, p. 111. See also, Waithe, *op. cit.*

57. Mario Meunier, *Femmes Pythagoriciennes: Fragments et Lettres de Theano, Perictione, Phyntis, Melissa et Myia* (Paris: L'Artisan du livre, MCMXXXII), p. 49. Translated by Odile Hellman, as are all passages from this text.

58. *Ibid.*, p. 52.

59. *Ibid.*, p. 53.

60. *Ibid.*, p. 59.

61. *Ibid.*, p. 60.

62. *Ibid.*, p. 61.

63. *Ibid.*, pp. 55-56.

64. Thesleff, *op. cit.*, p. 106.

65. Meunier, *op. cit.*, frag. i, p. 39. This fragment is translated by Odile Hellman, as are all other fragments from Theano I.

66. Thesleff, *op. cit.*, p. 25.

67. Meunier, *op. cit.*, frag. viii. p. 44.

68. *Ibid.*, frag. ii, p. 40.

69. *Ibid.*, frag. iv, p. 41.

70. *Ibid.*, frag. iii, p. 41.

71. *Ibid.*, frag. vii, p. 42.

72. *Ibid.*, frags. ix, v, vi, pp. 42-44.

73. See Thesleff, *op. cit.*, pp. 18, 59, 76 and 110; and Waithe, *op. cit.*

74. Meunier, *op. cit.*, pp. 63-64. This passage was translated by Odile Hellman, as are all other fragments from Phyntis.

75. *Ibid.*, pp. 64-65.

76. *Ibid.*, pp. 65-66.

77. *Ibid.*, pp. 67-68.

78. *Ibid.*, pp. 68-70.

79. *Ibid.*, p. 71.

80. *Ibid.*, p. 72.

81. *Ibid.*, p. 119. This passage was translated by Odile Hellman, as are all other fragments from Melissa.

82. *Ibid.*

83. Thesleff, *op. cit.*, p. 17.

84. Meunier, *op. cit.*, pp. 45-48. This passage was translated by Odile Hellman, as are all other passages by Perictione II.

85. Holger Thesleff, *The Pythagorean Texts of the Hellenistic Period* in *Acta Academiae Aboensis, Ser. A., Humaniora* (Abo: Abo Akademi, 1965), Vol. 30, nr. 1, frag. 266, p. 48. This passage was translated by Anne Dale, as are all other passages from Aesara.

86. I am grateful to Mary Ellen Waithe for bringing my attention to Aesara.

87. Thesleff, *The Pythagorean Texts*, *op. cit.*, p. 48. See also the translation by Vickie Lynn which was presented to the Minnesota Philosophical Society, October 29, 1983 and printed in the forthcoming Project on *Women in the History of Philosophy*, *op. cit.*

88. *Ibid.*, p. 49.

89. *Ibid.*, p. 50.

90. Thesleff, *An Introduction to Pythagorean Writings,. . .* *op. cit.*, p. 102.

91. Meunier, *op. cit.*, pp. 113-114. This passage is translated by Odile Hellman.

92. *Ibid.*, p. 81. This passage is translated by Odile Hellman, as are all other fragments from Theano II.

93. *Ibid.*, pp. 82-84.

94. *Ibid.*, p. 87.

95. *Ibid.*, p. 88.

96. *Ibid.*, p. 89.

97. *Ibid.*, p. 90.

98. *Ibid.*, pp. 92-93.

99. *Ibid.*, p. 101.

100. *Ibid.*, p. 117.

101. *Ibid.*, p. 95.

102. *Ibid.*, p. 96.

103. *Ibid.*, p. 97.

104. *Ibid.*

105. *Ibid.*, p. 98.

106. *Ibid.*

107. Diogenes Laertius, *op. cit.* VII, 6.

108. *Ibid.*, VII, 131.

109. Margaret E. Ressor, *The Political Theory of the Old and Middle Stoa* (New York: J.J. Augustin Publisher, 1952), pp. 12-13.

110. Diogenes Laertius, *op. cit.* VII, 121.

111. *Ibid.*, VII, 34.

112. Gilles Ménage, *op. cit*, Chapter X, pp. 45-6.

113. Athenaeus, *op. cit.*, XIII, 563 E, Vol. VI, p. 45.

114. Diogenes Laertius, *op. cit.*, VII, 13.

115. *Ibid.*, VII, 18.

116. *Ibid.*, VII, 130.

117. *Ibid.*, VII, 83. See also, 40-48.

118. *Ibid.*, VII, 111-118.

119. *Ibid.*, VII, 159.

120. *The Fragments of Zeno and Cleanthes* (New York: Arno Press, 1973), Fragment 107, p. 153. Translated by Diane Gordon.

121. Diogenes Laertius, *op. cit.*, VII, 18.

122. *Ibid.*, VII, 133.

123. *Ibid.*, VII, 135-136. See, David Hahn, *The Origins of Stoic Cosmology* (Ohio: Ohio State University Press, 1977), pp. 68-90 for a thorough discussion of the relation between Stoic cosmology and Aristotelian biological theory.

124. *Ibid.*, VII, 147.

125. Hahn, *op. cit.*, 79-80.

126. Diogenes Laertius, *op. cit.*, VII, 175.

127. *Ibid.*, VII, 188.

128. Joannes ab Arnim, *Stoicorum Verterum Fragmenta* (Lipsiae: B.G. Teubneri, MCMIII), Vol. III, Frag. 253, p. 59. Translated by Diane Gordon, as are other fragments from this text.

129. *Ibid.*, Fragment 254.

130. Diogenes Laertius, *op. cit.*, VII, 188.

131. *Ibid.*, VII, 188.

132. Hahn, *op. cit.*, pp. 71-72.

133. Philip Merlan, "Greek Philosophy from Plato to Plotinus" in *The Cambridge History of Later Greek and Early Medieval Philosophy*, A.H. Armstrong, ed. (Cambridge: The University Press, 1970), p. 126.

134. Marcus Tullius Cicero, *Academica* (Cambridge, Mass. and London: Harvard University Press and William Heinemann Ltd., 1941) (Lucullus), II, xxxviii, p. 621; II, cliii, p. 639; and *De Finibus Bonorum et Malorum* (London and New York: William Heinemann Ltd. and G.P. Putnam's Sons, 1939), V, iv, 9, p. 401.

135. Cicero, *Academica, ibid.*, I, iv, 17-18, pp. 427-429; see also, Letter to Marcus on Moral Goodness, in *De Officiis* (Cambridge, Mass. and London: Harvard University Press and William Heinemann Ltd., 1945), p. 3.

136. Cicero, *De Officiis, ibid.*, I, xvii, pp. 54-55. See also, *De Finibus, op. cit.*, (Cato) III, xix, 62-63, p. 283.

137. Cicero, *De Republica, De Legibus* (Cambridge, Mass. and London: Harvard University Press and William Heinemann Ltd., 1959) (Laelius) V, 6, p. 237.

138. *Ibid.*, (Philus) X, 17-XI, 18.

139. Cicero, *De Amicitia* (Cambridge, Mass. and London: Harvard University Press and William Heinemann Ltd., 1959), XII, 46, p. 157. This work became the basis for Heloise's appeal to Abelard for a relationship of friendship. See also, XX, 71, p. 87.

140. Cicero, *Academica, op. cit.* (Lucullus) II, ix, p. 501. For Wisdom as 'she,' see also II, viii, p. 499; and for Nature as 'she,' see *De Legibus, op. cit.*, I, viii, 24-ix, 26, pp. 325-327.

141. Cicero, *De Amicitia, op. cit.*, XXVII, 100, p. 207.

142. Cicero, *De Divinatione* (Cambridge, Mass. and London: Harvard University Press and William Heinemann Ltd., 1945), I, xxxi, 65, p. 298. Cicero discussed the prophetess rather that the philosopher in this context.

143. Cicero, *De Officiis, op. cit.*, I, iv, 14.

144. *Ibid.*, I, 130, pp. 131-133.

145. Immanuel Kant, *Observations on the Feeling of the Beautiful and Sublime* (Berkeley: University of California Press, 1960).

146. Seneca, *Ad Lucilium Epistulae Morales* (New York and London: G.P. Putnam's Sons and William Heinemann Ltd., 1925), Letter XCV 10-12, pp. 65-67 and Letter xv, iv 45, p. 41.

147. *Ibid.*, Letter LXXV, ix 10-11, pp. 384-385.

148. *Ibid.*, Letter LXV, ii, p. 451.

149. Seneca, "On Anger" in *Moral Essays* (New York and London: C.P. Putnam's Sons and William Heinemann Ltd., 1928-32), XXIV, 4, p. 317.

150. Seneca, "On Firmness" in *Moral Essays, ibid.*, XIV, 1, p. 89.

151. Seneca, "To Marcia on Consolation" in *Moral Essays, ibid.*, VI, 1, p. 3.

152. *Ibid.*, I, 5, p. 7.

153. *Ibid.*, II, 2, p. 9.

154. *Ibid.*, V, 4-5, pp. 19-21.

155. *Ibid.*, VII, 3, pp. 23-25.

156. *Ibid.*, XI, 1, p. 33.

157. *Ibid.*, XVI, 1, p. 49.

158. Seneca, "To Helvia on Consolation" in *Moral Essays, ibid.*, VI, v, 1, p. 425.

159. *Ibid.*, XI, 6-7, pp. 457-459.

160. *Ibid.*, XVI, 1-5, pp. 477-479.

161. *Ibid.*, XVII, 3-5, p. 477.

162. Seneca, "On Anger" in *Moral Essays, ibid.*, II, 16, 1-2, p. 471.

163. Seneca, *Ad Lucilium Epistulae Morales, op. cit.*, Letter XCIV, 26, p. 29. See also, Seneca, "On Benefits" in *Moral Essays, op. cit.*, III, xvi, 1-3, pp. 155-157; I, ix, 4-5, pp. 29-31.

164. Seneca, "On Benefits," *ibid.*, II, xviii, 1-2, pp. 85-87.

165. Pliny, *The Natural History* (London: Henry G. Bohn, 1855-7), Book VII, Chapter 13, (15), pp. 152-153.

166. *Ibid.*, Chapter 5, (6), p. 141.

167. *Ibid.*, Chapter 7, (9), p. 143. See also Pliny's infamous ridicule of menstruation. "It would indeed be a difficult matter to find anything which is productive of more marvelous effects than the menstrual discharge. On the approach of a woman in this state, the milk will become sour, seeds which are touched by her will become sterile, grafts will wither away, garden plants are parched up, and the fruit will fall from the tree beneath which she sits. Her very look, even, will dim the brightness of mirrors, blunt the edge of steel, and take away the polish from ivory."

168. *Ibid.*, Chapter 3, pp. 138-139.

169. *Ibid.*, Chapter 10 (12), p. 146.

170. *Father Malebranche's Treatise Concerning the Search After Truth* (Oxford: L. Lichfield, 1694), See, Chapter III, "Porphyry and Marcella."

171. For an excellent discussion of the sources available to Musonius Rufus see A.C. von Geytenbeek, *Musonius Rufus and Greek Diatribe* (Assen: Van Gorcum and Comp., 1963), Xenophon, pp. 89, 161; Plato, p. 57; Zeno, pp. 120, 162; Middle Stoa, p. 70; and Seneca, p. 162.

172. Rufus Musonius, *Deux prédicateurs de l'antiquité: Teles et Musonius* (Paris: Librarie Philosophique J. Vrin, 1978), XIII A 1-3, p. 96. Translated by Dominique Deslandres as are all passages from this text. See also, Linda Bell, *Visions of Women* (Clifton, New Jersey: Humana Press, 1983), p. 75. This text contains a complete translation of some of the writings of Musonius Rufus.

173. *Ibid.*, XIV, 6-7, p. 99.

174. *Ibid.*, XIV, 1-3, p. 98.

175. *Ibid.*, III, 1-3, p. 58.

176. *Ibid.*, IV, 1-2, p. 63.

177. *Ibid.*, IV, 9-10, p. 64.

178. *Ibid.*, III, 11-12, p. 59.

179. *Ibid.*, IV, 17-19, p. 66.

180. *Ibid.*, IV, 3-5, p. 63-64.

181. *Ibid.*, IV, 6-8, p. 64.

182. *Ibid.*, III, 4-5, p. 58.

183. *Ibid.*, III, 6, p. 59.

184. *Ibid.*, IV, 15, pp. 65-66.

185. *Ibid.*, XII, 8, p. 95.

186. *Ibid.*, IV, 11-12, p. 65.

187. *Ibid.*, IV, 13-14, p. 65.

188. *Ibid.*, XXI, 2, 32 and XXII, 4, pp. 126-127.

189. Epictetus, *Discourses*, in Oates, Whitney J., ed., *The Stoic and Epicurean Philosophers* (New York: Random House, 1940), III, i, pp. 345-6.

190. *Ibid.*, I, xvii, p. 253.

191. *Ibid.*, III, i, pp. 436-437.

192. Epictetus, *The Manual*, in Oates, *op. cit.*, no. 40, p. 480.

193. Epictetus, *Fragments*, in Oates, *op. cit.*, 10, p. 463.

194. Epictetus, *Discourses*, in Oates, *op. cit.*, II, iv, pp. 287-288.

195. *Ibid.*, IV, i, pp. 416-417.

196. *Ibid.*, IV, i, p. 407; IV, ix, p. 444; IV, x, p. 449.

197. Gilbert Highet, *Juvenal the Satirist* (Oxford: The Clarendon Press, 1960), pp. 198-199. He also appears to have influenced Boccaccio, see, p. 204.

198. E. Courtney, *A Commentary on the Satires of Juvenal* (London: The Athlone Press, 1980), pp. 260-261.

199. *The Satires of Juvenal* (Bloomington and London: Indiana University Press, 1958), VI, 135-137, p. 68.

200. *Ibid.*, 347-349, p. 76.

201. *Ibid.*, 42-58, p. 65.

202. *Ibid.*, 162-168, p. 69.

203. *Ibid.*, 200-292, p. 70.

204. *Ibid.*, 30-32, p. 64; 45, p. 65; 206-213, p. 71.

205. *Ibid.*, 245-260, pp. 72-73.

206. *Ibid.*, 185-192, p. 70.

207. *Ibid.*, 430-460, pp. 81-82.

208. *Ibid.*, 485-486, p. 83.

209. Marcus Aurelius, *Meditations*, in Oates, *op. cit.*, X, no. 26, p. 567.

210. *Ibid.*, IX, no. 3, p. 554.

211. *Ibid.*, VI, no. 12, p. 527.

212. Seneca, "On the Firmness of Wise Men," *op. cit.*, 18, 5, p. 102.

213. Epictetus, *Discourses*, in Oates, *op. cit.*, IV, v, p. 432.

214. Marcus Aurelius, *Meditations*, in Oates, *op. cit.*, XI, no. 28 p. 577.

215. *Ibid.*, IV, no. 28, p. 512.

216. Galen, *On the Passions and Errors of the Soul* (Columbus: Ohio State University Press, 1975), VIII, p. 57. See also, pp. 28, 49 and 51.

217. *Ibid.*, IX, p. 61.

218. Galen, *On the Doctrines of Hippocrates and Plato* (Berlin: Akademie-Verlag, 1978), III, 4, 23-26, pp. 197-199; III, 3, 18-22, p. 191.

219. Galen, *On the Usefulness of the Parts of the Body* (Ithaca: Cornell University Press, 1968), B14 (11, 296). For a discussion of the relation of Hippocrates and Aristotle to Galen on hot and cold, see, Galen, *On the Natural Faculties* (New York: G.P. Putnam's Sons, 1916), Book II, iv, 88-89, p. 139. Maimonides observed the centrality of this view of Galen: "In many places he [Galen] asserts that the male is warmer than the female. It is upon this [Assertion] that he bases the fundamentals of all medicine." See, *The Medical Aphorisms of Maimonides* (New York: Yeshiva University Press, 19–), 25, 29, p. 184.

220. Galen, *On the Usefulness of the Parts of the Body*, *op. cit.*, B14 (11, 288).

221. *Ibid.*, B14 (11, 300).

222. Galen, *On the Natural Faculties*, *op. cit.*, Book II, iii, 85-86, p. 135.

223. Galen, *On the Usefulness of the Parts of the Body*, *op. cit.*, B14 (11, 288).

224. *Ibid.*, B 14 (11, 300).

225. Galen, *On the Natural Faculties*, *op. cit.*, Book II, iii, p. 85.

226. *Ibid.*

227. Galen, *On the Usefulness of the Parts of the Body*, *op. cit.*, B 14 (11, 321).

228. *Ibid.*, B 14 (11, 303).

229. *Ibid.*

230. *Ibid.*, B 14 (11, 299).

231. *Ibid.*, "It provides no small usefulness in inciting the female to the sexual act and in opening wide the neck of the uterus during coitus," B 14 (11, 323-324) and B 14 (11, 319).

232. *Ibid.*, B 14 (11, 32).

233. *Ibid.*, B 14 (11, 29). Galen argued further that it was better for the female to be created colder because she would then retain the nutrient needed in generation.

234. Philo, *Questions and Answers on Genesis* (Cambridge, Mass. and London: Harvard University Press and William Heinemann, Ltd., 1963), Book III, 47, pp. 241-242.

235. Philo, *Questions on Exodus* in Philo (Cambridge, Mass. and London: Harvard University Press and William Heinemann, Ltd., 1929-62), I, 8, p. 46.

236. Philo, *Questions and Answers on Genesis, op. cit.*, I, 37, p. 22. Philo follows Plato's division of soul into parts, rather than functions; but he echoes Aristotle's identification of the levels of function with male and female. See also, "The serpent is a symbol of desire,. . . and woman is a symbol of sense, and man of mind." I, 47, p. 37.

237. *Ibid.*, IV, 38, pp. 312-313.

238. *Ibid.*, IV, 15, p. 288.

239. *Ibid.*, II, 49, pp. 130-131.

240. Philo did not always divide the mind into male and female parts. Sometimes he divided it into two different orders of male parts: the rational man and the sensible man. See, *Questions and Answers on Genesis, op. cit.*, I, 4, p. 3 and I, 8, p. 5. He also sometimes divided the soul into two different orders of female parts: the higher part symbolized by Sarah and Leah and the lower part symbolized by Hagar or Rachel. See, *On Mating with the Preliminary Studies* in *Philo, op. cit.*, no. 26-28, pp. 471-473; no. 181, p. 551; and no. 11-12, p. 463. He also referred to a "mistress of philosophy" and her hand-maidens of the lower sciences. See, no. 144-145, pp. 333-335.

241. Philo, *Questions and Answers on Genesis,* op. cit., *I, 33, p. 20.*

242. *Ibid.*, I, 46, p. 26.

243. Philo, *On Abraham*, in *Philo, op. cit.*, 98-102, pp. 53-55.

244. Philo, *Questions and Answers on Genesis, op. cit.*, Book III, 18, p. 203.

245. *Ibid.*, I, 26, pp. 15-16. The passage cointinues: "The lack of her is ruin, but her being near at hand constitutes household management."

246. *Ibid.*, IV, 67, p. 347. Philo did, however, use Sarah as a symbol of virtue in *On Mating with the Preliminary Studies, op. cit.*, 6-7, p. 461.

247. See, Richard A. Baer, *Philo's Use of the Categories of Male and Female* (Leiden: E.J. Brill, 1970); and Joan Engelsman, "The Repression of Sophia in the Writings of Philo" in *The Feminine Dimension of the Divine* (Philadelphia: Westminster Press, 1979), pp. 95-106.

248. Richard Baer, *ibid.*, p. 21.

249. Philo, *Who is the Heir?* in *Philo, op. cit.*, 164, p. 365.

250. Philo, *Questions and Answers on Genesis, op. cit.*, I, 27, p. 16. Philo argued that in generation it took 80 days for the female to be formed and 40 for the male. "Whereas the imperfect woman, who is, so to speak, a half-section of man, requires twice as many days, namely eighty."

251. Agrippa von Nettesheim, Heinrich Cornelius, *On the Superiority of Woman Over Man* (New York: American News Company, 1873), p. 10.

252. See, Chapter IV: "Hildegard of Bingen." More recently, Pope John Paul II developed this interpretation. See, *On the Original Unity of Woman and Man* (Boston: St. Paul Editions, 1983).

253. Plutarch, *Isis and Osiris* in *Moralia* I-V (Cambridge, Mass. and London: Harvard University Press and William Heinemann, Ltd., 1927-37), V, 374D-375A, p. 141.

254. Plutarch (Florus) in *Tabletalk III* in *Morilia* VIII (Cambridge, Mass. and London: Harvard University Press and William Heinemann, Ltd., 1969), 651A-651E, pp. 155-157.

255. *Ibid.*, 637D-E. See also, Plutarch, *On Affection for Offspring* in *Moralia* VI (Cambridge, Mass. and London: Harvard University Press and William Heinemann, Ltd., 1939), 495C-496D, pp. 345-349.

256. Plutarch, *Fragments* in *Moralia XV and Fragments* (Cambridge, Mass. and London: Harvard University Press and William Heinemann, Ltd., 1969), no. 97, p. 203.

257. Plutarch, *Roman Questions* in *Moralia* IV, *op. cit.*, 288C-E, no. 102, pp. 153-155.

258. Plutarch, *Table Talk II* in *Moralia* VIII, *op. cit.*, 636D.

259. Plutarch, *Isis and Osiris*, *op. cit.*, 373F-374A.

260. *Ibid.*

261. *Ibid.*

262. Plutarch wrote the text *Isis and Isiris* for the priestess Clea. "For you are at the head of the inspired maidens of Delphi, and have been consecrated by your father and mother in the holy rites of Isiris," 364A, p. 85. Plutarch was a priest of Apollo at Delphi.

263. *Ibid.*, 368, p. 105.

264. *Ibid.*, 375C-D, p. 143; 376A-B, p. 147.

265. *Ibid.*, 351F-352A, p. 9.

266. Plutarch, *On the Fortune of Romans* in *Moralia* IV, *op. cit.*, 38E-39A, p. 337.

267. *Ibid.*, 317C, p. 329; 316D, p. 323.

268. *Ibid.*, 317E, p. 331. See also, *On the Fortune or Virtue of Alexander* in *Moralia* IV, *op. cit.*, 326D, p. 383; and *Can Vice Cause Unhappiness?* in *Moralia* VI, *op. cit.*, 498F-499A, pp. 367-369.

269. Plutarch, *On the Control of Anger* in *Moralia* VI, *op. cit.*, 457A-B, p. 117. For an example of an association of weakness in the concept of woman see, "But the lyre of Paris gave forth an altogether weak and womanish strain" in *On the Fortune or Virtue of Alexander*, *op. cit.*, 331E, p. 441. See also, "If anger is present in a home, husbands cannot endure even their wife's chastity, nor wives their husband's love." *On the Control of Anger*, *op. cit.*, 462A, p. 145.

270. Plutarch, *Advice to Bride and Groom* in *Moralia* II, *op. cit.*, 139D, p. 11; 145A, pp. 47-48.

271. Plutarch, *Sayings of Spartan Women* in *Moralia* III, *op. cit.*, 240, 5, p. 457.

272. Plutarch, *Bravery of Women* in *Moralia* III, *ibid.*, 243A-D, pp. 475-479.

273. *Ibid.*, 245D-F, pp. 489-491.

274. *Ibid.*, 245C, p. 493.

275. *Ibid.*, 142F, 34-143A, pp. 323-325.

276. Plutarch, *Roman Questions*, *op. cit.*, 263E-F, p. 7.

277. Plutarch, *Can Virtue Be Taught?* in *Moralia*, *op. cit.*, 439E, p. 9.

278. Plutarch, *Advice to Bride and Groom*, *op. cit.*, 138B-C, p. 138.

279. *Ibid.*, 145E-146A, pp. 341-342.

280. *Ibid.*, 145C-48D, pp. 337-339.

281. Plutarch, *Dinner of Seven Wise Men* in *Moralia* II, *op. cit.*, 148D, p. 361. A woman named Melissa was also present. At the end of the essay Eumetis' riddle was turned against the guest. See, 154B, pp. 391-393.

282. A.H. Armstrong, *The Cambridge History of Later Greek and Early Medieval Philosophy* (Cambridge: The University Press, 1970), p. 214.

283. Porphyry, "Life of Plotinus" in *Plotinus* (London and Cambridge, Mass.: William Heinemann Ltd. and Harvard University Press, 1966), Vol. I, p. 41.

284. Plotinus, *Enneads* in *Plotinus*, *op. cit.*, Vol. III, 6, 21-26.

285. *Ibid.*, III, 6, 30-38.

286. *Ibid.*, III, 5, 9, 45-53, Vol. III, p. 203.

287. *Ibid.*, III, 5, 2, 20-25, Vol. III, p. 175.

288. *Ibid.*, III, 6, 19, 47-53, Vol. III, p. 285.

289. *Ibid.*, III, 1, 30-55, Vol. III, pp. 12-13.

290. *Ibid.*, II, 4, 16, 5-15, Vol. II, p. 149.

291. *Ibid.*, I, 8, 5, 5-10, Vol. 1, p. 289. "If someone calls matter evil, he would speak the truth if he meant that it was unaffected by the good," III, 6, 11, 42-44, Vol. III, p. 256.

292. *Ibid.*, I, 8, 4, 1-5, Vol. I, p. 287.

293. *Ibid.*, I, 4, 14, 5-10, Vol. I, p. 25.

294. *Ibid.*, I, 1, 10, 5-10, Vol. I, p. 115.

295. *Ibid.*, III, 3,4 53-55, p. 125.

296. *Ibid.*, III, 4, pp. 145-147.

297. Porphyry, "Life of Plotinus" in *Plotinus*, *op. cit.*, Vol. I, p. 31.

298. Plotinus, *Enneads*, *op. cit.*, III, 8, pp. 385-390.

299. A.H. Armstrong, *The Cambridge History of Later Greek and Early Medieval Philosophy*, *op. cit.*, p. 284.

300. Porphyry, *Pros Gauron* in André Marie Festugière, *La Révelation d'Hermès Trismégiste* (Paris: Lecoffre, 1944-54), Vol. 3, Appendix II, pp. 265-305.

301. *Ibid.*, X, 1, 4, 47 (16-24), p. 284. Translated by the author as are all passages from this text. Porphyry describes the relation of the mother to the embryo in an analogy with the process of grafting a branch on to a tree. See, X, 1, 46 (12-21), pp. 282-283. He insisted by this analogy that the two souls were separate entities in a kind of union which maintained their unique separateness.

302. *Ibid.*, II, X, 1, 46 (12-21), pp. 282-283.

303. *Ibid.*, II, V, 1, 41 (19-24), p. 276.

304. *Ibid.*, X, 5, 48 (1-5), p. 285.

305. *Ibid.*, XVII, 1, 2, 58 (20-22), p. 299.

306. *Ibid.*, II, 4, 35 (23-36), p. 269.

307. *Ibid.*, II, 5, 36 (4-10), p. 269.

308. "Yes, taking a witness to the truth of the discourse of Plato, and with him, Aristotle, I will maintain that the intellect survives later with men and not with everything simple like that, but that it is rare, and it is only given to those things for which the soul is fit to be united to," *ibid.*, XII, 2 (11-16), p. 288.

309. *Ibid.*, II, 2, 35 (6-22), pp. 268-269.

310. *Ibid.*, XVI, 1, 56 (9-12), p. 296.

311. Porphyry, *The Philosopher to His Wife, Marcella* (London: George Redway, 1896).

312. *Ibid.*, (8), p. 60.

313. *Ibid.*, (32), p. 76. See also, (5), p. 56 and (8), p. 60.

314. *Ibid.*, (33), pp. 77-78.

315. *Ibid.*

316. *Ibid.*, (7), pp. 59.

317. *Ibid.*, (5), p. 57.

318. *Ibid.*, (3), p. 55.

319. *Ibid.*

320. *Ibid.*

321. The medieval *Organon* contained the following nine works: Porphyry's *Isagoge*, and Aristotle's *Categories*, *De Interpretatione*, *Prior Analytics*, *Posterior Analytics*, *Topics*, *De Sophisticis Elenchi*, *Rhetoric* and *Poetics*.

322. Porphyry, *Isagoge* (London: H.G. Bohn, 1853), Vol. II, Chapter ii, p. 612; see also Chapter iii, p. 618.

323. *Ibid.*, Chapter xv, pp. 631-632.

324. 'The one brilliant period of neo-Platonism at Alexandria was when it was expounded there by Hypatia." Thomas Whittaker, *The Neo-Platonists; A Study in the History of Hellenism* (Cambridge: The University Press, 1928), p. 27. This opinion is contested by other scholars. See Armstrong, *op. cit.*, p. 314: "Hypatia (d. 415) a mathematician who was also a professor of philosophy but 'inferior to Isodorus not only as a woman is to a man but as a geometer is to a philosopher,' according to his biographer."

325. Ivor Thomas, *Greek Mathematics* (Cambridge, Mass. and London: Harvard University Press and William Heinemann, Ltd., 1939), Vol. I, 48, n.a., II 285, II 517, n.b.

326. John Toland, *Tetradymus* (London: J. Brotherton and W. Meadows, 1720), p. 106. The language has been changed into modern English by the author.

327. *Ibid.*

328. *Ibid.*, p. 109.

329. *Ibid.*, p. 117.

330. *Ibid.*, p. 130.

331. *Ibid.*, p. 131.

332. "Neo-Platonism" in *The Catholic Encyclopedia*, 1913 edition. Proclus' Elements of Theology was used as a basis for the spurious *Theology of Aristotle (Liber de Causis)*, see Chapter V: "Theology of Aristotle".

333. Theon of Alexandria, "Commentaire sur les Tables Manuelles astronomique de Ptolemée" in *Oeuvres de Ptolemée* (Paris: Chez Merlin, Librairie, 1821), Vol. 5.

334. Wolfgang Alexander Meyer, *Hypatia von Alexandria* (Heidelberg: 6 Weis, 1886). This work was originally published in 1853. Charles Kingsley, *Hypatia* (New York: Garland Publishers, 1975).

335. Dora Russell, *Hypatia: Or, Woman and Knowledge* (Folcroft, Pa.: Folcroft Library Editions, 1976). This work was originally published in 1925.

336. *Hypatia: A Journal of Feminist Philosophy*, Azizah a-Hibri, ed. (Dept. of Philosophy, University of Pennsylvania, 1983).

337. *The Life of St. Katherine* (London: H. Trubner and Co., 1884), Basil in introduction to Royal MS A xxvii, p. viii.

338. *Ibid.*, pp. 34-42. This version has been changed into modern English by the author.

339. *Ibid.*, Basil in the introduction, p. viii.

340. *Ibid.*, p. 61.

341. "Catherine of Alexandria" in *The Catholic Encyclopedia*, 1913 edition.

342. *Life of St. Katherine, op. cit.*, p. 118.

343. Augustine, *The City of God Against the Pagans* (London and Cambridge, Mass.: William Heinemann, Ltd., and Harvard University Press, 1966), IV, 16.

344. Augustine, *Confessions* (Great Britain: Cox and Wyman Ltd., Penguin, 1981), IV, 16, p. 88.

345. Augustine, *The City of God, op. cit.*, XIII, 19.

346. *Ibid.*, XII, 17.

347. *Ibid.* See also, "What our Lord said was that in the resurrection there would be no marriage. He did not say that there would be no women." *Ibid.*

348. *De Libero Arbitrio* (The Free Choice of the Will) (Philadelphia: The Peter Reilly Company, 1937), Chapter 21, p. 379.

349. Augustine, *The City of God, op. cit.*, XII, 27. See also, XIII, 19.

350. *Ibid.*, XIII, 24.

351. Augustine, *The Trinity* (Washington, D.C.: The Catholic University of America Press, 1963), Book XII, Chapter 7, 12, p. 354.

352. Augustine, *Confessions, op. cit.*, Book XII, 23.

353. Augustine, *The Trinity, op. cit.*, Book XII, Chapter 7, 10, p. 352.

354. *Ibid.*, XX, p. 355.

355. Augustine, *De Genesis ad Litteram* ("La Genèse au sense littéral") in *Oeuvres* (Paris: Desclée, De Brouwer, 1936). Translated by the author as are all other passages from this text, XI, x1ii, 58, pp. 323-325.

356. Augustine, *The Trinity, op. cit.*, Book XII, Chapter 7, p. 351.

357. I am indebted to Fr. Robert Sokolowski for this articulation of the radical shift in Christian thought about God. See, Robert Sokolowski, *The God of Faith and Reason* (Notre Dame: University of Notre Dame Press, 1982).

358. Augustine, *Confessions, op. cit.*, Book V, 10.

359. *Ibid.*, Book X, 6.

360. *Ibid.*, Book XIII, 5.

361. Augustine, *The Trinity, op. cit.*, Book XII, Chapter 5.

362. See Chapter IV, "*St. Albert The Great*": "Mariology."

363. Augustine, *Letters* (New York: Fathers of the Church, Inc., 1951), No. 243, p. 224.

364. Augustine, *The Trinity, op. cit.*, III, Chapter 9.

365. Augustine, *De Genesis ad Litteram, op. cit.*, VI, v, 8, p. 455.

366. *Ibid.*

367. *Ibid.*, VI, vi, 10, pp. 457-459.

368. Augustine, *The Trinity, op. cit.*, Book XII, Chapter 7, p. 351.

369. Augustine, *De Genesis ad Litteram, op. cit.*, IX, v, 9, p. 101. See also, IX, ix, 15, p. 111 and Augustine, *The City of God., op. cit.*, XIV, 22.

370. Augustine, *The City of God., ibid.*, XII, 17.

371. *Ibid.*, XIV, 24.

372. Augustine, *Letters, op. cit.*, No. 190, Vol. IV, pp. 279-280.

373. Augustine, *De Genesis ad Litteram, op. cit.*, X, xxi, 47, pp. 213-215. This doubt is repeated in a letter to Honoratus: "Who would care to launch himself rashly upon the opinion, when the method of the coming or origin of soul lies hid in such an abyss of nature, that it is better to seek it out always as long as we are in this life than at any time to assume that we have found it?" See, *Letters, op. cit.*, Vol. III, No. 140, pp. 84-85.

374. Augustine, *The City of God, op. cit.*, XII, 26.

375. Augustine, *Confessions, op. cit.*, III, 4.

376. Augustine, *The City of God, op. cit.*, VII, 1.

377. Augustine, *De Ordine* (Divine Providence and the Problem of Evil) (New York: Cosmopolitan Science and Art Service Co., Inc., 1942), II, 18, 47.

378. Augustine, *De Libero Arbitrio, op. cit.*, 12, p. 61.

379. Augustine, *De Ordine, op. cit.*, I, 11, 31.

380. *Ibid.*, I, 11, 32.

381. *Ibid.*, II, 17, 45.

382. *Ibid.*, II, 20, 52.

383. *Ibid.*, II, 1, 1.

384. Augustine, *De Beata Vita* (Happiness—A Study) (Philadelphia: The Peter Reilly Company, 1937), 27.

385. *Ibid.*, 8, 10, 11, 16, 35.

386. *Ibid.*, 10. See also, "My mother" had the weak body of a woman but the strong faith of a man." Augustine, *Confessions, op. cit.*, IX, 4.

387. Augustine, *Confessions, op. cit.*, XIII, 32.

388. Augustine, *De Genesis ad Litteram, op. cit.*, XI, x1ii, 58, pp. 323. See also, III, xxii, 34, pp. 267-269.

389. Augustine, *The Trinity, op. cit.*, Book XII, Chapter 18, 13.

390. See, *Beatification and Canonization* in *The Catholic Encyclopedia*, 1913 edition.

391. See Augustine, *De Libero Arbitrio, op. cit.*, I, 13; and Augustine, *De Beata Vita, op. cit.*, 36.

392. Augustine, *De Genesis ad Litteram, op. cit.*, XI, xxxvii, p. 50.

393. Augustine, *The City of God, op. cit.*, XIV, 121, p. 397.

394. Augustine, "Letter to Consecrated Virgins," in *Letters, op. cit.*, No. 211.

395. *Ibid.*, No. 35.

396. Augustine, *The City of God, op. cit.*, II, 19. See also, I, 16, 18, 28, and II, 2.

397. Augustine, *Confessions, op. cit.*, VIII, 7.

398. *Ibid.*, VIII, 9.

399. Augustine, *The Soliloques of St. Augustine* (New York: Cosmopolitan Science and Art Service, Inc., 19–), I, X, 417, p. 41.

400. Augustine, *De Libero Arbitrio, op. cit.*, III, 10.

401. Augustine, "Homilies sur l'évangile de St. Jean" in *Oeuvres, op. cit.*, II, 14, pp. 201-203. Translated by the author as are all passages from this work.

402. *Ibid.*

403. Augustine, *Confessions, op. cit.*, I, p. 16. See also, Augustine, *Treatises on Marriage* (New York: Fathers of the Church, 1955), Chapter 23, pp. 45-46.

404. Augustine, *Confessions, op. cit.*, XIII, 34.

405. Augustine, *De Genesis ad Litteram, op. cit.*, II, xxii, p. 267 and VIII, xxiii, 44, p. 277.

406. Augustine, "Letters to Consecrated Virgins" in *Letters, op. cit.,* no 211.

407. Boethius, "A Treatise Against Euthuches and Nestorius' in *The Theological Tractates* (Cambridge, Mass. and London: Harvard University Press and William Heinemann, Ltd., 1918), III, 5, p. 85.

408. *Ibid.*, II, 50, p. 85.

409. Boethius, *The Consolation of Philosophy* (Indianopolis: Bobbs-Merrill, 1962), Book I, Prose I, p. 3.

410. *Ibid.*, Book I, Prose 3, pp. 7-8.

411. *Ibid.*, Book I, Prose 2, p. 6.

412. *Ibid.*, Book I, Prose 5, p. 16.

413. *Ibid.*, Book I, Prose 6, p. 18.

414. *Ibid.*, Book II, Prose 4, p. 29.

415. *Ibid.*, Book II, Prose 6, p. 35.

416. *Ibid.*, Book III, Prose 12, p. 71.

417. *Ibid.*, Book V, Prose 6, p. 119.

418. *Ibid.*, Book V, Prose 3, p. 105.

419. *Ibid.*, Book V, Prose 6, p. 119.

420. "He wrote *The Consolation of Philosophy*, a work read by every educated man for more than 1000 years." See, "Boethius" in *The New Catholic Encyclopedia*, 1967 edition.

421. Boethius, *The Consolation of Philosophy*, *op. cit.*, Book V, Prose 1, p. 102.

421. John Scotus Erigena, *Periphyseon: De Divisione Naturae* (Dublin: The Dublin Institute for Advanced Studies, 1972), Book II, 532c, 33-37.

422. John Scotus Erigena, *Periphyseon* (On the Division of Nature) (Indianapolis: Bobbs-Merrill Co., 1976), 532d 1.

423. *Ibid.*, (1972), 532b 25-28.

424. *Ibid.*, (1976), 533a 11.

425. *Ibid.*, 536c 31; 532a 15-532c35.

426. *Ibid.*, 540a 20-540b 33.

427. *Ibid.*, 532a 15-18.

428. *Ibid.*, Book V, 20.

429. *Ibid.*, (1972), 537d 11-13; 537b 32.

430. *Ibid.*, 541a 22-30.

Chapter IV

1. Hastings Rashdall, *The Universities of Europe in the Middle Ages* (London: Oxford University Press, 1931), Vol. 1, p. 26.

2. Richard William Southern, *Western Society and the Church in the Middle Ages* (Great Britain: Penguin, 1982), pp. 309-310.

3. "Hilda of Whitby, St." in *New Catholic Encyclopedia*, 1967 edition.

4. Lina Eckenstein, *Women Under Monasticism; Chapters on Saint-Lore and Convent Life between A.D. 500 and A.D. 1500* (New York: Russell and Russell, 1963), p. 91.

5. *Ibid.*, p. 90.

6. Rashdall, *op. cit.*, p. 39.

7. *The Non-Dramatic Works of Hroswitha; Text, Translation, and Commentary.* Dissertation by Sister M. Gonsalva Weigand, O.S.F. (St. Louis, Missouri, 1936), Introduction, pp. xx-xxi.

8. Alice Kemp-Welch, *Of Six Medieval Women* (London: Macmillan and Co., 1913), pp. 24-5.

9. *The Non-Dramatic Works of Hroswitha, op. cit.*, p. xvii.

10. *Hrosvithae Liber Tertius: A Text with Translation, Introduction and Commentary.* Dissertation by Sister Mary Bernardine Bergman (St. Louis, Missouri: 1942).

11. *Ibid.*, p. 41.

12. *Ibid.*, p. 57.

13. *The Non-Dramatic Works of Hrosvitha, op. cit.*, pp. 7-9.

14. *Ibid.*, p. 7.

15. In the Fall and Conversion of Theophilius', Roswitha gave one of the earliest statements of the theme of Faust in which a man makes a pact with the devil.

16. *The Plays of Roswitha* (New York: Cooper Square Publishers, Inc., 1966), p. xxvi.

17. *Ibid.*, pp. xxix-xxx.

18. Boethius, *The Consolation of Philosophy* (Indianapolis: Bobbs-Merrill, 1962). "This robe had been torn, however, by the hands of violent men, who had ripped away what they could. In her right hand, the woman held certain books; in her left hand, a scepter." Book I, Prose I, p. 4.

19. *The Plays of Roswitha, op. cit.*, pp. xxviii, xxix.

20. *Ibid.*, p. 96.

21. *Ibid.*, p. 97.

22. *Ibid.*, p. 100.

23. See Chapter V, "Early Institutions of Higher Learning and the University of Paris," for a discussion on the history of other forms of medieval education.

24. *The Plays of Roswitha, op. cit.*, pp. 136-7.

25. *Ibid.*, pp. 137-8.

26. *Ibid.*, pp. 138-9.

27. *Ibid.*, p. 140.

28. *Ibid.*, pp. 152-3.

29. "Anselm of Canterbury" in *New Catholic Encyclopedia*, 1967 edition.

30. Anselm used Aristotle's definition of substance in the *Monologium* and *De Incarnatione Verbi.* A short work entitled *De Grammatico* contained constant reference to Aristotle's theory of definition and syllogism. All these texts are contained in *Anselm of Canterbury*, Vols. I-IV (Toronto and New York: Edwin Mellen Press, 1976). See, *De Grammatico*, Vol. II, no. 10, p. 52; no. 17, p. 62, and no. 18, pp. 63-4.

31. Anselm, *Proslogium* in *Anselm of Canterbury op. cit.*, Vol. I, Chapter xv.

32. Anselm, *De Incarnation Verbi*, *op. cit.*, no. 16, Vol. III, p. 37.

33. Anselm, *Monologium*, *op. cit.*, Chapter 42, Vol. I, pp. 55-6.

34. See Chapter III, "St. Augustine: Generation."

35. Anselm, *Monologium*, *op. cit.*, p. 56.

36. *Ibid.* See also Chapter 56, p. 66.

37. *Ibid.*

38. Anselm, *De Processione Spiritus Sancti* in *Anselm of Canterbury*, Vol. 3, pp. 183-230.

39. Anselm, *Monologium*, *op. cit.*, Preface, p. 4.

40. Anselm, "Prayer to St. Paul" in *The Prayers and Meditations of St. Anselm* (Great Britain: Penguin Books, 1973), 395-415, pp. 153-4.

41. *Ibid.*, 415-425, p. 154.

42. *Ibid.*, 432-457, pp. 154-5.

43. *Ibid.*, 470-485, pp. 155-6.

44. For a further development of the motherhood of Jesus, see Julian of Norwich, *The Revelations of Divine Love* (London: Burns and Oaks, 1961); and Christine Allen, "Christ Our Mother in Julian of Norwich" in *Studies in Religion*, Vol. 10, no. 4, (Fall 1981), pp. 32-39.

45. "Prayer to Mary" in *The Prayers and Meditations of St. Anselm*, *op. cit.*, 175-197, pp. 120-121.

46. *Ibid.*, 240-270, pp. 122-3.

47. *Ibid.*, 305-325, pp. 124-5.

48. *Ibid.*, 363-370, p. 126.

49. *The Prayers and Meditations of St. Anselm*, *op. cit.*, p. 90.

50. *Lettres spirituelles choisies de Saint Anselme* (Paris: Desclée de Brouwer et Cie., 1926), XXIV, (1, 37), pp. 52-3.

51. *Ibid.*, LXXII, p. 151.

52. *Ibid.*, LXXIII, pp. 151-55.

53. Anselm, *Cur Deus Homo* in *Anselm of Canterbury*, *op. cit.*, Vol. II, no. 18, pp. 131-2.

54. Anselm, "Philosophical Fragments" in *Anselm of Canterbury*, *op. cit.*, Vol. II, nos. 36-7, p. 20.

55. Echenstein, *op. cit.*, pp. 210-211.

56. *Lettres spirituelles choisie de St. Anselm, op. cit.*, nos. CI, CII, CIII, CX, CXVI, CXVIII, CXXVII, CXXVIII.

57. *Ibid.*, no. CXVII, pp. 244-5.

58. Another interesting area to explore is Anselm's philosophy of sex identity in his descriptions of the relation of Adam and Eve. He argued that he can use 'Adam' to refer to both Adam and Eve. See *De Conceptu Virginali*, in *Anselm of Canterbury, op. cit.*, Vol. III, Chapter 9, p. 155. Anselm carried forward this neglect of Eve in his extensive discussions of original sin. See *De Liberate Arbitrii* in *Anselm of Canterbury, op. cit.*, Vol. II, pp. 105-126. However, Anselm did not always ignore Eve, for he referred to her different way of generation in *Cur Deus Homo, op. cit.*, Vol. II, Chapter 8, pp. 105-106.

59. John F. Benton, "Fraud, Fiction and Borrowing in the Correspondence of Abelard and Heloise" in *Pierre Abélard, Pierre le Vénérable: Les Courants Philosophiques, Littéraires et Artistiques en Occident au milieu de XIIe siècle* (Paris: Éditions du Centre National de la Recherche Scientifique, 1975), p. 498.

60. Etienne Gilson, *Heloise and Abelard* (Ann Arbor: The University of Michigan Press, 1960), p. 166.

61. Charlotte Charrier, *Héloïse dans l'histoire et dans la légende* (Paris: Librairie Ancienne Honoré Champion, 1933), pp. 368-395.

62. Peter Abelard, *Historia Calamitatum: The Story of My Misfortunes* (St. Paul: Thomas A. Boyd, 1922), pp. 1-2.

63. "Abelard" in the *New Catholic Encyclopedia*, 1967 edition.

64. *Ibid.*, see also, Rashdall, *op. cit.*, Vol. I, p. 43.

65. Abelard, *Historia Calamitatum, op. cit.*, p. 14.

66. See, Peter Abelard, *Dialectica* (Assen: Vangorcum and Co., 1956), and D.E. Luscombe, *Peter Abelard's Ethics* (Oxford: Clarendon Press, 1971).

67. *The Letters of Abelard and Héloise* (New York: Alfred A. Knopf, 1926), p. 131.

68. *Ibid.*, p. 145.

69. Mary Martin McLaughlin, "Peter Abelard and the Dignity of Women: Twelfth Century 'Feminism' in Theory and Practice" in *Pierre Abélard, Pierre le Vénérable, op. cit.*, p. 305.

70. *The Letters of Abelard and Heloise, op. cit.*, p. 137.

71. Abelard, *Historia Calamitatum, op. cit.*, p. 71.

72. *Ibid.*, pp. 71-2.

73. *The Letters of Abelard and Heloise, op. cit.*, p. 201.

74. McLaughlin, *op. cit.*, pp. 305-306. See, note 57.

75. Luscombe, *Peter Abelard's Ethics, op. cit.*, p. 33.

76. *Ibid.*

77. *Ibid.*, pp. 33-4.

78. Abelard, *Historia Calamitatum, op. cit.*, p. 21.

79. *The Letters of Abelard and Heloise*, pp. 78-9.

80. *Ibid.*, p. 104.

81. Abelard, *Historia Calamitatum, op. cit.*, p. 16.

82. *The Letters of Abelard and Heloise*, p. 97.

83. *Ibid.*, p. 156. See also, McLaughlin, *op. cit.*, p. 302.

84. *Ibid.*, p. 100.

85. *Ibid.*, p. 156.

86. McLaughlin, *op. cit.*, p. 291.

87. *The Letters of Abelard and Heloise, op. cit.*, p. 134.

88. *Ibid.*, p. 133.

89. *Ibid.*, p. 136.

90. *Ibid.*, p. 139.

91. McLaughlin, *op. cit.*, p. 296, note 20. She notes that the epithet 'the Apostle of the Apostles' was commonly applied to Magdalene in the twelfth century and that it has been used by St. Odo of Cluny in the tenth century.

92. *The Letters of Abelard and Heloise, op. cit.*, pp. 156-7.

93. *Ibid.*, p. 158.

94. *Ibid.*, p. 155.

95. *Ibid.*, p. 96. See also, Abelard, *Historia Calimitatum, op. cit.*, p. 16.

96. *Ibid.*, p. 193.

97. *Ibid.*, p. 194.

98. *Ibid.*, p. 203.

99. *Ibid.*, p. 205.

100. *Ibid.*, pp. 206-207.

101. *Ibid.*, p. 208.

102. *Ibid.*, p. 209. See also: "And let him be like a steward in a king's palace, who does not oppress the mistress with his power, but acts providently towards her, that he may straightway obey her in things needful, and in harmful things not give ear to her, and so minister to all things without that he may never, unless ordered, enter into the secrecy of the bride-chamber," p. 208.

103. *Ibid.*, p. 208.

104. *Ibid.*, pp. 213-5.

105. *Ibid.*, p. 207.

106. *Ibid.*, pp. 220.

107. *Ibid.*, p. 230.

108. *Ibid.*, p. 241. See Benton, *op. cit.*, pp. 477-8, for a consideration of how this issue relates to the question of forgery.

109. *Ibid.*, pp. 244-5.

110. *Ibid.*, p. 183.

111. Petrus Abelardus, *Patrologiae* (Paris: J.P. Migne, 1885), Vol. 178, p. 33. Translated by Paul Widdows.

112. *The Letters of Abelard and Heloise, op. cit.*, p. 196.

113. *Ibid.*, p. 197.

114. *Ibid.*, pp. 210-4.

115. *Ibid.*, p. 215.

116. *Ibid.*, p. 258.

117. *Ibid.*, p. 59.

118. *Ibid.*, pp. 65, 75.

119. *Ibid.*, p. 87.

120. *Ibid.*, p. 82.

121. *Ibid.*, p. 83.

122. *Ibid.*, pp. 81-2.

123. *Ibid.*, p. 55.

124. *Ibid.*, p. 111.

125. *Ibid.*, p. 59.

126. *Ibid.*, p. 57. See also, p. 60.

127. *Ibid.*, p. 82.

128. *Ibid.*, p. 57.

129. *Ibid.*, pp. 57-8.

130. Abelard, *Historia Calamitatum*, *op. cit.*, p. 23.

131. *Ibid.*, p. 24.

132. *Ibid.*, p. 25.

133. *Ibid.*, p. 27.

134. *Ibid.*, p. 28.

135. *Ibid.*, p. 24. Theophrastus's arguments were transmitted by Jerome's text "Adversus Jovinianus" in Hieronymus, *Patrologiae* (Paris: J.P. Migne, 1885).

136. See, David S. Wiesen, *St. Jerome as a Satirist* (Ithaca, New York: Cornell University Press, 1964), p. 119. See also "Advice to Eustochium" in *Selected Letters of St. Jerome* (Cambridge, Mass. and London: Harvard University Press and William Heinemann Ltd., 1954), pp. 53-159.

137. Abelard, *Historia Calamitatum*, *op. cit.*, p. 25.

138. *Ibid.*, p. 19.

139. *Ibid.*, p. 28.

140. *Ibid.*

141. *Ibid.*, p. 16.

142. *The Letters of Abelard and Heloise* (Harmondsworth: Penguin Books, 1974), "Letter of Peter the Venerable," no. 115, pp. 277-8.

143. Abelard, *Historia Calamitatum*, *op. cit.*, p. 15.

144. *The Letters of Abelard and Heloise* (Penguin edition), *op. cit.*, "Letter of Peter the Venerable," no. 115, p. 178.

145. *The Letters of Abelard and Heloise* (Knopf edition), *op. cit.*, p. 110.

146. *Ibid.*

147. *Ibid.*, p. 112.

148. *Ibid.*

149. *Ibid.*, p. 113.

150. *Ibid.*, pp. 115-6. Heloise was the first to introduce the secondary source reference to Aristotle in this context. "Macrobius Theodosius, in the seventh book of the Saturnalia, reminds us in these words: Aristotle says that women are rarely inebriated, old men often. The woman is of an extremely humid body... The woman's body is cleansed by frequent purgations, it is pierced with many holes... By these holes the vapour of wine is speedily released... And so, considering these things, perpend how much more safely and rightly to our nature and informity any food and drink may be allowed.... The quality of the female body, as I have said, protects us."

151. *Ibid.*

152. *Ibid.*, p. 123.

153. D.E. Luscombe, *Peter Abelard* (London: The Historical Association, 1979), p. 27.

154. McLaughlin, *op. cit.*, p. 330. Note that the earliest copy of this work is not known until the thirteenth century. See Luscombe, *ibid.*, p. 28. It can be located in *Patrilogiae, op. cit.*, Vol. 178.

155. Peter Dronke, *Abelard and Heloise in Medieval Testimonies* (Glasgow: The University of Glasgow Press, 1976), p. 55.

156. Charrier, *op. cit.*, pp. 371, 388-391. This phrase was developed into "La très sage Heloys" by Francois Villon.

157. Dronke, *op. cit.*, pp. 56-7. See also, Charrier, *op. cit.*, pp. 391-4.

158. *Ibid.*, p. 29.

159. Charrier, *op. cit.*, p. 320. Translation by the author.

160. "Hildegarde of Bingen," *New Catholic Encyclopedia*, 1967 edition.

161. Charles Joseph Singer, *From Magic to Science: Essays on the Scientific Twilight* (New York: Dover Publications, 1958), pp. 235-8; see also, Frances and Joseph Gies, *Women in the Middle Ages* (New York: Thomas Y. Crowell, 1978), p. 79.

162. Francesca Maria Steele, *The Life and Visions of St. Hildegard* (London: Heath, Cranton and Ousely, Ltd., 1914), p. 132. See also, Barbara Newman, *O Feminea Forma: God and Woman in the Works of St. Hildegard*, Ph.D. Dissertation, Yale, 1981. This work will be published in a revised text entitled *Sister of Wisdom: St. Hildegard's Theology of the Feminine* (University of California Press, forthcoming 1985). I am indebted to Barbara Newman for many clarifications and sources concerning Hildegard of Bingen.

163. Hildegard of Bingen, *Scivias* (CCCM 43-43a). See *Wisse die Wege* (Salzburg: Otto Müller Verlag, 1975), Translated by Barbara Newman and printed in "Hildegard of Bingen: Visions and Validation" presented at the American Academy of Religion, Dallas, December 1983 and appearing in a forthcoming issue of *Church History*, pp. 4-5 of manuscript, footnote 8.

164. Hildegard of Bingen, *Vita* (II.17, 104A), printed in Newman, "Hildegard of Bingen: Visions and Validation," p. 5 of manuscript, footnote 9.

165. At present her works are available in Latin and German only. However, a translation of the *Scivias* is being completed by Mother Columba Hart, O.S.B., to be published in the *Classics of Western Philosophy* (New York: Ramsay; Toronto: Paulist Press, forthcoming).

166. "Hildegard of Bingen," *New Catholic Encyclopedia*, 1967 edition. Her hymns have recently been recorded by Christopher Page, a Hyperion recording. See a review of this recording by Barbara Grant, "A Feather on the Breath of God" in *Parabola Magazine*, published by the Society for the Study of Myth and Tradition, New York City, New York, Vol. IX, no. 2 (Summer 1984), pp. 94-8. For the written text of her hymns see, *Lieder* (Salzburg: Otto Müller Verlag, 1969).

167. Hildegard of Bingen, *Heilkunde: das Buch von den Grund und Wesen und der Heilung der Krankheiten (Causae et curae)* (Salzburg: O. Müller Verlag, 1972), p. 97. Translated from the German by Jasmin el Kordi-Schmitt, as are all subsequent passages from this text.

168. *Ibid.*, p. 103.

169. *Ibid.*, p. 124.

170. *Ibid.*, p. 93. "That the man wears a beard and has more hair all over his body than does the woman, hence comes because the man was formed of earth." See also, "And since they [the second kind of woman] do have a somewhat manly nature, and a great deal of procreative power, they often grow a down around their chin," p. 144.

171. Barbara Newman, "Divine Power Made Perfect in Weakness: St. Hildegard on the Frail Sex," *Medieval Religious Women* (Cistercian Publications, forthcoming 1985), p. 18 of manuscript, footnote 54.

172. *Ibid.*, p. 21 of manuscript, footnote 60.

173. *Ibid.* See also footnotes 61-66 of the manuscript for other examples of Hildegard's description of this theory.

174. Hildegard, *Heilkunde, op. cit.*, p. 178.

175. *Ibid.*, p. 92. See also, "Not until Adam's transgression was the extraordinary power in his sexual member changed into this poison-like foam. The woman's blood was likewise altered into yonder unnatural discharge," p. 104; and "When Adam, through his sin was blinded and in a state of insensibility, his generative power went with him into exile and transferred to another organ. It fled so to speak secretly to the above-mentioned genitals and remained there," p. 138.

176. *Ibid.*, p. 125.

177. *Ibid.*

178. *Ibid.*

179. *Ibid.*, p. 126.

180. Steele, *op. cit.*, p. 213.

181. Hildegard, *Heilkunde, op. cit.*, p. 102.

182. *Ibid.*

183. Steele, *op. cit.*, p. 176.

184. Hildegard of Bingen, *Der Mensch in der Verantwortung, das Buch der Lebensverdienste* (*Liber vitae Meritorum*) (Salzburg: Otto Müller Verlag, 1972), 69. Translated by Jasmin el Kordi-Schmitt as are all other passages from this text.

185. Hildegard, *Heilkunde, op. cit.*, p. 142.

186. *Ibid.*, p. 143.

187. *Ibid.*, see especially Chapters IV-XII.

188. *Ibid.*, p. 138.

189. *Ibid.*, p. 140.

190. *Ibid.*

191. *Ibid.*, p. 141.

192. *Ibid.*, p. 142.

193. *Ibid.*, p. 144.

194. *Ibid.*

195. *Ibid.*, p. 145.

196. *Ibid.*, p. 146.

197. *Ibid.*, p. 139.

198. *Ibid.*, p. 140.

199. See, Jerome, "Letter to Eustochium, no. 22," *op. cit.*, Juvenal, "Satire Against Women" in Chapter III, and Lucretius, *The Nature of Things*," in Chapter III.

200. Hildegard of Bingen, *Heilkunde*, *op. cit.*, p. 140.

201. *Ibid.*

202. *Ibid.*

203. *Ibid.*, p. 141.

204. *Ibid.*, p. 142.

205. *Ibid.*, p. 143.

206. *Ibid.*, p. 144.

207. *Ibid.*, p. 145.

208. *Ibid.*

209. *Ibid.*, p. 140. See also, "The reason within them knows its extraction and therefore modesty and a humane attitude are prevailing. Such men are entitled to marry with manly discipline, for the female nature is of more gentleness and tenderness than that of man," p. 139.

210. Bruce William Hozeski, *Ordo Virtutum: Hildegard of Bingen's Liturgical Morality Play*, Ph.D. Dissertation, Michigan State University, 1969, p. ii.

211. *Ibid.*, p. 6. Translated by Bruce Hozeski as are all other passages from this text.

212. *Ibid.*, pp. 9-10.

213. *Ibid.*, p. 32.

214. Hildegard of Bingen, *Heilkunde*, *op. cit.*, p. 93.

215. Hildegard of Bingen, *Der Mensch in der Verantwortung*, p. 69.

216. Steele, *op. cit.*, pp. 32-40.

217. Gies, *op. cit.*, pp. 84-5. See also, Jacques Christophe, *Sainte Hildegard* (Paris: Gallimard, 1942), pp. 52-54.

218. Newman, "Divine Power," *op. cit.*, page 5 of the manuscript, footnote 12. An unofficial fragment (IV, 28).

219. Newman, "Visions and Validation," *op. cit.*, p. 15 of manuscript, note 39 (*Liber visionum*, I, 1).

220. Newman, "Divine Power," *op. cit.*, footnote 4, p. 28 of manuscript.

221. "Hildegard of Bingen," *New Catholic Encyclopedia*, 1967 edition.

222. S. Hildegardis, Abbatissae, *Opera Omnia, Patrologiae* (Paris: J.P. Migne, 1882, vol. 197.

223. "Hildegard of Bingen," *New Catholic Encyclopedia,* 1967 edition.

224. Christophe, *op. cit.,* pp. 49-53.

225. Steele, *op. cit.*, p. 75.

226. Marianna Schroder and Adelgundis Führkötter, *Die Echtheit des Schrifttums der heiligen Hildegard von Bingen* (Köln-Graz: Böhlau-Verlag, 1956), pp. 151-3. I am grateful to Barbara Newman for bringing this theory to my attention.

227. Herrad of Hohenbourg, *Hortus Deliciarum: Commentary* (New Rochelle, New York: Caratzas Brothers Publishers, 1971), p. 226. Translated by Paul Widdows, as are all inscriptions registered in this text.

228. Eckenstein, *op. cit.*, p. 233.

229. *Ibid.*, p. 242.

230. *Ibid.*, p. 240.

231. Herrad of Hohenbourg, *Hortus Deliciarum: Commentary*, *op. cit.*, p. 23.

232. Herrad of Hohenbourg, *Hortus Deliciarum: Reconstruction* by Rosalie Green et al. (London: Warbourg Institute, 1979), p. 36. Translated by Paul Widdows as are all passages from this text.

233. Herrad of Hohenbourg, *Hortus Deliciarum: Commentary*, *op. cit.*, p. 23.

234. *Ibid.*, p. 30.

235. Herrad of Hohenbourg, *Hortus Deliciarum: Reconstruction*, *op. cit.*, pp. 231-2.

236. *Ibid.*

237. *Ibid.*, p. 37.

238. *Ibid.*, p. 29.

239. *Ibid.*, p. 37.

240. Herrad of Hohenbourg, *Hortus Deliciarum: Commentary*, *op. cit.*, p. 96. The centrality of the body to human identity is reaffirmed by Herrad in her claim that in the resurrection women and men will receive the same bodies they had on earth. See *Reconstruction*, p. 24. "It will be concluded when the saints recover their bodies and possess the doubles of their earthly ones."

241. Herrad of Hohenbourg, *Hortus Deliciarum: Commentary*, *op. cit.*, p. 96.

242. *Ibid.*, p. 224.

243. Herrad of Hohenbourg, *Hortus Deliciarum: Reconstruction*, *op. cit.*, p. 40.

244. Herrad of Hohenbourg, *Hortus Deliciarum: Commentary*, *op. cit.*, p. 103.

245. Herrad of Hohenbourg, *Hortus Deliciarum: Reconstruction*, *op. cit.*, p. 54.

246. Herrad of Hohenbourg, *Hortus Deliciarum: Commentary, op. cit.*, p. 104.

247. *Ibid.*

248. *Ibid.*

249. Herrad of Hohenbourg, *Hortus Deliciarum: Reconstruction, op. cit.*, p. 37.

250. *Ibid.*, p. 353.

251. *Ibid.*

252. *Ibid.*

253. Herrad of Hohenbourg, *Hortus Deliciarum: Commentary, op. cit.*, p. 201.

254. *Ibid.*

255. *Ibid.*

256. *Ibid.*

257. *Ibid.*

258. *Ibid.*, p. 192.

259. *Ibid.*

260. See Chapter III, "Greek Schools of Philosophy."

261. It was proclaimed by Pope Clement on November 27, 1095 and began in 1096.

262. "Crusades" in *Encyclopedia Britannica*, 1968 edition.

263. James Brundage, *Medieval Canon Law and the Crusader* (Madison, Milwaukee, and London: The University of Wisconsin Press, 1969), p. 32.

264. *Ibid.*, p. 44. For a history of the relation of canon law to the concept of woman see Chapter V, "The Faculty of Law."

265. *Ibid.*, p. 77.

266. *Ibid.*, pp. 110-111. See also, Chapter IV, "St. Albert the Great."

267. Meg Bogin, *The Women Troubadours: An Introduction to the Women Poets of the 12th-century Provence and a Collection of their Poems* (Toronto: George J. McLeod Limited, 1976), p. 81.

268. *Ibid.*, pp. 83-7.

269. *Ibid.*, p. 125.

270. *Ibid.*, pp. 99-101.

271. Robert Briffault, *The Troubadours* (Bloomington: Indiana University Press, 1965), p. 142.

272. Andreas Capellanus, *The Art of Courtly Love* (New York: Frederick Ungar Publishing Co., 1957), Book I, Chapter i, p. 2.

273. *Ibid.*, p. 3.

274. *Ibid.*, Chapter ii, p. 4.

275. See, Chapter IV, "The Crusades and Courtly Love."

276. Capellanus, *op. cit.*, Chapter V, p. 6.

277. *Ibid.*, first dialogue, p. 8.

278. *Ibid.*, second dialogue, pp. 9-10.

279. *Ibid.*, third dialogue, pp. 12-13.

280. *Ibid.*, seventh dialogue, pp. 17-18.

281. *Ibid.*, Book II, pp. 42-3.

282. *Ibid.*, Book III, p. 44.

283. *Ibid.*, pp. 48-9.

284. *Ibid.*, p. 49.

285. *Ibid.*, p. 50.

286. *Ibid.*

287. *Ibid.*, pp. 50-51.

288. *Ibid.*, p. 51.

289. *Ibid.*

290. *Ibid.*, p. 53.

291. Dronke, *op. cit.*, p. 29. (Dronke states that the illuminated manuscript is mentioned by G.F. Warner and J.P. Wilson in *Catalogue of Western MSS.* in the Old Royal and Kings' Collection II-1921, pp. 203-204).

292. Walter Map, *De Nugis Curialium* (Courtiers' Trifles) (London: Chatto and Windus, 1924), 5-8, p. 197.

293. *Ibid.*, 28-30, p. 184.

294. *Ibid.*, 19-27, p. 185.

295. *Ibid.*, 21-35, p. 186.

296. *Ibid.*, 8-10, p. 187.

297. See Chapter IV, 'Heloise and Abelard,'' and St. Jerome's *Adversus Jovinianum* in Hieronymus, *Patrologiae*, *op. cit.*

298. Map, *op. cit.*, 18-20, p. 190. In one passage Plato is described as being generated by the union of Perictione and Apollo. See 15-25, p. 194.

299. *Ibid.*, 2-10, p. 192.

300. See, Chapter III, "Epicureanism" and "Juvenal."

301. *The Latin Poems Commonly Attributed to Walter Mapes*, edited by Thomas Wright (Hildesheim: Georg Olms Verlagsbuchhandlung, 1968), 40-50, p. 79. Wright states: "This poem, which appears to have been extremely popular is a remarkable specimen of the gross satirical attacks upon the female sex which were common in the middle ages," note p. 79.

302. Map, *De Nugis Curialium*, *op. cit.*, 5-8, p. 193.

303. *Ibid.*, 28-30, p. 196.

304. *Ibid.*, Introduction, p. 8.

305. Avicenna, *The Metaphysics of Avicenna (Ibn Sina)* (New York: Columbia University Press, 1973), (38), p. 76.

306. Avicenna, *The Life of Ibn Sina* (Albany: State University of New York Press, 1974), pp. 34-5.

307. *Ibid.*

308. Al-Farabi, *On the Perfect State* (Oxford: Clarendon Press, 1985), especially chapter 12, pp. 187-97 and Alfarabi, *The Political Regime,* in *Medieval Political Philosophy: A Sourcebook,* Ralph Lerner and Muhsin Mahdi, eds. (Ithaca, New York: Cornell University Press, 1963), chapter 6, pp. 50-53.

309. Avicenna, *Healing: Metaphysics in Medieval Political Philosophy, op. cit.,* pp. 98-111.

310. Avicenna, *Avicenna's Psychology: An English Translation of Kitab al-Najat, Book II, Chapter VI* (London: Oxford University Press, 1952), Chapter XII, p. 57.

311. *Ibid.,* p. 58.

312. Avicenna, *Livre des définitions* (Cairo: Publications de l'institut français d'archéologie orientale du Caire, 1903), "The complete description includes things nonessential but proper to X,—but a definition is of the essence," Chap. 3, p. 12.

313. Avicenna, *The Metaphysics of Avicenna (Ibn Sina), op. cit.,* (13), p. 38, and *Healing: Metaphysics X,* in *Medieval Political Philosophy,* Chapter 4, pp. 105-6.

314. Avicenna, *A Treatise on the 'Canon of Medicine' of Avicenna* (New York: AMS Press, 1973), Book I, Part III, Preface no. 679, p. 359. See also, I, I, Thesis V, no. 123.

315. *Ibid.*, I, I, ii, no. 20, p. 34. The translator of this text carried out the implications of this view in his own commentary: "Light, equivalents: weak, male (because conferring or inceptive), positive, active, Heaven. Heavy, equivalents: strong, female (because recipient), negative, passive, Earth," p. 35.

316. *Ibid.*, I, I, ii, no. 21, p. 35.

317. *Ibid.*, I, I, Thesis V, no. 125, p. 99. See also, M. Meyerhof and D. Joannides, *La gynécologie et l'obstétrique chez Avicenne (Ibn Sina) et leur rapports avec celles des grecs* (Cairo: Imprimerie E. and R. Schindler, 1938), p. 23.

318. *Ibid.*, I, I, Thesis VI, no. 145, p. 119.

319. *Ibid.*, I, I, Thesis V, no. 125. p. 99.

320. *Ibid.*, natural abortion: I, II, no. 328-9; pulse in pregnancy: I, II, no. 597; urine in pregnancy: I, II, iii, no. 672; diseases in pregnancy: III, V; and lactation: I, III, i, no. 696-712.

321. *Ibid.*, "The generative organs some of which are essential and others auxiliary. The essential function is that of forming generative elements; the auxiliary functions are those of giving the masculine and feminine form and temperament. These functions are inseparable from the race, and yet play no part in the essence of life," I, I, V, no. 123. For other descriptions of primary reproductive activity, see *Avicenna's Psychology, op. cit.*, Chapter I, pp. 24-5; and Avicenna, *A Compendium on the Soul* (Verona: Stamperia di N. Paderno, 1906), Chapter IV, no. 40.

322. F.E. Peters, *Aristotle and the Arabs* (New York: NYU Press, 1968), p. 217. "The falsafah tradition had been moving chiefly under the influence of Ibn Sina, away from the texts in the direction of general works of synthesis (of Aristotle). . . with Ibn Rushd there is a return to the text."

323. *Ibid.*, p. 218. From Marrakushi, *History of Maghrib*, "If someone would tackle those books, summarize them, and expound their aims, after understanding them thoroughly, it would be easier for people to grasp them. . . (Ibn Rushd) said: "This is what led me to summarize the books of the philosopher Aristotle."

324. *Colliget* is a derivative of *Kulliyat.*

325. Averroes, "Colliget" in *Aristotelis Opera cum Averrois Commentariis* (Frankfurt: Minerva Verlag, 1962), II, 10, Suppl. I, p. 23. Translated by Fr. Andrew Murray, O.M. as are all passages from this text.

326. *Ibid.*, Averroes also mentioned as a further example a woman who swore she was impregnated in bath water in which men had previously bathed.

327. *Ibid.*

328. *Ibid.*, "It is not credible that the seed adds anything qualitatively, but it adds to the heat qualitatively."

329. *Ibid.*, see also, "Because of all these reasons therefore it is not credible that the seed of the woman is the matter or form of the embryo but the seed of man stands in the place of form and the menstrual blood in the place of matter," p. 24.

330. Averroes, "Commentariis et epitome Aristotelis Metaphysicorum" in *Aristotelis Opera, op. cit.*, Book X, Chapter 8, Vol. III, p. 275. It must be noted that Averroes' chapters do not exactly match Aristotle's (X, 9) for the same passage.

331. *Ibid.*

332. *Ibid.*

333. Averroes, "In Moralia Nicomachia Expositione" in *Aristotelis Opera, op. cit.*, Vol. III, Book VII, Chapter 7, p. 118.

334. See Chapter IV, "Maimonides," for a fuller discussion of this process.

335. Averroes, "Peripateticorum Principis Politicorum" in *Aristotelis Opera, op. cit.*, Vol. III, Book I, Chapter 8, p. 233. This corresponds to Aristotle's *Politics*, Book I, Chapter 12.

336. *Ibid.*, compare with Aristotle's *Politics*, Book I, Chapter 12.

337. *Ibid.*, p. 234.

338. Averroes, *On Plato's 'Republic'* (Ithaca: Cornell University Press, 1974), 22, 34-6, p. 4. "The first part of this is. . . also in this book of Plato's that we intend to explain since Aristotle's book of governance has not yet fallen into our hands."

339. *Ibid.*, 53, 9-10, p. 57.

340. *Ibid.*, 53, 25, p. 58.

341. *Ibid.*, 54, 5-10, p. 59. Averroes was considering women soldiers in this passage.

342. *Ibid.*, see "All this being as we have characterized it and since the cities whose association we wish to be virtuous ought to be of this kind, why it is evident that the community of children and women of which we have spoken is one of the most necessary things," pp. 60-65.

343. Averroes's view went further than Avicenna's which had held that while the active intellect was one in all persons, the passive intellect was differentiated.

344. Averroes, *Tahafut al-Tahafut (The Incoherence of the Incoherence)* (London: Luzac, 1954), first discussion 28, 16-29, p. 15. In another place in the same work, Averroes mentioned that the body of a dead person could become matter in the form of a plant, then through digestion and nutrition either seed or menstrual blood, and therefore part of another human being. See, 269, 5-11, p. 159.

345. Isaac Husik, *A History of Medieval Jewish Philosophy* (New York: The Macmillan Co., 1916). Maimonides' works were translated into Latin in the twelfth century and into Hebrew in the thirteenth century.

346. Avicebron, *Fountain of Life* (Philadelphia, 1954), I, no. 5, p. (no. 5, p. 6;) IV, no. 20, p. 225; V, no. 11, p. 245.

347. Avicebron, *Choice of Pearls* (New York: Bloch Publishing Co., 1925).

348. *Selected Religious Poems of Solomon Ibn Gabirol* (New York: Arno Press, 1973), no. 2, p. 3. See also, Avicebron, *The Kingly Crown* (London: Valentine and Mitchell, 1961), "Knowledge is her glory, and therefore decay has no rule over her, and she endures with the endurance of her foundation, this is her state and her secret," XXX, p. 50.

349. Solomon Ibn Gabirol, *The Kingly Crown*, *op. cit.*, XXXV, p. 56.

350. *Selected Religious Poems of Solomon Ibn Gabirol*, *op. cit.*, "How can I forsake wisdom, and the spirit of God has made a covenant between me and her? How can she forsake me when she is to me like a mother and I to her as a child of old age?" p. xx.

351. Avicebron, *Fountain of Life*, *op. cit.*, III, no. 47, p. 166.

352. *Ibid.*

353. *Ibid.*, IV, no. 1, p. 189.

354. *Ibid.*, V, no. 12, p. 247.

355. *Ibid.*, III, 49, p. 170. See also, III, no. 58, p. 187.

356. Isaac Myer, *Qabbalah (The Philosophical Writings of Solomon Ben Yehudah Ibn Gabirol and their connection with the Hebrew Qabbalah)* (New York: Ktav Publishing House, 1970), V, p. 117.

357. *Ibid.*, VI, p. 123.

358. Husik, *op. cit.*, pp. 78-9.

359. Avicebron, *Choice of Pearls*, *op. cit.*, no. 268, p. 67.

360. *Ibid.*, nos. 302-4, 456, p. 98.

361. *Ibid.*, no. 374, pp. 83-4.

362. "Maimonides" in *New Catholic Encyclopedia*, 1967 edition.

363. Husik, *op. cit.*, p. 60.

364. Moses Maimonides, *The Guide of the Perplexed* (Chicago: University of Chicago Press, 1963), I, 17, p. 43.

365. *Ibid.*, III, 8, pp. 431-2.

366. *Ibid.*, I, 6, p. 31.

367. *The Medical Aphorisms of Maimonides* (New York: Yeshiva University Press, 19–), 25, 29, p. 184.

368. *Ibid.*, 25, 29, pp. 184-5.

369. Maimonides, *The Commandments: Sefer Ha-Mitzvoth of Maimonides* (London and New York: Soncino, 1967), Negative Commandment no. 346, Vol. II, p. 311. Maimonides qualifies the taboos that are associated with menstruating women in other cultures. "It is generally known that according to the usages observed up to our times by the Sabians in the lands of the West. . . the *menstruating* woman remains isolated in her house; the places upon which she treads are burnt; whoever speaks with her becomes unclean; and if a wind that blows

passes over a menstruating woman and a clean individual, the latter becomes unclean. See how great the difference is between this and our dictum: All the various kinds of work that a wife does for her husband, are also done by a menstruating woman for her husband, except for washing his face, and so on. It is only forbidden to have intercourse with her in the days in which she is unclean and defiled." *The Guide of the Perplexed, op. cit.*, III, 47, p. 595.

370. *The Medical Aphorisms of Mainonides, op. cit.*, 16, 7, p. 33.

371. *Ibid.*, 16, 8, p. 34. "If any woman's nature tends to be transformed to the nature of a man, this does not arise from medications, but is caused by heavy menstrual activity." The hidden implication here is that the outpouring of impure blood leaves a residue of pure blood that would allow for the development of male identity.

372. *Ibid.*, 16, 31, p. 39. "During pregnancy, the creative and growth prompting forces of the fetuses attract the best blood, and leave the worst thereof in the vessels of the woman."

373. *Maimonides, The Eight Chapters on Ethics (Shemorak perakim); A Psychological and Ethical Treatise* (New York: Columbia University, Ph.D. Dissertation, 1912), Chapter IV, p. 67.

374. Maimonides "Discourse on Sexual Intercourse" in *Essays on Maimonides, The Medical Works of Maimonides*, Appendix II, edited by Salo Wittmayer Baron (New York: Columbia University Press, 1941), p. 290.

375. *The Medical Aphorisms of Maimonides, op. cit.*, 11, 37, p. 40.

376. Maimonides, *The Commandments, op. cit.*, Positive Commandment, no. 75, Vol. I, p. 87.

377. Maimonides, *The Guide of the Perplexed, op. cit.*, III, 8, p. 436.

378. Maimonides, *Book of Women* in *The Code of Maimonides* (New Haven: Yale University Press, 1949), no. 2, p. 93. See also, *The Commandments, op. cit.*, "It does not apply to women: the Talmud says explicitly: The duty to be fruitful and multiply is laid on the man, not on the woman." Positive Commandment, no. 212, Vol. I, p. 228.

379. *The Medical Aphorisms of Maimonides, op. cit.*, 24, 18, p. 158. However, Maimonides is reputed to have criticized Hippocrates in another work for arguing that a boy is born from the right ovary, a girl from the left. See *Commentary on the Aphorisms of Hippocrates* (Jerusalem: Mossad Harav Kook, 1961), p. xiii.

380. *Ibid.*, 16, 25, p. 38.

381. Maimonides, "Laws concerning Character Traits" in *Ethical Writings of Maimonides* (New York: New York University Press, 1975), IV, 19, p. 40. See also, *The Eight Chapters on Ethics, op. cit.*, Chapter IV, pp. 64-5.

382. *Ibid.*, V, 4, p. 43. Maimonides allowed more frequent intercourse for medical reasons. See, III, 2, p. 35.

383. Maimonides, *The Guide of the Perplexed, op. cit.*, III, 8, p. 436.

384. Maimonides, *Ethical Writings, op. cit.*, V, 4, p. 43. Compare this passage with Maimonides' statements that sexual desires should be carefully checked, see, *The Guide of the Perplexed, op. cit.*, III, 8, pp. 432-5.

385. Maimonides, *The Guide of the Perplexed, op. cit.*, III, 54, pp. 632-8.

386. *Ibid.*, p. 632.

387. Maimonides, *The Commandments, op. cit.*, Positive Commandment, no. 13, Vol. I, p. 20.

388. Maimonides, "On the Management of Health" in *Ethical Writings, op. cit.*, Chapter III, p. 106.

389. *Ibid.*, p. 108.

390. Maimonides, *The Guide of the Perplexed, op. cit.*, III, 8, pp. 433-4.

391. Maimonides, *Introduction to the Talmud* (New York: Judaica Press, 1975), p. 152.

392. Maimonides, *The Guide of the Perplexed, op. cit.*, III, 48, p. 600.

393. *Ibid.*, III, 8, p. 433.

394. *Ibid.*, III, 49, p. 608. This misappropriation of Aristotle may have come by way of the spurious work: *The Apple or Aristotle's Death.* See Chapter V, "The Apple or Aristotle's Death".

395. For a detailed explanation of the processes of translation see, Fernand von Steenberghen, *Aristotle in the West* (Louvain: E. Navwelaerts, 1955); John Patrick Lynch, *Aristotle's School* (Berkeley: University of Chicago Press, 1972); and Gordon Leff, *Paris and Oxford Universities in the Thirteenth and Fourteenth Centuries* (New York: John Wiley and Sons Inc., 1968), pp. 128-137.

396. Hieronymus Wilms, *Albert the Great: Saint and Doctor of the Church* (London: Burns, Oates and Washbourne, Ltd., 1933), p. 67.

397. *Ibid.*, p. 66.

398. Rashdall, *op. cit.*

399. S.M. Alpert, *Albert the Great* (Oxford: Blackfriars Publications, 1948), p. 67. See also Thomas Maria Schwertner, *St. Albert the Great* (New York: The Bruce Publishing Co., 1932), pp. 210-229. Albert apparently influenced the following major scientific works: Bartholoumarius Anglicus, *Encyclopedia of Natural History*, Konrad von Megenberg, *Book of Nature*, and Meineu, *The Natural History of Medicine.* See "Albertus Magnus" in *The Catholic Encyclopedia*, 1913 edition.

400. The lack of discussion of opposites, generation, and virtue on the theological level is simply due to the fact that wisdom is selected as a sample category. It is not meant to imply that St. Albert did not consider the other aspects of Mary's existence.

401. Albertus Magnus, *Metaphysics* in *Opera Omnia*, Borgnet, ed. (Paris: Apud Ludovicum Vives, 1890-99), Chapter 10. Translated by Sister M. Therese Dougherty.

402. *Ibid.*

403. Albertus Magnus, *Quaestiones Super de Animalibus*, in *Opera Omnia, op. cit.*, Book XV, Quest. 3. Translated by Diane Gordon as are all passages from this text unless noted otherwise.

404. Albertus Magnus, *Summa de Creaturis*, in *Opera Omnia, op. cit.*, Part 2, Quest. 7, Art. 2, translated by Sister M. Therese Dougherty.

405. Albertus Magnus, *Quaestiones Super de Animalibus, op. cit.*, Book VI, Quest 6-13.

406. *Ibid.*, Book IX, Quest. 16-17.

407. *Ibid.*

408. *Ibid.*, Book IX, Quest. 24-8.

409. *Ibid.*, Book V, Quest. 11-14.

410. *Ibid.*, Book XV, Quest. 8.

411. *Ibid.*, Book V, Quest. 10.

412. *Ibid.*, Book XV, Quest. 19. For a detailed study of Albert's views on female seed, see Danielle Jacquart and Claude Thomosset, "Albert le Grand et les problèmes de la sexualité," in *Pubblicazioni della stazione zoologica di Napoli*, section II, "History and Philosophy of the Life Sciences," Vol. 3, no. 1, 1981, pp. 74-94.

413. *Ibid.* If heat is superior to cold, this would imply that black women are superior to white women.

414. *Ibid.*

415. *Ibid.*, Book VI, Quest. 3.

416. *Ibid.*, Book XV, Quest. 19. "Thus Albert adopts from Galen via Avicenna, the division of the female contribution, which Aristotle had left undifferentiated as the catamenia, into a nourishing and material component." See L. Demaitre and A.A. Traville, "Human Embryology and Development in the Works of Albertus Magnus" in *Albert Magnus and the Sciences* (Toronto: Pontifical Institute for Medieval Studies, 1980), p. 417.

417. *Ibid.*, Book XV, Quest. 20.

418. *Ibid.*

419. *Ibid.*, Book XVI, Quest. 3.

420. *Ibid.*, Book XVI, Quest. 1.

421. Albertus Magnus, *Summa de Creaturis*, *op. cit.*, p. 159.

422. Albertus Magnus, *De Natura et Origine Animae*, in *Opera Omnia*, *op. cit.* Chapter 4, translated by Sister M. Therese Dougherty. This work was originally planned by St. Albert as Book XX of *Quaestiones Super de Animalibus*.

423. Albertus Magnus, *Summa de Creaturis*, *op. cit.*, Part 2, Quest. 17, Art. 2.

424. Albertus Magnus, *Quaestiones Super de Animalibus*, *op. cit.*, Book IX, Quest. 18.

425. *Ibid.*, Book VI, Quest. 19-22.

426. *Ibid.*, Book XVIII, Quest. 1.

427. *Ibid.*, Book XV, Quest. 4-5.

428. *Ibid.*

429. *Ibid.*, Book XVIII, Quest. 2.

430. *Ibid.*, Book XV, Quest. 2.

431. *Ibid.*

432. *Ibid.*, Book XVIII, Quest. 1.

433. *Ibid.*, Book XVIII, Quest. 3.

434. *Ibid.*

435. *Ibid.*, Book XVIII, Quest. 4.

436. *Ibid.*, Book XV, Quest. 1.

437. *Ibid.*, Book V, Quest. 6.

438. *Ibid.*, Book V, Quest. 4. Translated by Sister M. Therese Dougherty.

439. *Ibid.*, Book XV, Quest. 11.

440. Albertus Magnus, *Politicorum*, in *Opera Omnia*, *op. cit.*, Book 9, a. Translated by Diane Gordon as are all passages from this text.

441. *Ibid.*, Book 9, g.

442. *Ibid.*, Book 9, i.

443. Albertus Magnus, *Quaestiones Super de Animalibus*, *op. cit.*, Book XV, Quest. 8.

444. Albertus Magnus, *Politicorum*, *op. cit.*, Book 9, h.

445. Albertus Magnus, *Quaestiones Super de Animalibus*, *op. cit.*, Book V, Quest. 4. Translated by Sister M. Therese Dougherty.

446. *Ibid.*, Book XV, Quest. 8.

447. *Ibid.*, Book XV, Quest. 11.

448. *Ibid.*

449. See Chapters III, "Juvenal," and IV, "Andreas Capellanus" and "Walter Map."

450. To compare Albert's views on Mary with other medieval theologians see, Kari Elisabeth Børrensen, *Anthropologie médiévale et théologie Mariale* (Oslo: Bergen-Troms Universitetsforlaget, 1971).

451. Thomas Heath in Appendix I to *Summa Theologiae* by St. Thomas Aquinas (New York: McGraw Hill Book Co., 1964), Vol. 51, p. 86.

452. See, Questions 96-110.

453. Albertus Magnus, *Mariale sive Questiones super Evangelium*, in *Opera Omnia*, *op. cit.*, Quest. 96, p. 157.

454. *Ibid.*

455. *Ibid.*, Quest. 97, p. 18.

456. *Ibid.*, Quest. 98, p. 159.

457. *Ibid.*

458. *Ibid.*, Quest. 99, p. 159.

459. *Ibid.*, p. 160.

460. *Ibid.*, Quest. 101, p. 160.

461. *Ibid.*

462. *Ibid.*

463. *Ibid.*, Quest. 102, p. 161.

464. *Ibid.*, Quest. 103, pp. 161-2.

465. *Ibid.*, p. 162.

466. *Ibid.*, Quest. 104, p. 162.

467. *Ibid.*, Quest. 105-8, pp. 163-4.

468. *Ibid.*, Quest. 109, p. 165.

469. *Ibid.*

470. *Ibid.*, Quest. 110, p. 166. For a more detailed discussion of the *Sentences* see Chapter IV, "Averroes."

471. *Ibid.*

472. *Ibid.*

473. *Ibid.* St. Albert anticipated the twentieth century dogma of the Assumption of Mary, see Børrensen, *op. cit.*, pp. 102-112.

474. *Ibid.*

475. Robert J. Buschmiller, *The Maternity of Mary in the Mariology of St. Albert the Great* (Ph.D. Dissertation, University of Fribourg, Switzerland, 1959), p. 20.

476. Albert argues that Mary's spiritual conception by the Holy Spirit precedes the second conception in the body. This would bring the relation with the Holy Spirit back more directly. See Buschmiller, p. 63.

477. "Albertus Magnus," *Encyclopedia Britannica*, 1945 edition.

478. See, Chapter V, "*De Secretis Mulierum.*"

479. Thomas Heath, in *Summa Theologiae, op. cit.*, Vol. 52, p. 86.

480. James Weisheipl, "Thomas d'Aquino and Albert his Teacher," in *The Etienne Gilson Series*, 2 (Toronto: Pontifical Institute for Medieval Studies, 1980), pp. 10-11.

481. Thomas Aquinas, *Summa Theologiae* (New York: McGraw Hill Book Co., 1964), 1a, 3, 2. See also, la, 3, 8 and *The Soul* (St. Louis: B. Herder, 1949), Art. 1, Reply to Obj. 5, p. 12. All references to the *Summa Theologiae* will be taken from this edition unless otherwise stipulated.

482. *Ibid.*, 1a, 92, 1 and 2.

483. Thomas Aquinas, *Petri Lombardi Sentiarum Libri Quattuor* (Paris: J.P. Migne, 1853), Book 2, Dist., 18, Quest. 1. Translated by Sister Therese Marie Dougherty. "That particular rib pertained to Adam's completeness not as one individual man but as the source of the human species; just as seed pertains to the male's perfection as procreator." See also, *Summa Theologiae, op. cit.*, 1a, 92, 3.

484. Thomas Aquinas, *Summa Theologiae, op. cit.*, 1a, 28, 4.

485. *Ibid.*, 1a, 93, 6.

486. *Ibid.*

487. See Kari Elizabeth Børrensen, *Subordination and Equivalence: The Nature of the Role of Woman in Augustine and Thomas Aquinas* (Washington, D.C.: University Press of America, 1981), pp. 133-8.

488. Thomas Aquinas, *Summa Theologiae, op. cit.*, 1a, 93, 4.

489. *Ibid.*

490. Thomas Aquinas, *Summa Contra Gentiles* (New York: Benzinger Bros., 1923-29), II, 62, 7.

491. Ibid. See also, Thomas Aquinas, *Summa Theologiae, op. cit.*, 1a, 99, 2.

492. Thomas Aquinas, *Commentary on the "Metaphysics" of Aristotle* (Chicago: Henry Regnery, 1961), No. 2127 XL 11c and 2134 XL 11C.

493. Thomas Aquinas, *De Anima* (New Haven: Yale University Press, 1951), II v, no. 366, p. 242.

494. Thomas Aquinas, *Summa Contra Gentiles, op. cit.*, II, 58, 14.

495. Thomas Aquinas, *On the Power of God* (Westminster, Maryland: Newman Press, 1952), Quest. 9, Art. 1, reply to 3rd objection, p. 100.

496. *Ibid.*, Quest. 9, Art. 4, p. 116.

497. Thomas Aquinas, *Summa Theologiae, op. cit.*, 1a, 75, 4.

498. See, Chapter III, "John Scotus Erigena," "Poryphry and Marcella," and Chapter I, "Plato."

499. Thomas Aquinas, *Summa Contra Gentiles, op. cit.*, Book IV, 79, 10.

500. *Ibid.*, Book II, 44, 7.

501. Thomas Aquinas, *On the Power of God, op. cit.*, Quest. 5, Art. 10. See also Quest. 3, Art. 10, Quest. 2, Art. 2, and *Summa Theologiae, op. cit.*, 1a, 76, 1.

502. Thomas Aquinas, *Summa Contra Gentiles, op. cit.*, IV, 88, 3.

503. *Ibid.*, see, IV, 83, 5 where St. Thomas argued that the generative organs will not be used: "Among those who rise there will be no sexual union."

504. Thomas Aquinas, *Summa Theologiae* (New York: Benziger Brothers, 1948), Suppl. Q. 81, Art. 3.

505. *Ibid.*

506. Weisheipl, "Thomas d'Aquino and Albert His Teacher," *op. cit.*, pp. 10-11.

507. Thomas Aquinas, *Truth* (Chicago: Henry Regnery Co., 1952), Art. 9, p. 245. See also an outstanding summary of St. Thomas's theory of generation in Rev. Mark Toon, O.S.B., M.A., *The Philosophy of Sex According to St. Thomas Aquinas*. Ph.D. dissertation, The Catholic University of America, 1954.

508. Thomas Aquinas, *Summa Theologiae, op. cit.*, 1a, 75, 4.

509. Thomas Aquinas, *Petri Lombardi Sentiorum Libri Quattuor, op. cit.*

510. *Ibid.*, no. 1.

511. Thomas Aquinas, *Summa Theologiae, op. cit.*, 1a, 75, 4.

512. *Ibid.*, 1a, 99, 1.

513. Weisheipl, *op. cit.*, p. 14. "It turns out that many instruments of Thomas' research were in fact tabulae excerpted from the *Libri Naturales* and *Ethics* of St. Albert."

514. Thomas Aquinas, *Summa Theologiae, op. cit.*, 1a, 118, 1.

515. Thomas Aquinas, *Truth, op. cit.*, Quest. 3, Art. 8, p. 167. In this passage St. Thomas explained that males were generated because the material was outside the species of seed.

516. Thomas Aquinas, *On the Power of God, op. cit.*, Quest. 3, Art. 9, p. 158. See also, Quest. 3, Art. 12, 183, "It follows then that there is not a soul in semen, but a certain energy derived from the soul, which prepares the way for the soul's advent."

517. Thomas Aquinas, *Summa Theologiae, op. cit.*, 1a, 118, 2.

518. *Ibid.*, 1a, 118, 1.

519. *Ibid.*

520. *Ibid.*

521. Thomas Aquinas, *Summa Contra Gentiles, op. cit.*, II, 89.

522. Weisheipl, *op. cit.*, p. 15. "Albert devoted considerable thought to the development of the human embryo and held it to be a natural process of one higher form succeding a lower form — all in the natural course of biological development. Thomas, on the other hand, thought that such a development looked too much like alteration, an accidental change, rather than substantial change, and he insisted on a multiplicity of corruptions and generations in the embryological process. Albert's explanation sounded too natural to Thomas, while Thomas' explanation was not natural enough for Albert."

523. Thomas Aquinas, *On the Power of God*, *op. cit.*, Quest. 3, Art. 9, p. 158.

524. For this reason some have claimed Thomas as support for the view that abortions may be performed in the first trimester.

525. Thomas Aquinas, *Summa Theologiae*, *op. cit.*, 1a, 92, 1.

526. *Ibid.*, 1a, 98, 1 and 2.

527. Thomas Aquinas, *The Soul, op. cit.*, Art. xi, 5, Reply to Obj. 2, p. 146.

528. Thomas Aquinas, *Summa Contra Gentiles*, *op. cit.*, IV, 11, 1a.

529. Thomas Aquinas, *Truth*, *op. cit.*, Quest. 5, Art. 9, p. 245.

530. Thomas Aquinas, *Summa Theologiae*, *op. cit.*, 3a, 28, 1.

531. *Ibid.*, 3a, 32, 4.

532. *Ibid.*, see also, *Summa Contra Gentiles*, *op. cit.*, IV, 45, 3, 6, 7.

533. Thomas Aquinas, *Summa Theologiae*, *op. cit.*, 1a, 2ae, 81, 1.

534. *Ibid.*, 1a, 2ae, 81, 5. St. Thomas recognized the philosophical problem that this theory presented in the light of his previous claim that the rational soul was given not by the father but by God. He argued that the father nonetheless made the fetus ready to receive its rational soul, and thereby formed the condition for human nature which transmitted its tendency to disorder. See, 1a, 2ae, 81, 1.

535. Thomas Aquinas, *Summa Contra Gentiles, op. cit.*, IV, 52.

536. See Thomas R. Heath, "The Immaculate Conception," Appendix 3, *Summa Theologiae, op. cit.*, Vol. 51, pp. 111-118.

537. Thomas Aquinas, *On the Power of God*, *op. cit.*, Quest. 1, Art. 4, p. 24. See also, *Summa Theologiae op. cit.*, 1a, i, 1.

538. Thomas Aquinas, *Summa Theogogiae*, *op. cit.*, 1a, 1, 8.

539. *Ibid.*, 1a, 5-6.

540. Thomas Aquinas, *Compendium of Theology* (St. Louis: Herder, 1947), Chapter 38. See also Chapter 39.

541. Thomas Aquinas, *Summa Theologiae, op. cit.*, 2a, 2ae, 45, 2.

542. Thomas Aquinas, *In Octo Libros Policorum Aristotelis* (Quebec: Tremblay and Dion, 1940), Book 1, p. 51. Translated by Diane Gordon as are all passages from this text.

543. Thomas Aquinas, *Summa Theologiae*, *op. cit.*, 1a, 1, 6.

544. *Ibid.*, 1a, 92, 1.

545. Thomas Aquinas, *In Octo Libros Policorum Aristotelis*, *op. cit.*, Book 1, p. 51.

546. *Ibid.*

547. Thomas Aquinas, *Summa Theologiae*, *op. cit.*, 2a, 2ae, 45, 2.

548. *Ibid.*, 3a, 27, 6.

549. *Ibid.*, 2a, 2ae, 45, 3.

550. James Weisheipl, *Friar Thomas d'Aquino: His Life, Thought and Work* (New York: Doubleday and Co., 1974), p. 322.

551. Thomas Aquinas, *Summa Theologiae*, *op. cit.*, 1a, 2ae, 61.

552. *Ibid.*, 1a, 2ae, 63.

553. *Ibid.*, 1a, 2ae, 63, 1.

554. *Ibid.*, 1a, 2ae, 63, 3.

555. *Ibid.*, 1a, 2ae, 55, 4. "The righteousness which means order to a due end and to the divine law, which is the rule of the human will, is. . . common to all virtues"; see also, 1a, 2ae, 75, 1, "The disorder of sin, and evil generally, is not a simple negation but the absence of something which ought to be there."

556. Aristotle, *Nicomachean Ethics*, in *The Basic Works of Aristotle* (New York: Random House, 1949), 1148, 31-3. "Now those in whom nature is the cause of such a state no one would call incontinent any more than one would apply the epithet to women because of the passive part they play in copulation."

557. Thomas Aquinas, *In Octo Libros Policorum Aristotelis*, *op. cit.*, Book 1, x, p. 51.

558. *Ibid.*

559. *Ibid.*

560. Thomas Aquinas, *Summa Contra Gentiles,* op. cit., *III, II, 123, 3.*

561. Thomas Aquinas, *Summa Theologiae*, *op. cit.*, 1a, 92, 2.

562. *Ibid.*, 1a, 92, 1.

563. *Ibid.* (Benzinger Brothers edition), Suppl. Q. 81, Art. 3, Obj. 2.

564. Thomas Aquinas, *On Kingship* (Toronto: Pontifical Institute of Medieval Studies, 1949), Book 1, 2, no. 19, pp. 12-13. The Latin word *rex*, which is translated here as *king*, is more usually translated in the feminine as *queen*. Therefore, no conclusions for the philosophy of sex identity can be drawn from this translation. I am very grateful to Father Joseph Owens, C.Ss.R., for clarification on this point. See, Weisheipl, *Friar Thomas d'Aquino*, *op. cit.* for a defence of the authenticity of this book up to II, 4, pp. 388-9.

565. Thomas Aquinas, *On Kingship*, *op. cit.*, I, i, no. 14, p. 10. In this passage, St. Thomas also contains a footnote reference to Aristotle, *Nicomachean Ethics*, 1160a, 24.

566. Thomas Aquinas, *Summa Theologiae*, *op. cit.*, Suppl., Quest. 39, Art. 1.

567. Thomas Aquinas, *Petri Lombardi Sentiarum*, *op. cit.*, Book 2, Dist. 18, Q. 1.

568. See Chapter V, "Oeconomicus."

569. Thomas Aquinas, *Petri Lombardi Sentiarum*, *op. cit.*, II, II, Q. 26, Art. 10.

570. Thomas Aquinas, *Summa Contra Gentiles*, *op. cit.*, III, II, 123, 6.

571. *Ibid.*, III, II, 124-5.

572. *Ibid.*

573. Thomas Aquinas, *Summa Theologiae*, 1a, 2ae, 73, 6.

574. Thomas Aquinas, *Summa Contra Gentiles*, *op. cit.*, III, II, 123, 4.

575. *Ibid.*

576. Thomas Aquinas, *Summa Theologiae, op. cit.*, 2a, 2ae, 153, 2.

577. See, Thomas Aquinas, *Summa Contra Gentiles, op. cit.*, III, 9, 3.

578. Thomas Aquinas, *Summa Theologiae* (Benziger Bros. edition), II, II, Q. 17, Art. 6.

579. Thomas Heath, *Summa Theologiae, op. cit.*, Vol. 51, Appendix I (p. 101).

580. Weisheipl, "Thomas d'Aquino and Albert His Teacher," *op. cit.*, pp. 20-21.

Chapter V

1. Plato's Academy 386 B.C., Aristotle's Lyceum 335 B.C., the Stoa of Zeno 308 B.C., and Epicurus's School 306 B.C. See, William A. Smith, *Ancient Education* (New York: Greenwood Press, 1969), pp. 142-3.

2. *Ibid.*, p. 187. The Stoic philosopher Crates of Mallos lectured in Rome in 169 B.C.

3. Vespasian endowed Greek and Latin chairs of rhetoric in 69-70 A.D.

4. Stanley F. Bonner, *Education in Ancient Rome: From the Elder Cato to the Younger Pliny* (London: Methuen and Co., 1977), p. 125. See also, Smith, *op. cit.*, p. 124.

5. Thomas Whittaker, *The Neo-Platonists; a Study in the History of Hellenism* (Cambridge: The University Press, 1928), p. 27.

6. F.E. Peters, *Aristotle and the Arabs: The Aristotelian Tradition in Islam* (New York: New York University Press, 1968), p. 9.

7. *Ibid.*, p. 23.

8. *Ibid.*, p. 60. These translations were procured in great part through a research center established in Bagdad, c. 813-833.

9. Smith, *op. cit.*, p. 248.

10. Hastings Rashdall, *The Universities of Europe in the Middle Ages* (London: Oxford University Press, 1958), Vol. 1, p. 26. "[The Benedictine Age] exactly expresses its position in the history of education; it was the age, and the only age, during which European education was mainly in the hands of monks." The first women's abbey was founded in 512 by the Bishop Caessaries of Arles. See Frances and Joseph Gies, *Women in the Middle Ages* (New York: Thomas Y. Crowell, 1978), p. 65.

11. Gies, *op. cit.*, p. 64.

12. Rashdall, *op. cit.*, Vol. 1, p. 275.

13. This school at St. Geneviève was in this period the most famous school in Europe.

14. Gordon Leff, *Paris and Oxford Universities in the Thirteenth and Fourteenth Centuries: An Institutional and Intellectual History* (New York: John Wiley and Sons Inc., 1968), p. 23. See also Rashdall, *op. cit.*, Vol. 1, p. 161. "To appreciate the fact that the university was in its origin nothing more than a guild of foreign students is the key to the real origin and nature of the institution."

15. Leff, *op. cit.*, p. 52.

16. Rashdall, *op. cit.*, Vol. 1, p. 298.

17. *Ibid.*, p. 287.

18. Leff, *op. cit.*,, pp. 36-7.

19. Gies, *op. cit.*, p. 110. See also, Rashdall, *op. cit.*, Vol. 1, p. 335.

20. Rashdall, *op. cit.*, p. 353.

21. *Ibid.*, p. 356. Rashdall also mentioned the Aristotelianism in John Scotus Erigena's pantheism as a possible third source for the condemnation.

22. Gabriel Compayré, *Abelard and the Origin and Early History of Universities* (New York: Greenwood Press, 1969), pp. 176-7.

23. Leff, *op. cit.*, p. 120.

24. Rashdall, *op. cit.*, p. 357.

25. Compayré, *op. cit.*, p. 179.

26. I am indebted to Fr. John Wippel of the Catholic University of America for insights into this process.

27. This reflected the tradition in Oxford where Aristotle had never been banned.

28. Rashdall, *op. cit.*, p. 441.

29. Hieronymus Wilms, *Albert the Great: Saint and Doctor of the Church* (London: Burns, Oates and Washbourne, Ltd., 1933), p. 199.

30. Rashdall, *op. cit.*, p. 365.

31. Compayré, *op. cit.*, p. 179.

32. Rashdall, *op. cit.*, p. 442.

33. Leff, *op. cit.*, p. 127.

34. Stewart C. Easton, *Roger Bacon and His Search for a Universal Science* (New York: Russell and Russell, 1952), p. 45. "We know that if not in 1241-44, at least very soon afterwards, Bacon was lecturing publicly on Aristotle at Paris."

35. *Ibid.*, p. 21. See also p. 3, "An exlusive study of the early *Quaestiones* given at the University of Paris,. . . will tell us much about the curriculum of the Faculty of Arts in Paris about the year 1245, and about Bacon himself as he was at that time. But they cannot be supposed to embody his final philosophical views."

36. Roger Bacon, "Quaestiones supra undecimum prime philosophie Aristotelis *Metaphysics* X, " in *Opera Hacterus Inedita Rogeri Baconi* (Oxford: The Clarendon Press, 1909-40), pp. 125-173. In the same context Bacon discussed other kinds of contraries.

37. See, Chapter V, "*Secretum Secretorum*"

38. Spurious, *Secretus Secretorum*, in Roger Bacon, *Opera*, *op. cit.*, Vol. V, Discourse X, pp. 252-3. See also, Easton, *op. cit.*, p. 24. He argued that the *Secretum Secretorum* was the most influential book in Bacon's life.

39. Roger Bacon, *Opus Majus* (Frankfurt: Minerva-Verlag, 1964), Vol. I, Part IV, Chap. 1, p. 116. "Of these sciences [math, optics, experimental science and ethics] the gate and key is mathematics."

40. Easton, *op. cit.*, p. 177. 'Bacon viewed himself as another Aristotle, trying to do for his own time that Aristotle had done in his."

41. Bacon, *Opus Majus*, *op. cit.*, II, VI, xii, p. 617.

42. *Ibid.*, II, I, iii, p. 10.

43. *Ibid.*, I, III, p. 77. "For so great is their perverseness, crudity, and terrible difficulty in the translated works of Aristotle that no one can understand them, but each one contradicts another." See also p. 22, "For we know that in our own times objection had been raised in Paris to the natural philosophy and metaphysics of Aristotle as set forth by Avicenna and Averroes, and through dense ignorance of their books and those using them were excommunicated for quite long periods."

44. Easton, *op. cit.*, p. 60.

45. René Descartes, *La Formation du Foetus* in *Oeuvres* (Paris: Librairie Philosophique, 1969), Vol. 11.

46. Bacon, *Opus Majus*, *op. cit.*, I, V, xvi, p. 413.

47. *Ibid.*, I, IV, v, p. 159.

48. *Ibid.*, II, VI, xii, p. 618.

49. *Ibid.*, I, V, xvi, p. 308. See also, p. 394, "Aristotle says in his book on *Vegetation* that the sun is the father of the plants and the moon their mother, and in the case of men and of animals he says that man begets man with the help of the sun. But Averroes says that the sun does more than man in producing a thing. For the force of the sun continues in the seed from the beginning of generation to the end, while that of a father does not, but is confined to one act only."

50. See Chapter V, "The Popularization of Aristotle," for a more detailed account of this use of Aristotle.

51. Bacon, *Opus Majus*, *op. cit.*, VII, IV, p. 675. "Aristotle, the greatest of philosophers, accordingly is the most conspicuous example, who in contempt of the world and all its riches and honors and pleasures left his native land and ended his life in exile."

52. *Ibid.*, I, V, xvii, p. 241.

53. Leff, *op. cit.*, p. 163.

54. J. Guy Bougerol, *Introduction to the Works of Bonaventura* (Patterson, New Jersey, 1964), p. 172. See also Compayré, *op. cit.* The usual age for the Doctor of Theology was thirty-five, p. 202.

55. Leff, *op. cit.*, p. 165.

56. Compayré, *op. cit.*, p. 207. See also, Rashdall, *op. cit.*, Vol. I, pp. 474-7.

57. D.E. Luscombe, *The School of Peter Abelard: The Influence of Abelard's Thought in the Early Scholastic Period* (Cambridge: The University Press, 1969), p. 261.

58. For example, The Catholic University of America has at least forty different commentaries in its holdings.

59. See, Chapter IV, "St-Albert the Great: Generation," and "St-Thomas Aquinas: Generation."

60. Peter Lombard, *Libri IV Sentiarum* (Florence: Claras Aquas, 1916), II, 18.1 (140). Translated by Sr. Therese Marie Dougherty as are all other passages from this text.

61. *Ibid.* (141).

62. *Ibid.* (148). "The Catholic Church teaches that they [souls] are. . . poured into bodies when they are begotten and formed through intercourse and are created with that inpouring."

63. *Ibid.*, II, 22.3 (180).

64. Bougerol, *op. cit.*, pp. 25-31.

65. Bonaventure, *Commentary on the Sentences* in *Opera Omnia* (Florence: Claras Aquas [Quaracchi], 1882), II, 16.2, p. 403. Translated by Sr. Therese Marie Dougherty as are all other passages from this work unless otherwise stated.

66. *Ibid.*, p. 404.

67. *Ibid.*, II, 18.1.1, p. 432.

68. Emma Therese Healy, Sister, *Women According to Saint Bonaventure* (New York: Georgian Press, 1955), III, *Sent.* d 12 1 3 9, p. 3.

69. Bonaventure, *Commentary on the Sentences, op. cit.*, II, 20, 1, 6. Sister Healy heralds this passage as a rejection of Aristotle, *op. cit.*, p. 11. "The deficiency is a deficiency of measure; hence, no real deficiency and the authority of Aristotle disappears." However, the sex polarity of Aristotle, while qualified, nonetheless remained, for each woman was, singularly considered, a defective man.

70. Bonaventure, *Commentary on the Sentences, op. cit.*, II, 20, 1, 6.

71. *Ibid.*

72. Sister Healy argues that Bonaventure held the correct double-seed theory, *op. cit.*, p. 25. "St. Bonaventure's view is more in keeping with that of modern physiologists who hold that human generation takes place by union of the male seed with the female germ cell or ovum with which it must grow into one body."

73. Bonaventure, *Commentary on the Sentences, op. cit.*, II 20, 1, 6.

74. Healy, *op. cit.*, p. 19; IV, *Sent.* d 36 a 2 g 1.

75. Bonaventure, *Breviloquium* (St. Louis, Mo. and London: B. Herder, 1946), p. 271.

76. Bonaventure, *Commentary on the Sentences, op. cit.*, II, 22, 1, 3. See also, Healy, *op. cit.*, pp. 39-40. "Original sin is an inheritance from Adam not from Eve, from the father not from the mother. If Eve alone had fallen, we should have had the first sinful woman, but not a race of sinful women."

77. John F. Wippel, "The Condemnation of 1270 and 1277 at Paris" in *The Journal of Medieval and Renaissance Studies* 7 (1977), pp. 169-201.

78. James Weisheipl, *Friar Thomas d'Aquino: His Life, Thought and Work* (New York: Doubleday and Co., 1974), p. 349.

79. Wippel, *op. cit.*, p. 184.

80. Maude Glasgow, *The Subjection of Women and the Traditional Men* (New York: published by author, 1940).

81. Compayré, *op. cit.*, pp. 242-3. "It seems that its first beginnings must be sought for in the Abbey of Monte-Cassino, founded by the Benedictines in 528, at some distance from Salerno. Medicine was first studied in this monastery with marked devotion. The monks copied and recopied the works of Hippocrates and Galen, which had been translated into Latin as early as the sixth century."

82. See Chapter IV, "Hildegard of Bingen."

83. Compayré, *op. cit.*, pp. 244-5.

84. *Ibid.*, p. 246. Other names include Abella, Rebecca de Guarna, and Mercuriade. See also H.J. Mozans, *Woman in Science* (Cambridge: M.I.T. Press, 1974), pp. 284-6.

85. *Ibid.*

86. Charles Singer, *From Magic to Science: Essays on the Scientific Twilight* (New York: Dover Publications, 1958), p. 286.

87. Mozans, *op. cit.*, p. 286.

88. Joseph Needham, *A History of Embryology* (Cambridge: University Press, 1959), pp. 85-6. A modern English translation of this text is: *Medieval Woman's Guide to Health*, trans. Beryl Rowland (Kent, Ohio: Kent State University Press, 1981).

89. Glasgow, *op. cit.*, p. 217.

90. Mozans, *op. cit.*, p. 289. See also, Glasgow, *op. cit.*, p. 218.

91. Rashdall, *op. cit.*, Vol. 1, p. 127. See also Compayré, *op. cit.*, pp. 247-250. The Archbishop of Mainz is reputed to have studied medicine there around 1140, Rabelais from 1520-1530, and John Locke in the seventeenth century.

92. Rashdall, *op. cit.*, p. 235. He mentions that in Bologna students had to pay 40 *solidi* to take a course in the *De Animalibus* and 4 *solidi* for the spurious *Oeconomica.*

93. *Ibid.*, p. 245. "Mondino da Luzzi (1276-1328), sometimes styled the father of modern anatomy, was one of the earliest teachers of surgery at Bologna, and his *Anatomia* remained the standard text book on the subject for more than two centuries."

94. Mondino da Luzzi, *Anathomia* in *The Fasciculus Medicinae of Joannes de Ketham* (Milan: R. Lier and Co., 1924), p. 75. "As Avicenna saith in the Canon, II fer. 20 and 21, on the anatomy of the womb, the vasa spermatica in man and in woman. . . etc."

95. *Ibid.*, p. 75.

96. Compayré, *op. cit.*, p. 251.

97. Rashdall, *op. cit.*, pp. 436-7.

98. M. Anthony Hewson, *Giles of Rome and the Medieval Theory of Conception (A Study of the De Formatione Corporus Humani in Utero)* (London: The Athlone Press, 1975), p. 67. As shown previously in Chapter III, "Galen", this view was falsely attributed to Galen who had actually argued that the female seed had no formative function.

99. *Ibid.*, p. 69.

100. *Ibid.*, p. 86.

101. *Ibid.*, p. 137.

102. *Ibid.*, p. 85.

103. *Ibid.*, p. 109. See also p. 115. "The body of the mother is the cause of her child's body, by the action of the soul of the father using the seed as intermediary."

104. *Ibid.*, p. 198. See also, pp. 182-3.

105. *Ibid.*, pp. 179-97.

106. *Ibid.*, p. 183. See also, p. 70.

107. *Ibid.*

108. *Ibid.*, p. 176.

109. *Ibid.*, p. 116.

110. Giles of Rome, *De Regime Principum*, trans. John Treorsa, Bodleian MS. Digby 233, cols. 1-182.

111. Hewson, *op. cit.*, pp. 201-230. See also, p. 204. "They all read the *De Formatione Corporis* and all take it seriously."

112. "Medicine and Canon Law" in *The Catholic Encyclopedia*, 1967 edition.

113. See also, Jacques le Goff, *Les intellectuels au moyen âge* (Paris: Éditions du Seuil, 1957), pp. 121, 129, 131, and 149.

114. "Medicine and Canon Law" in *The Catholic Encyclopedia*, *op. cit.*, "Priests are reminded that it is preferable to study theology and become expert physicians of souls rather than to cure bodies which is a secular profession."

115. Max Hamburger, *The Awakening of Western Legal Thought* (New York: Biblo and Tanner, 1969), pp. 115-8, 158. See also, *Morals and Law: The Growth of Aristotle's Legal Theory* (New York: Biblo and Tanner, 1955).

116. Compayré, *op. cit.*, p. 225. "What was the method of Ireneus, the dominating method of the twelfth and thirteenth centuries? It consited essentially, in submitting the legal texts to very nearly the same laborous exploration and perpetual commentary to which the contemporary professors of logic and philosophy subjected the texts of Aristotle."

117. Rashdall, *op. cit.*, Vol. I, pp. 127-28. "It may be considered as an attempt to do for Canon Law what Peter Lombard did a little later (1150-2) for theology proper by the publication of the *Sentences*. Both works are only fresh applications of the method inaugurated by Abelard."

118. Stanley Chodorow, *Christian Political Theory and Christian Politics in the Mid-Twelfth Century: The Ecclesiology of Gratian's Decretum* (Berkeley: University of California Press, 1972), p. 2.

119. Ida Raming, *The Exclusion of Women from the Priesthood: Divine Law or Sex Discrimination?* (Metuchen, New Jersey: The Scarecrow Press, 1970), Canon 968, no. 1, p. 28.

120. *Ibid.*, p. 29.

121. Rashdall, *op. cit.*, Vol. I, pp. 119-120. Rashdall suggests that Matilda was motivated by the desire to acquire a lawyer who could assist her in anti-papist activities.

122. Compayré, *op. cit.*, p. 229. *The Code of Justinian, the Digest, Institutes,* and *Authenticum* of Irnerius are mentioned as the basic law texts at Bologna.

123. *Ibid.*, pp. 214-5, 236.

124. *Ibid.*, p. 217.

125. John A. Abbo and Jerome D. Hannan, *The Sacred Canons: A Concise Presentation of the Current Disciplinary Norms of the Church* (London and St. Louis: B. Herder Book Co., 1957), no. 88, Vol. I, p. 128. See also, David J. Morrison, *The Juridic Status of Women in Canonical Law and in United States Law: A Comparative Socio-Juridical Study* (Rome: Pontificia Universitas Lateranensis, 1965), p. 41.

126. *The Legal Status of Women from 2250 B.C.* (Des Moines, Iowa: U.S. Works Project Administration, 1938), Justinian *Digest* 29, Vol. I, p. 289. See also, Abbo, *op. cit.*, no. 90, Vol. I, pp. 130-1.

127. *Ibid.*, Justinian *Institutes*, Book 3, sect. 2, title 2, Vol. 1, p. 276.

128. *Ibid.*, Book 2, title 8, sect. 19, Vol. I, p. 265.

129. *Ibid.*, Book 3, title 1, sect. 15, Vol. I, p. 294.

130. *Ibid.*, Book 1, title 11, sect. 10, Vol. I, p. 259.

131. *Ibid.*, Book 1, title 12, Vol. I, p. 251.

132. Abbo, *op. cit.*, no. 1129-1130, Vol. II, p. 392.

133. *Ibid.*, no. 1111, Vol. II, pp. 369-70.

134. *Ibid.*

135. *Ibid.*, no. 1081 and 1074. See also Morrison, *op. cit.*, pp. 35, 60.

136. *The Legal Status of Women from 2250 B.C.*, *op. cit.*, Justinian, *Digest*, Part 2, Book 9, sect. 11, no. 9, p. 309.

137. *Ibid.*, Part 1, Book 2, sect. 8, p. 29.

138. *Ibid.*, Justinian, *Institutes*, sect. 6, Book 2, title 10, p. 266.

139. Morrison, *op. cit.*, p. 30, 50-52. See also, Abbo, *op. cit.*, no. 107, Vol. I, p. 157.

140. *Ibid.*, no. 87, Vol. 1, pp. 124-7.

141. *Ibid.*, no. 108, Vol. I, pp. 159-60.

142. Chodorow, *op. cit.*

143. Abbo, *op. cit.*, no. 118, Vol. I, p. 172.

144. See, Joan Morris, *The Lady was a Bishop: the Hidden History of Women with Clerical Ordination and the Jurisdiction of Bishops* (New York: The Macmillan Co., 1973), and Raming, *op. cit.*

145. Morris, *op. cit.*, pp. 18-23, 151. Note that some Abbesses were also allowed to plea court cases at the request of the Holy See, pp. 75-6.

146. Raming, *op. cit.*, pp. 8-9.

147. *Ibid.*, p. 71.

148. *Ibid.*, Preface, p. xiii. See also Abbo, *op. cit.*, no. 1327, Vol. II, p. 565. "Bishops are obliged by the duty of personally preaching the gospel, unless prevented by a justifying impediment; moreover, they should call to their assistance for the purpose of effectively fulfilling this duty of preaching not only pastors but also other qualified men."

149. Compayré, *op. cit.*, pp. 50-53.

150. *Ibid.*

151. *Ibid.*, pp. 181-2.

152. Rashdall, *op. cit.*, Vol. II, p. 238.

153. "Aristotelianism" in *The New Catholic Encyclopedia*, 1967 edition.

154. Rashdall, *op. cit.*, Vol. I, p. 540.

155. *Ibid.*, p. 542.

156. *Ibid.*, p. 548.

157. *Ibid.*, p. 549.

158. Hewson, *op. cit.*, pp. 212-3. In another case a lawyer appealed to the view that the female fetus matures more slowly than the male, pp. 213-9.

159. John Leofric Stocks, *Aristotelianism* (New York: Cooper Square Publishers, 1963), pp. 133-4.

160. *Ibid.*

161. E.R. Dodds, in Proclus, *The Elements of Theology* (Oxford: Clarendon Press, 1931), introduction pp. xxix-xxx. Albert the Great believed this work to be genuine. See also Leff, *op. cit.*, p. 132.

161′. For further information about these texts see *The Book of Causes*, trans. from Latin by Dennis J. Brand (Milwaukee: Marquette University Press, 1984); Christine d' Ancona Costa, *Recherches sur le Liber de causis* (Paris: Vrin, 1995); and Charles H. Lohr, "The Pseudo-Aristotelian *Liber de causis* and Latin Theories of Science in the Twelfth and Thirteenth Centuries," in *Pseudo-Aristotle in the Middle Ages: the Theology and and other texts*, eds. Jill Kraye, W. F. Ryan, and D. B. Schmitt (London: Warburg Institute, 1986), pp. 53-62.

162. Proclus, *The Elements of Theology, op. cit.*, p. 175.

162′. See F. W. Zimmermann, "The Origins of the so-Called *Theology of Aristotle*," in *Pseudo-Aristotle in the Middle Ages, op. cit.*, pp. 110-240.

163. *The Apple or Aristotle's Death*, ed. Mary Rosseau (Milwaukee: Marquette University Press, 1968), p. 76.

164. *Ibid.*, p. 59.

165. *Ibid.*, p. 76.

166. *Ibid.*, pp. 3-47.

167. *Ibid.*, p. 45.

168. *Ibid.*, p. 33.

169. *Ibid.*, p. 61.

170. *Secretum Secretorum* in *Opera Hactenus Inedita Rogeri Baconi, op. cit.*, introduction by Robert Steele, pp. viii-xvi. See also Easton, *op. cit.*, pp. 73-8.

171. *Ibid.*, p. xlviii.

172. Easton, *op. cit.*, pp. 86, 110-1.

173. See Chapter IV, "Avicenna."

174. *Secretum Secretorum, op. cit.*, p. 176.

175. *Ibid.*

176. *Ibid.*, p. 280. See also Bacon, *The Opus Majus, op. cit.*, Vol. II, part vi, p. 261. Here Aristotle is described as following in a line of prophets which began with Adam.

177. *Secretum Secretorum, op. cit.*, p. 187.

178. *Ibid.*, p. 209.

179. Bacon, *The Opus Majus, op. cit.*, Vol. II, part vi, p. 682.

180. *Secretum Secretorum, op. cit.*, p. 191.

181. *Ibid.*

182. *Ibid.*

183. *Ibid.*, pp. 200-202.

184. *Ibid.*, pp. 228-9.

185. *Ibid.*, p. 262.

186. *Ibid.*, p. 263

187. *Ibid.*, p. 283.

188. *Ibid.*, p. 233.

189. See, Chapter I, "Xenophon."

190. Aristotle (spurious), *Économique* (Paris: Les Belles Lettres, 1968), introduction by B.A. van Groningen, pp. xi-xxviii.

191. Aristotle (spurious), *The Politics and Economics of Aristotle* (London: Henry G. Bohm, 1853), Book I, Chap. viii, pp. 299-300.

192. *Ibid.*, Book I, Chap. ix, p. 301. Book II appears to have a different author. It contains nothing of significance for the concept of women.

193. *Ibid.*, Book I, Chap. ii, p. 291. See also, Book I, Chap. ix, p. 302. Here the positive consequences of such harmony in a marriage are described.

194. *Ibid.*, Book I, Chap. ix, p. 300.

195. *Ibid.*, Book I, Chap. iv, p. 292.

196. *Ibid.*, Book I, Chap. vii, p. 297.

197. *Ibid.*

198. *Ibid.*, Book I, Chap. ii, p. 290.

199. *Ibid.*, Book I, Chap. v, p. 293.

200. *Ibid.*, Book I, Chap. vii, p. 297.

201. *Ibid.*, Book I, Chap. viii, p. 299.

202. *Ibid.*, Book I, Chap. iii, pp. 291-2.

203. *Ibid.*, p. 292.

204. *Ibid.*, Book I, Chap. vii, p. 296.

205. *Ibid.*

206. Thomas Maria Schwertner, *St. Albert the Great* (New York: The Bruce Publishing Co., 1932), p. 237.

207. I am grateful to Fr. James Weisheipl, University of Toronto for clarification of this point.

208. Needham, *op. cit.*, pp. 91-2.

209. Albert the Great (spurious), *De Secretis Mulierum, or the Mystery of Human Generation Fully Revealed* (London: Curil, 1725), Introduction by John Quincy, pp. 1-2.

210. *Ibid.*, Chap. L, p. 7.

211. *Ibid.*, Chap. XIII, pp. 1-4.

212. *Ibid.*, Chap. V, pp. 53-4.

213. *Ibid.*, Chap. XI, p. 92.

214. *Ibid.*, Chap. V, pp. 60-1.

215. *Ibid.*, Chap. VI, pp. 73-4.

216. *Ibid.*, Chap. VI, p. 72.

217. See, Chapter I, "The Pythagoreans."

218. *De Secretis Mulierum, op. cit.*, Chap. VIII, pp. 81-5, Chap. XII, p. 100.

219. Aristotle (spurious), *The Works of Aristotle, The Famous Philosopher* (New York: Arno Press, 1974), introduction by Charles and Carroll Rosenberg, p. 1.

220. Needham, *op. cit.*, p. 92.

221. Sir D'Arcy Power, *The Foundations of Medical History* (Baltimore: Williams and Wilkins, 1931), p. 149. Power suggests 1503 as the date. Rosenberg, however, suggests 1684 in *The Works of Aristotle, The Famous Philosopher, op. cit.*, p. 1.

222. See, *The Works of Aristotle, The Famous Philosopher, op. cit.*, pp. 5-70 for the complete text.

223. *Ibid.*, p. 3.

224. *Ibid.*, Part I, Chapter I, sect. ii, p. 13.

225. *Ibid.*, Part I, Chapter I, sect. iii, p. 14, "The use and action of the clitoris in women is like that of the penis or yard in men, that is erecting its extreme end, being like that of the glands in the men, the seat of the greatest pleasure in the act of copulation, is this of the clitoris in women, and therefore called the sweetness of love and the fury of venery." This recognition of the function of the clitoris was repeated in subsequent spurious works, see *Experienced Midwife*, Part I, Chapter I, sect. ii, p. 80; and *Aristotle's Last Legacy*, Chapter II, pp. 235-6.

226. *Ibid.*, Part I, Chapter I, sect. ii, p. 12.

227. *Ibid.*, p. 13.

228. *Ibid.*, Part II, Chapter II, sect. iii, p. 17. "If you ask why a woman is sooner barren than a man? Let such know that the natural heat, which is the cause of generation is more predominant in men than in women."

229. *Ibid.*, Part I, Chapter I, sect. i, pp. 7-8.

230. *Ibid.*, Part II, Chapter I, sect. i, p. 21.

231. *Ibid.*, pp. 21-2.

232. *Ibid.*, Part III, Chapter I, sect. i, p. 57.

233. *Ibid.*, Part II, Chapter VI, sect. i, p. 86.

234. *Ibid.*, Part II, Chapter I, sect. v, pp. 24-5.

235. Power, *op. cit.*, pp. 169-70.

236. *Ibid.*, p. 171. "The author, editor, or compiler of this precious rubbish was William Salmon, a well known sixteenth century quack."

237. See, *The Works of Aristotle, The Famous Philosopher*, *op. cit.*, pp. 74-164.

238. *Ibid.*, p. 85.

239. *Ibid.*

240. *Ibid.*, p. 86.

241. *Ibid.*, p. 87. These arguments were taken nearly verbatum from the *Masterpiece.*

242. *Ibid.*, p. 87.

243. *Ibid.*, p. 75.

244. *Ibid.*, p. 157.

245. *Ibid.*, p. 141.

246. *Ibid.*, pp. 90-1.

247. *Ibid.*, pp. 99-100.

248. Aristotle (spurious), *Problems* (Cambridge, Mass. and London: Harvard University Press and William Heinemann, Ltd., 1936). Introduction by W.S. Hett, Vol. I. p. viii.

249. Power, *op. cit.*, pp. 149-150. These are also now believed to be spurious.

250. Aristotle, *Problems*, *op. cit.*, I, 9, Vol. I, p. 9.

251. *Ibid.*, IV, 4, Vol. I, p. 113.

252. *Ibid.*, 7, Vol. II, p. 207.

253. *Ibid.*, XIV, 5, Vol. I, p. 315.

254. *Ibid.*, IV, 25, Vol. I, p. 127. See also IV, 28, Vol. I, p. 131.

255. *Ibid.*, IV, 26, Vol. I, p. 129.

256. *Ibid.*, XXIX, 11, Vol. II, pp. 141-3.

257. Aristotle's *Problems* in *The Works of Aristotle: The Famous Philosopher*, *op. cit.*, p. 170.

258. *Ibid.*, p. 177.

259. *Ibid.*, p. 181. See also, p. 207.

260. *Ibid.*, p. 183. A man is ambidextrous "by reason of the great heat of the heart; for that makes a man as nimble of the left hand as of the right."

261. *Ibid.*, p. 206.

262. *Ibid.*, p. 193.

263. *Ibid.*, p. 184.

264. *Ibid.*, p. 196.

265. *Ibid.*, p. 197.

266. *Ibid.*, p. 198.

267. *Ibid.*, p. 199.

268. *Ibid.*, p. 200.

269. *Ibid.*, pp. 196-7. This example so interested people that it was often used as the design for the cover of *Aristotle's Masterpiece.* See, *Power, op. cit.*, p. 166.

270. *Aristotle's Masterpiece* in *The Works of Aristotle: The Famous Philosopher, op. cit.*, Part I, Chapter II, sect. 1, pp. 25-6.

271. *Experienced Midwife* in *The Works of Aristotle: The Famous Philosopher, op. cit.*, Part I, Chapter III, sect. iv, pp. 92-3.

272. *Zimara's Problems* in *The Works of Aristotle: The Famous Philosopher, op. cit.*, p. 212.

273. *Ibid.*

274. *Ibid.*, p. 213.

275. *Ibid.*, p. 215.

276. Power, *op. cit.*, p. 168.

277. See, *The Works of Aristotle: The Famous Philosopher, op. cit.*, pp. 231-264.

278. Albert the Great, *De Secretis Mulierum, op. cit.*, Chapter X, p. 86. A further test involving the quality of the woman's urine is also mentioned, pp. 88-9.

279. *Masterpiece*, in *The Works of Aristotle: The Famous Philosopher, op. cit.*, Part I, Chapter III, sect. ii, p. 19.

280. *Experienced Midwife* in *The Works of Aristotle: The Famous Philosopher, op. cit.*, Part I, Chapter I, sect. ii, p. 81.

281. *Last Legacy* in *The Works of Aristotle: The Famous Philosopher, op. cit.*, Chapter I, p. 235.

282. *Ibid.*, p. 233.

283. For the signs of a male child see *ibid.*, Chapter V, p. 244. For a description of a midwife see *ibid.*, Chapter IX, p. 259.

284. *Ibid.*, Chapter IV, p. 24.

BIBLIOGRAPHY

N.B. The name of an author as recorded in the Library of Congress listing is noted by LCC:

Abbo, John A., and Hannan, Jerome D. *The Sacred Canons: A Concise Presentation of the Current Disciplinary Norms of the Church*. Revised edition. 2 vols. London and St. Louis: B. Herder Book Co., 1957.

Abelard, Peter — LCC: (Abelaird, Pierre).

__________ . *Dialectica: First Complete Edition of the Parisian Manuscript*. By L. M. De Rijk. Assen: Van Gorcum and Co., 1956.

__________ . *Ethics*. Edited by D.E. Luscombe; translated with an introduction by J. Ramsey McCallum; foreword by Kenneth E. Kirk. Oxford: Basil Blackwell, 1935.

__________ . *Historia Calamitatum. The Story of My Misfortunes, an Autobiography by Peter Abelard*. Translated by Henry Adams Bellows; introduction by Ralph Adams Cram. St. Paul: T.A. Boyd, 1922.

__________ . *The Letters of Abelard and Heloise*. Translated, with an introduction, by Betty Radice. Harmondsworth: Penguin Books, 1974.

Aeschylus. *Tragedies and Fragments*. Translated by E. H. Plumptre with notes and rhymed choral odes. London: Ballantyne, Hanson and Co., 1901.

Agonito, Rosemary, ed. *History of Ideas on Women*. New York: G. P. Putnam's Sons, 1977.

Agrippa von Nettesheim, Heinrich Cornelius. *On the Superiority of Woman over Man*. Translated by Amaudin. New York: American News Company, 1873.

Albert, the Great — LCC: (Albertus Magnus, Saint, Bishop of Ratisbon).

__________ . *Opera Omnia*. Vol. 18. Bernhardo Creyer, praeside. Monasterii Westfalorum, in aedibus Aschendorff, 1951-78.

__________ . *Opera Omnia*. Curac ac Labora Augusti Borgnet, 38 vols. Paris: Apud Ludovicum Vives, Bibliopolam Editorem, 1890-99.

__________ . (Spurious). *De Secretis Mulierum, or The Mystery of Human Generation Fully Revealed*. Edited by John Quincy. London: Curll, 1725.

Alfarabi — LCC: (al-Farabi).

__________ . *Alfarabi's Philosophy of Plato and Aristotle*. Translated with an introduction, by Muhsin Mahdi. New York: The Free Press of Glencoe, 1962.

Allen, Christine. (Christine Garside). "Can a Woman Be Good in the Same Way as a Man?" In *Dialogue* 10, 2 (1971): 534-544.

__________ . "Christ Our Mother in Julian of Norwich." In *Studies in Religion* 10, 4 (Fall, 1981): 32-39.

__________ . "Conceptual History as a Methodology in Women's Studies." In *McGill Journal of Education* X, 1 (Spring, 1975): 49-58.

__________ . "Good and Evil for Women." In *Women and Religion* I, pp. 104-127. Edited by Judith Goldenberg and Joan Romero. Montana: Scholars' Press, 1973.

__________ . "Ideology Separates While the Heart Binds: Response to Lonergan's 'Prolegomena.'" In *Studies in Religion* 911 (Winter, 1980): 20-24.

__________ . "Nietzsche's Ambivalence about Women." In *Sexism in Political Theory*, pp. 117-131. Edited by Lorenne Clark and Lynda Lange. Toronto: University of Toronto Press, 1979.

__________ . "On Me Be The Curse, My Son!" In *Encounter with the Text: Form and History in the Hebrew Bible*, pp. 159-172. Edited by Martin J. Buss. Missoula, Montana: Scholars' Press, 1979.

__________ . "Plato on Women." *Feminist Studies* 2, 213 (1975): 133-138.

__________ . "Self-Creation and Loss of Self." In *Studies in Religion* 6, 1 (1976): 93-125.

———. "Sex Identity and Personal Identity." In *Contemporary Canadian Philosophy Series: Philosophy and the Quality of Life* I, pp. 93-125. Edited by W. Shea and J. King Farlow. Neal Watson, Academic Publications, Inc., 1976.

———. "Sex Unity, Polarity, or Complementarity?" *International Journal of Women's Studies* 6, 4 (Sept./Oct., 1983): 311-325.

———. "Woman's Liberation Movement: Some Effects on Women, Men, and Children." In *Configurations*, pp. 103-113. Edited by Raymond Prince. Lexington and Toronto: D. C. Heath and Company, 1974.

———. "Women and Persons." *Mother Was Not A Person*, pp. 194-204. Edited by Margaret Anderson. Montreal: Content Publishing, 1972.

Alpert, S. M. *Albert the Great*. Oxford: Blackfriars Publications, 1948.

Anaxagoras. *The Philosophy of Anaxagoras; An Attempt at Reconstruction*. Felix M. Cleve. New York: King's Crown Press, 1949.

Anselm — LCC: (Anselm, Saint, Archbishop of Canterbury).

———. *Anselm of Canterbury*. 4 vols. Edited and translated by Jasper Hopkins and Herbert Richardson. Toronto and New York: Edwin Mellen Press, 1976.

———. *The Prayers and Meditations of St. Anselm*. Great Britain: Penguin Books, 1973.

The Apple or Aristotle's Death. Translated by Mary F. Rousseau. Milwaukee: Marquette University Press, 1968.

Arendt, Hanna. *The Human Condition*. Chicago: University of Chicago Press, 1958.

Aristotle — LCC: (Aristoteles).

———. *The Art of Rhetoric*. Cambridge, Mass: Harvard University Press, 1965.

———. *The Athenian Constitution, The Eudemian Ethics*, and *On Virtues and Vices*. With an English translation by H. Rackham. London and Cambridge, Mass.: The Loeb Classical Library, 1935.

———. *The Basic Works of Aristotle*. Edited and with an introduction by Richard McKeon. New York: Random House, 1941.

———. (Spurious). *Économique*. Texte établi par B. Van Groningen et André Wartelle. Paris: Les Belles Lettres, 1968.

———. *Generation of Animals*. With an English translation by A. L. Peck. Cambridge, Mass. and London: Harvard University Press and William Heinemann, Ltd., 1943.

———. *On the Heavens*. With an English translation by W. K. C. Guthrie. Cambridge, Mass. and London: Harvard University Press and William Heinemann, 1939.

———. *Historia Animalium*. 3 vols. With an English translation by A. L. Peck. Cambridge, Mass. and London: Harvard University Press and William Heinemann, Ltd., 1965.

———. *History of Animals*. Cambridge, Mass. and London: Harvard University Press and William Heinemann Ltd., 1943.

———. '*Metaphysics*.' 2 vols. A revised text with introduction and commentary by W. D. Ross. Oxford: At the Clarendon Press, 1924.

———. *Meteorologica*. With an English translation by H. D. P. Lee. Cambridge, Mass. and London: Harvard University Press and William Heinemann, 1952.

———. *On Sophistical Refutations*. Cambridge, Mass.: Harvard University Press, 1965.

———. *The Organon*. Including *The Categories, On Interpretation*. By Harold P. Cooke, and *Prior Analytics*, by Hugh Tredennick. Cambridge, Mass. and London: Harvard University Press and William Heinemann, 1938.

———. *Parts of Animals*. With an English translation by A. L. Peck. *Movement of Animals, Progression of Animals*. With an English translation by E. S. Forster. London and Cambridge, Mass.: William Heinemann and Harvard University Press, 1937.

———. *Physics*. 2 vols. With an English translation by Philip Wickstead and Francis M. Cornford. London and Cambridge, Mass.: William Heinemann and Harvard University Press, 1934.

———. *The Politics of Aristotle*. With English notes by Richard Congreve, second edition. London: Longmans, Green and Company, 1874.

———. (Spurious). *The Politics and Economics of Aristotle*. Translated with notes, original and selected, and analyses, by Edward Walford. London: Henry G. Bohn, 1853.

———. *Posterior Analytics*. With an English translation by Hugh Tredennick. *Topica*. With an English translation by E. S. Forster. Cambridge, Mass. and London: Harvard University Press and William Heinemann Ltd., 1960.

———. (Spurious). *Problems* I, 1-21. With an English translation by W. S. Hett. London and Cambridge, Mass.: William Heinemann Ltd. and Harvard University Press, 1936.

———. *Problems* II, 22-38. With an English translation by W. S. Hett. *Rhetorica ad Alexandrum*. With an English translation by W. Rackham. London and Cambridge, Mass.: William Heinemann Ltd. and Harvard University Press, 1937.

———. *Topics*. Cambridge, Mass. and London: Harvard University Press and William Heinemann Ltd., 1936.

———. (Spurious). *The Works of Aristotle, the Famous Philosopher*. Edited by Charles and Carroll Rosenberg. New York: Arno Press, 1974.

Arnim, Joannes ab. *Stoicorum Veterum Fragmenta*. Lipsiae: B.G. Teubneri, 1905. Reprinted, Vols. 1-IV, Dubuque, Iowa: William C. Brown, 1967.

Athenaeus. *The Deipnosophists*. Translated by Charles Burton Gulik. Cambridge, Mass. and London: Harvard University Press and William Heinemann Ltd., 1959.

Augustine — LCC: (Augustinus, Aurelius, Saint).

———. *The Catholic and Manichean Ways of Life*. Translated by Donald A. Gallagher and Idella J. Gallagher. Washington, D.C.: Catholic University of America Press, 1966.

———. *The City of God*. Translated by Gerald O. Walsh and Mother Grace Monahan. New York: Fathers of the Church, Inc., 1952.

———. *The City of God against the Pagans*. 7 vols. With an English translation by Philip Levine. London and Cambridge, Mass.: William Heinemann Ltd. and Harvard University Press, 1966.

———. *Confessions*. R. S. Pine-Coffin, ed. Great Britain: Penguin Books Ltd., 1981.

———. *De Beata Vita (Happiness—A Study). Translated by Francis E. Tourscher. Philadelphia: The Peter Reilly Company, 1937.*

———. *De Libero Arbitrio. The Free Choice of the Will* (Three Books). Latin text with English translation and notes by Francis E. Tourschez, Philadelphia: The Peter Reilly Company, 1937.

———. *De Ordine* (*Divine Providence and the Problem of Evil*). Translated by Robert P. Russell. New York: Cosmopolitan Science and Art Service Co., Inc., 1942.

———. *Letters*. Vols. 1-5. Translated by Sister Wilfred Parsons. New York: Fathers of the Church, Inc., 1951.

———. *Oeuvres*. Texte, traduction, introduction et notes par B. Roland-Gosselin (et al.). Paris: Descleé, De Brouwer, 1936.

———. *The Retractions*. Translated by Sister Mary Ines Bogan, R.S.M. Washington, D.C.: Catholic University of America Press, 1968.

———. *The Soliloquies of St. Augustine*. Translation and notes by Thomas F. Gilligan. Introduction by Robert P. Russell. New York: Cosmopolitan Science and Art Service, Inc., 19–.

__________ . *Treatises on Marriage and Other Subjects*. Translated by Charles T. Wilcox (and others). Edited by Roy J. Defarrari. New York: Fathers of the Church, Inc., 1955.

__________ . *The Trinity*. Translated by Stephen McKenna. Washington, D.C.: The Catholic University of America Press, 1963.

Averroes. *Aristotelis Opera cum Averrois Commentariis*. Venice: Apud Junctas, 1562-1574. Frankfurt: Minerva-Verlag, 1962.

__________ . *Averroes on Plato's 'Republic.'* Translated, with an introduction and notes by Ralph Lerner. Ithaca: Cornell University Press, 1974.

__________ . *Epitome of 'Parva Naturalia.'* Translated from the original Abrabic, and the Hebrew and Latin versions, with notes and an introduction by Henry Blumberg. Cambridge, Mass.: The Medieval Academy of America, 1961.

__________ . *On the Harmony of Religion and Philosophy*. A translation, with introduction and notes, by George F. Hourani. E. J. W. Gibbs Memorial Series XXI. London: Luzac, 1961.

__________ . *Middle Commentary and Epitome on Aristotle's "De generatione et corruptione."* Translated by Samuel Kirkland. Cambridge, Mass.: Medieval Academy of America, 1958.

__________ . *Middle Commentary on Porphyry's Isagoge and Aristotle's Categoniae*. Translated by Herbert A. Davidson. Los Angeles: University of California Press, 1969.

__________ . *The Philosophy and Theology of Averroes*. Tractata translated from the Arabic by Mohammad Jamil-ur-Rehman. Baroda: A.G. Widgery, 1921.

__________ . *Tahafut al-Tahafut (The Incoherence of the Incoherence)*. Vol. 1. Translated from the Arabic with introduction and notes by Simon van den Bergh. E. J. W. Gibbs Memorial Series XIX. London: Luzac, 1954.

Avicebron. (See Ibn Gabirol, Solomon ben Judah).

Avicenna. *Avicenna's Psychology: An English Translation of Kitab al Najat, Book II, Chapter VI*. With historicophilosophical notes and textual improvements on the Cairo edition. London: Oxford University Press, 1952.

__________ . *A Compendium on the Soul*. Translated from the Arabic original by Edmund Abbott van Dyck. Verona: Stamperia di N. Paderno, 1906.

__________ . *The Life of Ibn Sina: A Critical and Annotated Translation*. By William E. Gohlman. Albany: State University of New York Press, 1974.

__________ . *Livre des définitions*. Édité, traduit, et annoté par A. M. Goichon. Cairo: Publications de l'institut français d'archéologie orientale du Caire, 1903.

__________ . *The Metaphysics of Avicenna (Ibn Sina): A Critical Translation-Commentary and Analysis of the Fundamental Arguments in Avicenna's 'Metaphysics' in the Danish nama-i Alai (The Book of Scientific Knowledge)* by Parviz Morewedge. New York: Columbia University Press, 1973.

__________ . *A Treatise on the 'Canon of Medicine' of Avicenna, Incorporating a Translation of the First Book*. By O. Cameron Gruner. New York: AMS Press, 1973.

Bacon, Roger. *Opera Hacternus Inedita Rogeri Baconi*. 16 vols. Edited by Robert Steele. Oxford: At the Clarendon Press, 1909-40.

__________ . *The Opus Majus*. Edited with an introduction and analytical tables by John Henry Bridges. Frankfurt: Minerva-Verlag, 1964.

Baer, Richard A. *Philo's Use of the Categories of Male and Female*. Leiden: E.J. Brill, 1970.

Barber, Richard. *The Knight and Chivalry*. Ipswich: The Boydell Press, 1974.

Baron, Salo Wittmayer. *Essays on Maimonides: An Octocentennial Volume*. New York: Columbia University Press, 1941.

Beard, Mary. *Women as Force in History*. New York: Collier Books, 1971.

Beauvoir, Simone de. *The Second Sex*. Translated and edited by H. M. Parshley. New York: Vintage Books, 1974.

Bell, Linda. *Visions of Women*. Clifton, New Jersey: Humana Press, 1983.

Bell, Susan G. *Women, from the Greeks to the French Revolution*. Stanford: Stanford University Press, 1980.

Benton, John F. "Fraud, Fiction and Borrowing in the Correspondence of Abelard and Heloise." In *Pierre Abélard, Pierre le Vénérable: Les Courants Philosophiques, Littéraires et Artistiques au Occident au Milieu de XIIe Siècle*. Paris: Éditions du Centre National de la Recherche Scientifique, 1975.

Bernard, Jessie. *The Female World*. New York: The Free Press, 1981.

__________. *The Future of Motherhood*. New York and Baltimore: Penguin Books, Inc., 1975.

Boethius. *The Consolation of Philosophy*. Translated with introduction and notes by Richard Green. Indianapolis: Bobbs-Merrill, 1962.

__________. *The Theological Tractates*. With an English translation by H.F. Stewart and E.K. Rand. Cambridge, Mass. and London: Harvard University Press and William Heinemann, 1918.

Bogin, Meg. *The Women Troubadours: An Introduction to the Women Poets of 12th Century Provence and a Collection of Their Poems*. Toronto: George J. McLeod Limited, 1976.

Bonaventure, Saint — LCC: (Bonaventura, Saint).

__________. *Breviloquium*. Translated by Erwin Esser Nemmers. St. Louis, Mo. and London: B. Herder, 1946.

__________. *Opera Omnia*. Edita, Studio et cura pp. Collegii a S. Bonaventura. Ad plurimos codices mss. emendata. Florence: Claras Aquas (Quaracchi), 1882.

__________. *The Works of Bonaventure: Cardinal, Seraphic Doctor, and Saint*. 5 vols. Translated from the Latin by José de Vinck. Patterson, New Jersey: St. Anthony Guild Press, 1960-70.

Bonner, Stanley Frederick. *Education in Ancient Rome: From the Elder Cato to the Younger Pliny*. London: Methuen and Co., Ltd., 1977.

Bornstein, Diane. *Mirrors of Courtesy*. Hamden, Conn.: Anchor Books, 1975.

Børrensen, Kari Elizabeth. *Anthropologie médiévale et théologie Mariale*. Oslo: Bergen-Troms Universitetsforlaget, 1971.

__________. *Subordination and Equivalence: The Nature and Role of Women in Augustine and Thomas Aquinas*. Washington, D.C.: University Press of America, 1981.

Bougerol, J. Guy. *Introduction to the Works of Bonaventure*. Translated from the French by José de Vinck. Patterson, New Jersey: Anthony Guild Press, 1964.

Boyance, Pierre. *Le Culte des Muses chez les Philosophes Grecs; études d'histoire et de psychologie religieuses*. Paris: E. de Brocard, 1972.

Briffault, Robert S. *The Troubadours*. Bloomington: Indiana University Press, 1965.

Brundage, James A. *Medieval Canon Law and the Crusader*. Madison, Milwaukee, and London: The University of Wisconsin Press, 1969.

Buschmiller, Robert J. *The Maternity of Mary in the Mariology of St. Albert the Great*. Ph. D. dissertation, University of Fribourg, Switzerland, 1959.

Catherina, Saint of Alexandria, Legend. *The Life of St. Katherine*. Edited, with introduction, notes and glossary by Dr. Eugen Einenkel. London: H. Trubner and Co., 1884.

Caldwell, Taylor. *The Glory and the Lightning*. First ed. Garden City, New York: Doubleday, 1974.

The Cambridge History of Later Greek and Early Medieval Philosophy. Edited by A. H. Armstrong. Cambridge: The University Press, 1970.

The Cambridge History of Latin Medieval Philosophy (1100-1600). Edited by Norman Kretzmann et al. Cambridge: The University Press, 1982.

Capellanus, Andreas. *The Art of Courtly Love.* Edited by Frederick W. Locke. United States: Frederick Ungar Publishing Co., 1957.

Catholic Encyclopedia, 1913. New York: The Encyclopedia Press, Inc.

The Characters of Theophrastus. Translated by J. M. Edmonds. London and Cambridge, Mass.: William Heinemann Ltd. and Harvard University Press, 1946.

Charrier, Charlotte. *Héloïse dans l'histoire et dans la légende.* Thèse présentée à la Faculté des Lettres de l'Université de Paris. Paris: Librairie Ancienne Honoré Champion, 1933.

Chodorow, Stanley. *Christian Political Theory and Christian Politics in the Mid-Twelfth Century: The Ecclesiology of Gratian's Decreum.* Berkeley: University of California Press, 1972.

Christophe, Jacques. *Sainte Hildegard.* Paris: Gallimard, 1942.

Cicero, Marcus Tullius. *De Finibus Bonorum et Malorum.* With an English translation by H. Rackham. The Loeb Classical Library. London and New York: William Heinemann Ltd. and G. P. Putnam's Sons, 1939.

———. *De Officiis.* With an English translation by Walter Miller. Cambridge, Mass. and London: Harvard University Press and William Heinemann Ltd., 1941.

———. *De Natura Deorum. Academica.* With an English translation by H. Rackham. Cambridge, Mass. and London: Harvard University Press and William Heinemann Ltd., 1956.

———. *De Republica. De Legibus.* With an English translation by Clinton Walker Keyes. Cambridge, Mass. and London: Harvard University Press and William Heinemann Ltd., 1945.

———. *De Senectute. De Amicitia. De Divinatione.* With an English translation by William Amisted Falconer. Cambridge, Mass. and London: Harvard University Press and William Heinemann Ltd., 1959.

Clark, Lorenne M.G., and Lange, Lynda, eds. *The Sexism of Social and Political Theory.* Woman and Reproduction from Plato to Nietzsche. Toronto, Buffalo, and London: University of Toronto Press, 1979.

Cleve, Felix M. *The Philosophy of Anaxagoras; an Attempt at Reconstruction.* New York: King's Crown Press, 1949.

Compayré, Gabriel. *Abelard and the Origin and Early History of Universities.* New York: Greenwood Press, 1969.

Courtney, E. *A Commentary on the Satires of Juvenal.* London: The Athlone Press, 1980.

Daly, Mary. *Gyn/Ecology: The Metaethics of Radical Feminism.* Boston: Beavon Press, 1978.

Demaitre, L. and Traville, A. A. "Human Embryology and Development in the Works of Albertus Magnus." In *Albert Magnus and the Sciences.* Toronto: Pontifical Institute for Medieval Studies, 1980.

Descartes, René. *L'Homme. La Formation du Foetus.* In *Oeuvres*, Tome 11. Publiées par Charles Adam et Paul Tannery. Paris: Librairie Philosophique, 1969.

Detienne, Marcel. *De la pensée religieuse à la pensée philosophique: la notion de daimôn dans le pythagorisme ancien.* Pref. de J. P. Vernant. Paris: Les Belles Lettres, 1963.

Diels, Hermann. *Die Fragments der Vorsokratiker.* Vol. I. Dublin/Zürich: Weidman, 1966.

———. *Die Fragmente der Vorsokratiker.* Vol. II. Berlin: Weidmanische Buchhandlung, 1935.

———. *Die Fragmente der Vorsokratiker.* Vol. III. Dublin/Zürich: Weidman, 1967.

Dinnerstein, Dorothy. *The Mermaid and the Minotaur.* New York: Harper and Row, 1976.

Diogenes, Laertius. *Lives of Eminent Philosophers.* 2 vols. With an English translation by H. D. Hicks. Cambridge, Mass. and London: Harvard University Press and William Heinemann, Ltd., 1941.

Dronke, Peter. *Abelard and Heloise in Medieval Testimonies.* Glasgow: University of Glasgow Press, 1976.

Easton, Stewart C. *Roger Bacon and His Search for a Universal Science.* New York: Russell and Russell, 1952.

Eckenstein, Lina. *Women under Monasticism; Chapters on Saint-Lore and Convent Life between A.D. 500 and A.D. 1500.* New York: Russell and Russell, 1963.

Elsthain, Jean Bethke. *Public Man, Private Woman: Women In Social and Political Thought.* Princeton, New Jersey: Princeton University Press, 1981.

Empedocles. *Empedocles' Cosmic Cycle: A Reconstruction from the Fragments and Secondary Sources.* Edited by D. O'Brien. Cambridge: The University Press, 1969.

__________. *The Fragments of Empedocles.* Translated into English verse by William E. Leonard. Illinois: Open Court Publishing Co., 1973.

__________. *The Proem of Empedocles' 'Peri Physios': Towards a New Edition of All the Fragments.* Edited by N. van der Bern. Amsterdam: B. R. Gruner, 1975.

Encyclopedia Britannica. 1968.

Engels, Friedrich. *The Origin of the Family, Private Property, and the State.* Introduction by Evelyn Reed. New York: Pathfinder Press, 1972.

Engelsman, Joan Chamberlain. *The Feminine Dimension of the Divine.* First edition. Philadelphia: Westminster Press, 1979.

English, Jane. "Review Essay on Philosophy." In *Signs: Journal of Women and Society* 3, 4 (1978): 823-931.

Epicurus. *Epicurus' Morals.* Translated by John Digby. New York: A.M.S. Press, 1975.

Erigena. (See Johannes Scotus, Erigena).

The Fasciculus Medicinae of Joannes de Ketham. Facsimile of the first Venetian edition of 1491. With introduction by Karl Sudhoff, translated and adapted by Charles Singer, with XIII plates. Milan: R. Lier and Co., 1924.

Father Malebranche's Treatise Concerning the Search After Truth. Oxford: L. Lichfield, 1964.

Festugière, André Marie Jean. *La révélation d'Hermès Trismégiste.* Avec un appendice sur l'hermétisme arabe par Louis Massignon. 4 vols. Paris: Lecoffre, 1944-54. Appendice II. Porphyre. Sur la manière dont l'embryon reçoit l'âme.

Firestone, Shulamith. *The Dialectic of Sex: The Case for a Feminist Revolution.* New York: Morrow, 1970.

The Fragments of Zeno and Cleanthes. New York: Arno Press, 1973.

Frazer, Sir James George. *The Golden Bough; a Study in Magic and Religion.* 2 vols., 3rd edition. London: Macmillan and Co., Ltd., 1936-37.

Freeman, Kathleen. *Ancilla to the Pre-Socratic Philosophers. (A complete translation of the Fragments in Diels, 'Die Fragmente der Vorsokratiker').* Oxford: Basil Blackwell, 1948.

__________. *The Pre-Socratic Philosophers, A Companion to Diels, 'Die Fragmente der Vorsokratiker.'* Oxford: Basil Blackwell, 1946.

Freud, Sigmund. *New Introductory Lectures on Psychoanalysis.* Middlesex, England: Penguin Books, 1973.

Friedan, Betty. *The Feminine Mystique.* New York: Norton, 1963.

__________. *The Second Stage.* New York: Summit Books, 1981.

Friedlander, Paul. *Plato.* 2 vols. Translated from the German by Hans Meyerhoff. New York: Pantheon Books (Bollingen Series LIX), 1964.

———. *Plato: An Introduction.* Translated from the German by Hans Meyerhoff. New York and Evanston: Harper Torch Books, 1958.

Führkötter, O.S.B., Adelgundis. *Das Leben der heiligen Hildegard von Bingen: Herausgegeben, eingeleitet und übersetzt.* Düsseldorf: Patmos-Verlag, 1968.

Galen — LCC: (Galenus).

———. *On Anatomical Procedures; the Later Books.* A translation by W. L. H. Duckworth. Edited by M. C. Lyons and B. Towers. Cambridge: The University Press, 1962.

———. *On the Doctrines of Hippocrates and Plato.* Edited, translated and commentary by Phillip de Lacy. Berlin: Akademie-Verlag, 1978.

———. *On the Natural Faculties.* Translated by Arthur John Brook. New York: G. P. Putnam's Sons, 1916.

———. *On the Passions and Errors of the Soul.* Translated by Paul Harkins. With an introduction and interpretation by Walter Riese. Columbus: Ohio State University Press, 1965.

———. *A Translation of Galen's 'Hygiene' (De sanitate tuenda).* By Robert Montraville Green. With an introduction by Henry E. Sigerist. Springfield, Ill.: Charles C. Thomas, 1951.

———. *On the Usefulness of the Parts of the Body.* 2 vols. Translated from the Greek with an introduction and commentary by Margaret Tallmadge May. Ithaca: Cornell University Press, 1968.

Garside, Christine (see, Allen, Christine).

Geach, P.T. *The Virtues.* London, New York, Melbourne: Cambridge University Press, 1979.

Gershenson, Daniel, and Greenberg, Daniel A. *Anaxagoras and the Birth of Physics.* With an introduction by Ernest Nagel. New York: Blaisdell Publishing Co., 1964.

Geytenbeek, A.C. van. *Musonius Rufus and Greek Diatribe.* Translated by B. L. Hijmans. Assen: Van Gorcum and Company, N.V. 1963.

Gies, Frances and Joseph. *Women in the Middle Ages.* New York: Thomas Y. Crowell, 1978.

Giles of Rome — LCC: (Aegidivs Romanus, Archbishop of Bourges).

———. *Errores Philosophorum.* Critical text with notes and introduction. By Josef Kock. English translation by John O. Riedl. Milwaukee: Marquette University Press, 1944.

———. "De Formationis Corporis." In *Giles of Rome and the Medieval Theory of Conception.* A study of *De Formatione Corporis Humani in Utero.* M. Anthony Hewson. London: The Athlone Press, 1975.

———. *De Regime Principum.* Translated by John Treorsa. Bodleian MS. Digby 233.

———. *Theorems on Existence and Essence (Theormata de Esse et Essentia).* Translated from the Latin with an introduction and preface by Michael V. Murray. Milwaukee: Marquette University Press, 1952.

Gilligan, Carole. *In a Different Voice.* Cambridge, Mass.: and London: Harvard University Press and William Heinemann, 1982.

Gilson, Etienne. *Heloise and Abelard.* Authorized translation by L.K. Shook. Chicago: Henry Regnery Co., 1951.

———. *Heloise and Abelard.* Ann Arbor: The University of Michigan Press, 1960.

Glasgow, Maude. *The Subjection of Women and the Traditional Men.* New York: published by author 360 Central Park W., 1940.

Goldberg, Stephen. *The New Inevitability of Patriarchy.* New York: Macmillan, 1953.

Goldenberg, Naomi. *The Changing of the Gods: Feminism and the End of Traditional Religions.* Boston: Beacon Press, 1979.

Gouges (Marie Gouze, dite Olympe de). *Les Droits de la Femme. À la Reine.* 1792.

Gournay, Marie de Jars de (fille d'alliance de Michel de Montaigne). *Égalité des hommes et des femmes*. À la reyne. 1622.
Grant, Barbara. "A Feather on the Breath of God." In *Parabola Magazine* IX, 2 (Summer, 1984).
Graves, Robert. *The Greek Myths*. Great Britain: Penguin Books, 1960.
———. *The White Goddess: A Historical Grammar of Poetic Myth*. Amended and enlarged. New York: The Noonday Press, 1969.
A Greek-English Lexicon. 9th edition. Compiled by Henry George Liddell and Robert Scott. Revised and augmented throughout by Sir Henry Stuart Jones. With a supplement, 1968. Oxford: At the Clarendon Press, 1968.
Grayleff, Felix. *Aristotle and His School*. London: Duckworth, 1974.
Guthrie, W. K. C. *The Sophists*. Cambridge: The University Press, 1971.
Hadzsits, George Depue. *Lucretius and His Influence*. New York: Longmans, Green and Co., 1935.
Hahn, David. *The Origins of Stoic Cosmology*. Ohio: Ohio State University Press, 1977.
Hamburger, Max. *The Awakening of Western Legal Thought*. Translated by Bernard Miall, with a new introduction by the author. New York: Biblo and Tanner, 1969.
———. *Morals and Law: The Growth of Aristotle's Legal Theory*. New York: Biblo and Tanner, 1965.
Harding, Sandra and Hintikka, Merrill B., eds. *Discovering Reality*. Dordrecht, Holland/ Boston, U.S.A./ London: England: D. Reidel Publishing Company, 1983.
Healy, Emma Therese, Sister. *Women According to Saint Bonaventure*. New York: Georgian Press, 1955.
Heidegger, Martin. *Early Greek Thinking*. Translated by David Farrell Krell and Frank A. Capuzzi. First edition. New York: Harper and Row, 1975.
———. *The End of Philosophy*. New York: Harper and Row Publishers, 1973.
———. *The Question Concerning Technology and Other Essays*. Translated with an introduction by William Louitt. New York: Harper and Row Publishers, 1977.
———. *What Is Called Thinking*. Translated by J. Glenn Gray. New York: Harper and Row Publishers, 1972.
Heraclitus. *The Cosmic Fragments*. Edited with an introduction and commentary by G. S. Kirk. Cambridge: The University Press, 1954.
———. *Heraclitus of Ephesus*. An edition combining in one volume the fragments of Heraclitus of Ephesus 'On Nature,' translated from the Greek text of Bywater with introduction and critical notes by G. T. W. Patrick. Chicago: Augonaut, 1969.
Herrad of Hohenbourg, *Hortus Deliciarum: Commentary*. New Rochelle, N.Y.: Caratzas Brothers Publishers, 1971.
———. *Hortus Deliciarum: Reconstruction*. By Rosalie Green et al.; London: The Warburg Institute; Leiden: E.J. Brill, 1979.
Hesiod — LCC: (Hesiodus).
Hesiod. Cambridge, Mass.: Harvard University Press, 1967.
———. *Theogony*. Translated, with an introduction by Norman O. Brown. Indianopolis, Indiana: Bobbs-Merrill Company, Inc., 1953.
———. *Theogony*. Translated with an introduction by Norman O. Brown. New York: Liberal Arts Press, 1953.
———. "The Works and Days." In *Theogony, The Shield of Herakles*. Translated by Richmond Lattimore. Ann Arbor: The University of Michigan Press, 1959.
Hewson, M. Anthony (See, Giles of Rome).
Hieronymus. *Patrologiae*. Paris: J. P. Migne, 1885.

Highet, Gilbert. *Juvenal the Satirist.* Oxford: The Clarendon Press, 1960.

Hildegard von Bingen — LCC: (Hildegardis, Saint).

__________. *Das Buch von den Steinen.* Nach den Quellen übersetzt und erläutert von Peter Riethe. Salzburg: Otto Müller Verlag, 1979.

__________. *Heilkunde; das Buch von dem Grund und Wesen und der Heilung der Krankheiten (Causae et Curae).* Nach den Quellen übersetzt und erläutert von Heinrich Schipperges. Salzburg: Otto Müller Verlag, 1957.

__________. *Lieder.* Nach den Handschriften herausgegeben von Prudtiana Barth, O.S.B., M. Immaculata Ritscher, O.S.B., und Joseph Schmidt-Görg. Salzburg: Otto Müller Verlag, 1969.

__________. *Der Mensch in der Verantwortung, das Buch der Lebensverdienste (Liber Vitae Meritorum).* Nach den Quellen übersetzt und erläutert von Heinrich Schipperges. Salzburg: Otto Müller Verlag, 1972.

__________. *Naturkunde; das Buch von dem inneren Wesen der verschieden Naturen in der Schöpfung.* Nach den Quellen übersetzt und erläutert von Peter Riethe. Salzburg: Otto Müeller Verlag, 1959.

__________. *Scivias.* Translated by Mother Columba Hart, O.S.B. In *Classic of Western Spirituality.* New York: Ramsay; Toronto: Paulist Press (forthcoming).

__________. *Wisse die Wege: Scivias.* Nach den Quellen übersetzt und erläutert von Maura Böckeler. Salzburg: Otto Müller Verlag, 1954.

Hildegardis, Abbess (S.). *Opera Omnia. Patrologiae Latina.* Tomus 197. Paris: J.P. Migne, 1882.

Hippocrates. *The Aphorisms of Hippocrates.* From the Latin version of Verhoofd, with a literal translation on the opposite page, and explanatory notes. By Elias Marks. New York: Collins and Co., 1817.

__________. *The Genuine Works of Hippocrates.* 2 vols. Translated from the Greek, with a preliminary discourse and annotations by Francis Adams. New York: W. Wood and Co., 1886.

__________. *Hippocrate.* "De la Génération," "De la Nature de l'Enfant." Texte établi et traduit par Robert Joly. Paris: Société d'édition "les belles lettres," Tome XI, 1970.

__________. *Hippocrates.* Translated by W. H. S. Jones. Cambridge and London: Harvard University Press and William Heinemann Ltd., 1967. Vols. I, II, IV.

__________. *Hippocrates.* Translated by W. H. S. Jones. London and New York: William Heinemann Ltd. and G. P. Putnam's Sons, 1931. Vols. I, II, and IV.

__________. *Hippocrates.* London and New York: William Heinemann and G. P. Putnam's Sons, 1923.

__________. *Hippocrates.* Translated by E.T. Withington. Cambridge, Mass. and London: Harvard University Press and William Heinemann Ltd., 1959. Vol. III.

__________. *The Medical Works of Hippocrates.* Translated by John Chadwick and W. H. Mann. Oxford: Basil Blackwell, 1950.

__________. *Traduction des oeuvres médicales d'Hippocrate, sur le texte grec, d'après l'édition de Foës.* 4 vols. Translated by J. B. Gardeil and edited by D. J. Tournon. Toulouse: Fages, Meilhac et Compagnie, 1801.

Horowitz, Marilyn. "Aristotle and Women." *Journal of the History of Biology* 9, 2 (Fall, 1976): 194 ff.

Hozeski, Bruce William. *Ordo Virtutum: Hildegard of Bingen's Liturgical Morality Play.* Ph.D. Dissertation, Michigan State University, 1969.

Hrotsuit (See, Roswitha of Gandersheim).

Husik, Isaac. *A History of Medieval Jewish Philosophy.* New York: The Macmillan Co., 1916.

Hypatia. *Hypathia: A Journal of Feminist Philosophy*. Vol. 1. Philadelphia: University of Pennsylvania Press, 1983.

Ibn Gabirol, Solomon — LCC: (Ibn Gabirol, Solomon ben Judah).

__________. *Choice of Pearls (Mivhar ha perrinim)*. From the Hebrew with introduction and annotations by the Rev. A. Cohen. New York: Bloch Publishing Co., 1925.

__________. *Fountain of Life (Fons Vitae)*. Translated from the Latin by Alfred B. Jacob. Philadelphia, 1954.

__________. *The Kingly Crown (Malkhut)*. Newly translated with an introduction and notes by Bernard Lewis. London: Valentine and Mitchell, 1961.

__________. *Qabbalah: The Philosophical Writings of Solomon ben Yehudah Ibn Gabirol and their Connection with the Hebrew Qabbalah*. By Isaac Myer. New York: Ktav Publishing House, 1970.

__________. *Selected Religious Poems of Solomon Ibn Gabirol*. From a critical text edited by Israel Davidson. New York: Arno Press, 1973.

Jacquart, Danielle, and Claude Thomasset. "Albert le Grand et les problèmes de la sexualité." In *Pubblicazioni della stazione zoologica di Napoli*. Section II, "History and Philosophy of the Life Sciences." Vol. 3, no. 1 (1981), pp. 73-93.

Jaspers, Karl. *The Way to Wisdom: An Introduction to Philosophy*. Translated by Ralph Mannheim. New Haven and London: Yale University Press, 1969.

Jenkyns, Richard. *Three Classical Poets: Sappho, Catullus and Juvenal*. London: Unwin Brothers Limited, 1982.

Jerome. "Advice to Eustochium." In *Selected Letters of St. Jerome*. Cambridge, Mass. and London: Harvard University Press and William Heinemann Ltd., 1954.

John Paul II (See also, Wojtyla, Cardinal Karol).

__________. *The Original Unity of Man and Woman*. Boston: St. Paul Editions, 1981.

John the Scot — LCC: (Johannes Scotus, Erigena).

__________. *Periphyseon: De Divisione Naturae*. Edited by I. P. Sheldon-Williams. Dublin: The Dublin Institute for Advanced Studies, 1972.

__________. *Periphyseon (On the Division of Nature)*. Translated by Myra L. Uhlfelder. With summaries by Jean A. Potter. Indianapolis: The Bobbs-Merrill Co., 1976.

Johnson, Jill. *Lesbian Nation*. New York: Simon and Schuster, 1973.

Julian of Norwich. *The Revelations of Divine Love*. London: Burns and Oaks, 1961.

Jung, Carl Gustav. *Collected Works*. Edited by Herbert Read, Michael Fordham and Gerhard Adler. New York: Pantheon Books, 1953.

Kahn, Charles. *Anaximander and the Origins of Greek Cosmology*. New York: Columbia University Press, 1960.

Kant, Immanuel. *Observations on the Feeling of the Beautiful and Sublime*. Translated by John T. Goldthwait. Berkeley: University of California Press, 1960.

Katzenellenbogen, Adolf. *Allegories of the Virtues and Vices in Medieval Art*. New York: W. W. Norton and Company, Inc., 1964.

Kemp-Welch, Alice. *Of Six Medieval Women to Which is Added a Note on Medieval Gardens*. London: Macmillan and Co., 1913.

Kerferd. G. B. *The Sophistic Movement*. Cambridge: The University Press, 1981.

Ketham, Joannes de Mondinode Luzzi. *The Fasciculodi Medicina, Venice 1493*. With an introduction, etc. by Charles Singer. Florence: R. Lier and Co., 1924.

Kingsley, Charles. *Hypatia*. New York: Garland Publishing, 1975.

Krapiec, Mieczytaw A. *I-Man: An Outline of Philosophical Anthropology*. New Britain, Conn.: Marial Publications, 1983.

The Ladies' Dictionary, Being a General Entertainment for the Fair-Sex: A Work Never Attempted Before in English. Edited by N. H. London: J. Dunton, 1694.
Lakoff, Robin T. *Language and Woman's Place.* New York: Harper and Row, 1975.
The Latin Poems Commonly Attributed to Walter Mapes. Edited by Thomas Wright. Hildesheim: Georg Olms Verlagsbuch-handlung, 1968.
Leff, Gordon. *Paris and Oxford Universities in the Thirteenth and Fourteenth Centuries: An Institutional and Intellectual History.* New York: John Wiley and Sons Inc., 1968.
The Legal Status of Women from 2250 B.C. 2 vols. Des Moines, Iowa: U.S. Works Project Administration, 1938.
Le Goff, Jacques. *Les Intellectuels au moyen âges.* Paris: Éditions du Seuil, 1957.
The Letters of Abelard and Heloise. Translated by C. K. Scott Moncrieff. New York: Alfred A. Knopf, 1926.
Lettres Spirituelles Choisies de Saint Anselme. Traduites par les moniales du Monastère de Ste-Croix de Poitiers. Paris: Desclée de Brouwer et cie., 1926.
Lindsay, Jack. *The Troubadours and Their World of the Twelfth and Thirteenth Centuries.* London: Frederick Muller Limited, 1976.
Lobel, Edgar and Page, Denys, eds. *Poetarum Lesbiorum Fragmenta.* Oxford: At the University Press, 1955.
Lombard, Peter — LCC: (Petrus Lombardus).
__________. *Libri IV Sententiarum.* Studio et cura PP. collegii S. Bonaventurae. Secundo editio. Florence; Claras Aquas, 1916.
Long, A. A. *Hellenistic Philosophy: Stoics, Epicureans, Sceptics.* New York: Charles Scribner's Sons, 1974.
The Love Songs of Sappho. Translated with an introduction by Paul Roche. Toronto: Mentor Books, 1966.
Lucretius. *The Nature of Things.* New York: W. W. Norton and Company, Inc., 1977.
Luscombe, D. E. *Peter Abelard.* London: The Historical Association, 1958.
__________. *Peter Abelard.* London: The Historical Association, 1979.
__________. *Peter Abelard's Ethics.* An edition with introduction, English translation and notes. Oxford: At the Clarendon Press, 1971.
__________. *The School of Peter Abelard: The Influence of Abelard's Thought in the Early Scholastic Period.* Cambridge: The University Press, 1969.
Lynch, John Patrick. *Aristotle's School: A Study of a Greek Educational Institution.* Berkeley: University of California Press, 1972.
Mahowald, Mary Briody, ed. *Philosophy of Woman: Classical to Current Concepts.* Indianapolis: Hacket Publishing Co., 1978.
McLaughlin, Mary Martin. "Peter Abelard and the Dignity of Women: Twelfth Century 'Feminism' in Theory and Practice." In *Pierre Abélard, Pierre le Vénérable: Les Courants Philosophiques, Littéraires et Artistiques en Occident au milieu de XIIe siècle* (Paris: Éditions du Centre National de la Recherche Scientifique, 1975).
Maimonides — LCC: (Moses ben Maimon).
__________. *The Code of Maimonides.* New Haven: Yale University Press, 1949.
__________. *The Commandments: Sefer Ha-Mitzvoth of Maimonides.* 2 vols. Translated from the Hebrew with foreword, notes, glossary, appendices and indices by Rabbi Dr. Charles B. Chavel. London and New York: Soncino, 1967.
__________. *Commentary on the Aphorisms of Hippocrates.* Hebrew translation by Moshe Ibn Tibbon. Edited, with an introduction (in English) by Suessmann Muntner. Jerusalem: Mossad Harav Kook, 1961.

__________. "Discourse on Sexual Intercourse." In *Essays on Maimonides, The Medical Works of Maimonides*, Appendix II, edited by Salo Wittmayer Baron. New York: Columbia University Press, 1941.

__________. *The Eight Chapters on Ethics (Shemorak perakim); a Psychological and Ethical Treatise.* Edited, annotated and translated, with an introduction by Joseph I. Gorfinkle. New York: Columbia University (Ph.D. dissertation), 1912.

__________. *Ethical Writings of Maimonides.* Translated by Raymond L. Weiss, with Charles E. Butterworth. New York: New York University Press, 1975.

__________. *The Guide of the Perplexed.* Translated with an introduction and notes by Shlomo Pines. With an introductory essay by Leo Strauss. Chicago: University of Chicago Press, 1963.

__________. *Introduction to the Talmud; A Translation of the Ramban's Introduction to his Commentary of the 'Mishna.'* Translated and annotated by Zvi L. Lampel. New York: Judaica Press, 1975.

__________. *The Medical Aphorisms of Maimonides.* Translated and edited by Fred Rosner and Suessman Muntner. New York: Yeshiva University Press, 19–.

__________. *Rambam Readings in the Philosophy of Moses Maimonides.* Selected and edited, with introduction and commentary, by Lenn Evan Goodman. New York: Viking Press, 1976.

Malebranche, Nicolas. *Treatise Concerning the Search after Truth.* Ohio: Ohio State University Press, 1980.

Map, Walter. *De Nugis Curialium* (Courtiers' Trifles). Translated by Frederick Tupper and Marbury Bladen Ogle. London: Chatto and Windus, 1924.

Marx, Karl. *Doktordissertation von Karl Marx (1841).* ('Differenz der democratischen und epikurischen Naturphilosophie'). Eingeleitet und bearbeitet von Georg Mende under Mitwirkung von Ernst Günther Schmidt. Jena: Friedrich-Schiller Universität, 1964.

McKeough, Michael J. *The Meaning of Rationes Seminales in St. Augustine.* Ph.D. dissertation, Catholic University of America, Washington, D.C., 1926.

McMillan, Carol. *Women, Reason, and Nature.* Princeton, New Jersey: Princeton University Press, 1982.

The Medical Aphorisms of Maimomides. Edited by Rossner and Muntner. New York: Yeshiva University Press, 19–.

Medieval Woman's Guide to Health, trans. Beryl Rowland Kent. Ohio: Kent State University Press, 1981.

Ménage, Gilles. *Historia Mulierum Philosophorum.* Amsterdam: Henricum Wetsternium, 1692.

__________. *The History of Women Philosophers.* Translated from the Latin with an introduction by Beatrice H. Zedler. Lanham, Mo.: University Press of America, 1984.

Merchant, Carolyn. *The Death of Nature: Women, Ecology, and the Scientific Revolution.* San Francisco: Harper and Row Publishers, 1980.

Merlan, Philip. "Greek Philosophy from Plato to Plotinus." In *The Cambridge History of Later Greek and Early Medieval Philosophy*, edited by A.H. Armstrong. Cambridge: At the University Press, 1970.

Meunier, Mario. *Femmes Pythagoriciennes: fragments et lettres de Théano, Périctioné, Phintys, Mélissa, et Myia.* Traduction nouvelle avec prolégomènes et notes. Paris: L'Artisan du livre, 1932.

Meyer, Wolfgang Alexander. *Hypatia von Alexandria.* Ein Beitrag zur Geschichte des Neoplatonismus. Heidelberg: 6 Weis. 1886.

Meyerhof, M., and Joannides, D. *La gynécologie et l'obstétrique chez Avicenne (Ibn Sina) et leurs rapports avec celles des grecs.* Cairo: Imprimerie E. and R. Schindler, 1938.

Miles, Margaret Ruth. *Augustine on the Body*. Missoula, Montana: Scholars' Press, 1979.

Mill, John Stuart. *The Subjection of Women*. Cambridge, Mass. and London, England: The M.I.T. Press, 1970.

Mondino de Luzzi (See, Ketham, Joannes de).

Montagu, Ashley. *The Natural Superiority of Woman*. New York: Macmillan, 1953.

Morgan, Robin, ed. *Sisterhood Is Powerful: An Anthology of Writings from the Women's Liberation Movement*. New York: Random House, 1970.

Morris, Joan. *The Lady Was a Bishop: The Hidden History of Women with Clerical Ordination and the Jurisdiction of Bishops*. New York: The Macmillan Co., 1973.

Morrison, David J. *The Juridic Status of Women in Canonical Law and in United States Law: A Comparative Socio-juridical Study*. Rome: Pontificia Universitas Lateranensis, 1965.

Mozans, H. J. — (Zahm, John Augustine). *Women in Science*. Cambridge: The M.I.T. Press, 1974.

Musonius, Rufus. *Deux prédicateurs de l'antiquité: Teles et Musonius*. Paris: Librairie Philosophique J. Vrin, 1978.

Myer (See, Ibn Gabirol, Solomon).

Needham, Joseph. *A History of Embryology*. Second ed. revised with the assistance of Arthur Hughes. Cambridge: University Press, 1959.

Neumann, Erich. *The Great Mother: An Analysis of the Archetype*. Translated from the German by Ralph Mannheim. Second edition. New York: Bollingen Foundation, 1963.

The New Catholic Encyclopedia, 1967-79 edition.

New Encyclopedia Britannica, 15th edition.

Newman, Barbara. "Divine Power Made Perfect in Weakness: St. Hildegard on the Frail Sex." In *Medieval Religious Women*. Cistercian Publications, forthcoming 1985.

__________ . *O Feminea Forma: God and Woman in the Works of St. Hildegard*. Ph.D. dissertation, Yale, 1981.

__________ . *Sister of Wisdom: St. Hildegard's Theology of the Feminine* University of California Press, forthcoming.

Newcastle, Margaret Cavendish, duchess of. "Female Orations." In *Orations of Divers Sorts*, 1662.

Nietzsche, Friedrich Wilhelm. "The Greek Woman." *The Complete Works of Friedrich Nietzsche*. Vol. 2. Edited by Oscar Levy. New York: Russell and Russell, 1964.

__________ . *The Portable Nietzsche*. Selected and translated, with an introduction, prefaces and notes by Walter Kaufmann. New York: Viking Press, 1954.

Oates, Whitney J., ed. *The Stoic and Epicurean Philosophers: The Complete Extant Writings of Epicurus, Epictetus, Lucretius (and) Marcus Aurelius*. With an introduction. New York: Random House, 1940.

Okin, Susan Moller, *Women in Western Political Thought*. Princeton, New Jersey: Princeton University Press, 1979.

O'Toole, Christopher J. *The Philosophy of Creation in the Writings of St. Augustine*. Washington, D.C.: Catholic University Press, 1944.

Owens, Joseph. *The Doctrine of Being in the Aristotelian Metaphysics*. With a preface by Etienne Gilson. Third ed., rev. Toronto: Pontifical Institute of Mediaeval Studies, 1978.

Parmenides. *Eleates*. A text with translation, commentary and critical essays by Leonardo Tarán. Princeton: Princeton University Press, 1965.

__________ . *The Fragments of Parmenides*. Translated into English hexameters, with introduction and notes by Thomas Davidson. New York: Wiley and Sons, 1869.

Peters, F. E. *Aristotle and the Arabs; the Aristotelian Tradition in Islam*. New York: New York University Press, 1968.

Petri Lombardi Sentiarum Libri Quattuor. Lutetiae Parisiorum: J.P. Migne, 1853.
Petrus Abaelardus. *Patrologiae.* Vol. 178. Paris: J.P. Migne, 1885.
Petrus Lombardus (Peter Lombard). *Libri IV Sentiarium* (Florence: Claras Aquas, 1916.
Philip, J. A. *Pythagoras and Early Pythagoreanism.* Toronto: University of Toronto Press, 1966.
Philo — LCC: (Philo Judaeus)
__________. *Philo.* 10 vols. With an English translation by F. H. Colson and G. H. Whitaker. Cambridge, Mass. and London: Harvard University Press and William Heinemann, Ltd., 1929-62.
__________. *Philo: Supplement I. Questions and Answers on Genesis.* Translated from the ancient Armenian version of the original Greek by Ralph Marcus. Cambridge, Mass. and London: Harvard University Press and William Heinemann Ltd., 1953.
The Philosophy of Epicurus. Edited by George F. Strodach. Evanston, I11.: Northwestern University Press, 1963.
Philostratus and Europius. The Lives of the Sophists. Translated by Wilmer Cabe Wright. Cambridge, Mass. and London: Harvard University Press and William Heinemann, Ltd., 1949.
Pierce, Christine. "Review Essay on Philosophy." *Signs: Journal of Women and Society* 1, 2 (1975): 487-501.
Pierre Abelard. *Pierre le Vénérable: Les courants philosophiques, littéraires et artistiques en occident au milieu du xiie siècle,* Colloques internationaux du centre national de la recherche scientifique, no. 346, Abbaye de Cluny, 2 au 9 juillet, 1972. Paris: Éditions du centre national de la recherche scientifique, 1975.
Plato. *The Collected Dialogues of Plato, Including the Letters.* Edited by Edith Hamilton and Huntington Cairns. With an introduction and prefatory notes. New York: Pantheon Books (Bollingen Series, 71), 1961.
__________. *Symposium.* Indianapolis: The Bobbs-Merrill Company, 1956.
Pliny. *The Natural History of Pliny.* 6 vols. Translated, with copious notes and illustrations by John Bostock and H. T. Riley London: Henry G. Bohn, 1855-57.
Plotinus. *Enneads* in *Plotinus 1-III.* With an English translation by A. H. Armstrong. London and Cambridge, Mass.: William Heinemann, Ltd. and Harvard University Press, 1966.
Plutarch. *Moralia.* Vols. 1-5. With an English translation by Frank Cole Babbitt. Cambridge, Mass. and London: Harvard University Press and William Heinemann, Ltd., 1927-37.
__________. *Moralia VI.* With an English translation by W.C. Helmbold. Cambridge, Mass. and London: Harvard University Press and William Heinemann, Ltd., 1939.
__________. *Moralia VII.* With an English translation by Phillip de Lacy and Benedict Einarson. Cambridge, Mass. and London: Harvard University Press and William Heinemann, Ltd., 1959.
__________. *Moralia VIII.* With an English translation by Paul Clement and Herbert B. Hoffleit. Cambridge, Mass. and London: Harvard University Press and William Heinemann, Ltd., 1969.
__________. *Moralia XIII, Part I.* With an English translation by Harold Cherniss. Cambridge, Mass. and London: Harvard University Press and William Heinemann, Ltd., 1976.
__________. *Moralia XV and Fragments.* With an English translation by F. H. Sandbach. Cambridge, Mass. and London: Harvard University Press and William Heinemann, Ltd., 1969.
Pomeroy, Susan. *Goddesses, Whores, Wives and Slaves: Women in Classical Antiquity.* New York: Schocken Books, 1975.

Porphyry — LCC: (Porphyrius).
__________. *Isagoge.* In *The Organon, or Logical Treatises of Aristotle.* 2 vols. Literally translated, with notes, syllogistic examples, analysis and introduction by Octavius Freire Owen. London: H. G. Bohn, 1853.
__________. *The Philosopher to His Wife, Marcella.* Translated, with an introduction by Alice Zimmern. London: George Redway, 1896.
Poullain de La Barre, François. *De l'égalité des deux sexes, discours physique et moral où l'on voit l'importance de défaire des préjugés.* Paris: J. Du Puis, 1673.
Power, Sir D'Arcy. *The Foundations of Medical History.* Baltimore: Williams and Wilkins, 1931.
The Prayers and Meditations of St. Anselm. Translated by Sister Benedicta Ward, S.L.G. Great Britain, Penguin Books, 1973.
Proclus — LCC: (Proclus Diadochus).
__________. *The Elements of Theology.* A revised text, with translation, introduction and commentary by E. R. Dodds. Oxford: At the Clarendon Press, 1931.
Protagoras. *The Older Sophists,* ed. Rosamond Kent Sprague. Columbia, South Carolina: University of South Carolina Press, 1972.
Pythagoras. *The Golden Verses of Pythagoras.* Translated from the Greek by Nicholas Rowe. London, 1746.
Raming, Ida. *The Exclusion of Women from the Priesthood: Divine Law or Sex Discrimination?* Translated by Norman R. Adams. With a preface by Arlene and Leonard Swindler. Metuchen, New Jersey: The Scarecrow Press, Inc., 1970.
Rashdall, Hastings. *The Universities of Europe in the Middle Ages.* London: Oxford University Press, 1931.
__________. *The Universities of Europe in the Middle Ages.* 3 vols. A new edition, edited by F. M. Powicke and A. B. Emden. London: Oxford University Press, 1958.
Reilly, George C. "The Psychology of St. Albert the Great." Ph.D. dissertation. The Catholic University of America, 1934.
Ressor, Margaret E. *The Political Theory of the Old and Middle Stoa.* New York: J. J. Augustin Publisher, 1952.
de Riencourt, Amaury. *Sex and Power in History.* New York: Della Books, 1975.
Robinson, David. *The Songs of Sappho.* Kentucky: The Maxwelton Co., 1925.
Roswitha of Gandersheim — LCC (Hrotsvit, of Gandersheim)
__________. *Hrosvithae Liber Tertius.* A text with translation, introduction, and commentary by Sister Mary Bernardine Bergman, a dissertation presented to the Faculty of the Graduate School of Saint Louis University, 1942.
__________. *Hroswitha of Gandersheim, Her Life, Times, and Works, and A Comprehensive Bibliography.* Edited by Anne Lyon Haight. New York: The Hroswitha Club, 1965.
__________. *The Non-Dramatic Works of Hroswitha, Text, Translation, and Commentary.* Dissertation by Sister M. Gonsalva Wiegand, O.S.F., St. Louis, Missouri, 1936.
__________. *The Plays of Roswitha.* Translated by Christopher St. John with an introduction by Cardinal Gasquet and a critical preface by the translator. New York: Cooper Square Publishers, Inc., 1966.
Rousseau, Jean Jacques. *Emile: or, on Education.* Introduction, translation, and notes by Allan Bloom. New York: Basic Books, 1979.
Ruether, Rosemary. *New Woman, New Earth: Sexist Ideologies, and Human Liberation.* New York: The Seabury Press, 1951.
Russell, Dora Winifred Black (Russell, Countess). *Hypatia: On Woman and Knowledge.* Folcroft, Pa.: Folcroft Library Editions, 1976. (Original 1925.)

Sappho. *The Songs of Sappho, Including the Recent Egyptian Discoveries; the Poems of Erinna* (etc.). Greek texts prepared and annotated and literally translated in prose by David Moore Robinson. New York: Frank-Maurice, Inc., 1925.

__________ . *Poems and Fragments.* Translated, with an introduction by Guy Davenport. Ann Arbor: University of Michigan Press, 1957, 1965.

Sartre, Jean Paul. *Being and Nothingness.* Translated by Hazel E. Barnes. New York: Philosophical Library, 1950.

The Satires of Juvenal. Translated by Rolfe Humphries. Bloomington and London: Indiana University Press, 1958.

Schroder, Marianna and Führkotter, Adelgundis. *Die Echtheit des Schrifttums der heiligen Hildegard von Bingen.* Köl/Graz: Böhlau-Verlag, 1956.

Schurman, Anna Maria von. *The Learned Maid; or, Whether a Maid Can Be a Scholar: A Logick Exercise.* London: John Redmayne, 1659.

Schwertner, Thomas Maria. *St. Albert the Great.* New York: The Bruce Publishing Co., 1932.

Seneca — LCC: (Seneca, Lucius Annoeus).

__________ . *Ad Lucilium Epistulae Morales.* 3 vols. With an English translation by Richard M. Gummere. The Loeb Classical Library. London and New York: William Heinemann, Ltd, and G. P. Putnam's Sons, 1925.

__________ . *Moral Essays.* 3 vols. With an English translation by John W. Basore. New York and London: G. P. Putnam's Sons and William Heinemann, Ltd., 1928-32.

__________ . *Naturales Quaestiones.* Vol. 1. With an English translation by Thomas H. Corcoran. The Loeb Classical Library. Cambridge, Mass. and London: Harvard University Press and William Heinemann, Ltd., 1971.

She Said/He Said: An Annotated Bibliography of Sex Differences in Language, Speech, and Nonverbal Communication, eds. Nancy Henley and Barrie Thorne. Pittsburgh: Know, Inc., 1975.

Singer, Charles. *From Magic to Science; Essays on the Scientific Twilight.* New York: Dover Publications, 1958.

Slater, Philip. *The Glory of Hera: Greek Mythology and Greek Family.* Boston: Beacon Press, 1968.

Smith, Philip. *Languages, the Sexes and Society.* Oxford: Basil Blackwell, 1984.

Smith, William A. *Ancient Education* New York: Greenwood Press, 1969.

Sokolowski, Robert. *The God of Faith and Reason: Foundation of Christian Theology.* Notre Dame: University of Notre Dame Press, 1982.

Solanis, Valerie. *Sisterhood Is Powerful.* New York: Random House, 1974.

Southern, Richard William. *Western Society and the Church in the Middle Ages.* Great Britain: Penguin, 1982.

Sprague, Rosamond Kent, ed. *The Older Sophists: A Complete Translation by Several Hands of the Fragments in Diels, "Die Fragmente der Vorsokratiker."* First edition. South Carolina: University of South Carolina Press, 1972.

Steele, Francesca Maria (Darley Dale). *The Life and Visions of St. Hildegarde.* With a preface by the very Rev. Vincent McNabb. London: Heath, Cranton and Ousely, Ltd. 1914.

Steenberghen, Fernand van. *Aristotle in the West; the Origins of Latin Averroism.* Translated by Leonard Johnston. Louvain: E. Navwelaerts, 1955.

Stein, Edith. *Die Frau; ihre Aufgabe nach Natur und Grade.* Herausgegeben von Dr. L. Gerber. Louvain and Freiburg: E. Nauwelaerts and Verlag Herder, 1959.

Stocks, John Leofric. *Aristotelianism.* New York: Cooper Square Publishers, 1963.

Stone, Merlin. *When God Was a Woman.* New York: The Dial Press, 1976.

Strauss, Leo. *Xenophon's Socratic Discourse; an Interpretation of the 'Oeconomicus.'* With a new, literal translation of the 'Oeconomicus' by Carnes Lord. Ithaca: Cornell University Press, 1970.

Swidler, Leonard J. *Biblical Affirmations of Women*, First edition. Philadelphia: Westminster Press, 1979.

Taran, Leonardo. *Speusippus of Athens, A Critical Study with a Collection of the Related Texts and Commentary*. Leiden: E. J. Brill, 1981.

Teilhard de Chardin, Pierre. *Human Energy*. Translated by J. M. Cohen. New York: Harcourt Brace Jovanovich, 1971.

Télès et Musonius: Deux prédicateurs de l'antiquité. Traduit par A. J. Festugière. Paris: Librairie Philosophique, J. Vrin, 1978.

Theon, of Alexandria. "Commentaire sur les Tables Manvelles astronomiques de Ptolemée." *Oeuvres de Ptolemée*, Tome V. Traduites par M. l'abbé Halma. Paris: Chez Merlin, Librairie, 1921.

Theophrastos: Περι Συζεβειασ (Griechischer Text). Herausgegeben, übersetzt und eingeleitet von Walter Pötscher. Leiden: E. J. Brill, 1964.

Thesleff, Holger. *An Introduction to the Pythagonean Writings of the Hellenistic Period*. In *Acta Academiae Aboenis Humaniora*. Abo: Akademi, 1961.

__________. *The Pythagorean Texts of the Hellenistic Period*. In *Acta Academiae Aboensis, Ser. A., Humaniora*. Abo: Akademi, 1965.

Thomas Aquinas, Saint. *Commentary on the 'Nicomachean Ethics.'* Translated by C. I. Litzinger. Chicago: Henry Regnery Co., 1964.

__________. *Commentary on the "Metaphysics" of Aristotle*. Translated by John P. Rowan. Chicago: Henry Regnery, 1961.

__________. *Compendium of Theology*. Cyril Vollert, translator. St. Louis: Herder, 1947.

__________. *'De Anima' in the Version of William of Moerbeke; and the Commentary of Saint Thomas Aquinas*. Translated by Knelm Foster and Silvester Humphries, with an introduction by Ivor Thomas. New Haven: Yale University Press, 1951.

__________. *De Principii Naturae*. Latin text and English translation by P. J. Henle and V. J. Bourke. St. Louis: St. Louis University, 1947.

__________. *In Octo Libros Policorum Aristotelis Expositio Sev. de Rebus Civilibus*. Peculiaris editio Alumnis Universitatis Lavallensis. Quebec: Tremblay and Dion, 1940.

__________. *On the Power of God. (Quaestiones Disputatae de Potentia Dei)*. Literally translated by the English Dominican Fathers. Westminster, Maryland: Newman Press, 1952.

__________. *On Kingship, to the King of Cyprus*. Done into English by Gerald B. Phelan. Revised with introduction and notes by I. Th. Eschmann. Toronto: Pontifical Institute of Mediaeval Studies, 1949.

__________. *Petri Lombardi Sentiarum Libri Quattuor*. Paris: J.P. Migne, 1853.

__________. *The Soul; A Translation of St. Thomas Aquinas' 'De Anima.'* By John Patrick Rowan. St. Louis: B. Herder, 1949.

__________. *The 'Summa Contra Gentiles' of Saint Thomas Aquinas*. 4 vols. Literally translated by the English Dominican Fathers. New York: Benzinger Bros., 1923-29.

__________. *Summa Theologiae*. Vols. 1-60. Latin text and English translation, with introductions, notes, appendices and glossaries. Blackfriars edition. New York: McGraw-Hill Book Co., 1964.

__________. *Summa Theologiae*: Vols. 1-3. Translated by the English Dominican Fathers. New York: Benzinger Bros., 1948.

__________. *Truth*. 3 vol. Translated from the definitive Leonine text by R. W. Mulligan, J. V. McGlynn, and R. W. Schmidt. Chicago: Henry Regnery Co., 1952.

Thomas, Ivor. *Greek Mathematics*. Cambridge, Mass. and London: Harvard University Press and William Heinemann, Ltd., 1939.

———. trans. *Selections Illustrating the History of Greek Mathematics.* 2 vols. With an English translation. Cambridge, Mass. and London: Harvard University Press and William Heinemann, Ltd., 1939.

Toland, John. *Tetradymus.* London: J. Brotherton and W. Meadows, 1720.

Toon, Reverend Mark, O.S.B., M.A. *The Philosophy of Sex According to the St Thomas Aquinas.* Ph.D. dissertation, The Catholic University of America, 1954.

Torrence, Ridgley. *Abelard and Heloise.* New York: Charles Scribner's Sons, 1907.

Visions of Women. Edited by Linda A. Bell. Clifton, N.J.: Humana Press, Inc., 1958.

Vogel, Cornelia J. de. *Pythagoras and Early Pythagoreanism; An Interpretation of Neglected Evidence of the Philosophger Pythagoras.* Assen: Van Gorcum, 1966.

Waithe, Mary Ellen. "Authenticating the Fragments and Letters." In *The Project on the History of Women in Philosophy.* St. Paul, Minn.: forthcoming.

Warren, Mary Ann. *The Nature of Woman: An Encyclopedia and Guide to the Literature.* Inverness, Calif.: Edgepress, 1980.

Weisheipl, James A., ed. *Albertus Magnus and the Sciences; Commemorative Essays, 1980.* Toronto: Pontifical Institute of Mediaeval Studies, 1979.

———. *Friar Thomas D'Aquino: His Life, Thought and Work.* New York: Doubleday and Co., 1974.

———. "Thomas D'Aquino and Albert His Teacher." *The Etienne Gilson Series,* 2. Toronto: Pontifical Institute for Mediaeval Studies, 1980.

Whittaker, Thomas. *The Neo-Platonists; a Study in the History of Hellenism.* 2nd ed., with a supplement on the *Commentaries of Proclus.* Cambridge: The University Press, 1928.

Wiesen, David S. *St. Jerome As A Satirist: A Study in Christian Latin Thought and Letters.* Ithaca, N.Y.: Cornell University Press, 1964.

Wilms, Hieronymous. *Albert the Great: Saint and Doctor of the Church.* London: Burns, Oates and Washbourne, Ltd., 1933.

Wippel, John F. "The Condemnation of 1270 and 1277 at Paris." In *The Journal of Medieval and Renaissance Studies,* 7, 2 (1977): 169-201.

Wojtyla, Cardinal Karol. *The Acting Person.* Dordrecht, Holland/Boston, U.S.A./London, England: D. Reidel Publishing Company, 1979.

ADDITIONAL SOURCES TO THE SECOND EDITION

N.B. The items in the bibliography are listed alphabetically by chapter.

GENERAL SOURCES

Ashley, Benedict, O.P. *Theologies of the Body: Humanist and Christian.* 2nd printing. Braintree, Mass.: The Pope John Center, 1995.

Grimshaw, Jean. *Feminist Philosophers: Women's Perspectives on Philosophical Traditions.* Brighton, Sussex: Wheatsheaf Books Ltd., 1986. Same text with different title: *Philosophy and Feminist Thinking.* Minneapolis: University of Minnesota Press, 1986.

Harding, Sandra. *The Science Question in Feminism.* Ithaca: Cornell University Press, 1986.

Kersey, Ethel M. *Women Philosophers: A Bio-Critical Source Book.* New York: Greenwood Press, 1989.

Kilpatrick, William K. *Why Johnny Can't Tell Right from Wrong.* New York: Simon & Schuster, 1992.

Lloyd, Genevieve. *The Man of Reason: "Male" and "Female" in Western Philosophy.* Minneapolis: University of Minnesota Press, 1984.

Phillips, John A. *Eve: The History of an Idea.* New York: Harper and Row, 1984.

Tarnas, Richard. *The Passion of the Western Mind: Understanding the Ideas That Have Shaped Our World View.* New York: Harmony Books, 1991.

Taylor, Charles. *Sources of the Self: The Making of the Modern Identity.* Cambridge, Mass.: Harvard University Press, 1989.

Waithe, Mary Ellen, ed. *A History of Women Philosophers: Ancient Women Philosophers, 600 B.C.-500 A.D.* Vol. 1. Dordrecht, Boston, and Lancaster: Martinus Nijhoff Publishers, 1987.

———. *A History of Women Philosophers: Medieval, Renaissance and Enlightenment Women Philosophers, A.D. 500-1600.* Vol. 2. Dordrecht, Boston, and London: Klewer Academic Publishers, 1989.

Walker, Barbara. *The Woman's Encyclopedia of Myths and Secrets.* New York: Harper & Row, 1983.

Young-Bruehl, Elisabeth. "The Education of Women as Philosophers." *Signs: Journal of Women in Culture and Society* 12, 2 (1987): 207-221.

PREFACE TO THE SECOND EDITION

Allen, R.S.M., Sr. Prudence. "Analogy and Human Community in Lublin Existential Personalism." *The Toronto Journal of Theology* 5, 2 (Fall 1989): 236-46.

———. *Synergetics* and Sex Complementarity." *International Philosophical Quarterly* 32, 1 (March 1992): 3-16.

———. "Integral Sex Complementarity and the Theology of Communion." *Communio: International Catholic Review* 17 (Winter 1990): 523-44.

———. "Metaphysics of Form, Matter, and Gender." *Lonergan Workshop* 12 (1996): 1-26.

———. "Rationality, Gender, and History." *American Catholic Philosophical Quarterly.* Proceedings of 1994 Annual Conference, 68 (1994): 271-88.

———. "A Woman and a Man as Prime Analogical Beings." *American Catholic Philosophical Quarterly* 66, 4 (1992): 456-82.

Clarke, W. Norris, S.J. *Person and Being: The Aquinas Lecture, 1993.* Milwaukee: Marquette University Press, 1993.

Damico, Linda. "Book Review: *The Concept of Woman.*" *Hypatia: Journal of the Society for Women in Philosophy, American Philosophical Association* 4, 1 (Spring 1989): 171-75.

Flax Jane. "Postmodernism and Gender Relations in Feminist Theory." *Signs: Journal of Women in Culture and Society* 12, 4 (1987): 3-19.

Foucault, Michel. *The History of Sexuality.* Vol. 1. Translated by Robert Hurley. New York: Random House, 1980.

———. *The Use of Pleasure: The History of Sexuality.* Vol. 2. Translated by Robert Hurley. New York: Random House, 1986.

Gill, Christopher, ed. *The Person and the Human Mind: Issues in Ancient and Modern Philosophy.* Oxford: Clarendon Press, 1990.

Harding, Sandra. "Is Gender a Variable in Conceptions of Rationality? A Survey of Issues." In *Beyond Domination: New Perspectives on Women and Philosophy.* Edited by Carole C. Gould. Lanham, Md.: Rowman and Allanheld, 1984, 43-63.

Illich, Ivan. *Gender.* New York: Pantheon Books, 1982.

Jaggar, Allison, and Susan Bordo, eds. *Gender/Body/Knowledge: Feminist Reconstructions of Being and Knowing.* New Brunswick and London: Rutgers University Press, 1989.

Lauretis, Teresa de. *Technologies of Gender.* Bloomington and Indianapolis: Indiana University Press, 1987.

Maritain, Jacques. *The Person and the Common Good.* Translated by John J. Fitzgerald. Notre Dame, Ind.: University of Notre Dame Press, 1985.

Rousseau, Mary F. *Community: The Tie That Binds.* Lanham, Md.: University Press of America, 1991.

Rubin, Gayle. "The Traffic in Women: Notes on the 'Political Economy of Sex.' " In *Towards an Anthropology of Women.* Edited by Rayna R. Reigner. New York: Monthly Review Press, 1975, 157-210.

Schmitz, Kenneth L. "The Geography of the Human Person." *Communio* 13 (Spring 1986): 27-48.

———. "Selves and Persons: A Difference in Loves?" *Communio* 18 (Summer 1991): 183-206.

Stein, Edith. *Essays on Woman.* Translated by Freda Mary Oben. The Collected Works of Edith Stein, vol. 2. Washington, D.C.: ICS Publications, 1987.

Taylor, Charles. *The Malaise of Modernity.* CBC Massey lectures series, 1991. Concord, Ont.: House of Anansi Press Limited, 1991.

Tiles, Mary. "Book Review: *The Concept of Woman.*" *Philosophy: The Journal of the Royal Institute of Philosophy, London* 61, 237 (July 1986): 414-18.

Wittig, Monique. "The Mark of Gender." *Feminist Issues* 5, 2 (1985): 3-12.

Wojtyla, Karol. *Person and Community: Selected Essays.* Translated by Theresa Sandok, O.S.M. Catholic Thought from Lublin, vol. 4. New York: Peter Lang, 1993.

Zedler, Beatrice. "Book Review: *The Concept of Woman.*" *Speculum: A Journal of Medieval Studies* 62, 4 (October 1987): 898-900.

CHAPTER I

Allen, R.S.M., Sr. Prudence. "Foundational Virtues for Community." *Etudes maritainiennes/Maritain Studies* 12 (1996): 133-49.

Bar On, Bat-Ami, ed. *Engendering Origins: A Collection of Feminist Essays about Plato and Aristotle.* Albany: SUNY Press, 1994.

Bluestone, Natalie Harris. *Women and the Ideal Society: Plato's "Republic" and Modern Myths of Gender.* Amherst: University of Massachusetts Press, 1987.

———. "Why Women Cannot Rule: Sexism in Plato Scholarship." *Philosophy of Social Science* 18 (March 1988): 41-60.

Brown, Wendy. " 'Supposing Truth Were a Woman . . .': Plato's Subversion of Masculine Discourse." *Political Theory* 16, 4 (November 1988): 594-616.

Code, Lorraine. *What Can She Know? Feminist Theory and the Construction of Knowledge.* Ithaca: Cornell University Press, 1991.

Darling, John. "Are Women Good Enough: Plato's Feminism Re-examined." *Journal of the Philosophy of Education* 20 (Summer 1996): 123-28.

Egan, Edmund J. "The Transformation of Ethics and Heterosexual Consciousness." *Cross Currents* (Summer 1975): 159-72.

Keller, Evelyn Fox. *Reflections on Gender and Science.* New Haven: Yale University Press, 1985.

Scaltas, Patricia Ward. "Virtue without Gender in Socrates." *Hypatia* 7, 3 (Summer 1992): 126-37.

Smith, Nicholas D. "Plato and Aristotle on the Nature of Women." *Journal of the History of Philosophy* 21 (October 1983): 467-78.

Tauna, Nancy, ed. *Feminist Interpretations of Plato.* University Park, Pa.: The Pennsylvania State University Press, 1994.

Walker, Michelle. "Silence and Reason: Woman's Voice in Philosophy." *Australasian Journal of Philosophy* 71, 4 (December 1993): 400-424.

Wider, Kathleen, "Women Philosophers in the Ancient Greek World: Donning the Mantle." *Hypatia: A Journal of Feminist Philosophy* 1, 1 (Spring 1986): 21-62.

CHAPTER II

Allen, R.S.M., Sr. Prudence. "The Influence of Plato and Aristotle on the Concept of Woman in Medieval Jewish Philosophy" *Florilegium* 9 (1987): 89-111.

Clark, Stephen. "Aristotle's Woman." *History of Political Thought* 3 (Summer 1982): 177-92.

Crowe, Michael J. *Theories of the World from Antiquity to the Copernican Revolution.* New York: Dover Publications, 1990.

Fausto-Sterling, Anne. *Myths of Gender: Biological Theories about Women and Men.* Second Edition. New York: Harper Collins Publishers, 1992.

Fememias, Maria Luisa. "Women and Natural Hierarchy in Aristotle." *Hypatia* 9, 1 (Winter 1994): 164-72.

Green, Judith M. "Aristotle on Necessary Verticality, Body Heat, and Gendered Proper Places in the Polis: A Feminist Critique." *Hypatia* 7, 1 (Winter 1992): 70-96.

Lange, Lynda. "Woman Is Not a Rational Animal: On Aristotle's Biology of Reproduction." In *Discovering Feminist Perspectives on Epistemology, Metaphysics, Methodology, and Philosophy of Science.* Edited by Sandra Harding and Merrill B. Hintikka. Dordrecht, Holland, Boston, U.S.A., and London, England: D. Reidel Publishing Company, 1983, 1-16.

MacIntyre, Alasdair. *After Virtue: A Study in Moral Theory.* Second Edition. Notre Dame, Ind.: University of Notre Dame Press, 1984.

————. *Whose Justice? Which Rationality?* Notre Dame, Ind.: University of Notre Dame Press, 1988.

Matthews, Gareth B. "Gender and Essence in Aristotle." *Australian Journal of Philosophy*, supplement 64 (June 86): 16-25.

Schott, Robin. "Aristotle on Women." *Kinesis* 11 (Spring 1982): 69-84.

Spelman, Elizabeth V., "Aristotle and the Politicization of the Soul." In *Discovering Reality: Feminist Perspectives on Epistemology, Metaphysics, Methodology, and Philosophy of Science.* Edited by Sandra Harding and Merrill B. Hintikka. Dordrecht, Holland, Boston, U.S.A., and London, England: D. Reidel Publishing Company, 1983, 17-30.

Swanson, Judith A. *The Public and the Private in Aristotle's Political Philosophy.* Ithaca: Cornell University Press, 1992.

Tumulty, Peter. "Aristotle, Feminism and Natural Law Theory." *New Scholasticism* 55 (Autumn 1981): 450-64.

CHAPTER III

Alexander, William M. "Sex and Philosophy in Augustine." *Augustinian Studies* 5 (1974): 197-208.

Elshtain, Jean Bethke. "Christianity and Patriarchy: The Odd Alliance." *Modern Theology* 9, 2 (April 1993): 109-22.

———. "Thinking about Women, Christianity, and Rights." In *Religious Human Rights in Global Perspective: Religious Perspectives.* Chicago: Cathedral Graphics, 1996, 141-53.

———. *Women and War.* Chicago: The University of Chicago Press, 1995.

McAlister, Linda Lopez, ed. *Hypatia: A Journal of Feminist Philosophy. Special Issue: The History of Women in Philosophy* 4, 1 (Spring 1989).

Olsen, Glenn W. "St. Augustine and the Problem of the Medieval Discovery of the Individual." *Word and Spirit* 9 (1987): 129-56.

Porphyry. *Porphyry the Philosopher to Marcella.* Translated, with an Introduction and Notes, by Kathleen O'Brien Wicker. Index Verborum by Lee E. Klosinski (Texts and Translations 28; Graeco-Roman Religion Series 10). Atlanta, Ga.: Scholars Press, 1988.

———. *Porphyry's Letter to His Wife Marcella concerning the Life of Philosophy and the Ascent to the Gods.* Translation from Greek by Alice Zimmern with Introduction by David R. Fideler. Grand Rapids: Phanes Press, 1986.

Ramsey, Paul. "Human Sexuality in the History of Redemption" *The Journal of Religious Ethics* 16, 1 (Spring 1988): 56-86.

Weaver, E. Ellen, and Jean Laporte. "Augustine and Women: Relationships and Teaching." *Augustinian Studies* 12 (1981): 115-31.

CHAPTER IV

Allen, R.S.M., Sr. Prudence. "Two Medieval Views on Woman's Identity." *Studies in Religion/Sciences Religieuses* 16, 1 (1987): 21-36.

———. "Hildegard of Bingen's Philosophy of Sex Identity." *Thought: A Review of Culture and Idea* 64, 254 (September 1989): 231-41.

———. "Sex and Gender Differentiation in Hildegard of Bingen and Edith Stein." *Communio: International Catholic Review* 20, 2 (Summer 1993): 389-414.

Al-Farabi. *On the Perfect State.* Edited, translated, and with commentary by Richard Walzer. Oxford: Clarendon Press, 1985.

Bonn, Caecilia. *Mut zur Ganzheitlichkeit: Aspekte bei Hildegard von Bingen.* Eibingen: Abtei St. Hildegard, 1990.

Clarke, W. Norris, "Person, Being, and St. Thomas." *Communio* 19 (Winter 1992): 601-18.

Ellis, Peter Berresford. *Celtic Women: Women in Celtic Society and Literature.* Grand Rapids: Eerdmans, 1995.

Flanagan, Sabina. *Hildegard of Bingen: A Visionary Life.* London: Routledge, 1990.

Gossmann, Elisabeth. "The Image of the Human Being according to Scholastic Theology and the Reaction of Contemporary Women." *Ultimate Reality and Meaning: Interdisciplinary Studies in the Philosophy of Understanding* 11, 3 (September 1988): 183-95.

Hildegard von Bingen — LCC: (Hildegardis, Saint)

———. *Hildegard of Bingen: An Anthology.* Edited by Fiona Bowie and Oliver Davies. Translated by Robert Carver. London: SPCK, 1990.

———. *Hildegard of Bingen's Book of Divine Works with Letters and Songs.* Edited by Matthew Fox. Santa Fe: Bear & Company, 1987.

———. *Scivias.* Translated by Mother Columba Hart, O.S.B., and Jane Bishop. Mahwah, N.J.: Paulist Press, 1990.

———. *Scivias.* Translated by Bruce Hozeski. Santa Fe: Bear & Company, 1986.

———. *The Letters of Hildegard of Bingen.* Vol. 1. Translated by Joseph L. Baird and Radd K. Ehrman. Oxford: Oxford University Press, 1994.

Krapiec, M. A. *Person and Natural Law.* Translated by Maria Szymanska. New York: Peter Lang, 1993.

John, Helen J. "Hildegard of Bingen: A New Twelfth-Century Woman Philosopher?" Review Essay, *Hypatia* 7, 1 (Winter 1992): 115-23.

Lauter, Werner. *Hildegard—Bibliographie.* Alzey: Verlag der Rheinhessuschen Druckwerkstätte, 1984.

Lerner, Ralph, and Mahdi Muhsin, eds. *Medieval Political Philosophy: A Source Book.* Ithaca N.Y.: Cornell University Press, 1963.

Martin, Francis. *The Feminist Question: Feminist Theology in the Light of Christian Tradition.* Grand Rapids, Mich.: Eerdmans, 1994.

McCool, S.J., Gerald A. "Why St. Thomas Stays Alive." *International Philosophical Quarterly* 30, 3 (September 1990): 275-87.

Newman, Barbara. *Sister of Wisdom: St. Hildegard's Theology of the Feminine.* Berkeley: University of California Press, 1987.

———. "Some Mediaeval Theologians and the Sophia Tradition." *The Downside Review* 108 (April 1990): 111-30.

Nolan, Michael. *Defective Tales: The Story of Three Myths* ["The Council of Macon held that a Woman does not have a Soul," "Aquinas said that a Female is a Defective Male," and "Aristotle said a Female is a Deformed Male"]. Reprinted with revisions. Oxford: New Blackfriars, 1995.

Nye, Andrea. "A Woman's Thought or a Man's Discipline? The Letters of Abelard and Heloise." *Hypatia* 7, 3 (Summer 1992): 1-22.

Petroff, Elizabeth Alvilda, ed. *Medieval Women's Visionary Literature.* Oxford: Oxford University Press, 1986.

Popik, Kristin Mary. "The Philosophy of Woman of St. Thomas Aquinas." Pars dissertations ad lauream in facultate philosophiae apud pontificiam universitatem s. thomae de urbe, 1979.

Schipperges, Heinrich, and Caecilia Bonn. *Hildegard von Bingen und ihre Impulse für die moderne Welt.* Eibingen, 1984.

Scholz, Bernhard W. "Hildegard Von Bingen on the Nature of Woman." *American Benedictine Review* 31, 4 (1980): 361-83.

Wilson, Katharina, ed. *Medieval Women Writers.* Athens, Ga.: University of Georgia Press, 1984.

CHAPTER V

Allen, R.S.M., Sr. Prudence, "Aristotelian and Cartesian Revolutions in the Philosophy of Man and Woman" and "Response." *Dialogue: Journal of the Canadian Philosophical Association* 26, 2 (Summer 1987): 263-79.

———. "Descartes, The Concept of Woman, and The French Revolution." In *Revolution, Violence, and Equality.* Edited by Yaeger Hudson and Creighton Peden. Studies in Social and Political Theory, Vol. 10, no. 3. Lewiston, Queenston, and Lampeter: The Edwin Mellen Press, 1990, 61-78.

———, and Filippo Salvatore. "Lucrezia Marinelli and Woman's Identity in Late Italian Renaissance." *Renaissance and Reformation,* new series 28, 4 (1992): 5-39.

Ashworth, E. J. *Language and Logic in the Post-Medieval Period.* Dordrecht, Holland, and Boston, U.S.A: D. Reidel Publishing Company, 1974.

———. *The Tradition of Medieval Logic and Speculative Grammar.* Toronto: Pontifical Institute of Medieval Studies, 1978.

Ancona, Christine d'. *Recherches sur le Liber de causis.* Paris: Vrin, 1995.

Bloom, Allan. *The Closing of the American Mind.* New York: Simon and Schuster, 1987.

The Book of Causes. Translated from the Latin by D. J. Brand. Milwaukee: Marquette University Press, 1984.

Crysdale, Cynthia. "Horizons That Differ: Women and Men and the Flight from Understanding." *Cross Currents* 44, 3 (Fall 1994): 345-61.

Fowlkes, Diane L., et al. *Feminist Visions: Toward a Transformation of the Liberal Arts Curriculum.* University, Ala.: The University of Alabama Press, 1984.

Gabriel, Astrik L. "The College System in the Fourteenth-Century Universities." In *The Forward Movement of the Fourteenth Century.* Edited by Francis Lee Utley. Columbus: Ohio State University Press, 1961.

Klein, Julie. *Interdisciplinarity: History, Theory, and Practice.* Detroit: Wayne State University Press, 1990.

Kraue, Jill, W. F. Ryan, and D. B. Schmitt, eds. *Pseudo-Aristotle in the Middle Ages: The Theology and Other Texts.* London: Warburg Institute, 1986.

Nye, Andrea. *Words of Power: A Feminist Reading of the History of Logic.* New York and London: Routledge, 1990.

INDEX